Evidence-Based Applied Sport Psychology

Roland A. Carlstedt, PhD, is a licensed clinical psychologist, board-certified sport psychologist, is board certified in applied clinical psychophysiology and biofeedback, and chairman of the American Board of Sport Psychology. He is also licensed as an applied psychologist in the State of Virginia. Dr. Carlstedt earned his doctorate in psychology with honors from Saybrook Graduate School (with emphases in health and sport psychology and psychophysiology) in San Francisco, under the renowned personality psychologist and behavioral geneticist Dr. Auke Tellegen. He has completed postdoctoral continuing education in psychiatric neuroscience through Harvard Medical School. He also received training in the joint Massachusetts General Hospital–Massachusetts Institute of Technology–Harvard Medical School Athinoula A. Martinos Center for Biomedical Imaging Functional Magnetic Resonance Imaging (fMRI) Visiting Fellowship program and its NIH-sponsored program in multi-modal brain imaging. Dr. Carlstedt is a member of the Massachusetts General Hospital Psychiatry Academy and a research fellow in applied neuroscience with the Brain Resource Company. He is also the clinical and research director of Integrative Psychological Services of New York City.

Dr. Carlstedt's dissertation on neuropsychological, personality, and performance processes in highly skilled athletes across seven different sports was the recipient of the American Psychological Association's Division 47 (Exercise and Sport Psychology) 2001 Award for Best Dissertation in Sport Psychology. It was also the basis for his book *Critical Moments During Competition: A Mind–Body Model of Sport Performance When it Counts the Most* (2004, Psychology Press). His edited book, *Handbook of Integrative Clinical Psychology, Psychiatry and Behavioral Medicine: Perspectives, Practices and Research* was released in 2009 (Springer Publishing Company). Dr. Carlstedt's research has been published in *Biofeedback, Cortex, Brain and Cognition*, and the *Journal of the American Board of Sport Psychology*. He has also presented papers and chaired symposia at numerous American Psychological Association and Association for Applied Psychophysiology and Biofeedback conventions and has co-authored chapters in five academic books. He also served on Division 47's science committee.

In his capacity as founder and chairman of the American Board of Sport Psychology (ABSP), Dr. Carlstedt has mentored dozens of practitioners pursuing certification in sport psychology, and over 100 undergraduate and graduate students in the ABSP annual summer research and visiting fellowship programs. He has also consulted with numerous athletes, teams, and organizations worldwide, including the Harlequins Professional Rugby Union Team (London, UK) and the Polish Tennis Federation, and has mentored and trained many international sport psychology practitioners, including India's 2012 Olympic shooting team mental training coach. He is involved in numerous ongoing research projects in sport psychology, including in vivo qEEG and HRV studies of athletes from the sports of baseball, golf, tennis, basketball, football, and rugby. A former professional tennis player and full-time consultant and coach on the professional tennis tours, Dr. Carlstedt has been published and featured in the popular media over 500 times, appearing in magazines, radio, and television extending into more than 40 countries. Dr. Carlstedt has consulted with Niki Pilic, captain of the champion German Davis Cup Team and with Rohan Goetzke, coach of former Wimbledon Champion Richard Krajicek. He has also coached numerous top-ranked juniors and professionals, including Ronald Agenor, former world-ranked #22 and French Open quarter-finalist.

Evidence-Based Applied Sport Psychology

A Practitioner's Manual

Roland A. Carlstedt, PhD

SPRINGER PUBLISHING COMPANY

NEW YORK

Springer Publishing Company, LLC
11 West 42nd Street
New York, NY 10036
www.springerpub.com

Acquisitions Editor: Nancy S. Hale
Senior Production Editor: Joe Stubenrauch
Composition: Techset

ISBN: 978-0-8261-0317-8
E-book ISBN: 978-0-8261-0553-0

12 13 14 15/ 5 4 3 2 1

The author and the publisher of this Work have made every effort to use sources believed to be reliable to provide information that is accurate and compatible with the standards generally accepted at the time of publication. The author and publisher shall not be liable for any special, consequential, or exemplary damages resulting, in whole or in part, from the readers' use of, or reliance on, the information contained in this book. The publisher has no responsibility for the persistence or accuracy of URLs for external or third-party Internet websites referred to in this publication and does not guarantee that any content on such websites is, or will remain, accurate or appropriate.

Library of Congress Cataloging-in-Publication Data

Carlstedt, Roland A.
  Evidence-based applied sport psychology : a practitioner's manual / Roland
A. Carlstedt.
   p. cm.
  Includes bibliographical references and index.
  ISBN 978-0-8261-0317-8—ISBN 978-0-8261-0553-0
  1. Sports—Psychological aspects. 2. Psychology, Applied. I. Title.
  GV706.4.C3644 2012
  796.01 – dc23

                                        2012025706

Special discounts on bulk quantities of our books are available to corporations, professional associations, pharmaceutical companies, health care organizations, and other qualifying groups.

If you are interested in a custom book, including chapters from more than one of our titles, we can provide that service as well.

For details, please contact:
Special Sales Department, Springer Publishing Company, LLC
11 West 42nd Street, 15th Floor, New York, NY 10036-8002s
Phone: 877-687-7476 or 212-431-4370; Fax: 212-941-7842
Email: sales@springerpub.com

Printed in the United States of America by Bradford and Bigelow.

This book is dedicated to all of the American Board of Sport Psychology certificate holders, and especially undergraduate and graduate students and practitioners who have attended the annual ABSP summer visiting fellowship and research program and in the process helped acquire much of the data upon which this book is based.

Contents

Foreword

Systematic, higher evidentiary approaches to integrative athlete assessment and intervention are scarce in applied sport psychology, especially ones that have been validated and subjected to extensive accountability metrics. While numerous systems of athlete evaluation and mental training continue to be propagated among practitioners and researchers, most can be called into question when scrutinized in the context of gold-standard efficacy testing. *Evidence-Based Applied Sport Psychology* addresses this limitation head on by providing systematic, validated, step-by-step research and a data-driven road map for practitioners; from the initial intake session to the final report. Its author, Dr. Roland A. Carlstedt, convincingly argues that the practice of applied sport psychology has been given a "pass" as far as accountability is concerned. The field's maxim, he contends, continues to assume treatment efficacy in the absence of determining to what extent the use of an array of mental training strategies and approaches to athlete assessment are valid and reliable predictors of improved performance. The efficacy of a recommended mental training method is often absent. The current practitioner-centered sport psychology services delivery paradigm makes it very difficult to practice gold-standard requisite comprehensive athlete assessment and intervention efficacy testing. The result is that sport psychology services often lack credibility, calling into question notions of intervention efficacy. Dr. Carlstedt correctly suggests that practitioners rarely leave the office and directly observe athletic performance, especially during the crucial stages of athlete assessment, mental training, and intervention efficacy testing. He contends that consulting sessions cannot be compartmentalized incrementally to accommodate practice and financial realities. Ultimately, effective consulting is about the science, and science cannot always be neatly packaged.

The book confronts practitioners with the question of whether verifiable changes in an athlete's thoughts, emotions, or behaviors as a function of an intervention can be attained when administered in an ad hoc manner devoid of ecological validity. It is doubtful whether performance-relevant psychological deficiencies or maladaptive behaviors that have become habitual over many years can be eradicated or even remediated through infrequent and low intensity mental training intervention. If the answer is affirmative, then where is the evidence? Claims of high success rates seem pervasive, but where is the efficacy data?

Dr. Carlstedt's book encourages and teaches practitioners to reexamine their practices critically and to go well beyond mere intuition and mythology, and to explore the *causes*, or mechanisms, of intervention outcomes. He presents an elaborate client-centered assessment and intervention paradigm, one that is marked by technology-supported systematic, step-by-step methods and procedures, and followed by efficacy testing. He maintains that if a sport psychology practitioner is not trained in a host of high-tech applied neuropsychophysiological and advanced analytic procedures and methodologies, and does not devote sufficient time to comprehensive diagnostics, mental training, and outcome testing, athletes, coaches, and teams are being short-changed. The sport psychology practitioner must be able to distinguish himself or herself from the athlete's coach, parent, friend, peer, colleague, or other advisor beyond the type of relationship or credential. Reputable professional services require empirical scrutiny.

The book presents a plethora of potent procedures, methodologies, and technologies for delving into mind–body processes that drive peak performance, psychological performance deficiencies, and the mental training process. For example, instead of requiring athletes to engage exclusively in visualization, the "Carlstedt Protocol" contains a visualization "efficiency" test paradigm that uses heart rate variability (HRV) to detect autonomic nervous system changes as a function of the manipulation of mental images. Then, in the context of time-outs during training and actual competition, visualization efficiency is assessed ecologically using HRV in real time. Subsequently, visualization efficacy is determined on the basis of visualization-mediated HRV changes and micro-outcome measures, such as critical moment analyses. What often emerges from this methodological procedure is that differential responding can be predicted on the basis of the athlete's profile model of psychological peak performance. The presented paradigms and procedures provide practitioners with procedures that are novel, innovative, advanced, and methodologically sound that take guesswork out of typical assessment and mental training.

Evidence-Based Applied Sport Psychology is not a "guru"-driven book. That is, this is not a book that is based on some "expert's" notion of how to "do" sport psychology. It is based on scientific approaches and principles that mark more mature and innovative fields in the behavioral sciences. Highest evidentiary methods, approaches, and procedures were used to develop an extensive practitioner-based database of psychological and mind–body predictor variables and micro-level outcome measures that span the last 25 years. These components form the book's basis, critique, and recommendations. The bottom-line message of this ongoing extensive database project is that not everything one was told about athlete

psychological performance is necessarily true, and that a major paradigm shift in the field of applied sport psychology is welcomed, needed, and timely. The extensive data–sets on personality, behavioral tendencies, mind–body responses, and performance outcome that the book presents convincingly makes clear that an intervention is just as likely to exhibit low to no efficacy (and even negative efficacy) as positive efficacy, making mental training a 50:50 proposition. Carlstedt contends that group studies that tout positive outcomes must be viewed with caution. Needed are extensive longitudinal single-case studies with repeated measures and concurrent psychophysiological monitoring to individualize psychological performance assessment and intervention efficacy testing.

The book presents compelling evidence in support of the extensive points of critique that it makes. Central to the advanced protocol's evidence acquisition pursuits is using practitioner-friendly regression and statistical modeling to determine the amount of variance in an outcome measure that can be attributed to an intervention-based predictor or mediating variables. Working with an athlete can no longer just involve talking and other procedures devoid of accountability. A specific form of mental training, for instance, must be empirically justified, he claims. It is not tenable to merely "do what one does" without extensive high evidentiary efficacy testing supporting the use of a particular method with a particular athlete. In other words, the validation of mental training procedures must be an ongoing pursuit at the intra-individual level; each athlete's mental training regime must be tested for efficacy, irrespective of global, group-based outcome studies. Hence, a practitioner must glean how much of the variance in an outcome measure can be attributed to an intervention-based predictor variable before ever remotely claiming "success." To advance the applied perspective for graduate-level study and as a practitioner's manual, the book is replete with actual data–sets, individual and team case studies, challenging practitioner questions, and advanced step-by-step methods and procedures.

Evidence-Based Applied Sport Psychology can be considered a seminal, watershed book, and a major contribution to the field. Ultimately, the book should mobilize practitioners to challenge the status quo in applied sport psychology by going well beyond the cursory, and become more critical thinkers and practitioners. The book calls on all practitioners to be trained in the presented procedures and methodologies in order to become more credible practitioner-researchers, something that is crucial to the field's credibility and long-term viability. Doing so is also vital to client-athletes, who must be sure they are being exposed to high evidentiary procedures and reliable information, and not mere "dual-placebo beliefs" (see Carlstedt, 2009) that do not hold up to empirical scrutiny. This book represents a significant advancement of the field of applied sport psychology.

Mark H. Anshel, PhD
Professor
Department of Health and Human Performance
Middle Tennessee State University

Acknowledgments

This book was first conceptualized in 2007. In 2008 I received a contract from Springer Publishing Company to prepare the manuscript. It was finally finished in late 2011 and has now, at last, been published, for which I thank Springer and Nancy S. Hale, who supported my project unwaveringly despite missing many deadlines. These deadlines were not missed due to laziness. They could not be met because of the fluid nature of my research and the need to continually integrate and analyze constantly acquired data and information that were crucial to advancing the message of evidence-based athlete assessment and intervention. In the process I learned many new things that had to be conveyed, including the use of methodological and analytic approaches, procedures, and new technology to better illuminate, delineate, and investigate vexing issues associated with athlete assessment and intervention. The adage "you don't know how much you don't know" had to be asked often throughout the research, analysis, and writing process, a question my first graduate school advisor Ian Wickramasekera[1] demanded that his students continually ask themselves, which I did and continue to do. Doing so delayed the completion of this project, but in the end a much better book was produced.

The following people, even if they might not know it, in their unique ways contributed to the end product and some of the discoveries that it contains. So I thank them (some again) for their known and unknown contributions to my knowledge base, skills and, especially my motivation and drive, to do the work that is necessary to make discoveries. First, Auke Tellegen of the University of Minnesota, my dissertation committee chairman, along with Stanley Krippner (Saybrook University) and Eugene Taylor (Harvard University and Saybrook University; also my master's thesis advisor), long-time mentors and dissertation committee members who taught me to think critically in the context of multiple research approaches.

In more recent years, Itay Perlstein, a distinguished scientist, has provided invaluable advice pertaining to heart rate variability, advanced methodology, and statistics in his capacity as Director of Statistics with ABSP. I have also had the pleasure of interacting with Fred Schiffer and Martin Teicher of McLean Hospital and Harvard Medical School. Dr. Schiffer's contestation of simplistic conventional thinking regarding cerebral laterality led me to consider alternative assessment approaches to brain localization of strategic planning and emotions (affect) in the context of pre-action preparation and performance outcome. Dr. Teicher, a pioneer in the arena of psychopharmacology and the effects of psychotropic medication, AD/HD, and trauma, made me keenly aware of advanced biomarker-based approaches to intervention efficiency and efficacy testing, inspiring me to adopt and adapt his scientific philosophy and investigative strategies to the study of sport performance. I also found a kindred spirit in Ajay Wasan, a psychiatrist and researcher with Brigham & Women's Hospital and Harvard Medical

---

[1]Dr. Wickramasekera's High Risk Model of Threat Perception provides the foundational basis for much of my research.

School, an avid tennis player who underwent my protocol and in the process provided me with important scientific insights.

I'd also like to thank Mark Anshel of Middle Tennessee State University, a stalwart in the field of sport and exercise psychology, for his support and courage in challenging the status quo and the American Board of Sport Psychology's quest to improve standards in applied sport psychology.

I would also like to thank Evian Gordon of the Brain Resource Company. His extraordinary work and vision in applied neuroscience has enabled myself and ABSP to develop one of the largest databases of athlete brain–mind–body and outcome measures. Thanks also goes out to BioCom Technologies and the Polar corporation for their technical and product support in the realm of heart rate variability.

Last, but not least, I'd like to thank my significant other, Denise Fortino, a clinical psychologist and addiction expert, my personal expert, who is always available to answer a question, look at my writing, provide critical advice, and keep me on the right track.

SECTION I

Conceptual, Methodological, and Practice Foundations of Integrative Evidence-Based Athlete Assessment and Intervention

1

Introduction: Perspectives on Evidence-Based Practice

Evidence-based practice and *empirically validated* assessment and interventions have become catch-phrases in psychology. However, what do they really mean, and what minimum standard or threshold is necessary before "meaningful" evidence-based practice in applied sport psychology has been established? Can we even talk about evidence-based interventions, assessment, and practice unless the most rigorous criteria for what constitutes such evidence are used? Although the American Psychological Association's quest for empirically validated approaches to intervention and outcome assessment is commendable and necessary and should be heeded, one must ask to what extent this pursuit has become a reality and whether it is even attainable, especially in the realm of applied sport psychology. Can mental training interventions be considered evidence based if an outcome assessment fails to address the ecological validity of data emanating from the office only or on the basis of mere self-report? Without real-world monitoring and measurements in the context of salient stimuli and stressors, do we really know if an intervention is having more than a cursory effect? Because a large body of research contests the generalizability of data/responses obtained in the practice (office or lab) to the real world, is the field of sport psychology being too hasty when it professes the efficacy of certain interventions (e.g., mental imagery)? What about the longitudinal staying power of a particular mental training method? Have our empirically validated interventions really demonstrated their potency over time, and if so, on the basis of what evidence at the intra-individual athlete level? What is the minimum benchmark for constituting evidence? Does *evidence based* mean merely conveying the impression that one is "doing sport psychology" by pursuing intervention and efficacy research in a perfunctory manner? Or should the standard be much higher and based on hierarchical criteria that rank the potency of evidence in accord with accepted scientific guidelines, an approach this book advocates and advances?

Although "empirically validated" assessment and intervention should drive the practice of sport psychology, the reality is that few practitioners strictly adhere to scientifically based and validated mental training protocols or engage in outcome studies to assess the efficacy of the methods that they are using. This is understandable considering the practical constraints, financial realities, and methodological requirements associated with systematic or controlled approaches to applied sport psychology. In the context of private practice, it can be difficult to adhere to the rigorous demands of a scientifically derived intervention protocol and assessment model. This presents a problem for researchers seeking to generalize findings and protocols to the real world of applied practice. Without the participation of sufficient numbers of practitioners and athletes in using certain protocols, it is difficult to concurrently validate or replicate their utility and substantiate their efficacy. Since the essence of replication or validation is control, it is imperative that your "average" practitioner be given the tools and support necessary to participate in empirically validated approaches to treatment. This is vital to the credibility of the field of applied sport psychology.

Consequently, the main purpose of this book is to expose practitioners, educators, and students to an integrative, interdisciplinary, and systematized approach to athlete assessment and intervention. Too many sport psychology practitioners work within a vacuum; becoming too comfortable with approaches they were trained in, that may be, at least to a certain extent, no longer adequate or qualify as being evidence based. For example, mental imagery or visualization, the most widely advocated and used mental training method, may not even work for many athletes. Although practitioners may argue that meta-analyses of mental imagery research have shown this intervention modality to be efficacious, effect sizes have been moderate at best and based on group results. Interventions need to be individualized and based on intra-individual longitudinal outcome research using objective repeated measures that are cognizant of key personality and behavioral measures that drive performance and intervention amenability. Yet, practitioners continue to apply methods that are cursory, lack integration, and are not well controlled or rarely, if ever, tested for efficacy.

While grass-roots practitioners on the front line of applied sport psychology provide an invaluable service, in the rapidly advancing world of research and practice it is almost impossible to keep up with key findings and methods in numerous subfields of psychology that are highly relevant to athlete assessment and optimum performance. Although most credentialed sport psychology practitioners are required to participate in continuing education, course offerings have become so vast, diffuse, and even trivial that is easy to overlook or remain unexposed to sophisticated and potent procedures and research in the field. Crucial findings and approaches frequently go unnoticed beyond press releases and superficial presentations on television or radio. Moreover, many, if not the vast majority, of training programs in applied sport psychology have training gaps or oversights that preclude practicing at the highest levels in the evidence-chain hierarchy. Most have yet to integrate advanced methods and instruments that are vital to evidence-based athlete assessment and interventions. There is also an information and training gap that needs to be closed if we are to practice high-level evidence-based applied sport psychology. The field must advance beyond anecdotal and antiquated assessment and practice models and integrate multifaceted approaches and modalities.

This manual will facilitate these goals by exposing practitioners in applied sport psychology to cutting-edge assessment methods, intervention procedures, and research that are critical to evidence-based practice. Importantly, practitioners will be given a systematized, evidence-based blueprint for becoming integrative practitioners. A longitudinal and ecologically valid approach to applied sport psychology that incorporates objective predictor and outcome measures that have been shown to reflect behavioral change and improvement will be emphasized. This book was also designed to foster interdisciplinary understanding, information sharing, and integrative approaches to athlete assessment, mental training, and outcome research. It is made necessary by the fact that while applied sport psychology is booming, the majority of practitioners work in relative isolation and in the context of unidimensional assessment and intervention approaches that may no longer meet the gold standard for client services.

Practitioners tend to practice the way they were trained and often go through an entire career married to an assessment and intervention approach that is either antiquated, obsolete, or needs to be augmented with the best emerging evidence-based practices. While many practitioners would welcome being able to upgrade their training and approach to practice, most are mired in the realities associated with having to survive as a practitioner. Time is scarce, with little available to keep up with advances across numerous subdomains of psychology. In the end, we all suffer from this state of affairs, especially coaches and athletes who are not being exposed to the most advanced approaches to assessment and intervention that are now available. As a result, a road map is needed; a blueprint for a truly integrative applied evidence-based sport psychology that is designed to disseminate critical emerging research in an efficient and understandable manner, as well as expose practitioners to sophisticated methods and procedures that need to be integrated into *all* practices. Practitioners need to be aware that sophisticated brain imaging techniques are revealing things that are important to decision making about intervention selection. They need to know about practices being used by psychologists in the clinical realm who are demonstrating that heart rate variability biofeedback may be *the* treatment modality of choice for dealing with competitive anxiety or that neurofeedback can be used in attempts to enhance focus in athletes.

Sport psychology practitioners must be exposed to and trained in validated alternative evidence-based interventions that can help athletes deal with psychologically mediated performance issues in the moment, on the playing field, including respiratory sinus arrhythmia (RSA) biofeedback, active-alert self-hypnosis, and manipulation of brain hemispheric activation to better control cognitive processing. They need to consider ecological validity and the temporal dynamics of an intervention or longitudinal impact of certain mental training methods before marrying themselves to an intervention approach. Advanced assessment and monitoring methods such as quantitative electroencephalography (qEEG) and in-the-field ambulatory wireless monitoring of psychophysiological processes are capable of revealing things that previously were unobservable, allowing a practitioner insight in athlete performance tendencies at the beginning of a working relationship with an athlete to better guide subsequent mental training and predict its course.

These are a few of the many methods that this book presents, information and approaches that are critical to high-standard evidence-based applied sport psychology.

This manual will also illuminate select research, data, and methods from various subfields in psychology that are relevant to applied sport psychology but have yet to be considered or adopted as standard procedures. An applied integrative practice template will be presented, making it possible for practitioners to draw on methods, procedures, research, and practical advice at the highest level in the evidence hierarchy. Practitioners will be taught how to work within an integrative model; how to acquire and share data for the greater good of their clients and thereby contribute to the advancement of evidence-based applied sport psychology. It will consolidate the most sophisticated methods, cutting-edge research, and potent data to give practitioners of any persuasion and training background practical insight into how to provide best-evidence-based approaches to applied sport psychology. The book will foster a systematized and interdisciplinary approach to athlete assessment and mental training and facilitate a move toward integrative evidence-based practice.

Too many books in sport and applied sport psychology merely reformulate, reword, or present what has already been published numerous times before. They lack innovation, continue to propagate myth and anecdote, and fail to provide practitioners with an integrated, coherent, and, importantly, evidence-based practice template. Such a template is missing in the landscape of publications in applied sport psychology and in the real world of practice. This manual fills that gap. The procedures, methods, and applications that will be advanced in this book have been field-tested on hundreds of athletes and practitioners.

One of the motivating factors in writing this book was the fact that practitioners who have gone through the American Board of Sport Psychology training and certification program continued to comment that this was the first time they felt that they were practicing sport psychology in a competent manner. Many of these practitioners held graduate degrees in sport psychology, postgraduate training, and certification in applied sport psychology and were active practitioners who worked with athletes. Yet, almost all expressed that something was missing. They admitted to a training gap, and even though they were credentialed on paper and were able to present themselves as competent and confident practitioners to their clients, privately they conveyed their reservations about their training, what they were doing, or not doing, and stated they needed a systematized approach to working with athletes in which standardized methods and procedures could be applied that took the guesswork out of consulting with athletes.

The evidence-based athlete assessment and intervention protocol upon which this book is based gave these practitioners a systematized approach to applied sport psychology that made sense. It includes tools that make practitioners confident and more effective, something that is crucial to building rapport with athletes and coaches and for demonstrating the efficacy of one's methods. Practitioners who are trained in these methods become part of a large network of sport psychology practitioner–researchers who have access to sophisticated methods, allowing them to contribute to the advancement of our knowledge of athlete psychological responding by submitting their findings and data to a database on athlete mind–body functioning. The methods taught in this book have been found to motivate practitioners to use evidence-based procedures, something that will help to advance the field.

It should be noted that although this book focuses on the American Board of Sport Psychology–Carlstedt Protocol (ABSP-CP), a system of athlete assessment and intervention that since originally being conceptualized (around 1995) has been applied to hundreds of athletes, leading to its validation; the main mission of this book is not to advertise or advocate for this model. Rather, the goal of this book is to raise awareness of critical issues in applied sport psychology pertaining to athlete assessment and intervention that all practitioners need to seriously contemplate and ultimately apply the herein recommended higher evidentiary approaches to the mental game. The

Accountability Challenge in Chapter 3 challenges practitioners to question and test their own approaches in each individual athlete with whom they work, and not rely on assessment and intervention approaches merely on the basis of group research findings or other influences of which they may be aware, such as educational background, training, or anecdotal beliefs.

The ABSP-CP approach provides a systematic methodological and procedural road map containing numerous validated assessment and intervention components. It is predicated not on claims, but demonstrated intervention efficiency and efficacy and valid and reliable comprehensive athlete assessments having strong predictive validity. It is an approach that should be considered by all practitioners. The protocol's greatest strength lies in its methodological and accountability framework.

Active Participation

Readers of this practitioner's manual have the opportunity to actively participate in the presented American Board of Sport Psychology–Carlstedt Protocol in the form of *Practitioner, Practitioner-Researcher*, and *Student Challenges* that are highlighted in black boxes throughout this book. Practitioners, researchers, and students are encouraged to take the challenge by responding to questions that are posed or completing data analysis and specific experiential tasks. Doing so will not only be a learning experience but can count toward American Board of Sport Psychology certification. Readers are encouraged to submit their responses and analyses for credit (submit to: rcarlstedt@americanboardofsportpsychology.org).

The book is also replete with extensive case studies of actual athlete assessment and intervention, bringing to life the perspectives, models, methodologies, and procedures that are presented in the form of real data sets and their step-by-step acquisition, analysis, and interpretation. The availability of such "real" assessment, intervention, and performance data allows readers to reanalyze and interpret the provided information as though they were these case study athletes' sport psychologist.

Another unique component of the comprehensive athlete assessment and intervention protocol is that practitioners, researchers, and students can participate in the continued development of the ABSP assessment and intervention databases in the context of its Universal Applied Sport Psychology and Clinical trials and Accountability Challenge (see Chapter 3), the goal of which is to expand the already large and extensive database of athlete brain–heart–mind–body–motor and outcome responses emanating from the higher evidentiary assessment and intervention methodologies and modalities that are presented throughout this book.

2

Construct Validity in Evidence-Based Applied Sport Psychology: Integrative Mind–Body Bases of Peak Psychological Performance

Construct validity in sport psychology refers to the extent to which a test measures an actual underlying psychological, behavioral, or mind–body process (construct) that is hypothesized to influence or is related to the derived score on an assessment instrument (Anastassi, 1988). For example, a score of 10 on the Stanford Scale of Hypnotic Susceptibility (SSHS; Weitzenhoffer & Hilgard, 1959), indicative of high hypnotic susceptibility (HHS), should be reflected in specific electroencephalography (EEG) activity that is different from that of an individual who scores a 3 on the HSHS under baseline and test conditions; or an individual who scores high on a test of neuroticism should exhibit greater physiological reactivity as reflected in, for example, more sympathetic nervous system (SNS) activity during a stress test than someone who scores low. In both examples, a construct that is assessed using a test instrument (self-report questionnaire, behavioral or performance test) is incrementally validated on the basis of neuropsychophysiological responses that are shown to underlie differential behavior, symptoms, cognitive activity, performance, and a host of other psychological variables of interest.

The establishment of construct validity in the context of sport psychological assessment and intervention requires the identification of valid functional mind–body origins or bases of athlete psychological responses and associated performance tendencies during training or competition. Validating the theoretical or conceptual precepts of performance through hypotheses or observational testing might involve, for example, demonstrating that pre-action heart rate deceleration (HRD) actually exists and is differentially associated with reaction time (RT) and subsequent performance outcome.[1] Finding additional links between HRD and concomitant brain activity parameters leading up to action that are also associated with performance outcome would be an extension finding in the construct validation process. The stronger and conceptually consistent associations between and among mind–body–motor–performance responses and outcome, the greater the construct validity of a model of peak performance.

Evaluative testing and interventions should be based on a foundation of strong construct validity. Relative to the ABSP-Carlstedt Protocol (CP; Carlstedt, 2004a, 2004b), specific brain–heart–mind–motor and performance dynamics that have been isolated in a long line of research investigating what happens neuropsychophysiologically, prior to, during, and after sport-specific action phases constitute its construct validity. These dynamics are explicated in the Athlete's Profile (AP) and "Theory of Critical Moments" (CM) models of peak performance that are presented in this chapter and throughout this book. Over the last 15 years, validation, extension, and replication research on these models of peak performance have further solidified the empirical merit of what is called the *Brain–Heart–Mind–Body–Motor* (BHMBM) construct validity model of peak performance. Findings attesting to this model's mediating role in the performance equation are presented in numerous chapters.

Irrespective of whether a practitioner subscribes to the BHMBM and its interrelated AP and CM models of peak performance, construct validity should be considered when deciding what assessment instrument to use or intervention to apply. Strong construct validity increases the probability that a test instrument will not only demonstrate strong criterion-referenced, but high predictive validity, as well, along with greater sensitivity in detecting psychological influences on performance, especially micro-level (critical moment) outcome. Strong construct validity is also crucial to intervention selection, since it makes much more sense to apply an intervention that has known and validated BHMBM responses that are associated with performance gain, than employing a mental training method whose BHMBM responses are unknown or not linked to positive performance outcome. However, practitioners need to be cautious and not assume that globally established construct validity will hold up in each individual athlete. It should be emphasized that construct validity can reveal differential responding and outcome as a function of individual differences variables, not just global (group-based) positive associations between an assessment or intervention predictor measure and outcome. What this means, for example, is that if HRD is a consistent peak performance BHMBM response biomarker, parameters of this heart rate variability (HRV) measure may still vary as a function of positive and negative performance (more or less HRD) and that HRD response tendencies can differ as a function of an Athlete's Profile of primary higher-order (PHO) constellation of mediating psychological traits and behaviors (evidence of strong construct validity).

The following points pertaining to construct validity should be taken into account when designing an assessment and intervention plan for an athlete:

1. **What should be measured and what constitutes peak psychological performance?**
   If a practitioner asserts, for example, that motivation is the key to his or her client's ability to attain peak performance, how can this hypothesis be tested and validated? What BHMBM measure(s) reflect or underlie motivation and what outcome performance measures are associated with motivation?

2. **What are the mind–body–motor underpinnings of peak psychological performance?**
   Practitioners who talk about peak psychological performance must differentiate global statistical outcome from BHMBM measures. The former metric, say, games won versus games lost, even if highly positively skewed (more games won), may not reflect the essence of peak psychological performance that may instead be revealed through specific micro-BHMBM measures independent of global outcome measures, even if they are negative, especially in sports that have an opponent factor (like tennis, baseball, etc.). For example, even though a tennis player loses a match by a score of 6-3, 6-3, his or her BHMBM response parameters may reflect better psychological control than such a score line would suggest.

3. **What assessment measures predict peak psychological performance?**
   Assessment instruments and measures, ultimately, should predict peak psychological performance. Obtaining, for example, a competitive anxiety or style of attention score is of limited

value if such scores do not predict at least macro-level performance outcome. By contrast, the value of a test or test battery increases if it predicts micro-level performance outcome, and even more so if a test score is consistently associated, at the intra-individual level, with specific performance facilitative BHMBM responses.

4. **Why construct validity, if of a high level, should determine what intervention to use**
An intervention should not be used merely because group study findings suggest that a mental training method will work. Instead, the selection of a mental training procedure should be predicated on its ability to induce replicable performance facilitative BHMBM responses at the intra-individual level, for example, pre-action HRD that is associated with better focus and motor control. An intervention that, for example, induces a relaxation response that is inconsistent with established performance facilitative responses that are marked by greater physiological reactivity (activation as opposed to relaxation) is useless and would be analogous to a physician prescribing Valium when Ritalin is indicated. Construct validity should guide assessment and intervention-provided higher evidentiary methodologies were used to validate applied approaches to athlete evaluation and mental training.

5. **Construct validity and intervention efficacy**
Strong construct validity increases the probability that an intervention will elicit a BHMBM response that is performance facilitative if the construct validity at hand is not based on group study findings alone and has been validated at the intra-individual level. Inducing a species-wide BHMBM response like pre-action HRD that consistently occurs prior to action should be the goal of all interventions, especially in athletes whose AP PHO constellations are associated with negative performance tendencies. Linking BHMBM measures to an intervention helps determine the efficacy of mental training independent of macro-outcome measures that may be less sensitive to and not isolate psychological influences on performance.

6. **What constitutes strong construct validity?**
Strong construct validity is reflected in consistent BHMBM responses that are also associated with consistent outcome at the macro- and micro-levels. These responses and associated outcomes can be different, that is, successful and unsuccessful performance can both be marked by consistent BHMBM responses. For example, if greater amounts and magnitude of HRD are associated with better critical moment performance over a longitudinal course that generates a sufficient number of repeated measures (HRD and critical moment performance) upon which statistical inferences can be made (statistical power), HRD can be considered to have strong construct validity in the assessment, intervention, and performance equation. Construct validity would be further strengthened if it was discovered that less amounts and magnitude of HRD or the existence of heart rate acceleration (HRA) instead of HRD prior to action was associated with worse performance over time.

High evidentiary athlete assessment and intervention is predicated on a practitioner's thorough knowledge and understanding of the construct validity of the tests and mental training measures that are being used. It also requires extensive training in procedures and methods that frequently involve the use of high technology to evaluate an athlete beyond mere self-report to determine the extent that an intervention is inducing responses that are consistent with what would be predicted on the basis of a mental training modality's construct or conceptual model. The rest of this chapter presents a comprehensive and integrative explication of key components of the CP's validated athlete assessment and intervention system. Arguably, this protocol can be considered of high evidentiary value whose methodologies are consistent with gold standard empirical approaches to assessment and the structured manipulation of behavior and performance (intervention). It is recommended that all practitioners use the methodologies that are presented in this chapter and throughout this book in an attempt to establish the construct validity of any psychological approach that they may apply to athletes. If strong construct validity cannot be demonstrated, it is likely that an assessment or intervention system will have low predictive validity. That would warrant discarding such a system or not using it in the first place.

Brain–Mind–Heart–Motor Construct Validity Model of Peak Performance: Key Components

This section presents key components of the CP construct validity model, starting with an illustration that depicts known and hypothesized mind–body correlates of performance prior to the initiation of action (Figure 2.1).

During routine phases of competition, the following dynamics tend to occur automatically, free from intrusive disruptions. In the immediate seconds leading up to action, the left-brain hemisphere is more activated, a response that is hypothesized to reflect strategic planning that then gives way to motor priming as reflected in greater right hemispheric activation (motor cortex region). Concomitant to the rightward hemispheric shift, HRD has been shown to occur as cognitive quieting (cessation of strategic planning) commences (relative left hemispheric deactivation), up to the onset of purposeful motor or technical action when HRA takes place to support and sustain the metabolic demands associated with the task demands of specific sport action phases.

This interaction of brain–heart and motor responding has been demonstrated in a number of sports, including marksmanship, golf, tennis, and baseball, and will likely occur in pre-action phases of all sports that involve the self-paced volitional initiation of a sport-specific task, or when waiting to respond to an opponent's initiation of action (e.g., when pitching [self-paced volitional action or batting [waiting to respond]). It is also hypothesized that HRD and concomitant left-to-right brain shifts will occur at the micro-level, as reflected in millisecond changes in cardiovascular metabolic activity and resultant hemodynamic changes in the frontal lobe and motor cortex regions of the brain. This latter proposition is based on Dietrich's (2003) *Transient Hypofrontality Hypothesis* (THH), which accounts for zone states on the basis of a reallocation of cortical resources from the frontal-lobe area of the brain to the motor cortex as a function of changes in metabolic demands in these regions.

Ultimately, peak psychological performance will be mediated by the above mind–body dynamics. Peak psychological performance allows an athlete to exhibit his or her highest technical level or motor ability. As such, the end effect of mental training interventions that are designed to enhance or maintain peak psychological performance should be the inducement of known sport-specific mind–body response dynamics that are associated with optimum technical and motor control and positive outcome. Validated construct validity models should guide intervention. Practitioners need to know what mental training is doing, what mind–body responses a method elicits, and their impact on performance outcome. It is not sufficient, for example, to merely tell an athlete to visualize about winning. Instead, visualization as an intervention should be structured in such a manner that responses to mental imagery can be measured in the context of known performance-facilitative mind–body dynamics. An athlete whose visualization attempts are associated with the generation of heart and brain responses that are inconsistent with what has been shown to occur prior to action and successful outcome may be engaging in counterproductive mental training. Consequently, practitioners and athletes alike need to know what it is they are trying to manipulate when an intervention procedure is used. To date, the construct validity of peak or zone performance

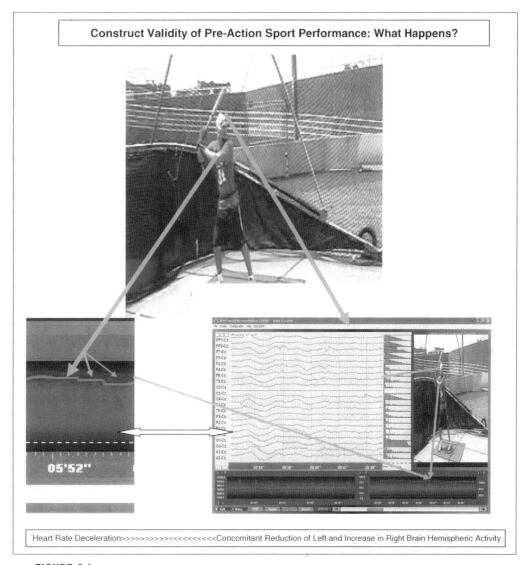

FIGURE 2.1   Construct bases of Athlete's Profile and BHMBM models of peak performance.

can be best traced to the above HRD-brain response dynamics. They are elaborated in the next section. Thereafter, an extension of the CP construct validity model that accounts for breakdowns in HRD-brain responses and peak performance in the most critical of competitive situations on the basis of PHO psychological factors will be presented.

Component I: Heart Rate Variability—HRD and Brain Activity

HRV is an important psychologically mediated performance response.

In addition to reflecting emotions and other psychological states (e.g., motivation), heart activity has been found to vary as a function of attention and cognitive activity (Sandman, Walker, & Berka, 1982). In reviewing research on heart activity, these researchers concluded that heart rate (HR) and blood pressure (BP) were the physiological parameters that best differentiated the cognitive-perceptual process. Their observation is based on Lacey and Lacey's (1964) work, which discovered that HR decreased during tasks demanding attention to the environment, and increased during tasks that required mental concentration (or, rejection of the environment). These findings were attributed to neurophysiological evidence that indicated that decelerating HR (i.e., HRD) released the cortex from the inhibitory control of the baroreceptors (circulation regulatory cells located in the vasculature of the neck), as reflected in fast frequency (i.e., beta waves in the 14–30+ Hz range) electroencephalographic (EEG) activity (14–30+ Hz EEG activity has been associated with vigilant or attentive behavior; Lindsley, 1969; Sandman et al., 1982). Conversely, HRA is thought to stimulate baroreceptor activity and thereby inhibit cortical activity. This is reflected in slower wave EEG (8–12 Hz) activity that has been associated with cognitive activity (e.g., problem solving) and decreased perceptual processing (Sandman et al., 1982; Wolk & Velden, 1987).

Galin (1974) suggested that heart activity is more useful than EEG for analyzing attentional processes, because EEG only represents activity at the dorsal convexity of the brain but does not reflect activity in deep medial brain areas such as the hippocampus and the amygdala, a hypothesis that was supported by Pribram and McGuiness's (1975) research that implicated these areas in the context of attention. Not surprisingly, attention and cognitive activity play central roles in the anecdotal literature of sport performance (Gallwey, 1974; Waller, 1988). As might be expected, attention (e.g., focusing on an incoming ball) is considered a desirable psychological state, whereas temporally inappropriate cognitive activity (e.g., thinking about winning during a point) is thought to disrupt sport performance. Gallwey (1974), in his classic work, *The Inner Game of Tennis*, propagates letting things flow, or happen naturally, by focusing on the ball, and warns of thinking too much about the consequences of hitting the ball. His notions appear to have found acceptance, with Ravizza (1977) reporting that 95% of the athletes he surveyed believed that thinking hinders performance. In addition, Waller (1988) reported that reduced levels of cognitive activity were experienced by athletes during peak performance episodes. Since heart activity (i.e., HRV and HRD/HRA) has been shown to reflect many psychological states (e.g., attention and cognition), its importance to models of peak performance should be emphasized and is highly relevant to the establishment of their construct validity. HRV may be the ideal measure for operationalizing psychological constructs (construct validity) that have yet to be delineated beyond anecdotal conjecture in sports (e.g., attention, cognitive activity, activation). Consequently, in the context of the development of the construct validity model of the CP, attention was operationalized on the basis of differential HRD, with greater amounts and magnitude of this measure of HRV hypothesized to reflect better attention prior to and during action. Conversely, loss of attention or focus due to intrusive and negative subliminal cognitive activity was operationalized on the basis of the manifestation of HRA prior to action, a psychophysiological response that is hypothesized to adversely affect performance.

HRV/HRD AND CONCOMITANT BRAIN ACTIVITY RESEARCH: A REVIEW

Heart activity, the original component of the CP construct validity model, contains two lines of research that have performance implications. The first emanates from Lacey and Lacey's (1964, 1978) studies of cardiac deceleration (HRD) using the simple reaction time (RT) paradigm (see Andreassi, 1996). The second line can be traced to Akselrod's (1981) mathematical quantification of the physiologic mechanisms of beat-to-beat fluctuations in HRV, or spectrum analyses of

HRV. Although research on HRD and HRV has been extensive, important performance-relevant findings have not been widely disseminated or universally recognized by practitioners in applied sport psychology. HRD, despite a plethora of strong findings, validating its existence as a reliable bio-marker of pre-action attention and subsequent impact on performance (in numerous sports) remains a fringe topic, with the vast majority of practitioners being unaware of this crucial mind–body peak performance response phenomenon (e.g., Boutcher & Zinsser, 1990; Carlstedt, 1998; Hatfield, Landers, & Ray, 1984, 1987).[2]

HRD RESEARCH

Research of HRD fall into two categories: (1) mechanistic studies or investigations that have delineated the properties of HRD within experimental variations of the simple RT paradigm. These studies have demonstrated the species-wide existence of HRD prior to the appearance of an expected or unexpected stimulus, and (2) performance studies that have investigated the effects of HRD on performance. This latter class of research has associated HRD with differential RT and task performance, both in the laboratory and in sport settings.

MECHANISTIC STUDIES OF HRD

HRD has been demonstrated in a variety of studies, with Lacey and Lacey (1964) being the first to show that HR decreased in response to an imperative (i.e., imminent or impending) stimulus. The Laceys' work introduced the simple RT paradigm in which subjects were required to press a key after the appearance of a ready signal (a green circle in a display box), hold the key down until the imperative signal (a white cross) was superimposed on the green circle, and respond as quickly as possible to the white cross by releasing the key. The so-called fixed foreperiod, or time offset, between the time of initial key depression and the presentation of the imperative signal, lasted 4 seconds. Results of this study showed a progressive slowing of the heart (i.e., HRD) from the time of the ready signal (i.e., pressing the key) to when the imperative signal was presented (as reflected in the lengthening of successive inter-beat-intervals [IBI] prior to the imperative signal). In an extension of their original research, the Laceys (1977) measured heart period (HP) as a function of time, in which the imperative stimulus was presented in the cardiac cycle. They found that the magnitude of HRD during the fixed foreperiod depended on where in the cardiac cycle the imperative stimulus was presented. If it occurred early (4th decile) in the cycle, HRD was significantly greater than if the imperative signal came late (10th decile) in the cycle. The Laceys (1970) also reported anticipatory slowing (i.e., HRD) in experiments requiring self-initiated responses (choice RT paradigm). For example, subjects having a prior knowledge of the onset of a significant stimulus tended to exhibit increasingly greater heart rate slowing (HRD) as the time of voluntary motor response approached. The simple RT paradigm and variations thereof (e.g., choice RT paradigm), lend themselves well to studying HRD in settings where persons are waiting to respond to a stimulus, such as sport situations that have a distinct pre-action phase, like waiting to serve or return in tennis, putting or driving in golf, at the free-throw line in basketball, or a penalty kick in soccer. The Laceys' mechanistic studies of HRD have been replicated numerous times, supporting the validity of HRD as a species-wide response in anticipation of an impending stimulus (Andreassi, 1996; Edwards & Alsip, 1969; Heslegrave, Olgilvie, & Furedy, 1979; Nowlin, Eisdorfer, Whalen, & Troyer, 1970; Surwillo, 1971; Walter & Porges, 1976).

PERFORMANCE STUDIES OF HRD AND CONCOMITANT BRAIN ACTIVITY

Performance studies in sports have also demonstrated the existence of HRD and performance relationships. Wang and Landers (as cited in Boutcher & Zinsser, 1990), comparing highly and moderately skilled archers, reported HRD in both subject groups prior to shooting (i.e., in the preparation [pre-action] phase before arrow release). They also found phasic differences in heart activity between groups. For example, although both groups exhibited HRD patterns, highly skilled archers demonstrated significantly greater HRD in comparison to lesser skilled archers during the aiming phase. In a similar study of golfers, Boutcher and Zinsser (1990) replicated the basic findings of Wang and Landers. In a comparison of elite and beginning golfers during putting, they also reported individual differences in HRD-performance effects. Specifically, they showed that both elite and beginning golfers exhibited significant HRD compared to baseline HR prior to putting. In addition, elite golfers were found to experience significantly less HRD immediately before, during, and after the ball was putted than beginning golfers. This may be attributable to shorter "wait" time before putting that most elite golfers exhibit, that is, they initiate the hitting action sooner than less-confident novices. By contrast, Carlstedt (1998) reported greater amounts and magnitude of HRD in a nationally ranked junior tennis player whose heart activity was monitored during an official tournament in matches that he won compared to a match that he lost.

In a more mechanistic study, Hatfield et al. (1984) also reported that elite rifle shooters exhibited HRD prior to shooting. Although this study did not differentiate performance proficiency, it did provide evidence in support of previous electrophysiological and neurocardiologic explanations of psychologically mediated HRD (e.g., Armour, 1994; Lacey & Lacey, 1978; McCraty & Watkins, 1996; Sandman et al., 1982). For example, it was found that increased right hemispheric EEG activity was concomitant to HRD prior to shooting. This finding is in line with previous research associating HRD with increased cortical activity (Lacey & Lacey, 1978; Sandman et al., 1982). These researchers proposed that elite marksmen have developed attentional focus to the extent that they are capable, subliminally, of reducing cognitive activity in the left hemisphere (i.e., left half of the brain). Left hemispheric cognitive activity has been associated with the disruption of motor performance (Langer & Imber, 1979; Hatfield et al., 1984). The preceding investigations are important because they clearly established that the magnitude of HRD during self-paced sports is associated with a performer's level of skill and provided evidence that HRD is not only a species-wide physiological response, but that it also reflects individual differences in athletic ability and performance outcome.

Taken at face value, the preceding review of HRD and its concomitant brain activity suggests that pre-action cardiac slowing, along with specific shifts in cortical activity, is a species-wide performance relevant response that will always be exhibited as an athlete attends to an impending stimulus, such as an incoming ball or when contemplating and focusing on the initiation of a sport-specific technical motor response (like hitting a gold ball). However, this is not always the case, as indicated by differential amounts and magnitude of HRD and variations in brain activity and their association with differential subsequent performance outcome (better or worse) that this research revealed. This again highlights the limitations that are inherent in findings that are derived from group studies, and points to the need to delineate mind–body responses like HRD at the intra-individual level to more accurately evaluate their influences on technical performance and outcome. This can be best done using regression statistical procedures to determine how much of the variance in performance outcome measures can be attributed to, in this instance, HRD and concomitant brain activity as a function of individual differences factors.

The issue of influences of individual differences variables such as traits, behaviors, and neuropsychophysiological responding on performance outcome is crucial to construct validity models, since they are mediating predictor variables that can help account for response and performance tendencies that are inconsistent with mean group findings. Rather than just accept group findings as the gospel on the basis of significance testing (hypothesis testing), for example, that HRD and left-to-right hemispheric cortical shifts do indeed occur prior to action and are associated with better outcomes, attempts need to be made to isolate individual differences variables that are most likely to impact performance, such as disrupting or facilitating species-wide BHMBM responses that are linked to peak performance. Doing so is another step up in the evidence hierarchy and imperative to the development of a strong construct validity model to guide practice.

Such attempts were undertaken by the ABSP-CP to explain discrepant individual variability in the vast majority of performance-related psychological and neuropsychophysiological studies of athlete performance. It was hypothesized that select psychological factors (traits and behaviors) that are intimately related to key components of peak performance, namely, intense attention, physiological reactivity (differential activation or intensity) and cognitive coping/strategic planning, if they could be isolated, would emerge as critical psychological mediators of differential HRD and brain activity responses and the resultant performance. In the course of a comprehensive review of the literature of sport and performance psychology and behavioral medicine, three measures were identified as the strongest mediators of not only clinical symptoms, but performance, as well, especially in the context of increasing competitive stress or pressure (criticality).

CRITICAL MOMENTS DURING COMPETITION: THE THEORY OF CRITICAL MOMENTS

HRD and simultaneous brain activity are established and validated responses in pre-action phases of numerous sports. As such, ultimately, anything that is done to enhance, manipulate, or sustain peak performance should be guided by these measures. Peak performance is likely to be associated with HRD and the described left-to-right cortical shift, whereas unsuccessful or error-laden performance is likely to be associated with a disruption of HRD and concurrent brain activity. These BHMBM response phenomena encapsulate the essence of performance upon which athlete assessment and evaluative judgments, interventions, and intervention efficacy testing should be based. Despite the central role BHMBM responses play in the performance equation, the mere knowledge of their presence has limited value without additional insight into psychological processes that may impact these peak performance responses, both facilitative and detrimental BHMBM responding. In other words, there has to be a conceptual or explanatory framework within a comprehensive construct validity model that accounts for both positive and negative performance tendencies and outcome. This can be found in the Theory of Critical Moments.

The _Theory of Critical Moments_ (TCM) proposes that psychological factors are most likely to differentially impact sport performance when competitive pressure is at its greatest. The theory advances the perspective that to determine and understand influences of an athlete's psyche on performance and account for more of the statistical variance in outcome measures that can be attributed to psychological factors, performance must be investigated at the micro-level in the context of performance relevant PHO personality, behavioral, and psychophysiological variables and repeated longitudinal outcome measures that are derived from analyses of critical moments of competition.

While a plethora of psychological measures have been investigated in athletes, most research has been unidimensional and not attempted to associate psychological factors with longitudinal micro-operationalizations of objective performance outcome measures. As a result, little is known about relationships between psychological factors and performance during pressure phases of competition. Previous research, in its totality, has been unable to explain more than 1% to 3% (per predictor measure and less than 10% on the basis of all psychological factors combined) of the variance in the performance equation that can be attributed to psychological factors, despite anecdotal notions that sport performance is mostly "mental."

The failure of previous research to account for more of the variance in the performance equation can be attributed to the inability to identify and analyze specific psychological measures that are most vital to performance during critical moments of competition, when competitive stress levels are elevated and attention, physiological reactivity, and technical skills are most vulnerable to disruptive psychological influences.

TCM is central to the development of the construct validity of the Athlete's Profile (AP) model of peak performance since it establishes the conceptual foundation upon which the AP is based. Predictions from the TCM evolved from new theoretical and methodological approaches to the study of psychological factors and performance, some of which are discussed in this chapter. Its components and lines of inquiry include:

1. **The isolation of specific PHO psychological predictor or independent variables that have been shown to mediate performance and the effects of secondary lower-order (SLO) psychological variables on performance and neuropsychophysiological concomitants of these PHO variables.**

   Primary higher-order psychological variables should not be confused with factor analytic *order* concepts. Instead, in the context of the TCM, they refer to the impact specific psychological measures or constructs have on mediating or influencing behavior, psychophysiology, and, ultimately, performance as reflected in variance explained.

   Psychological measures that influence the effects of other psychological measures and subsequent physiological responses and performance are considered PHO variables, while psychological measures that are affected by PHO variables are considered SLO variables. For example, although psychological measures like anxiety or attention are central to theories of performance such as the Zone of Optimum Functioning (Hanin, 2006), the fact that these and many other psychological measures have not been able to explain much of the variance in the performance equation calls their verifiable impact on performance into question. Although intuitively one might expect anxiety, attention, and various other psychological predictor variables to affect performance, it is difficult to determine the empirical and practical, or "real" effects most psychological predictor variables have on performance *independently* without analyzing the influence PHO variables have on secondary predictor (SLO) variables (e.g., anxiety and attention), especially in the context of pressure situations.

   The inability of most psychological predictor variables to explain much of the variance in criterion or outcome measures leads to uncertainty regarding the real impact many psychological variables (SLO) have on performance and the role other overlooked psychological factors (PHO) play in moderating, facilitating, and/or suppressing the effects of SLO psychological measures on performance. In other words, if attention, a psychological variable that, anecdotally, is thought to mediate performance, yet cannot be more precisely delineated or quantified in an assessment and/or intervention context, its performance-relevant impact remains in the realm of conjecture. The TCM maintains that most psychological measures that have been investigated in relationship to performance are SLO measures that are subordinate to select higher-order (primary) psychological processes in terms of their ability to impact performance. Thus, although it is widely accepted that measures such as attention and anxiety, to name a few, have an effect on performance, they can be disrupted or facilitated, especially during critical moments and by Athlete's Profile PHO measures.

The TCM further posits that the low levels of variance in the performance equation that can be explained by any given psychological measure can be traced in part to the suppressive effects that PHO measures exert on psychological processes that can mediate or affect performance. Should the effects of PHO processes emerge during competition, an occurrence that is most likely to happen during critical moments, the potential positive or negative influences of secondary measures, or SLO variables, on performance may be attenuated or potentiated as a function of the level or strength of a singular constellation or interaction of PHO measure(s). This dynamic will reveal itself in statistical analyses that are presented and discussed later, demonstrating that PHO psychological processes can act as suppressors or enhancers of the effects of SLO psychological processes on psychophysiology and performance. For example, in the case of anxiety or attention, the fact that even such obvious performance-relevant measures have been unable to explain much of the variance in the performance equation strongly suggests that other psychological factors are involved and that criterion or dependent outcome measures are too *global* in nature to reflect psychological influences on performance.

Numerous other constructs that have been investigated, including intensity, self-confidence, and determination also lose their PHO status in the performance equation when addressed in terms of variance explained, as research has revealed that these and virtually every psychological variable investigated in relation to objective macro-global outcome measures of performance have been minimally revealing at best.

TCM, Athlete's Profile findings strongly suggests that research on athletes must be multifactorial or multidimensional in its structure; otherwise revealing relationships between and among psychological factors and performance are unlikely to emerge. Research must also be cognizant of the potential effects of PHO factors on most SLO predictor and independent variables and psychophysiological responses, especially when SLO predictor or independent variables explain little of the variance in the performance equation (e.g., the impact of PHO measure high HS/SA on SLO measure attention).

The TCM states further that weak SLO predictors or independent variables can no longer be considered central to peak sport performance unless such measures can be shown empirically to play a primary role in mediating and predicting performance as reflected in objective micro-level outcome measures. PHO factors that have been shown to affect SLO constructs that are considered critical to peak performance, including attention, anxiety, and cognition, must be integrated into future research in an attempt to establish the real effects these and other SLO psychological factors have on performance that appear to have been inflated and anecdote driven.

The TCM hypothesizes that PHO predictor factors are intrinsically involved in mediating mind–body processes associated with peak performance, zone, and/or flow states. These PHO measures are thought to be located in specific regions of the brain and most likely to functionally manifest themselves in response to the perception of threat during critical moments of competition. The activation of PHO measures can independently or interactively facilitate or hinder performance by directly mediating physiological reactivity and motor ability. The TCM maintains that during critical moments of competition, an Athlete's Profile of brain and psychophysiological functioning drives successful performance that is reflected in specific EEG activity and HRV responses.

2. **The study of psychological factors and performance at the micro-level by isolating and investigating criterion or dependent-outcome measures in the context of critical moments of competition.**

Analyzing performance outcome measures (criterion/dependent variables) at the micro level during critical moments of competition is central to determining the impact psychological factors have on performance.

Previous attempts to link psychological factors with performance have not sufficiently reduced performance outcome measures to the micro-level or differentiated critical moments from routine phases of competition. As a result, potential relationships between and among psychological and performance outcome measures may have gone unnoticed. Past research on performance outcome measures for the most part have been (1) too global in nature, (2) contained contrived indices of performance, and/or (3) used comparisons of one psychological construct with another and devoid of objective sport-specific statistical outcome measures. Global measures have included basic performance statistics of specific sports, including won-loss percentage or shooting percentage. Contrived measures have consisted of, for example, distance from the hole when putting (in golf) or other practice tasks and post-hoc self-ratings of performance. Comparisons of the effect of one psychological construct on another using self-report have included comparing the effects of pre-competitive anxiety with post-competition anxiety. The comparison of psychological measures obtained from one self-report with another self-report test is an especially weak predictor of real and objective performance outcomes, since rarely have attempts been made to link associations between psychological constructs that such tests purportedly measure with objective micro-level performance outcome measures. For example, even though the level of self-reported pre-competition anxiety may be associated with the recall of an athlete's perceived competitive anxiety after a match or game, such subjective feedback, unless empirically associated with objective sport-specific micro-level performance outcome measures, remains highly equivocal in terms of what self-report comparisons actually predict (performance outcome).

Unfortunately, researchers have come to rely on contrived macro and/or global criterion (outcome) measures when attempting to investigate psychological influences on performance, even though until the emergence of the Athlete's Profile PHO factors, no psychological measures have been able to explain much of the variance in the performance equation. In that the practice of applied sport psychology is predicated on being able to reliably identify psychological influences on performance, the failure to make significant inroads toward isolating the effects of psychological measures on objective measures of performance outcome is troubling and calls for new approaches to the analysis of athlete mental performance in the context of predictor-criterion variable relationships. An analysis of micro-level moments of competition using advanced methodological and procedural paradigms is predicted to better illuminate the role select psychological and behavioral factors play in differentially facilitating or hindering performance, especially during critical competitive situations that are most likely to induce psychologically mediated performance problems.

3. **The study of psychological factors longitudinally and in the context of multiple objective performance outcome measures.**
Longitudinal and multiple criterion measure approaches to the study of performance are designed to increase the probability that meaningful relationships between psychological predictor and performance outcome (criterion) variables will emerge. Such relationships are not likely to be revealed in singular research or applied attempts to determine if personality traits, specific behavior, and/or psychophysiological activity may have on performance. The discovery of new relationships between and among psychological factors and performance is contingent on the selection of potent psychological predictor variables and reliable performance outcome measures that must be repeatedly documented at the intra-individual level. Reliable predictor and criterion measures are crucial to the predictive capability of any regression model. In studying the influence psychological factors have on performance, one must be sure that performance outcome measures reflect the influences of psychological processes on a sport-specific task. This is

more likely to occur at the micro-level. Longitudinal analyses of critical moments over the course of many games or matches are expected to be the most sensitive for finding strong relationships between psychological factors and performance outcome measure.

POTENT AND MEANINGFUL OBJECTIVE MICRO-OPERATIONALIZATIONS OF PERFORMANCE OUTCOME

Psychological predictor measures, including those that the TCM has identified as the most important predictors of performance, ultimately are most revealing in the context of objective longitudinal micro-operationalizations of performance outcomes, or critical moments of competition. This becomes apparent when one attempts to associate psychological predictor measures with macro- or global measures of performance, where previous research has failed to account for much of the variance in the performance equation on the basis of psychological factors. PHO psychological measures are most likely to demonstrate their effects on performance when outcome measures are sensitive to psychological influences. This will most likely occur at the micro-level or critical moments when attention, physiological reactivity, and thought processes are most vulnerable to being disrupted by psychological influences.

WHAT ARE CRITICAL MOMENTS?

Critical moments can be defined as instances or situations that are pivotal to the successful outcome of a competition. These moments test athletes' ability to perform their best when it counts the most and demands superior control over mind–body processes. In a tennis match, a critical moment could be points in a tie-breaker. In golf, a critical moment might be having to sink a short birdie putt to win a match. In basketball, a critical moment might be a free throw with the game on the line. In football, a less obvious critical moment might occur when a lineman has to block a rusher to prevent pressure from being put on the quarterback at a key juncture of a game.

The TCM hypothesizes that athletes will be more or less vulnerable to psychological influences on performance during critical moments as a function of their Athlete's Profile constellation of PHO factors. The "mentally toughest" athletes are predicted to be those who are capable of suppressing negative psychological influences when it counts the most, a capability that is facilitated by an "ideal" athlete's profile of TCM-isolated PHO factors. These have been elaborated and will be revisited throughout the book.

Critical moments can be operationalized quantitatively using a hierarchical system that rates the impact critical moments are expected to exert on an athlete's psyche, or to what extent certain psychological factors either facilitate or hinder performance. The *Carlstedt Critical Moment Psychological Proficiency Index* (CCMPP-I) uses expert raters consisting of coaches and highly skilled athletes to establish criteria for defining what constitutes a critical moment in specific sports. This involves identifying situations during competition and numerically weighing them in terms of their criticality. The CCMPP-I assigns a *Criticality Weight* (CW; 1–5, with 5 being the most critical) to each point, situation, or play during competition in the context of what an athlete is expected to do in a certain situation (varies as a function of being a team or individual sport). Applied to tennis, the first point of a match might have a CW of 1, whereas a 15–30 point, i.e., when playing against a powerful and efficient server, could receive a CW of 4. An example of a hierarchy of micro-level events or critical moments in baseball might include the following instances (numbered in order of psychological significance from 1 [less critical or global macro event] to 5 [extremely critical micro event]): (1) Batting Average for Season, (2) Batting Average with Player in Scoring Position, (3) Batting Average with Player in Scoring Position with Game Outcome on the Line, (4) Batting

Average with Player in Scoring Position with 2 Outs and Game Outcome on the Line, (5) Batting Average with Player in Scoring Position with Outcome of Playoff Game on the Line.

The criticality level of a competitive moment is not necessarily constant. It can fluctuate dynamically as a function of constantly changing conditions. For example, using the preceding example from tennis, the criticality level 4 associated with a break point opportunity against a good server on a grass court might only receive a level 3 rating during the same situation on a slower surface such as clay, where it is easier to return a serve.

The magnitude of a micro-level critical moment can be used as a predictor variable or as a criterion (outcome) variable, depending upon the design of a study. For example, one could investigate the effect of encountering a magnitude 5 critical moment on HRV, or determine whether persons with more pronounced slow-macro brain potentials (ERPs; see Andreassi, 1995) perform better when encountering magnitude 5 critical moments (e.g., higher batting or shooting average during such moments). Analyses of performance outcome at the micro-level are designed to distinguish more routine moments (macro-moments) of competition that elicit normal or baseline levels of psychophysiological responses from micro-level critical moments that demand the utmost mind–body control or self-regulation. Such distinctions are necessary to better quantify mental toughness. For example, a baseball player with a .350 batting average, a golfer who reaches the green in regulation 85% of the time, or a tennis player ranked in the top 10 in the world may not necessarily be mentally tougher than an athlete having weaker macro-level statistical performance outcome, since macro performance statistics reflect global performance proficiency without sufficiently taking into account performance during micro-level critical moments, when pressure is the greatest and performance counts the most. Without analyzing performance at the micro-level, it is difficult to determine whether a 60% field goal shooter in basketball is really mentally tougher than a 40% shooter or is merely a great technician. An analysis of performance during critical moments might reveal a drop in shooting to 35% in the 60% shooter, while the 40% shooter hits at a rate of 80% during critical moments.

The study of psychological factors and performance at the micro-level involves isolating and investigating competitive moments that are critical to performance outcome or winning. Analyzing micro-level critical moments helps to partition out physical, technical, and motor-ability (talent) variables that drive global performance during routine phases of competition, while isolating and analyzing the impact select psychological factors have on physical, technical, and motor talent variables during critical moments. An analysis of micro-level critical moments is expected to better illuminate the role of psychological factors in differentially facilitating or hindering performance during competitive situations that are most likely to be associated with psychological stress.

The failure to analyze performance outcome measures at the micro-level, or critical moment, can lead to inaccurate evaluations of an athlete's mental toughness by overemphasizing and not controlling confounding physical and technical factors that may be disrupted by psychological influences during critical moments of competition.

It should be noted that one of the reasons for the failure to investigate psychological factors and performance relationships in the context of micro-level outcome measures is that conventional statistics used in most sports are too global in nature. With the exception of baseball, few sports analyze performance statistically at the micro-level, although even statistics from this sport do not extend to the most micro-levels of criticality. Unfortunately, researchers attempting to associate psychological factors with performance have had to rely on available outcome statistics that may not be sensitive enough to reflect the influence of most psychological measures on performance. This problem was acknowledged by Piedmont, Hill, and Blanco (1999), who in an attempt to link personality traits with objective performance outcome measures, had trouble finding meaningful and sensitive statistics that were kept on soccer players that reflected psychological performance. As such, they were only able to account for about 5% of the variance in the performance equations that could be attributed to the Big-5 psychological traits that they were investigating.

Future studies of psychological factors and performance outcome statistics should integrate psychological, or micro-level critical moment statistics, to increase the probability of explaining more of the statistical variance in the performance equation that can be attributed to psychological factors.

MEDIATORS OF CRITICAL MOMENT PERFORMANCE

The TCM attributes how critical moments are dealt with or mastered by athletes to conscious and/or unconscious/subliminal thought processes that differentially facilitate or hinder performance. The TCM hypothesizes that select PHO personality and behavioral measures that have been shown to mediate thought processes and subsequent physiological and motor responding in clinical situations can also affect performance (see HRMTP). Interactions or constellations of these PHO measures are thought to impact performance by differentially influencing the cognition and psychophysiology of athletes, especially as a function of increasing sport-situational criticality. These PHO factors, which form the Athlete's Profile, induce susceptible athletes to either fixate on or ignore intrusive and negative thoughts that occur during a game's most critical moments as a function of their specific profile. Fixation on negative intrusive thoughts leading to undesirable shifts in relative brain hemispheric activation, physiological functioning, and motor responses are thought more likely to occur in athletes exhibiting the most negative constellation of PHO factors. By contrast, athletes who possess the most performance-facilitative constellation of PHO factors are more likely to focus on strategic planning and carrying out effective motor and tactical responses and are capable of suppressing negative intrusive thoughts. This latter response tendency facilitates shifts in cerebral laterality that are associated with optimal cardiovascular and motor responding and performance (see HRD).

Potential negative manifestations of certain constellations of PHO factors are expected to remain relatively dormant until critical moments during competition when the conscious or unconscious perception of threat leads to the disruption of attention and motor skills. Conversely, ideal constellations of PHO factors that also lie relatively dormant during routine phases of competition will insulate athletes from the conscious or unconscious perception of threat during critical moments and facilitate peak physical, tactical, and technical performance. Athletes who have the most negative PHO constellations are more likely to perceive threat during critical moments and experience autonomic nervous system (ANS)-mediated disruptions of attention and motor skills. Moreover, they will be less likely to recover and overcome episodic poorer performance compared to athletes who have an ideal athlete's profile of PHO personality and behavioral measures.

The TCM also maintains that successful athletes cannot automatically be considered mentally tough, since technically proficient and physically superior athletes are often capable of dominating competition to such an extent that they infrequently encounter critical moments during competition. By contrast, technically and physically weaker athletes who possess the ideal Athlete's Profile of PHO traits and behaviors can compensate psychologically for technical and physical deficiencies during critical moments. For example, a highly ranked or rated athlete not in possession of an ideal PHO constellation might still routinely defeat less-skilled opponents who possess an ideal PHO constellation, but remain vulnerable to defeat or to being outplayed during critical moments of competition and eventually lose to lesser opponents who are mentally tougher when it counts.

However, this does not preclude that successful athletes can excel both technically and mentally and exhibit an ideal Athlete's Profile as well. There is not a linear relationship between success as an athlete as measured in conventional terms (e.g., won-loss record) and mental toughness.

The High-Risk Model of Threat Perception: Conceptual Origin of the Athlete's Profile Model

Emerging and converging evidence support the perspective that the mind and body are inextricably linked and function in an integrative manner to mediate the manifestation of maladaptive autonomic nervous system (ANS) responses that can result in symptoms and eventual illness, and in the realm of sports, drive competitive anxiety, reduced attention, diminished motor control, and consequent poor performance. In addition, similar psychological profiles consisting of traits and behavioral tendencies that have been isolated as playing an important role in the etiology of disease and mental disorders have been found to differentially impact performance. Identifiable mind–body processes and interactions that have been harnessed therapeutically to ameliorate symptoms and promote well-being have also been shown to enhance self-regulation and improve performance (Carlstedt, 2009; Moss, McGrady, Davies, & Wickramasekera, 2003).

While this may be common knowledge to some, what has not been *adequately explicated* and *disseminated* to frontline practitioners are plausible integrative conceptual/explanatory frameworks that guide athlete assessment and intervention beyond the cursory. For example, a sport psychologist could readily arrive at a diagnosis of competitive anxiety on the basis of self-report and subsequently initiate cognitive behavioral therapy (CBT) in an attempt to eliminate symptoms that an athlete may have. However, what is the probability that a specific athlete will be amenable to CBT or capable of engaging in, let alone benefitting from it? What can be done to obtain greater insight into key psychological processes and behaviors that are crucial to the athlete assessment and intervention that is not readily apparent at face value? Could a practitioner, using a conceptually sound or relevant assessment battery or strategy, at intake, be able to predict intervention amenability and compliance as well as mind–body response tendencies at baseline and in response to an intervention? Moreover, to what extent could a course of intervention be tracked, monitored, and analyzed in the context of real-world stimuli and stressors to establish the efficacy of a mental training modality? Importantly, what analytic methods can be used to determine statistically at the level of the individual athlete, longitudinal changes in mind–body responses, especially in ecological settings, for future comparative purposes and the development of individualized databases of neuropsychophysiological functioning, symptom manifestation during training and competition, cognitive and motor performance, well-being, and performance outcome (intervention efficacy).

Increasing levels (in terms of evidentiary value) of assessment, intervention, efficacy testing, and general analysis of mind–body functioning are necessary to adequately address critical sport psychological issues that can impact the athlete evaluation and mental training process. Reaching diagnostic conclusions on the basis of athlete self-report and practitioner intuition, without further testing and insight into what are often subliminal mind–body processes and cognitions that can affect the accuracy of a diagnosis, intervention selection, and efficacy, is no longer tenable.

An integrative and conceptually (construct validity) based approach extends beyond initial impressions and practitioner assumptions to higher levels in the information, analytic, and evidence hierarchy. It includes multifaceted assessment batteries and intervention procedures, efficacy testing, longitudinal monitoring, and data acquisition and storage methods for descriptive–exploratory–diagnostic, inferential-analytic and clinical research purposes.

Central to such an all-encompassing integrative approach are models that enhance the accuracy of the investigative/diagnostic process and potency/efficacy of interventions. Such models should have isolated predictor/independent and criterion/outcome variables and interactions among PHO individual differences factors that are intimately associated with or linked to key components or mediators in performance equation, including external attending to stimuli (attention), physiological reactivity (ANS activation) and internal/subliminal cognitive processing/strategic planning/coping (subliminal attention).

One particular promising model, the High Risk Model of Threat Perception (HRMTP) is explicated below (Wickramasekera, 1988). The Athlete's Profile and Brain–Mind–Heart–Motor models of peak performance emanate from the HRMTP. Conceptualized in the 1980s on the basis of independent lines of research in the realm of psychophysiology, health and personality psychology, behavioral medicine, and genetics, this model has generated over 100 peer-reviewed publications, but as is frequently the case in the mental health, behavioral medicine, and sport psychological realm, sometimes the best models and research are not adequately disseminated across disciplines and end up languishing in the archives (Addis, 2002). However, since the HRMTP is integrative and highly plausible in accounting for a host of clinical issues and phenomena relating to patient diagnosis and intervention, it should be revisited and seriously considered by researchers and practitioners alike. Clinicians who have used the HRMTP to guide practice have come to appreciate its diagnostic sensitivity and ability to predict intervention amenability and outcome (McGrady, Lynch, Nagel, & Zsembik, 1999). As such, it has become a niche/insider research and practice model that should be receiving wider scrutiny and consideration by researchers and practitioners alike.

INTRODUCTION: BACKGROUND

The High Risk Model of Threat Perception (HRMTP; Wickramasekera, 1988) is a theoretical and applied model that attempts to assess and predict the risks specific mind–body interactions pose for the development of psychological and physical symptoms and illness. It has isolated a set of PHO risk factors (predictor variables) that have been shown to increase stress, drive physical symptoms, and influence intervention amenability, compliance, and efficacy. These factors are (1) hypnotic susceptibility (HS), (2) neuroticism (N), and repressive coping (RC). In contrast to more well-known guiding conceptual foundations that have made their way into clinical manuals and handbooks, including the Stress-Moderation, Constitutional Predisposition, and Illness-Behavior models, along with independent/singular constructs such as Type-A personality, neuroticism, hardiness, and optimism that tend to be unidimensional in their composition, the HRMTP advances multidimensional (integrative) driving hypotheses, predictions, research designs, and clinical procedures (see Hogan, Johnson, & Briggs, 1997, for an overview of the earlier-cited competing models and constructs). The HRMTP emerged from a comprehensive review of competing insular models in health psychology and behavioral medicine. It led to the isolation of the earlier-mentioned PHO individual differences factors, using an integrative diagnostic and intervention framework as being primary mediators in the health and mental health equation. The preceding measures have also emerged as PHO factors in the performance equation and will be presented in a sport psychological context throughout this book.

In addition to its comprehensive system of patient evaluation, the HRMTP also advances an eclectic multifaceted approach to intervention consisting of psychophysiological psychotherapy, hypnosis, biofeedback, and cognitive-behavioral therapy (Wickramasekera, 1988). Adaptations of these interventions made their way into the mental training arena as well. The application of these interventions is based on constellations of the so-called risk factors (see below) that have been shown to predict intervention amenability. For example, a patient or athlete who is high in HS and N and low in RC would not be given the same intervention as a patient or athlete exhibiting the opposite profile. The HRMTP approach does not assume that everyone will necessarily benefit from the same intervention and has demonstrated that a discriminating and individual-differences-based approach to treatment is more effective than the application of interventions *en masse*.

A major goal of the HRMTP approach to intervention is to illuminate and document *incongruence* between verbal reports of distress and the actual underlying psychophysiology of patients during episodes of dysfunctional behavior, somatic complaints and illness, or, in the case of athletes, determining the validity of expressed performance complaints on the basis of mind–body response patterns.

Depending on a patient's constellation of risk factors, his or her verbal report of pain or distress is more or less likely to be consistent with actual medical tests and/or psychophysiological data. For example, somaticizers and hypochondriacs, most of whom appear to be high in HS and N and low in RC, often report acute pain and distress that cannot be substantiated or validated on the basis of objective clinical tests. By contrast, many patients who are low in HS and N and high in RC tend to not report symptoms or psychological distress, yet tests reveal that they have medical disorders or psychological problems that they were not consciously aware of. Exposing such mind–body incongruence is accomplished by continuously monitoring the physiology of patients during psychotherapy, or by comparing self-report with objective medical tests. Ultimately, psychophysiological and medical data is used to validate concurrently or refute a patient's self-report to arrive at a more accurate diagnosis and to intervene appropriately to alleviate symptoms and maladaptive behavior. The same preceding profiles frequently exert their effects in a unique manner in athletes. For example, an athlete who is high in HS and N and low in RC is prone to psychological complaints related to competition. By contrast, athletes who are low in HS and N and high in RC tend to be more impervious to psychological distress during competition.

The ability to expose mind–body incongruence is central to the HRMTP intervention strategy, since there is a tendency on the part of practitioners to readily believe that "what you see is what you get" when it comes to patient body language, verbalizations, and self-report, despite documented inconsistencies between external behavior, behavioral cues, and actual internal (subliminal) psychophysiological reactivity (Wickramasekera, 1988). Inaccurate interpretations of the meaning of patients' body language, verbalizations, and self-report can lead to faulty diagnoses and clinical decisions, as well as inappropriate application of interventions. For example, just because a patient or athlete exhibits supposedly normal body language does not necessarily mean that he or she is not experiencing underlying elevated SNS reactivity or hypertension. Overtly noticeable body language also can be a temporally isolated (post-facto) reaction to a preceding event, a response that is often fleeting that does not accurately reflect a patient's or athlete's predominant autonomic nervous system state. For example, patients and athletes who verbally express anger are not necessarily out of control psychologically. An inciting incident during competition or animated response to therapist questioning does not necessarily warrant an immediate diagnosis of, say, anger management disorder. It is presumptuous to assume that body language, verbalizations, or self-report will reveal the same thing in all patients and athletes, as though a facial expression or verbal emoting in one patient or athlete will have the same concomitant physiological responses in another one (Carlstedt, 2004a, 2004b). Consequently, according to the HRMTP, it is important to continuously monitor and analyze the physiology of patients (and athletes) during psychotherapy before attaching clinical meaning to patient body language, verbalizations, and self-report. Unfortunately, physiological monitoring of patients and athletes is rarely done, making it difficult to validate concurrently or criterion reference practitioner analyses of patients' and athlete behavior or self-report. However, without knowing the underlying physiology of a patient or athlete, it is speculative to assume congruence exists between the observable behavior and what a practitioner believes it to mean.

The HRMTP approach to interventions has shown that in addition to revealing mind–body incongruence, shifts in physiological reactivity that are elicited during psychotherapy or mental training reflect the *perception of threat* moving from unconscious to conscious memory, an event that is thought to occur when conflict is brought to the consciousness (Wickramasekera, 1988). The concept of perception of threat is another central tenet of the HRMTP, with differential interactions of HS, N, and RC and their manifestations on health and performance expected to be the greatest under conditions of high stress, when one's perceived well-being is threatened (e.g., sense of fear and loss of control during competition). Dramatic change in physiological reactivity in response to stimuli that is presented during psychotherapy or mental training is thought to reflect unconscious conflict or perception of threat reaching conscious awareness. Such an occurrence is associated with an increase in psychological distress, but also frequently leads to an attenuation of maladaptive physiological reactivity, behavior, and symptoms (Wickramasekera, 1988). For example, a patient or athlete being monitored during psychotherapy or mental training, and even at intake when being questioned, may exhibit a highly reactive physiological profile (e.g., high HR at baseline, excessive sweat activity) yet admit to no psychological distress, and then suddenly, upon acknowledging previously repressed trauma, conflict, or performance issues, experience sudden reduced physiological reactivity. A person who finally reveals a previously unacknowledged emotion (e.g., being unhappy about a relationship, or poor play during a match) often exhibits an immediate reduction in baseline and chronically present levels of SNS arousal and accompanying physical complaints (e.g., excessive muscle tension, fatigue) as suppressed feelings and thoughts come to consciousness. Immediately thereafter, the person may feel conscious psychological distress associated with a new awareness of an issue he or she did not want to confront, but is nevertheless pleasantly surprised when the chronic symptoms attenuate (Wickramasekera, 1988). Once this occurs, patients are on their way to achieving or restoring mind–body harmony or homeostasis.

According to Wickramasekera (1988), the previously described dynamic psychophysiological processes reflect *secrets that are kept from the mind, but not the body*. In other words, you can try to fool yourself, but you cannot fool your body. The HRMTP predicts that specific interactions or constellations of risk factors (hypnotic susceptibility, neuroticism, and repressive coping) are sufficient to account for somatic complaints, or positive physical findings. Similarly, PHO Athlete's Profile constellations have emerged as potent predictors of peak performance. However, performance problems of a psychological nature can be more complex because of the motor or technical components that must be controlled concomitant to a mental training intervention. Instead of just trying to control one's emotions in an attempt to reduce stress or distress, which almost always requires the inducement of a relaxation response, in sports, interventions should attempt to manipulate and control activation or physiological reactivity at a level that is higher than in a relaxation response (i.e., more SNS activation). Nevertheless, irrespective of interventional fine tuning as a function of a client population, the conceptual foundation (construct validity) of the HRMTP and the sister Athlete's Profile model of peak performance that evolved from it, essentially use the same methods and procedures to ultimately arrive at a diagnosis or facilitate positive functional change through intervention (clinical) or assess and illuminate the etiology of performance issues and improve performance through mental training (sport psychological).

Conceptual Basis of the HRMTP

INTRODUCTION

To fully appreciate and understand the HRMTP and its adaptation to sports and athletes, it should be thoroughly reviewed. While some readers may wonder why a book on sport psychology is devoting so much space to a clinical model, it cannot be stressed enough that the royal road to high evidentiary, gold standard athlete assessment and intervention is a long and complex one. It is integrative and encompasses key research, procedures, and methods from the domains of clinical psychology, behavioral medicine, neuropsychology, psychophysiology, and neuroscience to name a few. Practitioners would be well advised to go far beyond the arena of sport psychology in their quest to provide high-level evidence-based practice. As previously mentioned, the field of sport psychology has been remiss in not being more integrative, and as a result has tended to advance and propagate assessment and interventions that are in many cases substandard and antiquated. It is suggested that when reading the, for the most part, clinical research background of the HRMTP, an attempt should be made to view the presented material creatively and imagine it being integrated into sport psychological and athlete scenarios. Such a process was engaged in when adapting this model to athletes and developing the construct validity of the HRMTP. Sport or athlete relevant comments are presented in bold to help link, what may seem to some, as disparate findings and information to performance.

BACKGROUND

The conceptual origins of the HRMTP can be traced to a wide-ranging body of theory and research that has implicated chronic stress as a primary mediator of cardiovascular disease and cancer, which are today's major causes of debilitation and death (Oeppen & Vaupel, 2002).[3] Whereas earlier in the century mortality was the greatest for infectious diseases (e.g., the plague, polio, small pox, etc.), or what Wickramasekera (1988) refers to as "diseases of chance," today, behavioral and environmental factors are recognized as key mediators of morbidity and mortality. It has been estimated that about 80% of the visits to primary care physicians involve chronic diseases such as arthritis, asthma, diabetes, and cardiovascular disease, with 50% of all deaths being attributable to an unhealthy lifestyle or so-called diseases of choice (Wickramasekera, 1988). The landscape of illness today is marked more by chronic stress-related diseases in which psychological factors and behavioral choices are central to their prevention and treatment. Mounting evidence suggests that cognition and emotion interact to affect behavior and lifestyle choices that can exacerbate, alleviate, or prevent and protect individuals from chronic medical disorders (e.g., House, Landis, & Umberson, 1988; Lepore, Mata, & Evans, 1993; O'Leary, 1990).

Wickramasekera (1988, 2003), in advancing the HRMTP, originally isolated nine factors that are hypothesized to increase the risk for developing stress-related physical symptoms and disease, including "subject variables," which are thought to predispose an individual to illness, "situational variables" or inciting "trigger" events that often precipitate illness, and "buffers" that play a protective role in preventing symptoms and illness. Subject variables include (1) hypnotic susceptibility (HS), (2) neuroticism (N), and (3) repressive coping (RC). Depending upon their constellation and interactions (e.g., high HS, high N, and low RC) these measures have been found to be potent predictors of symptom and illness onset, intervention amenability, and compliance and efficacy (Wickramasekera, 1988, 2003). Situational variables that include triggers, such as major life changes (e.g., loss of one's job; a divorce) and/or multiple "hassles" that occur over a short period of time (e.g., family issues; conflict with one's boss) are thought to increase the negative effects of select subject variable constellations. By contrast, protective buffers, including social support systems (e.g., positive interpersonal relationship; friends) and advanced coping skills for managing psychosocial stressors (e.g., proficiency in meditation) are predicted to attenuate the negative influence of constellations of subject variables and serve a protective role in staving off illness (Wickramasekera, 1988, 2003; Weinberger, 1990).

Although is it conceivable that the preceding situational variables can impact sport performance, only the HRMTP subject variables have been investigated in athletes because of methodological issues relating to establishing longitudinal links between variables that cannot be repeatedly measured on a daily basis and multiple times during training and competition. However, this does not detract from the potential clinical or diagnostic utility relative to athlete assessment, and further research into their possible performance-related dynamics is encouraged. It should be emphasized that the ABSP-CP approach is primarily concerned with assessing and manipulating performance in the moment during actual training and competition, irrespective of or despite off-the-playing-field psychological life issues that have to be diffused for periods of competition, otherwise there is little point in an athlete showing up if personal situation factors are so overwhelming that peak performance is virtually impossible. If that is the case, we are getting more into the clinical realm. It is conceivable that an extension of the ABSP-CP assessment battery will measure these situational and other variables of interest, provided they can measured repeatedly prior to, during, and after training and competition (e.g., using a stated measure of the impact of buffers prior to competition).

In order to better understand how the preceding risk and protective factors interact to impact the course of symptoms and illness, an overview of the conceptual bases of these measures is presented.

Subject Variables

The following measures will also be discussed in a sport performance context after an elaboration of the HRMTP.

HIGH HYPNOTIC SUSCEPTIBILITY (HSS)

Hypnotic susceptibility (HS) is considered a stable individual difference trait that may be partially genetically determined (Fromm & Nash, 2003). An individual's level of HS is crucial to hypnosis, which can be defined as a psychophysiological state that is marked by an alteration of attention and reduction of cognitive awareness and critical-analytic thinking, and leads to major distortions in perception, mood, and memory, as well as significant behavioral and biological changes (Wickramasekera, 1988).

Research suggests that HS is a mode of information processing occurring under various conditions, but most often during states of high or low physiological arousal (Wickramasekera, 1988). HS can be viewed as an omnipresent and ongoing cognitive state independent of actually being hypnotized. About 10% to 15% of the population can either readily access the hypnotic mode of information processing, or are incapable of doing so, which also reflects the distribution of population extremes in this trait (High HS [HHS] vs. Low [LHS] HS; ca. 10%–15%; Wickramasekera, 1988).

While people who are high in HS possess an increased ability to intensely focus on the task at hand, in the context of health, HHS can lead to maladaptive cognitive responses, including the belief that minor physical sensations signal major illness. Such distorted attending is thought more likely to occur if an individual is concurrently high in the second subject variable, N. The interaction of high HS and high N is thought to lead to fixation on negative and catastrophic cognitions and associated visceral sensations and symptoms that occur in high neurotics, especially as a function of heightened stress. By contrast, people who are low in HS attend too little to physical sensations and physiological responses and are less attuned to emotions and cognitions that may precede or occur, concurrent to bodily reactions (Wickramasekera, 1988).

In athletes, HHS can interact with high N to disrupt performance, especially as competitive pressure (critical moments) increases or when threat is perceived.

The neuropsychophysiological mechanisms of HS appear to have clinical implications with Wickramasekera (1988), finding that 85% of a sample of 103 patients who exhibited somatic symptoms were either very high or very low in HS. Three features of both high and low HS are thought to increase the risk for developing psychophysiological (mind–body) disorders. First, the ability to hallucinate voluntarily and generate rich and vivid images of seeing, hearing, feeling, and smelling and engaging in fantasy activity up to 50% of waking time that is common to HHS is thought to have physiological consequences and likely to lead to somatic conditions.

A second feature contributing to risk in people who are high in HS is hypersensitivity to psychological and physiological change. Hypersensitivity is thought to be a learned process of symptom induction, whereby an individual who is high in HS exhibits a superior sensory memory or ability to transfer information from sensory to short-term memory (Ingram, Saccuzzo, McNeil, & McDonald, 1979; Saccuzzo, Safnan, Anderson, & McNeil, 1982). Wickramasekera (1988) hypothesizes that people who are high in HS learn, remember, and consolidate the experience of acute symptoms and pain too well, thereby allowing it to become a chronic pain disorder. On the basis of this interpretation, one could predict, for example, that, patients with chronic or refractory back pain of a functional nature are likely to be high in HS.

The preceding suggests that athletes who are high in HS may be more likely to consolidate the events, thoughts, and emotions that were associated with poor performance, especially if they are concurrently high in N. By contrast, if they are low in N, athletes may use their superior sensory memory to readily recall instances of peak performance and its concomitant performance facilitative thoughts, emotions, and technical responses.

Another possible learning mechanism of symptom induction may be the HHS individual's hypersensitivity to sensory stimuli and a superior ability to discriminate between visceral sensations. For example, without analgesic suggestions, people who are high in HS are less tolerant of pain than people who are low in HS (Barabaez, 1983; Wickramasekera, 1988). People who are high in HS also have been found to have an unusual capacity for attention to and absorption in subjective events like pain and fear (Tellegen & Atkinson, 1974). This ability may be used to magnify their response to even minimal sensory and visceral stimuli (Wickramasekera, 1988). The preceding not only highlights maladaptive attention to pain and symptoms on the part of individuals who are high in HS, but their ability to attenuate pain and symptoms by using their enhanced focusing ability, provided they are administered or engage in an intervention modality that is ideally suited to them (e.g., clinical hypnosis).

> *The preceding suggests that athletes who are high in HS are less tolerant of pain, a characteristic that could impact the ability to perform for long periods of time that can be associated with muscle pain and tiredness.*

A third feature contributing to risk in people who are high in HS is their ability to voluntarily alter states of consciousness and memory functions (Evans, 1977; Kilhstrom, 1987). These abilities may be a protective reflex for dealing with biological hypersensitivity (Wickramasekera, 1988). For example, people who are high in HS can easily induce sleep at different times in diverse locations, can wake up at preselected times without an alarm, and are capable of learning during sleep without waking up. Retention of simple information from such state-dependent learning has been demonstrated up to 6 months (Evans, 1977). It appears that maladaptive and/or aversive physiological responses can be learned in states of hyperarousal or hypoarousal (such as sleep). Wickramasekera (1988) proposes that negative-aversive expectations may alter the content of REM dreams and establish maladaptive patterns of muscular and vascular responses in sleep. Furthermore, people who are high in HS can readily learn fear and pain responses, but are unaware of what was learned and where it was learned. Thus, the phenomena of incidental learning, source amnesia, or state-dependent learning that is associated with HHS may be the basis of the strong resistance to extinction of overlearned and consolidated maladaptive responses associated with the development of somatic illness (Wickramasekera, 1988).

LOW HYPNOTIC SUSCEPTIBILITY (LHS)

People who are low in HS also display three features putting them at increased risk for developing somatic symptoms or illness. These include (1) hyposensitivity to psychological and physiological changes; (2) a tendency to deny psychological causation of symptoms and feelings; and (3) delay in seeking medical investigation (Wickramasekera, 1988).

People who are low in HS are relatively insensitive to or deficient in attention to interrelationships between psychological (verbal-emotional) and physiological (proprioceptive-interoceptive) states (Wickramasekera, 1988). They tend to engage a skeptical, critical, and analytic mode of information processing, and tend to deny or attenuate minimal sensory cues from their bodies. They tend to lack or do not want to use verbal fantasy and imagination, and prefer to think in specific and distinct terms. LHS appears to be linked to alexithymia, a disorder that is characterized by an individual's lack of ability to use words to describe moods and emotions. It was first identified in people with psychosomatic disorders by Sifneos, Apfel-Savitz, and Frankel (1977), who found that 73% of individuals who were classified as being low in HS were alexithymic compared to only 8% of individuals who were high in HS. Alexithymics tend to attribute psychological changes to external physical changes and are likely to verbally inhibit or deny their feelings. When viewed in the context of trauma, their verbal inhibition has been associated with higher levels of physiological reactivity (Pennebaker, 1985). Consequently, for individuals who are low in HS, somatic symptoms may be the physiological manifestation of the verbal inhibition of trauma and psychosocial conflicts (Wickramasekera, 1988).

People who are low in HS may also be inhibited in resetting dysfunctional neurogenic (hypothalmic–pituitary–adrenal) feedback systems after stress incidents. That is, arousal levels or excessive SNS reactivity only slowly return to baseline states. Wickramasekera (1988) hypothesizes that the ability to enter states of altered consciousness that of which persons of HHS are capable (e.g., hypnosis), may facilitate the use of central nervous system (CNS) processes like suggestion to reset dysfunctional peripheral (autonomic nervous system; ANS) feedback systems. For example, the neurogenic regulation of BP through the resetting of baroreceptors, thereby restoring homeostasis after a stress incident, may involve such dynamics (Cannon, 1932). Individuals who are low in HS also appear to be more susceptible to psychosocial stress disorders because they are less aware of psychological stressors and deny the role of psychological factors in driving physical dysfunction (Wickramasekera, 1988).

Athletes who are low in HS may benefit from a more critical and analytic style of information process and appear to be less vulnerable to negative intrusive thoughts than athletes who are high in HS. The physiological manifestation of verbal inhibition of distress may actually be beneficial for attaining states of activation that are performance facilitative. While a slow return to baseline has health implications in more sedentary individuals who are low in HS, athletes, at least over the course of their career, seem not to be impacted by this response tendency. This may be attributable to physiological mechanisms associated with constant, intense movement (exercise).

NEUROTICISM

The second risk factor for developing somatic illness or symptomology in the HRMTP triad is neuroticism (N). A high level of N is associated with the tendency to recognize and recall predominantly aversive past memories (Wickramasekera, 1988). N is considered to be a longitudinally stable trait independent of objective stress. In clinical samples, there is frequently large incongruence between self-report of distress and direct psychophysiological measures of stress (Wickramasekera, 1988). High neuroticism is associated with lability of the autonomic nervous system (ANS) and hyper-reactivity of the SNS and appears to have a genetic origin (Eysenck, 1960; Shields, 1962). Self-report of N has been linked to the limbic system by Eysenck (1983) and is manifested psychophysiologically by elevated baseline levels of muscle tension (EMG), skin conductance (EDA), HR, BP, and delays in returning to baseline after episodes of stress (Eysenck, 1983). High N appears to be an unjustified and exaggerated amplification of physical concerns and manifestation of functional symptoms as opposed to a sign of physical disease per se (Geen 1997; Wickramasekera, 1988).

The tendency to exhibit a consistently elevated ANS response profile appears to have clinical implications. For example, people showing maximum physiological reactivity in the cardiovascular system may be at high risk for developing myocardial infarction or stroke (Krantz & Manuck, 1984) whereas those who exhibit hyper-reactive responses in specific muscles may be at greatest risk for chronic back pain or tension headache conditions (Flor, Turk, & Birbaumer, 1985; Philips, 1977).

Wickramasekera (1988) views the most physiological reactive system as an individual's "window of maximum vulnerability" for developing clinical symptoms when under stress (p. 17).

High N frequently leads to catastrophizing. In earlier conceptualizations of the HRMTP, catastrophizing was presented in its own right as an independent risk factor (Wickramasekera, 1988). However, more recently, catastrophizing, which is marked by a tendency to expect the worst to happen when looking at the future, has been viewed more as a consequence of interactions between HHS and high N (Wickramasekera, 1988). Catastrophizing can involve becoming frequently and intensely absorbed in negative psychological or sensory events and exaggerating aversive properties of such events with negative self-talk or auto-suggestion. Catastrophizing has at least two response components. First, attentional focus is kept on the sensory or visceral events that are associated with symptoms and, second, remembering or anticipating a wide variety of negative physical and psychosocial consequences and antecedents of the aversive or symptomatic event (Wickramasekera, 1988). It is hypothesized that many internal and/or external cues that trigger catastrophizing are outside of conscious awareness (Dixon, 1981). Numerous studies have linked catastrophizing to somatic complaints. For example, Chaves and Brown (1978) found that the majority of chronic pain patients are catastrophizers and have higher pain ratings than the so-called copers. In addition, 86% of catastrophizers requested antianxiety or antidepressant medication to deal with psychological stress that was associated with their pain, compared to only 12% of copers (Chaves & Brown, 1978). Wickramasekera (1988) proposed that the predisposition to experience spontaneous panic attacks that is central to the formation of phobias is mediated by catastrophizing cognitions that subjectively reduce pain tolerance, spiral anxiety, and generate self-report of hopelessness. Moreover, it appears that chronic pain, panic, fear disorders, and depression may have common biological bases involving serotonin and norepinephrine metabolism (Sternbach, Janowsky, Huey, & Segal, 1976).

> *The preceding psychological and cognitive processes that are associated with high N can impact sport performance negatively. As such, high N can be considered the "great" disrupter of peak performance, since the fear and worry that pervades the high N's life, in an athlete, transfers to the playing field to undermine focus and motor control; even more so in the presence of high HS.*

REPRESSIVE COPING

Repressive coping (RC) is the third risk factor in the HRMTP triad. It is characterized by implicit (unconscious) defensiveness and the tendency to inhibit affect. The Malowe Crown scale is frequently used to measure this capacity for blocking negative perceptions, memories, and moods from consciousness, a style of coping that appears to promote inattention to aversive situations and the amplification of positive situations (Crowne & Marlowe, 1960; Wickramasekera, 1988). Individuals who are high in RC frequently exhibit incongruence between subjective positive self-report and physiological and behavioral indicators of distress, and tend to have a poor memory for negative emotional experiences (Lane, Merikangas, Schwarz, Huang, & Pushoff, 1990; Weinberger, Schwartz, & Davidson, 1979; Wickramasekera, 1996). The self-deception associated with RC appears to make individuals who are high in this trait susceptible to developing somatic and/or behavioral symptoms (Lane et al., 1990). By contrast, people who are low in RC are considered less adept at self-deception, appear more likely to experience psychological symptoms such as depression and anxiety, but less likely to experience psychophysiological symptoms (Lane et al., 1990; Wickramasekera, 1988).

Repressive coping has also been viewed as a "self-enhancing cognitive style" that promotes the rapid dampening of negative affective responses to stressors, maintenance, or enhancement of self-esteem and a lowered risk for psychopathology (Tomarken & Davidson, 1994, p. 339). Neurophysiological studies of RC have led some researchers to characterize repressive coping as a "functional disconnection syndrome" between the left hemisphere and other cortical or subcortical regions that mediate autonomic and neuroendocrine components of affective responsivity (Davidson, 1984; Schwartz, 1990). For example, Davidson (1984) demonstrated relative deficits in interhemispheric transfer of negative affect from the right to the left hemisphere. This deficit in reduced cross-callosal transfer of aversive information is thought to account for reduced psychopathology in people who are high in RC (Tomarken & Davidson, 1994). The heightened ANS and endocrine activation that is frequently exhibited by individuals who are high in RC is thought to reflect the mobilization of processes that inhibit distress, facilitate goal-oriented behavior, or both (Tomarken & Davidson, 1994). Repressive and defensive coping styles have also been associated with impaired immune function and increased risk and worsened prognosis in neoplastic diseases. In their opioid-peptide hypothesis of repression, Jammer, Schwarz, and Leigh (1988) propose that repressive coping is associated with increases in the level of endorphin in the brain and can lead to diminished immunocompetence and hyperglycemia. In support of their hypothesis, they found that repressive and high-anxious patients demonstrated significantly decreased monocyte counts, elevated eosinophil and serum glucose levels, and increased self-report of reactions to medications.

Specific to the HRMTP, mechanisms of RC are hypothesized to block the perception of threat from consciousness and is considered a psychological mechanism that can increase the incongruence between subjective perception (consciousness of threat) and physiological or behavioral markers of threat perception (Wickramasekera, Davies, & Davies, 1996).

> High RC can be viewed as the "great" facilitator of zone states. Athletes who are high in RC appear impervious to psychological distress during competition, even when pressure is thought to be the greatest (critical moments). Similar to low HS, in non-athletes, high RC has negative health consequences. Active athletes, however, seem not to be impacted. Instead, the mechanisms that block perceptions of threat from reaching consciousness and promote the repression of negative intrusive thoughts appear to facilitate psychological performance in athletes.

It should be noted that HRMTP subject variables are hypothesized to primarily exert their influence as risk factors in the context of the perception of threat of both objective and subjectively perceived and subliminal stressors.

> This is a very important tenet of the HRMTP. During life situations and psychological states that are pleasant or innocuous and devoid of overt stress, HRMTP subject or PHO measures are more likely to exert positive effects that are associated with them. For example, if an individual with high HS starts to read a book or watch a film, he or she may become so absorbed to the point of being oblivious to, for example, someone arguing loudly in the near vicinity. Consequently, this ability to become intensely engaged in a salient task of interest is what makes the person who is high in HS an ideal candidate for hypnosis as an intervention to attenuate symptoms. Essentially, it takes actual situational-induced stress or the perception of stress (a subliminal

process) to set off a cascade of interactions between and among subject of PHO that can lead to symptoms or distress. If the person reading the book who is high in HS happens to also be high in N, the intense focus on what is being read can be quickly diverted to the external noise and lead to catastrophic cognitions of fear that sets off a panic attack. In such a case, HS, if a threshold is met, can lead to fixation on a situation that may not be that dangerous, but in the mind of the high HS and high N individual, it is magnified to the point of eliciting great fear and concomitant excessive physiological reactivity and symptoms. The same dynamic is evident in sports, where PHO measures have been found to remain dormant until critical moments during competition occur.

Original Predictions from the HRMTP

In addition to the preceding hypothesized processes associated with PHO subject variables, the HRMTP makes the following specific predictions:

1. The development of somatic symptomology and illness is *always* a function of multidimensional interactions among psychological risk factors and genetics.

This prediction can be considered the PHO tenet of the HRMTP. It states that specific constellations of HRMTP-identified risk factors are potent enough to mediate differential neuropsychophysiological responses to stress and that these factors have primacy or higher-order functional and mediating dominance over all other psychological factors in affecting ANS reactivity. Isolated HRMTP subject variables are expected to strongly influence symptomology, morbidity, and clinical outcome.

The preceding applies similarly to athlete performance issues with psychological problems during competition being mediated by interactions of specific PHO traits and behaviors. All psychological factors, including those that may appear to be or are related to HS, N, and RC, are subordinate to and mediated by these PHO measures. For example, the construct competitive anxiety (CA) can be considered a lower-order factor of N, which ultimately drives the manifestation of symptoms associated with the aforementioned performance measure (CA).

2. The trait neuroticism and state of negative affect are essential but not sufficient for the development of psychosomatic symptoms and illness.

This implies that neuroticism and negative affect play central roles in the etiology of symptoms and illness and can be referred to as the "Great Mediators" of maladaptive neuropsychophysiological responses to stress. However, maladaptive manifestations of N are most likely to occur in the context of the perception of threat to real or perceived stress, in the presence of high HS.

Similarly, in the context of athletes, high N plays a critical role in mediating performance detrimental BMHM responses. In the absence of actual and perceived competitive stress, however, it may remain dormant. High N can also be potentiated and is more likely to manifest itself in the presence of high HS.

3. Individuals who are high in HS and low in RC are more likely to develop both psychological and somatic symptoms. By contrast, those who are low in HS and high in RC will develop primarily somatic symptoms.

Individuals who are high in HS and low in RC can be expected to consciously experience psychological distress and the perception of threat during periods of heightened stress. This dynamic will be strengthened in the presence of high N and its associated negative and catastrophizing cognitions that people who are concurrently high in HS tend to intensely focus on. The result of unmitigated attending to negative thoughts and subsequent generation of symptoms that frequently occur in high N can be chronic vasoconstriction and consequent inability to relax or return to a baseline state of homeostasis. By contrast, individuals who are low in HS and high in RC are less likely to experience psychological distress or perceive stress, especially if they are low in N. RC, which in earlier conceptualizations of the HRMTP (Wickramasekera, 1988) was referred to as Covert Neuroticism, is associated with higher states of SNS activation at baseline, a dynamic that is found in people who are high in RC. Psychological imperviousness or unawareness of psychological factors and influences in one's life can serve to protect an individual from mental distress or stress, but with a trade-off, namely chronic hyper-physiological reactivity.

High HS and low RC in athletes can similarly be associated with psychological distress and even physical symptoms like nervousness and fatigue, especially in the presence of critical moments of competition. High HS independently and in the presence of high RC and low N, by contrast, can be performance facilitative with high RC exerting a protective influence by preventing negative intrusive thoughts that are associated with N from manifesting themselves.

4. Individuals who are high in HS and experiencing somatic symptoms are more likely to seek help for their problem in a mental health setting as opposed to a medical setting, since they are more likely to recognize the influence of mind–body interactions in the disease process.

Such behavior would be consistent with the known dynamics of HHS patients who are more attuned to psychological influences and are more cognizant of stress and distress that may lead to symptoms, especially as a function of high N. Going to a psychotherapist instead of a physician can have health consequences if a mental health provider is not trained to recognize and assess psychophysiological symptoms/disorders in the context of behavioral medicine/medical diagnostic and intervention procedures. Knowledge of HRMTP PHO factors can be crucial to treating a patient appropriately on the basis of mind–body response tendencies that are endemic to a specific constellation (e.g., HHS and HN).

This is a very important observation and prediction that can be extended to sport psychology, where it, too, can be expected that the majority of athletes seeking help for psychologically mediated performance problems will be high in HS. High HS is associated with openness to critique, feedback, and input and self-awareness or being in tune with mind–body interactions, or in athletes, acknowledgement that the psyche can influence motor or technical performance.

5. The majority of patients in primary medical care settings will be low in HS and high in RC and are more likely to avoid referral to mental health settings.

By contrast, patients who are low in hypnotic susceptibility (LHS) are less likely to seek assistance from mental health practitioners/psychotherapists. LHS is associated with a skeptical cognitive style and unawareness or denial of mind–body influences/effects on symptoms and health. This skeptical cognitive style is compounded by high RC. These patients can benefit from intervention modalities that provide objective information about psychophysiological processes (e.g., biofeedback). However, because patients who are low in HS and high in RC can be difficult to motivate to engage interventions, especially psychological ones, the HRMTP advocates a "Trojan Horse" approach for the purpose of covertly and subtly introducing potentially beneficial treatment procedures (Wickramasekera, 1988).

> *Similarly, athletes who are low in HS and low in RC even in the presence of psychological performance issues tend not to recognize or admit mind–body connections and are far more likely to seek help from a coach than a sport psychology practitioner (analogous to an individual with psychological issues [that are not self-recognized] seeking out a physician for symptoms [that are not of a physiological origin].*

These predictions have much anecdotal and emerging research support and serve a valuable utility in both clinical and sport psychological contexts. HRMTP PHO subject factors, depending on their constellation, are potent predictors of cognitive style, perception of threat, and autonomic nervous system (ANS) response tendencies to stress, as well as intervention amenability and compliance. They provide valuable clues and insight into subliminal mind–body processes that are not readily apparent or discernible alone through body/facial language, self-report, or clinical intuition or gleaned from medical or psychological tests that do not tap the unconscious dynamics and behavioral tendencies that have been associated with these measures (Wickramasekera, 1988).

Additional Predictions: Extending the HRMTP

In addition to the preceding hypothesized relationships between PHO subject variables and symptoms, intervention, and treatment choices (medical vs. mental; health domain), the following predictions are made on the basis of known dynamics of HRMTP PHO-isolated individual differences measures, additional clinical and performance observations, and supportive research.

DELAYS IN DIAGNOSIS AND TREATMENT ONSET

Individuals with symptoms seek help differentially. Not everyone who feels ill, experiences pain, or psychological distress goes to the emergency room, makes an appointment with a physician, or contacts a psychotherapist. In the extreme, hypochondriacs may arrange to be evaluated daily, whereas other people rarely admit to being sick or experiencing pain (even in the presence of objective evidence to the contrary) and therefore never schedule a consultation with a doctor or psychologist.

This latter type of individual is expected to face a greater risk of experiencing an acute medical incident or developing a chronic disorder that becomes threatening disease. The ability to discern and predict which person is likely to undergo regular physical examinations or respond appropriately upon pain or symptom onset by seeking out a physician and who does not, can have important consequences for patients, physicians, and the broader health care system. For one, symptoms that are addressed and treated early usually increase the probability that a disorder can be eradicated. In best-case scenarios, some illnesses and disorders can be averted on the basis of preemptive medical responses. Identifying those individuals who are more likely to deny symptoms, in addition to being potentially life saving, also has practical and financial implications, since illnesses that can be staved off or ameliorated in their early stages are usually less costly for all entities in the disease and health care equation, including patients themselves, hospitals, insurance companies, and an affected person's family and micro-economy.

On the basis of the characteristics of HRMTP PHO subject variables (individual differences risk factors), it may be possible to screen individuals for what can be referred to as diagnostic aversion (DA) or clinical denial (CD) behaviors. The extent of DA/CD is hypothesized to vary as a function of the level of HS and RC, with high RC being the primary mediator of denial of symptoms, pain and psychological discomfort, and the consequent failure to seek medical or psychological assistance. Low HS is expected to reinforce the tendency of high RC toward denial and feelings of imperviousness or indestructibility through the suppression of cognitive mechanisms that facilitate openness or recognition of feelings and sensations that are associated with symptoms that should not be ignored. While low HS can be involved in the DA/CD process, high RC is of primary importance, especially since this PHO subject variable has also been associated with heightened pain tolerance and the tendency to rationalize away or dismiss the existence of what would normally be considered objective potential threats to one's wellbeing (e.g., chest pain or a noticeable lump) that warrant further investigation (Wickramasekera, 1988).

> *Similarly, in sports, the ability to accurately identify athletes that are more or less likely to experience and admit psychological performance issues is crucial to informed assessment. As in clinical contexts, high RC in athletes is expected to mediate the denial of performance issues, whether psychological or motor (technical related). Low HS is expected to accentuate diagnostic aversion and clinical denial behaviors that hinder athletes from being assessed comprehensively and admitting to issues that may impact performance. In sports, diagnostic aversion can be referred to as* assessment avoidance *and clinical denial,* performance issue denial.

INTERVENTION AMENABILITY AND COMPLIANCE

The propensity toward diagnostic aversion and clinical denial in individuals who are high in RC (or low in HS and high in RC) increases the probability that such people are more likely to not be amenable to most interventions and therefore apt to be noncompliant should an intervention be forced upon them due to an acute medical event that requires hospitalization (after being discharged). Behavioral tendencies associated with RC can function as major confounds in clinical and research contexts. For example, a patient who is high in RC, when hospitalized, may have no choice but to take medication that is administered with oversight and experience symptom amelioration and eventually be released. Thereafter, doctors might assume that such a patient will comply with a drug schedule that was prescribed at the time of discharge. However, by not screening for PHO subject variables and having knowledge of behaviors (intervention compliance) that are associated with RC, physicians may be surprised days or weeks later when the same patient is readmitted (which is usually a serious matter, since the high RC patient is not likely to voluntarily admit him- or herself to a hospital). Such a scenario may perplex attending physicians who have no explanation for why a drug that usually works did not in this and other patients (up to 33% of the population) who are unknowingly high in RC or low in HS and high in RC. While non- or faulty compliance may be assumed in such instances, it is doubtful that patients who are high in RC would admit to not following treatment orders, since doing so would signal mental weakness and be at odds with heightened self-perceived sense of psychological control and high self-esteem that characterizes this PHO measure.

> *One of the clinical strengths of the HRMTP is the isolation of specific PHO subject variables that are strong predictors of intervention amenability. Specifically, HS and RC have been found to interact to mediate mental training compliance in athletes, with low HS and high RC being most associated with poor compliance. HS tends to drive intervention amenability in athletes, as in clinical patients, with high levels of HS being associated with the ability to learn, use, and benefit from imagery-based mental training, including hypnosis, whereas athletes who are low in HS and high in RC and levels in between (who tend to be more skeptical and averse to mental training), assuming that they can be persuaded to participate in a course of intervention, appear to benefit more from biofeedback and data-driven methods whose generated numbers helps allay their skepticism through objective demonstrations of mind–body interactions that they may otherwise not believe.*

DUAL-PLACEBO–NOCEBO EFFECTS: PRACTITIONER–PATIENT DYNAMICS

The success of psychotherapy and other interventions that are designed to ameliorate symptoms and conditions that have mental or psychological components is predicated, at minimum, on the belief that they work. The belief that a treatment works may be more important than objective evidence that substantiates notions of intervention efficacy, especially in more nebulous areas like psychotherapy, although the placebo effect is well established in medical circles. While beliefs may be important, especially in the immediate context of an actual psychotherapy session and perhaps shortly thereafter and then again prior to the next scheduled session, they may in the long run hinder more substantive and real measures of outcome success. For example, a patient with depression may week after week see a psychotherapist that is convinced that existential issues are at the heart of his or her client's somber affect, hopelessness, and gloomy outcome. In the course of therapy, as early as the intake and onset of an existential psychotherapeutic intervention, the patient may become convinced that his or her therapist is not only right, but caring, and will succeed in bringing joy back into his or her life. In this scenario, both the patient and practitioner are on the same page, they see eye-to-eye, and are committed to a clinical goal through the use of an insight-based approach and treatment strategy and technique.

However, is the patient really getting better, or does the patient merely "feel" better just before, during, and for a short period after therapy, only to relapse 2 days later before feeling good again knowing the next session is just around the corner? And, is such a rhythm conducive to averting the potential medical consequences that are associated with chronic depression, even with the occasional escape from its most debilitating symptoms? Are the therapist and patient even aware of these potential medical consequences, or is the therapeutic goal just a matter of feeling better for longer stretches of time than previously?

What the preceding case is meant to illustrate is that a mutual belief system may be at the heart of many therapeutic alliances and, although well-intentioned, may result in little more than a therapist–patient-mediated dual-placebo effect that in the end leads to temporally isolated bursts of symptom amelioration that makes the patient feel good but does little to alter maladaptive ANS functioning that may eventually lead to medical conditions.

The probability of such a dual placebo effect from occurring and resulting in feelings or beliefs of success, in the context of the HRMTP, could be predicted to hinge on mutually high levels of hypnotic susceptibility in both the psychotherapist and patient. High HS is associated with increased openness to new experiences, intellectual and analytic exploration, the kind that psychodynamic and insight-oriented therapies are known to advance and engage in. Alone, the likelihood that an individual will seek out a psychologist or physician may be increased and predicted on the basis of an individual's level of HS. Couple a patient's high HS with a physician's or psychologist's similar level of this trait, and both are likely to interact cooperatively and in the context of a HS-mediated belief system that fosters confidence that treatment will work.

Again, on the basis of the normal distribution theorem, one would expect that about 15% to 30% of all patients and clinical practitioners to be high in HS. Should such individuals be paired through chance clinical encounters, one could predict that physician-driven placebo responses will occur in predisposed patients in up to 30% of all therapeutic relationships and efforts.

The preceding hypotheses warrant investigation, since the implications of dual-placebo-mediated clinical dynamics can have important consequences relative to intervention efficacy, morbidity, and even mortality; more so when pathophysiology goes undetected, because a faulty belief system leads to false-positive or false-negative outcome. For example, it may be false to assume that depression has been ameliorated if medical tests were not administered to substantiate such. To further illustrate: with the dual-placebo effect in play, both the therapist and patient may be convinced that depression no longer exists, yet a test of HRV might reveal an SDNN or HRV index of less than 30 that can reflect depression-mediated reduced cardiac resiliency (Malik & Camm, 1995). In such an instance, a dual-placebo effect-mediated false-negative intervention conclusion may have been reached (no depression), yet underlying mind–body (ANS) responses suggest otherwise (low SDNN can be a symptom of depression or residual consequences of this disorder; Lederbogen et al., 2001) or at least indicates that a cardiologic deficit may exist that would have gone undetected, irrespective of whether a patient's depression had been successfully treated.

A dual-nocebo[4] effect can also occur between a patient and practitioner who are both low in hypnotic susceptibility and high in repressive coping, assuming that an individual who is high in RC would actually schedule and show up for an appointment. Should this occur (this is more likely in the course of involuntary hospitalization), both the practitioner and patient are apt to be hypercritical, skeptical, and overly analytical and diametrically opposite in their interactions, responses, and beliefs compared to a dual-placebo-prone clinician and patient who are high in HS.

The low HS and high RC practitioner may order too many tests to the point of overkill because he or she is overcautious and as such may even be demanded by the high RC patient who needs more and more evidence to even remotely allay his or her skepticism and disbelief that illness or disease exists. In the intervention stage of such a relationship, both parties are likely to believe that a therapy or intervention will not work, with the patient believing that there is nothing wrong and the practitioner employing a vast array of treatment modalities before arriving at a diagnosis.[5]

Both the dual placebo and nocebo patient–practitioner dynamic can have practical and financial consequences, not to mention getting in the way of efficient patient evaluation and intervention. It further points to the need to assess patients and practitioners alike on HRMTP-PHO subject measures for clinical exploratory and research purposes.

Just substitute the term patient *with* client *or* clinical *with* sport psychology *and almost all of that is conveyed from before about the dual-placebo-effect transfers to athletes and their relationship with sport psychology practitioners. This, for the most part unrecognized (or acknowledged) therapeutic or interventional phenomenon, plays a crucial role in the mental training outcome or efficacy equation in that it can bias the consulting process, influencing practitioners and athletes alike to believe a method works even if it does not. Athletes and practitioners, upon commencement of a working relationship, should be assessed for HS, or at minimum, absorption, a correlate of HS to appraise whether the dual-placebo effect can impact practitioner and athlete perceptions about intervention efficacy. It is predicted that the vast majority of sport psychology practitioners and athletes who seek their services voluntarily will be in the higher range for HS and N and lower range for RC. Practitioners and their athlete clients need to be aware of potent manipulative properties of, especially, high HS, lest they both fall victim to a dual belief system that leads to false-positive conclusions about an intervention's efficacy.*

The HRMTP and Individualized Interventions: Psychophysiological Psychotherapy

The HRMTP approach to interventions relies heavily on physiological monitoring and has been referred to as Psychophysiological Psychotherapy (PPT; Wickramasekera, 1988). PPT is an integrative investigative procedure designed to analyze and reveal mind–body interactions and incongruence between patient verbal-report and actual underlying autonomic nervous system responses during psychotherapy. It is composed of six stages of continuous physiological monitoring (Wickramasekera, 1988). The goal of PPT is to reduce ANS measures of threat perception and expand cognitive flexibility and adaptability in an attempt to reduce or eliminate somatic symptoms (Wickramasekera, 1988). The inhibition or disruption of dysfunctional cognitions or cognitive style and resultant perception of threat is addressed using hypnosis, self-hypnosis, other cognitive-behavioral methods, and/or biofeedback in an attempt to reduce ANS correlates of threat perception, including elevated BP and cardiac hyper-reactivity at baseline (Wickramasekera, 1994). It is based on the premise that PPT procedures will disengage subliminal and consciously consolidated dysfunctional memories, images, and emotions, and thereby facilitate new and adaptive cognitive responses to real and perceived threat (Wickramasekera, 1988). PPT is indicated when patients presenting physical complaints without underlying disease cannot be effectively treated medically. It attempts to challenge previous notions and myths regarding the etiology of a patient's somatic complaints by illuminating the extent to which a person's thoughts can mediate the development of symptoms (Wickramasekera, 1988).

PPT has been shown effective in treating a wide variety of somatic afflictions, including vasovagal syncopy, headaches, clinical pain, Raynauds disease, fecal and urinary incontinence, hypertension, and functional arrhythmias (Wickramasekera, 1988; Wickramasekera, Davies, & Davies, 1996). Individualized applications of PPT and hypnosis are applied on the basis of the following HRMTP PHO subject to variable constellations (Wickramasekera, 1988).

PPT can readily be adapted to athletes. The conceptual or construct basis of the CP's use of psychophysiological monitoring and biofeedback as an intervention was initially explicated in the previous section on HRD-Brain responses and will be further elaborated in various chapters.

HHS, LOW NEUROTICISM, AND HIGH REPRESSIVE COPING

While these types of patients tend to score in the normal range or below on widely used psychological tests (e.g., MMPI-2), they are at risk for "transducing" the perception of threat into somatic symptoms, yet are often unaware of clinical pain and anxiety (Wickramasekera, 1988). Patients exhibiting this profile are thought to have at least two mechanisms that suppress pain or fear from conscious perception, including HHS and HRC. In patients with this profile, who are adept at suppressing psychological stress, perception of stress, fear, and pain, chronic ANS hyper-reactivity and concomitant vasoconstriction is thought to occur implicitly or unconsciously as reflected in increases in BP, very-low-frequency HRV, and/or electrodermal responses. This type of patient is considered vulnerable to serious medical disorders, including cancer and heart disease, especially during middle age, when unhealthy lifestyle factors can override whatever protective genetic attributes they may possess (Wickramasekera, 1988). According to Wickramasekera (1988), the H/A-LN-HRC patient will benefit the most from hypnotherapy with a psychodynamic or Gestalt orientation and delayed biofeedback.

Paradoxically, in light of the poor health prognosis that is associated with the HHS-LN-HRC profile, this constellation of HRMTP subject variables is one of two ideal Athlete's Profiles. This may be attributable to mind–body response dynamics that in the absence of physical activity induce levels of physiological reactivity that are maladaptive or inappropriate, especially in the context of sedentary activities. Psychological mediators of such hyper-reactivity, including the suppression of psychological stress and distress, by contrast, during competitive sports, foster mental and emotional control by sublimating and actually blocking the generation of negative intrusive thoughts that can disrupt motor performance. Moreover, the heightened physiological reactivity that has deleterious health consequences in more sedentary individuals, in an athlete is associated with levels of activation that are required to initiate and sustain optimum states of attention, intensity, cognitive coping, strategic planning, and technical performance. Stress hormones such as cortisol and adrenaline, mediators, and by-products of excessive reactivity that lead to unhealthy chronic vasoconstriction in nonathletes, in athletes may be broken down and expelled faster and more efficiently by the body as a function of the consistent rigorous physical activity that is associated with sport training and competition. So, on one hand, what could be considered abnormal psychophysiological responding, in athletes appears to be adaptive and performance facilitative. Nevertheless, and as anecdotal evidence suggests, once an athlete's career is over, he or she would be well advised to maintain a regime of physical training comparable to his or her active days to further suppress hazardous response tendencies that may manifest themselves once a certain inactivity threshold is reached. Relative to intervention amenability and compliance hypnosis, self-hypnosis, active-alert hypnosis, and biofeedback are the recommended modality of choices with ongoing psychophysiological monitoring for assessment and intervention efficacy testing purposes.

LOW HYPNOTIC SUSCEPTIBILITY, LOW NEUROTICISM, AND HIGH REPRESSIVE COPING

This type of patient appears to be best served by a treatment modality that allows a rapid and reliable shift into a state of low physiological arousal that facilitates the subjective perception of muscular and vascular changes (e.g., reduction of muscle tension, peripheral temperature manipulation).

Consequently, immediate biofeedback is indicated, not least because it provides the LHS and HRC patient objective feedback on mind–body interactions that is often needed to convince the skeptical HRC patient that something is actually wrong. As previously mentioned, getting the LHS/HRC patient to participate in psychotherapy or medical interventions can be challenging. As such, the *Trojan horse* role induction method, a covert method of getting a patient with this profile to recognize the effects that emotions and cognitions can exert on psychophysiology, is used with individuals who are low in HS and high in RC to verbalize and experience changes in perception that are necessary to participate in conventional psychotherapy (Wickramasekera, 1988). The failure to prepare and make the skeptical LHS and HRC patient aware that alterations in physiological arousal and somatic sensations can be cognitively induced often results in their terminating treatment.

Again, paradoxically, the LHS-LN-HRC profile is the other ideal Athlete's Profile; however, one can rightly assume that the clinical dynamics of HRMTP measures, although highly relevant to peak performance, can manifest themselves differently with responses that could be considered maladaptive in the context of health, actually being performance facilitative. This can be attributed to attention, intensity, and cognitive demands that, although mediated by the same neuropsychophysiological mechanisms in clinical and sport contexts, vary in terms of how they interact and the extent to which individual to which PHO measures exert their effects as a function of level of activity. Relative to this PHO profile, in athletes, biofeedback, too, is the first intervention of choice for the same reasons that have been noted.

HHS, HIGH NEUROTICISM, AND HIGH REPRESSIVE COPING

Since high N and RC are characteristics of "explicit defensiveness" (i.e., repression), this type of patient requires a gradual approach to psychotherapy. Initially these patients should receive cognitive-behavioral therapy that focuses on somatic symptoms and the reduction of catastrophizing cognitions (Wickramasekera, 1988). Once a trusting therapeutic relationship has developed, hypnotherapy can be introduced (to which HHS patients are amenable). Hypnotic suggestions that selectively focus on and retain positive memories and emotions should be used to restructure such patients' propensity to over-attend to especially threatening cognitive stimuli (e.g., negative internal thoughts). After defensive barriers are reduced, hypnoanalysis can be introduced to access unconscious resistance to greater levels of social intimacy, social support, and interpersonal vulnerability (Wickramasekera, 1988). Essentially, psycho-and-hypnotherapy with these patients strives to "boost psychological immunity" by increasing cognitive and behavioral adaptive coping skills and reducing "acting out" (Wickramasekera, 1988).

The HHS–HN–HRC profile is one of the rarest. It is seen in less than 5% of all athletes. Athletes with this profile present challenges because, on one hand, they are high in the performance facilitative behavior RC, but on the other they also have a high level of N. The issue of whether and/or when the protective measure (RC) will be able to exert its strength to the extent that it can suppress even high levels of neuroticism has not been resolved and warrants further study, for example, determining whether one or the other measure will predominate as a function of variations in the actual level RC and N (more precise calibrations) and level and amount of competitive pressure or stress (criticality). As far as intervention amenability is concerned, this profile is also paradoxical in that HHS facilitates imagery and hypnosis-based mental training methods, yet high RC is associated with skepticism and diagnostic aversion and an overriding belief that intervention is not necessary or would not do any good anyway. Wickramsekera's (1988) Trojan Horse method should be used to introduce athletes who are high in RC to mental training in a more indirect manner, telling them that psychophysiological monitoring will be used to gain better insight into mind–body responses that are associated with performance and competitive stress, and then, if indicated, incorporate biofeedback in an attempt to enhance performance. Since athletes with this profile are also high in HS, eventually imagery and hypnotic methods can be used, preferably, in conjunction with ongoing psychophysiological monitoring.

HHS, HIGH NEUROTICISM, AND LOW REPRESSIVE COPING

Because of its known and hypothesized characteristics and ANS correlates, it is expected that this HRMTP-PHO subject variable profile will be exhibited by the vast majority of patients who present due to mind–body symptoms and complaints, both in medical and psychological settings. High N, in the presence of HHS and low RC, and concurrent external or internal perception of threat, is thought to lead to excessive SNS activity. Over time, such chronic hyperactivation can lead to chronic symptoms, pain, psychological distress, and eventual pathophysiology. Consequently, it is important that physicians and mental health practitioners screen patients using HRMTP-prescribed test instruments for diagnostic and intervention guidance. This class of patients is very treatable because they are usually aware of or admit to having a motivation to rid themselves of debilitating psychologically mediated symptoms (such openness is associated with high HS). They are also amenable to most interventions, especially those that are imagery or hypnosis-based. Monitoring their physiology during an intake session, ongoing psychotherapy will frequently reveal strong SNS spikes in response to directed questioning that conjures up memories or pain, symptoms, and, often, psychosocial mediators such as a poor marriage or conflict with a coworker.

The high HS, high N, and low RC profile is the most performance detrimental PHO profile. Athletes who are have this profile comprise the vast majority of athletes who seek help for psychologically mediated performance issues, in line with their clinical counterparts who make up the largest group of psychotherapy patients. Fortunately, helping these athletes is straightforward. They are aware of and readily admit to performance-related problems and are willing and motivated to try almost any intervention; they are especially amenable to hypnosis and imagery-based mental training modalities.

SYSTEMS OF PSYCHOTHERAPY: MATCHING INTERVENTIONS WITH PHO PROFILE

The following chart (Figure 2.2) pairs HRMTP PHO subject variable profile with ideal intervention modality. More neutral profiles in which middle levels of HS, N, and RC predominate are more ambiguous regarding intervention amenability and must be teased out empirically. To that end, continuous monitoring of HRV during intake, therapy sessions and in vivo ecological settings (real world) can help determine ANS responses to stressors and take precedence over self-report-based instruments that the HRMTP uses.

> *The intervention amenability chart (Figure 2.2) entries for the most part apply to athletes as well. However, interventions with athletes should be carried out on the playing field in the context of training and competition and should be delivered within a methodological paradigm that allows for controlled efficacy testing. This matter is discussed in numerous other chapters.*

It should be noted that the preceding intervention modalities are recommended on the basis of their known ability to reduce excessive ANS-SNS activation through cognitive mediation or direct feedback (biofeedback). However, it should not be assumed that any intervention will work. The devil's advocate perspective should drive treatment strategies where the maxim "show me the data" rules and determines an intervention's efficacy, since whenever self-reporting is involved in the assessment process, false positives and negatives are bound to occur. PHO and other profiling can be fallible. Consequently, an inappropriate treatment procedure can at times be applied to a misdiagnosed patient. Hence, ultimately, objective longitudinal, repeated predictor (mind–body measures such as HRV) and criterion outcome (changes in mind–body measures pre- compared to post-intervention and/or performance or symptom differences) measures should be turned to for highest evidentiary guidance regarding profiling conclusions, intervention selection decisions, and determining incongruence/congruence between practitioner intuition and patient self-report/test results. That is why ongoing psychophysiological monitoring during psychotherapy, at home and in the real world, should routinely be engaged.

Constellation	Intervention 1	Intervention 2	Intervention 3
HHS-HN-LRC hypothesized most common profile in medical-therapy context	Hypnosis–self-hypnosis with biofeedback	Mental imagery with biofeedback	Physical exercise as an adjunct intervention in all high N patients
LHS-HN-LRC using Trojan Horse (TH) induction approach	Biofeedback—in office—with cognitive component	Biofeedback-at home-with cognitive component	Biofeedback-real world situation-with cognitive component; physical exercise
HHS-LN-LRC infrequent constellation	Hypnosis–insight-talk therapy		
HHS-HN-HRC with TH	Hypnosis–biofeedback	Physical exercise	Physical exercise

FIGURE 2.2   HRMTP constellation and matched intervention modalities.

As recommended with clinical patients, intervention efficacy should always be determined in athletes as well. The remark about the reduction of excessive ANS–SNS activity does not necessarily apply to athletes. The goal of athlete-based interventions is to induce responses that are consistent with an athlete's empirically determined Individual Zone of Optimum Functioning (IZOF) and/or facilitate the generation of pre-action HRD and concomitant brain activity (construct validity based).

SUMMARY

The HRMTP is a multidimensional model composed of quantifiable measures, including PHO individual differences risk factors that in isolation or independently may be weak predictors of a clinical outcome. However, in the presence of a real or perceived threat, specific constellations of HS, N, and RC are hypothesized to be strong predictors of the complex mind–body interactions that have been shown to underlie various medical and psychological disorders. People at greatest risk for developing symptoms and eventual disease are those who are positive for all predisposing features, deficient in support systems and coping skills, and have experienced multiple major life changes and/or hassles over a short time. Individuals at lowest risk are those who have none of the isolated risk factors and effective multiple support systems and coping skills (Wickramasekera, 1988).

As previously mentioned, the CP Athlete's Profile model of peak performance traces its origins to the HRMTP. The isolated PHO measures have been shown to exert potent effects in both clinical and sport psychological contexts, impacting attention, physiological reactivity, and cognitive coping mechanisms, key components in the etiology of symptoms and disease as well as the performance equation. The HRMTP's relevance to sports and athletes was noted in an ancillary manner throughout the previous section. In the next section, the Athlete's Profile model will be elaborated.

Component II: The Athlete's Profile and Critical Moments Model of Peak Performance

Construct validity is in part established by criterion-referencing test scores with mind–body responses. Responses that are consistent with what would be predicted on the basis of a psychological variable's (e.g., test score for neuroticism) hypothesized impact on specific outcome measures such as a symptom checklist or sport-specific statistical outcome measure (e.g., batting average) usually suggest strong construct validity. In the context of sport performance, especially pre-action responding, specific parameters of HRD, and concomitant brain activity have been isolated. These response tendencies constitute *the* primary component of the overall construct validity model (BHMBM) of peak sport performance. However, since performance does not occur in a vacuum or in the absence of disruptive psychological forces, it must also be investigated in the context of what hinders and facilitates peak performance. Individual variability in performance outcome must be explained on the basis of mediating psychological variables, factors that can contribute to a breakdown of primary construct validity model derived measures, in this case, HRD and associated brain functioning. Doing so does not detract from a model's overall construct validity, since consistency works both ways; responses being differentially stable as a function of both successful and unsuccessful outcomes. If HRD occurs concomitant to success but does not manifest itself when performance outcome is negative, such would be consistent responding and indicative of good construct validity. By contrast, if HRD were present irrespective of outcome, that would be inconsistent with ABSP-CP construct validity model tenets.

Previously, the HRMTP was explicated to better understand the impact of the specific so-called PHO traits and behaviors that the model had isolated that are intimately involved in psychological processes that drive performance (attention, intensity, and cognitive coping/strategic planning). These measures were found to exert their influences as a function of increasing competitive pressure (criticality), with debilitating constellations or PHO factors leading to the disruption of known mind–body dynamics that occur prior to action, whereas facilitative constellations of PHO factors helped maintain mind–body control that is associated with peak performance, even during the most critical moments of competition. These factors comprise the second level of construct validity components, with athlete-specific PHO constellations offering a validated explanatory framework to account for individual variability in performance as a function of criticality.

ATHLETE'S PROFILE PHO MEASURES AND THEIR PROPERTIES

Hypnotic susceptibility (HS), neuroticism, (N) and repressive coping (RC) are primary order measures that have been found to mediate a host of subordinate lower-order psychological factors, mind–body responses, and performance. In the context of sport and athletes, analogue measures that are derived from the Carlstedt Subliminal Attention, Reactivity and Coping Scale-Athlete version (CSARCS-A) can be used in place of the HRMTP clinical measures. The CSARCS-A PHO measures have high convergent validity with test instruments that measure HS, N, and RC and are used mostly to increase the face validity of question items that ask athletes about performance-related issues and responses. These measures will be used interchangeably with subliminal attention being abbreviated as (SA), subliminal reactivity (SR), and subliminal coping (SC).

HS/SA, N/SR, and RC/SC are considered traits and behaviors that have distinct mind–body correlates and dynamics. Research has localized them in specific brain regions and functionality with distinct patterns of EEG, HRV, and muscle tension (Carlstedt, 2004a, 2004b, 2006; Davidson, 1984; Wickramasekera, 1988; Davidson, Schwartz, & Rothman, 1976; Tomarken & Davidson, 1994). These measures have emerged as *Primary Higher Order* (PHO) factors in mediating performance, especially during critical moments of competition when the perception of threat and competitive stress are thought to be the greatest, instances when certain athletes are expected to be most vulnerable to negative intrusive thoughts. When interacting together, these measures have been shown empirically to supersede all other psychological variables in affecting and predicting psychological performance in athletes, especially during critical moments of competition (Carlstedt, 2001, 2004a, 2004b, 2007a, 2007b). These isolated PHO measures have been found to be intimately linked to key components of peak performance, including attention (focus), intensity (physiological reactivity), cognitive processing/strategic planning, motor readiness, and emotional control. A recent longitudinal study of tennis (spanning 5 y) and baseball players (season-long; presented herein) has found these traits and behaviors to be strongly associated with objective performance outcome measures as well as neurocognitive responses that have well-established functional and anatomical cortical concomitants. In addition, they have been found to influence pre-and post-competition HRV responses. In one form or another (interacting or singularly), HS/SA-N/SR-RC/SC have accounted

	Outcome	N	N	N	N	N	N & HRV	N & HRV	HRV	HRV
HS/SA	.36	-.68 N13	-.58-N21	-.68- N25	.58-N21	.52-N22	-.55 N36	-.57 N44	.28 HR-sdnn/pre	.31 L/H-post
N/SR	.48	.52-N12	-.52- N14	.79-N17	-.40-N30	-.62-N34	-.31 HR-pre	.41 VL-pre	-.24 Hr-post	-35 HR-pre
RC/SC	-.41	-.72-N12	.89-N14	-.54-N17	.73-N30	.53-N30	.43 HR-pre	.35 L/H-pre	.37 LF-post	.29 Power-post

Key: HS/SA = hypnotic susceptibility/subliminal attention; N/SR = neuroticism/subliminal reactivity; RC/SC = repressive coping/subliminal coping; Outcome Measures: statistical performance measure (games lost); N12-pre-frontal/parietal/occipital; N13-pre-frontal/frontal/temporal/basal ganglia/ thalamus; N14-same as 13; N17-frontal; N21-pre-frontal/parietal/occipital/anterior cingulate; N22-same as 21; N25-same as 21; N30-pre-frontal/frontal/motor/parietal/occipital; N34-pre-frontal/frontal; N36-same as 34; N44-same as 34 and anterior cingulate. HRV Measures: HR = heart rate; VL = very low frequency; LF = low frequency; L/H = low/high frequency ratio. NOTE: N measures are associated with implicated brain regions.

FIGURE 2.3 Sample outtake of correlations between primary higher order factors and performance outcome, neurocognition and heart rate variability.

for up to 70% of the variance in specific neurocognitive and HRV criterion measures and up to 40% of the variance in the performance equation that can be attributed to psychological factors (personality traits, behaviors, and psychophysiological responding; Carlstedt, 2001, 2004a, 2004b, 2007a, 2007b; Figure 2.3).[6]

These statistics are but a handful of a plethora of revealing findings that strongly support the contention that HS/SA-N/SR-RC/SC are the most potent psychological mediators of performance under pressure. Athletes should be routinely assessed on these measures as part of the consulting process. In addition to its utility as an assessment instrument, the established Athlete's Profile is a strong predictor of intervention amenability and compliance tendencies, pain threshold, attentional control during competitive stress, coachability, and the placebo–nocebo effects (Carlstedt, 2004a, 2004b, 2009; Wickramasekera, 1988).

PHO Factors and Their Relevance to Performance

HYPNOTIC SUSCEPTIBILITY/SUBLIMINAL ATTENTION

Hypnotic susceptibility/subliminal attention (HS/SA) is an omnipresent mode of information processing independent of actually being hypnotized. In other words, one does not have to be formally inducted to experience a hypnotic response or state. HS/SA is a cognitive style that can occur unconsciously and lead to intense periods of attention. HS/SA and peak performance experiences (e.g., zone or flow) have been described in similar terms with anecdotal descriptions and reports of being in the zone, replete with adjectives that similarly characterize the cognitive and perceptual experiences of persons who are also high in HS/SA, including intense focus, effortlessness, and involuntariness. High HS/SA is hypothesized to mediate flow and in-the-zone experiences reported by athletes.

Although the intense and effortless focus that is associated with high HS/SA is thought to facilitate zone states, being in the zone can also be short-lived, elusive, and easily disrupted. High HS/SA can come at a cost, since attending to or focusing on the wrong thing at the wrong time can impact performance negatively and actually undermine flow or zone states. While high HS/SA when directed toward the task at hand may drive the feeling of dissociation athletes have reported when experiencing being in the zone, the flow feeling appears only to remain active so long as intrusive negative thoughts remain dormant. The chances of HS/SA subverting peak performance increases substantially if an athlete is concurrently high in neuroticism (N). As such, although high HS/SA is still likely to facilitate performance during routine phases of competition irrespective of level of N, once the going gets tough, especially during critical moments, in the presence of high N, the enhanced task-directed focus that is associated with high HS/SA can be diverted, locking on to negative intrusive thoughts that are associated with high N and disrupting performance.

HYPNOTIC SUSCEPTIBILITY/SUBLIMINAL ATTENTION IN ATHLETES

HS/SA has been understudied in athletes with limited research on its mind–body dynamics and performance relationships having been published. It is important to distinguish HS/SA from hypnosis and investigations of hypnosis as an intervention. There are lines of research on hypnosis in sports that have for the most part generated equivocal results regarding its efficacy as a mental training modality (see Morgan, in Van Raalte & Brewer (1996), for a review). The equivocal nature of sport hypnosis research findings may in part be attributable to the failure to assess the level of the study subject's HS/SA, a potential extraneous, confounding, or moderating variable that should be routinely assessed in the context of investigations of hypnosis and in the context of practice (consulting). One needs to keep in mind that HS/SA, in addition to being a psychophysiological trait, is also a cognitive style of information and perceptual processing independent of being hypnotized. Consequently, research on hypnosis in sports can be called into question if it failed to control for level HS/SA. Practitioners in sport psychology, who for the most part gained exposure to hypnosis more in passing than as a serious academic, research, and practice pursuit, tend also not to be aware of HS/SA and its relevance to athlete assessment and intervention, which is unfortunate in light of its performance mediating properties.

Hypnotic Susceptibility: General and Athlete-Specific Characteristics

This chart compares and contrasts high HS/SA with low HS/SA. A discussion follows.

High Hypnotic Susceptibility (General Characteristics)	High Hypnotic Susceptibility (Performance Relevance)	Low Hypnotic Susceptibility (General Characteristics)	Low Hypnotic Susceptibility (Performance Relevance)
1. Attends too much to physical symptoms	1. Excessive concern with technical aspects	1. Ignores physical symptoms	1. Less concern about technical aspects
2. Exaggerates significance of physical symptoms	2. Motor complaints and breakdown in technique	2. Underestimates significance of symptoms	2. Less concern about technique and technical problems
3. Rich images of seeing, hearing, and feeling	3. Surplus pattern recognition, excess awareness of crowd, noise, opponent, and other distractions and superior imagery ability	3. Skeptical, critical, and analytic mode of information processing	3. More focused in the here and now, less distractible, reality oriented

(Continued)

High Hypnotic Susceptibility (General Characteristics)	High Hypnotic Susceptibility (Performance Relevance)	Low Hypnotic Susceptibility (General Characteristics)	Low Hypnotic Susceptibility (Performance Relevance)
4. Hypersensitivity to psychological and physical change	4. Need for ideal conditions to perform at best	4. Deny sensory cues from their bodies	4. Not as sensitive to psychological and physical changes
5. Less pain tolerance, heightened awareness of fear (more likely to perceive threat)	5. Problems when encountering pain, fear of critical moments	5. Greater pain tolerance	5. Plays through pain, less likely to fear critical moments
6. Superior sensory memory and transfer from short- to long-term memory	6. Heightened motor learning ability, rapid learning consolidation, talent	6. Less efficient transfer from short- to long-term procedural memory	6. Longer learning process to integrate physical aspects of game
7. Deep absorption and focus	7. Superior concentration, vulnerable to selective inattention	7. Reality-oriented focus	7. Incremental goal-oriented focus
8. Cognitive flexibility	8. Ability to alter mental states to suit the situation	8. More rigid cognitive style	8. Less ability to shift focus in accord with changing demands

1. and 2.   HS/SA Trait Characteristics and Response Manifestations
Attends too much to physical symptoms/exaggerates physical symptoms

High HS/SA and Sport Performance
Excessive attention to technique and physical sensations/vulnerable to motor complaints

Athletes who are high (highs) in HS can be perfectionists regarding technical aspects of their game. They tend to be more concerned with how their game or technique looks than actual performance or outcome. They are often more interested in style than substance (results). Highs have a keen awareness of physical sensations and body positions associated with technique and know what their technique looks like and how it feels when it goes awry and are capable of quickly making and feeling corrections. Aspiring athletes who are high in HS/SA are quick to learn technical aspects of a sport; they have an enhanced ability to feel and visualize their technique both internally and externally. However, if things don't go right, technical complaints can be frequent. Dissatisfaction with technique that does not correspond with an internal image of what it should look like can be deflating. Satisfaction is not so much attained by winning as when a perfect technique has been demonstrated or perceived.

3. HS/SA Trait Characteristics and Response Manifestations
Rich images of seeing, hearing, and smelling, especially threatening perceptions

HS/SA and Sport Performance
Surplus pattern recognition, excess awareness of crowd, noise, opponent and other distractions as well as superior imagery ability

While non-athletes and patients often use their rich ability to imagine, see, hear, and smell to focus on threatening perceptions, including symptoms and fears, athletes who are high in HS/SA can be hypersensitive to the presence of a crowd, noise, their opponent, and other distractions and lose focus. Their tendency toward surplus pattern recognition (fixating on noise of the superfluous) can undermine their natural propensity or ability to enter zone or flow states. However, if they learn to harness their tendency for surplus pattern recognition, they may be able to see the big picture or the whole playing field, the movements of their opponent(s), be able to anticipate where they have to move, or whom or what to avoid. Surplus pattern recognition can facilitate strategic planning and tactical execution.

4. Trait Characteristics and Response Manifestations

Hypersensitivity to physical and psychological change

HS/SA and Sport Performance

Hypersensitivity to changes in playing conditions, progression of competition, and personal performance

High hypnotizables (HS/SA) are too aware of changes in their environment and tend to be on "red alert" as they monitor symptoms and pain that affect their ability to maintain the homeostasis that they so desire. Athletes who are high in hypnotic ability also tend to thrive when conditions remain constant or they can anticipate change in advance. They have an enhanced ability to focus and concentrate on maintaining a high level of technical and tactical performance, something that they like to monitor. If things go well they can dominate and stay in the zone, but if things go wrong with their technique, conditions change (e.g., weather; critical moments), or temporal patterns they are familiar with are disrupted, they can readily experience a major drop in performance, something that is more likely to occur if they are concurrently high in N.

5. Trait Characteristics and Response Manifestations

Less tolerance for pain, heightened awareness of fear (more likely to perceive threat)

HS/SA and Sport Performance

Less tolerance for pain, greater fear of critical moments

Persons who are high in hypnotic ability tend to be very aware of bodily sensations and exaggerate mild discomfort as being major pain. They are also more likely to attach meaning to pain, fearing that even minor pain is a precursor of catastrophic consequences. Athletes who are high in HS/SA ability may have less tolerance for pain occurring during intense competition. This tendency can lead to psychosomatic reactions, such as sudden stomach problems and vomiting, muscle cramps, and other symptoms of pain and subsequent defaulting or being taken out of the game.

6. Trait Characteristics and Manifestations

Superior sensory memory and transfer from short- to long-term memory

HS/SA and Sport Performance

Heightened motor learning ability, rapid learning consolidation, talent

Although the superior sensory memory and memory can foster maladaptive behaviors, in athletes, this quality may facilitate motor learning and underlie talent. Athletes who are high in hypnotic ability may require less practice to maintain motor skills once a high level of proficiency (motor consolidation) has been reached.

7. Trait Characteristics and Manifestations

Deep absorption and focus capability

HS/SA and Sport Performance

Superior concentration, vulnerable to selective inattention

Athletes who are high in HS/SA can become deeply absorbed in tasks that they find salient, including those that are sport specific. They have a superior potential to attend or focus. However, highs can also lose their task-specific focus if they become interested in competing stimuli, whether internal (e.g., an intrusive thought) or external (e.g., noise of the crowd). Selective inattention can inexplicably occur in apparently highly focused athletes who are high in HS/SA, especially if they are also high in N.

8. Trait Characteristics and Clinical Manifestations

Cognitive flexibility

Sport Psychology Analogy

Ability to readily alter mental states

Athletes who are high in HS/SA often shift their focus or attention from one stimulus to the other. Although this characteristic can have an adaptive function in nonthreatening situations (at baseline/routine moments), it can lead to mental chaos during stress-laden periods of competition, especially if an athlete is high in neuroticism. Highs who become upset during routine moments of competition usually can quickly regain their composure by shifting attention back to the task at hand, even if they are high in neuroticism.

Low HS/SA and Sport Performance

1. and 2.   Trait Characteristics and Clinical Manifestations

Ignores Physical Symptoms/Underestimates Their Significance

Sport Psychology Analogy

Less concerned with technique and technical problems

Athletes who are low in HS/SA tend to be less concerned about the technical aspects of their game during actual competition. Lows are usually more concerned with results rather than the process. They are often more interested in substance than style. However, this does not necessarily mean that lows cannot have excellent technique; it's just that they are not as aware of their technique or how it looks. Lows tend to be unaware of physical sensations and exact body positions associated with their technique. As a result, they are less capable of making and feeling technical corrections without intense practice. Aspiring athletes who are low in HS/SA need time and patience to learn technique because of their reduced ability to feel and see technique internally and externally (lack of visual orientation, poor at visualizing). An advantage lows have over highs in this is that they tend to just do it as opposed to being hyperaware of the process. Lows obtain more satisfaction from winning than performing well or looking good. They have nothing against "winning ugly" or getting "dirty" so long as they win. Lows usually need to work harder to maintain their skills and be prepared to compete.

3. Trait Characteristics and Clinical Manifestations

Skeptical, critical, and analytic mode of information processing

Sport Psychology Analogy

More focused in the here and now, less distractible, reality oriented

Although athletes who are low in HS/SA have more difficulty achieving the effortless, intense levels of focus that highs can, with effort and practice, lows are capable of maintaining focus on the task at hand and are less burdened with the high's tendency to shift focus from one stimulus to the next. Even though highs at baseline are more likely to achieve flow, lows are less vulnerable to being distracted over the course of competition. In other words, although highs can focus more intensely without trying, they are more likely than lows to experience fluctuations in attention as competing internal or external stimuli are encountered during critical moments of competition. Lows need to practice and train and learn to increase focus thresholds and intervals using mental training methods that are more concrete. For example, instead of visualization, the low HS/SA athlete should be trained more directly and engage in attention drills. The skeptical, critical, and analytic cognitive style of lows makes them poor candidates for imagery or hypnosis-based interventions. Lows can benefit from behavioral procedures and simulation training that are data-driven (providing statistical feedback regarding outcome).

4. Trait Characteristics and Clinical Manifestations

Deny sensory cues from their bodies

Sport Psychology Analogy

Not as sensitive to psychological and physical changes

Athletes who are low in HS/SA tend to be less aware of psychological and technical issues associated with performance. They have more difficulty recognizing root causes of technical problems and correcting them as they occur. Lows are also less adept at recognizing or admitting that psychological factors may be affecting their performance; for example, not admitting that outbursts of anger contribute to subsequent errors, even if evidence suggests that it does.

5. Trait Characteristics and Clinical Manifestations

Greater tolerance for pain

Sport Psychology Analogy

Plays through pain, less likely to fear critical moments

Athletes who are low in HS/SA tend to have a greater tolerance for pain and are more likely to play through bouts of minor injuries and fatigue, rarely admitting that they are psychologically distressed. Their tendency to ignore physical and psychological stress, although considered admirable by some coaches, can lead to excessive physiological reactivity even in the face of no apparent psychological stress. Lows frequently exhibit the previously described (HRMTP section) incongruence between body language and verbalizations and underlying physiology, which can disrupt motor performance; for example, controlled body language does not necessarily mean that stress exists.

6. Trait Characteristics and Clinical Manifestations

Less efficient transfer from short- to long-term memory

Sport Psychology Analogy

Longer learning process for integrating physical aspects of game into procedural memory

Athletes who are low in HS/SA may train more to achieve and maintain motor skills. They are generally less adept than highs at using tactile feedback and sensory cues to better consolidate motor learning in long-term procedural memory.

7. Trait Characteristic and Clinical Manifestations

Reality-oriented focus

<u>Sport Psychology Analogy</u>

Incremental goal-oriented focus/Reality-based focus

Athletes who are low in HS/SA have a more reality-oriented cognitive style. Although highs can achieve intense focus more effortlessly than lows, lows are less affected by surplus pattern recognition (e.g., noise of the crowd, changes in the environment) that can shift the focus of highs away from the task at hand. Lows tend to have a more consistent level of focus but have more difficulty entering flow or zone states that are associated with intense, but effortlessly achieved focus.

8. Trait Characteristics and Clinical Manifestations

More rigid cognitive style

<u>Sport Psychology Analogy</u>

Less ability to shift focus in accord with changing demands

Lows are less capable of shifting focus, even when such might be warranted, for example, during a phase of poor play. Their tendency to rigidly adhere to familiar routines, behavior, and thought patterns can get in the way of creative problem solving in a crisis situation or critical moments. Lows are more comfortable with fixed patterns of training and when competing. They are less capable of altering an entrenched pattern of play when it is not working.

NEUROTICISM/SUBLIMINAL REACTIVITY

If HS/SA can be viewed as the flow or zone trait, then neuroticism (N) can be seen as the flow or zone buster since it is associated with numerous response tendencies that have been shown to undermine peak performance, including a tendency to generate negative intrusive thoughts that can disrupt the pre-action HRD and the seamless shift from left brain hemispheric strategic planning to motor priming that has been associated with successful outcomes. Athletes who are high in N tend to exhibit a slow return to baseline (homeostasis) after episodes of cognitive stress and concomitant hyper-reactivity. They appear to be more susceptible to episodes of competitive anxiety, a maladaptive response that is most likely to occur during critical moments when psychological stress is the greatest. High N individuals also tend to catastrophize or anticipate the worst possible outcomes when thinking about the future (Wickramasekera, 1988). Catastrophizing is a cognitive style of becoming intensely and frequently absorbed in negative psychological or sensory events and talking or thinking about them in ways that increase their aversive properties. Catastrophizing has indirectly been associated with the disruption of attention in the anecdotal literature and research of sports. Gallwey (1974), in his classic work, the *Inner Game of Tennis*, warns that negative thoughts can interfere with performance. Waller (1988) reported that a lack of thinking and absence of negative intrusive thoughts characterized episodes of peak performance in athletes she studied. The catastrophizing athlete can often be heard engaging in negative self-talk during competition. Statements such as "I'm no good" or "I can't hit a ball today" often precipitate spiraling feelings of losing control.

Although there are references to neuroticism in the literature of sport psychology, most research has failed or not attempted to link this trait with specific outcomes or operationalizations of performance during actual competition. In essence, these studies merely describe mean values for N in certain populations of athletes but do not demonstrate how this trait may affect performance. For example, Daino (1984) reported that adolescent male and female tennis players were less neurotic than teenagers who did not participate in sports but did not show or suggest how this finding might be relevant to performance. Geron, Furst, and Rotstein (1986) investigated manifest anxiety (a lower-order factor of neuroticism; Watson & Clark, 1984) among other traits in heterogeneous groups of athletes participating in various sports. Again, although differences in levels of this trait were found between and within groups, N was not investigated in the context of specific objective performance outcome criteria (e.g., won-loss record, ranking, etc.). In general, research suggests that athletes may be lower in N than in non-athletes, although this finding is far from being unequivocal (Becker, 1986; Egloff & Gruhn, 1996; Eysenck, Nias, & Cox, 1982). While these studies are descriptive and have established limited norms for N in certain populations of athletes, they appear to have minimal predictive validity. An exception to this more demographic and descriptive research is Carlstedt's (2001) dissertation research that investigated N among numerous other psychological factors in which great N was associated with negative outcomes. Extension and replication studies in the context of the Athlete's Profile and Theory of Critical Moments have generated additional support regarding Ns', deleterious performance influences (Carlstedt, 2004).

REPRESSIVE COPING/SUBLIMINAL COPING

High repressive coping (RC/SC) is characterized by a self-enhancing cognitive style that promotes the perception and maintenance of high self-esteem and appears to be common in most athletes who are deemed mentally tough on the basis of criticality analyses. Mentally tough athletes are known for having high levels of self-confidence and ego strength, characteristics that also mark high RC/SC (Carlstedt, 2001, 2004a, 2004b; Tomarken & Davidson, 1994). Athletes who are high in RC/SC have a developed ability to prevent negative cognitions, memories, and affect from reaching awareness. This capability has been documented in EEG studies that revealed that people who are high in RC/SC actually functionally inhibit the inter-hemispheric transfer of negative affect (N/SR) from the right to the left frontal brain hemispheres (Tomarken & Davidson, 1994). Essentially, this performance-enhancing brain response functions to prevent negative intrusive thoughts that are associated with high N from manifesting themselves. Athletes who are high in RC/SC appear to have developed neuronal response systems that are linked to high self-esteem, self-confidence, positive affect and goal-oriented motivation, and the suppression of negative cognitions. Athletes who are high in this behavior seem impervious to (or do not even generate) negative intrusive thoughts and are more likely to successfully master critical moments during competition than athletes who are low in RC/SC, tendencies that can be traced to what Tomarken and Davidson (1994) refer to as the "functional disconnection" syndrome.

The ability of high RC/SC individuals to focus away from aversive situations and memories and the propensity to amplify positive thoughts and self-perception can have a positive effect on performance. Since negative intrusive cognitions have been associated with right-brain hemisphere activity, the ability of highs to functionally disconnect the right from the left hemisphere and other cortical or subcortical regions that are implicated in mediating autonomic and neuroendocrine components of affective responsivity may insulate them from the potential disruptive consequences of such thoughts (Davidson, 1984; Fox & Davidson, 1984). Moreover, the tendency of highs to have poor memory for negative emotional experiences may help them maintain a positive outlook even after episodes of poor performance during competition (Lane et al., 1990; Wickramasekera, 1996; Weinberger et al., 1979). For example, rather than catastrophize about an easy error, highs may more readily forget such an incident and move on to the next task.

Although the self-deception mechanisms and concurrent increases in physiological reactivity that underlie high RC/SC are thought to make highs more susceptible to developing somatic and/or behavioral symptoms in clinical contexts, increased activation in the absence of high neuroticism may be beneficial to sport performance. Indeed, heightened autonomic activation in highs is thought to reflect the mobilization of processes that inhibit distress, facilitate goal-oriented behavior, or both, factors that are thought to have an adaptive and positive function in athletes (Bonanno, Davis, Singer, & Schwartz, 1991; Taylor, 1996; Tomarken & Davidson, 1994). However, this self-deception component of high RC/SC may also have adverse developmental consequences. For example, highly skilled athletes can be difficult to coach at times (Carlstedt, 1995). There is a tendency among some elite athletes to "know it all," with those who get to the top of their sport liking to portray themselves as perfect in the physical and technical sense, and want to be thought of as mentally tough and free of psychological weaknesses (Carlstedt, 1995). High RC/SC athletes can fail to recognize or admit their frailties and have a tendency to reject constructive criticism from coaches (Carlstedt, 1995). This may arrest or limit the technical progress and advancement of these athletes, especially those who need to develop better skills or are trying to break out of a slump (Carlstedt, 1995, 2004a, 2004b).

When working with athletes who are high in RC/SC (who can be resistant, skeptical, and noncompliant; and assuming one ever presents for consultation voluntarily [a rarity]), one must convince them of the potential benefits of a mental training method. This can be achieved by providing them with objective evidence that an intervention works or show them how a mental training modality affects mind–body–motor responses to enhance performance (see the Trojan Horse approach in the HRMTP section). Biofeedback is an excellent procedure for convincing the unbelieving, skeptical athlete that the mind (usually the high RC/SC athlete) indeed can influence the body and motor control since self-generated response tendencies are readily apparent on a screen or in the form of visual and audio feedback (Carlstedt, 2001, 2004a, 2004b). The high RC/SC athlete may actually view the biofeedback process as some sort of internal or personal competition at which they want to succeed (e.g., readily demonstrate a prescribed biofeedback response).

Repressive coping had not previously been studied in athletes until Carlstedt's (2001) dissertation.

PREDICTIONS: CONSTELLATIONS OF PHO FACTORS AND PERFORMANCE

Consistent with predictions from the HRMTP in clinical settings, it is expected that specific constellations of H/A, N, and RC in athletes will be more powerful predictors of performance than these individual measures alone, especially during critical moments of competition. The following predictions emanate from an extension of the HRMTP to sport performance and athletes and were tested and continue to be in the context of the original Athlete's Profile and Theory of Critical Moments models of peak performance.

1. Hypnotic susceptibility/subliminal attention (HS/SA) is the PHO factor that is most directly related to sport-specific attention (focus) and cognitive/perceptual processes in athletes. Athletes who are high in HS/SA, in the presence of high neuroticism/subliminal reactivity (N/SR) and low repressive/subliminal coping (RC/SC), will be the most vulnerable to negative intrusive thoughts during competition.
2. High RC/SC will protect athletes who are high in HS/SA from intrusive thoughts that are associated with high neuroticism/subliminal reactivity (N/SR), thereby facilitating their capacity for sustained focused attention, even when under pressure.

3. High RC/SC will modulate negative cognitive activity that is associated with high N/SR by preventing negative intrusive thoughts from reaching consciousness during critical moments of competition, regardless of an athlete's level of HS/SA and N/SR.

4. High RC/SC mediates intensity levels, or physiological reactivity that is necessary for optimum performance. High RC/SC will help stabilize physiological reactivity in athletes who are high in N/SR by preventing negative intrusive thoughts from raising physiological reactivity to levels outside an athlete's IZOF. Conversely, high RC/SC will raise levels of physiological reactivity in athletes who are low in N/SR.

5. The most mentally tough athletes will be high or low in HS/SA, low in N/SR, and high in RC/SC. Athletes possessing this constellation of PHO factors will have a distinct psychological advantage during critical moments of competition.

6. The most performance detrimental PHO constellation will be high HS/SA, high N/SR, and low RC/SC. Athletes possessing this PHO constellation will be at a distinct psychological disadvantage during critical moments of competition.

7. Specific neuropsychophysiological responses will occur as a function of an Athlete's Profile constellation of PHO factors during critical moments of competition, including shifts from left-to-right relative brain hemispheric activation, increased HRD, and decreased muscle tension in secondary (nontask essential) muscles, including the frontalis muscle during critical moments in athletes possessing the ideal Athlete's Profile constellation of PHO measures (see number 5).

SUMMARY: KNOWN AND HYPOTHESIZED ATHLETE'S PROFILE MIND–BODY DYNAMICS

As previously noted, high HS/SA is associated with the heightened capacity for sustained focused attention, an important component of optimum performance. High HS/SA has also been linked to increased cardiac vagal tone, a physiological response related to HRD, which is mediated by the parasympathetic nervous system (PNS; Carlstedt, 1998, 2001; Harris, Porges, Clemenson-Carpenter, & Vincenz, 1992). Since HRD is an important marker of attention, cognition, and physiological reactivity that occurs most frequently during episodes of intense focus on a salient, external stimulus (such as a ball during competition), a state more easily attained by athletes who are high in HS/SA, these athletes may have a psychological performance advantage, especially if they are concurrently low in N/SR and high in RC/SC. High HS/SA in the presence of low N/SR and high RC/SC has emerged as one of two ideal Athlete's Profiles, mediating and sustaining zone states even during critical moments of competition.

Although athletes who are low in HS/SA may not have an inherent advantage when it comes to focus or readily be able to attain flow or zone states, these athletes may be less vulnerable to internal and external distractions (surplus pattern recognition). Athletes who are low in HS/SA, especially if they are low in N/SR and high in RC/SC, are as likely to benefit from the positive effects of these latter PHO measures (N/SR & RC/SC) in a manner similar to highs. The type of focus associated with low HS/SA is more of an instrumental or reality and goal-oriented focus that differs from that of athletes who are high in HS/SA, who tend have a more visually based, imagery-laden style of attention. In essence, the less distractibility associated with athletes who are low in HS/SA may be just as advantageous as the enhanced ability to rapidly enter states of intense focus that is seen in athletes who are high in HS/SA and may account for the emergence of the low HS/SA, low N/SR, and high RC/SC Athlete's Profile as the co-ideal constellation of PHO measures.

The presence of high RC/SC coping in an athlete's PHO constellation functions not only to suppress the inter-hemispheric transfer of negative intrusive thoughts but also to regulate intensity as a function of an athlete's level of N/SR. In athletes who are low in N/SR, at baseline, RC/SC may exert its influence to drive motivation and goal orientation, thereby facilitating levels of physiological reactivity that are necessary for peak performance.

Just as it is predicted that there are ideal constellations of PHO measures, certain Athlete's Profile constellations can put athletes at a distinct disadvantage during critical moments of competition. The PHO constellation that has been shown to be most detrimental to performance when it counts the most is high HS/SA, high N/SR, and low RC/SC. Its disadvantage can be attributed to high HS/SA, high N/SR, and low RC/SC exerting their effects. In the context of situational competitive pressure (critical moments), this profile is associated with the generation of negative intrusive thoughts. In this scenario, the normally superior focusing ability of athletes who are high in HS/SA shifts from being task-specific to these internally manifested negative cognitions, leading to a breakdown in motor performance when utmost control is necessary. This tendency on the part of athletes who are high in HS/SA, who are concurrently high in N/SR, to generate and attend excessively on negative intrusive thoughts and visceral sensations of something not feeling right, is hypothesized to interfere with pre-action HRD and concomitant shifts in cerebral laterality. Superfluous and context-inappropriate cognitive activity have been associated with HRA and continued increased left brain hemispheric activity when a rightward shift to more motor cortex activity should be occurring: neuropsychophysiological responses that are considered undesirable immediately prior to action. In the absence of high RC/SC to help suppress or prevent the generation of negative intrusive thoughts and their transfer from the right to the left cerebral hemisphere (the suppression of relative left-brain hemispheric and shift to right-brain hemispheric activity immediately prior to action after the cessation of left hemispheric strategic planning and motor priming is associated with increases in HRD), athletes with this profile are likely to be negatively impacted (high N/SR mediated) by excessive physiological reactivity that are not conducive to peak performance.

VISUAL OVERVIEW OF ATHLETE'S PROFILE MIND–BODY DYNAMICS

Reading, studying, and retaining the multiple interactions between and among Athlete's Profile PHO constellations is an exercise in focus and concentration in itself, not necessarily for an athlete, but the reader of this book. As such, the following charts (Figures 2.4–2.6) are provided as visual aids to help better understand the dynamics of the BHMB and Athlete's Profile models of peak performance along with a consolidating discussion of what each chart reveals. Although there is some redundancy, until one fully understands these validated models, review and repetition is the maxim, and that will be the case with readers being continually exposed to models in the context of numerous topics throughout this book's chapters.

The mind–body dynamics (HRD and cortical shifts) that are depicted in the following charts (Figures 2.4–2.6) have been well documented in numerous studies of athletes performing during routine phases of competition (irrespective of an athlete's PHO profile), whereby spectral analyses of total power (brain frequencies and their amplitudes) have revealed differential levels of activation between brain hemispheres as a function of internal or external focus or task orientation (e.g., strategic planning versus visuoperceptual attending). An observed seamless relative left-to-right brain hemispheric shift just prior to the commencement of action has been associated with faster RTs, motor/technical control, and better outcomes (see Carlstedt, 2001, 2004a, 2004b for a review of EEG studies on athletes; Landers et al., 1994).

By contrast, in negatively predisposed players (high HS/SA, high N/SR, low RC/SC), whenever critical moments occur or when stress increases (whether real or self-perceived), this seamless left-to-right brain hemispheric shift that usually takes place during routine moments in all athletes (athlete populations and species-wide response) is disrupted. A cascade of emotional responses that

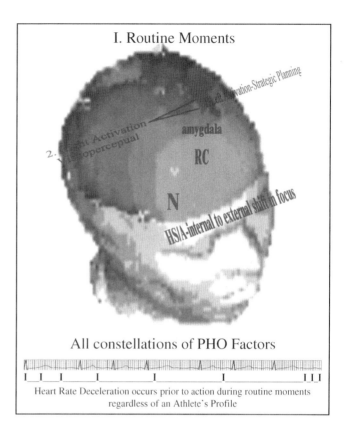

FIGURE 2.4 Cortical dynamics and heart rate variability during a routine pre-action phase.

is hypothesized to originate in the amygdala (the brain's repository for emotion, fear, and failure of memory), is thought to set off a "fight or flight" response (excessive [SNS] physiological activation) that is mediated by negative, catastrophic, and chaotic thinking. Negative affect (right frontal region-based neuronal ensembles) that normally remain dormant during routine moments of competition become active and infiltrate the left frontal region of the brain. This occurrence is thought to disrupt an athlete's strategic planning phase and the subsequent shift to more right frontal hemispheric and motor cortex brain activity that is associated with focusing and visuoperceptual demands of a particular impending technical action (priming of task-specific motor pathways).

These negative intrusive thoughts (e.g., "I hope I don't lose this point") take over, leading an athlete to fixate on negative emotions and images instead of preparing for action. As a result, one no longer observes the previously described relative left-to-right shift in brain activity. Instead, sustained increased activation (varying levels of beta EEG activity) in the left frontal hemisphere has been found to occur. Essentially, athletes who are burdened with high neuroticism/subliminal reactivity and low repressive coping/subliminal coping remain stuck in the ruminative left-brain hemisphere and are often rendered incapable of exhibiting peak motor or technical ability. If they are concurrently high in hypnotic susceptibility/subliminal attention, their potentially superior ability to concentrate suddenly is directed inward toward negative thoughts and images and not on the competitive tasks at hand. Such athletes are likely to see their games fall apart (see Figure 2.5).

On the other hand, athletes who thrive on and actually look forward to critical moments during competition usually have high levels of repressive/subliminal coping (left-hemisphere-based), are low in neuroticism/subliminal reactivity, and either high or low in hypnotic susceptibility/subliminal attention (Carlstedt, 2004a, 2004b). These athletes have developed a protective psychological

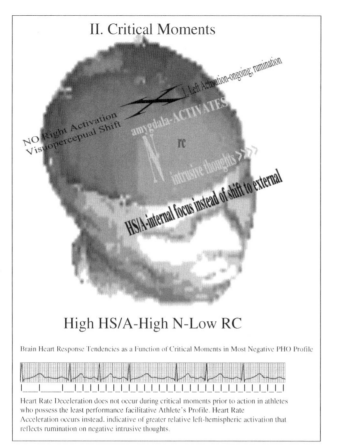

FIGURE 2.5 Cortical dynamics and heart rate variability during critical moment pre-action phase.

mechanism over the course of their career. Rarely, if ever, do they experience negative or self-defeating intrusive thoughts. They are self-assured and confident even in the most precarious of situations. If they are also concurrently high in hypnotic susceptibility/subliminal attention, their focus on task demands can be so intense they may not even recognize that a critical moment is imminent (indicative of flow or being in the zone), allowing them to play free from constraining pressure and associated negative intrusive thoughts and general lack of focus. In such athletes, the left-to-right shift that is observed during routine moments also occurs during critical moments. The fight-or-flight response is suppressed and negative thoughts are not generated. These athletes remain in total mind–body control that is marked by focused strategic planning (left frontal region activation) followed (immediately prior to action) by visuoperceptual attention to the impending task and motor priming (right frontal and motor cortex activation). This dynamic increases the probability that athletes will perform to their maximum physical and technical capabilities even during critical moments (Carlstedt, 2004a, 2004b; Figure 2.6).

Athletes possessing the ideal constellation of high repressive/subliminal coping, low neuroticism/subliminal reactivity, and high or low hypnotic susceptibility/subliminal attention appear to be less vulnerable to negative intrusive thoughts, whereas athletes who are low in repressive/subliminal coping, high in neuroticism/subliminal reactivity, and high in hypnotic susceptibility/subliminal attention are more vulnerable to disruptive cognitions, especially during critical moments of competition (Carlstedt, 2004a, 2004b).

Concomitant to shifts in brain hemispheric activity are specific parameters of HRV. Most notably, during routine phases of competition, athletes in most sports exhibit HRD immediately

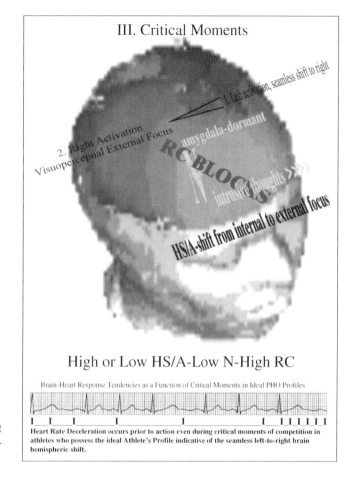

FIGURE 2.6 Cortical dynamics and heart rate variability during critical moment pre-action phase.

prior to action (e.g., before serving, putting, or shooting a free throw, batting, and pitching in base-ball) regardless of their constellation of PHO measures. By contrast, during critical moments, ath-letes possessing the most negative or disruptive constellation of PHO factors exhibit HRA prior to action, while those having the most facilitative or protective constellation continue to demonstrate HRD. HRA is associated with cognitive activity (e.g., thinking; intrusive thoughts) whereas HRD is associated with visuoperceptual processing or orienting on or toward an important stimulus (like the ball). HRD is also more pronounced when right-brain hemisphere and motor cortex activity increases after motor priming and strategic planning have taken place in the left frontal region (see heart activity tracers in the brain illustrations [Figures 2.4–2.6]). Negatively predisposed ath-letes also exhibit increased muscle tension in secondary muscles that are not relevant to a specific technical demand (e.g., increased frontalis muscle activity when batting; see Carlstedt, 2004a, 2004b, for a review and references pertaining to the preceding mind–body dynamics).

Summary

This chapter explicated the concept of construct validity in the context of the ABSP-CP approach to higher evidentiary athlete assessment and intervention. The conceptual bases of the ABSP-CP models of peak performance origins were traced to the High Risk Model of Threat Perception, a multifaceted integrative clinical model containing specific mind–body measures that have been found to mediate brain–heart–mind–body–motor responses associated with critical moment performance. It was emphasized that athlete assessment and intervention approaches must have strong conceptual and construct bases to reach valid and reliable evaluations concerning athlete performance tendencies in addition to predicting performance outcomes as well as guide the intervention process to increase mental training amenability, efficiency, and efficacy.

The presented Athlete's Profile, Theory of Critical Moments and Brain–Heart–Mind–Body–Motor models of peak performance will be repeatedly encountered in a number of subsequent chapters. *This is not an oversight or exercise in redundancy, rather, since specific components, methods, and procedures within these models are crucial to virtually all approaches to athlete assessment and intervention, they must be continually reviewed, as they are integrated into specific evaluation and mental training analytic procedures.*

Notes

1. As conceptualized or hypothesized and then shown to actually occur in relevant research.
2. This can be attributed to the vast majority of training and certification programs failing to educate practitioners in psychophysiology, applied psychophysiology, and biofeedback. As a result, practitioners are not being exposed to advanced procedures and methodologies that are crucial to high evidentiary practice.
3. Readers may notice that many of the following references date back decades. Nevertheless, such does not detract from their quality, since much of the cited research was of a seminal nature and still has an important place in the developmental history of various independent lines of research in behavioral medicine. They also point to the fact that the HRMTP has been understudied in recent years for reasons that were elucidated in a general context in Chapter 1.
4. A nocebo effect is the opposite of a placebo effect; it is marked by a strong belief that treatment will not work (Wickramasekera, 1988).
5. This may be good in many cases, especially in the realm of psychotherapy, where the dual-placebo response effect may be pervasive and exceed what would be expected on the basis of the normal distribution, thereby reducing due diligence and a thorough diagnostic process.
6. Variance explained on the basis of numerous combinations of PHO factors, neurocognition, and heart rate variability (predictor variables) in objective statistical performance outcome measures ranged from circa .30 to .70 (adjusted r).

Toward a Gold Standard System of Accountability: Advanced Methodologies in Athlete Assessment and Intervention Efficacy Testing

Do athletes really know whether an assessment or evaluation of their psychological or behavioral tendencies has validity, especially when test findings are extrapolated or generalized to sport performance? Can coaches, talent scouts, and general managers be confident that a report regarding an athlete's personality traits, neurocognitive functioning, or expected ability to master pressure situations is reliable? Should practitioner impressions and intuition about an athlete be accepted at face value?

After all, we are talking about psychological tests, "scientific" findings, and the opinion of expert sport psychology practitioners who have been trained to analyze an athlete's psyche and are thus capable of predicting subsequent performance tendencies, right? Not necessarily! What about interventions or mental training? Athletes are taught mental training techniques that supposedly will enhance their performance by practitioners who with great zeal and confidence attest to the potency of visualization, breathing, relaxation, and numerous other methods. But do they really work, and if so, on the basis of what evidence? Is self-report feedback from an athlete sufficient to conclude that an intervention is working, or not? Perhaps a practitioner's interpretation of observed "positive" changes in body language or an athlete's attitude is enough to conclude that mental training is having a performance facilitative impact. But is it? Are anecdotal accounts and interpretations that are devoid of sensitive objective outcome measures sufficient to conclude that an assessment instrument is a reliable predictor of performance or that an intervention is efficacious? Absolutely not!

So what can be done to bring gold standard, high evidentiary accountability to the field of applied sport psychology? Can this even be done? What will practitioners say? Will they be willing to adopt methodologies that will turn the prevalent practice paradigm upside down, an approach to athlete assessment and intervention that is more practitioner (office-based) centered than it is athlete centered? The current practice paradigm was born out of "clinical," economic, and temporal realities that still drive approaches to mental training. Practitioners for the most part are based in an office. They have to pay rent; to do so they must have a steady stream of clients every day. A client load of six or more athletes (or patients) can for the most part be efficiently handled only in the context of the 50 to 60-minute session time framework. Concomitant to these practitioner realities are client financial issues that very frequently preclude seeing a practitioner more than once a week, if that much. This is an inherently flawed practice dynamic, one that primarily caters to the practitioner's timeline and economic needs, a consulting model that can also be adversely impacted by an athlete's financial situation that rarely, if ever, can be mitigated through insurance reimbursement.[1] This service delivery model is also endemic to sport organizations such as colleges and professional sport teams where sport psychology practitioners see athletes in a similar manner, in the office for testing and training purposes for the most part, an approach that is devoid of a high evidentiary accountability system.

Such a state of affairs, marked by a practice model that does not elevate crucial scientific considerations to the forefront, is not conducive to gold standard practice and the advancement of accountability, since an arbitrarily constructed and constrained approach to athlete assessment and intervention precludes the acquirement of sufficient requisite high evidentiary information, data, and findings pertaining to athlete functioning and intervention efficacy. In other words, an athlete cannot expect to receive gold standard, accountability-driven applied sport psychological services in the context of a consulting framework that is dictated by practitioner or organizational realities, along with athlete impediments, like a lack of personal or organizational funding to finance a more extensive and intensive sport psychological regime.[2] Practitioners who unwittingly engage in the prevalent "consultant-centered" model will be extremely constrained in what they can provide an athlete client in terms of evidence-based approaches, and this has ethical implications that the field can no longer ignore.

So what can be done? This book and introductory chapter addresses this important question and presents a solution in the form of advanced methodologies that were designed to bring accountability to the athlete assessment and intervention process. The higher evidentiary procedures that will be advanced have been applied on hundreds of athletes over the last 15 years. They evolved out of dissatisfaction with eclectic, anecdotal, intuition-driven, status quo approaches to athlete evaluation and mental training whose main outcome measures are claims of success with faulty causal associations, dual-placebo mediated client-practitioner beliefs, and media and guru propagated self-proclamations of working wonders with athletes pervading. An argument can be made that the field of applied sport psychology rests on a deck of cards, with its tenuous claims and methods being on the verge of collapse. This collapse can only be averted if the field finally and collectively[3] exercises self-critique and institutes a systematic approach to applied sport psychology and the enhancement of psychological performance, one that is marked by high evidentiary accountability.

Gold Standard Accountability

The best way to demonstrate the validity of an assessment battery or efficacy of an intervention is through an accountability process. Accountability can be operationalized as the derivation of a quantifiable outcome measure (e.g., correlation coefficient, adjusted r^2 or t statistic) through the observation or manipulation and statistical documentation of relationships between independent/predictor and dependent/criterion measures.

Relative to athlete assessment, accountability can and should be demonstrated in the construct validity of a specific psychological, behavioral, or psychophysiological measure that is being assessed. For example, the Athlete's Profile, and one of its underlying primary higher order (PHO) factors, neuroticism/subliminal reactivity, has been linked, conceptually, to elevated sympathetic nervous system (SNS) reactivity even in an innocuous baseline condition, like just sitting still and doing nothing. Rather than just accept this to be true, at the intra-individual level an attempt should made to validate and/or replicate this component of the construct or conceptual basis of this measure. To do this, a practitioner would repeatedly (longitudinally) use, say, heart rate variability monitoring (HRV) to ascertain whether an individual who is high in neuroticism indeed exhibits elevated SNS activity at baseline. If that is the case, then one component of the construct validity of high neuroticism would have been validated in the specific individual who was tested. In this case, neuroticism was the predictor and SNS level at baseline, the criterion measure, since no attempts were made to manipulate variables as researchers do in experimental paradigms, in which case neuroticism would have been the independent and SNS the dependent variable. The eventual outcome measure in such a longitudinal, observational, single-case study with repeated measures is a correlation coefficient. The astute reader may wonder how neuroticism, being a stable trait, can be measured repeatedly in an individual, since variability is necessary to determine the extent of a relationship between a predictor and criterion measure. The answer is that even though neuroticism is considered to be a trait, and while group studies have found that high neuroticism is associated with greater SNS activity at baseline, high neuroticism is a score range and is not expected to be exhibited at its most intense level in all individuals, all of the time, as group studies might suggest. Hence, to better glean daily and situational fluctuations of neuroticism, even at baseline, the Positive Affect–Negative Affect Schedule (Watson, Clark & Tellegen, 1988), a test of affect whose negative affect (NA) measure is strongly correlated with neuroticism, can be used to arrive at level of state of neuroticism. Since it can be expected that daily NA scores will vary, over time one can determine to what extent state NA or neuroticism will influence baseline SNS activity, if at all. Psychometric and statistical issues aside, what is meant to be conveyed through this example is that if a particular psychological measure or trait is being assessed in an athlete, it should not be assumed because of group findings that psychophysiological responses in all athletes will be consistent with what would be expected on the basis of a measure's conceptual origins or construct validity.

One might say, "So what, why do I, as a practitioner need to know whether an assessment score for a particular trait is associated with some level of brain or physiological functioning?" The reason is that testing athletes should not be a random or arbitrary exercise, or "doing" sport psychology, just for the sake of doing something. A high neuroticism score in and of itself is merely a self-report, questionnaire-based value that may or may not be associated with behaviors or mind–body responses that are predicted for score ranges of this measure. That has to be established through criterion-referencing procedures or concurrently or externally validating the psychological measure at hand with functional mind–body measures that are associated with its construct validity (of the psychological measure). Doing so increases the probability that a psychological construct is actually measuring what it purports to (validity), and that will increase the probability that a measure will reliably predict performance. High predictive validity is the ultimate benchmark of psychological, behavioral, and mind–body measures; after all, if they do not predict performance, are they really relevant to the performance equation?

Accountability in the context of interventions is perhaps even more important than in the assessment phase of the consulting process, since it is vital to know whether any intervention is having an effect. The efficacy of a mental training procedure can be determined through the direct and indirect quantification of an intervention variable, for example, the quality of visualization prior to a golf or tennis match and its relationship to an outcome measure, say, golf round score or games won in a tennis match. Over time, a practitioner is able to determine statistically how much of the variance in an outcome measure, like a golf score, can be attributed to the quality of visualization. Numerous predictor or independent variables can be added to the mix, for example, in addition to quality of visualization (based on self-report), amount of time engaged in visualization, time of day when visualization takes place, and visualization lag time (time elapsed from intervention to start of competition) are additional factors that may influence or predict an outcome.

Accountability Procedures: Key Components

The field of applied sport psychology is replete with research-based systems, eclectic and hybrid athlete evaluation, and mental training methods, as well as extreme Guru-propagated, "analyze and cure-all" schemes that promise or guarantee incredible success. They all have one thing in common: the failure to routinely engage in gold standard accountability procedures to validate findings, theories, hypotheses, and claims at the intra-individual level. Certified sport psychology practitioners, many with doctorates and clinical licensure, are just as likely to believe in their systems as Gurus, yet, like their often rogue counterparts, fail to bring high evidentiary accountability to the assessment and intervention process. Athletes are told that if they visualize correctly, they will improve their game. One Guru swears that your "brain type" predicts with 100% certainty how you will perform and your chances of success as an athlete. While so-called credible and professionally liable sport psychology practitioners are not likely to buy into such extreme claims, one could argue that telling an athlete that visualization will work is just as extreme, especially when such a claim is sweeping in nature and devoid of evidence at the level of each individual athlete. It is just not credible to state or claim that an intervention will work, period! Just as the null hypothesis is negatively formulated, that is, it assumes and states that an effect will not be found between two populations, so, too, should athletes be told that an intervention might not work. Practitioners must determine empirically whether an intervention impacts performance and to what extent, and that can only happen if accountability procedures are used as a matter of routine.

Accountability methodology is the key to high evidentiary, gold standard sport psychological services. It is crucial for establishing the construct and predictive validity of specific athlete assessment and intervention systems and approaches and is critical for ethical and professional practice.

The Universal Claim: Accountability Enlightens, Substantiates, and Refutes

Although untested and unchallenged claims are the scourge of science and antithetical to evidence-based practice, here is a claim that can be advanced and tested. It is hereby claimed:

> that the validity and reliability of any assessment instrument and intervention procedure, especially its predictive validity, can and must be established through high-level evidentiary accountability methodologies and that the failure to do so **at the intra-individual level** (every single athlete in a sport psychology consulting context) can be considered malpractice and renders any intervention suspect as to its efficacy.

Irrespective of a practitioner's theoretical orientation, educational, and training background or extant applied approach to working with athletes, be it Guru-driven "Brain Typing," guided imagery, The Attentional and Interpersonal Style inventory (TAIS; Nideffer, 1976) assessment approach or the Critical Moments and Athlete's Profile models that are advanced in this book, ultimately, the validity and legitimacy of these and other diverse and disparate ways of evaluating athletes and conducting mental training hinge on high-level accountability methodologies and any and all inventors, purveyors, practitioners, Gurus, and zealots who use and advocate a particular system of applied sport psychology must accept the *Accountability Challenge* or their motives, ethics, and/or credibility can be called into question.

The Accountability Challenge

The *Accountability Challenge* can be considered a kind of a practitioner's "competition." It is a call to challenge and attempt to validate systems of athlete assessment and intervention, especially specific approaches that are used, advocated, and sold or conveyed to athletes and other consumers of sport psychological services as being of a high standard and highly efficacious. Essentially, the *Accountability Challenge* asks practitioners to put up or shutup. Using accountability methodologies that are presented in this chapter and throughout this book, practitioners accepting the challenge would be required empirically to test, analyze, and quantify their applied sport psychological approaches to athlete assessment and intervention. The following validity measures would be reported for assessment measures:

1. Construct validity
2. Criterion referenced or external validity
3. Predictive validity

Intervention efficacy would be established on the basis of the predictive validity coefficient.

Construct Validity

A system's conceptual basis and construct validity should be identified and incrementally validated through criterion, concurrent, and external referencing methods. It is not to be expected that the construct validity of an assessment or intervention model will or can be fully established, but as part of the challenge a practitioner would at least attempt to isolate an association between an assessed psychological measure and functional mind–body responding (e.g., if the TAIS were used to assess style of attention, then an identified style should be associated with functional brain, heart, or other neuropsychophysiological responses).

Criterion Referenced Validity

Construct validity drives the criterion referencing process. Here, practitioners would attempt to demonstrate that any assessment measure they deem to be highly relevant to peak performance actually measures what it purports to. For example, the Athlete's Profile model that is advanced in this book consists of three measures that have been shown to influence performance as a function of increasing criticality (pressure-laden critical moments of competition). A protective factor, high repressive/subliminal coping has been shown (construct/conceptual validity) to inhibit the inter-hemispheric transfer of negative emotions from the right frontal to left frontal lobe brain regions, thereby preventing negative intrusive thoughts from infiltrating the ruminative left frontal lobe area and negatively impacting strategic planning, eventual motor priming, and the onset of right brain hemisphere-based motor cortex mediated coordinated technical action responses. If this indeed occurs, then it must be demonstrated that athletes who are high in this measure are actually capable of shutting down internal and external distractions, be they intrusive thoughts or an opponent's trash talk. The *Accountability Challenge* demands of practitioners that they externally or concurrently validate or criterion reference what they claim about a measure with performance-relevant evidence. In this case, one might attempt to show to what extent brain wave or HRV activity changes as a function of the induction of internal negative messages or visual prompts from a baseline condition that fosters a neutral state and another experimental condition that attempts to foster a positive mental state in the moment.

Predictive Validity

While the preceding criterion referenced or external validity example may reveal brain and heart activity responses that are consistent with repressive/subliminal coping's conceptual basis or construct validity, ultimately, a psychological measure's sport performance relevance or potency is reflected in its predictive validity. That is, how much of the variance in a sport-specific statistical outcome measure can be attributed to the psychological measure of interest (the predictor variable). As part of the *Accountability Challenge*, practitioners must establish the predictive validity (the most important) of any psychological measures that they purport to be crucial to assessing athletes and predicting their subsequent performance. The predictive validity of any intervention must also be determined. The predictive validity coefficient (e.g., Pearson's r or adjusted r^2; i.e., variance explained) reflects or expresses intervention efficacy.

The Accountability Challenge: Rating Systems

So how does a practitioner win the *Accountability Challenge*? When it comes to this challenge, it really is all about accepting the challenge and competing. This means applying the recommended accountability methodologies to generate a validity profile for any assessment and intervention that a practitioner might use on an athlete. Completing a comprehensive validity profile is sort of like finishing a marathon. Establishing a validity profile is a longitudinal task that must be carried out on each athlete client. Sufficient repeated measures must be generated to achieve acceptable levels of statistical power to be able to arrive at empirical inferences about relationships about, say, the effect of an intervention (visualization) on a performance outcome measure (e.g., getting out of the block start in a 100 m race; about 60 repeated predictor and outcome measures per athlete). Once a validity profile has been established (at the intra-individual level and group or collective level [multiple athlete single-cases with repeated measures]), it must be submitted for review. If it is approved (reviewer validated) on the basis of an analysis of the submitted methodology, data, and findings, a validity profile is entered into an appropriate database category (e.g., a validity profile of a specific visualization protocol would be placed in the Imagery section under Interventions) and made accessible to *Accountability Challenge* participants (practitioners/researchers).

While the main goal of the *Accountability Challenge* is to motivate and inspire practitioners to engage in higher evidentiary gold standard approaches to athlete assessment and intervention and take a serious and critical look at what it is that they are doing (a more qualitative exercise that should have intrinsic value), the challenge will also produce a rating or ranking of systems of assessment and interventions that is based on the variance explained (predictive validity) metric, both at the intra-individual and conglomerate level (pooling all athlete single-case validity profiles). Importantly, the challenge will also highlight negative findings and validity profiles that call into question a particular procedure or approach, not necessarily globally, but for those specific athletes who did not benefit from a particular intervention or whose test measures did not predict performance in a manner that would have been predicted on the basis of group studies that are often used to guide practice (both assessment and intervention). Practitioners who report negative findings will be rewarded and recognized in the database of negative findings and allied ratings and rankings. The reporting of negative findings is crucial to the credibility of any scientific field of inquiry and should be highlighted.

Sample Ratings: Validity Profiles

Here's what a practitioner validity profile rating might look like:

Athlete/ AP[4]	Intervention	Criterion Reference	Variance Explained (Criticality)
A-H-L-H	Pregame imagery	L: H .2	.16
C-M-M-L	Same	2.5	.12
F-L-L-M	Same	3.8	.11
K-M-M-M	Same	.4	.04
L-L-M-L	Same	1.6	.01
W-H-M-L	Same	3.7	$-.03$
R-M-H-M	Same	.5	$-.05$
B-M-H-L	Same	.8	$-.08$

The above data set depicts HRV responses during a visualization intervention. Athletes are ranked in accord with how much of the variance in a pressure performance statistical outcome measure (criticality-critical moments) could be attributed to the imagery induced Low:High-frequency (L:H) ratio HRV activity. This visualization paradigm has been validated and is elaborated elsewhere in the book (Chapter 17). Briefly, it has been demonstrated that HRV is a reliable indicator of imagery mediated psychophysiological responding (changes from a baseline to a specified imagery scenario condition) and can be used to assess the vividness, intensity, and sustainability of a specific visualization scenario. The following charts (Figures 3.1 and 3.2) emanate from a world-class tennis player whose amenability and ability to induce visualization scenarios was assessed. They show HRV in the baseline condition (Figure 3.1) and HRV during a positive visualization scenario (Figure 3.2).

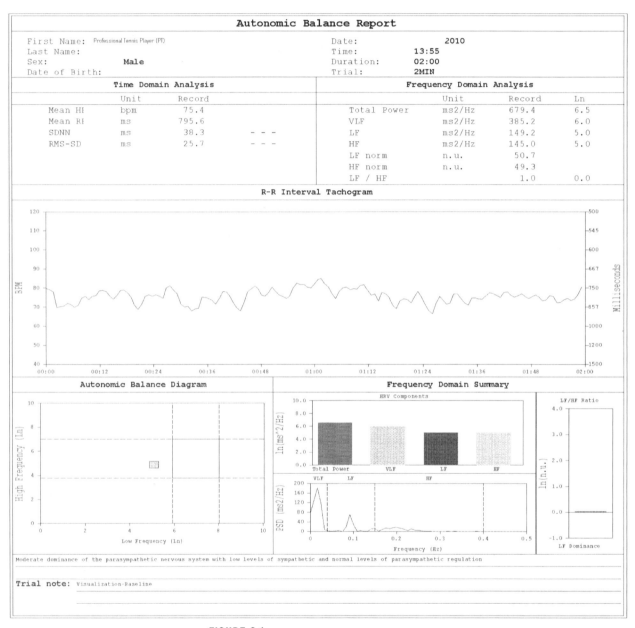

FIGURE 3.1   HRV in the baseline condition.

Notice that in the baseline condition, this athlete's L:H frequency ratio is 1.0, reflective of a state of autonomic nervous system (ANS) balance. By contrast, in the visualization scenario in which this tennis player attempted to generate positive imagery related to his match play, his L:H ratio increased to 8.8, indicative of a greater state of activation that may or may not be associated with a better outcome. The impact of a change in HRV responding across conditions on actual performance would still have been determined using intervention efficacy testing methods. Irrespective thereof, HRV is emerging as a reliable biomarker of visualization or imagery-induced neuropsycho-physiological changes.

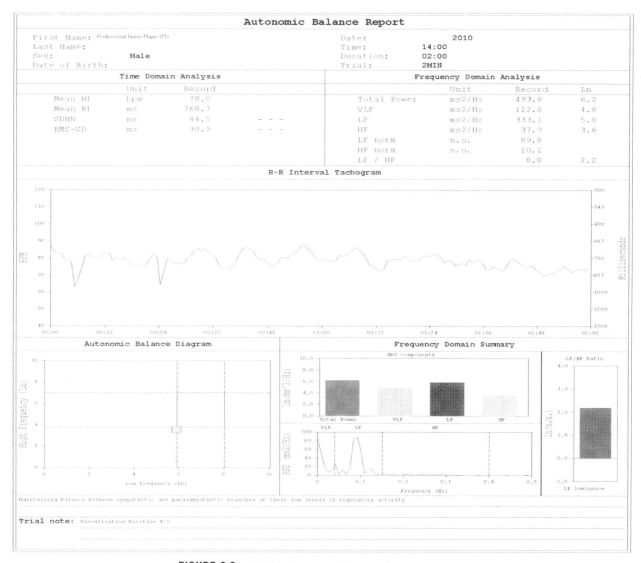

FIGURE 3.2   HRV during a positive visualization scenario.

In addition to reflecting imagery-mediated changes, HRV serves as a predictor variable in the intervention efficacy testing process. Since HRV is conceptually associated with key components of various models of peak performance, including attention, physiological reactivity/intensity, and cognitive coping/strategic planning, as expected, it has emerged as a potent predictor measure in the intervention efficacy testing process.

The preceding data set is consistent with individual athlete differential mind–body responses that have been observed in extensive previous intervention efficacy research. It was modeled for illustrative purposes and reflects response variability in a psychophysiological measure (HRV) that would be expected to emerge in the context of the Individual Zone of Optimum Functioning (IZOF; Hanin, 2006) and Athlete's Profile models of peak performance. These models maintain that peak performance is differentially mediated by constellations of specific personality, behavior, and psychophysiological measures (Athlete's Profile model) and that each individual athlete will exhibit a unique zone of optimum functioning (IZOF model).

The Athlete's Profile extends on the IZOF model by predicting and attributing variation in individual response to an athlete's constellation of PHO factors. The preceding findings reveal *Intervention Efficacy Quotients* ranging from $+.16$ to $-.08$, which is the amount of variance explained in the outcome measure (Criticality) that can be attributed to the pregame imagery induced L:H HRV frequency ratio. Conceptually, and as modeled earlier, the Athlete's Profile predicts performance outcome (intervention efficacy) consistent with what would be expected on the basis of pressure performance dynamics and tendencies that are hypothesized in relation to specific Athlete's Profile PHO constellations.

Practitioners should generate and maintain an accountability database throughout the course of their work with an athlete. It is insufficient to merely assume that an assessment is accurate or that an intervention will work. Many times an assessment finding cannot be validated and interventions, much more often than practitioners would like to admit or even want to know, do not work, or at best have a negligible impact on performance, and in many cases, have actually been shown to exert a negative influence on performance (see above data set).

Accountability should be mandated by professional societies in psychology and sport psychology, its educators, certification and licensing boards, and demanded of its practitioners by athletes, coaches, and other stakeholders in amateur and professional sports. It is hoped that the *Accountability Challenge* will help usher in a new paradigm in the field of applied sport psychology, one that is predicated on rigorous methodologies that will provide unprecedented insight into peak psychological performance processes and the efficacy of interventions.

Accountability Methodologies

Accountability methodologies should be systematically applied to assessment and intervention components of the athlete consulting process. Tests that are administered to athletes should be evaluated in terms of their criterion referenced and predictive validity, while the efficacy of an intervention should be established by determining to what extent a mental training method influences performance. The following section will discuss the components of the American Board of Sport Psychology-Carlstedt Protocol (ABSP-CP) in the context of accountability methodology. The presented methods and procedures should routinely be applied or adapted to all assessment and intervention approaches in applied sport psychology.

Accountability in the Assessment Process

THE ATHLETE'S PROFILE

Personality and behavioral measures, to have demonstrated empirical relevance to performance, must ultimately have predictive potency. That is, they must predict performance outcomes, otherwise assessing them may be nothing more than a trivial exercise that leads to information about an athlete's psyche that is at best ancillary to the performance equation. Consequently, to make a strong case for routinely assessing specific psychological measures, a practitioner must generate data and findings that are supportive of a guiding conceptual model (construct validity). Regarding the Athlete's Profile, the interactional predictions that are associated with it must be tested in a hierarchical manner. For example, an athlete with an Athlete's Profile of high hypnotic susceptibility/subliminal attention, low neuroticism/subliminal reactivity, and high repressive coping/subliminal coping (H-L-H), one of two ideal performance facilitative profiles, would need to have performance predictions relating to his or her profile validated on the basis of criterion or external referencing. Here's how that would be done.

Criterion Referencing of an Athlete's Profile Constellation

CONCEPTUAL VALIDATION WITH PSYCHOPHYSIOLOGICAL MEASURES

The first step in the evidence hierarchy is to determine to what extent an Athlete's Profile mediates a stress response that would be expected on the basis of its hypothesized and/or known neuropsychophysiological response tendencies. In the case of an athlete with an H-L-H profile, one could expect the athlete to remain relatively calm in the context of a validation stress test, such as the *Serial 7s Backward Counting Test.* However, since "calm" is a qualitative and anecdotal descriptor, in an accountability paradigm, "calm" or "less reactive" needs to be operationalized, for example, using HRV or other mind–body measures like brain waves electroencephalography (EEG) or electrodermal activity (EDA) to determine whether a particular Athlete's Profile is associated with expected neuropsychophysiological responses. In an athlete with the H-L-H profile, we would expect a fairly stable level of SNS activity across the baseline and task condition, with HRV measures that are associated with emotional and cognitive control, like a L:H frequency ratio, being 1.0 or less in the stress condition.

While the manifestation of a global criterion-referenced measure such as a Serial 7s Stress test HRV response that is consistent with what one would expect on the basis of an Athlete's Profile constellation may be reassuring, there are important and sensitive micro-level criteria and outcome measures that have more credence in the validation process. These include actual performance in criticality assessment test paradigms during training and criticality analyses during actual matches, the ultimate and definitive test of concordance between an Athlete's Profile and performance outcome (the predictive validity of an Athlete's Profile).

Flow Chart of the Athlete's Profile Assessment Accountability Process

Figure 3.3 depicts three levels of assessment in the Athlete's Profile validation testing process, the goal of which is to determine to what extent predictions regarding peak performance, especially performance during critical moments during competition, are consistent with what would be expected on the basis of this athlete's profile. The data set was again modeled to illustrate what has been observed with actual athletes who possess this particular Athlete's Profile (H-L-H). The first component of the validation process, Level I (Serial 7s Stress Test), revealed a .9 L:H frequency ratio in the stressor (task) condition, a response that is consistent with the vast majority of athletes who exhibit the following profile (a less reactive cognitively mediated HRV SNS response when encountering stress). This counts as a *PASS* and 1 point toward a *Valid Profile* assessment verdict regarding the validity of the self-report-derived Athlete's Profile in a specific athlete.

The Serial 7s Stress Test is considered a macro-level test that in and of itself is insufficient to validate an Athlete's Profile. Consequently, a micro-level validation test is necessary to further discern whether an athlete will exhibit a similarly controlled psychophysiological response profile as in the stress test during an actual performance test, on the playing field (a behavioral test). A Level II validation test attempts to determine the effect of psychophysiological responses on performance outcome. The provided data in the pressure performance "Money Ball" paradigm (see Figure 3.3) is again consistent with what one would expect of an athlete with the H-L-H Athlete's Profile, namely, a fairly high Money Ball success rate (70%). Money Balls are points or event/task moments in sports that *must* be successfully mastered. For example, in tennis, a Money Ball task might involve requiring a player to hit his or her first serve to a precise area of the service box whenever they are told a particular serve is a Money Ball serve. Or, when they hear "Money Ball," they must win the impending point. In other words, however Money Ball is operationalized, it must be successfully handled to receive statistical credit.

In this tennis-specific paradigm upon which the data set was modeled, changeovers or time-outs were also incorporated into the testing. During a 1-minute changeover, HRV was monitored. HRV responding has emerged as a sensitive predictor of performance subsequent (prospective) to being monitored for 1 to 2 minutes during time-outs. It has also been found to reflect performance (retrospectively) prior to a time-out (performance prior to a time-out). In the data set below (Figure 3.3),

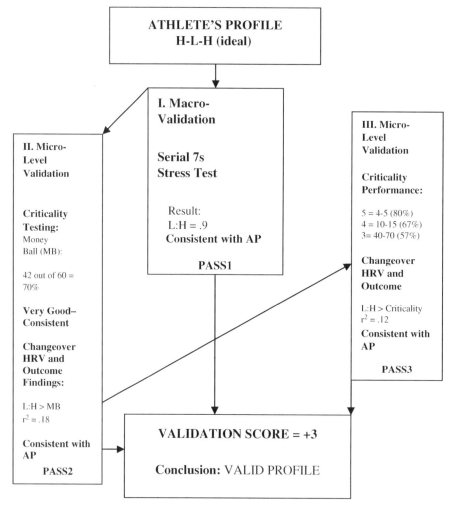

FIGURE 3.3 Accountability hierarchical pathways.

the Validation Level II Money Ball test, HRV during the changeover or time-out, explained .18 of the variance in pressure performance that could be attributed to the L:H frequency ratio response. This would be a very high level of variance explained that is more likely to be manifested in athletes with a more ideal Athlete's Profile. Thus, an athlete with an H-L-H profile who exhibits such Money Ball and concomitant HRV-performance outcome numbers would receive another *PASS* and validation point.

Finally, and most importantly (except for actual official tournament competition), a Level III validation test (superseding Validation levels I and II), in this case, a practice tennis match (2 out of 3 sets) revealed a high level of successful critical moment performance (80% of criticality level 5 points won, 67% of criticality level 4 points won; the lower rate of level 3 points won [52%], if anything, shows how much better the player performed as a function of the highest level of pressure [CM 3 is one of the most common point pressure ratings]). In addition, the player's changeover L:H frequency ratio explained .12 of the variance in critical moment performance that could be attributed to a psychophysiological measure (HRV) that is known conceptually (and empirically) to mediate pressure/stress responses. This, again, would be considered a high amount of variance explained. Consistency or high test-retest reliability of a HRV measure that then also emerges to impact performance; here, the L:H ratio in both the Money Ball test condition and in the actual match are thought to reflect a high level of mind–body control that is hypothesized to characterize athletes with more ideal Athlete's Profile PHO constellations, as in this case.

In this scenario, the data set illustrates a triple validation pass. Three criterion-external referencing validation tests were associated with performance and psychophysiological responses that would be considered consistent with what one would expect on the basis of this athlete's AP. In cases when athletes with a specific profile do not pass any of the criterion or external referencing validation tests, the self-report-derived Athlete's Profile can be called into question with the likelihood of a false-positive reading for a specific profile being greater. By contrast, weaker or less performance facilitative Athlete's Profiles can be negated when athletes exhibit their best performance and psychophysiological response-performance associations in Level III of the validation process. For example, an athlete with the most pressure performance detrimental Athlete's Profile (the high-high-low PHO constellation), who then, unexpectedly and paradoxically, performs in a superior manner during the Money Ball paradigm or during critical moments of actual matches or games and exhibits performance facilitative psychophysiological responses, is likely to possess a false-negative Athlete's Profile. In such a case, actual performance during training and competition supersedes self-report, test instrument generated findings that can be considered preliminary and must always be validated using accountability methodologies.

It should be noted that false-positive and false-negative Athlete's Profiles are rare, in the neighborhood of 30%, which is very low for self-report test instrument-generated psychological performance predictor measures. One might maintain that a 70% positive hit rate is actually quite poor, that would indeed be true if a test instrument that purports to measure a personality trait and behavioral tendency resulted in invalid measures or profiles 30% of the time. But it is not about merely determining an athlete's psychological, personality, or behavioral profile, it is about using such a profile to actually predict performance at the micro-levels of competition and, in attempting to do so, the Athlete's Profile that is generated using the Carlstedt Subliminal Attention, Reactivity and Coping Scale-Athlete Version (CSARCS-A), and clinical analogues Harvard Scale of Hypnotic Susceptibility, Tellegen Absorption Scale, Eysenck Personality Inventory, Positive-Negative Affect Schedule (PANAS), and Marlowe-Crown Scale has demonstrated an unprecedented level of predictive validity (see Carlstedt, 2001, 2004a, 2004b; Crowne & Marlowe, 1960; Eysenck & Eysenck, 1975; Watson, Clark, & Tellegen, 1988).

Nevertheless, individualized and integrative high evidentiary athlete assessment and intervention demands accountability. As such, the presented three-step validation process should be applied to every athlete when undergoing assessment and mental training, irrespective of preliminary self-report psychological findings and/or practitioner intuition regarding an athlete's psychological and behavioral tendencies.

Predictor Measures: Assessment and Intervention Efficacy

The validity of an assessment instrument is predicated on its predictive validity, otherwise the derived psychological information is of limited value in the context of the performance or performance enhancement equation. For example, let's say a practitioner or researcher is interested in an athlete's emotional intelligence and its impact on performance or whether a particular brain wave response, say, theta activity, is associated with better golf putting. The conventional approach to ascertaining whether the aforementioned predictor measures (emotional intelligence or theta EEG activity) influence performance would be to design a group study with a sufficient sample size to achieve a desired level of statistical power and then analyze the data and see if the level of emotional intelligence is linearly associated with, for example, batting average, or whether more theta EEG activity prior to putting is related to fewer putts per hole.

What tends to emerge in these sorts of group studies is that a significance (p value) threshold is or is not exceeded, and on the basis of such a probability cut-off, a declaration is made or conclusion is reached about the influence of a psychological measure on performance. What the group approach fails to adequately consider, both in cases when the null hypothesis is rejected or supported, is that wide variability often exists among study participants, that is, intra-individual trait scores or psychophysiological responses that are not consistent with the group mean. Nevertheless, group studies continue to guide practitioner assessment and intervention decisions, despite being inherently flawed. They have unduly influenced practitioner decisions about athlete assessment approaches and mental training. For example, visualization, the "Holy Grail" intervention, stands out as an intervention that is routinely prescribed to just about every athlete on the basis of a plethora of positive group study findings. Yet data that has been derived from over 15 years of research on imagery as an intervention in athletes has found visualization procedures to be highly equivocal relative to their efficacy, and even more so when hierarchical evidence-based outcome testing standards are used to determine the effectiveness of imagery at the intra-individual level (ABSP database). What has been found is that the more rigorous the accountability criteria, the less likely it is that group findings will hold up or generalize to the individual athlete. Similarly, with EEG and neurofeedback (the manipulation of brain waves in an attempt to improve sport performance), what few group studies there are also reveal wide variability in targeted brain responses and their manipulation, yet proponents loudly advocate for their universal application (see Chapter 18).

Accountability methodology focuses primarily on the individual athlete, with findings from multiple single-case studies with repeated measures (longitudinal) being the equivalent of a group study, but one that is better controlled (each individual serves as his or her own control). The single-case, longitudinal, with repeated measures design methodology, is the most rigorous, controlled, and sensitive investigative approach when it relates to determining neuropsychophysiological response tendencies and intervention efficacy at the intra-individual level and should routinely be administered by practitioners.

Single-Case With Repeated Measures Methodology: Step by Step

PRE-INTERVENTION ASSESSMENT PHASE

The utility of any test ultimately is contingent on the predictive validity of the psychological variables it purportedly measures. For example, if a practitioner hypothesizes or believes (based on previous group studies) that motivation, state anxiety, and self-confidence are crucial mediators of performance outcome, it takes more than a belief, hunch, intuition, or group study finding to validate that these measures indeed have a significant impact on performance. It cannot be assumed that a one-shot score on some test will predict performance. While psychological and related tests that attempt to arrive at trait levels of a particular measure may tell a practitioner something about an athlete, the influence of traits on performance usually can, at best, be inferred, but not quantified. Inferences and beliefs about trait-performance relationships are arrived at through group studies, because a trait by definition is a longitudinally stable and pervasive way of acting, behaving, or responding. The stability of a trait is established by high test-retest reliability coefficients; consequently, instruments that arrive at a trait level or score are of limited use in the context of single-case longitudinal, repeated measures assessment models, since if a trait-test were administered daily or prior to every training session or competition, it is highly unlikely that sufficient variability would exist to determine whether low or high levels of a particular trait would differentially predict performance outcome. As a result, practitioners must be very cautious about attributing predictive potency to findings on traits that were derived from group research to the individual athlete, even if strong performance relationships were found to exist between a specific trait and a performance outcome measure (at the group level). One might think that in light of the preceding limitations that place constraints on the extent to which one can make inferences about traits and performance outcome, how is it that the Athlete's Profile and its varying constellations of specific traits and behavioral measures can be lifted to prominence and deemed PHO factors if their predictive validity was established on the basis of group studies? The answer lies in the predictive potency of a trait or trait-like behavioral. It is one thing to determine that, say, motivation, in one study was found to predict, for example, 2% of the variance in athlete self-perception of competiveness. In this example, one self-report measure predicted another self-report measure, but neither actually predicted performance. By contrast, predictive potency takes on an entirely new dimension when a trait or behavior predicts micro-level, objective, sport-specific statistically based performance outcomes; like the effect of high hypnotic susceptibility/subliminal attention, high neuroticism/subliminal reactivity, and low repressive coping/subliminal coping, to a high degree (high variance explained), repeatedly across numerous group studies over time, with the same and different athlete populations and in numerous diverse sports. The Athlete's Profile and Critical Moment models can lay claim to these research accomplishments. It should be noted that the variance explained in the performance equation that can be attributed to psychological measures in their totality has not exceeded 10%, with single measures being hard pressed to show that they even explain 1% to 2% of the variance. This can be attributed to a lack of sensitivity or more global, macrolevel statistical performance outcome measure in detecting psychological influences and the fact that psychological, self-report measures have, for the most part, been investigated in group studies and not intra-individual case studies with repeated measures. Conceptual and construct validity and methodological issues also very likely have contributed to the inability to isolate potent psychological factors in the performance equation. The Athlete's Profile and Critical Moments models of peak performance were conceptualized cognizant of the aforementioned methodological weaknesses and, as a result, in a series of replication and extension studies, established unprecedented levels of *variance explained* in outcome measures that could be attributed to psychological factors (ranging from adjusted r^2 of ca. $.30 - .70$). Nevertheless, even such group predictive validity potency does not negate the necessity of determining to what extent such findings hold-up at the intra-individual level. This is not an easy task when it comes to traits due to the previously mentioned longitudinal stability and pervasiveness of such measures and lack of test–retest variability. As such, other measures that are conceptually related to, or are concomitants of manifested responses or behaviors that emanate from stable psychological traits, can be used as repeated predictor measures by proxy. For example, since we cannot expect trait or trait-like behavioral measures to vary much, if at all, from one measurement occasion to the next, in the context of the proposed high evidentiary accountability methodology, ersatz measures that are known to vary as a function of external and internal stimuli, including HRV and other neuropsychophysiological measures, can be used daily in an attempt to assess pretraining and competitive states and over time determine their predictive validity. Alternatively or concurrently, any trait or trait-like behavioral measure that has a *state* analogue, for example, a state correlate of neuroticism is the NA score on the PANAS and can also be administered to an athlete prior to training or competition. What one will frequently find is that a neuropsychophysiological measure like HRV, if administered prior to competition, will reveal a specific ANS response profile that is consistent with a state score for NA.

What this all means is that in order to reliably ascertain the effect(s) of a psychological and related mind–body and other assessment measures, it must be repeatedly measured prior to, during (where feasible), and after practice or competition in the context of a specifically operationalized evaluation, experimental, or intervention efficacy paradigm. Statistical considerations determine how many repeated measures there should be for each predictor measure. When correlation statistics are used, 64 repeated measures are needed to achieve sufficient power or balance (probability) between a Type I and Type II error (.80 based on a medium effect size forecast).[5] When using linear regression, the rule of thumb is a sample size of 10 for every predictor variable (or 10 repeated measures per predictor variable). For example, in the CP accountability paradigm, Athlete's Profile analogue state measures for its PHO measures could include HRV profile in the context of prepractice visualization assessment scenarios to assess state hypnotic susceptibility or subliminal attention, NA score on the PANAS state version to assess neuroticism/subliminal reactivity, and HRV-mediated subliminal coping response (repressive coping; undergoing validation). The obtained predictor measure scores would then be analyzed relative to various outcome measures that might include games won, games lost, points won, points lost (matches won and lost), criticality (critical moments) performance, and other sport-specific macro- and micro-level performance statistics.

Single-Case With Repeated Measures: Assessment Paradigm

If a practitioner is interested in discerning to what extent Athlete's Profile PHO measures and a host of other mind–body measures predict or influence performance, the following steps would need to be carried out:

1. Administer state psychological test prior to a match or game (keep constant the time of administration) to quantify the psychological state.
2. Administer psychophysiological test prior to match or game, such as HRV, EEG, or electromyography (EMG) or all others to determine mind–body state.
3. Administer same tests during time-outs or changeovers.

4. Administer the same tests immediately after a match or game.
5. Acquire sport-specific outcome and critical moment statistics throughout competition.
6. Enter data into Excel (sample below) or other spreadsheet and analyze in statistical package for social sciences (SPSS) or other analysis program when sufficient power has been reached (64 repeated measures or ca. 10 repeated measures per predictor variable for regression procedures).

Figure 3.4 is a screenshot of an Excel spreadsheet containing specific pre-golf shot psychological and psychophysiological predictor variables along with subsequent statistical outcome measures. Psychological measures include Athlete's Profile PHO state measures (trait analogues); Focus = hypnotic susceptibility/subliminal attention; Comfort = neuroticism/subliminal reactivity; and Control = repressive coping/subliminal coping. Psychophysiological measures include pre-shot HRV (heart rate [HR], standard deviation of the normal cardiac cycle [SDNN], very low frequency heart rate variability [VLF], low frequency HRV [LF], high frequency HRV [HF], L:H ratio). Outcome measures include score on hole, direction, distance and location of shot, quality of shot, and two types of shot criticality (1) based on probability of attaining par or better and (2) based on situational and contextual considerations, including a player's Athlete's Profile.

Hole #	Par (yds.)	Score	Shot #	Scan	Direction	Distance (yds.)	Location	Quality	Shot Type (Club)	Focus	Comfort	Control	CM prob.	CM sit.	HR	SDNN	VLF	LF	HF	LF/HF
Pre-round				Y											65.6	68.6	1397.5	334.8	83.9	4
	1 4 (390)		1	Y	S	280	Fairway	5	Drive (D)	5	5	4	2	2	65.5	84.4	68.2	699.3	194.3	3.6
			2	Y	S	110	Green	4	Approach (SW)	5	5	4	3	3	956.9	72	956.9	1221	122.9	9.9
MB			3	N		25'	Green	4	Putt	5	5	5	3	4						
		4	4	Y		2'	Green	4	Putt	5	5	5	3	3	69.8	49	309.8	158.1	111.3	1.4
	2 4 (377)		1	Y	S	265	Rough	5	Drive (D)	5	5	4	2	2	67	73.9	40.6	933.9	126.5	7.4
			2	Y	S	115	Green	4	Approach (52)	5	5	4	3	3	67.4	62.1	374.6	333.4	62.7	5.3
			3	N		20'	Green	4	Putt	5	4	4	3	3						
		4	4	Y		1'	Green	4	Putt	5	4	4	3	3	66.3	99.5	592.9	495.3	273.9	1.8
	3 3 (192)		1	Y	R	190	Sand	3	Tee Shot (5i)	5	4	4	3	3	67	79.1	92.4	618.9	111.4	5.6
MB			2	Y	S	25	Green	3	Sand Shot (SW)	4	4	3	3	3	71.7	106.2	577.5	689.8	296.3	2.3
			3	N		12'	Green	4	Putt	5	4	4	4	5						
		4	4	Y		6"	Green	4	Putt	5	4	4	3	3	67.1	101.9	79.8	248.3	108	2.3
	4 4 (336)		1	Y	S	280	Rough	4	Drive (D)	5	5	4	2	3	63.9	78	273.8	36.4		
			2	Y	S	64	Green	5	Approach (SW)	5	5	4	3	4	64.8	75.3	522.7	428.7	131.8	3.3
		3	3	Y		3'	Green	5	Putt	5	5	5	4	5	68.5	83.4	145.5	153.1	44.4	3.4
	5 4 (379)		1	Y	S	280	Fairway	5	Drive (D)	5	5	4	2	2	70.3	78.7	77.2	395.3	67.7	5.8
			2	Y	S	100	Green	5	Approach (SW)	5	5	5	3	3	65.1	101.2	669.1	808.2	76.4	10.6
			3	N		8'	Green	5	Putt	5	5	5	3	4						
		4	4	Y		2"	Green	3	Putt	5	5	5	3	3	68.2	106.6	252.9	522.6	265.7	2
	6 4 (420)		1	Y	R	240	Rough	2	Drive (D)	4	3	3	2	2	71.5	63.3	120.2	176.1	87	2
			2	Y	S	65	Rough	2	Approach (6)	3	3	2	3	3	61.6	59.4	51.3	135	107.7	1.3
MB			3	Y	S	100	Fairway	3	Approach (SW)	4	4	4	4	5	68.2	49.4	517.3	323	71.2	4.5
			4	N		25'	Green	4	Putt	5	5	5	5	5						
		5	5	Y		1'	Green	5	Putt	5	5	5	3	3	64.4	90.3	153.2	587	115.3	5.1
	7 5 (533)		1	Y	R	275	Rough	2	Drive (D)	5	4	3	1	3	65.3	57.3	341.7	123.3	72.2	1.7
			2	Y	S	163	Rough	3	Layup (6i)	4	4	3	2	3	74.5	33.9	56.7	43.6	28.7	1.5
			3	Y	S	95	Green	4	Approach (SW)	5	4	4	3	4	76.3	60	65.6	864.9	130.9	6.6
MB			4	N		15'	Green	4	Putt	5	5	5	4	5						
		5	5	Y		1'	Green	5	Putt	5	5	5	3	3	66.7	76.6	68.7	286.8	147.3	1.9
	8 4 (332)		1	Y	S	265	Fairway	4	Drive (D)	5	4	4	2	3	70.8	138.9	465.5	3191.8	1725.9	1.8
			2	Y	S	75	Green	4	Approach (SW)	4	4	3	3	4	74.8	88.3	1133.6	448.3	803	0.6
		3	3	Y		20'	Green	5	Putt	5	5	5	4	5	61.2	51.8	140.7	318.8	104.2	3.1
MB 9	3 (212)		1	Y	S	200	Fringe	4	Tee Shot (3i)	5	4	4	3	5	68.3	66.7	137.9	169.8	73.3	2.3
			2	N		26'	Green	2	Putt	3	3	3	4	4						

Sheet1 / Sheet2 / Sheet3

FIGURE 3.4 Pre-intervention performance assessment template: Golf-related, psychological, and mind–body measures.

The above data is real and emanates from the pre-intervention phase of consulting that was done with a South American professional touring golf professional with a Medium-Medium-Medium Athlete's Profile. This case study is explicated in Chapter 8 on *Sport Psychological Performance Analysis and Statistics II: Criticality Analyses During Training and Competition.*

In order to reach the .80−.85 power level in golf, one round usually suffices, since even zero handicap (scratch) golfers will hit at least 65 shots a round. However, since one can efficiently arrive at a pre-intervention assessment profile, it is prudent, when possible, to do additional full round assessments, to replicate or validate initial findings, especially in athletes (such as this one with more ambiguous Athlete's Profiles).

The goal of pre-intervention or general evaluation assessment is to determine the impact psychological and psychophysiological factors have on real performance; for example, HRV and PHO measures, independently or interactively. Outcome measures ranging from a macrolevel metric, like the score on a hole to micro-level situational level of criticality or quality of shot as a function of level of criticality serve as criterion variables that can eventually be compared across baseline (preintervention) and intervention conditions.

Figure 3.5 depicts the accountability process as it pertains to intervention efficacy testing:

I. The Athlete's Profile constellation of PHO measures sets the stage conceptually regarding what one could expect to happen with a particular athlete as a result of an intervention (predicts intervention efficacy). It is instrumental to intervention selection and predicting amenability to and compliance with a specific mental-training method.

II. The Athlete's Profile and Critical Moment model's conceptual origin and construct validity are revisited and retested in the context of ongoing assessment, neuropsychophysiological monitoring, and intra-individual derived associations and findings between and among baseline and intervention-manipulated (induced) mind–body and PHO (state) measures and objective sport-specific statistical performance outcome measures (III–VII).

III. Athlete's Profile self-report generated analogue state measures are used to further test the models depicted in Figures 3.3 and 3.5 construct validity through criterion referencing/external validation methodology and attempts to establish their predictive validity and mediating role in the intervention process.

IV. Neuropsychophysiological measures such as HRV serve to externally and concurrently validate the models' construct validity as well as reflect the impact of an intervention on mind–body–motor responses (compared to baseline [pre-intervention]) and determine the extent to which intervention-induced or accompanying response-changes are differentially associated with outcome (intervention efficacy).

V. Macro-outcome or criterion measures (or in some cases, dependent variables) are a first and global level of outcome, a lower evidentiary level that may reveal associations between any number of predictor variables and performance outcome and can be suggestive of intervention efficacy.

VI. Microlevel outcome measures should also be built into the intervention efficacy testing equation since they are of a higher evidentiary value. They should be designed to get to the essence of peak psychological performance, namely, an athlete's ability to master critical moments during competition when pressure and stress are expected to be the greatest. Being able to empirically demonstrate the extent to which an intervention has effected performance (if at all) when it counts the most should be a central goal of a practitioner.

VII. The *Intervention Efficacy Quotient* expresses how much of the variance in an outcome measure can be attributed to an intervention-manipulated neuropsychophysiological

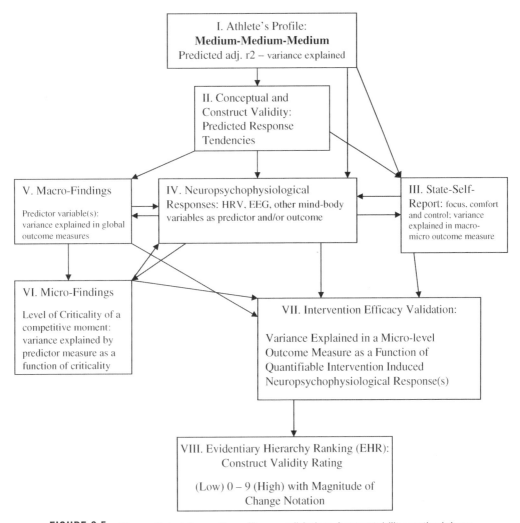

FIGURE 3.5   The path to intervention efficacy validation: Accountability methodology.

response. For example, to test the effect of visualization on critical moment performance (as with the aforementioned golfer), changes in pre-intervention/baseline HRV and state PHO responses are compared to the imagery condition prior to each golf shot, and the impact of such a response change is investigated using correlation and regression procedures.

VIII. The *Evidentiary Hierarchy Ranking* (EHR) is a qualitative metric based on the extent to which the efficacy of an intervention can be sequentially explained statistically (I-VII) in the context of an Athlete's Profile expected neuropsychophysiological response tendencies (construct validity) and as a function of increasing criticality. The EHR ranges from 1 (lowest evidentiary value) to 5 (greatest evidentiary value). The EHR is always calculated at the intra-individual level, since it is imperative that practitioners and each individual athlete client are aware of the empirical impact an intervention may have on performance. While aggregate EHR for a team or group research purposes can be calculated, ultimately, it's all about the individual athlete client.

Evidence Hierarchy Ranking: Criteria[6]

The following criteria are used to determine the potency of an intervention at the intra-individual level. They can also be adapted to group studies and athlete assessment instruments.

1. Intervention-induced neuropsychophysiological change from nonintervention baseline phase in the direction that is conceptually associated with expected changes and hypothesized positive outcome (enhanced performance). For example, visualization or imagery scenarios are designed to induce positive mind–body–motor states and such states are thought to improve performance.

   EHR Point: 1 if an intervention results in a statistically or practically significant positive change that is consistent, conceptually, with what would be expected or predicted.

   Example: visualization scenario that induces desired change (e.g., VLF of 120 in the baseline and 550 in the intervention condition) suggests that the intervention exerted an effect in the expected direction (greater SNS activation).

2. Self-report feedback after an intervention is consistent with what would be expected; for example, greater reported levels of focus, comfort, and control, and neuropsychophysioloical responses that are consistent with an athlete's established IZOF for a specific mind–body measure.

   EHR Point: 1 if an athlete who's previously reported focus, comfort, and control levels in a nonintervention phase or in the context of poor performance after an intervention were exceeded by two levels or reached level 4 (for all measures).

   Example: an athlete going from 1-3-2 to 3-4-4 for focus, comfort, and control.

3. An intervention, independent of any documentable neuropsychophysiological change, is statistically associated with macro-level positive performance outcome gains from the pre-intervention to the intervention phase.

   EHR Point: 2 if an athlete, in the intervention phase, exhibits performance gains as reflected in greater sport-specific macro-global outcome measures, exceeding those in the pre-intervention phase.

   Example: an athlete's batting average goes from .250 in the pre-intervention to .300 in the intervention phase.

4. An intervention, independent of any documentable neuropsychophysiological change, is statistically associated with micro-level positive performance outcome gains from the preintervention to the intervention phase.

   EHR Point: 3 if an athlete in the intervention phase exhibits performance gains as reflected in greater sport-specific micro-outcome measures than in the preintervention phase.

   Example: an athlete's quality of at-bats, 3, during criticality level 4 at-bats, increase to 6 in the intervention phase.

5. Intervention-induced neuropsychophysiological changes are statistically associated with positive sport-specific macro- or micro-performance statistical outcome gains.

   EHR Point: 4 if an intervention induced change, for example, an increase in HR from 85 at baseline to 100 after an intervention, is statistically associated with a macro-level performance gain.

   Example: an athlete's games-won total in tennis increases in the intervention phase compared to the pre-intervention phase as a function of increased HR (HR is correlated with more games won).

EHR Point: 5, if an intervention-induced change, for example, a decrease in HR from 85 at baseline to 60 is statistically associated with a macro-level performance gain, for example, an increase in Criticality Level 4 performance.

Example: an athlete's putting proficiency during Criticality Level 4 putts increases from 55% to 75% in the intervention phase.

Magnitude of Change

Magnitude of change (MOC) from the baseline (pre-intervention) to the intervention phase is also noted and is part of the final EHR. It is expressed as a variance explained coefficient and is derived from VII mentioned earlier. It reflects the amount of variance in a sport-specific statistical outcome measure that can be attributed to an intervention and/or intervention-induced predictor variable. The highest obtained association between an intervention predictor and outcome measure is attached to the final EHR; for example, 8 to .11 (an EHR of 8% and 11% of the variance explained).

Summary

Ultimately, an intervention that is designed to improve on-the-field performance must establish its worth empirically. It must be demonstrated that it works. "Works" means that an intervention reliably induces positive, documentable psychological, behavioral, neuropsychophysiological, technical, and tactical changes. Works, however, does not mean that an intervention is efficacious. Efficacy is determined on the basis of macro- and/or micro-level gains from the pre-intervention to intervention phase of the consulting process. Macro gains are global in nature, and although the pre–post improvement, for example, improving an athlete's shooting percentage from .45 to .68, may be significant, the causality of such a gain can, at best, be inferred. Nevertheless, at the intra-individual level in the context of a controlled intervention delivery paradigm, such a gain would be highly suggestive that an intervention has exerted a positive effect. However, the gold standard benchmark of intervention efficacy is variance explained. When obtaining the variance explained metric for intervention efficacy, a practitioner must structure his or her work with an athlete over time (longitudinally) with a pre-intervention and intervention phase and must operationalize interventional predictor and outcome variables to allow for on-the-playing-field, real competition-based analyses of intervention-induced responses and objective sport-specific statistical outcome measures.

This chapter presented an introduction to advanced gold standard accountability procedures for athlete assessment and intervention. There are almost limitless iterations and examples of how accountability procedures can be and have been applied. Serious, concerned practitioners must move away from the pervasive consulting paradigm in which an athlete comes to the office, is interviewed, analyzed, and taught interventions in an eclectic manner, and sent on his or her way in the hope that an evaluation is accurate and an intervention is efficacious. Advanced, gold standard athlete assessment and intervention must be athlete centered in terms of its temporal structure (how often, how long, and how much is an athlete seen and worked with), analytic components (in-office, during-training and real competition assessment, monitoring, data acquisition, database input, statistical analyses, conclusions, and reporting), and the manner in which interventions are administered (in-office, at-home, on-the-playing field validation and intervention ability, effectiveness, and efficacy testing).

Notes

1. It is very difficult to obtain insurance for sport psychological services to enhance performance per se.
2. Although in the context of current practice paradigms, more does not necessarily equate with better or greater intervention efficacy.
3. Organizations, educators, researchers, and practitioners in applied sport psychology.
4. AP = Athlete's Profile.
5. The reader is referred to *G Power*, a free software application that calculates power and effect size in a user-friendly manner.
6. If a specific criterion threshold is met, the designated point amount is awarded only one time. For example, if the intervention is associated with better batting average, better on-base percentage, better slugging percentage, and increased home runs (Criterion 3; Intervention predicts macro-level gains) 2 points (see criterion 3) would be counted toward the EHR, not 8 (2×4 statistical categories showing improvement). In addition, the higher point total is always allotted. For example, even if macro- and micro-criteria are met, only the higher point amount (micro) counts toward the EHR. Moreover, if criterion 5 (micro-level) is met, its point total (5) supersedes points allotted for criteria 3, 4, and 5 (macro). If criterion 3 (macro-micro), 4 (macro-micro), and 5 (macro-micro) are met, only the 5 points that are allotted for criterion 5 (micro) count toward the EHR. The count rule relative to criteria 3, 4, and 5 states that only the highest point amount counts toward the EHR. For example, if criteria 3 and 4 are met, criterion 4 supersedes criterion 3, and 3 points count toward the HER (points for 3 & 4 are not cumulative; the higher point amount only counts toward the EHR).

The Athlete's Profile Model: Primary Higher Order Psychological Mediators of Peak Performance

This chapter presents the Athlete's Profile (AP) in an applied context and will cover the following topics after a brief review of the Primary Higher Order (PHO) measures that it encompasses and their impact on performance:[1]

1. Test instruments, applications/administration, psychometrics, methodology
2. AP scores and their meaning in assessment and intervention contexts
3. Generation of AP-based reports: sample brief and comprehensive reports
4. Case studies: individual athletes and teams

The Athlete's Profile Model: An Overview

The AP model is a conceptual and explanatory framework that predicts athlete psychological performance tendencies during pressure situations of competition. It was previously explicated and is encountered repeatedly throughout the book, since establishing and interpreting resulting AP constellations of PHO factors are central to the assessment, intervention, and intervention efficacy testing process. The model will be briefly reviewed but not elaborated upon in this chapter. Readers are advised to thoroughly review Chapter 2 to better familiarize themselves with the intricacies of this model of peak performance. Based on initial, extension, and replication findings spanning 10 years, it is strongly recommended that practitioners use test instruments that are associated with their athlete's AP as their primary athlete assessment battery or to augment their current approach.

Background

The AP emerged out of an attempt to explain and predict peak psychological performance during pressure situations when competitive stress is expected to be the greatest. The conceptual origins of the AP can be traced to the High Risk Model of Threat Perception (HRMTP; Wickramasekera, 1988) and its isolation of the three so-called subject variables, hypnotic susceptibility (HS), neuroticism (N), and repressive coping (RC). These measures were shown to interact to mediate maladaptive cognitive processing/attention, physiological reactivity, and subliminal coping and resulting symptoms and/or illness (Wickramasekera, 1988). Since attention, physiological reactivity, and mental control (coping) are key components of peak performance, it was hypothesized that these measures would interact to mediate and predict pressure performance tendencies in athletes. Initial findings (Carlstedt, 2001) on these mind–body measures in athletes were consistent with predictions that emanated from the Theory of Critical Moments (see Chapter 2) that linked specific AP PHO constellations with better or worse performance as a function of increasing criticality (on a 1–5 scale, 5 is the greatest level of criticality or situational pressure). Over the last decade, extension and replication investigations have established the above HRMTP and their analogue athlete specific measures (subliminal attention = HS; subliminal reactivity = N; and subliminal coping = RC) as PHO factors that drive numerous psychological and mind–body responses (e.g., neuroticism and hypnotic susceptibility mediate state anxiety and attention, respectively). They have also been found to predict pressure performance tendencies with a high degree of accuracy and variance explained in objective statistical outcome measures that can be attributed to these measures (Carlstedt, 2004).

The dynamics of AP PHO constellations can be illustrated as follows:

During routine phases or moments of competition, most athletes are capable of exhibiting peak motor and technical performance. This means that a golfer who can regularly drive the ball about 250 yards down the center of the fairway will usually be able to demonstrate such length and direction consistently, even when under pressure, if he or she happens to possess an ideal AP constellation of PHO factors. By contrast, if burdened with the most detrimental AP, as situational (objectively operationalized) or perceived pressure increases, the likelihood that a golfer will display his or her best, normatively expected performance parameters decreases significantly.

Here is what is expected to happen in the vast majority of athletes during routine moments of competition leading up to the onset of action irrespective of their AP PHO constellation:

1. Strategic planning commences, a left frontal brain lobe localized preparatory response.
2. Just prior to the onset of action, a cortical shift is observed with strategic planning giving way to motor priming that is reflected in increased brain activity in the right-brain hemisphere motor cortex region and a "quieting," or strong reduction, in left frontal activity.
3. Concomitant with this cortical left-to-right shift is the onset of heart rate deceleration (HRD).
4. This dynamic sets the stage for the seamless activation of motor neural pathways and subsequent peak motor performance (commensurate with an athlete's technical competency) I_I__I__I____I____I_____I (depiction of HRD, longer/slower cardiac cycle/leading up to the onset of action (see Chapter 2).
5. AP PHO measures and/or their specific constellations remain relatively dormant or exert positive effects if a particular PHO measure is inherently associated with a peak performance component. For example, hypnotic susceptibility/subliminal attention is involved in the attention/focus-strategic planning process and, as such, will manifest itself in a performance facilitative manner during routine moments of competition. By contrast, neuroticism/subliminal reactivity is almost exclusively associated with the disruption of performance if an athlete's stress or pressure threshold is reached (a much lower threshold in athletes who are high in N/SR); however, during routine moments or phases of competition, N/SR will usually remain uninvolved in the performance process (that can change instantaneously, though, in an athlete who is high in N/SR). While high repressive coping/subliminal coping is a performance-facilitating PHO measure, it serves primarily to suppress the generation or manifestation of negative intrusive thoughts or mental "chatter" that is associated with N/SR, something that is less prevalent during routine moments of competition.

Once critical moments are encountered, AP PHO measures are activated in accordance with their mediating properties as follows:

1. Depending upon an athlete's AP constellation, the aforementioned described brain–heart–mind–body dynamics (Figure 4.1) will either continue to be manifested even during pressure-laden critical moments or they will be disrupted.
2. Two ideal APs have been isolated. Athletes who are high or low in HS/SA, low in N/SR, and high in RC/SC usually have a higher competitive stress tolerance level and, as such, are more likely to exhibit neuropsychophysiological responses that are consistent with those that are manifested during routine moments of competition, even in the presence of rising criticality.
3. Athletes possessing the most performance debilitating AP of high HS/SA, high N/SR, and low RC/SC, as competitive stress or pressure increases, are likely to experience a disruption of the neuropsychophysiological response dynamic that occurs during routine moments of competition (Figure 4.2).
4. Instead, rather than strategic planning (reflected relative greater left-frontal brain activation) giving way to motor priming and relatively greater right-brain hemispheric activation along with concomitant HRD prior to action, relatively greater left-frontal brain activity continues through the pre-action phase. This is indicative of excessive rumination and attending to internal mental chatter or negative intrusive thoughts predominating when pre-action motor priming should be occurring. Heart rate acceleration (HRA) also manifests itself, a response that in contrast to HRD reflects cognitive activity when a reduction in thinking should be taking place.

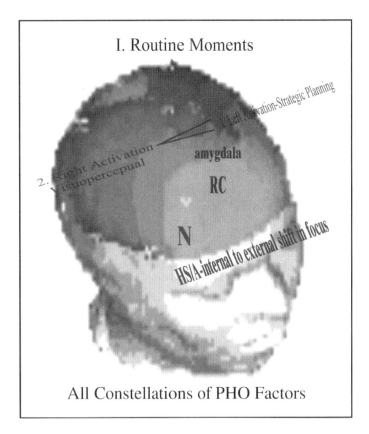

FIGURE 4.1 AP PHO measures and cortical dynamics during routine moments of competition.

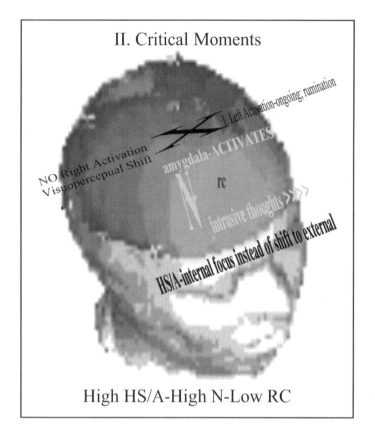

FIGURE 4.2   Worst AP PHO constellation and cortical dynamics during critical moments of competition.

HRA: **I_I I I I_I I I** (shorter cardiac cycle/nonlinear faster heart rate leading up to action; see Chapter 2).

5. These intrusive thoughts are thought to originate from the amygdala, the seat of negative emotions, fear, and anxiety memories. In athletes who are high in N/SR and low in RC/SC, in the presence of high HS/SA and competitive stress or critical moments (whether self-perceived or an objective reality), a cascade of responses occur that ultimately can disrupt motor ability and peak performance as follows: (1) critical moment occurs and is recognized, (2) amygdala is activated, (3) neuronal pathways from the amygdala to the right-frontal-lobe region where negative cognitions that are associated with high N/SR are activated, (4) these negative cognitions become intrusive, making their way into the left-frontal-lobe region, leading to the disruption of strategic planning and motor priming and subsequent pre-action relative left-to-right hemispheric cortical shift. Athletes who are high in HS/SA, high in N/SR, and low in RC/SC do not benefit from the potentially protective high RC/SC.

Athletes who have the ideal AP benefit from RC/SC, a subliminal behavior that has been shown to functionally disconnect the inter-hemispheric transfer of negative affect (negative cognitions; Tomarken & Davidson, 1994). In the context of competition and athletes, high RC/SC serves to suppress negative affect and enhance motivation, self-belief, and confidence even during the most critical of competitive situations. Athletes who are high in this measure have greater stress tolerance and are likely to display peak performance consistently, whether during routine or critical moments of competition (Figure 4.3).

FIGURE 4.3   Ideal AP PHO constellation and cortical dynamics during critical moments of competition.

Why Should the Athlete's Profile Test Battery Be Administered to All Athletes?

The rationale for using the AP model of peak performance and its allied test battery to guide the athlete assessment and evaluation process can be found in Chapter 2 on Construct Validity. It can be summarized as follows:

1. The AP has emerged as the most potent predictor of micro-level pressure performance, having explained up to 70% of the variance in the performance equation that can be attributed to specific associated psychological and mind–body measures.

2. Isolated AP measures have emerged as PHO measures that mediate the manifestation of almost all performance-relevant psychological, personality, and behavioral measures and constructs. For example, concentration or focus is not a unique stand-alone performance response. The strength or intensity of sport-specific attention, whether it is referred to as focus or concentration, is ultimately mediated by interactions of HS/SA, N/SR and RC/SC, rendering singular or independent assessments of attention inadequate and of limited predictive value.

3. The AP is the most reliable predictor of intervention amenability, intervention compliance, receptivity to coaching and pain, focus (attention), and technical or motor control thresholds. HS/SA and RC/SC strongly influence whether an athlete will and can engage in the predominant intervention in sport psychology, imagery, or visualization-based mental training modalities. Specific AP PHO constellations also predict with a high degree of probability whether an athlete

will seek out sport psychological assistance or mental training, with the vast majority of athletes who personally seek out a sport psychology practitioner being high in HS/SA and high in N/SR.

Administering the Athlete's Profile Test Battery

The AP battery consists of two separate but related and cross-validated sets of tests. The original battery contains independently validated test instruments that are used as part of the High Risk Model of Threat Perception (HRMTP, Wickramasekera, 1988) diagnostic process (establishment of the so-called subject variables), including the Stanford Scale of Hypnotic Susceptibility-A (SSHS-A) or the Tellegen Absorption Scale (TAS) that can be substituted for the SSHS-A, Eysenck Personality Inventory (EPI; neuroticism scale), and Marlowe-Crowne scale (MC; also known as the Marlowe Crowne Social Desirability scale). Original research pertaining to the Theory of Critical Moments (TCM) and AP models of peak performance used the preceding test instruments to investigate various hypotheses and develop the construct validity of these models. In 2004, the Carlstedt Subliminal Attention, Reactivity and Coping-Athlete scale was conceptualized, developed, and validated over the next 3 years (CSARCS-A; Carlstedt, 2004a, 2004b). The CSARCS-A was formulated to address various psychometric issues pertaining to face validity or how apparent or transparent test items are in the eyes of test takers. This test's items (questions) were tweaked to have higher face validity than its HRMTP analogue instruments in an attempt to mitigate possible response sets that may be endemic to athletes and the tendency of some athletes to discount test questions that do not seem to be relevant to sport performance and thereby not answer them honestly or take them seriously.

The TAS, EPI, and MC test instruments are self-report questionnaires that are usually administered and scored in an office or large room if an entire team is to take the battery. The SSHS-A, by contrast, is a behavioral test that takes about 40 minutes to administer (per individual). There is a group version of the SSHS allowing for its administration to entire teams in a more efficient manner. Practitioners also need to be trained in hypnosis and how to administer and score the SSHS. Consequently, the TAS can be substituted for the SSHS, since individuals who score high for absorption (the TAS generated measure) almost always score high in HS.

The ABSP-Carlstedt Protocol (ABSP-CP) is an integrative evidence-based approach to athlete assessment and intervention. As such, the AP battery should only be administered in the context of a comprehensive athlete evaluation and intervention efficacy testing process. It is not recommended that these tests are administered independently, nor should they be given to practitioners to use unless they have been trained and certified by the American Board of Sport Psychology to do so (see Chapter 22). In general, the TAS, EPI, and MC tests are administered secondary to the CSARCS-A if this latter battery is not revealing or ambiguous regarding athlete psychological tendencies. The former tests are also indicated if an athlete client's issues are more of a clinical nature.

The CSARCS-A is Internet-based and can easily be accessed by practitioners, coaches, and athletes. Its administration and scoring is done by computer. A report, analysis, and interpretation service is also available for individuals who have not been trained or certified by the ABSP to use the test. The CSARCS-A is an integrated instrument encompassing the three AP PHO factors, SA, SR, and SC, the sport-specific analogues of HS/A, N, and RC. The CSARCS-A has high convergent validity with its sister HRMTP tests, exceeding .85 for each construct that both batteries measure.

The CSARCS-A is a central assessment component of the Brain Resource Company's Web-Neuro Sport comprehensive psychological, neurocognitive, and health/mental health assessment

WebNeuro Sport

CSARCS-A, Cognition, DASS, Sleep, EI, Personality.

Client: CARL-SQFRE-00209   (birth date 14 Dec 1989; age 18 years; male)

Test	Level	Function Measured	Functional Significance
Carlstedt Subliminal Attention, Reactivity and Coping Scale-Athlete Version (CSARCS-A)			
	High Low High	Subliminal Attention Subliminal Reactivity Subliminal Coping	Ability to attain peak performance during critical moments
General Cognition			
Memory	Average	Working memory recall and recognition	Ability to attend to, learn, remember, store, retrieve and manipulate new information. It includes long and short term memory
Attention, Behavioral	Average	Sustained attention Focussed attention Impulsivity Cognitive flexibility	Ability to selectively concentrate during cognitive tasks, detect and respond to change in the environment, sustain attention over time and control impulses
Sensory-Motor/Spatial	Average	Hand/eye coordination Accuracy of selecting an appropriate response	Ability to perform motor skills and respond to information in a timely fashion. It includes reaction time
Language	Average	Word comprehension Verbal fluency Verbal memory	Ability to recognize words, access words and remember what has been heard
Executive Function	Borderline	Planning Abstraction Error correction	Ability to plan, strategize, execute complex tasks, abstract thinking, rule acquisition, inhibiting inappropriate actions and ignoring irrelevant sensory information
Emotion Recognition	Average	Emotional expressions	Ability to recognize interpersonal emotions through facial expression
Depression Anxiety Stress Scales (DASS)			
	Normal Normal Normal	Depression Stress Anxiety	Screening for Depression and Anxiety
Sleep			
	No	Probable Sleep Apnea	Screening for Sleep Apnea

Deficit	≤-2 standard deviation	Average	>-1 and <1 standard deviation
Borderline	>-2 and ≤-1 standard deviation	Superior	≥1 standard deviation

The Brain Resource Company©
BRC Operations Pty Limited ABN 45 098 619 115
Email: info@brainresource.com URL: www.brainresource.com

FIGURE 4.4   Summary report of WebNeuro Sport Battery with CSARCS-A summary classification for PHO measures.

CSARCS-A

Carlstedt Subliminal Attention, Reactivity and Coping Scale
Client: CARL-SQFRE-00209

The Carlstedt Subliminal Attention, Reactivity and Coping Scale-Athlete Version (CSARCS-A) contains measures that reflect the following neuropsychophysiological processes (Mind-Body processes):

I. *Subliminal Attention (SA)*: this measure reflects an athlete's subliminal or unconscious focusing or concentration tendencies. It can be viewed as the "Zone" facilitator in athletes who score high on this dimension (23-35). They possess an enhanced ability to focus intensely on task-relevant activities (sport-specific action/movement, etc). Paradoxically, low SA can also be performance facilitating.

II. *Subliminal Reactivity (SR)*: this measure reflects an athletes subliminal autonomic nervous system or "fight" or "flight" tendencies. It can be viewed as the "Great Disrupter" of peak performance in athletes who are high on this dimension (16-25). They are likely to exhibit increased psychophysiological reactivity (nervousness; muscle tension) that is mediated by catastrophic and negative intrusive thoughts, especially during critical moments of competition.

III. *Subliminal Coping (SC)*: this measure reflects an athletes subliminal or unconscious ability to fend off negative intrusive thoughts associated with high Subliminal Reactivity. It can be viewed as the "Great Facilitator" of "Zone" states and peak performance in athletes who are high in this measure (22-34).

Measure	Client Score	Range
Subliminal Attention	27	High
Subliminal Reactivity	7	Low
Subliminal Coping	23	High

This client has a "**Ideal**" profile as measured by the CSARCS-A.

It should be noted that the above measures interact to affect performance as a function of the criticality of a competitive moment. In other words the more critical the moment as established by the Carlstedt Critical Moment Analysis System (CCMAS) the greater the probability that an athlete's combination of the above measures will influence performance either positively or negatively. In isolation and outside the context of critical moments or competitive stress singular measures are expected to exert their positive effects. Their negative influences will remain relatively dormant until actual or perceived critical moments or competitive stress are encountered (see Critical Moments During Competition: A Mind-Body Model of Sport Performance When it Counts the Most; Carlstedt [2004] Psychology Press for a complete analysis of the dynamics of the above constructs).

Follow-up Report Service: It is recommended that athletes, coaches and practitioners who use this test battery consult with Dr. Roland A. Carlstedt to further inform the interpretation and implementation. Contact: RCarlstedt@americanboardofsportpsychology.org or DrRCarlstedt@aol.com. See the website: www.americanboardofsportpsychology.org

FIGURE 4.5   Brief report of CSARCS-A findings with raw scores for each PHO measure.

battery. It can also be taken independently via the American Board of Sport Psychology test center. In both cases, pre-registration by email is required (provision of access codes and passwords via info@americanboardofsportpsychology.org). Although only the CSARCS-A has established high predictive validity, other tests were included in WebNeuro Sport for research, demographic, epidemiological, and clinical diagnostic purposes. Its neurocognitive test battery is also still being investigated in the context of hypotheses that were derived from the AP and TCM conceptual and

Client: CARL-SQFRE-00209
Client ID: CARL-SQFRE-00209

Test Date: 27 Jul 2008
Page 3 of 16

NEO-FFI Data Table

Scale	Raw Score	*T* Score	Range
(N) Neuroticism	10	31	Very Low
(E) Extraversion	39	65	High
(O) Openness	22	40	Low
(A) Agreeableness	36	61	High
(C) Conscientiousness	37	59	High

FIGURE 4.6 NEO sub-scales from WebNeuro Sport battery (BRC, 2007).

construct validity models. These ancillary tests are presented here but will not be elaborated. The neurocognitive test battery will be discussed in Chapter 6. WebNeuro Sport also contains the NEO test battery (Brain Resource Company, Web NeuroSport, 2007) and can be used to cross-validate the CSARCS-A neuroticism analogue measure, SR, with the NEO-generated neuroticism score as well as criterion reference RC/SC with the NEO's "style of defense" dimension (see Figure 4.7).

CSARCS-A and WebNeuro Sport: Test Battery Components and Sample Outtakes

Figure 4.4 depicts a summary overview of CSARCS-A and other WebNeuro Sport integrated tests. It should be again noted that *only* the CSARCS-A PHO measures SA, SR, and SC have established predictive validity relative to pressure performance. Practitioners must exercise caution when attempting to interpret the performance or athlete-specific relevance of all other listed scores and/or classifications. It is possible to investigate any ancillary neuropsychophysiological measure in the context of performance outcome provided that one uses gold standard methodological approaches that are advanced by the ABSP-CP. Regarding this particular athlete (an NCAA Division 1 baseball player), what stands out at first glance is his CSARCS-A AP PHO constellation classification of High-Low-High (high in SR, low in SR and high in SC), one of two ideal Athlete's Profiles.

Figure 4.5 presents a brief report that elaborates the athlete's previously revealed CSARCS-A qualitative AP PHO constellation classification (High-Low-High) numerically (Figure 4.4). The actual raw score for each measure is important and supersedes the qualitative classification descriptors alone. In this case, the athlete's scores of 27 for SA, 7 for SR, and 23 for SC make him a "true" high for SA and low for SR, whereas his score of 23 for SC puts him at the lower end of the high spectrum for this measure. While still being high in SC he may not benefit from this performance facilitative response to the extent that an athlete who is on the high end of the high spectrum for SC, for example, as someone who scores 30, would.

In cases where an athlete has a more ambiguous or performance-neutral AP constellation or a PHO measure is on the cusp of another classification, as with this athlete, who scored 23 for SC (close to having the medium classification), it can be helpful to criterion or cross-reference a CSARCS-A score with that of an analogue test. Since the WebNeuro Sport battery also contains

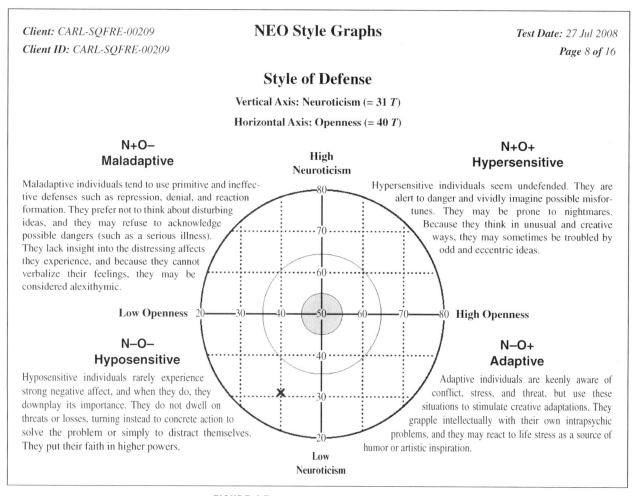

FIGURE 4.7   NEO style of defense chart.

the NEO, one can use its neuroticism and style of defense scales to help better determine an athlete's true classification for SR and RC, respectively. The Openness construct can also be used to help clear up any ambiguity about SA.

On the preceding page, Figure 4.6 reveals that this athlete's SR indeed is reflective of low N (very low N).

Figure 4.7 indicates further that the athlete is also likely to be a true high for SC. The hyposensitivity to negative affect and tendency not to dwell on threat or losses is consistent with high SC/RC.

Figure 4.8 depicts this athlete's neurocognitive standardized normative performance results. This test battery will be elaborated upon in Chapter 6.

WebNeuro Sport contains various clinical scales as seen in Figures 4.9 and 4.10. They are mentioned here since clinical measures and responses can be used as outcome variables in relationship to AP PHO constellation predictor measures; for example, to determine to what extent a specific AP constellation or individual PHO measure is associated with any of the previously listed symptoms, disorders, or responses.

Figure 4.11 is another ancillary test battery within WebNeuro Sport that purports to measure emotional intelligence (EI). As with many psychological constructs, EI has not emerged as a

Cognition

Client: CARL-SQFRE-00209

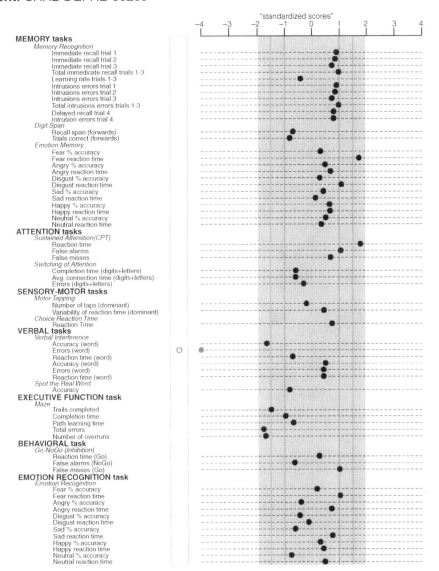

For convenience, the tasks are organized by broad cognitive groupings. The circles on the indicate statistically significant differences Compared with the normal control. The "standardized scores" on the right are normalized for age and gender, which means differences from zero reflect differences from 'average peer' (also known an z-scores). Positive "standardized scores" indicate strengths, negative "standardized scores" indicate potential deficits (Avg = average). "Standardized scores" beyond –2 to +2 are statistically significant. False alarms (respond when should not) = false positive; errors of commission. False misses (not respond when should) = false negatives; errors of omission. Instrusion = words not on the list. Specialist interpretation is required.

FIGURE 4.8   WebNeuro Sport neurocognitive test battery.

Depression Anxiety Stress Scales

Client: CARL-SQFRE-00209

Unresolved anxiety and stress are closely coupled with the cycle of decline in depression. Depression Anxiety Stress Scales provide a screening for Depression and Anxiety.

Measure	Client Score	Severity Rating
Depression	0	Normal
Stress	0	Normal
Anxiety	0	Normal

FIGURE 4.9   Clinical scales: Depression, stress, anxiety.

potent predictor of performance. As such, its relevance or utility in the context of the AP and TCM models of peak performance is that of an additional outcome measure, that, in line with the AP's PHO tenet, is expected to be mediated or predicted by specific AP PHO constellations or individual

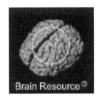

Sleep

Client: CARL-SQFRE-00209

This questionnaire provides a screen for a possible sleep difficulty.

Measure	Client Score
Total sleep score	9
Excessive daytime sleepiness symptom	1
Difficulty sleeping symptom	2
Narcolepsy symptom	1
Sleep Apnea symptom	1

Probable Sleep Apnea	No

The total sleep score indicates the likelihood for a sleep difficulty. The score for each symptom is scaled from 0 to 10 such that the higher the score, the more likelihood for that specific symptom. Scores for each symptom are summed from individual questions which range from 0 to 4 (0 = Never; 1 = Rarely, Less than once per week; 2 = 1-2 times per week; 3 = 3-4 times per week; 4 = 5-7 times per week).

FIGURE 4.10   Clinical scales: Sleep.

Emotional Intelligence

Client: CARL-SQFRE-00209

Trait	Client Score	Standardized Score	Range
Empathy/intuition	24	1.19	Superior
Social relationships	14	0.07	Average
Self esteem	15	0.99	Average
Total	53	1.18	Superior

The "standardized scores" on the right are normalized for age and gender, which means differences from zero reflect differences from 'average peer' (also known as z-scores).

Empathy/intuition:

Client CARL-SQFRE-00209 is rated as having a good capacity to perceive and understand the emotions in others. He is viewed as having a highly developed ability to use the understanding of those emotions when relating to others.

Social relationships:

Client CARL-SQFRE-00209 is perceived to have a good capacity to initiate and maintain positive relationships with others. He is seen to have a good level of confidence in a social environment.

Self esteem:

Client CARL-SQFRE-00209 illustrates a good ability to modify self presentation based on understanding the emotions of others. He indicates a highly developed capacity to experience positive emotions when confronted by challenges.

FIGURE 4.11   WebNeuro Sport emotional intelligence scale.

measures (e.g., high HS mediating EI). While intuitively, as with a plethora of psychological constructs that seem like they would be associated with peak performance, there is sparse, if any, evidence that EI impacts micro-level pressure performance outcome.

Comprehensive Report: Actual Athlete

In addition to the WebNeuro Sport computer-generated reports, practitioners and clients can be provided with a more extensive personal report regarding an athlete's AP PHO constellation, when possible, in the context of training and/or actual game/match performance outcome measures. The following customized report pertains to client *CARL*-SQFRE-00209 (name: DA; note, *CARL* does not refer to the name of any athlete client).

Client Report/DA-2007

INTERPRETIVE REPORT

Athlete: **DA**   Sport/Level: **Tennis/Professional**

Carlstedt Subliminal Attention, Reactivity and Coping Scale-Athlete Version (CSARCS-A)

Content

1. CSARCS-A Cover Page with Score Summary
2. WebNeuro Sport Test Summaries
3. WebNeuro Sport CSARCS-A Brief Report
4. Athlete's PHO Measures Overview
5. Narrative Report of CSARCS-A Findings
6. Neurocognitive Findings
7. NEO and Ancillary Tests

CSARCS-A ATHLETE'S PROFILE CONSTELLATION

SUBLIMINAL ATTENTION (Absorption/Hypnotic Susceptibility): **20**
Hypnotic Susceptibility Stanford Scale Hypnotic Susceptibility: A (SSHS-A): **6** (Medium Range)

SUBLIMINAL REACTIVITY (NEUROTICISM): **23**

SUBLIMINAL COPING (REPRESSIVE COPING): **22**

SUMMARY CLASSIFICATION: **MEDIUM-HIGH-HIGH**

WebNeuro Sport

CSARCS-A, Cognition, DASS, Sleep, EI, Personality.

Client: CARL-SQWEB-00030   (birth date 17 Jul 1989; age 18 years; male)

Test	Level	Function Measured	Functional Significance
Carlstedt Subliminal Attention, Reactivity and Coping Scale-Athlete Version (CSARCS-A)			
	Medium	Subliminal Attention	Ability to attain peak performance during critical moments
	High	Subliminal Reactivity	
	High	Subliminal Coping	
General Cognition			
Memory	Average	Working memory recall and recognition	Ability to attend to, learn, remember, store, retrieve and manipulate new information. It includes long and short term memory
Attention, Behavioral	Average	Sustained attention Focussed attention Impulsivity Cognitive flexibility	Ability to selectively concentrate during cognitive tasks, detect and respond to change in the environment, sustain attention over time and control impulses
Sensory-Motor/Spatial	Average	Hand/eye coordination Accuracy of selecting an appropriate response	Ability to perform motor skills and respond to information in a timely fashion. It includes reaction time
Language	Average	Word comprehension Verbal fluency Verbal memory	Ability to recognize words, access words and remember what has been heard
Executive Function	Average	Planning Abstraction Error correction	Ability to plan, strategize, execute complex tasks, abstract thinking, rule acquisition, inhibiting inappropriate actions and ignoring irrelevant sensory information
Emotion Recognition	Superior	Emotional expressions	Ability to recognize interpersonal emotions through facial expression
Depression Anxiety Stress Scales (DASS)			
	Moderate	Depression	Screening for Depression and Anxiety
	Normal	Stress	
	Extremely severe	Anxiety	
Sleep			
	No	Probable Sleep Apnea	Screening for Sleep Apnea

Deficit	≤-2 standard deviation	Average	>-1 and <1 standard deviation
Borderline	>-2 and ≤-1 standard deviation	Superior	≥1 standard deviation

The Brain Resource Company©
BRC Operations Pty Limited ABN 45 098 619 115
Email: info@brainresource.com URL: www.brainresource.com

CSARCS-A

Carlstedt Subliminal Attention, Reactivity and Coping Scale

Client: CARL-SQWEB-00030

The Carlstedt Subliminal Attention, Reactivity and Coping Scale-Athlete Version (CSARCS-A) contains measures that reflect the following neuropsychophysiological processes (Mind-Body processes):

I. *Subliminal Attention (SA)*: this measure reflects an athlete's subliminal or unconscious focusing or concentration tendencies. It can be viewed as the "Zone" facilitator in athletes who score high on this dimension (23-35). They possess an enhanced ability to focus intensely on task-relevant activities (sport-specific action/movement, etc). Paradoxically, low SA can also be performance facilitating.

II. *Subliminal Reactivity (SR)*: this measure reflects an athletes subliminal autonomic nervous system or "fight" or "flight" tendencies. It can be viewed as the "Great Disrupter" of peak performance in athletes who are high on this dimension (16-25). They are likely to exhibit increased psychophysiological reactivity (nervousness; muscle tension) that is mediated by catastrophic and negative intrusive thoughts, especially during critical moments of competition.

III. *Subliminal Coping (SC)*: this measure reflects an athletes subliminal or unconscious ability to fend off negative intrusive thoughts associated with high Subliminal Reactivity. It can be viewed as the "Great Facilitator" of "Zone" states and peak performance in athletes who are high in this measure (22-34).

Measure	Client Score	Range
Subliminal Attention	20	Medium
Subliminal Reactivity	23	High
Subliminal Coping	22	High

This client has a "**Red Flags**" profile as measured by the CSARCS-A.

It should be noted that the above measures interact to affect performance as a function of the criticality of a competitive moment. In other words the more critical the moment as established by the Carlstedt Critical Moment Analysis System (CCMAS) the greater the probability that an athlete's combination of the above measures will influence performance either positively or negatively. In isolation and outside the context of critical moments or competitive stress singular measures are expected to exert their positive effects. Their negative influences will remain relatively dormant until actual or perceived critical moments or competitive stress are encountered (see Critical Moments During Competition: A Mind-Body Model of Sport Performance When it Counts the Most; Carlstedt [2004] Psychology Press for a complete analysis of the dynamics of the above constructs).

Follow-up Report Service: It is recommended that athletes, coaches and practitioners who use this test battery consult with Dr. Roland A. Carlstedt to further inform the interpretation and implementation. Contact: RCarlstedt@americanboardofsportpsychology.org or DrRCarlstedt@aol.com. See the website: www.americanboardofsportpsychology.org

CSARCS-A: PHO MEASURE CHARACTERISTICS

The following important performance-relevant measures function to regulate focus, intensity, and thought processes, key elements of athletic success. They can work independently or in combination to exert an influence on the way athletes respond to various competitive situations. During more routine moments of competition these measures manifest themselves more subtly and are not likely to overly facilitate or disrupt performance. However, when competitive stress increases or critical moments are encountered, they can interact to enhance or hinder performance, depending upon their combination or constellation.

These measures also help determine what mode of mental training is most amenable to a particular athlete.

SUBLIMINAL ATTENTION (Hypnotic Susceptibility/Absorption)

Subliminal Attention is a psychological measure associated with the way we attend to external (real-world) and internal (our thoughts) stimuli. It can be considered a cognitive style relative to how we perceive the environment, people we encounter, focus on tasks at hand, and our own thoughts. This measure is also related to absorption and hypnotic susceptibility.

In the context of sports, Subliminal Attention can be considered the focus or zone factor in that high levels of this construct have been shown to facilitate intense attention or concentration on what needs to be done (task at hand). It helps athletes enter that "just do it" mode, especially in the absence of high Subliminal Reactivity or neuroticism (see next construct) by directing attention/focus toward sport-specific actions and away from distractions (e.g., intrusive thoughts). Research has shown that athletes who are high in Subliminal attention are capable of concentrating intensely in the absence of competitive stress. Paradoxically, athletes who are low in these measures also have an enhanced ability to focus situationally, especially if they are concurrently low in Subliminal Reactivity (neuroticism) when critical moments arise.

SUBLIMINAL REACTIVITY (Neuroticism)

Subliminal Reactivity (neuroticism) is associated with emotional reactivity and intensity. It can be considered the "great disrupter" of zone states in that negative intrusive thoughts that are associated with high levels of this measure tend to disrupt sensitive mind–body processes that occur during sports (e.g., waiting to serve or hit a pitch; putt; shoot a free-throw). Especially in athletes who are high in Subliminal Attention (hypnotic susceptibility), high levels of neuroticism can induce a shift in focus away from important tasks at hand and toward internal thoughts (e.g., fear of losing or failing). This is most likely to occur during critical moments of competition when athletes who are high in Subliminal Reactivity (neuroticism) are very likely to experience competitive anxiety.

SUBLIMINAL COPING (Repressive Coping)

Subliminal Coping can be considered the "great protector" of focus or zone states in that it has been shown to shut down negative intrusive thoughts associated with high neuroticism. Studies have demonstrated that Subliminal Coping (repressive coping) actually inhibits the inter-hemispheric transfer of negative affect from the right-to-left brain hemisphere, thereby facilitating the mind–body dynamics associated with peak performance.

OVERVIEW: Athlete's Profile Combinations/Constellations/Interactions

The following combinations/interactions of an athlete's level of Subliminal Attention (absorption/hypnotic susceptibility), Subliminal Reactivity (neuroticism), Subliminal Coping (repressive coping) have been shown to influence critical moment performance to varying degrees. This athlete's AP is highlighted in **bold** and elaborated after this chart.

SA/HS	SR/N	SC/RC	Critical Moment Tendency
Low	Low	Low	Neutral to Positive
Low	Low	Medium	Positive Tendencies
Low	Low	High	Ideal
Low	Medium	Low	Neutral
Low	Medium	Medium	Neutral
Low	Medium	High	Neutral to Positive
Low	High	Low	Red Flags (2)
Low	High	Medium	Red Flags (1)
Low	High	High	Red Flags (1)
Medium	Low	Low	Neutral to Positive
Medium	Low	Medium	Neutral to Positive
Medium	Low	High	Positive Tendencies
Medium	Medium	Low	Negative Tendencies
Medium	Medium	Medium	Neutral
Medium	Medium	High	Neutral
Medium	High	Low	Red Flags (2)
Medium	High	Medium	Red Flags (1)
Medium	**High**	**High**	**Red Flags (1)**
High	Low	Low	Positive Tendencies
High	Low	Medium	Positive Tendencies
High	Low	High	Ideal
High	Medium	Low	Red Flags (2)
High	Medium	Medium	Positive Tendencies

(Continued)

SA/HS	SR/N	SC/RC	**Critical Moment Tendency**
High	Medium	High	Positive Tendencies
High	High	Low	Least Desirable
High	High	Medium	Red Flags (1)
High	High	High	Red Flags (1)

Practitioner Challenge: Compare and contrast the two Ideal Athlete's Profiles with the "Worst Athlete's Profile. What does an Ideal Profile predict?

CLIENT ATHLETE'S PROFILE: ANALYSIS

CLIENT-ATHLETE-DA: MEDIUM-HIGH-HIGH

The AP PHO constellation **Medium Subliminal Attention** (Absorption/Hypnotic Susceptibility), **High Subliminal Reactivity** (High Neuroticism) and **High Subliminal Coping** (Repressive Coping) is considered a **1 RED FLAG PROFILE** that is rarely seen, since high subliminal reactivity/neuroticism and high subliminal/repressive coping have diametrically opposite construct bases (underlying mind–body responses). This profile is associated with potential performance disruptions, especially when stress occurs or increases during competition (e.g., critical moments). Although athletes who are high in Subliminal Attention tend to have a greater ability to focus intensely on the task at hand, once stress is perceived, whether consciously or subliminally (as reflected in physiological measures that are monitored), especially if they are concurrently high in Subliminal Reactivity (neuroticism), tend to focus on intrusive thoughts that are associated with this latter measure. These intrusive, negative and catastrophic thoughts get in the way of the so-called just-do-it mode that athletes who are high in Subliminal Attention can easily generate during routine moments of competition. Instead, thinking takes over, which can lead to a disruption of motor/technical skills. Although this athlete has a summary classification of **Medium** for Subliminal Attention, he is in the high–medium range (20) and is approaching the cut-off for the high classification (23) and is thus more likely to be negatively impacted by the pressure/stress-mediated Subliminal Attention-Neuroticism interaction (focus on intrusive thoughts) than an athlete who scores in the lower medium range for Subliminal Attention. It should also be noted that the summary classification of High Subliminal Coping (repressive coping) is on the cusp of being in the medium range for this potentially protective measure (a score of 22 for Subliminal Coping is the lowest in the high summary classification). As such, this athlete may be closer to having an AP of High–High–Medium than Medium–High–High. To better determine whether this is the case, additional assessments were evaluated. They are presented later in the report.

Neurocognitive Findings

There were no performance-relevant neurocognitive findings and it remains to be seen whether two significant test results have clinical implications (see following chart).

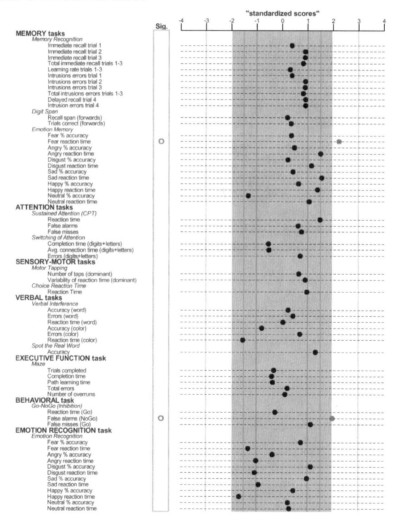

For convenience, the tasks are organized by broad cognitive groupings. The circles on the left indicate statistically significant differences compared with the normal control. The "standardized scores" on the right are normalized for age and gender, which means differences from zero reflect differences from 'average peer' (also known as z-scores). Positive "standardized scores" indicate strengths, negative "standardized scores" indicate potential deficits (Avg = average). "Standardized scores" beyond -2 to +2 are statistically significant. False alarms (respond when should not) = false positive; errors of commission. False misses (not respond when should) = false negatives; errors of omission. Intrusion = words not on the list. Specialist interpretation is required.

NEO and Ancillary Tests

The NEO is an ancillary test whose measures have not been found to impact performance with the exception of Neuroticism and perhaps Openness (a lower order factor of Absorption/Subliminal Attention). The results of this test can be used in the context of an overall evaluation but not necessarily for performance predictive services (SEE NEO narrative and findings). In the case of DA, his very low level of conscientiousness stands out and may have a negative impact on his off-the-court training habits and adherence to coach or sport psychologist instructions (see Concluding Analysis).

Client: CARL-SQWEB-00030
Client ID: CARL-SQWEB-00030

Test Date: 12 Aug 2007
Page 3 of 16

NEO-FFI Data Table

	Scale	Raw Score	T Score	Range
(N)	Neuroticism	27	53	Average
(E)	Extraversion	21	34	Very Low
(O)	Openness	30	54	Average
(A)	Agreeableness	31	52	Average
(C)	Conscientiousness	20	34	Very Low

Comments: Although the NEO neuroticism classification is not in the high range, as with its CSARCS-A analogue measure for neuroticism (Subliminal Reactivity), very low extraversion is associated with elevated neuroticism. Openness, which is correlated with Subliminal Attention (hypnotic susceptibility) is also in the average (medium) range in the NEO and does not provide convergent validity supportive that DA is a true high for Subliminal Attention, increasing the probability that he is a true medium for this measure.

 Brain Resource ⑨

Depression Anxiety Stress Scales

Client: CARL-SQWEB-00030

Unresolved anxiety and stress are closely coupled with the cycle of decline in depression.

Depression Anxiety Stress Scales provide a screening for Depression and Anxiety.

Measure	Client Score	Severity Rating
Depression	18	Moderate
Stress	6	Normal
Anxiety	20	Extremely severe

Comments: While the NEO neuroticism classification for WO is average, the extremely severe anxiety score on the BRC Anxiety Stress Scales is more consistent with the CSARCS-A Subliminal Reactivity (neuroticism) classification than the NEO neuroticism scale, and as such provides convergent validity evidence in support of the classification High Subliminal Reactivity/Neuroticism, that is, WO being a true High Subliminal Reactivity (high neuroticism) individual.

Emotional Intelligence

Client: CARL-SQWEB-00030

Trait	Client Score	Standardized Score	Range
Empathy/intuition	20	-0.07	Average
Social relationships	10	-1.49	Borderline
Self esteem	11	-0.98	Average
Total	41	-1.04	Borderline

The "standardized scores" on the right are normalized for age and gender, which means differences from zero reflect differences from 'average peer' (also known as z-scores).

Comments: Emotional Intelligence may have clinical implications but it remains to be seen to what extent, if any, it has an impact on objective performance outcome measures.

NEO Interactions

In cases of rare and paradoxical AP PHO constellations and/or when clinical issues appear to exist as in the case of DA (moderate depression and extremely severe anxiety), attempts to criterion reference CSARCS-A scores and PHO constellations with external measures should be pursued. Convergent validity analyses were undertaken to better determine WO's true AP PHO classifications due to the borderline and ambiguous nature of some of his PHO measures. In this case, his Subliminal Coping (repressive coping) score was compared with the NEO Style of Defense analysis to arrive at a true Subliminal Coping (repressive coping) classification.

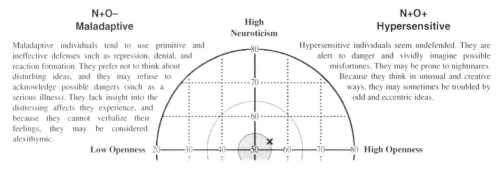

Style of Defense

Vertical Axis: Neuroticism (= 53 *T*)

Horizontal Axis: Openness (= 54 *T*)

N+O−
Maladaptive

High Neuroticism

N+O+
Hypersensitive

Maladaptive individuals tend to use primitive and ineffective defenses such as repression, denial, and reaction formation. They prefer not to think about disturbing ideas, and they may refuse to acknowledge possible dangers (such as a serious illness). They lack insight into the distressing affects they experience, and because they cannot verbalize their feelings, they may be considered alexithymic.

Hypersensitive individuals seem undefended. They are alert to danger and vividly imagine possible misfortunes. They may be prone to nightmares. Because they think in unusual and creative ways, they may sometimes be troubled by odd and eccentric ideas.

Low Openness   **High Openness**

Comments: DA's Style of Defense as described is inconsistent with true high Subliminal Coping (repressive coping). Consequently, his CSARCS-A score of 22 (the lowest possible score in the high range) may have been inflated because of the high face validity of the sport-specific test's items (questions). The clinical issues that were revealed by his WebNeuro Sport ancillary results for the most part are incompatible with high Subliminal Coping (repressive coping).

> Conclusion: DA's "true" AP PHO constellation is more likely to be **Medium (high range) to High-Medium** than the CSARCS-A generated rare and paradoxical **Medium-High to High** classification. This adjusted AP constellation is more consistent with his overall clinical psychological issues that may negatively impact his performance, even during routine moments of competition.

It must again be emphasized that when encountering a rare and paradoxical Athlete's Profile, a hierarchical evidence procurement strategy is employed to arrive at a more valid diagnosis. While the establishment of strong convergent validity on the basis of comparing scores from conceptually related test instruments (e.g., NEO neuroticism and CSARCS-A subliminal reactivity scales) is a necessary first step in the hierarchical evidence evaluation process, ultimately criterion referencing AP PHO and related (or any) psychological predictor measures with objective sport-specific micro-level pressure (criticality) performance is the gold standard final evidentiary benchmark for determining the psychological performance proficiency or mental toughness of an athlete. In other words, actual performance outcome supersedes any diagnostic or assessment classification of an athlete. However, relative to the CP, because of its strong construct validity, actual AP PHO constellations have very good predictive validity. As such, the AP classification has been found to be very revealing in terms of expected performance tendencies, especially when PHO constellations are or approach being the most or least performance facilitative (at the extremes of a normal distribution of PHO constellations).

Athlete's Profile and Performance Outcome

Since it is unlikely that DA is high in Subliminal Coping (repressive coping), his high level of Subliminal Reactivity (neuroticism) is expected to be the central mediator of pressure performance tendencies and he likely will manifest negative intrusive thoughts that will disrupt mind–body–motor responses when they count the most (during critical moments of competition). This observation and performance expectations can be tested in the context of outcome measures that were derived over the course of numerous tennis matches.

NOTE: The case study of DA is represented in Chapter 9 on heart rate variability monitoring and analysis paradigms. In that chapter, his HRV response profile and outcome measures are discussed.

The Athlete's Profile: Methodological and Analytic Procedures

An athlete-specific assessment measure is only as good as what it predicts. In other words, if a psychological construct and resultant score that is derived from a test instrument does not have strong predictive validity, its utility in the context of sport performance is questionable. Mere knowledge of the existence, on some level, of a trait, behavior, or response in an athlete that cannot be empirically linked to an objective sport-specific performance outcome measure renders it superfluous to the actual performance equation.[2] To establish the predictive validity of a psychological or mind–body measure, as with AP PHO constellations, it must be investigated in the context of objective, sport-specific performance outcome measures. If a measure is then found to explain "x" amount of the variance in a criterion measure (outcome measure), it can be said that the selected psychological or mind–body predictor measure has established predictive validity.

With traits, which are considered longitudinally stable and enduring and thus cannot be reliably repeatedly[3] measured in the context of outcome studies of a single athlete's performance, it can be difficult to accurately assess the impact of a trait on performance. Consequently, unless valid and reliable state version instruments are available that measure in-the-moment or day-to-day changes in a psychological or mind–body measure that is related to a trait of interest, it is difficult to directly empirically implicate a trait (that by definition does not change significantly) as being a performance mediator at the intra-individual level.

Virtually all that is known or assumed about psychological trait measures and their association with performance outcome is based on one-shot group studies, including performance predictions or response expectations that pertain to AP PHO measures and constellations. Thus, a two-pronged methodological approach should be used to investigate AP PHO measures and constellations in both individual athletes and multiple individual athletes on teams as follows by: (1) determining the impact of a team's aggregate AP PHO constellations on its performance and (2) using criterion- or external-referenced psychophysiological repeated measures (especially HRV) that are strongly associated with or reflective of specific AP PHO constellations, in place of AP trait measures that cannot be repeatedly measured, as HRV and other state measures that are variable over time can be.

Further on examples of AP PHO measures being applied to full teams of athletes are presented and discussed. AP PHO scores are analyzed in relationship to multiple outcome measures including global-macro and micro-performance (sport-specific statistical outcome and criticality) measures, raw scores from the BRC WebNeuro Sport neurocognitive test battery, and various neuropsychophysiological measures such as HRV that were obtained prior to, during, and after pre-intervention and intervention phases of competition. This methodology has led to a hypothesis that proposes that neuropsychophysiological measures can reliably blind or reverse-predict an athlete's PHO constellation independent of any prior knowledge of an athlete's psychological tendencies. Specifically, it is hypothesized that an athlete's AP PHO constellation can be predicted on the basis of HRV responses before, during, and after competition, without knowing an athlete's actual AP constellation (double-blind validation). This blind-reverse-validation (BRV) hypothesis attempts to address stability issues associated with psychological traits, including AP PHO factors that cannot be measured repeatedly in the context of longitudinal assessment and outcome studies at the intra-individual level. This methodology attempts to arrive at reliable statistical inferences about predictor-criterion variable relationships that involve psychological traits by substituting state measures that are hypothesized or shown to be related to specific trait measures. Since traits are longitudinally stable and unlikely to change if they were measured every day or prior to every competition, resulting in a restricted distribution of scores (insufficient variability), it is not possible to reliably test trait-predictor and performance outcome measures at the intra-individual level. Consequently, in the CP, HRV responses are used as a quasi-repeated analogue measure of AP PHO measures and constellations. Consistent with the conceptual and construct validity framework of the AP and TCM models of peak performance, it is posited that specific HRV measures will be associated with a differential outcome in accord with what one would expect on the basis of a particular AP PHO constellation. For example, an athlete with an ideal AP can be expected to generate replicable HRV responses that predict critical moment performance over the course of numerous games or matches (longitudinally) that are in line with response tendencies in pressure situations that one would expect in athletes with the most performance facilitative AP constellation. Conversely, HRV response patterns will emerge that distinguish athletes with an ideal from those having the most performance detrimental AP constellation. Essentially, HRV and other neuropsychophysiological measures serve as ersatz, quasi-AP PHO state analogue variables that are hypothesized to reflect actual underlying psychological influences on mind–body responses (e.g., HRV) and performance. This methodology allows for predictive validity trait/state studies of AP PHO measures at the intra-individual level that would not be possible using trait measures alone.

This repeated measure issue does not apply to team analyses of AP PHO measures and constellations since the AP measures are repeated in the form of multiple scores that are derived from each member of a team that usually generate sufficient variability in scores.[4]

The following series of charts depict data from an elite youth baseball. They are presented primarily to illustrate how AP PHO measures are aligned or linked to the outcome (criterion variables) that were previously mentioned and how data is managed prior to statistical analyses in SPSS or another program. Actual analysis and interpretations of these and other findings will be thoroughly discussed in Chapter 20.

Practitioner Challenge: Generate a fictional data set of HRV measures that could be used to blindly predict the two ideal and one worst Athlete's Profile constellations. Be sure to read Chapters 9 and 10 on HRV and HRD to prepare for this challenge.

In Figure 4.12, AP PHO individual measures expressed in raw scores can be found in columns C, D, and E. In this particular group (trait analysis paradigm), performance outcome measures include critical moment success rate (quality of at-bats; QAB) in the pre-intervention and intervention phases of competition. These outcome measures reflect averages based on all games during this team's season. Eventual data analyses would include determining the effect of AP PHO measures on the criticality-quality of at-bat success rate and success rate differences as a function of a no-intervention versus an intervention condition. Criticality and QAB would also be analyzed independent of AP PHO measures in the context of pre-intervention and intervention phases to determine whether team-wide gains in performance occurred in the intervention phase. In addition, all variables would be analyzed using regression and modeling statistical procedures to determine how much of the variance in the performance equation can be attributed to AP PHO and HRV measures.

Figure 4.13 depicts HRV measures that were obtained from the Serial 7s Stress Test (see Chapter 5). These measures are used for criterion-referencing and blind-reverse-validation purposes. AP PHO measures (to the left, seen in Figure 4.12) are analyzed as predictors (predictor variables) of stress test responses (criterion/outcome measures). AP PHO measures can also serve as criterion measures in blind-reverse-validation analyses in which stress test HRV responses are predictor variables in an attempt to establish neuropsychophysiologically stable response correlates of specific AP PHO constellations or individual AP PHO measures; for example, blindly predicting an athlete's AP PHO constellation on the basis of HRV change differences from a baseline to the stress condition (a cognitive task, see Chapter 5 and the Practitioner Challenge above).

Both of the preceding charts contain trait measures in a group (team) context. AP PHO and HRV stress test measures cannot be used repeatedly. Nor can the CM-QAB success rate outcome measure which, as previously mentioned, is an aggregate percentage that is based on multiple or repeated HRV measures that must be averaged when analyzed in the context of predictor or criterion measures that can only be noted or entered into the performance equation template once.

By contrast, Figure 4.14 depicts repeated measures upon which the aggregate performance outcome data noted in Figure 4.12 was derived (each athlete's data). Figure 4.14 contains repeated HRV data that was obtained prior to each at-bat for a series of games (partial outtake). The repeated measures methodological paradigm can be used to test the BRV hypothesis that expects specific

	ID	INT	SA/HS	SR/N	SC/RC	Cm-QabPre	Cm-QabInt	PreInQabDif	Cm-SucPre	Cm-SucInt	PreIntSucDif	Cm-QabTot	Cm-SucCom	Hrbase	SdnnBa	Vlbase	lowBa	highBa	I/hBas
2	CARL-SQFRE-00028	F												106	25	28	82	38	2.
3	CARL-SQFRE-00040	J	18	6	24	0.162	0.024	-0.138	0.165	0.035	-0.13	0.065	0.081	76	169	79	6880	1420	4.
4	CARL-SQFRE-00043	G	22	13	11	0.130	0.09	-0.04	-0.063	0.041	0.078	0.1	-0.013	74	75	58	340	339	
5	CARL-SQFRE-00046	K	19	8	6	0.232	0.165	-0.067	0.318	0.113	-0.205	-0.001	0.258	71	149	251	670	5460	0.
6	CARL-SQFRE-00053	Y	5	3	23	0.034	-0.052	-0.188	-0.04	-0.033	0.073	0.043	-0.032	85	55	227	498	281	1.
7	CARL-SQFRE-00054	R	18	2	17	0.061	0.718	0.657	-0.143	?	?	0.058	-0.136	91	142	1901	938	842	1.
8	CARL-SQFRE-00058	M	23	7	19	0.079	0.218	0.139	0.248	0.03	-0.218	0.227	0.166	68	54	152	452	369	1.
9	CARL-SQFRE-00059	J	15	4	25	-0.175	-0.022	0.153	-0.069	-0.154	-0.185	-0.152	-0.208	82	142	1684	290	237	1.
10	CARL-SQFRE-00065	YM	20	8	18	0.164	-0.102	-0.266	0.228	-0.233	-0.461	0.164	0.228	74	78	171	415	1033	0.
11	CARL-SQFRE-00067	RM	18	15	13	0.205	0.02	-0.185	0.116	-0.035	-0.151	0.315	-0.123	80	66	652	967	298	3.
12	CARL-SQFRE-00066	S	21	6	23	-0.074	0.104	0.11	-0.086	0.049	0.135	-0.001	-0.051	85	116	63	3407	729	4.
13	**MEAN**		**17.9**	**7.2**	**17.9**	**0.0818**	**0.1163**	**0.0175**	**0.0674**	**-0.0207778**	**-0.1182222**	**0.0818**	**0.017**						

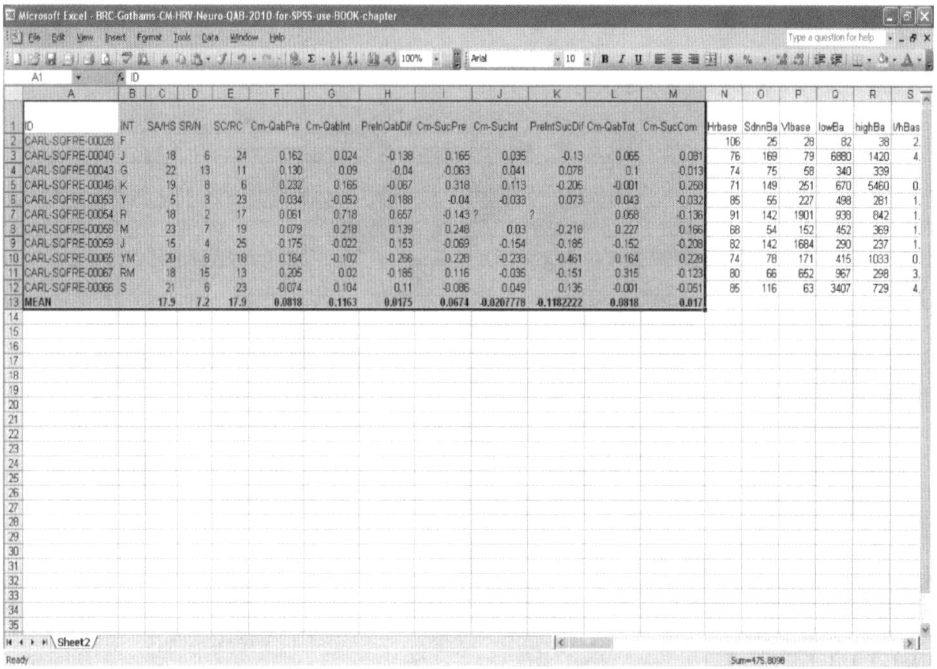

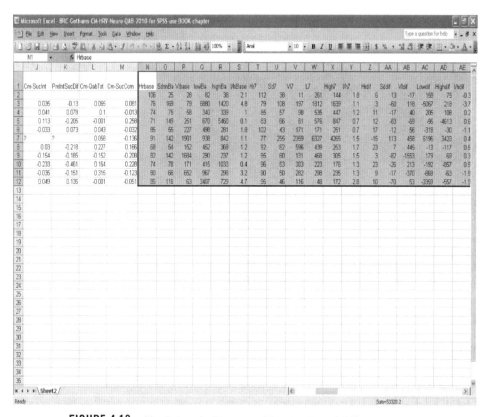

FIGURE 4.12 Youth baseball team Athlete's Profile PHO constellation and outcome measures.

	Cm-SucInt	PreIntSucDif	Cm-QabTot	Cm-SucCom	Hrbase	SdnnBa	Vlbase	lowBa	highBa	I/hBase	Hr7	Sd7	Vl7	L7	High7	I/h7	Hrdif	Sddif	Vldif	Lowdif	Highdif	I/hdif
2					106	25	28	82	38	2.1	112	38	11	261	144	1.8	6	13	-17	159	75	-0.3
3	0.035	-0.13	0.065	0.081	76	169	79	6880	1420	4.8	79	108	197	1812	1639	1.1	3	-60	118	-5067	218	-3.7
4	0.041	0.078	0.1	-0.013	74	75	58	340	339	1	85	57	98	535	447	1.2	11	-17	40	205	108	0.2
5	0.113	-0.205	-0.001	0.258	71	149	251	670	5460	0.1	83	66	81	576	847	0.7	12	-83	-69	-95	-4613	0.6
6	-0.033	0.073	0.043	-0.032	85	55	227	498	281	1.8	102	43	171	171	251	0.7	17	-12	56	-318	-30	-1.1
7	?	?	0.058	-0.136	91	142	1901	938	842	1.1	77	255	2359	6327	4265	1.5	-15	113	458	6196	3423	0.4
8	0.03	-0.218	0.227	0.166	68	54	152	452	369	1.2	92	62	596	439	253	1.7	23	7	445	-13	-117	0.5
9	-0.154	-0.185	-0.152	-0.208	82	142	1684	290	237	1.2	85	60	131	468	305	1.5	3	-82	-1553	179	69	0.3
10	-0.233	-0.461	0.164	0.228	74	78	171	415	1033	0.4	96	53	383	223	176	1.3	23	-26	213	-192	-857	0.9
11	-0.035	-0.151	0.315	-0.123	80	66	652	967	298	3.2	90	50	282	298	235	1.3	9	-17	-370	-869	-63	-1.9
12	0.049	0.135	-0.001	-0.051	85	116	63	3407	729	4.7	95	46	116	48	172	2.8	10	-70	53	-3359	-557	-1.9

FIGURE 4.13 Youth baseball team and heart rate variability measures.

HRV-OUTCOME-pre-intervention-G - SPSS Data Editor

File Edit View Data Transform Analyze Graphs Utilities Window Help

	hr	sdnn	power	vl	low	high	lh	scan	time	game	qab	success	cm	var	var	va
1	121.00	28.00	251.00	29.00	148.00	73.00	2.00	46.00	19.17		5.00	1.00	1.00			
2	114.00	26.00	62.00	9.00	37.00	16.00	2.20	47.00	19.40		5.00	1.00	1.00			
3	96.00	52.00	1047.00	81.00	762.00	204.00	3.70	47.00	20.18		5.00	1.00	1.00			
4	97.00	55.00	1070.00	4.00	659.00	407.00	1.60	47.00	20.45		1.00	.00	2.00			
5	104.00	26.00	162.00	16.00	61.00	85.00	.70	47.00	18.20		4.00	.00	1.00			
6	95.00	69.00	657.00	56.00	495.00	107.00	4.60	38.00	18.50		5.00	1.00	1.00			
7	83.00	46.00	616.00	47.00	378.00	191.00	2.00	51.00	19.13		2.00	.00	2.00			
8	105.00	45.00	465.00	11.00	186.00	268.00	.70	42.00	17.58	4.00	5.00	1.00	2.00			
9	104.00	38.00	329.00	47.00	122.00	159.00	.80	50.00	18.22		5.00	1.00	1.00			
10	117.00	48.00	430.00	20.00	147.00	263.00	.60	47.00	18.47		11.00	1.00	1.00			
11	105.00	40.00	182.00	12.00	113.00	57.00	2.00	47.00	19.07		5.00	1.00	1.00			
12	107.00	35.00	370.00	16.00	270.00	83.00	3.20	44.00	13.03	5.00	2.00	.00	4.00			
13	110.00	34.00	392.00	12.00	284.00	97.00	2.90	48.00	13.45		9.00	1.00	3.00			
14	117.00	38.00	507.00	73.00	224.00	210.00	1.10	44.00	14.19		4.00	.00	3.00			
15	127.00	30.00	249.00	6.00	54.00	190.00	.30	47.00	14.48		9.00	1.00	5.00			
16	108.00	24.00	117.00	14.00	78.00	25.00	3.10	41.00	16.19		4.00	.00	3.00			
17	117.00	34.00	103.00	33.00	56.00	15.00	3.90	39.00	16.30		5.00	1.00	1.00			
18	106.00	42.00	646.00	22.00	63.00	561.00	.10	35.00	17.14		4.00	.00	4.00			
19	107.00	39.00	200.00	79.00	94.00	28.00	3.40	47.00	8.54	7.00	1.00	.00	4.00			
20	95.00	29.00	186.00	4.00	111.00	71.00	1.60	48.00	9.31		1.00	.00	1.00			
21	107.00	51.00	678.00	1.00	219.00	458.00	.50	45.00	13.59	8.00	4.00	.00	1.00			
22	96.00	47.00	977.00	112.00	700.00	165.00	4.20	45.00	14.32		3.00	.00	1.00			
23	113.00	30.00	101.00	20.00	63.00	18.00	3.60	39.00	18.16	9.00	10.00	1.00	3.00			
24	109.00	26.00	181.00	9.00	98.00	74.00	1.30	44.00	18.47		10.00	1.00	3.00			
25	102.00	37.00	145.00	16.00	43.00	86.00	.50	46.00	19.28		9.00	1.00	3.00			
26	99.00	48.00	650.00	16.00	458.00	176.00	2.60	42.00	17.53	10.00	10.00	1.00	2.00			
27	112.00	23.00	226.00	31.00	175.00	20.00	8.60	48.00	18.14		10.00	1.00	1.00			
28	83.00	65.00	1029.00	81.00	764.00	184.00	4.20	45.00	19.08		2.00	.00	1.00			
29	85.00	68.00	1486.00	186.00	1014.00	285.00	3.60	45.00	19.38		9.00	1.00	1.00			
30	95.00	37.00	317.00	20.00	206.00	91.00	2.30	61.00	16.08	11.00	2.00	.00	1.00			
31	118.00	13.00	19.00	10.00	8.00	2.00	3.40	67.00	16.43		2.00	.00	2.00			
32	113.00	25.00	136.00	32.00	51.00	53.00	.90	67.00	17.44		4.00	.00	2.00			

Data View / Variable View

SPSS Processor is ready

FIGURE 4.14   SPSS outtake of one baseball player's longitudinal repeated measures data.

HRV response patterns to reliably predict or criterion-reference/externally validate AP PHO constellations on the basis of a neurophysiological response pattern's impact on repeated performance outcome measures, in the case of baseball, quality of at-bats and level of criticality outcome. For example, an outcome analysis of this athlete's pre-intervention HRV, quality of at-bats, criticality, and criticality success rate (Figure 4.14), independent of knowing his AP PHO constellation in advance should result in findings that would help predict his actual profile (BRV hypothesis). This particular athlete's AP PHO constellation classification is Medium-Medium-Low, with scores of 22 for subliminal attention (hypnotic susceptibility/absorption), 13 for subliminal reactivity (neuroticism), and 11 for subliminal coping (repressive coping) putting him on the cusp of the High-High-Low constellation. These two profiles are associated with, at best, negative tendencies and, at worst, two red flags that predict poor pressure situation psychological performance tendencies. So the question is, could these AP PHO constellations have been predicted on the basis of an analysis of this athlete's complete pre-intervention data (Figure 4.14 only reveals a portion of the pre-intervention games)? Let's see! In this player, situational criticality predicted about 2% of the variance in quality of at-bats ($r = .13$), meaning greater criticality (ranging from 1 to 5) was associated with relatively low-level batting performance, and in the context of the success outcome metric, there was a negative correlation between criticality and success. In other words, the greater the criticality, the worse the success rate ($-.06$). Both of these findings are consistent with what one would have expected of a player with the preceding AP PHO constellations and would likely have been predicted by practitioners who have been trained in the ABSP-CP and have sufficient experience using the CSARCS-A.

Without a repeated measures paradigm at the intra-individual, it would be difficult to determine to what extent an athlete's test (self-report) derived (CSARCS-A) AP PHO constellation could be empirically validated. Consequently, irrespective of what particular test or assessment instrument or battery a practitioner uses, the preceding methodology should be adopted and adapted as necessary (sport-specific) to ascertain whether a derived score or profile indeed predicts performance outcome in a manner that is consistent with a measure's conceptual bases. It should be noted that no HRV measures emerged as being associated with any outcome measures in this particular athlete. However, in the presence of clear and strong relationships between an objective sport-specific micro-level predictor variable (criticality rating) and outcome measures (quality of at-bats and success rate), the fact that the ersatz quasi-trait measure HRV did not predict performance is mitigated by the secondary trait replacement measure's impact (effect of criticality [pressure]) on performance in the direction that would be expected (consistent with this AP constellation poor pressure performance tendencies). HRV usually explains "x" amount of the variance in critical moment performance that can be attributed to AP PHO psychological factors, but not always, oftentimes, due to sample size and level of criticality distribution issues.[5] It is also possible that non-HRV findings will parallel a negative outcome, as in the case of this athlete where his poor critical moment-quality of at-bat relationships can be attributed to the absence of HRD prior to action, something that would be predicted in an athlete with a red flag profile. Thus, secondary and direct state response mediators like level of criticality should be integrated into all trait performance assessment analyses, since they are usually revealing independent of psychophysiological responding, with criticality–performance relationships actually being the most important pressure performance outcome measure, irrespective of mind–body responses.

Summary

1. AP PHO measures and constellations and all other psychological constructs and scores that are derived from assessment instruments that attempt to measure them must be analyzed in the context of longitudinal outcome studies at the intra-individual level to empirically determine their impact on performance.
2. It is insufficient to merely *assume* that a test score that purportedly reflects the level or potency of a psychological measure in the context of sport performance actually exerts an effect. An effect *must be demonstrated* using the methodological paradigms and procedures that are advanced in this chapter.
3. A selected psychological measure of interest should have established construct validity centering on key components of peak performance including attention (focus), physiological reactivity (intensity), and cognitive coping (through strategic planning, problem solving). The greater the construct validity of psychological measures that are used in the assessment process, the greater the probability that they will have high predictive validity.

Step-by-Step Validation of Athlete's Profile Psychological Measures: Procedures and Methodology

1. Administer the CSARCS-A via Brainresource.com or ABSP website.
2. Analyze the derived raw scores for each PHO measure to determine whether they are on the cusp of a higher or lower qualitative descriptor category (e.g., a 21 for SC would place an athlete in the Very High Medium category, a more accurate classification than just Medium).
3. Determine if the derived AP PHO constellation is close to being an "Ideal" or "Worst" profile.

4. In cases of ambiguous or paradoxical profiles or individual PHO measures (having weak predictive validity), highly correlated analogue tests (with the CSARCS-A) should be administered to arrive at a "second opinion." Analogue tests include the Harvard Scale of Hypnotic Susceptibility, Tellegen Absorption Scale, Eysenck Personality Inventory, the Marlowe-Crown Scale, and the NEO, to name a few.

5. Converging scores between the CSARCS-A and analogue tests suggest that a more ambiguous profile is valid as is; discrepant scores between test batteries indicate that further testing is necessary.

6. Irrespective of the derived AP PHO constellation, an attempt should be made to criterion-reference or externally validate a profile with the Serial 7s Stress Test to determine baseline and pressure condition mind–body states using HRV as the criterion (outcome) variable. HRV responses that are consistent with the underlying construct validity model of AP constellations and measures lend support that a derived AP PHO measures accurately assess an athlete's pressure performance tendencies.

7. A step up in the evidence hierarchy involves the further external validation of an AP PHO measure or constellations at the micro-level in the context of objective sport-specific criticality outcome measures. Established relationships between an AP PHO constellation or measure(s) and criticality outcome measures (adjusted r^2) constitutes the predictive validity of AP measures, the ultimate benchmark of the potency and mediating impact of psychological and mind–body measures on pressure performance.

Data Management and Analysis Procedures

1. Create a team and individual file for each athlete independently in Excel or SPSS (see Figures 4.12, 4.13, and 4.14).

2. Enter AP individual PHO measures into spreadsheet accordingly.

3. Enter any state measures that are related to AP PHO traits for each measurement occasion (e.g., self-report of level of comfort and control; see Chapter 9).

4. During training sessions, use experimental and assessment paradigms that simulate competitive pressure to obtain multiple repeated HRV predictor and performance outcome measures (remember that HRV responses are expected [hypothesized] to reflect AP PHO trait influences on performance). Enter HRV and outcome data accordingly (see Chapter 9).

5. Use the same procedures for actual practice games or matches, and if possible during real official competition (see Chapter 20).

6. Repeat procedures 3 to 5 until sufficient statistical power has been attained to enable reliable statistical inferences about predictor and criterion variable relationships. Depending upon the desired statistical power (.80–.90), usually 40 to 65 repeated measures are necessary. This means, for example, that 40 to 65 repeated HRV and/or state measure entries need to be made in the spreadsheet for an individual athlete.

7. Regarding team data, enter on separate lines in the spreadsheet each team member's AP PHO measures, and after an analysis epoch (e.g., 60 repeated measures or the entire pre-intervention or intervention phase of a team's season), average all predictor and outcome measures and enter the derived mean scores corresponding to the athlete whose data was analyzed (see Figures 4.13 and 4.14).

8. Once an analysis epoch has been concluded and all of the data has been entered into the spreadsheet, statistical analyses can commence. Correlational, regression, and modeling procedures as

well as *T*-tests are the most frequently used statistical analysis methods within the AP model assessment validation and intervention efficacy-testing paradigms.

Validation Challenge

It should be noted that the Carlstedt Protocol (CP) athlete and assessment model has been validated over the course of the last 15 years. Findings and resulting conclusions pertaining to the etiology of peak sport performance that have been derived from this system of applied sport psychology emanate from the only and longest (duration) ongoing longitudinal research trial of athlete psychological performance from a wide variety of sports. It has generated the largest and only repository of comprehensive brain–mind–body–motor response data[6] and their relationship to micro-level, objective, sport-specific outcome measures that was derived from actual training and official game/match competition. As such, rather than merely present and expound on theories, ideas, hypotheses, information, methods, and procedures in isolation (past and extant literature of the field), this book's topics are presented in an integrative manner in the context of ecological research and data that was obtained from daily work with actual athlete-clients and guided by a validated conceptual and construct validity framework (see Chapter 2). What has emerged is the first and, to date, only comprehensively validated applied sport psychological assessment and intervention protocol. This is not a boast or unsupportable claim. Rather, this is brought to light, not to somehow portend that the truth regarding athlete psychological performance can be found within this protocol, *but to encourage anyone who uses a particular method, procedure, or assessment and intervention approach to follow the empirical road map that is laid forth in this book in the interest of acquiring the best evidence, even if it is negative and non-supportive of a particular model or method.*

As readers will encounter in later chapters, interventions are also shown that do not work when they are subjected to rigorous gold standard efficacy testing analyses, and assessment instruments often fail to predict performance as they purport to be capable of doing. However, such outcome conclusions, despite being, in part, negative (and negative findings tend not to be reported by professional journals) have been validated and, as such, need to be at the forefront of the knowledge base of applied sport psychology and efficiently disseminated to frontline practitioners, many who believe all interventions always work and assessments never fail to measure and reveal what they claim to, in each individual athlete (there is a positive outcome bias or belief system that pervades the field; Carlstedt, 2011). Hence, it behooves all practitioners to be researchers as well in the context of consulting work with every athlete-client. Attempts should be made to validate assessment and intervention findings and claims and predictions that may guide their approach to practice, irrespective of group investigative outcome data and the conceptual origins of such research, test instruments, and intervention procedures that are used.

Open-minded practitioners are encouraged and challenged to approach athlete assessment and intervention from a high-evidentiary perspective and test, replicate, extend, amend, or even empirically refute tenets, hypotheses, and findings that define the ABSP-CP and any other model of peak performance. Alternatively, if a practitioner lays claim to having the answers to peak performance or best system of athlete assessment and intervention, if he or she is serious, competent, and concerned about professional ethics and best practices in the interest of client-athletes, as well as the field of sport psychology and performance science, he or she cannot allow personal claims or intense beliefs to supersede gold standard approaches to the investigation of evaluative instruments and mental training methods.

Practitioners are welcome to contribute to the ABSP-CP Universal Athlete Trial project, whose goal it is to raise practice and research standards among practitioners by advancing standardized and validated approaches to athlete assessment, intervention, and intervention efficacy testing by depositing data in a central repository for ongoing analysis.

Contact: rcarlstedt@americanboardofsportpsychology.org for more information.

Notes

1. The Athlete Profile model of peak performance will be presented throughout this book in the context of assessment and intervention approaches and procedures. It was also previously introduced in the chapter on construct validity and conceptual bases. Readers should thoroughly understand this model by the time they have finished this book, especially if they plan to use or test this model as practitioners, researchers, and/or students. Although its frequent appearance may seem redundant, it should be noted that each time it is mentioned or discussed it is in a specific context, whether in relationship to an assessment procedure or mental training method.

2. The performance equation expresses the amount of variance in an objective sport-specific outcome or multiple outcome measures that can be attributed to any number of predictor measures of interest, including psychological variables.

3. In the context of a longitudinal repeated measures investigation at the intra-individual level predictor, measures variability in responses are necessary, and traits, which are inherently stable, will not vary sufficiently for reliable inferential statistical analyses. As such, traits are not reliable predictor measures since they can be used only once.

4. It should be noted that the AP PHO trait-repeated measure issue at the intra-individual level is also being addressed by exploratory research pertaining to the development of state measures for SA/HS and SC/RC. State measures for SR/N already exist.

5. Instances of level 4 and 5 criticality are rarer than levels 1 to 3; however, HRV measures may be more sensitive to greater levels of pressure. As such, HRV as a predictor may remain dormant as a mediator when there is a low n for levels 3, 4, and 5.

6. A 2006 study of an elite youth baseball team in the context of actual consulting services contains the only complete data set of psychometric stress test HRV responses, neurocognitive and HRV activity obtained on the bench prior to every at-bat for every starting player during all official games for an entire season. The HRV data was acquired during pre-intervention and intervention phases that were administered during these real games, making this study the only one in the annals of research in sport psychology to amass a comprehensive array of predictor and outcome measures on all players during official league competition. This study is explicated in Chapter 20.

Psychophysiological Stress Testing: Validating Mind–Body Responses[1]

Once an Athlete's Profile (AP) Primary Higher Order (PHO) constellation has been established, it is desirable to go up a level in the evidence hierarchy and determine to what extent hypnotic susceptibility/subliminal attention (HS/SA), neuroticism/subliminal reactivity (N/SR), and repressive coping/subliminal coping (RC/SC) mediate levels of autonomic nervous system (ANS) reactivity that would be expected on the basis of his or her AP. This should be done as a matter of routine and due diligence, since the vast majority of self-report tests are prone to response sets and measurement error and are thus, to a certain degree, fallible. Although up to 70% of the variance in the performance equation has been explained by specific AP constellations, 100% predictive accuracy can rarely, if ever, be attained when psychological tests, especially self-report, questionnaire-based assessment instruments are used to evaluate people. As a result, false-positive and false-negative findings will occur no matter how predictive a test battery has been found to be. Another reason for criterion-referencing with conceptually relevant external measures is that while APs are highly predictive of critical moment performance and other psychological tendencies at the extremes of a sample's distribution, "ideal" and "worst" PHO constellations are much less prevalent, with the most performance impacting profiles being found in only about 15% to 30% of all athletes (the two ideal and one worst profile). The majority of athletes tend to have a more neutral or less revealing AP (one of 25 remaining profile constellations; see Figure 5.1). Since most athletes possess more ambiguous profiles in terms of their pressure or critical moment response tendencies, it is important to assess psychophysiological reactivity using more direct stress response measures, initially in a controlled laboratory and, later, in an ecological on-the-playing-field-based stress test paradigm.

Serial 7s Stress Test Paradigm: Conceptual and Construct Validity

Psychophysiological stress testing is an assessment approach that attempts to predict an athlete's future performance during critical moments of competition on the basis of cognitively mediated changes in specific (ANS) responses that are derived *a priori* using procedures that try to induce psychological pressure. Since mental engagement has been associated with heart rate acceleration

A/HS	NA/N	RC	Critical Moment Tendency and Select Frequency %
Low	Low	Low	Neutral to Positive
Low	Low	Medium	Positive Tendencies
Low	Low	High	**Ideal up to 15%**
Low	Medium	Low	Neutral
Low	Medium	Medium	Neutral
Low	Medium	High	Neutral to Positive
Low	High	Low	Red Flags (2)
Low	High	Medium	Red Flags (1)
Low	High	High	Red Flags (1)
Medium	Low	Low	Neutral to Positive
Medium	Low	Medium	Neutral to Positive
Medium	Low	High	Positive Tendencies
Medium	Medium	Low	Negative Tendencies
Medium	Medium	Medium	Neutral
Medium	Medium	High	Neutral
Medium	High	Low	Red Flags (2)
Medium	High	Medium	Red Flags (1)
Medium	High	High	Red Flags (1)
High	Low	Low	Positive Tendencies
High	Low	Medium	Positive Tendencies
High	Low	High	**Ideal up to 15%**
High	Medium	Low	Red Flags (2)
High	Medium	Medium	Positive Tendencies
High	Medium	High	Positive Tendencies
High	High	Low	**Least Desirable up to 15%**
High	High	Medium	Red Flags (1)
High	High	High	Red Flags (1)

FIGURE 5.1   Athlete's Profile constellations.

(HRA) and concomitant sympathetic nervous system (SNS) activation (Andreassi, 1995), it is hypothesized that athletes who exhibit excessive SNS responses to a psychological challenge in a static nonsport-specific setting will be less likely to elicit the pre-action heart rate deceleration (HRD) and simultaneous, relative, left-to-right brain hemispheric shift that is associated with peak performance when under pressure (higher criticality) during real competition (Andreassi, 1995; Carlstedt, 2004a, 2004b). Instead, in more vulnerable athletes, similar or proportionate levels of SNS-mediated HRA and concurrent increases in heart rate variability (HRV), very low frequency (VLF) and low–high (L/H) frequency ratio activities that are induced by a stress test, are expected to manifest themselves during competition and disrupt performance.

Adaptive stress test responses that predict and facilitate actual critical moment performance (during real competition) are thought more likely to occur in athletes with the ideal AP PHO constellation or profiles that approach the high or low subliminal attention/hypnotic susceptibility (SA/HS)-low subliminal reactivity/neuroticism (SR/N)-subliminal coping/high repressive coping (SC/RC) most performance facilitative profile. By contrast, the most detrimental AP, high SA/HS-high SR/N and low SC/RC, as well as high SR/N independently (regardless of AP), are likely to mediate stress test responses that are incompatible with peak pressure performance responses (pre-action HRA instead of HRD and concomitant cortical shifts).

Conceptually, the HRV stress test generated measure that is expected to be most predictive of future responding to stress during competition is the LF/HF ratio. This measure of autonomic balance, expressed as the ratio of LF/HF ANS activity, tends to change differentially (as a function of AP PHO constellation) in response to cognitive challenges such as the unexpected and novel subtraction task of the S7s stress test. Other HRV measures of interest include VLF a measure that is most associated with SNS activation and hyper-reactivity, as well as rapidly accelerating HR that can suddenly commence when faced with unexpected cognitive, physical, and/or competitive stressors. High-frequency (HF) activity is also a measure of interest since it is a pure parasympathetic nervous system (PNS)-mediated deactivation or relaxation response that one would not necessarily expect in the presence of mental activity and stress. SDNN, the HRV index, is also analyzed. SDNN usually decreases as a function of increasing HR and vice versa in people who are relatively physically fit (Andreassi, 1995; Carlstedt, 2004a, 2004b; Malik & Camm, 1995).

HRV measures also interact. For example, a large increase in HR in the S7s task condition, an SNS-mediated response, can impact LF, VLF, HF, L/H ratio, and SDNN. As such, an analysis of stress test HRV responses must take numerous ANS response tendencies and interactions into account, and importantly, influences of AP PHO measures and constellations that are thought to mediate pressure or critical moment HRV responses.

Serial 7s Psychophysiological Stress Testing Paradigm: Procedures

Psychophysiological stress testing (PST) should be routinely administered to all athletes at intake. This test provides an additional layer in the evidence hierarchy (Rosenthal, 2004) by extending AP PHO constellation self-report and behavioral measures to underlying mind–body responding (criterion referenced validation). A stress test paradigm that has been extensively used and validated involves a cognitive task in which an individual is asked to count backward from 1000 by 7s (Serial 7s stress test; S7; Carlstedt, 2004a, 2004b) for a period of 2 minutes while heart activity is being monitored. A 2-minute baseline precedes the backward counting condition. Differences between various HRV measures in the baseline and backward counting task are then calculated and analyzed.

The S7 test should be administered in the presence of a few people, preferably coaches, teachers, trainers, and/or teammates. An audience serves as an additional source of stress, since test takers do not want to appear foolish and make mistakes, especially during a supposedly easy mathematical task. The goal of a stress test is to make an individual feel as uncomfortable as possible.

Feelings of discomfort, worry, nervousness, and overall stress are expected to heighten in athletes with the most detrimental AP PHO constellation or in athletes who score high for N/SR, and induce changes in HRV that are associated with increases in SNS activity. Athletes who possess one of two ideal AP PHO constellations or who are low in N/SR are expected to be relatively impervious to the audience effect and are expected to exhibit, at worst, only minor increases in SNS-mediated ANS measures and, at best, will exhibit ANS responses that are associated with SNS deactivation or PNS activation, including reductions in HR, VLF, and L/H ratio activity and increases in HF activity. By contrast, AP vulnerable athletes are expected to respond more reactively in the task condition as reflected in greater HR, VLF, and L/H ratio HRV activity compared to baseline.

Step-by-Step Administration

Instrumentation: Research grade-approved HRV monitoring and analysis software and compatible recording sensor such as the BioCom Technologies HRV. Heart Rate Scanner system should be used.

FIGURE 5.2 Baseball player undergoing baseline HRV testing for stress test.

PROCEDURE

1. Inform athlete that he or she will take a test to measure "heart activity." Do not reveal any conceptual details or task condition instructions initially.
2. Bring athlete into a testing area with a prearranged audience of two to five people who should be told not to interact in any way with the test taker, make comments, or show affect of any kind. Seat the athlete in a chair with a hard back.
3. Explain baseline condition to the athlete as follows:

   I am going to monitor your heart activity for a period of two minutes. Just sit upright, try to remain as still as possible, and not do or think of anything in particular.
4. Connect HRV ear sensor to client and computer and start 2-minutes baseline recording (see Figure 5.2).
5. Explain Serial 7s backward counting task to athlete as follows:

   Now I want you to perform a mental task while your heart activity is being monitored. When I say "start," I want you to count backward from 1000 by 7s, for example, say 1000, then 993, and so on, out loud at a level of volume similar to just talking. If you feel that you have made a mistake, just pick up from where you stopped. After two minutes, I will say "stop."
6. Debrief the athlete after data have been analyzed in the context of the ABSP-CP comprehensive assessment analysis battery.

SERIAL 7S STRESS TEST: ANALYSIS AND INTERPRETATION

The following Serial 7s stress test findings offer some interpretive challenges, illustrating that athlete assessment is not necessarily a straightforward process. Too often only positive findings based on significant but tenuous *p* values or data that is supportive of a particular theory or practice model are presented or published in professional journals (Hall, de Antueno, & Webber, 2007). This can give consumers of research, including other researchers, educators, students, athletes, coaches, and practitioners the impression that a test instrument, procedure, or intervention is infallible or 100% accurate. This can lead, often unknowingly, to the use and misuse of test batteries and interventions, that in the end, when analyzed at the intra-individual level, turn out not to be revealing in terms of what is purported about an athlete's psychological tendencies. The failure to meticulously manage and analyze test data in relationship to sport-specific outcome measures can render an assessment instrument useless in terms of predictive capability. To increase the probability that an assessment instrument or procedure will generate valid and reliable information on athlete psychological performance propensities, it is necessary to go well beyond merely administrating and scoring them. While group findings can guide the assessment process, it is crucial that each individual athlete's score is analyzed independent of an entire team's mean score or mean findings from previous research that may have led to decisions to use a particular test in the first place. Unfortunately, the vast majority of practitioners tend to use a test and accept what is known about the test at face value, without engaging in an elaborate analysis process that is crucial to high evidentiary athlete assessment that will lead to more accurate insight regarding the predictive validity of a test instrument.

The data and findings that are presented in this chapter were derived from two groups of athletes, a professional soccer team from Europe and an elite youth baseball team from the United States. Athletes on these teams were administered the Serial 7s stress test prior to their seasons. Baseline, stress condition, and differences in HRV responses between these two conditions were compared and analyzed in relationship to AP PHO constellations and, with the baseball players, critical moment performance. In contrast to the baseball team, whose players' every pre-at-bat HRV was monitored in a pre-intervention and intervention phase during all official games, providing a plethora of objective sport-specific outcome measures, the soccer team's sport psychologist could provide only subjective impressions regarding performance and macro-level outcome measures (goals scored versus goals against). These latter outcome measures are typically the only ones used, with practitioners tending to rely solely on global macro-level outcome measures such as personal impressions, coach ratings, and final score or game won/game lost statistics to determine whether a test instrument is accurate in assessing athletes or predicting performance. Such limited, subjective, and macro criterion variables are wanting and usually are not sensitive enough to discern important psychological influences on performance.

At this point, data from both teams will be analyzed in a step-by-step manner. Commentary will be interjected to make readers aware of methodological issues that are relevant to specific data sets and findings. Practitioners are encouraged to contemplate how they could apply the following procedures and methodologies to tests that they use in an attempt to better determine the extent to which a score reflects what it is supposed to measure and predictions about performance outcome.

The following charts (Figure 5.3 and 5.4) depict the BioCom Technologies Heart Rate Scanner Autonomic Balance report that was automatically generated after one baseball player's Serial 7s stress test. The first report contains data from the baseline condition, the second, HRV responses from the task or stress condition (backward counting-subtraction).

Measures of interest include Mean HR, SDNN, VLF, LF, HF, and LF/HF. Data that is derived from the report is then entered into an Excel spreadsheet and eventually transferred to SPSS for statistical analysis.

Figure 5.5 contains the professional soccer team's individual player AP PHO measure scores and HRV responses from the baseline and task condition, along with changes in HRV as a function of the task condition. As an aside, it is interesting to note a team's mean AP PHO score, since ongoing research is attempting to determine to what extent the distribution of an entire team's AP constellations interact to influence team performance and eventual outcome (team dynamics). This soccer team's level of SA/HS was 23 (high level), SR/N = 12 (not visible in Figure 5.5), in the medium

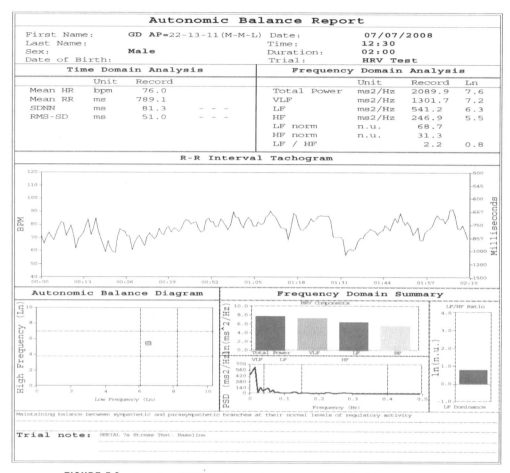

FIGURE 5.3   Baseline HRV readout and report as part of Serial 7s stress test.

range and SC/RC = 19 (upper medium level). This conglomerate chart, at face value, does not reveal much. However, when the response numbers are systematically organized, they reveal a wealth of information about AP PHO relationships with stress test HRV responding and allow for *preliminary* interpretations regarding the construct validity of the AP model and CSARCS-A and analogue measures on the basis of differential HRV across test conditions (baseline versus stress).

Figure 5.6 contains the most AP-HRV relevant data in a format that allows for initial screening pertaining to whether a specific AP PHO constellation is associated with HRV responses that would be expected in accordance with an APs construct bases. Each AP PHO measure that corresponds with a specific soccer player's name is rated qualitatively using a five-star system (* = most performance detrimental; and ***** = ideal profile: most performance facilitative). Based on the hypothetical tenets of the AP model and AP PHO measures and constellations, it is to be expected or could be predicted that the more performance facilitative (more stars) an AP constellation is, the more likely it will mediate the elicitation of an HRV stress response that is consistent with specifically operationalized levels of mind–body control that have been associated with peak performance, including:[2]

1. A decrease in L/H frequency from the baseline condition as a function of the stress task.
2. A decrease or minimal increase in HR in the stress task condition compared to baseline.
3. An increase in SDNN in the stress task condition compared to the baseline.

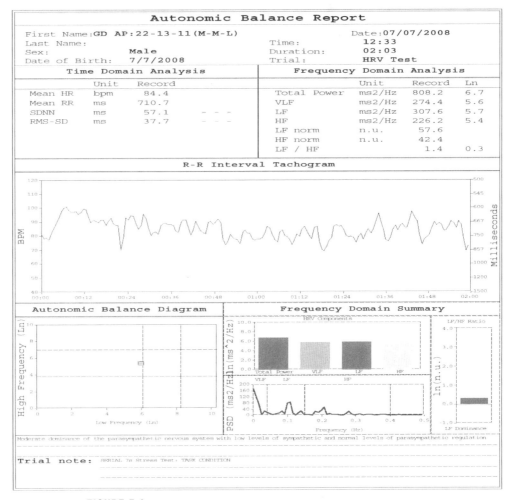

FIGURE 5.4   Serial 7s stress test task condition read-out and report.

4. A decrease in VL frequency in the stress task condition compared to baseline.
5. An increase in HF in the stress task condition compared to baseline.

The L/H frequency ratio reflects ANS balance. LF activity contains a mixture or interplay of both SNS (activation) and PNS (reduction in activation) while HF activity reflects a PNS exclusively. While differential levels of activation are usually necessary for sport performance, in the context of a static situation (no movement) and cognitive stressors, greater LF and accompanying SNS is hypothesized to be disruptive and interfere with mental tasks, such as strategic planning as a precursor to motor action. Greater L/H frequency HRV activity is also frequently associated with HRA or increases in HR (an SNS-mediated response) and reductions in SDNN (the HRV index). In more reactive individuals, the Serial 7s stress test task condition can induce significantly more VL frequency activity (SNS mediated) compared to baseline, a response that would be expected in athletes with the most performance detrimental AP PHO constellation. By contrast, greater HF activity (PNS mediated) would be more likely to occur in athletes with the Ideal AP PHO constellation and also contribute to a lower L/H frequency ratio. Relative to the stress response, it is hypothesized that the *magnitude of change* from the baseline to stress test task condition, in a performance-adaptive

Microsoft Excel - Martin-Pro-Soccer-HRV-CSARCS-A-SCORED-for-Chap5

PROFESSIONAL SOCCER TEAM and ATHLETE'S PROFILE STRESS TEST HRV RESPONSES

	Name	SA	SR	SC	BASELINE HR	SDNN	VLF	LF	HF	LF/HF	TEST 1 (-7 TEST) HR	SDNN	VLF	LF	HF	LF/HF	Counts	Change HR	Change SDNN	Change VLF	Change LF	Change HF	Change LF/HF
1	O	24	16	22	57.50	49.00	60.90	58.20	137.50	0.40	63.50	67.60	144.40	965.50	318.00	3.00	6.00	6.00	18.60	83.5	907.30	180.5	2.60
2	L	22	17	20	46.60	93.30	1095.10	1283.30	375.80	3.40	66.30	68.00	247.00	398.90	595.10	0.70	27.00	19.70	-25.30	-848.1	-884.40	219.3	-2.70
3	E	18	10	17	57.50	68.00	93.40	275.80	464.40	0.60	65.90	93.60	70.70	628.00	301.70	0.70	33.00	8.40	25.60	-22.7	352.20	-162.7	0.10
4	T	25	14	21	50.90	39.40	57.80	143.70	154.70	0.90	62.90	55.80	103.30	686.20	161.50	4.20	30.00	12.00	16.40	45.5	542.50	6.8	3.30
5	R	28	12	25	60.30	114.00	415.00	1388.50	190.50	7.30	98.40	66.20	221.60	645.90	172.80	3.70	74.00	38.10	-47.80	-193.4	-742.60	-17.7	-3.60
6	A	23	12	15	55.30	102.20	217.70	2098.90	546.70	3.80	69.60	119.50	1019.40	703.10	548.00	1.30	29.00	14.30	17.30	801.7	-1395.80	1.3	-2.50
7	S	31	15	19	59.80	85.60	325.30	325.00	1675.10	0.20	78.00	58.80	44.10	237.40	245.80	1.00	28.00	18.20	-26.80	-281.2	-87.60	-1429.3	0.80
8	C	21	9	23	50.20	63.50	458.60	286.40	336.40	0.90	64.30	71.30	328.50	542.50	108.80	5.00	31.00	14.10	7.80	-130.1	256.10	-227.6	4.10
9	D	21	10	21	60.50	69.60	604.30	669.00	396.90	1.70	78.20	68.90	496.10	544.90	188.60	2.90	18.00	17.70	-0.70	-108.2	-124.10	-208.3	1.20
10	U	14	4	17	46.70	50.70	121.30	57.00	278.00	0.20	60.80	124.90	716.60	841.90	218.40	3.90	32.00	14.10	74.20	595.3	784.90	-59.6	3.70
11	I	23	14	17	55.90	149.40	590.00	2677.60	1621.00	1.70	73.40	81.70	103.50	773.60	484.70	1.60	15.00	17.50	-67.70	-486.5	-1904.00	-1136.3	-0.10
12	K	28	14	23	51.60	71.70	561.30	197.10	514.90	0.40	64.40	111.40	429.20	1023.70	991.70	1.00	16.00	12.80	39.70	-132.1	826.60	476.8	0.60
13	P	19	17	20	56.40	38.50	162.20	120.10	77.60	1.50	63.50	79.80	475.60	610.70	178.70	3.40	27.00	7.10	41.30	313.4	490.60	101.1	1.90
14	G	23	12	19	63.20	93.50	506.30	1698.50	510.70	3.30	71.60	93.10	339.80	1142.00	419.40	2.70	32.00	8.40	-0.40	-166.5	-556.50	-91.3	-0.60
15	V	24	21	11	85.10	86.50	139.10	2472.40	122.70	20.10	96.10	66.00	98.90	1100.60	398.60	2.80	41.00	11.00	-20.50	-40.2	-1371.80	275.9	-17.30
16	H	30	16	13	71.60	82.70	778.70	431.00	225.90	1.90	97.80	44.60	226.10	120.80	103.10	1.20	56.00	26.20	-38.10	-552.6	-310.00	-122.8	-0.70
17	CI	21	11	16	68.00	53.00	379.80	299.40	113.00	2.60	78.10	81.20	403.70	1243.40	387.70	3.20	16.00	10.10	28.20	23.9	944.00	274.7	0.60
18	RC	21	8	24	73.50	43.90	243.10	171.90	195.10	0.90	77.10	51.10	234.80	623.00	67.00	9.20	32.00	3.60	7.20	-8.3	451.00	-128.1	8.30
19	NP	8	7	15	66.00	76.60	651.20	916.00	701.90	1.30	78.50	56.10	136.50	473.80	101.80	4.70	22.00	12.50	-20.50	-514.7	-442.20	-600.1	3.40
20	VK	32	9	20	64.10	97.80	78.30	2009.80	1339.20	1.50	85.90	59.90	53.30	477.50	145.70	3.30	37.00	21.80	-37.90	-25.0	-1532.30	-1193.5	1.80
	Total				1200.70	#####	7539.40	17579.60	9978.00	54.60	1494.30	1519.50	5893.10	13783.40	6137.10	56.50	602.00	293.60	-9.40	-1646.30	-3796.10	######	4.90
	Mean	23.00	###	18.9	60.00	76.40	376.97	878.98	498.90	2.73	74.71	75.98	294.60	689.10	306.80	2.82	30.10	14.68	-0.47	-82.31	-189.80	-192.00	0.24

List1 / List2 / List3

FIGURE 5.5 Professional soccer team player's database of stress test baseline, task, and change responses.

or facilitative ANS HRV measure, is a more important biomarker of pressure performance tendencies than an absolute value for a specific ANS measure. For example, an athlete whose *baseline* L/F frequency and HR (SNS predominant), who then experiences a reduction in these SNS-mediated responses during the stress test task condition, would be credited as exhibiting a reduction in activation as a function of a cognitive stressor, even if his or her task condition HRV response

Microsoft Excel - PRO-SOCCER-NEW CHART all HRV Change and PHO-USE

	Name	CSARCS-A SA	SR	RC	Rating	HRV CHANGE FROM BASELINE to STRESS TASK CONDITION L/H +/-	Rank-Prd	HR	Rank-Prd	SD	Rank-Prd	VL	Rank-Prd	H	Rank-Prd
1	O	24H	16H	22H	**	2.60	14-C	6.00	2-C	18.60	5-IC	83.50	17-HC	180.50	5-IC
2	L	22M	17H	20M	**	-2.70	3-HIC	19.70	17-HC	-25.30	14-IC	-848.10	1-HIC	219.30	4-IC
3	E	18M	10M	17M	***	0.10	7-N	8.40	4-N	25.60	3-N	-22.70	14-C	-162.70	14-N
4	T	25H	14M	21M	***	3.30	15-C	12.00	8-N	16.40	7-N	45.50	16-C	6.80	6-N
5	R	28H	12M	25H	****	-3.60	2-C	38.10	20-HIC	-47.80	18-HIC	-193.40	6-HC	-17.70	8-IC
6	A	23H	12M	15M	***	-2.50	4-N	14.30	13-N	17.30	6-N	801.70	20-N	1.30	7-N
7	S	31H	15M	19M	***	0.80	10-N	18.20	16-C	-26.80	15C	-281.20	5-IC	-1429.30	20-HC
8	C	21M	9L	23H	****	4.10	18-HIC	14.10	11-IC	7.80	8-C	-130.10	9-HC	-227.60	16-HIC
9	D	21M	10M	21M	***	1.20	11-N	17.70	15-IC	-0.70	11-N	-108.20	10-HC	-208.30	15-HIC
10	U	14L	4L	17M	***	3.70	17-IC	14.10	11-IC	74.20	1-C	595.30	19-HIC	-59.60	9-HIC
11	I	23H	14M	17M	***	-0.10	7-IC	17.50	14-N	-67.70	19-N	-486.50	4-IC	-1136.30	18-C
12	K	28H	14M	23H	***	0.60	8-N	12.80	10-N	39.70	3-N	-132.10	8-N	476.80	1-IC
13	P	19M	17H	20M	**	1.90	13-C	7.10	3-C	41.30	2-IC	313.40	18-C	101.10	11-IC
14	G	23H	12M	19M	***	-0.60	6-N	8.40	4-N	-0.40	10-N	-166.50	7-N	-91.30	10-IC
15	V	24H	21H	11M	**	-17.30	1-HIC	11.00	7-C	-20.50	12-HC	-40.20	11-HIC	275.90	2-HIC
16	H	30H	16H	13M	**	-0.70	5-IC	26.20	19-HC	-38.10	17-C	-552.60	2-HIC	-122.80	12-HC
17	CI	21M	11M	16M	***	0.60	8-N	10.10	6-N	28.20	4-C	23.90	13-N	274.70	3-C
18	RC	21M	8L	24H	****	8.30	19-HIC	3.60	1-HC	7.20	9-C	-8.30	15-C	-128.10	13-HIC
19	NP	8L	7L	15M	***	3.40	16-IC	12.50	9-IC	-20.50	12-IC	-514.70	3-HC	-600.10	17-HIC
20	VK	32H	9L	20M	****	1.80	12-IC	21.80	18-HIC	-37.90	16-IC	-25.00	12-C	-1193.50	19-HIC
	Mean	22.80	12.40	18.9	Mean	0.24		14.68		-0.47		-82.32		-192.05	

KEY: CSARCS-A Rating: ***** = Ideal Athlete's Profile Constellation; **** = Next Best; *** Average; ** Poor; * Worst Athlete's Profile Constellation

Prd: HC = Highly Consistent with Athlete Profile; C = Consistent; HIC = Highly Inconsistent; IC = Inconsistent; N = Neutral

HRV Change Rank: L/H = less; HR = less; SDNN = more; VL = less; H = more

List1 (2) / List1 / List2 / List3

FIGURE 5.6 Professional soccer team player's AP and stress test HRV relationships.

values remained in the SNS range (e.g., a drop in the L/H ratio from a baseline value of, say, 7.3 to 5.0 in the stress task condition, even though still SNS predominant, is a reduction in activation in a stress condition that is hypothesized to reflect an increase in mental control in context of a stress test). By contrast, an apparently relaxed athlete in the baseline condition as reflected in greater HF activity and a lower L/H ratio (PNS predominant) who stress task-mediated response results in less HF and a higher L/H ratio, even if still in the PNS range, would be credited with less of a performance facilitative response than an athlete with a greater initial baseline SNS response that transitions to lower levels of SNS activity in the stress task condition, even if his or her final absolute values are still in the SNS range. In essence, the psychophysiological "law of initial values" (Andreassi, 1995), a concept that may be related to the Individual Zone of Optimum Functioning (IZOF; Hanin, 2006), drives individual baseline HRV response parameters with subsequent HRV changes being measured against an athlete's initial values (baseline). Stress task condition-related changes are then analyzed in terms of the magnitude of their performance-facilitative directionality, with reductions in SNS activity in a baseline SNS predominant athlete in the stress task condition, being equivalent to a reduced PNS response in the stress condition, in an athlete whose baseline HRV response profile is PNS predominant.[3]

A review of the professional soccer team player's AP PHO measures/constellations and HRV responses in the baseline and stress task condition (Figure 5.5), reveals the following:

1. Four players had a **** (4-star) AP. These athletes would be expected to elicit HRV responses across test conditions that were consistent with the aforementioned hypothesized responses. All **** players exhibited decreases in VLF activity in the stress condition consistent with what would have been expected. By contrast, all **** players also showed disparate and inconsistent HRV responses in the stress condition (L/H, SDNN, HR, and HF). Five players had a ** AP (next to worst). Of these athletes, HRV response change consistency (CC) was as follows: 3 yes (consistent) and 2 no (inconsistent) for L/H ratio, 4-1 for HR, 2-3 for SDNN, 2-3 for VLF, and 1-4 for HF.

2. The remainder of the players had a *** AP. *** athletes have more ambiguous PHO constellations. As such, the Serial 7s stress test can be used to help better discern ANS response tendencies independent of an AP in these athletes. In doing so, special attention should be paid to SR/N and SC/RC raw scores, since higher or lower levels of these two PHO measures may differentially mediate stress condition HRV responses independent of a full AP constellation (all three PHO measures interacting).

3. *** AP players exhibited the following CC: 1 (yes)-3 (no)-7 (neutral) for L/H ratio, 1-3-7 for HR, 3-1-7 for SDNN, 4-3-4 for VLF, and 3-5-3. Consistent with middle-range AP, ambiguity predominated, with "neutral" CC ratings standing out the most.

The preceding findings and subsequent results of a youth baseball team will be further interpreted and discussed in the last section of this chapter.

GROUP FINDINGS

When working with an entire team, each individual player's AP PHO measures contribute to a collective (group) analysis of performance outcome, in this case, stress test HRV. While individual athlete outcomes supersede group findings in terms of their practical validity, data and results from entire teams are added to a database and used in ongoing analyses and meta-analyses to further validate, extend, amend, and, if necessary, refute and revise predictive components of the TCM and AP

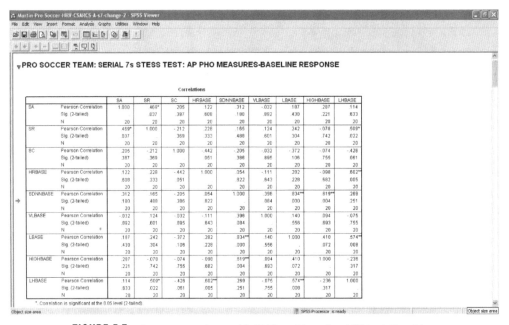

FIGURE 5.7   Pro soccer players AP PHO and baseline HRV relationships.

models of peak performance. The following series of figures present group data and findings on AP PHO measures and HRV relationships and performance outcome (pro soccer team).

Figure 5.7 revealed the following:

1. Subliminal/Repressive coping was negatively correlated with Serial 7s stress test baseline HR (−.44), which explains 19% of the variance in this HRV measure that can be attributed to this AP PHO measure. This finding can be considered conceptually ambiguous since higher levels of SC/RC are usually associated with greater SNS activation at baseline.
2. SC/RC was also negatively correlated with LF (−.37), explaining 13% of the variance in this HRV measure that can be attributed to this AP PHO measure. This finding can be considered conceptually inconsistent, since greater baseline LF contains a mixture of SNS/PNS activity that is not necessarily SC/RC mediated.
3. Subliminal reactivity/neuroticism was correlated with baseline L/H ratio (.51), explaining 26% of the variance in this HRV measure that could be attributed to this AP PHO measure and SC/RC was negatively correlated (−.43) with the same HRV measure. These two findings are highly conceptually consistent in that SR/N and SC/RC in almost all data analyses that result in statistically significant findings involving these two AP PHO measures reveal them to be orthogonal as reflected in correlations that are opposite (negative vs. positive, or vice versa). These findings are also consistent with greater SR/N being known to mediate the SNS activity that is associated with increased LF activity. Conversely, greater SC/RC would be expected to mitigate the SNS response and thereby mediate a lower L/H ratio.

Figure 5.8, the stress test task condition, reveals the following:

1. AP PHO measures were correlated with and predicted varying amounts of variance in the L/H ratio stress task response, as would be predicted by the AP model of peak performance. All AP

SERIAL 7s STESS TEST: AP PHO MEASURES-STRESS-TASK HRV RESPONSE

Correlations

		SA	SR	SC	HR7	SDNN7	VL7	L7	HIGH7	LH7
SA	Pearson Correlation	1.000	.469*	.205	.395	-.250	-.249	-.158	.176	-.318
	Sig. (2-tailed)		.037	.387	.085	.287	.290	.511	.457	.172
	N	20	20	20	20	20	20	20	20	20
SR	Pearson Correlation	.469*	1.000	-.212	.209	-.252	-.263	.053	.349	-.466*
	Sig. (2-tailed)	.037		.369	.377	.284	.262	.823	.131	.038
	N	20	20	20	20	20	20	20	20	20
SC	Pearson Correlation	.205	-.212	1.000	-.299	-.092	-.070	-.046	-.039	.376
	Sig. (2-tailed)	.387	.369		.201	.700	.768	.846	.871	.102
	N	20	20	20	20	20	20	20	20	20
HR7	Pearson Correlation	.395	.209	-.299	1.000	-.515*	-.314	-.203	-.281	.019
	Sig. (2-tailed)	.085	.377	.201		.020	.177	.391	.229	.935
	N	20	20	20	20	20	20	20	20	20
SDNN7	Pearson Correlation	-.250	-.252	-.092	-.515*	1.000	.717**	.497*	.585**	-.322
	Sig. (2-tailed)	.287	.284	.700	.020		.000	.026	.007	.166
	N	20	20	20	20	20	20	20	20	20
VL7	Pearson Correlation	-.249	-.263	-.070	-.314	.717**	1.000	.207	.263	-.046
	Sig. (2-tailed)	.290	.262	.768	.177	.000		.382	.263	.847
	N	20	20	20	20	20	20	20	20	20
L7	Pearson Correlation	-.158	.053	-.046	-.203	.497*	.207	1.000	.466*	.069
	Sig. (2-tailed)	.511	.823	.846	.391	.026	.382		.039	.773
	N	20	20	20	20	20	20	20	20	20
HIGH7	Pearson Correlation	.176	.349	-.039	-.281	.585**	.263	.466*	1.000	-.577**
	Sig. (2-tailed)	.457	.131	.871	.229	.007	.263	.039		.008
	N	20	20	20	20	20	20	20	20	20
LH7	Pearson Correlation	-.318	-.466*	.376	.019	-.322	-.046	.069	-.577**	1.000
	Sig. (2-tailed)	.172	.038	.102	.935	.166	.847	.773	.008	
	N	20	20	20	20	20	20	20	20	20

* Correlation is significant at the 0.05 level (2-tailed).

FIGURE 5.8   Pro soccer players AP PHO and stress task HRV relationships.

PHO measures emerged to influence the AP PHO-HRV relationship. SA/HS was negatively correlated ($-.31$) with L/H ratio, explaining 9% of the variance in this HRV measure that could be attributed to this AP PHO measure. In addition, and highly conceptually consistent, SR/N was also negatively correlated ($-.47$) with L/H ratio, explaining 22% of the variance in this HRV measure that could be attributed to this AP PHO measure. In virtually all cases in which every AP PHO is statistically significantly correlated with a performance outcome measure, or more than 5% of the variance in an outcome measure can be attributed to each AP PHO measure, SA/HS and SR/N will have the same directional association, that is, both will either be positively or negatively correlated with a specific performance outcome measure. By contrast, SC/RC will almost always show a correlation coefficient that has a sign that is opposite to the SA/HS-SR/N combination. In this case, SC/RC was positively correlated with L/H ratio (.38), explaining 14% of the variance in this HRV measure that could be attributed to this AP PHO measure. This three-way finding supports the AP and TCM model's hypothesis that SA/HS and SR/N interact as a function of increased stress, the S7s stress task condition here. The directional relationships exhibited here are conceptually consistent with AP PHO measures and their mediation of HRV responses, since it can be expected that higher levels of SA/HS and SR/N will interact to impact HRV, it is not clear why lower levels of SA/HS-SR/N were associated with greater L/H ratio, whereas, greater SC/RC was associated with a greater L/H ratio. In respect to AP PHO predictions, although, SA/HS-SR-N virtually always exert the same directional effect, in this case it would have been predicted that these measures would have been positively correlated with L/H ratio and SC/RC would have been negatively correlated with L/H ratio.

2. Additional findings included SR/N being correlated (.35) with HF activity, explaining 12% of the variance in this HRV measure that could be attributed to this AP PHO measure. This finding is conceptually inconsistent with the AP model, since HF is a pure PNS deactivation response and SR/N are hypothesized to mediate increases in SNS activity, especially as a function of stress, pressure, or a stress test task. SA/HS was also correlated with HR (.40), explaining 16% of the

FIGURE 5.9   Pro soccer players AP PHO and stress test HRV change relationships.

variance in this HRV measure that could be attributed to this AP PHO measure. This is a conceptually neutral finding since, depending upon one's level and constellation of SR/N and SC/RC, SA/HS can influence HRV responses differentially.

Figure 5.9 reveals the following:

1. Subliminal attention (SA/HS), the focus AP PHO trait, was correlated with HR (.45), explaining 20% of the variance in this HRV measure that could be attributed to SA/HS. It was also negatively correlated with SDNN (−.41), explaining 16% of the variance in this HRV measure that could be attributed to SA/HS. These findings can be considered conceptually neutral.
2. SR/N was negatively correlated with HRV change L/H ratio (−.64), explaining 40% of the variance in this HRV measure that could be attributed to SR/N. This finding is inconsistent with the AP and TCM conceptual/construct bases in that it would be expected that higher levels of SR/N in a stress condition would generate more LF activity and thereby increase the L/H ratio, not reduce it. By contrast, SC/RC was positively correlated with HRV change, L/H ratio (.53) explaining 28% of the variance in this HRV measure that could be attributed to SC/RC. This latter finding is also inconsistent, since conceptually, one would expect higher levels of SC/RC to mediate increases in PNS (HF) activity, thereby decreasing the L/H ratio. Despite this inconsistency, the high amounts of variance explained is impressive and attests to the predictive potency of AP PHO measures. In addition, the orthogonal nature of SR/N and SC/RC is highly consistent with the conceptual bases of these measures (opposite direction of correlations as a function of SR/N-SC/RC). These and other inconsistent findings will be further addressed in the final section of this chapter.

The next page contains a synopsis of the pro soccer team's official games' outcome along with brief comments by their sport psychologist.[4] Outcome measures were limited to macro-global ones, including games won, games lost, goals for and against, and sport psychologist rating. These criterion variables are usually insufficient and very insensitive to finding strong associations between psychological factors such as AP PHO measures and performance outcome. As such, the ability to analyze performance is quite constrained. In addition, in the context of the Serial 7s Stress Test paradigm, it is not possible to directly implicate HRV responses in the performance equation, only in relationship to AP PHO measures. This is because stress test responses cannot be repeatedly obtained in association with repeated sport-specific outcome measures unless mean outcome statistics are available (see Baseball team case study below). This methodological issue is encountered in various chapters (including this one below; baseball team) and is elucidated in alternative ecological stress tests that are carried out during structured training (Chapters 7 and 8).

ABSP Study-Msk Zilina-Professional Soccer Team

Games—A-Team Spring 2009

- **Game 1.** March 4, 2009, 4 p.m., Slovak Cup-Semifinal game, **Zilina-Bratislava 1-2,** very bad performance
- **Game 2.** March 7, 2009, 5.30 p.m., Corgon League, **Zilina-B. Bystrica 1-0,** won game but not really good performance
- **Game 3.** March 14, 2009, 5.30 p.m., Corgon League, **Dubnica-Zilina 2-0**, very bad performance, players looked very tired and nervous
- **Game 4.** March 18, 2009, 5 p.m., Slovak Cup-Semifinal game, **Slovan-Zilina 0-0**, good performance but we would have to win in order to advance
- **Game 5.** March 22, 2009, 5.30 p.m., Corgon League game, **Zilina-DAC D.S. 5-1**, very good performance with lot of goals
- **Game 6.** March 28, 2009, 1 p.m., International Scrimmage game, **Zilina-Krakov (Poland) 1-0,** won but not really good performance
- **Game 7.** April 4, 2009, 7.30 p.m., Corgon League, **Zilina-Z.M. 2-1**, won but really bad performance
- **Game 8.** April 12, 2009, 5.15 p.m., Corgon League, **Artmedia-Zilina 0-0,** good performance
- **Game 9.** April 18, 2009, 7.30 p.m., Corgon League, **Zilina-Presov 2-2**, bad performance, coach fired
- **Game 10.** April 26, 2 p.m., Corgon League, **Zilina-Nitra 2-0**, very good performance with new coach

Figures 5.10 through 5.12 chart ANS measures that were derived from pre-match HRV assessments.

Figure 5.13 contains data from the outcome synopsis page and in Figures 5.10 to 5.12. No significant findings emerged from this data. They are presented for illustrative purposes and to emphasize that higher evidentiary analyses must contain sufficient amounts of repeated predictor and micro-level, sport-specific outcome measures to be able to arrive at meaningful statistical inferences about the impact of psychological factors on performance both at the group/team and individual level. This issue is further addressed in the following case study of an elite youth baseball team whose Serial 7s stress test data could be analyzed in the context of micro-level repeated outcome measures (criticality analysis).

Figure 5.14 contains AP PHO and Serial 7s stress test baseline, task, and change HRV data from starting players on an elite youth baseball team. Figure 5.15 contains AP PHO rating and HRV change rankings.

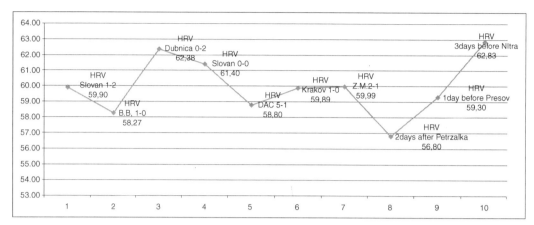

FIGURE 5.10 Mean HRV (below HRV = heart rate [HR]).

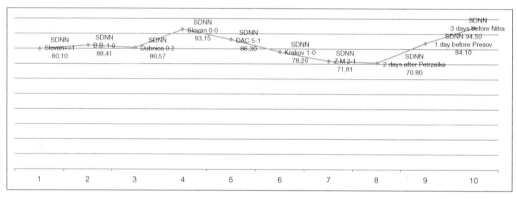

FIGURE 5.11 Mean SDNN.

A review of the preceding AP PHO measures/constellations and HRV responses in the baseline stress task and change condition reveals the following:

1. One player had an "Ideal" ***** (5-star; L-L-H) AP. Athletes with such an AP would be expected to elicit HRV responses across test conditions that are consistent the conceptual/construct bases of AP PHO measures. This ***** player exhibited a decrease in L/H ratio in the HRV change

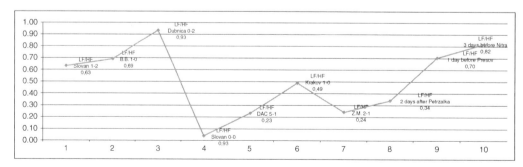

FIGURE 5.12 Mean L/H ratio.

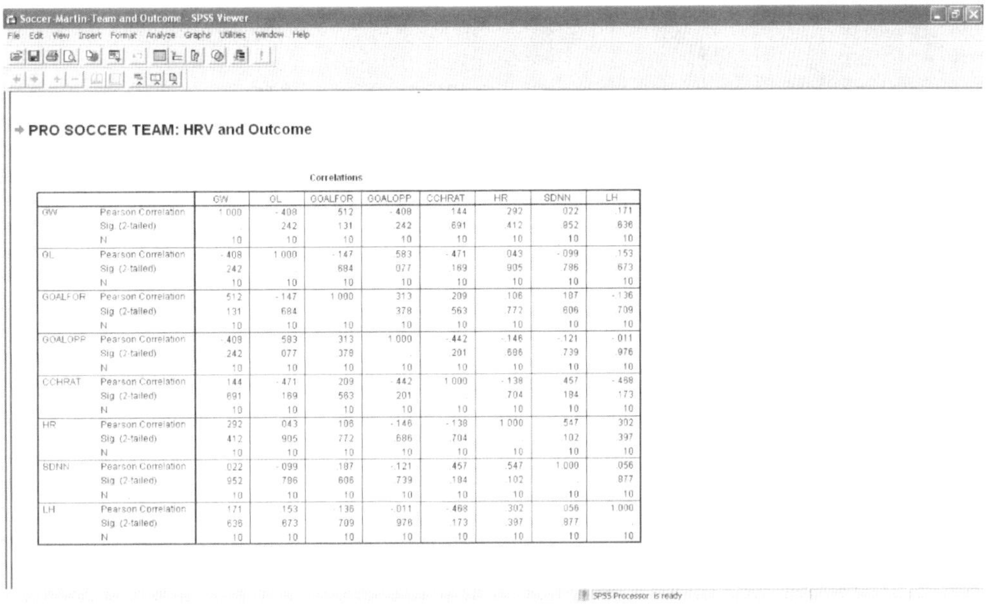

FIGURE 5.13   Pro soccer team's game outcome and select HRV measure relationships.

condition consistent with what would have been expected. By contrast, HR, SDNN, and VL increased and HF activity decreased in the change condition (conceptually inconsistent).

2. Six players had a **** AP (second best). Of these athletes, HRV response change consistency (CC) was as follows: 2 yes (consistent) and 4 no (inconsistent) for L/H ratio, 2-4 for HR, 1-5 for SDNN, 0-6 for VLF, and 3-3 for HF.

3. Two players had a ** AP (next to worst) with the following CC: 1-1 for L/H ratio, 2-0 for HR, 2-0 for SDNN, 0-2 for VLF, and 1-1 for HF.

4. Two players had *** AP, more ambiguous PHO constellations with the following CC: 0-1-1 (last 1 = neutral change range) for L/H, 1-1 for HR, 1-1 for SDNN, 1-1 for VLF, and 0-1-1 for HF.

These findings will be further addressed in a discussion section at the end of the chapter.

In contrast to the soccer team, the baseball team's AP PHO and stress test HRV measures could be further analyzed in the contact of critical moment performance, with criticality data being derived from all at-bats over the course of the entire season in a pre-intervention and intervention phase (ca. greater than 100 at-bats per starting player). Figures 5.16 to 5.22 present various outcome analyses.

Figure 5.16 depicts relationships between player AP PHO measures and critical moment performance as reflected in quality-of-at-bat and success outcome measures in the pre-intervention and intervention phases of the season. In the pre-intervention phase, SR/N was correlated (.56; 31% of the variance) with critical moment performance (CMP) and SC/RC was negatively correlated (−.70; 49% of the variance) with CMP. These findings are inconsistent with AP conceptual bases; however, these correlations and variance explained are quite high, and again attest to the potency of AP PHO measures as mediators of pressure performance.

Figure 5.17 depicts player AP PHO measures and their relationship with stress test HRV baseline HRV responding. It was found that SA/HS was negatively correlated (−.49; 24% of the

FIGURE 5.14   Elite youth baseball team player's database stress test baseline, task, and change responses.

YOUTH BASEBALL TEAM: AP PHO and SERIAL 7s STRESS TEST

Name	CSARCS-A			HRV-Baseline						SERIAL 7s STRESS TEST						HRV CHANGE					
	SA	SA	SC	HR	SDNN	VL	LOW	HIGH	L/H	HR	SDNN	VL	LOW	HIGH	L/H	HR	SDNN	VL	LOW	HIGH	L/H
F	9	15	15	106	25	28	82	38	2.1	112	38	11	261	144	1.8	6	13	-17	159	75	0.3
J	18	6	24	76	169	79	6880	1420	4.8	79	108	197	1812	1639	1.1	3	-60	118	.5067	218	-3.7
G	22	13	11	74	75	58	340	339	1	85	57	98	535	447	1.2	11	-17	40	205	108	0.2
K	19	8	6	71	149	251	670	5460	0.1	83	66	81	576	847	0.7	12	83	69	95	-4613	0.6
Y	5	3	23	85	55	227	498	281	1.8	102	43	171	171	251	0.7	17	-12	56	-318	-30	-1.1
R	18	2	17	91	142	1901	938	842	1.1	77	255	2359	6327	4265	1.5	-15	113	458	6196	3423	0.4
M	23	7	19	68	54	152	452	369	1.2	92	62	596	439	253	1.7	23	7	445	-13	-117	0.5
J	15	4	25	82	142	1684	290	237	1.2	85	60	131	468	305	1.5	3	.82	-1553	179	69	0.3
M	20	8	18	74	78	171	415	1033	0.4	96	53	383	223	176	1.3	23	-26	213	-192	-857	0.9
RM	18	15	13	80	66	652	967	298	3.2	90	50	282	298	235	1.3	9	-17	-370	-669	-63	-1.9
S	21	6	23	85	116	63	3407	729	4.7	95	46	116	48	172	2.8	10	-70	53	-3359	-557	-1.9
MEAN	17.091	7.909	17.64	81.09	97.36	478.7	1358	1004	1.964	90.55	76.18	402.3	1014	794	1.418	9.273	-21.27	-56.91	-270.4	-213.1	-0.545

FIGURE 5.15   Elite youth baseball team player's AP and stress test HRV relationships.

YOUTH BASEBALL TEAM ATHLETE'S PROFILE AP and HRV CHANGES from BASELINE to SERIAL 7s STRESS TASK

	Name	CSARCS-A			Rating	L/H	Rank-Prd	HR	Rank-Prd	SD	Rank-Prd	VL	Rank-Prd	H	Rank-Prd
		SA	SR	RC			CHANGE	FROM	BASELINE	TO	STRESS	TASK			
1	F	9L	15M	15M	***	-0.3	5-HIC	6	4-IC	13	1-IC	-17	4-IC	75	4-N
2	J	18M	6L	24H	****	-3.7	1-HC	3	2-C	-60	7-HIC	118	8-HIC	218	2-HC
3	G	22M	13M	11L	***	0.2	6-N	11	7-C	-17	4-C	40	5-C	108	3-IC
4	K	19M	8L	6L	**	0.6	10-C	12	8-C	-83	10-C	-69	3-IC	-4613	11-HIC
5	Y	5L	3L	23H	*****	-1.1	4-HC	17	9-HIC	-12	3-IC	56	7-HIC	-30	6-IC
6	R	18M	2L	17M	****	0.4	8-IC	-15	1-HC	113	11-HIC	458	11-HIC	3423	1-HC
7	M	23H	7L	19M	****	0.5	9-IC	23	10-IC	7	2-C	445	10-HIC	-117	8-HIC
8	J	15M	4L	25H	****	0.3	7-IC	3	2-C	-82	9-HIC	-1553	1-C	69	5-C
9	M	20M	8L	18M	****	0.9	11-IC	23	10-HIC	-26	6-IC	213	9-HIC	-857	10-HIC
10	RM	18M	15M	13M	**	-1.9	2-HIC	9	5-C	-17	4-C	-370	2-IC	-63	7-C
11	S	21M	6L	23H	****	-1.9	2-HC	10	6-IC	-70	8-HIC	53	6-IC	-557	9-HIC
	Mean	17.1	7.90	17.60		-0.545		9.2727		-21.3		-56.9		-213.1	

KEY: PRD= Predicted

Prd: HC = Highly Consistent with Athlete Profile; C = Consistent; HIC = Highly Inconsistent; IC = Inconsistent; N = Neutral

HRV Rank: L/H, better = greater negative change; HR: better = less positive change; SD: better = greater positive change; H: better = greater positive change

VL, better = less positive change

CSARCS-A Rating: ***** = Ideal Athlete's Profile Constellation; **** = Next Best; *** = Average; ** = Poor; * = Worst Athlete's Profile Constellation

variance) with stress test baseline HR, SR/N was also negatively correlated ($-.48$; 23% of the variance) with HR, and SC/RC was positively correlated (.41; 16% of the variance) with HR. These findings are consistent with AP-PHO conceptual bases regarding SA/HS, SR/N, and SC/RC directional effects (negative correlation for SA/HS-SR/N) and (positive correlation for SC/RC).

Youth Elite Baseball Team: CSARCS-A AP-PHO MEASURES and CRITICAL MOMENT PERFORMANCE

Correlations

		SA	SR	SC	CMQABPRE	CMQABINT	CMQABDIF	CMSUCPRE	CMSUCINT	CMSUCDIF
SA	Pearson Correlation	1.000	.450	-.369	.243	.242	.185	.302	.208	-.249
	Sig. (2-tailed)		.191	.294	.499	.501	.610	.396	.592	.518
	N	10	10	10	10	10	10	10	9	9
SR	Pearson Correlation	.450	1.000	-.603	.559	-.336	-.508	.318	.146	-.054
	Sig. (2-tailed)	.191		.065	.093	.342	.136	.370	.708	.889
	N	10	10	10	10	10	10	10	10	9
SC	Pearson Correlation	-.369	-.603	1.000	-.704*	-.216	.090	.386	-.383	.142
	Sig. (2-tailed)	.294	.065		.023	.549	.805	.271	.309	.715
	N	10	10	10	10	10	10	10	9	9
CMQABPRE	Pearson Correlation	.243	.559	-.704*	1.000	.006	-.420	.663*	.272	-.336
	Sig. (2-tailed)	.499	.093	.023		.988	.227	.037	.478	.376
	N	10	10	10	10	10	10	10	9	9
CMQABINT	Pearson Correlation	.242	-.336	-.216	.006	1.000	.897**	-.295	.796*	.215
	Sig. (2-tailed)	.501	.342	.549	.988		.000	.409	.010	.578
	N	10	10	10	10	10	10	10	9	9
CMQABDIF	Pearson Correlation	.185	-.508	.090	-.420	.897**	1.000	-.517	.289	.277
	Sig. (2-tailed)	.610	.136	.805	.227	.000		.126	.435	.470
	N	10	10	10	10	10	10	10	9	9
CMSUCPRE	Pearson Correlation	.302	.318	.386	.663*	-.295	-.517	1.000	.102	.735*
	Sig. (2-tailed)	.396	.370	.271	.037	.409	.126		.793	.024
	N	10	10	10	10	10	10	10	9	9
CMSUCINT	Pearson Correlation	.208	.146	-.383	.272	.796*	.289	.102	1.000	.564
	Sig. (2-tailed)	.592	.708	.309	.478	.010	.435	.793		.113
	N	9	9	9	9	9	9	9	9	9
CMSUCDIF	Pearson Correlation	-.249	-.054	.142	-.336	.215	.277	.735*	.564	1.000
	Sig. (2-tailed)	.518	.889	.715	.376	.578	.470	.024	.113	
	N	9	9	9	9	9	9	9	9	9

*. Correlation is significant at the 0.05 level (2-tailed).

FIGURE 5.16   Elite youth baseball team player's AP PHO measures and critical moment outcome.

Figure 5.18 depicts the player's AP PHO measures and their relationship with the Serial 7s stress test task. SR/N was negatively correlated (−.45; 20% of the variance) with SDNN, VLF (−.42; 16% of the variance) and HF (−.45), while SA/HS and SC/RC were positively correlated with L/H ratio (.47 and .38 respectively; 22% and 14% of the variance respectively). The SR/N findings can be considered conceptually inconsistent since it would be expected that greater levels of SR/N would induce an increase in VLF and decrease in HF activity in the stress condition. The findings on SA/HS-SC/RC are reconcilable with AP PHO conceptual bases and reflects at the group/team

YOUTH BASEBALL TEAM: CSARCS-A AP PHO MEASURES and HRV STRESS TEST BASELINE

Correlations

		SA	SR	SC	HR	SDNN	VL	LOW	HIGH	LH
SA	Pearson Correlation	1.000	.450	-.369	-.492	.093	-.180	.098	.133	-.001
	Sig. (2-tailed)		.191	.294	.149	.797	.619	.787	.713	.999
	N	10	10	10	10	10	10	10	10	10
SR	Pearson Correlation	.450	1.000	-.603	-.485	-.398	-.415	-.127	.009	.038
	Sig. (2-tailed)	.191		.065	.155	.255	.234	.727	.981	.917
	N	10	10	10	10	10	10	10	10	10
SC	Pearson Correlation	-.369	-.603	1.000	.406	.096	.148	.409	-.599	.496
	Sig. (2-tailed)	.294	.065		.244	.792	.682	.242	.067	.144
	N	10	10	10	10	10	10	10	10	10
HR	Pearson Correlation	-.492	-.485	.406	1.000	.206	.607	.056	-.363	.285
	Sig. (2-tailed)	.149	.155	.244		.569	.063	.877	.302	.424
	N	10	10	10	10	10	10	10	10	10
SDNN	Pearson Correlation	.093	-.398	.096	.206	1.000	.370	.546	.485	.209
	Sig. (2-tailed)	.797	.255	.792	.569		.292	.103	.156	.561
	N	10	10	10	10	10	10	10	10	10
VL	Pearson Correlation	-.180	-.415	.148	.607	.370	1.000	-.280	-.175	-.246
	Sig. (2-tailed)	.619	.234	.682	.063	.292		.432	.628	.493
	N	10	10	10	10	10	10	10	10	10
LOW	Pearson Correlation	.098	-.127	.409	.056	.546	-.280	1.000	.052	.826**
	Sig. (2-tailed)	.787	.727	.242	.877	.103	.432		.887	.003
	N	10	10	10	10	10	10	10	10	10
HIGH	Pearson Correlation	.133	.009	-.599	-.363	.485	-.175	.052	1.000	-.283
	Sig. (2-tailed)	.713	.981	.067	.302	.156	.628	.887		.429
	N	10	10	10	10	10	10	10	10	10
LH	Pearson Correlation	-.001	.038	.496	.285	.209	-.246	.826**	-.283	1.000
	Sig. (2-tailed)	.999	.917	.144	.424	.561	.493	.003	.429	
	N	10	10	10	10	10	10	10	10	10

**. Correlation is significant at the 0.01 level (2-tailed).

FIGURE 5.17   Elite youth baseball team player's AP PHO measures and stress test HRV baseline response.

YOUTH BASEBALL TEAM CSARCS-A AP PHO MEASURES and SERIAL 7S STRESS TEST TASK HRV

Correlations

		SA	SR	SC	HR7	SD7	VL7	L7	H7	LH7
SA	Pearson Correlation	1.000	.450	-.369	-.383	.064	.075	.034	.025	.468
	Sig. (2-tailed)		.191	.294	.302	.860	.836	.926	.946	.172
	N	10	10	10	10	10	10	10	10	10
SR	Pearson Correlation	.450	1.000	-.603	.034	-.453	-.418	-.443	-.445	-.084
	Sig. (2-tailed)	.191		.065	.925	.189	.229	.200	.197	.818
	N	10	10	10	10	10	10	10	10	10
SC	Pearson Correlation	-.369	-.603	1.000	.258	-.011	-.022	-.018	-.049	.382
	Sig. (2-tailed)	.294	.065		.471	.975	.952	.965	.893	.275
	N	10	10	10	10	10	10	10	10	10
HR7	Pearson Correlation	-.383	.034	.259	1.000	-.670*	-.430	-.653*	-.896*	.133
	Sig. (2-tailed)	.302	.925	.471		.034	.215	.041	.025	.715
	N	10	10	10	10	10	10	10	10	10
SD7	Pearson Correlation	.064	-.453	-.011	-.670*	1.000	.932**	.998**	.991**	.000
	Sig. (2-tailed)	.860	.189	.975	.034		.000	.000	.000	.999
	N	10	10	10	10	10	10	10	10	10
VL7	Pearson Correlation	.075	-.418	-.022	-.430	.932**	1.000	.935**	.889**	.096
	Sig. (2-tailed)	.836	.229	.952	.215	.000		.000	.001	.792
	N	10	10	10	10	10	10	10	10	10
L7	Pearson Correlation	.034	-.443	-.018	-.653*	.998**	.935**	1.000	.991**	-.013
	Sig. (2-tailed)	.926	.200	.965	.041	.000	.000		.000	.972
	N	10	10	10	10	10	10	10	10	10
H7	Pearson Correlation	.025	-.445	-.049	-.896*	.991**	.889**	.991**	1.000	-.085
	Sig. (2-tailed)	.946	.197	.893	.025	.000	.001	.000		.859
	N	10	10	10	10	10	10	10	10	10
LH7	Pearson Correlation	.468	-.084	.382	.133	.000	.096	-.013	-.085	1.000
	Sig. (2-tailed)	.172	.818	.275	.715	.999	.792	.972	.859	
	N	10	10	10	10	10	10	10	10	10

FIGURE 5.18   Elite youth baseball team player's AP PHO measures and stress test task condition HRV.

level the predominance of Ideal ***** and second best **** AP constellations in this baseball team (7 of 11 players had one of these profiles). SA/HS and SC/RC, here, appear to interact in the absence of SR/N to influence the stress test task condition generation of L/H ratio that may have been higher in a team composed of athletes who were predominant in SR/N (this team's SR/N mean = 7.9 a low level of this trait).

Figure 5.19 depicts the players HRV change from the baseline to task condition as a function of AP PHO measures. Here, findings were relatively sparse with only SC/RC emerging as a mediating trait. It was positively correlated (.49; about 25% of the variance) with HF activity and negatively correlated (−.41; 16% of the variance) with L/H ratio. These findings are highly conceptually consistent in that the AP and TCM models of peak performance predict that psychophysiological changes across baseline and stress conditions (increases in SNS-mediated responses) will be mitigated by higher levels of SC/RC or lead to greater levels of SC/RC-driven PNS responses like higher HF or lower L/H ratio activity.

Figure 5.20 depicts player's stress test baseline HRV and critical moment performance relationships an added layer of evidentiary information that was not available for the professional soccer team. Having repeated longitudinally derived micro-level outcome measures (critical moment performance) allows a practitioner or researcher to go beyond mere associations between AP PHO predictor and HRV outcome measures at both the group/team and individual level. They are particularly pertinent to analyses of athletes whose AP PHO constellations are more ambiguous (***) or stress responses are inconsistent with what would have been expected conceptually. AP PHO and HRV stress response relationships that are inconsistent can frequently be attributed to a host of methodological issues that will be discussed in the last section of this chapter. As such, interpretive limitations, caveats, and analytical issues can be avoided by just looking at associations between measures that can be repeatedly acquired (HRV and critical moment instances) to arrive at group/team and individual stress test responding HRV and competition outcome metrics (criticality performance). Eventual findings, if potent enough and conceptually consistent, can then be used

YOUTH BASEBALL TEAM CSARCS-A AP PHO MEASURES and HRV CHANGE: BASELINE vs. TASK

Correlations

		SA	SR	SC	HRDIF	SDDIF	VDIF	LOWDIF	HIGHDIF	LHDIF
SA	Pearson Correlation	1.000	.450	-.369	.052	.000	.257	-.049	-.093	.185
	Sig. (2-tailed)		.191	.294	.886	.999	.474	.892	.799	.608
	N	10	10	10	10	10	10	10	10	10
SR	Pearson Correlation	.450	1.000	-.603	.335	-.204	-.022	-.238	-.302	-.076
	Sig. (2-tailed)	.191		.065	.343	.573	.951	.507	.396	.835
	N	10	10	10	10	10	10	10	10	10
SC	Pearson Correlation	-.369	-.603	1.000	-.071	-.084	-.224	-.313	.458	-.406
	Sig. (2-tailed)	.294	.065		.846	.818	.534	.379	.183	.245
	N	10	10	10	10	10	10	10	10	10
HRDIF	Pearson Correlation	.052	.335	-.071	1.000	-.418	.131	-.436	-.571	.167
	Sig. (2-tailed)	.886	.343	.846		.229	.718	.208	.084	.644
	N	10	10	10	10	10	10	10	10	10
SDDIF	Pearson Correlation	.000	-.204	-.084	-.418	1.000	.537	.778**	.746*	.283
	Sig. (2-tailed)	.999	.573	.818	.229		.109	.008	.013	.463
	N	10	10	10	10	10	10	10	10	10
VDIF	Pearson Correlation	.257	-.022	-.224	.131	.537	1.000	.120	.142	-.018
	Sig. (2-tailed)	.474	.951	.534	.718	.109		.742	.696	.960
	N	10	10	10	10	10	10	10	10	10
LOWDIF	Pearson Correlation	-.049	-.238	-.313	-.436	.778**	.120	1.000	.437	.695*
	Sig. (2-tailed)	.892	.507	.379	.208	.008	.742		.207	.026
	N	10	10	10	10	10	10	10	10	10
HIGHDIF	Pearson Correlation	-.093	-.302	.458	-.571	.746*	.142	.437	1.000	-.120
	Sig. (2-tailed)	.799	.396	.183	.084	.013	.696	.207		.741
	N	10	10	10	10	10	10	10	10	10
LHDIF	Pearson Correlation	.185	-.076	-.406	.167	.283	-.018	.695*	-.120	1.000
	Sig. (2-tailed)	.608	.835	.245	.644	.463	.960	.026	.741	
	N	10	10	10	10	10	10	10	10	10

FIGURE 5.19 Elite youth baseball team player's AP PHO measures and stress test condition change HRV.

to reverse predict an approximation of an athlete's true AP PHO constellation. This methodology is elucidated in later chapters, including one on the complete case study of this baseball team.

Relative to the team's stress test baseline condition HRV, the following was found. In the pre-intervention phase of the baseball team's season, HR was negatively correlated ($-.51$; about 25% of the variance) with critical moment quality of at-bats (CMQAB), meaning that greater HR was

YOUTH BASEBALL TEAM: BASELINE HRV and Pre and Intervention Phase Critical Moment Perform.

Correlations

		CMQABPRE	CMQABINT	CMQABDIF	HR	SDNN	VL	LOW	HIGH	LH
CMQABPRE	Pearson Correlation	1.000	.006	-.420	-.505	-.123	-.443	.071	.477	-.143
	Sig. (2-tailed)		.988	.227	.136	.734	.200	.845	.163	.694
	N	10	10	10	10	10	10	10	10	10
CMQABINT	Pearson Correlation	.006	1.000	.897**	.371	.294	.545	-.079	.099	-.170
	Sig. (2-tailed)	.988		.000	.291	.409	.103	.828	.786	.639
	N	10	10	10	10	10	10	10	10	10
CMQABDIF	Pearson Correlation	-.420	.897**	1.000	.500	.354	.720*	-.109	-.112	-.121
	Sig. (2-tailed)	.227	.000		.141	.315	.019	.765	.757	.738
	N	10	10	10	10	10	10	10	10	10
HR	Pearson Correlation	-.505	.371	.500	1.000	.206	.607	.056	-.363	.285
	Sig. (2-tailed)	.136	.291	.141		.569	.063	.877	.302	.424
	N	10	10	10	10	10	10	10	10	10
SDNN	Pearson Correlation	-.123	.294	.354	.206	1.000	.370	.546	.485	.209
	Sig. (2-tailed)	.734	.409	.315	.569		.292	.103	.156	.561
	N	10	10	10	10	10	10	10	10	10
VL	Pearson Correlation	-.443	.545	.720*	.607	.370	1.000	-.280	-.175	-.246
	Sig. (2-tailed)	.200	.103	.019	.063	.292		.432	.628	.493
	N	10	10	10	10	10	10	10	10	10
LOW	Pearson Correlation	.071	-.079	-.109	.056	.546	-.280	1.000	.052	.826**
	Sig. (2-tailed)	.845	.828	.765	.877	.103	.432		.887	.003
	N	10	10	10	10	10	10	10	10	10
HIGH	Pearson Correlation	.477	.099	-.112	-.363	.485	-.175	.052	1.000	-.283
	Sig. (2-tailed)	.163	.786	.757	.302	.156	.628	.887		.429
	N	10	10	10	10	10	10	10	10	10
LH	Pearson Correlation	-.143	-.170	-.121	.285	.209	-.246	.826**	-.283	1.000
	Sig. (2-tailed)	.694	.639	.738	.424	.561	.493	.003	.429	
	N	10	10	10	10	10	10	10	10	10

FIGURE 5.20 Elite youth baseball team player's baseline HRV and critical moment performance.

associated with a decrease in CMQAB. Baseline VLF, similarly, was negatively correlated ($-.44$; 19% of the variance) with pre-intervention CMQAB, indicating that greater SNS-mediated HRV activity (VLF) was also associated with worse CMQAB performance. Increasing HR is associated with greater SNS-LF HRV activity, making these two findings highly conceptually consistent. Such a finding in an athlete whose AP PHO constellation is more ambiguous (***) or paradoxical (inconsistent with stress test baseline, task or change HRV) would be strongly suggestive of being a more performance detrimental one (marked by high SR/N, high SA/HS, and low SC/RC ** or * AP). Also, highly conceptually consistent was the finding that greater HF activity was positively correlated (.48; 23% of the variance) with CMQAB in the pre-intervention phase, since an increase in a PNS-mediated deactivation or stress reduction measure is predicted to be performance facilitative, especially during critical moments of competition.

In the intervention phase of the baseball team's season, players engaged in HRV biofeedback on the bench prior to every at-bat (during real official league games; see Chapter 20). Findings from the mental training phase include HR and VL being positively correlated with CMQAB (.37; 14% of the variance, and .55; 30% of the variance, respectively), diametrically opposite HRV effects than in the pre-intervention phase. These findings are highly conceptually inconsistent and may be explainable on the basis of actual criticality normative data (range of, etc.) that will be discussed in the final section.

Relative to HRV change as a function of baseline versus the stress test task greater HR and VLF were positively associated (.50; 25% of the variance, and .72; ca. 49% of the variance, respectively) with this outcome variable. It remains to be seen if increases in SNS activation as reflected in greater HR and VLF will consistently be associated with greater CM performance across a large population sample. It may also be irrelevant at the intra-individual level, where an athlete's unique IZOF, as opposed to such group findings from which he or she could make faulty inferences, take precedence in the assessment process.

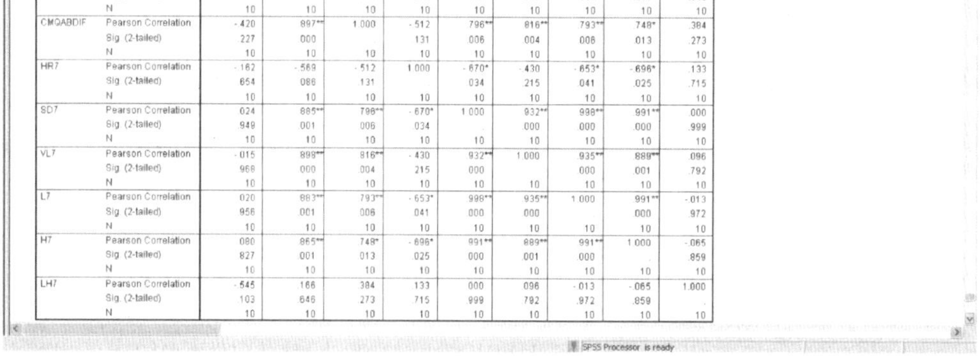

FIGURE 5.21 Elite youth baseball team player's stress test task condition HRV and critical moment performance.

Perhaps more important than baseline, HRV is the HRV stress test response that is depicted in Figure 5.21. Here, stress test baseline L/H was found to be negatively correlated (−.55; 30% of the variance) with pre-intervention CMQAB, a finding that is conceptually consistent, the only HRV finding in this condition. By contrast, the intervention phase replete with associations between HRV and outcome with HR being negatively correlated (−.51; 26% of the variance) with CMQAB; SDNN was highly correlated with CMQAB (.89; about 81% of the variance); VLF (.90; 81% of the variance with CMQAB); and HF (.87; 76% of the variance with CMQAB). These findings appear to be inflated and are in part paradoxical (e.g., same relationship between VLF and HF with performance outcome).

Stress test HRV changes from the baseline to the task condition as depicted in Figure 5.22 reveal that HR was negatively correlated (−.72; about 52% of the variance) with CMQAB, while SDNN and HF were positively correlated with CMQAB (.62; 38% of the variance and .59; about 34% of the variance, respectively). These findings are highly consistent conceptually.

FIGURE 5.22   Elite youth baseball team player's stress test HRV change and critical moment performance.

Discussion: Issues, Limitations, Caveats, and Considerations

These findings raise many questions. Change inconsistencies abounded across most AP constellations and individual change measures that could call into question certain conceptual tenets (construct validity components) of the TCM and AP models of peak performance, and the actual utility of the Serial 7s stress test. It is emphasized that incongruence between what is expected and predicted conceptually (hypothesized) must be addressed head-on. Negative findings will always occur in the context of self-report or questionnaire-based measures. They must be teased out when doing assessments and explained. It is not tenable or ethical to merely administer a test because group research findings suggest that it may reveal or predict something about future performance. Such predictions must be validated empirically using the methodologies that are espoused in this book, even at the risk of generating outcome data that may contradict what was hypothesized in the first place.

The following must be considered:

1. The TCM and AP model's predictions pertaining to ANS responding as a function of cognitive stress in both static and competitive situations do not necessarily allow for deviations from the original operationalizations of PHO constellations and what they predict. Doing so may lead to response inconsistencies like those that were observed. In their strictest form, TCM and AP predictions *may apply only to the exact Ideal Athlete's Profile PHO constellation of H-L-H or L-L-H and most performance detrimental PHO constellation (H-H-L). It may thus be inappropriate and methodologically flawed to attempt to make predictions about ANS stress test responses that are then extrapolated to pressure performance during competition on the basis of AP PHO constellations that do not meet the precise threshold for being the most potent predictors of optimum or worst peak pressure performance.* It may also be erroneous to assume that individual PHO measures such as SR/N and SC/RC will mediate ANS/HRV stress test responses independently, since the conceptual basis and construct validity of the AP model advances an interactional dynamic, in which, under stress, or situations involving competitive pressure (critical moments), PHO measures work synergistically (interact) to mediate brain–heart–mind–body responses.

2. Change inconsistencies may also be attributable to the "one-shot" test phenomenon in which a score can be reliably derived only once and does not reflect an athlete's actual predominant HRV responses to stressors across repeated occasions that are more reliable. Since the Serial 7s stress test can be administered only once (to an individual athlete) due to its surprise and unfamiliarity components, to which a test taker can quickly become habituated, and whose hypothesized resulting normative benchmarks for ideal and poor responses are derived from group and not individual-repeated measure norms, a more sensitive and higher evidentiary approach to the assessment of pressure performance should be used in cases where conceptually inconsistent stress responses occur. Specifically, the multiple individual case study and individual case study, repeated predictor-outcome measure (longitudinal) design is well suited to the investigation of AP PHO constellation-stress-/pressure-induced ANS changes in the context of more ecological stress test paradigms (see Chapters 7, 8, and 20).

3. Change consistency or inconsistencies as a function of AP PHO constellation can be addressed in relationship to eventual real performance outcome measures and IZOF profiles rather than a mere qualitative deviation rating. This was done with the soccer team's limited more global-macro level performance outcome measures and the baseball team stress test case study's data. More ambiguous AP PHO constellations (***AP) should be analyzed using stress test–mediated HRV changes in relationship to an actual performance outcome to determine whether an AP is valid or HRV stress test responses, independently, establishes an athlete's true AP PHO constellation. In other words, the HRV stress test response profile may reverse predict an athlete's AP PHO constellation directly. Psychophysiological measures that are consistent with a specific AP PHO constellation's conceptual components are used to replace an initial CSARCS-A or analogue self-report-generated test score with one that is derived from HRV and performance relationships during real competition. In such a case, ecological HRV responding supersedes a psychometric instrument-generated AP that is not linked externally (criterion referenced) to objective sport-specific outcome measures. For example, if excessive VLF that is repeatedly associated with poor high criticality performance in an athlete whose profile is a ****AP, marked by low SR/N, it is probable that his or her real level of competitive SR/N is high. As a result of such an ecological IZOF finding, this athlete's AP would be adjusted to high SR/N, with the level of SA/HS being kept as is (based on CSARCS-A) and SC/RC being changed to

low if it was high in the first place, since high SC/RC is not compatible with high SR/N and poor critical moment performance.

4. Inconsistent stress test responses in athletes who have an ideal or most detrimental AP, as with athletes who possess a more ambiguous profile, can nullify an initial self-report test-derived AP PHO constellation. However, an original CSARCS-A generated AP PHO constellation would still hold up if it mediates conceptually consistent HRV or other psychophysiological responses that predict micro-level sport-specific critical moment performance in the context of higher-evidentiary, repeated measures of longitudinal stress test designs, or on the basis of real competition critical moment performance, the ultimate benchmark of psychological performance proficiency (mental toughness). In other words, if an athlete has an AP of H-L-H (ideal constellation), yet exhibits, for example, an L/H ratio that goes from .8 in the baseline to 7.5 in the stress test task condition, would have his or her AP called into question, unless it was later determined that his or her criticality performance was stellar (e.g., .30 for quality of bat/criticality relationship when the norm is closer to .10). In this case, actual pressure performance outcome supersedes both self-report and static cognitive-based stress test scores and profiles. Such an occurrence could be attributable to the "threshold effect" in which a static stress test, which is devoid of context for an athlete, fails to induce responses and response relationships that would occur in ecological, real competition (face validity of a test must be equal to its ecological validity or it will not evoke serious consideration and focused attention to stress test task conditions).

5. Variance also factors into the stress testing process and helps account for change inconsistencies, since ultimately the predictive validity of a test measure is what makes a test a valuable assessment instrument (reason to use it). Depending upon the adjusted r^2 of stress test HRV responses, which is likely to be relatively low, one can estimate the probability of change consistency, without necessarily calling into question the validity of an AP PHO constellation. Since explaining 100% of the variance in objective performance outcome measures on the basis of a temporally removed test response (self-report or stress test) is a virtual impossibility, the probability of conceptually inconsistent stress test response can be high. In other words, measurement error can drive AP PHO-HRV-mediated inconsistencies, consequently, the gold standard outcome measure in cases of response inconsistencies is actual critical moment performance (see items 4 and 5) with highest variance explained r^2 coefficients being used to change original AP profiles accordingly.

6. A more straightforward reason for change inconsistencies is the fact that, in both case studies, sample size and power were low, calling into question the statistical integrity of some of the findings. However, the conceptual bases of AP and TCM predictions regarding stress and pressure performance were originally based on multiple studies having adequate sample size and power, and while assessment can be guided by group findings, as is continually stressed in this book, ultimately, reliable and valid athlete assessment must be conceptualized to address each athlete's response tendencies individually.

7. Another statistical issue that is easy to overlook are criticality ranges. Since the AP and TCM models maintain that the ideal and most detrimental AP PHO constellations will be potent predictors of critical moment performance at the micro-level, it is important to determine the criticality distribution of a sample.

As Figure 5.23 shows, of the 768 data points (at-bats) that composed the baseball players' HRV-criticality analyses, 369 were assigned level 1, 183 level 2, 127 level 3, 71 level 4, and 15 level 5 criticality. It is noticeable that this distribution contains vastly more level 1, 2, and 3 critical moments. As such, this team and its athletes did not encounter sufficient amounts of what are by far

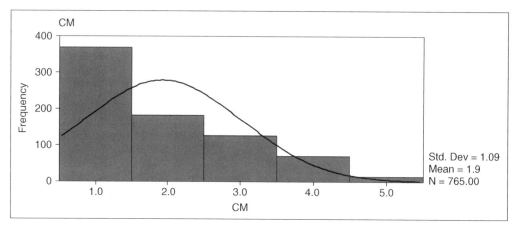

FIGURE 5.23 Distribution of criticality level 1–5.

the most critical of competitive moments, levels 4 and 5 criticality. A sample must have sufficient amounts of levels 4 and 5 critical moments to accurately gauge pressure performance tendencies as a function of both HRV stress test responses and AP PHO constellations. Relative to AP PHO constellations, original conceptualizations of their impact on critical moment performance were arrived at on the basis of multiple studies with sample sizes ranging from 200 to 1500 predictor and criterion variable data points, with sufficient levels 4 and 5 critical moments. Consequently, in the context of correlation and regression statistical analyses, one could erroneously reach the conclusion that a particular HRV response or AP PHO constellation, even if conceptually inconsistent, were associated with better critical moment performance despite the low criticality ceiling (ca. level 3). Level three is not a high level of criticality, yet, if the distribution inflates its stature, it can drive positive correlation or variance explained coefficients. This can make it appear that a conceptually inconsistent predictor variable such as an H-H-L AP PHO constellation or L/H ratio HRV response is associated with or predicts better pressure performance, when in fact accurate inferences regarding pressure performance tendencies cannot be made. So, what good are the Serial 7s stress tests, and any other test for that matter, if they reveal numerous inconsistent response profiles? First of all, assessments are oftentimes done independent of meticulous follow-up. In these cases, AP constellations and HRV stress test profiles provide qualified but not absolutely reliable insight into possible pressure performance tendencies, that when possible (and it must be in the context of a one-on-one consulting relationship with an individual client or team member) must be validated in a hierarchical manner.

Advanced Practitioner Challenge: Reverse validate or establish an Athlete's Profile constellation of PHO measures on the basis of baseline to stress test condition HRV responses. Create hypothetical data sets to do so. For example, if the S7 change in L:H frequency from baseline is +2 (1.4–3.4), what does that suggest, if such an increase is also found to predict poorer critical moment performance, about an athlete's AP or specific PHO measure that is known to mediate increases in SNS activity that would have led to such a change in L:H frequency activity?

Preliminary athlete evaluation is also often done in the context of group showcase events such as the NFL combine, team try-outs, and client consulting that does not evolve into an extended working relationship. The Serial 7s stress test or hybrids thereof provide a highly accurate assessment of ANS activity, irrespective of actual performance outcome. Its generated HRV measures can be clinically relevant and assist in the diagnosis of sleep, anxiety, and other psychophysiological disorders that may impact performance. The Serial

7s stress test is a valuable screening tool. As with all tests, it should be used as part of a comprehensive athlete assessment and intervention approach, cognizant of its strengths and limitations.

Notes

1. It is strongly recommended that readers thoroughly familiarize themselves with the Athlete's Profile Model Primary Higher Order Constellations and individual measures, the Theory of Critical Moments, and heart rate variability to best understand the content of this chapter and participate in the analysis of the presented data as an informed practitioner, researcher, educator, coach, and/or student (see Chapters 2, 5 and 9).
2. This approximation hypothesis extends on the TCM/AP models prediction that the most facilitative (*****) and detrimental (*) AP PHO profiles are most likely to elicit conceptually consistent directional psychophysiological responses. The provided data may or may not support this amending premise.
3. The preceding sections and content on HRV also apply to the second case study on a youth baseball team.
4. Dr. Martin Kramer, ABSP, served as the sport psychologist to the team. He collected all AP PHO and HRV data and administered the stress tests in context of the ABSP certification program final project.

6

Neurocognitive Testing and Quantitative Electroencephalography: Brain Functioning and Athlete Performance

Neurocognitive testing (NCT) and quantitative electroencephalography (qEEG) are brain assessment procedures that are used to investigate relationships between cortical functioning and context-specific outcome measures to arrive at clinical diagnoses or better informed patient and client evaluations. NCT, specifically, is part of the Brain Resource Internet–based test battery (BRC, 2007) that contains the Carlstedt Subliminal Attention, Reactivity and Coping Scale (CSARCS-A), the central and most predictive (pressure performance) psychological test of the ABSP-Carlstedt Protocol (ABSP-CP). Scores from NCT are routinely analyzed as part of the ABSP-CP athlete assessment/intake process and added to its comprehensive database of athlete brain–heart–mind–body–motor functioning. Its utility is primarily clinical since neurocognitive response deviations from validated norms for certain brain functioning parameters can be relevant to an individual's psychological integrity. NCT can also be used to assess athlete performance. However, since NCT is rarely administered more than once every few years, it is not a repeated measure per se. Readers may recall that in order to more reliably ascertain whether neuropsychophysiological predictor variables actually influence or mediate performance/pressure performance, a repeated predictor and outcome measures— longitudinal assessment/research design, at the intra-individual level, should be used. Consequently, it is difficult to directly implicate specific neurocognitive responses in the sport performance equation at the individual level. Nevertheless, at the group level, intriguing findings have emerged from the developing ABSP-CP datbase that are consistent with certain tenets of the Theory of Critical Moments (TCM) and Athletes Profile (AP) conceptual and construct validity bases.

In this chapter, results from pilot research encompassing over 50 athletes from the sports of baseball, tennis, and ice hockey will be reviewed prior to presenting a case study of an ex–world class professional tennis player who underwent NCT and qEEG as part of the ABSP-CP pre-intervention evaluation process. It should be noted that qEEG or brain mapping is an elaborate and advanced procedure that is used to assess actual real-time cortical functioning or electrical activity that is emitted by neurons as they fire in specific regions of the brain as a function of a particular task or stimulus that an individual encounters on a computer screen. By contrast, NCT involves task/stimulus-specific tests that are associated with the engagement or activation of specific brain regions (functional activation of neurons that have been localized in certain brain areas; see Figure 6.1) and whose resulting score(s) reflect differential abilities, strengths, and/or deficits, usually without simultaneous EEG or qEEG monitoring (although EEG can be derived concurrently as in the case study that follows).

NCT tests, including those in the brain resource company (BRC) battery have undergone an extensive validation process with qEEG/EEG and magnetic resonance imaging/functional magnetic resonance imaging (MRI; fMRI) serving as criterion referenced or external validation measures, while any number of life, education, job, psychopathology, or performance variables being used as outcome measures in a normative context (BRC normative database, 2007).

Neuropsychological Test Battery

Region	Motor tapping (1)	Choice Reaction time (2)	Timing (3)	Span of visual memory (4)	Digit span (5)	Memory recall and recog. (6)	Verbal interference (7)	Spot the real word (8)	Word generation (9)	Sustained attention (10)	Switching of attention (11)	Executive maze (12)
Prefrontal				●	●		○	●	●	●		○
Frontal		●				○		●	●	●	●	○
Motor	●	●		●					●			○
Parietal		●		●	●	○	○	●		●		○
Occipital		●					○	●				○
Temporal					●			●		●		
Ant. cingulate							○					
Hippocampus			●									
Basal ganglia	●									●		
Cerebellum	●		●									
Thalamus		●								●		

○ = deficit (compared to controls);   ● = no deficit

This matrix shows each test (1–12) and which region of the brain is preferentially associated with that test. This spatial information is indicative only and should be further assessed in the context of other neuroimaging methods.

The list below summarizes what the practical significance of that deficit is considered to be:

6. Ability to learn and remember new tasks based on verbal information. Critical, central everyday skill.
7. Part 1: Simple reading ability. Part 2: Ability to control impulses; behavioral control e.g., anger control.
12. Ability to plan, strategize and implement complex tasks involving visuospatial information.

FIGURE 6.1   Summary overview of neuropsychological test results with brain anatomical and regional localization (*Source*: Brain Resource Company).

NCT and qEEG and Sport Performance

An NCT and qEEG session can pose a competitive challenge for some people and athletes and may also be revealing in terms of what various scores predict regarding eventual macro- and micro-sport performance outcome measures. Although NCT and laboratory-based qEEG are temporally removed from actual competition (not time-locked to moment-to-moment action on the playing field), they may elicit brain responses that are similar to those that could be captured in the context of simulation and experimental paradigms that were designed to document and assess actual brain wave activity and their impact on performance. For example, an athlete who has an AP primary higher order (PHO) constellation of high subliminal attention/hypnotic susceptibility (SA/HS)-high subliminal reactivity/neuroticism (SR/N), and low subliminal coping/repressive coping (SC/RC), the least performance facilitative AP, primarily on the basis of the effects of high SR/N, would be expected to be nervous in any testing situation and as a result possibly experience competitive anxiety-like reactions, including elevated sympathetic nervous system (SNS) activation and concomitant reduced attention or focus that leads to poor performance on a cognitive task (e.g., a maze task) that is intended to assess brain regions that are associated with concentration and motor activity. In such a scenario, NCT and qEEG responses could be used to cross-validate or even predict an AP PHO constellation (on a blind basis or without having administered the CSARCS-A) or heart rate variability stress test response profile (HRV-S7s test). Research is ongoing to test the premise that NCT and qEEG can serve as reliable criterion-referenced measures for AP PHO constellations, HRV responding and eventually macro- and micro-(pressure/criticality) performance outcome.

Conceptual Bases/Construct Validity

The conceptual bases and construct validity of the TCM and AP models of peak sport performance have been and will be continually encountered throughout this book (see Chapters 2 and 4 for a thorough overview of the AP and TCM models). A brief bullet-point listing of their dynamics is presented here to reorient readers regarding relevant brain–heart–mind–body–motor measures and NCT task/stimuli responses that could be considered conceptually consistent (see the earlier AP PHO H-H-L example).

Here is what is expected to happen in the vast majority of athletes during routine moments of competition leading up to the onset of action, irrespective of their AP PHO constellation and what is predicted to occur in terms of NCT and qEEG outcome (in **bold; see Figure 6.1**):

1. Strategic planning commences, a left frontal brain lobe localized preparatory response.

   NCT Sensitive Test and Outcome: Verbal Interference and Executive Maze

   These tests activate the pre-frontal region of the brain, the area in which initial pre-action strategic planning also occurs.

2. Just prior to the onset of action, a cortical shift is observed, with strategic planning giving way to motor priming that is reflected in increased brain activity in the right brain hemisphere motor cortex region and a "quieting," or strong reduction, in left frontal activity.

   NCT Sensitive Test and Outcome: Motor Tapping, Choice Reaction Time, Span of Visual Memory, Executive Maze

   These tests activate the motor cortex and conceptually involve response mechanisms that may be similar to the shift from strategic planning and its visual components (also overt visualization as part of a conscious intervention or subliminal developed response) to motor priming and onset of a task having reaction and technical components.

3. Concomitant with this cortical left-to-right shift is the onset of heart rate deceleration.

NCT Sensitive Test and Outcome: Motor Tapping, Choice Reaction Time, Executive Maze

These tests activate brain regions and mechanisms similar to those in number 2. In the context of HRV monitoring, it is hypothesized that a reduction in very-low-frequency (VLF) and increase in high frequency (HF) and decrease in low-/high-frequency activity will be associated with scores on these tests.

4. This dynamic (# 3) sets the stage for the seamless activation of motor neural pathways and subsequent peak motor performance (commiserate with an athlete's technical competency) I_I__I___I_____I_____I_____I (depiction of heart rate deceleration [HRD], longer/slower cardiac cycle/leading up to the onset of action; see Chapter 3).

NCT Sensitive Test and Outcome: Motor Tapping, Choice Reaction Time, Executive Maze

Same as number 3.

5. AP PHO measures and/or their specific constellations remain relatively dormant or exert positive effects if a particular PHO measure is inherently associated with a peak performance component. For example, HS/SA is involved in the attention/focus-strategic planning process and, as such, will manifest itself in a performance-facilitative manner during routine moments of competition. By contrast, N/SR is almost exclusively associated with the disruption of performance if an athlete's stress or pressure threshold is reached (a much lower threshold in athletes who are high in N/SR); however, during routine moments or phases of competition, N/SR will usually remain uninvolved in the performance process (that can change instantaneously though, in an athlete who is high in N/SR). While high RC/SC is a performance-facilitating PHO measure, it serves primarily to suppress the generation or manifestation of negative intrusive thoughts or mental chatter that is associated with N/SR, something that is less prevalent during routine moments of competition.

Once critical moments (CMs) are encountered, AP PHO measures are activated in accord with their mediating properties as follows:

1. Depending upon an athlete's AP constellation, the brain–heart–mind–body dynamics described earlier will either continue to be manifested even during pressure-laden CMs, or they will be disrupted.
2. Two ideal APs have been isolated. Athletes who are high or low in HS/SA, low in N/SR, and high in RC/SC usually have a higher competitive stress tolerance level and, as such, are more likely to exhibit neuropsychophysiological responses that are consistent with those that are manifested during routine moments of competition, even in the presence of rising criticality.
3. Athletes possessing the most performance-debilitating AP of high HS/SA, high N/SR, and low RC/SC, as competitive stress or pressure increases, are likely to experience a disruption of the neuropsychophysiological response dynamic that occurs during routine moments of competition.
4. Instead, rather than strategic planning (reflected relative greater left-frontal brain activation) giving way to motor priming and relative greater right brain hemispheric activation along with concomitant HRD prior to action, relatively greater left-frontal brain activity continues through the pre-action phase. This is indicative of excessive rumination and attending to internal mental chatter, or negative intrusive thoughts predominating when pre-action motor priming

should be occurring. Heart rate acceleration (HRA) also manifests itself, a response that in contrast to HRD reflects cognitive activity when a reduction in thinking should be taking place. HRA: I__I_I_I_I__I_I_I (shorter cardiac cycle/nonlinear faster heart rate leading up to action; see Chapter 3).

5. These intrusive thoughts originate from the amygdala, the seat of negative emotions, fear, and anxiety memories. In athletes who are high in N/SR and low in RC/SC, in the presence of high HS/SA and competitive stress or CMs (whether self-perceived or an objective reality), a cascade of responses occur that can ultimately disrupt motor ability and peak performance as follows: (1) CM occurs and is recognized, (2) amygdala is activated, (3) neuronal pathways from the amydala to the right-frontal-lobe region where negative cognitions that are associated with high N/SR are activated, (4) these negative cognitions become intrusive, making their way into the left-frontal-lobe region, leading to the disruption of strategic planning and motor priming and subsequent pre-action relative left-to-right hemispheric cortical shift. Athletes who are high in HS/SA, high in N/SR, and low in RC/SC do not benefit from the potentially protective high RC/SC.

NCT Sensitive Test and Outcome: During critical moments as described in number 5, prefrontal/frontal lobe and motor cortex brain regions are expected to be differentially involved. In the context of NCT, it is hypothesized that most vulnerable AP PHO athletes will show deficits on some or all of the tests that are highlighted in bold in Figure 6.3 compared to athletes who have more performance-facilitative AP PHO profiles.

The hypothesized effects of the preceding tests and resulting scores and their relationship with AP PHO constellations and the performance equation (real competition and performance outcome) are based on the assumption that an athlete who sits in front of a computer screen and responds to a series of directed tasks (NCT) is engaging in psychological preparatory activity in an attempt to successfully master them, analogous to pre-action mental priming during real competition. While motor tasks during NCT do not involve complex technical motor responses that are associated with, for example, hitting a golf ball or shooting a jump shot, specific NCT tests, at times, can activate the same brain regions that are engaged during pre-action phases of sport-specific tasks.

It is also assumed that specific AP PHO constellations can impact NCT performance in a manner similar to how they influence or mediate performance during real sport competition. The following figure (Figure 6.2, a sample report for illustrative purposes only) depicts associations between specific neurocognitive tests and brain regions or anatomical structures.

Conceptually Relevant Findings

Findings on relationships between and among NCT, AP PHO constellations, HRV, and outcome (four elite level or pro teams) are presented in this section. Figure 6.2 is a sample report of one of the 54 athletes who were included in this pilot study. It will not be elaborated upon here. Later in this chapter, a single-case study will explicate an athlete's NCT and qEEG reports.

Neurocognitive, AP-PHO, HRV, and Outcome Findings

Figure 6.3 contains a list of neurocognitive tests and their abbreviations as they appear in the following statistical package for social sciences (SPSS) charts (significant findings).

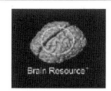

Cognition

Cognition: Client CARL-SQFRE-00054 compared to normal controls

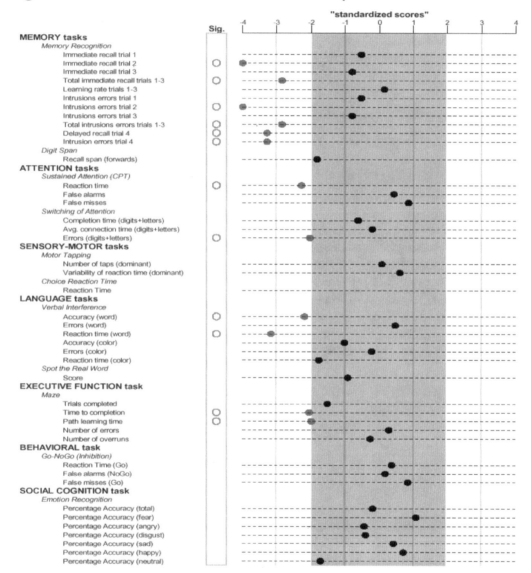

For convenience, the tasks are organized by broad cognitive groupings. The circles on the left indicate statistically significant differences compared with the normal control. The "standardized scores" on the right are normalized for age and gender, which means differences from zero reflect differences from 'average peer' (also known as z-scores). Positive "standardized scores" indicate above average scores, negative "standardized scores" are below average (Avg = average). "Standardized scores" beyond -2 to +2 are statistically significant. False alarms (respond when should not) = false positive; errors of commission. False misses (not respond when should) = false negatives; errors of omission. Intrusion = words not on the list. Specialist interpretation is required.

FIGURE 6.2   Neurocognitive report from ABSP-BRC Internet-based test center.

Memory Recognition - Immediate recall trial 1	mem1
Memory Recognition - Immediate recall trial 2	mem2
Memory Recognition - Immediate recall trial 3	mem3
Memory Recognition - Total immediate recall trials 1-3	memtot
Memory Recognition - Learning rate trials 1-3	mlearn13
Memory Recognition - Intrusions errors trial 1	mrcecin1
Memory Recognition - Intrusions errors trial 2	mrcecin2
Memory Recognition - Intrusions errors trial 3	mrcenin3
Memory Recognition - Total intrusions errors trials 1-3	mrectot
Memory Recognition - Delayed recall trial 4	mrdel4
Memory Recognition - Intrusion errors trial 4	mriner4
Digit Span - Recall span (forwards)	digitref
Sustained Attention (CPT) - Reaction time	susattrt
Sustained Attention (CPT) - False alarms	susattfa
Sustained Attention (CPT) - False misses	susattfm
Switching of Attention - Completion time (digits+letters)	switatct
Switching of Attention - Avg. connection time (digits+letters)	swattav
Switching of Attention - Errors (digits+letters)	swatter
Motor Tapping - Number of taps (dominant)	mtapdom
Motor Tapping - Variability of reaction time (dominant)	mtapvarrtd
Choice Reaction Time - Reaction Time	choicert
Verbal Interference - Accuracy (word)	verintac
Verbal Interference - Errors (word)	verinerr
Verbal Interference - Reaction time (word)	verinrtw
Verbal Interference - Accuracy (color)	verinc
Verbal Interference - Errors (color)	verintec
Verbal Interference - Reaction time (color)	verinrtc
Spot the Real Word - Accuracy	realwdac
Maze - Trials completed	mazetc
Maze - Completion time	mazect
Maze - Path learning time	mazelt
Maze - Total errors	mazete
Maze - Number of overruns	mazeover
Go-NoGo (Inhibition) - Reaction time (Go)	gngortgo
Go-NoGo (Inhibition) - False alarms (NoGo)	gngofang
Go-NoGo (Inhibition) - False misses (Go)	gngofmig
Emotion Recognition - Total % accuracy	erecognac
Emotion Recognition - Fear % accuracy	erefeara
Emotion Recognition - Angry % accuracy	ereanga
Emotion Recognition - Disgust % accuracy	eradisa
Emotion Recognition - Sad % accuracy	eresadac
Emotion Recognition - Happy % accuracy	erehapac
Emotion Recognition - Neutral % accuracy	ereneuac

LEGEND Figure 2. and SPSS charts: SA = Subliminal Attention; SR = Subliminal Reactivity; SC = Subliminal Coping; CPT = Completion time; Neurocognitive Testing Variables in Table; NCT tests in BOLD are considered conceptually relevant to TCM and AP models.

FIGURE 6.3   BRC WebNeuro Sport NCT test battery tests with key/legend.

The subsequent SPSS charts include the most conceptually relevant significant correlations between and among NCT test scores AP PHO constellations, stress test baseline, task condition, and differential (baseline versus stress task HRV).

Correlations: Neuro, PHO, and Outcome

COMMENTS: FINDINGS (FIGURES 6.4–6.6)

SR/N was positively correlated with the delayed recall task of the memory recognition task (trial 4; $r = .35$) and was negatively correlated with intrusion errors in trial 4 ($-.35$). These two findings are ambiguous in the context of sport performance but point to the disruptive impact of higher levels of SR/N in many other contexts including memory, especially when quick recall is demanded and stress may lead to intrusive cognitions.

Regarding sustained attention, a conceptually highly relevant NCT test task, SA/HS was negatively correlated with RT in this test condition ($.-31$). This can be explained on the basis of the surplus pattern recognition (Wickramasekera, 1988) phenomenon that is associated with high levels of SA/HS in which attention can shift from stimulus to stimulus when an individual is bored from the onset of a task or becomes distracted during a task; something people who are high in these measures are prone to. In the sustained attention paradigm, RT, a changing or new stimulus is measured. An individual who scores low (slower RT) is likely not focusing to peak potential. While people who are high in SA/HS have a heightened ability to intensely focus, they can be easily distracted if they are not intensely absorbed in a salient task or activity, something certain that neurocognitive tests may not be for these individuals.

Correlations

		Global Success across sports	SA	SR	SC	MRDEL4	MRINER4	SUSATTRT
Global Success across sports	Pearson Correlation	1.000	-.108	.087	-.210	.031	-.065	-.013
	Sig. (2-tailed)	.	.428	.523	.120	.823	.632	.924
	N	56	56	56	56	56	56	54
SA	Pearson Correlation	-.108	1.000	.249	-.174	.088	-.113	-.306*
	Sig. (2-tailed)	.428	.	.065	.199	.517	.408	.024
	N	56	56	56	56	56	56	54
SR	Pearson Correlation	.087	.249	1.000	-.334*	.353**	-.354**	-.011
	Sig. (2-tailed)	.523	.065	.	.012	.008	.007	.937
	N	56	56	56	56	56	56	54
SC	Pearson Correlation	-.210	-.174	-.334*	1.000	-.161	.173	-.070
	Sig. (2-tailed)	.120	.199	.012	.	.237	.203	.614
	N	56	56	56	56	56	56	54
MRDEL4	Pearson Correlation	.031	.088	.353**	-.161	1.000	-.979**	-.236
	Sig. (2-tailed)	.823	.517	.008	.237	.	.000	.086
	N	56	56	56	56	56	56	54
MRINER4	Pearson Correlation	-.065	-.113	-.354**	.173	-.979**	1.000	.216
	Sig. (2-tailed)	.632	.408	.007	.203	.000	.	.116
	N	56	56	56	56	56	56	54
SUSATTRT	Pearson Correlation	-.013	-.306*	-.011	-.070	-.236	.216	1.000
	Sig. (2-tailed)	.924	.024	.937	.614	.086	.116	.
	N	54	54	54	54	54	54	54

*Correlation is significant at the 0.05 level (2-tailed).

**Correlation is significant at the 0.01 level (2-tailed).

FIGURE 6.4   Partial listing of AP PHO measures and NCT test correlations.

Correlations

		Global Success across sports	SA	SR	SC	SWATTERR	MAZETC	GNGORTGO
Global Success across sports	Pearson Correlation	1.000	-.108	.087	-.210	-.023	.137	-.107
	Sig. (2-tailed)	.	.428	.523	.120	.869	.323	.434
	N	56	56	56	56	55	54	56
SA	Pearson Correlation	-.108	1.000	.249	-.174	.296*	.144	.085
	Sig. (2-tailed)	.428	.	.065	.199	.028	.300	.533
	N	56	56	56	56	55	54	56
SR	Pearson Correlation	.087	.249	1.000	-.334*	.267*	-.177	.045
	Sig. (2-tailed)	.523	.065	.	.012	.049	.199	.741
	N	56	56	56	56	55	54	56
SC	Pearson Correlation	-.210	-.174	-.334*	1.000	.147	.297*	-.364**
	Sig. (2-tailed)	.120	.199	.012	.	.283	.029	.006
	N	56	56	56	56	55	54	56
SWATTERR	Pearson Correlation	-.023	.296*	.267*	.147	1.000	.097	.010
	Sig. (2-tailed)	.869	.028	.049	.283	.	.489	.945
	N	55	55	55	55	55	53	55
MAZETC	Pearson Correlation	.137	.144	-.177	.297*	.097	1.000	-.027
	Sig. (2-tailed)	.323	.300	.199	.029	.489	.	.845
	N	54	54	54	54	53	54	54
GNGORTGO	Pearson Correlation	-.107	.085	.045	-.364**	.010	-.027	1.000
	Sig. (2-tailed)	.434	.533	.741	.006	.945	.845	.
	N	56	56	56	56	55	54	56

*Correlation is significant at the 0.05 level (2-tailed).

**Correlation is significant at the 0.01 level (2-tailed).

FIGURE 6.5   Partial listing of AP PHO measures and NCT test correlations.

SA/HS and SR/N were both correlated with switching of attention errors (.30 & .27, respectively), a finding that could be seen as being conceptually consistent with the tendency of these two AP PHO measures to operate synergistically (exerting a negative influence on performance), especially under stress conditions or CMs during competition, something NCT tests of attention may induce in AP PHO vulnerable athletes.

Correlations

		Global Success across sports	SA	SR	SC	EREANGA	ERECOGAC	ERESADAC	ERENEUAC
Global Success across sports	Pearson Correlation	1.000	-.108	.087	-.210	.330*	.363**	.364**	.345**
	Sig. (2-tailed)	.	.428	.523	.120	.013	.006	.006	.009
	N	56	56	56	56	56	56	56	56
SA	Pearson Correlation	-.108	1.000	.249	-.174	-.304*	-.157	-.197	-.217
	Sig. (2-tailed)	.428	.	.065	.199	.023	.248	.146	.108
	N	56	56	56	56	56	56	56	56
SR	Pearson Correlation	.087	.249	1.000	-.334*	.157	.203	.162	.119
	Sig. (2-tailed)	.523	.065	.	.012	.248	.134	.231	.382
	N	56	56	56	56	56	56	56	56
SC	Pearson Correlation	-.210	-.174	-.334*	1.000	-.361**	-.219	-.043	.020
	Sig. (2-tailed)	.120	.199	.012	.	.006	.105	.755	.886
	N	56	56	56	56	56	56	56	56
EREANGA	Pearson Correlation	.330*	-.304*	.157	-.361**	1.000	.584**	.214	.392**
	Sig. (2-tailed)	.013	.023	.248	.006	.	.000	.114	.003
	N	56	56	56	56	56	56	56	56
ERECOGAC	Pearson Correlation	.363**	-.157	.203	-.219	.584**	1.000	.666**	.541**
	Sig. (2-tailed)	.006	.248	.134	.105	.000	.	.000	.000
	N	56	56	56	56	56	56	56	56
ERESADAC	Pearson Correlation	.364**	-.197	.162	-.043	.214	.666**	1.000	.152
	Sig. (2-tailed)	.006	.146	.231	.755	.114	.000	.	.262
	N	56	56	56	56	56	56	56	56
ERENEUAC	Pearson Correlation	.345**	-.217	.119	.020	.392**	.541**	.152	1.000
	Sig. (2-tailed)	.009	.108	.382	.886	.003	.000	.262	.
	N	56	56	56	56	56	56	56	56

*Correlation is significant at the 0.05 level (2-tailed).

**Correlation is significant at the 0.01 level (2-tailed).

FIGURE 6.6   Partial listing of AP PHO measures and NCT test correlations.

SC/RC was correlated with maze test completion time, a conceptually consistent finding that is supportive of this AP PHO measure's performance facilitating dynamic. SC/RC was also negatively correlated ($-.36$) with the GO-NO-GO, GO condition-RT, a test of inhibition/inhibitory control that implicates the pre-frontal-lobe area of the brain and its ability to respond swiftly and appropriately to a correct stimulus. This, too, is a conceptually consistent finding in that greater levels of SC/RC are known to suppress intrusive thoughts when under stress, thereby enhancing attention and performance, in this case, as reflected in a reduction in RT (quicker response to correct stimulus via pressing a computer key). SC/RC, in concert with SA/HS, was negatively correlated with the emotional recognition of an anger test ($-.30$ & $-.36$, respectively). This is also a conceptually consistent finding, and although it may not be directly relevant to sport performance, a reduced recognition of anger as expressed facially or in the body language of an opponent, may serve an adaptive purpose and call into question the myth that body language will be recognized and differentially impact performance. In other words, athletes who are higher in SC/RC (they tend toward alexythymia and self-aggrandization/high self-esteem/confidence; Fortino, 2001) may be impervious to an opponent's emotional expressions and body language that are assumed to some how influence performance (either negatively or positively). It should be noted that high SA/HS and high SC/RC are two of three AP PHO measures that make up the Ideal AP.

Interestingly, the only NCT test measures that were correlated with the Global Outcome Measure, a standardized (across sport type: baseball, ice hockey, & tennis) score that reflects a sport-specific success percentage, involved emotional recognition (total emotional recognition, .36; anger, .33; sad, .36; and neutral, .36). This finding warrants further investigation.

AP PHO measures were not associated with Global Outcome.

Neurocognition and HRV Baseline and Serial 7s Stress Test

The following SPSS charts contain correlations between NCT test measures and baseline and stress test HRV measures. There were a plethora of findings of which not all will be commented on. Conceptually relevant findings will be highlighted, especially those that may reflect or be associated with pre-action HRD that marks enhanced strategic preparation, attention and RT, or those that are associated with elevated SNS (stress response that is associated with decreased performance on a NCT test). NCT tests that are most conceptually relevant to the HRD phenomenon are:

1. Attention domain tests: continuous attention
2. Response speed tests: motor tapping
3. Information processing efficiency: choice reaction time; switching of attention; verbal interference
4. Executive functioning: maze
5. Impulsivity: Go-no-go

Figures 6.7, 6.8, 6.9, and 6.10 depict NCT and HRV relationships. HRV measures were obtained from a psychophysiological stress test battery (Serial 7s; see Chapter 5) that was administered to athletes who were included in this study. The NCT and stress tests were temporally isolated, that is, not taken on the same day. This makes strong correlations noteworthy and points to the trait-like synergy between seemingly disparate mind–body measures that are not time-locked within a controlled experimental paradigm (e.g., monitoring HRV & EEG during an NCT test session as was done with the case study athlete later in this chapter).

The most conceptually relevant and/or consistent baseline-NCT test measure correlations include heart rate (HR) being positively associated with the switching of attention-completion

Correlations

		Global Success across sports	HR	SDNN	VL	LOW	HIGH	MEMTOT	MRECTOT	MRINER4
Global Success across sports	Pearson Correlation	1.000	.070	.042	-.213	.075	.228	-.102	.102	-.065
	Sig. (2-tailed)		.644	.783	.155	.622	.127	.453	.453	.632
	N	56	46	46	46	46	46	56	56	56
HR	Pearson Correlation	.070	1.000	.113	.065	.131	.021	-.352*	.352*	.346*
	Sig. (2-tailed)	.644		.456	.666	.384	.891	.017	.017	.018
	N	46	46	46	46	46	46	46	46	46
SDNN	Pearson Correlation	.042	.113	1.000	.480**	.703**	.775**	-.098	.098	.169
	Sig. (2-tailed)	.783	.456		.001	.000	.000	.515	.515	.262
	N	46	46	46	46	46	46	46	46	46
VL	Pearson Correlation	-.213	.065	.480**	1.000	.172	.095	-.102	.102	.399**
	Sig. (2-tailed)	.155	.666	.001		.254	.531	.499	.499	.006
	N	46	46	46	46	46	46	46	46	46
LOW	Pearson Correlation	.075	.131	.703**	.172	1.000	.411**	-.068	.068	-.091
	Sig. (2-tailed)	.622	.384	.000	.254		.005	.654	.654	.546
	N	46	46	46	46	46	46	46	46	46
HIGH	Pearson Correlation	.228	.021	.775**	.095	.411**	1.000	-.053	.053	-.103
	Sig. (2-tailed)	.127	.891	.000	.531	.005		.728	.728	.496
	N	46	46	46	46	46	46	46	46	46
MEMTOT	Pearson Correlation	-.102	-.352*	-.098	-.102	-.068	-.053	1.000	-1.000**	-.203
	Sig. (2-tailed)	.453	.017	.515	.499	.654	.728		.000	.133
	N	56	46	46	46	46	46	56	56	56
MRECTOT	Pearson Correlation	.102	.352*	.098	.102	.068	.053	-1.000**	1.000	.203
	Sig. (2-tailed)	.453	.017	.515	.499	.654	.728	.000		.133
	N	56	46	46	46	46	46	56	56	56
MRINER4	Pearson Correlation	-.065	.346*	.169	.399**	-.091	-.103	-.203	.203	1.000
	Sig. (2-tailed)	.632	.018	.262	.006	.546	.496	.133	.133	
	N	56	46	46	46	46	46	56	56	56

*Correlation is significant at the 0.05 level (2-tailed).
**Correlation is significant at the 0.01 level (2-tailed).

FIGURE 6.7   Partial listing of NCT test measure and HRV measure correlations.

Correlations

		Global Success across sports	HR	SDNN	VL	LOW	HIGH	SUSATTFA	SWITATCT	SWATTERR	CHOICERT
Global Success across sports	Pearson Correlation	1.000	.070	.042	-.213	.075	.228	.209	-.038	-.023	.025
	Sig. (2-tailed)		.644	.783	.155	.622	.127	.130	.784	.869	.863
	N	56	46	46	46	46	46	54	54	55	48
HR	Pearson Correlation	.070	1.000	.113	.065	.131	.021	.248	.587**	-.630**	-.116
	Sig. (2-tailed)	.644		.456	.666	.384	.891	.104	.000	.000	.469
	N	46	46	46	46	46	46	44	44	46	41
SDNN	Pearson Correlation	.042	.113	1.000	.480**	.703**	.775**	.202	.267	-.338*	.125
	Sig. (2-tailed)	.783	.456		.001	.000	.000	.189	.079	.022	.438
	N	46	46	46	46	46	46	44	44	46	41
VL	Pearson Correlation	-.213	.065	.480**	1.000	.172	.095	.380*	.157	-.197	.560**
	Sig. (2-tailed)	.155	.666	.001		.254	.531	.011	.309	.190	.000
	N	46	46	46	46	46	46	44	44	46	41
LOW	Pearson Correlation	.075	.131	.703**	.172	1.000	.411**	-.087	.172	-.236	.114
	Sig. (2-tailed)	.622	.384	.000	.254		.005	.576	.265	.115	.478
	N	46	46	46	46	46	46	44	44	46	41
HIGH	Pearson Correlation	.228	.021	.775**	.095	.411**	1.000	-.087	.151	-.176	.051
	Sig. (2-tailed)	.127	.891	.000	.531	.005		.573	.327	.243	.753
	N	46	46	46	46	46	46	44	44	46	41
SUSATTFA	Pearson Correlation	.209	.248	.202	.380*	-.087	-.087	1.000	-.113	.064	.205
	Sig. (2-tailed)	.130	.104	.189	.011	.576	.573		.416	.649	.173
	N	54	44	44	44	44	44	54	54	53	46
SWITATCT	Pearson Correlation	-.038	.587**	.267	.157	.172	.151	-.113	1.000	-.896**	-.134
	Sig. (2-tailed)	.784	.000	.079	.309	.265	.327	.416		.000	.374
	N	54	44	44	44	44	44	54	54	53	46
SWATTERR	Pearson Correlation	-.023	-.630**	-.338*	-.197	-.236	-.176	.064	-.896**	1.000	.208
	Sig. (2-tailed)	.869	.000	.022	.190	.115	.243	.649	.000		.160
	N	55	46	46	46	46	46	53	53	55	47
CHOICERT	Pearson Correlation	.025	-.116	.125	.560**	.114	.051	.205	-.134	.208	1.000
	Sig. (2-tailed)	.863	.469	.438	.000	.478	.753	.173	.374	.160	
	N	48	41	41	41	41	41	46	46	47	48

*Correlation is significant at the 0.05 level (2-tailed).
**Correlation is significant at the 0.01 level (2-tailed).

FIGURE 6.8   Partial listing of NCT test measure and HRV measure correlations.

Correlations

		Global Success across sports	HR	SDNN	VL	LOW	HIGH	VERINTAC	VERINRTW	VINTERTC	REALWDAC
Global Success across sports	Pearson Correlation	1.000	.070	.042	-.213	.075	.228	-.050	.068	-.206	-.124
	Sig. (2-tailed)	.	.644	.783	.155	.622	.127	.717	.624	.128	.361
	N	56	46	46	46	46	46	56	55	56	56
HR	Pearson Correlation	.070	1.000	.113	.065	.131	.021	.326*	-.224	-.458**	.361*
	Sig. (2-tailed)	.644	.	.456	.666	.384	.891	.027	.139	.001	.014
	N	46	46	46	46	46	46	46	46	46	46
SDNN	Pearson Correlation	.042	.113	1.000	.480**	.703**	.775**	.166	-.116	.006	.396**
	Sig. (2-tailed)	.783	.456	.	.001	.000	.000	.271	.448	.969	.006
	N	46	46	46	46	46	46	46	45	46	46
VL	Pearson Correlation	-.213	.065	.480**	1.000	.172	.095	-.304*	.374*	.383**	.202
	Sig. (2-tailed)	.155	.666	.001	.	.254	.531	.040	.011	.009	.178
	N	46	46	46	46	46	46	46	45	46	46
LOW	Pearson Correlation	.075	.131	.703**	.172	1.000	.411**	.042	.011	.018	.334*
	Sig. (2-tailed)	.622	.384	.000	.254	.	.005	.782	.940	.907	.023
	N	46	46	46	46	46	46	46	45	46	46
HIGH	Pearson Correlation	.228	.021	.775**	.095	.411**	1.000	.321*	-.210	-.077	.246
	Sig. (2-tailed)	.127	.891	.000	.531	.005	.	.030	.166	.610	.099
	N	46	46	46	46	46	46	46	45	46	46
VERINTAC	Pearson Correlation	-.050	.326*	.166	-.304*	.042	.321*	1.000	-.923**	-.304*	.357**
	Sig. (2-tailed)	.717	.027	.271	.040	.782	.030	.	.000	.023	.007
	N	56	46	46	46	46	46	56	55	56	56
VERINRTW	Pearson Correlation	.068	-.224	-.116	.374*	.011	-.210	-.923**	1.000	.526**	-.365**
	Sig. (2-tailed)	.624	.139	.448	.011	.940	.166	.000	.	.000	.006
	N	55	45	45	45	45	45	55	55	55	55
VINTERTC	Pearson Correlation	-.206	-.458**	.006	.383**	.018	-.077	-.304*	.526**	1.000	-.326*
	Sig. (2-tailed)	.128	.001	.969	.009	.907	.610	.023	.000	.	.014
	N	56	46	46	46	46	46	56	55	56	56
REALWDAC	Pearson Correlation	-.124	.361*	.396**	.202	.334*	.246	.357**	-.365**	-.326*	1.000
	Sig. (2-tailed)	.361	.014	.006	.178	.023	.099	.007	.006	.014	.
	N	56	46	46	46	46	46	56	55	56	56

*Correlation is significant at the 0.05 level (2-tailed).

**Correlation is significant at the 0.01 level (2-tailed).

FIGURE 6.9   Partial listing of NCT test measure and HRV measure correlations.

Correlations

		Global Success across sports	HR	SDNN	VL	LOW	HIGH	GNGORTGO	GNGOFANG	EREANGA
Global Success across sports	Pearson Correlation	1.000	.070	.042	-.213	.075	.228	-.107	.230	.330*
	Sig. (2-tailed)	.	.644	.783	.155	.622	.127	.434	.089	.013
	N	56	46	46	46	46	46	56	56	56
HR	Pearson Correlation	.070	1.000	.113	.065	.131	.021	-.355*	.132	.305*
	Sig. (2-tailed)	.644	.	.456	.666	.384	.891	.015	.383	.039
	N	46	46	46	46	46	46	46	46	46
SDNN	Pearson Correlation	.042	.113	1.000	.480**	.703**	.775**	-.031	.322*	.082
	Sig. (2-tailed)	.783	.456	.	.001	.000	.000	.839	.029	.586
	N	46	46	46	46	46	46	46	46	46
VL	Pearson Correlation	-.213	.065	.480**	1.000	.172	.095	.009	.070	.191
	Sig. (2-tailed)	.155	.666	.001	.	.254	.531	.955	.645	.203
	N	46	46	46	46	46	46	46	46	46
LOW	Pearson Correlation	.075	.131	.703**	.172	1.000	.411**	.040	.108	.062
	Sig. (2-tailed)	.622	.384	.000	.254	.	.005	.789	.475	.683
	N	46	46	46	46	46	46	46	46	46
HIGH	Pearson Correlation	.228	.021	.775**	.095	.411**	1.000	.065	.232	.084
	Sig. (2-tailed)	.127	.891	.000	.531	.005	.	.669	.122	.580
	N	46	46	46	46	46	46	46	46	46
GNGORTGO	Pearson Correlation	-.107	-.355*	-.031	.009	.040	.065	1.000	-.701**	.083
	Sig. (2-tailed)	.434	.015	.839	.955	.789	.669	.	.000	.541
	N	56	46	46	46	46	46	56	56	56
GNGOFANG	Pearson Correlation	.230	.132	.322*	.070	.108	.232	-.701**	1.000	.086
	Sig. (2-tailed)	.089	.383	.029	.645	.475	.122	.000	.	.528
	N	56	46	46	46	46	46	56	56	56
EREANGA	Pearson Correlation	.330*	.305*	.082	.191	.062	.084	.083	.086	1.000
	Sig. (2-tailed)	.013	.039	.586	.203	.683	.580	.541	.528	.
	N	56	46	46	46	46	46	56	56	56

*Correlation is significant at the 0.05 level (2-tailed).

**Correlation is significant at the 0.01 level (2-tailed).

FIGURE 6.10   Partial listing of NCT test measure and HRV measure correlations.

time (see Figure 6.8) indicative of a trait-like response in which greater baseline HR is linked to more time to switch attention across all trials. Very-low-frequency (VL) HRV was correlated with the choice reaction time test (see Figure 6.8), suggesting that trait levels of baseline-elevated SNS activity (VL) impacts RT negatively in a test of ability to respond correctly to a presented stimulus by correctly and swiftly pressing a computer key. These findings may be relevant to pre-action phases in sports where strategic planning that gives way to motor action has been associated with a reduction in SNS activation as HRD commences, a response that is mediated by the parasympathetic nervous system (PNS). These HR and VL responses were associated with negative outcome or poor performance on an NCT test task, whose dynamics may parallel those of pre-action epochs of competition (switching of attention being analogous to shift [switching] from strategic planning to impending stimulus [e.g., oncoming ball in tennis]).

In the stress test task condition (S7s backward counting), conceptually relevant findings again include HR being correlated with the switching of attention completion time (see Figure 6.11), which can be interpreted as was discussed earlier. HR was also negatively related to switching of attention error rate (see Figure 6.12), suggesting that lower heart rate was associated with better attention in this task condition (possibly mediated through a reduction in SNS activity or onset of PNS mediated HRD). In addition, it was implicated in the maze completion time task (see Figure 6.13), a test of executive functioning (frontal lobes) and maze path learning time (see Figure 6.13); with greater HR exerting a negative effect on performance (completion time & learning). The maze test may contain response components that are similar to pre-action phases in certain sports in which greater HR is not desirable. Finally, greater HR was negatively correlated (see Figure 6.13) with RT in the no-go condition of the go-no-go test, another conceptually consistent finding in this test of impulsivity, a measure that may differentially affect sport performance.

Low frequency (LF) HRV activity was also correlated with sustained attention reaction time (.52) (see Figure 6.11). LF reflects a balance between SNS and PNS activity and may play a role in HRD to HRA transitions during competition. This correlation explained about 25% of the variance in switching of attention RT that could be attributed to this HRV measure (the greater the LF, the longer the RT [poorer RT]).

Low/High (L/H) ratio is an even stronger measure of SNS/PNS balance with a lower ratio (less than 1.0) reflecting greater H frequency activity, a PNS response that predominates when HRD occurs. L/H was associated with numerous conceptually relevant NCT tests, including motor tapping variability (see Figure 6.12), motor tapping (number of taps; see Figure 6.12), switching of attention errors (.36), and switching of attention completion time (see Figure 6.11). These findings are conceptually consistent, since one could expect that more SNS HRV activity that is evident in larger L/H ratios to occur as a function of motor responding tasks that demand quick responses/reactions and that greater SNS activity can lead to more errors in cognitive-motor tasks whose successful completion is predicated on mental control. Mental control in pre-action phases of both laboratory and sport competition–based task situations is marked by the onset of HRD, which is associated with a lower L/H ratio (greater H frequency activity-PNS).

The L/H frequency was also implicated in the NCT executive maze test completion time score (see Figure 6.13), maze learning score (see Figure 6.13), and maze total errors (see Figure 6.13). The negative relationship between L/H frequency and maze measures suggest that in this cognitive-motor task more L frequency activity was performance facilitative relative to finishing time, learning correct paths, and error rate (less errors). These findings can be attributed to the continuous nature of this cognitive-motor task in which there is only one pre-action phase rendering the HRD that is associated with lower L/H ratios inert (HRD only occurs upon task onset, followed by SNS–PNS fluctuations as a function of mental processing and motor activity).

Correlations: Neuro and HRV Stress Test Task (S7s)

CORRELATIONS: NEURO-HRV-DIFFERENCE: BASELINE VERSUS STRESS TASK (S7S)

Figures 6.14 and 6.15 contain findings pertaining to NCT tests and the magnitude of change in select HRV measures from the baseline to the stress condition (change difference-CD). Here, L/F ratio again stood out. It was associated with switching of attention (average connection time; see Figure 6.14), switching of attention errors (see Figure 6.14), motor tapping (see Figure 6.14), and motor tapping variability (.31) in a conceptually consistent manner. The explanatory mechanisms of these findings are the same as in the Stress test condition (S7s stress test task; see Figures 6.11–6.13). In addition, L/H ratio was negatively correlated with NCT maze task as in the stress test condition (see Figure 6.13 with trials completed, see Figure 6.13 with completion time & see Figure 6.13 with total errors). These findings can also be attributed to the continuous nature of this cognitive-motor task in which there is only one pre-action phase rendering the HRD that is associated with lower L/H ratios inert (HRD only occurs upon task onset, followed by SNS–PNS fluctuations as a function of mental processing & motor activity); as with similar findings in the stress test condition.

VL frequency was found to be negatively correlated with choice reaction time (see Figure 6.14) and sustained attention-false alarms (see Figure 6.14). VL frequency, which is SNS mediated, if excessive, can result in impulsivity driven diminished motor control, a mind–body dynamic involving prefrontal and frontal-lobe disruptions and subsequent decreases in performance. By contrast, L frequency activity was associated with sustained attention-RT (see Figure 6.14), which could be

Correlations

		Global Success across sports	HR7	SD7	VL7	L7	H7	LH7	MEMTOT	MRECTOT	DIGITREF	SUSATTRT	SWATTAV
Global Success across sports	Pearson Correlation	1.000	.386**	-.208	-.020	-.207	-.113	-.251	-.102	.102	-.128	-.013	-.017
	Sig. (2-tailed)		.008	.165	.894	.168	.453	.093	.453	.453	.347	.924	.902
	N	56	46	46	46	46	46	46	56	56	56	54	56
HR7	Pearson Correlat	.386**	1.000	-.161	.007	-.182	-.004	-.298*	-.313*	.313*	.042	-.042	-.180
	Sig. (2-tailed)	.008		.285	.966	.227	.976	.044	.034	.034	.782	.786	.231
	N	46	46	46	46	46	46	46	46	46	46	44	46
SD7	Pearson Correlat	-.208	-.161	1.000	.765**	.922**	.890**	.022	-.070	.070	-.188	.369*	.007
	Sig. (2-tailed)	.165	.285		.000	.000	.000	.883	.643	.643	.212	.014	.961
	N	46	46	46	46	46	46	46	46	46	46	44	46
VL7	Pearson Correlat	-.020	.007	.765**	1.000	.696**	.608**	.040	-.264	.264	-.097	.180	-.094
	Sig. (2-tailed)	.894	.966	.000		.000	.000	.792	.076	.076	.522	.241	.536
	N	46	46	46	46	46	46	46	46	46	46	44	46
L7	Pearson Correlat	-.207	-.182	.922**	.696**	1.000	.874**	.133	-.099	.099	-.302*	.519**	.120
	Sig. (2-tailed)	.168	.227	.000	.000		.000	.379	.513	.513	.042	.000	.425
	N	46	46	46	46	46	46	46	46	46	46	44	46
H7	Pearson Correlat	-.113	-.004	.890**	.608**	.874**	1.000	-.206	-.154	.154	-.225	.362*	-.052
	Sig. (2-tailed)	.453	.976	.000	.000	.000		.169	.307	.307	.133	.016	.731
	N	46	46	46	46	46	46	46	46	46	46	44	46
LH7	Pearson Correlat	-.251	-.298*	.022	.040	.133	-.206	1.000	.181	-.181	.068	.182	.443**
	Sig. (2-tailed)	.093	.044	.883	.792	.379	.169		.229	.229	.655	.238	.002
	N	46	46	46	46	46	46	46	46	46	46	44	46
MEMTOT	Pearson Correlat	-.102	-.313*	-.070	-.264	-.099	-.154	.181	1.000	-1.000**	.174	.073	.173
	Sig. (2-tailed)	.453	.034	.643	.076	.513	.307	.229		.000	.199	.602	.202
	N	56	46	46	46	46	46	46	56	56	56	54	56
MRECTOT	Pearson Correlat	.102	.313*	.070	.264	.099	.154	-.181	-1.000**	1.000	-.174	-.073	-.173
	Sig. (2-tailed)	.453	.034	.643	.076	.513	.307	.229	.000		.199	.602	.202
	N	56	46	46	46	46	46	46	56	56	56	54	56
DIGITREF	Pearson Correlat	-.128	.042	-.188	-.097	-.302*	-.225	.068	.174	-.174	1.000	-.246	-.149
	Sig. (2-tailed)	.347	.782	.212	.522	.042	.133	.655	.199	.199		.073	.272
	N	56	46	46	46	46	46	46	56	56	56	54	56
SUSATTRT	Pearson Correlat	-.013	-.042	.369*	.180	.519**	.362*	.182	.073	-.073	-.246	1.000	.389**
	Sig. (2-tailed)	.924	.786	.014	.241	.000	.016	.238	.602	.602	.073		.004
	N	54	44	44	44	44	44	44	54	54	54	54	54
SWATTAV	Pearson Correlat	-.017	-.180	.007	-.094	.120	-.052	.443**	.173	-.173	-.149	.389**	1.000
	Sig. (2-tailed)	.902	.231	.961	.536	.425	.731	.002	.202	.202	.272	.004	
	N	56	46	46	46	46	46	46	56	56	56	54	56

*Correlation is significant at the 0.05 level (2-tailed).

**Correlation is significant at the 0.01 level (2-tailed).

FIGURE 6.11   Partial listing of NCT test measure and HRV measure correlations (stress task).

Correlations

		Global Success across sports	HR7	SD7	VL7	L7	H7	LH7	SWATTERR	MTAPDOM	MTVARRTD	VERINERR	VERINRTW	VERINC	VINTERTC
Global Success across sports	Pearson Correlation	1.000	.386**	-.208	.020	-.207	-.113	-.251	-.023	.226	-.175	.017	.068	.257	-.206
	Sig. (2-tailed)		.008	.165	.894	.168	.453	.093	.869	.094	.198	.902	.624	.056	.128
	N	56	46	46	46	46	46	55	56	56	56	56	55	56	56
HR7	Pearson Correlation	.386**	1.000	-.161	.007	-.182	-.004	-.298*	-.534**	.194	-.219	-.078	-.482**	.599**	-.601**
	Sig. (2-tailed)	.008		.285	.966	.227	.976	.044	.000	.197	.145	.604	.001	.000	.000
	N	46	46	46	46	46	46	46	46	46	46	46	45	46	46
SD7	Pearson Correlation	-.208	-.161	1.000	.765**	.922**	.890**	.022	-.128	-.082	.000	.085	-.098	-.202	.090
	Sig. (2-tailed)	.165	.285		.000	.000	.000	.883	.397	.588	1.000	.573	.522	.179	.554
	N	46	46	46	46	46	46	46	46	46	46	46	45	46	46
VL7	Pearson Correlation	-.020	.007	.765**	1.000	.696**	.608**	.040	-.190	.018	-.032	.422**	-.081	.037	-.085
	Sig. (2-tailed)	.894	.966	.000		.000	.000	.792	.207	.905	.834	.003	.598	.806	.573
	N	46	46	46	46	46	46	46	46	46	46	46	45	46	46
L7	Pearson Correlation	-.207	-.182	.922**	.696**	1.000	.874**	.133	-.101	-.024	.068	.078	-.013	-.235	.134
	Sig. (2-tailed)	.168	.227	.000	.000		.000	.379	.505	.876	.656	.606	.931	.115	.374
	N	46	46	46	46	46	46	46	46	46	46	46	45	46	46
H7	Pearson Correlation	-.113	-.004	.890**	.608**	.874**	1.000	-.206	-.337*	-.071	-.089	-.007	-.087	-.028	-.057
	Sig. (2-tailed)	.453	.976	.000	.000	.000		.169	.022	.638	.555	.962	.571	.854	.707
	N	46	46	46	46	46	46	46	46	46	46	46	45	46	46
LH7	Pearson Correlation	-.251	-.298*	.022	.040	.133	-.206	1.000	.361*	.297*	.316*	-.015	-.101	-.504**	.388**
	Sig. (2-tailed)	.093	.044	.883	.792	.379	.169		.014	.045	.033	.924	.510	.000	.008
	N	46	46	46	46	46	46	46	46	46	46	46	45	46	46
SWATTERR	Pearson Correlation	-.023	-.534**	-.128	-.190	-.101	-.337*	.361*	1.000	.124	.028	-.050	.293*	-.220	.346**
	Sig. (2-tailed)	.869	.000	.397	.207	.505	.022	.014		.366	.839	.719	.031	.107	.010
	N	55	46	46	46	46	46	46	55	55	55	55	54	55	55
MTAPDOM	Pearson Correlation	.226	.194	-.082	.018	-.024	-.071	.297*	.124	1.000	-.082	.022	-.042	.136	-.033
	Sig. (2-tailed)	.094	.197	.588	.905	.876	.638	.045	.366		.546	.871	.762	.318	.810
	N	56	46	46	46	46	46	46	55	56	56	56	55	56	56
MTVARRTD	Pearson Correlation	-.175	-.219	.000	-.032	.068	-.089	.316*	.028	-.082	1.000	.106	.113	-.336*	.129
	Sig. (2-tailed)	.198	.145	1.000	.834	.656	.555	.033	.839	.546		.437	.410	.011	.344
	N	56	46	46	46	46	46	46	55	56	56	56	55	56	56
VERINERR	Pearson Correlation	.017	-.078	.085	.422**	.078	-.007	-.015	-.050	.022	.106	1.000	.155	.190	-.144
	Sig. (2-tailed)	.902	.604	.573	.003	.606	.962	.924	.719	.871	.437		.258	.160	.291
	N	56	46	46	46	46	46	46	55	56	56	56	55	56	56
VERINRTW	Pearson Correlation	.068	-.482**	-.098	-.081	-.013	-.087	-.101	.293*	-.042	.113	.155	1.000	-.301*	.526**
	Sig. (2-tailed)	.624	.001	.522	.598	.931	.571	.510	.031	.762	.410	.258		.026	.000
	N	55	45	45	45	45	45	45	54	55	55	55	55	55	55
VERINC	Pearson Correlation	.257	.599**	-.202	.037	-.235	-.028	-.504**	-.220	.136	-.336*	.190	-.301*	1.000	-.792**
	Sig. (2-tailed)	.056	.000	.179	.806	.115	.854	.000	.107	.318	.011	.160	.026		.000
	N	56	46	46	46	46	46	46	55	56	56	56	55	56	56
VINTERTC	Pearson Correlation	-.206	-.601**	.090	-.085	.134	-.057	.388**	.346**	-.033	.129	-.144	.526**	-.792**	1.000
	Sig. (2-tailed)	.128	.000	.554	.573	.374	.707	.008	.010	.810	.344	.291	.000	.000	
	N	56	46	46	46	46	46	46	55	56	56	56	55	56	56

*Correlation is significant at the 0.05 level (2-tailed).
**Correlation is significant at the 0.01 level (2-tailed).

FIGURE 6.12   Partial listing of NCT test measure and HRV measure correlations (stress task).

Correlations

		Global Success across sports	HR7	SD7	VL7	L7	H7	LH7	REALWDAC	MAZETC	MAZELT	MAZETE	GNGOFANG	EREFEARA	EREANGA	EREDISA	EREHAPAC
Global Success across sports	Pearson Correlation	1.000	.386**	-.208	-.020	-.207	-.113	-.251	-.124	.137	-.034	.180	.230	-.090	.330*	.256	-.164
	Sig. (2-tailed)		.008	.165	.894	.168	.453	.093	.361	.323	.807	.192	.089	.508	.013	.057	.226
	N	56	46	46	46	46	46	46	56	54	54	54	56	56	56	56	56
HR7	Pearson Correlation	.386**	1.000	-.161	.007	-.182	-.004	-.298*	.340*	-.172	-.358*	-.025	.301*	-.202	.389**	.374*	-.126
	Sig. (2-tailed)	.008		.285	.966	.227	.976	.044	.021	.263	.017	.873	.042	.177	.008	.011	.403
	N	46	46	46	46	46	46	46	46	44	44	44	46	46	46	46	46
SD7	Pearson Correlation	-.208	-.161	1.000	.765**	.922**	.890**	.022	.182	.007	.016	.061	.180	.332*	-.149	-.054	.013
	Sig. (2-tailed)	.165	.285		.000	.000	.000	.883	.227	.964	.920	.695	.230	.024	.323	.720	.934
	N	46	46	46	46	46	46	46	46	44	44	44	46	46	46	46	46
VL7	Pearson Correlation	-.020	.007	.765**	1.000	.696**	.608**	.040	.204	.099	-.067	-.062	.246	.197	-.151	.160	.125
	Sig. (2-tailed)	.894	.966	.000		.000	.000	.792	.175	.521	.664	.689	.099	.189	.317	.288	.407
	N	46	46	46	46	46	46	46	46	44	44	44	46	46	46	46	46
L7	Pearson Correlation	-.207	-.182	.922**	.696**	1.000	.874**	.133	.062	.180	.182	.135	.181	.316*	-.210	-.031	-.054
	Sig. (2-tailed)	.168	.227	.000	.000		.000	.379	.680	.242	.237	.381	.230	.032	.160	.839	.723
	N	46	46	46	46	46	46	46	46	44	44	44	46	46	46	46	46
H7	Pearson Correlation	-.113	-.004	.890**	.608**	.874**	1.000	-.206	.202	.136	.164	.188	.181	.131	.055	-.088	.009
	Sig. (2-tailed)	.453	.976	.000	.000	.000		.169	.178	.379	.289	.221	.229	.386	.718	.562	.953
	N	46	46	46	46	46	46	46	46	44	44	44	46	46	46	46	46
LH7	Pearson Correlation	-.251	-.298*	.022	.040	.133	-.206	1.000	-.143	-.304*	-.325*	-.142	-.142	.453**	-.586**	.173	.031
	Sig. (2-tailed)	.093	.044	.883	.792	.379	.169		.345	.045	.031	.346	.346	.002	.000	.250	.836
	N	46	46	46	46	46	46	46	46	44	44	44	46	46	46	46	46
REALWDAC	Pearson Correlation	-.124	.340*	.182	.204	.062	.202	-.143	1.000	-.293*	-.306*	-.075	.141	.069	.155	.119	.105
	Sig. (2-tailed)	.361	.021	.227	.175	.680	.178	.345		.032	.024	.591	.300	.615	.253	.384	.443
	N	56	46	46	46	46	46	46	56	54	54	54	56	56	56	56	56
MAZETC	Pearson Correlation	.137	-.172	.007	.099	.180	.136	-.304*	-.293*	1.000	.804**	.665**	.032	-.302*	-.118	.036	-.063
	Sig. (2-tailed)	.323	.263	.964	.521	.242	.379	.045	.032		.000	.000	.817	.026	.395	.806	.649
	N	54	44	44	44	44	44	44	54	54	54	54	54	54	54	54	54
MAZELT	Pearson Correlation	-.034	-.358*	.016	-.067	.182	.164	-.325*	-.306*	.804**	1.000	.523**	-.226	-.328*	-.197	-.124	.048
	Sig. (2-tailed)	.807	.017	.920	.664	.237	.289	.031	.024	.000		.000	.101	.015	.153	.372	.728
	N	54	44	44	44	44	44	44	54	54	54	54	54	54	54	54	54
MAZETE	Pearson Correlation	.180	-.025	.061	-.062	.135	.188	-.142	-.075	.665**	.523**	1.000	.039	.032	-.052	.088	.003
	Sig. (2-tailed)	.192	.873	.695	.689	.381	.221	.346	.591	.000	.000		.782	.816	.711	.525	.981
	N	54	44	44	44	44	44	44	54	54	54	54	54	54	54	54	54
GNGOFANG	Pearson Correlation	.230	.301*	.180	.246	.181	.181	-.142	.141	.032	-.226	.039	1.000	.072	.086	.484**	-.275*
	Sig. (2-tailed)	.089	.042	.230	.099	.230	.229	.346	.300	.817	.101	.782		.597	.528	.000	.040
	N	56	46	46	46	46	46	46	56	54	54	54	56	56	56	56	56
EREFEARA	Pearson Correlation	-.090	-.202	.332*	.197	.316*	.131	.453**	.069	-.302*	-.328*	.032	.072	1.000	-.097	.029	-.112
	Sig. (2-tailed)	.508	.177	.024	.189	.032	.386	.002	.615	.026	.015	.816	.597		.479	.829	.411
	N	56	46	46	46	46	46	46	56	54	54	54	56	56	56	56	56
EREANGA	Pearson Correlation	.330*	.389**	-.149	-.151	-.210	.055	-.586**	.155	-.118	-.197	-.052	.086	-.097	1.000	-.050	.067
	Sig. (2-tailed)	.013	.008	.323	.317	.160	.718	.000	.253	.395	.153	.711	.528	.479		.713	.625
	N	56	46	46	46	46	46	46	56	54	54	54	56	56	56	56	56
EREDISA	Pearson Correlation	.256	.374*	-.054	.160	-.031	-.088	.173	.119	.036	-.124	.088	.484**	.029	-.050	1.000	.073
	Sig. (2-tailed)	.057	.011	.720	.288	.839	.562	.250	.384	.806	.372	.525	.000	.829	.713		.591
	N	56	46	46	46	46	46	46	56	54	54	54	56	56	56	56	56
EREHAPAC	Pearson Correlation	-.164	-.126	.013	.125	-.054	.009	.031	.105	-.063	.048	.003	-.275*	-.112	.067	.073	1.000
	Sig. (2-tailed)	.226	.403	.934	.407	.723	.953	.836	.443	.649	.728	.981	.040	.411	.625	.591	
	N	56	46	46	46	46	46	46	56	54	54	54	56	56	56	56	50

*Correlation is significant at the 0.05 level (2-tailed).
**Correlation is significant at the 0.01 level (2-tailed).

FIGURE 6.13   Partial listing of NCT test measure and HRV measure correlations (stress task).

Correlations

		Global Success across sports	HRDIF	VDIF	LOWDIF	LHDIF	SUSATTRT	SUSATTFA	SWATTAV	SWATTERR	MTAPDOM	MTVARRTD	CHOICERT	VERINRTW	VINTERTC
Global Success across sports	Pearson Correlation	1.000	.447**	.173	-.200	-.075	-.013	.209	-.017	-.023	.226	-.175	.025	.068	-.206
	Sig. (2-tailed)		.002	.250	.182	.619	.924	.130	.902	.869	.094	.198	.863	.624	.128
	N	56	46	46	46	46	54	54	56	55	56	56	48	55	56
HRDIF	Pearson Correlation	.447**	1.000	.265	-.187	.088	-.116	.002	.008	.009	.001	-.256	-.272	-.404**	-.289
	Sig. (2-tailed)	.002		.075	.213	.560	.455	.987	.957	.953	.992	.085	.085	.006	.051
	N	46	46	46	46	46	44	44	46	46	46	46	41	45	46
VDIF	Pearson Correlation	.173	.265	1.000	.328*	.296*	.044	-.331*	.006	-.003	.191	-.176	-.498**	-.396**	-.409**
	Sig. (2-tailed)	.250	.075		.026	.046	.775	.028	.970	.985	.204	.241	.001	.007	.005
	N	46	46	46	46	46	44	44	46	46	46	46	41	45	46
LOWDIF	Pearson Correlation	-.200	-.187	.328*	1.000	.432**	.465**	.027	.138	.105	-.057	.068	-.153	-.008	.075
	Sig. (2-tailed)	.182	.213	.026		.003	.001	.862	.361	.488	.706	.654	.339	.960	.622
	N	46	46	46	46	46	44	44	46	46	46	46	41	45	46
LHDIF	Pearson Correlation	-.075	.088	.296*	.432**	1.000	.238	.041	.333*	.307*	.308*	.164	.062	-.141	.321*
	Sig. (2-tailed)	.619	.560	.046	.003		.119	.790	.024	.038	.037	.275	.700	.354	.029
	N	46	46	46	46	46	44	44	46	46	46	46	41	45	46
SUSATTRT	Pearson Correlation	-.013	-.116	.044	.465**	.238	1.000	.057	.389**	-.078	-.104	.268*	-.074	.150	-.040
	Sig. (2-tailed)	.924	.455	.775	.001	.119		.684	.004	.576	.456	.050	.627	.284	.776
	N	54	44	44	44	44	54	54	54	53	54	54	46	53	54
SUSATTFA	Pearson Correlation	.209	.002	-.331*	.027	.041	.057	1.000	-.056	.064	.166	.204	.205	.009	-.017
	Sig. (2-tailed)	.130	.987	.028	.862	.790	.684		.689	.649	.229	.140	.173	.949	.904
	N	54	44	44	44	44	54	54	54	53	54	54	46	53	54
SWATTAV	Pearson Correlation	-.017	.008	.006	.138	.333*	.389**	-.056	1.000	.209	-.025	.221	.097	.124	.225
	Sig. (2-tailed)	.902	.957	.970	.361	.024	.004	.689		.126	.857	.102	.511	.368	.096
	N	56	46	46	46	46	54	54	56	55	56	56	48	55	56
SWATTERR	Pearson Correlation	-.023	.009	-.003	.105	.307*	-.078	.064	.209	1.000	.124	.028	.208	.293*	.346**
	Sig. (2-tailed)	.869	.953	.985	.488	.038	.576	.649	.126		.366	.839	.160	.031	.010
	N	55	46	46	46	46	53	53	55	55	55	55	47	54	55
MTAPDOM	Pearson Correlation	.226	.001	.191	-.057	.308*	-.104	.166	-.025	.124	1.000	-.082	.057	-.042	-.033
	Sig. (2-tailed)	.094	.992	.204	.706	.037	.456	.229	.857	.366		.546	.700	.762	.810
	N	56	46	46	46	46	54	54	56	55	56	56	48	55	56
MTVARRTD	Pearson Correlation	-.175	-.256	-.176	.068	.164	.268*	.204	.221	.028	-.082	1.000	-.123	.113	.129
	Sig. (2-tailed)	.198	.085	.241	.654	.275	.050	.140	.102	.839	.546		.406	.410	.344
	N	56	46	46	46	46	54	54	56	55	56	56	48	55	56
CHOICERT	Pearson Correlation	.025	-.272	-.498**	-.153	.062	-.074	.205	.097	.208	.057	-.123	1.000	.687**	.553**
	Sig. (2-tailed)	.863	.085	.001	.339	.700	.627	.173	.511	.160	.700	.406		.000	.000
	N	48	41	41	41	41	46	46	48	47	48	48	48	47	48
VERINRTW	Pearson Correlation	.068	-.404**	-.396**	-.008	-.141	.150	.009	.124	.293*	-.042	.113	.687**	1.000	.526**
	Sig. (2-tailed)	.624	.006	.007	.960	.354	.284	.949	.368	.031	.762	.410	.000		.000
	N	55	45	45	45	45	53	53	55	54	55	55	47	55	55
VINTERTC	Pearson Correlation	-.206	-.289	-.409**	.075	.321*	-.040	-.017	.225	.346**	-.033	.129	.553**	.526**	1.000
	Sig. (2-tailed)	.128	.051	.005	.622	.029	.776	.904	.096	.010	.810	.344	.000	.000	
	N	56	46	46	46	46	54	54	56	55	56	56	48	55	56

*Correlation is significant at the 0.05 level (2-tailed).
**Correlation is significant at the 0.01 level (2-tailed).

FIGURE 6.14 Partial listing of NCT test measure and HRV measure correlations (Dif).

Correlations

		Global Success across sports	HRDIF	VDIF	LOWDIF	LHDIF	MAZETC	MAZCT	MAZETE	EREANGA	EREDISA	ERENEUAC
Global Success across sports	Pearson Correlation	1.000	.447**	.173	-.200	-.075	.137	-.025	.180	.330*	.256	.345**
	Sig. (2-tailed)		.002	.250	.182	.619	.323	.860	.192	.013	.057	.009
	N	56	46	46	46	46	54	54	54	56	56	56
HRDIF	Pearson Correlation	.447**	1.000	.265	-.187	.088	-.312*	-.419**	-.134	.184	.392**	.177
	Sig. (2-tailed)	.002		.075	.213	.560	.039	.005	.386	.221	.007	.241
	N	46	46	46	46	46	44	44	44	46	46	46
VDIF	Pearson Correlation	.173	.265	1.000	.328*	.296*	-.010	-.144	-.072	-.285	.111	-.189
	Sig. (2-tailed)	.250	.075		.026	.046	.947	.352	.643	.055	.461	.209
	N	46	46	46	46	46	44	44	44	46	46	46
LOWDIF	Pearson Correlation	-.200	-.187	.328*	1.000	.432**	-.054	.020	-.312*	-.185	.020	-.268
	Sig. (2-tailed)	.182	.213	.026		.003	.730	.897	.039	.219	.897	.072
	N	46	46	46	46	46	44	44	44	46	46	46
LHDIF	Pearson Correlation	-.075	.088	.296*	.432**	1.000	-.302*	-.328*	-.327*	-.466**	.040	-.339*
	Sig. (2-tailed)	.619	.560	.046	.003		.047	.030	.030	.001	.793	.021
	N	46	46	46	46	46	44	44	44	46	46	46
MAZETC	Pearson Correlation	.137	-.312*	-.010	-.054	-.302*	1.000	.739**	.665**	-.118	.034	.206
	Sig. (2-tailed)	.323	.039	.947	.730	.047		.000	.000	.395	.806	.135
	N	54	44	44	44	44	54	54	54	54	54	54
MAZCT	Pearson Correlation	-.025	-.419**	-.144	.020	-.328*	.739**	1.000	.513**	-.174	-.131	.084
	Sig. (2-tailed)	.860	.005	.352	.897	.030	.000		.000	.208	.344	.547
	N	54	44	44	44	44	54	54	54	54	54	54
MAZETE	Pearson Correlation	.180	-.134	-.072	-.312*	-.327*	.665**	.513**	1.000	-.052	.088	.361**
	Sig. (2-tailed)	.192	.386	.643	.039	.030	.000	.000		.711	.525	.007
	N	54	44	44	44	44	54	54	54	54	54	54
EREANGA	Pearson Correlation	.330*	.184	-.285	-.185	-.466**	-.118	-.174	-.052	1.000	-.050	.392**
	Sig. (2-tailed)	.013	.221	.055	.219	.001	.395	.208	.711		.713	.003
	N	56	46	46	46	46	54	54	54	56	56	56
EREDISA	Pearson Correlation	.256	.392**	.111	.020	.040	.034	-.131	.088	-.050	1.000	.123
	Sig. (2-tailed)	.057	.007	.461	.897	.793	.806	.344	.525	.713		.367
	N	56	46	46	46	46	54	54	54	56	56	56
ERENEUAC	Pearson Correlation	.345**	.177	-.189	-.268	-.339*	.206	.084	.361**	.392**	.123	1.000
	Sig. (2-tailed)	.009	.241	.209	.072	.021	.135	.547	.007	.003	.367	
	N	56	46	46	46	46	54	54	54	56	56	56

*Correlation is significant at the 0.05 level (2-tailed).
**Correlation is significant at the 0.01 level (2-tailed).

FIGURE 6.15 Partial listing of NCT test measure and HRV measure correlations (Dif).

attributed to greater SNS/PNS balance and concomitant HRD (one slowing cardiac cycle) prior to each response motor task (pre-action HRD before each computer-key/bar/lever pressing response).

Multiple Regression: Neuro-PHO-HRV and Global Outcome: 4 Teams-3 Sports

In addition to correlation analyses, multiple regression was applied to the data in an attempt to discern any additive effects of PHO and HRV predictor variables on both global (macro) and micro (criticality-based) outcome measures. Findings were as follows in Figures 6.16 and 6.17.

The most potent regression model as seen in Figure 6.16 explained 67% of the variance in Global Success, a standardized performance outcome measure across baseball, tennis, and ice hockey. Predictor variables were HRV measures HR difference between the S7s stress test baseline and stress task conditions, baseline condition L/H ratio and NCT scores, maze total errors, sustained attention false misses, sustained attention RT, and motor tapping variability in the dominant hand. This is a very high amount of variance explained, although maze errors and false misses, intuitively, appear to have exerted effects on performance outcome that seem paradoxical and conceptually inconsistent. Nevertheless, this finding and other multiple regression results further on point to the need to further investigate neurocognition in the context of micro-level outcome measures to see whether the preceding and other strong findings hold up in other populations (via meta-analyses) and determine if influences of specific NCT measures can be reconciled with the TCM and AP models of peak performance.

NCT and AP PHO Measures

For exploratory purposes, NCT measures were analyzed in relationship to individual AP PHO measures to determine how much of the variance in SA/HS-SR/N-SC/RC can be attributed to neurocognitive tendencies and by extension brain location and functionality.

Model Summary

Model	R	R Square	Adjusted R Square	Std. Error of the Estimate
1	.470[a]	.221	.199	.8859
2	.623[b]	.388	.353	.7961
3	.722[c]	.521	.479	.7143
4	.785[d]	.616	.569	.6499
5	.822[e]	.675	.624	.6067
6	.849[f]	.720	.666	.5722

a. Predictors: (Constant), HRDIF

b. Predictors: (Constant), HRDIF, MAZETE

c. Predictors: (Constant), HRDIF, MAZETE, SUSATTFM

d. Predictors: (Constant), HRDIF, MAZETE, SUSATTFM, MTVARRTD

e. Predictors: (Constant), HRDIF, MAZETE, SUSATTFM, MTVARRTD, LH

f. Predictors: (Constant), HRDIF, MAZETE, SUSATTFM, MTVARRTD, LH, SUSATTRT

Criterion variable: GLOBAL SUCCESS

FIGURE 6.16 AP PHO, HRV, and sport performance outcome variance explained.

In the first multiple regression analysis (NCT-AP PHO; Figure 6.17), emotional recognition of anger, motor tapping variability in the dominant hand, total memory recognition, go-no-go, false misses in the go condition, digit span recall, and verbal interference RT (color condition) explained 72% of the variance in SA/HS. This is another strong finding that needs to be further analyzed relative to the conceptual basis and construct validity of SA and in the context of additional statistical modeling that is beyond the scope of this book. This and the following results on NCT-PHO relationships are presented to demonstrate that performance on select neurocognitive tests are associated with individual AP PHO measures. The next challenge is to determine to what extent such findings are conceptually relevant, support the TCM and AP construct validity models, and, importantly, predict actual sport performance macro- and micro-level outcomes.

While NCT test measures were not associated with SR/N, within this data set, differences between stress test baseline and stress test task conditions VL and L/H ratio HRV activity and stress test condition standard deviation of the normal cardiac cycle (HRV measure; SDNN) predicted 57% of the variance in this AP-PHO measure (SR; Figure 6.18). This is a conceptually consistent finding in that greater levels of SR/N are expected to elicit or be associated with greater SNS activity that are apparent in VL and greater L/H ratio HRV. This finding will be noted and entered into the ABSP database of athlete mind–body functioning (as would all other conceptually relevant findings).

Regarding the final AP-PHO measure, SC/RC, the strongest regression model in Figure 6.19, shows that NCT test measures, go-no-go false alarm, maze learning time, and emotional recognition of sad accuracy, along with stress test baseline H frequency, L frequency, and L/H ratio HRV differences between the baseline and stress test task condition, explained 74% of the variance in this behavioral measure, another very strong finding. Again, this result raises additional questions and requires further scrutiny to ascertain whether it is conceptually reconcilable.

Model Summary

Model	R	R Square	Adjusted R Square	Std. Error of the Estimate
1	.483[a]	.233	.212	4.0362
2	.637[b]	.405	.371	3.6051
3	.714[c]	.509	.466	3.3221
4	.762[d]	.581	.530	3.1167
5	.816[e]	.666	.614	2.8262
6	.850[f]	.722	.668	2.6194
7	.877[g]	.769	.715	2.4279

a. Predictors: (Constant), EREANGA

b. Predictors: (Constant), EREANGA, MTVARRTD

c. Predictors: (Constant), EREANGA, MTVARRTD, HR7

d. Predictors: (Constant), EREANGA, MTVARRTD, HR7, MEMTOT

e. Predictors: (Constant), EREANGA, MTVARRTD, HR7, MEMTOT, GNGOFMIG

f. Predictors: (Constant), EREANGA, MTVARRTD, HR7, MEMTOT, GNGOFMIG, DIGITREF

g. Predictors: (Constant), EREANGA, MTVARRTD, HR7, MEMTOT, GNGOFMIG, DIGITREF, VERINC

Criterion variable: Subliminal Attention

FIGURE 6.17   NCT test measures and individual AP PHO measures variance explained.

Model Summary

Model	R	R Square	Adjusted R Square	Std. Error of the Estimate
1	.583[a]	.340	.322	3.3515
2	.725[b]	.526	.498	2.8821
3	.777[c]	.604	.569	2.6729

a. Predictors: (Constant), VDIF

b. Predictors: (Constant), VDIF, LHDIF

c. Predictors: (Constant), VDIF, LHDIF, SD7

Criterion variable: Subliminal Reactivity

FIGURE 6.18   HRV test measures and individual AP PHO measures variance explained.

It should be noted that all of the preceding multiple regression findings were generated from samples having high statistical power and were associated with large effect sizes.

NCT and Pressure Performance

Only three of the four team's performance statistical benchmarks contained micro-level criticality outcome measures. These were standardized across baseball and hockey and subjected to a multiple regression analysis with NCT test measures serving as predictor variables (Figure 6.20).

Model Summary

Model	R	R Square	Adjusted R Square	Std. Error of the Estimate
1	.532[a]	.283	.263	3.6111
2	.662[b]	.438	.406	3.2423
3	.738[c]	.545	.505	2.9599
4	.797[d]	.636	.592	2.6887
5	.838[e]	.703	.657	2.4653
6	.863[f]	.745	.696	2.3198
7	.853[g]	.727	.685	2.3616
8	.884[h]	.781	.739	2.1508

a. Predictors: (Constant), HIGH

b. Predictors: (Constant), HIGH, EREANGA

c. Predictors: (Constant), HIGH, EREANGA, LOWDIF

d. Predictors: (Constant), HIGH, EREANGA, LOWDIF, LHDIF

e. Predictors: (Constant), HIGH, EREANGA, LOWDIF, LHDIF, GNGOFANG

f. Predictors: (Constant), HIGH, EREANGA, LOWDIF, LHDIF, GNGOFANG, MAZELT

g. Predictors: (Constant), HIGH, LOWDIF, LHDIF, GNGOFANG, MAZELT

h. Predictors: (Constant), HIGH, LOWDIF, LHDIF, GNGOFANG, MAZELT, ERESADAC

Criterion variable: Subliminal Coping

FIGURE 6.19   NCT test measures and individual AP PHO measures variance explained.

Model Summary

Model	R	R Square	Adjusted R Square	Std. Error of the Estimate
1	.333[a]	.111	.086	.8737

a. Predictors: (Constant), SWATTERR

Criterion variable: Critical Moment Success (across 3 sports)

FIGURE 6.20   NCT test measures and standardized criticality measure.

One NCT test measure, switching of attention error rate emerged as predictive of CM performance, explaining about 9% of the variance in pressure-outcome that could be attributed to this neurocognitive measure. A conceptually consistent finding, less cognitively mediated errors on an attention test being associated with better CM performance may play an analogous role in pre-action phases of sport competition where the ability to smoothly transition from frontal lobe–based strategic planning to action onset focusing and motor action demands (left-to-right brain hemispheric shift & HRD) is associated with better RT, technical control, and performance outcome. Although this finding does not remotely approach some of the very high variance explained coefficients that were revealed in other analyses of NCT-AP PHO and outcome relationships, 9% variance explained is still notable in the context of sport psychological performance outcome research, where 1% to 3% variance explained on the basis of psychological or behavioral measures tends to be the ceiling. This data will be added to the ABSP database for inclusion in eventual meta-analyses.

PHO and NCT Predict HRV

What also emerged from this pilot research of AP PHO, NCT, and HRV measures and their relationships were extremely strong variance-explained coefficients between select NCT and HRV measures. These are presented for illustrative and contemplative/interpretive purposes relative to the TCM and AP models conceptual and construct bases and the formulating of additional research involving these variables. These findings will not be elaborated here, but advanced readers are encouraged to study the following table and develop explanatory models for some of these findings. Note, the HRV measures were derived from the Serial 7s stress test baseline and stress task condition with the NCT measures being derived from separate measurement occasions (temporally removed from each other).

NCT, PHO, HRV, and Outcome

Advanced Practitioner-Researcher-Student Challenge: Based on your knowledge of the presented neurocognitive measures, heart rate variability, and Athlete's Profile model of peak performance, arrive at explanations for any findings of interest in Figure 6.21.

There were numerous other findings involving NCT, AP PHO, and HRV measures. Again, these findings are noteworthy considering the temporal distance (time separation of days to weeks) between tests, that at face value, would not necessarily be thought to be related or involve synergistic mediating mechanisms. This points to the need to engage in practice or research in an integrative and multimodal manner in the context of a guiding conceptual framework and construct validity model. While these findings and results from multiple regression are based on group samples and may, thus, not generalize to specific individual athletes (at the

HRV-Criterion Variable	Adjusted r^2 Variance Explained	PHO and NCT Predictor Variables
HR baseline	.96	VERINC, SWATTERR, MTAPDOM, EREHAPAC, CHOICERT, VERINRTW, MEMTOT, GNGOFANG, SC, SA, MTVARRT
SDNN baseline	.72	REALWDAC, MEM2, MRINER4, VERINC, SC, MAZETE, DIGITREF
VL baseline	.53	CHOICERT, ERESADAC, SC
L baseline	.43	MAZETE, REALWDAC, MEM2
H baseline	.61	SC, MEM2, MRINER4, SWATTAV, REALWDAC
L/H baseline	.21	REALWDAC, VERINTAC
HR-S7 stress task	.95	VERINC, ERESADAC, MRDEL4, MTAPDOM, SUSATTFM, SA, MAZETE, MAZEOVER, MTVARRTD, SR, SWATTAV
SDNN S7	.21	ERESADAC, EREFEARA
VL S7	.48	SUSATTFM, VERINTEC, ERESADAC, EREDISA
L S7	.13	EREANGA
H S7	.15	SC
L/H S7	.91	EREANGA, MAZELT, VINTERTC, SC, MRDEL4, SUSATTRT, EREFEARA, VERINTAC, SUSATTFM
HR DIF	1.00	EREDISA, SUSATTRT, VERINC,

FIGURE 6.21   NCT test measures and HRV: Multiple regression.

intra-individual level) they can inform practice and in the initial stages of an athlete evaluation provide insight regarding brain–heart–mind–body–motor functioning and their inter-relationships that can then be further tested in the context of assessment and intervention procedures and methodologies that the CP advocates.

The preceding findings also have potential importance for neurofeedback and mental training intervention (see Chapter 18). Established associations between and among NCT, HRV, AP PHO, and performance outcome measures that support the TCM and AP can be used to guide evidence-based individualized neurofeedback protocols, since neurocognitive measures that were found to be predictive have been localized anatomically and functionally in the specific brain regions.

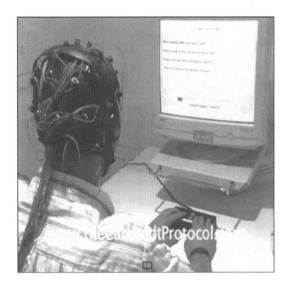

FIGURE 6.22   qEEG test session.

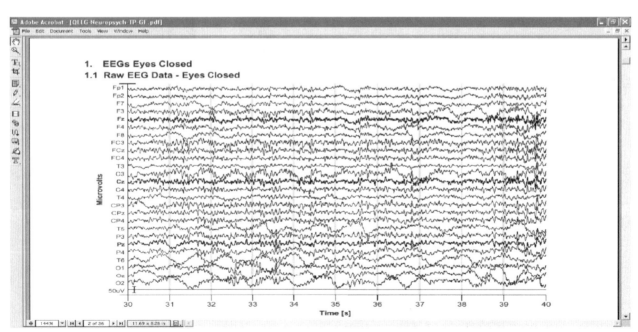

FIGURE 6.23   Raw brain waves: Eyes closed condition.

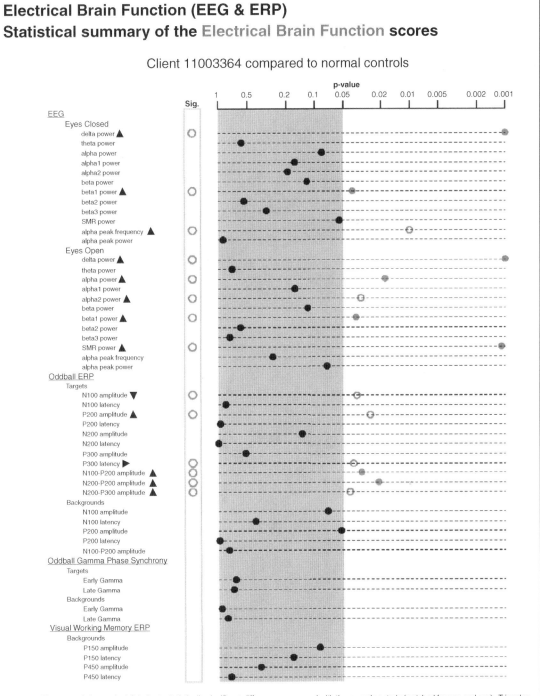

FIGURE 6.24   BRC qEEG paradigm: EEG activity measures.

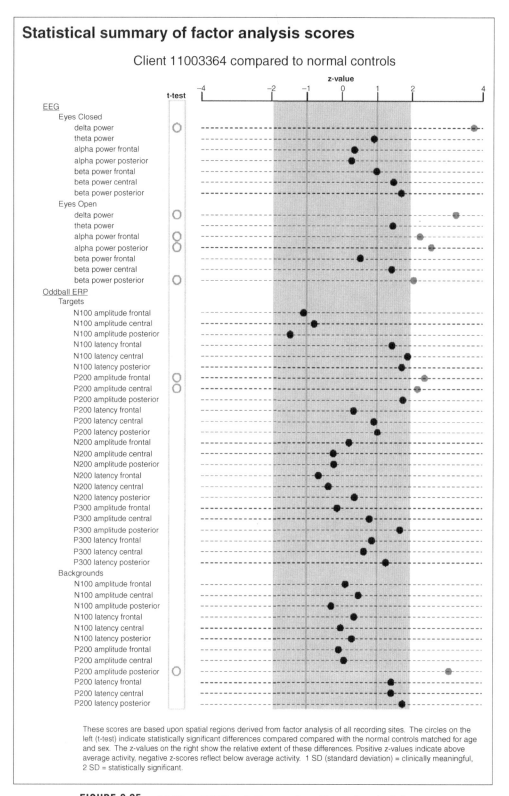

FIGURE 6.25   Additional EEG activity overview: Normative deviations.

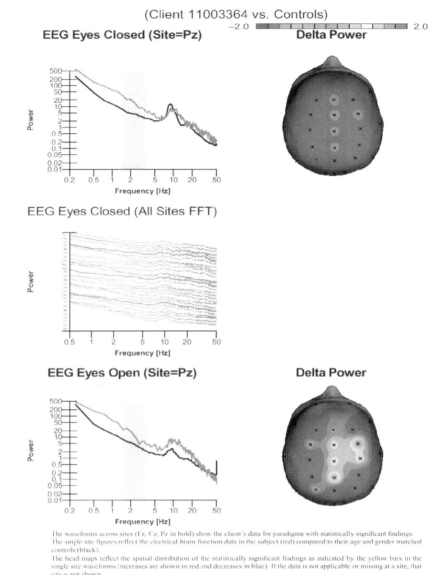

Visualization of THE most stastically significant result in each paradigm
(followed by all sites data)

(Client 11003364 vs. Controls)

The waveforms across sites (Fz, Cz, Pz in bold) show the client's data for paradigms with statistically significant findings. The single site figures reflect the electrical brain function data in the subject (red) compared to their age and gender matched controls (black).
The head maps reflect the spatial distribution of the statistically significant findings as indicated by the yellow bars in the single site waveforms (increases are shown in red and decreases in blue). If the data is not applicable or missing at a site, that site is not shown.

FIGURE 6.26   Illustration of significant numeric EEG findings.

qEEG and Performance: An Overview and Case Study

This section presents an overview of qEEG as it was applied in a case study of a former world-ranked professional tennis player. The use of qEEG/EEG is predicated on a practitioner having completed advanced training and having access to instrumentation or an affiliated laboratory that can carry out this procedure on his or her behalf. Figure 6.22 shows a person undergoing qEEG simultaneously to NCT.

It is beyond the scope of this book to thoroughly cover the intricacies of this procedure. Data presented in this section is shown for illustrative purposes. Findings that are relevant to sport

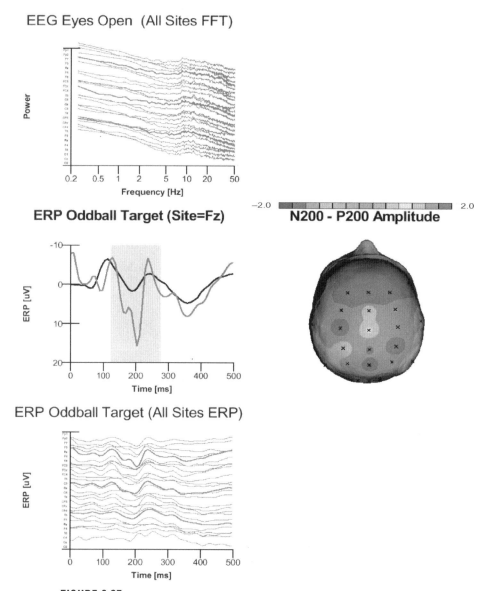

FIGURE 6.27   Illustrated significant EEG findings from stimulus paradigm.

performance or have clinical significance will be discussed. An actual full case report is also included at the end of this section.

Figure 6.23 depicts brain waves that emanated from 26 standardized head locations ("y" axis) per the International 10–20 system during the eyes-closed condition (see Andreassi, 1995).

Figure 6.24 contains a statistical summary of brain wave activity in the eyes open and closed conditions and as a function of various stimuli and whether derived EEG activity differed from the BRC normative database. Definitions of technical EEG terms, numbers, and designations can be found in Andreassi (1995).

Figure 6.25 depicts standard deviation scores. Note the excessive delta brain wave deviations that will be elaborated later in the case study.

Figure 6.26 depicts the most significant findings from Figures 6.24 and 6.25.

Neuropsychological Test Battery

Summary of Neuropsychological Test Battery **findings**

Neuropsychological Test Battery

Test	Deficit
1. Memory Recall and Recognition	
2. Digit Span	
3. Span of Visual Memory	
4. Sustained Attention	●
5. Switching of Attention	
6. Motor Tapping	
7. Choice Reaction Time	
8. Timing	
9. Verbal Interference	
10. Spot the Real Word	
11. Word Generation	
12. Maze	

● = deficit compared to matched controls

The table above shows deficit found in each test (1–12).

The list below summaries what the practical significance of that deficit is considered to be:

4. Ability to detect and respond to significant change under conditions requiring vigilance. Fundamental everyday skills e.g., train, plane, automobile, computer, and equivalent machine operations.

FIGURE 6.28   Neuropsychological (NCT) testing summary chart.

Figure 6.27 presents significant findings from stimuli paradigms.

As previously mentioned, neuropsychological/NCT can be built into qEEG/EEG assessment sessions. In the case of this athlete, a deficit in sustained attention emerged (Figure 6.28), which can also be seen in Figure 6.29. Continuous EEG is recorded during simultaneous NCT in contrast to non-EEG-based NCT that was elaborated in the first portion of this chapter. The advantage of concurrent monitoring of EEG is that real-time brain waves can be used to criterion-reference NCT test scores functionally at the group and individual level.

Figure 6.29 contains all neuropsychological test scores. Notice the red circles and open circles that represent clinically relevant statistical differences exhibited by the case study athlete. These findings are addressed in his report later in this section.

Figure 6.30 provides an overview of raw scores from the qEEG/EEG included neuropsychological test battery, along with normative scores from the BRC international database.

Client Report

The following is an actual client report (pages 172–178). The most performance and clinically relevant findings from the preceding qEEG and neuropsychological test batteries are addressed. The report is not limited to qEEG and NCT findings. It also discusses the Athlete's AP PHO Profile, HRV stress test, and outcome measures, consistent with the CP's integrative approach to athlete assessment. The report is personally directed toward the client (as opposed to a practitioner) and, as such, is less formal in terms of language used.

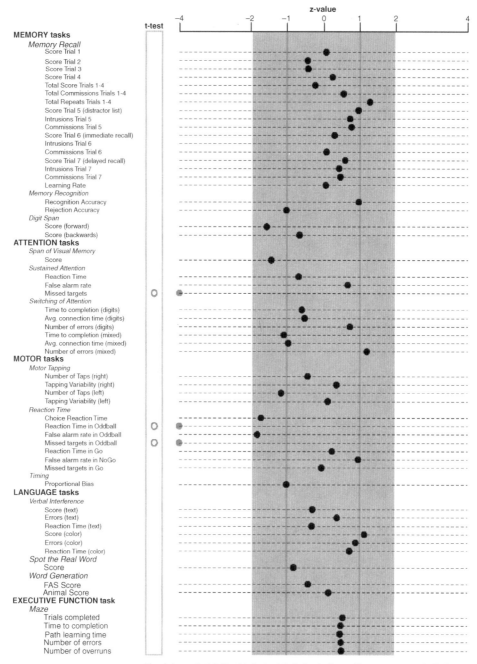

FIGURE 6.29   Neuropsychological test battery.

Details of the clients Neuropsychological Test Battery **scores**

Measure	Client	Int. Brain Database Average	Std. Dev	Z Score	Per.
Memory Recall					
Score Trial 1	6	5.9	1.4	0.07	53
Score Trial 2	7	7.5	1.2	-0.44	33
Score Trial 3	8	8.37	0.87	-0.42	33.7
Score Trial 4	9	8.7	1.1	0.25	59.7
Total Score Trials 1-4	30	30.7	2.8	-0.23	40.7
Total Commissions Trials 1-4	0	0.46	0.84	0.55	71
Total Repeats Trials 1-4	0	3.2	2.5	1.28	90
Score Trial 5 (distractor list)	6	4.5	1.6	0.97	83.3
Intrusions Trial 5	0	0.47	0.65	0.73	76.7
Commissions Trial 5	0	0.37	0.48	0.77	77.9
Score Trial 6 (immediate recall)	8	7.3	2.4	0.31	62.1
Intrusions Trial 6	0	0	0	0	0
Commissions Trial 6	0	0.02	0.23	0.08	53.4
Score Trial 7 (delayed recall)	8	6.6	2.4	0.59	72.3
Intrusions Trial 7	0	0.16	0.37	0.43	66.6
Commissions Trial 7	0	0.14	0.31	0.47	68
Learning Rate	1	0.96	0.62	0.06	52.4
Memory Recognition					
Recognition Accuracy	12	11.36	0.66	0.97	83.5
Rejection Accuracy	10	11.02	1	-1.02	15.4
Digit Span					
Score (forward)	5	6.8	1.2	-1.56	5.9
Score (backward)	4	5.1	1.7	-0.65	25.6
Span of Visual Memory					
Score	3	4.9	1.3	-1.43	7.6
Sustained Attention					
Reaction Time	590ms	513ms	113ms	-0.68	24.8
False alarm rate	0	0.7	1.1	0.67	74.7
* Missed targets	8	0.53	0.95	-7.84	0
Switching of Attention					
Time to completion (digits)	28.5s	24.6s	6.5s	-0.59	27.6
Avg. connection time (digits)	993ms	876ms	230ms	-0.51	30.5
Number of errors (digits)	0	1	1.3	0.73	76.8
Time to completion (mixed)	60s	50.4s	8.9s	-1.09	13.9
Avg. connection time (mixed)	2.48s	1.96s	0.54s	-0.96	16.9
Number of errors (mixed)	0	1.5	1.3	1.2	88.4
Motor Tapping					
Number of Taps (right)	162	173	25	-0.43	33.2
Tapping Variability (right)	18ms	28ms	27ms	0.36	64.2
Number of Taps (left)	136	162	23	-1.16	12.3
Tapping Variability (left)	32ms	40ms	65ms	0.12	54.9

Raw scores of the Cognitive findings (* = statistically significant; Std. Dev = standard deviation; Int = international; Per = percentile).

Measure	Client	Int. Brain Database Average	Std. Dev	Z Score	Per.
Reaction Time					
Choice Reaction Time	887ms	709ms	104ms	-1.71	4.3
* Reaction Time in Oddball	510ms	321ms	36ms	-5.26	0
False alarm rate in Oddball	3	1	1.1	-1.82	3.4
* Missed targets in Oddball	5	0.13	0.34	-14.16	0
Reaction Time in Go	289ms	298ms	39ms	0.24	59.4
False alarm rate in NoGo	1	2.3	1.3	0.96	83.2
Missed targets in Go	0	-0.01	0.11	-0.05	48.1
Timing					
Proportional Bias	0.5s	0.35s	0.15s	-1	15.8
Verbal Interference					
Score (text)	16	16.9	3	-0.3	38.3
Errors (text)	0	0.12	0.33	0.38	64.7
Reaction Time (text)	1190ms	1139ms	161ms	-0.31	37.7
Score (color)	13	8.6	3.9	1.13	87.2
Errors (color)	0	0.64	0.72	0.89	81.4
Reaction Time (color)	1530ms	1860ms	456ms	0.72	76.5
Spot the Real Word					
Score	50	53.5	4.3	-0.81	20.8
Word Generation					
FAS Score	15	16.9	4.6	-0.41	34
Animal Score	23	22.2	5.2	0.15	55.8
Maze					
Trials completed	7	9.8	5.3	0.54	70.4
Time to completion	203s	256s	110s	0.48	68.6
Path learning time	168s	216s	103s	0.47	67.9
Number of errors	29	55	52	0.49	68.8
Number of overruns	13	22	18	0.51	69.4

FIGURE 6.30 Raw scores on individual neuropsychological tests.

Raw scores of the Cognitive findings (* = statistically significant; Std. Dev = standard deviation; Int = international; Per = percentile).

Roland A. Carlstedt, Ph.D.

Licensed Clinical Psychologist Ψ Board Certified Sport Psychologist

Client Report

Name: GOF
Gender: 54
Age: confidential
Sport: Tennis
Ranking: Former Professional Tennis Player

COMPLAINTS:

Clinical: Depression, lack of joy, happiness, marital issues, job dissatisfaction

Performance: Inability to maximize what has always been a very good serve; closing out matches

Medication: Anti-depressant

<u>**Session Summary- 10 sessions**</u>

March 9	1:00–3:00	Sessions 1	Office/Intake
March 16	2:00–4:00	Sessions 2–3	On-Court
April 7	2:30–3:30	Session 4	Office
April 28	1:00–3:00	Sessions 5–6	On-Court
May 18	1:00–3:00	Sessions 7–8	On-Court
June 9	11:30–1:30	Sessions 9–10	On-Court

CSARCS-A-Psychological and Behavioral Measures

SUBLIMINAL ATTENTION-HYPNOTIC SUSCEPTIBILITY

You scored in the high range for SA. Athletes who score in the high range for this measure have potential advantages and disadvantages depending on how your level SA works together with two other performance relevant measures below. A high score on SA is associated with the ability to focus intensely on a task at hand, as long as an athlete scores low in SR/N, which you do; however, since you have complained about certain performance issues, including lapses in focus when serving and the inability to close out matches, your full neuropsychological and qEEG test findings, which are elaborated below, will be used in an attempt to account for your perceived and real match performance issues.

SUBLIMINAL REACTIVITY: NEUROTICISM

You scored in the extremely low range for SR/N. All-in-all this should bode well for your tennis game, since your emotional profile (SR/N) is associated with good mind–body control and less intrusive thoughts. However, low SR/N can give rise to hypo-activation, or a level of intensity that may lead to slow starts and inexplicable let-downs during matches. It should also be noted that your level of SR/N is inconsistent with a person suffering from depression, unless your emotional state is being well-regulated by the medication that you have been on for quite some time now.

SUBLIMINAL-REPRESSIVE COPING

You scored high in both SC/RC and, as previously mentioned, high in SA indicating that you have developed a protective ability to shutdown negative thoughts during competition, especially during CMs, which the CM analysis data supports (see below). However, since you came to me to deal with closing out matches and serving issues that you thought were psychologically mediated, you may be one of those rare or paradoxical cases in which the *AP* test measures are inconsistent or only partially inconsistent with actual psychological performance. Consequently, special attention will be given to your neuropsychological and qEEG battery to see what they reveal (see below).

RELATIVE BRAIN HEMISPHERIC PREDOMINANCE

You were found to be relative left brain-hemisphere predominant to a high degree, a tendency that highly skilled athletes exhibit overwhelmingly. This finding is consistent with your constellation of high SA/HS, low SR/N, and high SC/RC, is a profile exhibited by athletes who are actually the most "mentally tough."

HEART RATE VARIABILITY ANALYSIS

As you may recall, I was astounded by your HRV readings, especially your SDNN, the index of HRV. Your SDNN score throughout the assessment period both pre- and post- training were extremely high and more reflective of a person in their 20s than their 50s. This finding bodes well in the context of longevity and your tonic (overall) state of equilibrium or mind–body control, or at least your ability to induce change to feel and perform better. High SDNN is rarely seen in people who are depressed, in fact severely depressed individuals often have an SDNN lower than 30, something that can have cardiologic implications. Your HRV stress test task response was also consistent with an athlete who is mentally tough (a drop off in the activation/nervousness response and increase in the "relaxation" response; first chart is the baseline measurement; second chart, the stress response).

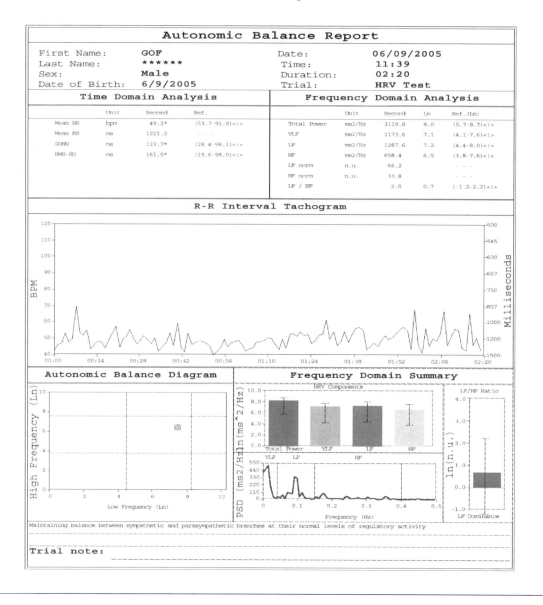

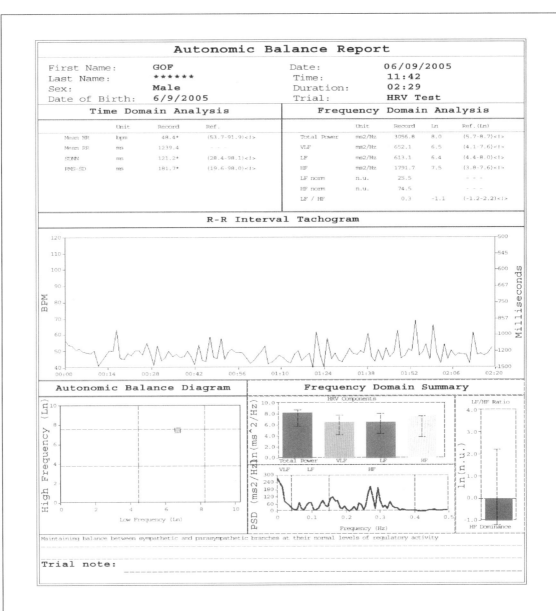

TECHNICAL ANALYSIS

Obviously, you are a world-class tennis player and always have been relative to your age-group, and, as such, your technique is excellent, but reflective of the type of game/technique that you were taught. As you know, I saw a few "weaknesses" that could be enough to potentially set off a cascade of negative psychological events or mind–body processes, especially during CMs, that may undo the protective psychological and behavioral tendencies that your profile suggests that you possess. I see these as being your serve, which I believe could be more of a weapon, especially come crunch-time. I suggested that you work on more upper-body rotation, greater racquet-head acceleration on both first and second serves, and not open up the shoulders and hips too soon. I felt that you could get about 25 to 30 more mph in serving pace. I also would like to see more variety off the ground, especially when you are being attacked. Although some feel it is difficult to change or amend the technical game of an established player, motor learning principles suggest otherwise. Because you have such a good foundation, you possess a motor or neuronal template(s) that will facilitate the learning of or integration of new components into your game. The technical game may very well be the royal road to your improved psychological game. As such, we should consider implementing a short- to mid-term training plan to address technical aspects of your game that could be enhanced.

CMS ANALYSES

You performed well during both matches that were analyzed relative to CM performance. You scored above 90% in mastering criticality level 4 and 5 points during the sets that were scored, demonstrating that you were capable of mastering the most critical points during these matches. Usually, there is a strong correlation between CMs performance in practice compared to CM performance during real competition, especially in mentally "weaker" athletes who tend to perform worse during CMs during both situations. Since you performed well during CMs in practice, the odds are that you will be a "good" CM performer during tournament competition, although this needs to be verified. Your CM performance appears consistent with your *AP*. However, it must be viewed in the context of your expressed performance issues.

CONSTELLATION OF TRAITS, BEHAVIORS, RESPONSES: IMPLICATIONS-PREDICTIONS

As previously mentioned, overall, your AP constellation is consistent with the "best" AP and at face-value would lead me to predict that you were/are a mentally tough tennis player who will perform well come crunch-time or during CMs. However, since this has not been the case recently, we will examine further to determine what may be underlying your current performance issues.

Neurophysiological Findings: qEEG

The following findings are of interest. Please note that unless you are experiencing specific clinical problems (beyond the mentioned depression and relationship issues) they need to be viewed with caution. We should discuss them in a clinical session. Relative to their performance implications, see my comments below:

Major Findings: Significantly more delta (slow brain waves) activity in the eyes open condition compared to normative age-matched database, especially in the frontal brain regions. In addition, increased eyes closed beta activity was found in certain frontal brain regions.
Clinical Implications: Increased slow-wave activity may be associated with reduced cognitive processing speed or mental dulling, fog-like states when awake. Delta activity usually increases when sleeping but occurs less when awake. Do you have sleep problems or trouble staying awake during the day? Any focus problems when at work?

Performance/Clinical Implications: Since you are obviously a top-notch tennis player who is in great physical shape (as attested to by your HRV SDNN index), it is highly unlikely that a delta "state" or predominance of slow brain waves is occurring during actual training or tournament matches, the delta finding must be looked at in a context-specific manner. It may be related to that "unhappy" tonic (enduring) state you told me about in that chronic malaise or sadness that you experience "dulls" you emotionally, leading to lessened cortical activity in the frontal lobes, which are responsible for contemplation, emotional interpretation, and knowledge of one's state of being. The delta manifestation could very well reflect or be a brain biomarker of the lack of "happiness" that you mentioned, and may be involved in your job dissatisfaction. Have things changed since you quit your job and started your business? Are you more excited about life now? Tennis is your therapy, as you told me, so an obvious prescription is to continue to play, perhaps even a bit more. You should also address your relationship issues. The delta findings may also be a psychopharmacological remnant or resulting change in frontal lobe brain activity or a neurophysiological biomarker of depression, which is associated with frontal lobe hypo-activation. Paradoxically, frontal hypo-frontality has also been associated with the "just do it" as opposed to "just think it" feeling, since reductions in frontal lobe activity (that are associated with delta activity) take the analytic mind out of the equation and free an athlete to perform without fear of consequences. The delta state, in the context of tennis, may actually underlie your good CM performance.

NEUROPSYCHOLOGICAL FINDINGS (NON-EEG)

The most significant neuropsychological finding was that your sustained attention score was 4SD (standard deviations) from the mean. This result could be seen as consistent with a person exhibiting increased levels of delta activity in a waking state and reported symptoms of emotional dulling and depression. As to whether this finding has implications for performance remains to be seen, since it appears that your psychological state changes for the better when you play tennis. As such, you may be exhibiting a much more balanced brain activity profile when engaged in things you really like to do. One finding that may have performance implications is that your RT in the so-called "odd-ball" task was well below the norm for your age group. This suggests that when encountering deviations from expected patterns during a rally, surprises during the match or even when serving (deciding when your motion has started, where and how to serve the ball), your RT and selective attention or commitment to an initial plan may become disrupted, leading to errors. This may be accompanied by intrusive thoughts and could explain your reports of having thoughts about outcome (winning a point or getting a good serve in) when you are serving.

CONCLUSION

Considering that you are a former world-class professional tennis player and have current technical and physical skills and advantages that would probably make you a top-5 in the world senior player, I tend to think that your performance issues may indeed be driven by clinical issues, aside from the serving technical consideration. Your off-the-court mood state (mild-managed depression and emotional malaise ["lack of joy"] combined with antidepression medication) may have led to functional brain changes, as reflected in increased slow-wave delta activity, left frontal-lobe hypo-activation, and other cortical tendencies that can get in the way of absolute peak performance. Nevertheless, there is no need to panic or let these findings worry you needlessly. The fact is, you are still a great tennis player, have had a successful business career, and are highly functional. So, do not let your quest for "perfection" take away from the reality of your talents and what you have accomplished.

I would recommend a combination of approaches, both clinically and performance enhancement oriented. Clinically, I would consider undergoing a neurofeedback regime to regulate your increased waking state delta activity as well as cognitive-behavioral methods to deal with your relationship and "joy" issues.

Relative to the performance issues, I suggest that we continue to work on technical elements that through improvement may help you overcome intrusive thoughts that may be affecting your game especially when CMs occur. We should also do additional on-the-court monitoring to see if your brain activity varies relative to what was revealed during testing in the laboratory.

Roland A. Carlstedt, PhD
Licensed Clinical and Applied Psychologist
Board Certified Sport Psychologist-Diplomate ABSP
Research Fellow in Applied Neuroscience-Brain Resource Company

Comments: Preceding Athlete Client Report

This case study is a complex one and again points to the need approach athlete assessment from an integrative and multimodal perspective. On one hand this athlete possesses an ideal AP PHO constellation, one that should facilitate CM performance, yet, he complains of not being able to serve out a match without difficulty, despite having a good serve. However, when tested, his CM performance was consistent with his profile. On the other hand, he exhibited neuropsychological and brain functioning deficits that, although not directly implicated in the performance equation, appear to be related to his psychological state off the tennis court. In fact, his excessive level of delta brain wave activity might lead a neurologist to conclude that he is suffering from organic brain dysfunction. Such a diagnosis, though, could be called into question due to his overall high level of functionality despite his current mild depression, lack of "joy," and marital problems. It is also possible that the medication he is taking has led to functional brain changes (excessive delta wave activity). It should be noted that high SC/RC, while performance facilitative in pressure performance situations during actual sport competition, in the context of overall health and well-being, especially after an elite athlete retires (especially if he or she does not remain physically as active during his or her career where intensive training was the norm), can have a negative effect. It is associated with increased physiological activation at baseline (similar to someone who is high in SR/N) and psychological imperviousness to negative life situations. While this latter characteristic of high SC/RC leads to less (if any) conscious psychological distress, subliminally (unconsciously) it may be involved in driving maladaptive autonomic nervous system (ANS) responses that eventually lead to symptoms and disease if not confronted. This dynamic may be involved in this athlete's suspected brain wave activity and depression. Interestingly, playing tennis continues to serve as an elixir for this athlete, consistent with an emerging body of literature (e.g. Anshel, 2006, 2009) that attests to the positive effects of exercise on depression and anxiety. This tennis player stated that he felt his best and full of life when he played tennis, almost like he did 25 years ago when he was a full-time professional.

Relevance of NCT and qEEG

Without NCT and qEEG, the above tennis player's self-report and AP PHO constellation would have remained paradoxical when viewed in relationship to his clinical issues and, especially, actual tennis performance. The administered tests of brain functioning provided an explanatory framework for clinical symptoms and issues that, although not directly implicated in his performance equation, did impact his personal life to a great extent. qEEG findings also suggested that medication for depression may have altered brain functioning as reflected in abnormal delta wave activity. Such an occurrence may not be that unusual (side effects are not uncommon with antidepressants), but goes often unnoticed since patients rarely undergo NCT and qEEG for most psychological (mental) disorders.

Irrespective of the etiology of his excessive delta wave manifestations, it is an important finding that would have gone unnoticed without brain-based qEEG assessment.

Methodologically, in an ideal scenario, such an athlete would have multiple qEEG's administered to determine whether context inappropriate excessive delta wave activity would diminish as a function of exercise, playing tennis, or engaging in any other activity that someone enjoys. Doing so would help to ascertain whether the observed delta wave activity occurred as a function of boredom or lack of interest/joy mediated depression. A medication moratorium involving an initial baseline qEEG prior to antidepressant cessation that could then be compared with one, say, 1 month later, could also help to discern whether a psychotropic agent played a role in the generation of his excessive delta wave activity.

Summary

NCT and qEEG are tests of brain functioning that are administered as part of the CP's evidence-based athlete assessment framework. While they do have limitations by not being repeated measures that can be directly linked to sport performance macro and micro outcome measures, data from a pilot study of over 50 athletes from three sports were revealing, supporting their use in the initial athlete intake/evaluation process.

Sport Psychological Performance Statistics and Analysis I: Technical and Focus Threshold Training

After an initial office or laboratory-based assessment of an athlete's constellation of PHO factors (CSARCS-A-Athlete's Profile), Serial 7s stress test, and neurocognitive/qEEG responses, it is time to move to the playing field. In a hierarchical approach to evidence-based practice and research, it is not assumed that test results that emanate from self-report will necessarily predict or influence actual sport performance. The same applies to psychophysiological and neurocognitive/neurophysiological (qEEG/EEG) response profiles that are obtained in static situations and settings (away from the playing field). Since virtually all assessment instruments and the scores that they generate are not direct measures or predictors of real sport performance, one can only make inferences about them and what they mean. While a conceptually sound construct and methodological frameworks can increase the probability that test-based findings will have higher predictive validity than models that are conceptually weak, false-positive and false-negative results will always emerge, even when testing the most plausible or potent models. For example, although 70% of the variance explained in a sport-specific outcome measure that can be attributed to a self-report test derived psychological trait or behavior, the strongest result from investigations of the Athlete's Profile (AP) and Theory of Critical Moments (TCM) models, is a very high level of predictive validity, 30% of the variance still remains unaccounted for. Consequently, despite the APs and TCM's strong conceptual bases, construct validity, and supportive findings that attest to its predictive capability, one still cannot rely solely on in-office and laboratory test scores to make definitive judgments about athlete performance. Ultimately, increasing levels of actual on-the-playing-field responding and performance scores supersede test results that do not directly measure sport-specific outcomes when attempting to assess athlete psychological performance tendencies and mental toughness. On-the-playing-field, ecological-valid psychological testing ranges from technical and focus threshold to critical moment analyses that are derived from pre- and intervention phases of competition and training.

Procuring and integrating multimodal sources of information allows for a hierarchical approach to the analysis of performance data. Level I data acquisition involves observing and analyzing basic technical parameters of an athlete (e.g., forehand and backhand in a tennis player) along with outcome (success or errors) pertaining to progressively increasing grades of task difficulty. Each practice session requires that an athlete demonstrate optimal technique as determined by his coach and conveyed to a sport psychology practitioner with expertise in the sport at hand during "accountability" sessions that can last from 30 minutes to 2 hours or longer. In addition to technical ratings, success/error ratios are calculated. Accountability sessions take athletes out of routine training situations and into the realm of structured pressure in which performance components are documented, forcing them to raise their focus and technical thresholds if they are to make a good impression on a coach. Thresholds are continually expanding upper limits of performance tolerance that athletes are systematically trained to attain. For example, if a basketball player's free-throw percentage is 55, the goal of a coach or sport psychology practitioner would be to help incrementally raise the success threshold for this particular skill, especially in pressure situations, using standardized and customized psychological and motor learning approaches. While athletes can get away with errors, breakdowns in technique, and diminished attention for the bulk of most training sessions, once a coach or sport psychology practitioner announces "accountability session," practice takes on more importance, since an athlete's psychological performance proficiency (PPP) will be established on the basis of success: error rates during this formal evaluation phase of training. For example, if a technical-stroke drill required that the player hit 10 basic cross-court backhands that landed beyond the service line and he or she needed five attempts to reach the 10-shot threshold, the PPP for this particular task would be 20% (one success out of five attempts). If he or she had succeeded on the first attempt, the PPP would have been 100% and would immediately allow the athlete to move on the next higher difficulty threshold task. The term "psychological" is added to performance and proficiency (PPP), since it can be inferred that a player possessing an advanced level of technical skills who either masters an easy task immediately (success) or after numerous attempts (reduced performance) does so as a function of mental effort and influences (e.g., motivation + attention + motor control + persistence + physical fitness = an increased probability of success on a task). Add to the equation criticality or pressure components and we delve into the realm of Critical Moment Psychological Performance Proficiency (CMPPP; mental toughness; more on this in Chapter 8).

To expand an athlete's technical and focus (attention) threshold level, it is crucial that he or she masters basic sport-specific performance tasks as soon as possible in the accountability session (fewer attempts to reach a target threshold level that is commensurate with level of technical ability). An athlete is not allowed to move on to the next progressively more difficult task (as mutually established by an athlete's coach and sport psychology practitioner) until the one before it has been completed. This system can be grueling, testing the limits of an athlete's ability to keep trying until success is achieved. In the most difficult threshold iterations, even professional athletes can break down and give up because they are incapable of mastering a particular technical and focus task (reaching their previously established highest threshold or PPP; see flow chart in Figure 7.1).

Figure 7.1 depicts two of a virtually endless list of technical and focus threshold tasks, in this case, specified amounts of tennis backhands that must be hit to a target area on the court before being able to move on to the next, higher level task (STOP or GO). Success and error decisions can be made not only on the basis of the stated outcome goal, but also in the context of technical proficiency (exhibiting technique in accord with parameters that are established by an athlete's coach); meaning that even if the target is hit but faulty technique was exhibited, the result would be considered an error.

In addition to specific technical and focus threshold task iterations, global or overall PPP can be calculated longitudinally. For example, during the season, in formal practice (coach supervised), the player in this case study hit 1550 forehands, of which 1040 were successful and 510 resulted in errors (a forehand PPP of .666). The following figures provide a breakdown of numerous stroke categories or combinations for this particular player.

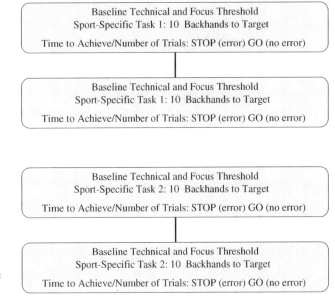

FIGURE 7.1 Two of many sport-specific threshold task iterations.

While these numbers may seem far removed from the mental game, inferences about psychological influences on performance can still be made. Even basic Level I data can be revealing since trends in performance, such as success streaks during which error rates may be much lower than a player's aggregate average, can indicate heightened concentration (attention-focus) or inexplicable errors during a drill on a particular day (or time of day) that normally should be easily mastered by a tournament player and may signal lack of interest or motivation and resultant diminished attention. The documentation of what might be considered routine practice tasks can be illuminating, by providing initial clues about psychological tendencies during training that may later impact performance during actual competition. For example, in our case study, player (EN) made more errors during practice than would be expected on the basis of his level of skill. He especially had difficulty with hitting many balls consecutively without making an error, a requisite for success when playing matches on slower surfaces like clay. Consequently, a direct link could be established between specific poor practice statistics and losing matches that were played on clay.

Tracking global performance statistics during practice can also provide insight into the effects of mental training. For example, EN's season included a pre-intervention phase, or period during which he was observed at every practice session but was not provided with any psychological advice or mental training. In the second portion of the season, the player was taught an intervention, in this case, heart rate variability (HRV) and respiratory biofeedback, that he was told to employ before action (after a drill ceased and before subsequently resuming action). The mental training protocol was taught[1] in an office-laboratory setting and reinforced prior to training (courtside) via a computer screen that showed self-induced responses that were shaped in an attempt to help transfer them from the office to the playing field (pre-action HRV-heart rate deceleration [HRD] see Chapters 2, 9, and 12).

What can be gleaned from global performance statistics are differences between pre-intervention and post-intervention (intervention) success or error outcome. If performance gains can be documented in the intervention phase (compared to the pre-intervention phase), preliminary, lower-level evidence of positive mental training effects can be established. Such information can help inform and guide the evaluation process but still must be viewed with caution, since practice effects, independent of any psychological intervention, may in fact have contributed to improved performance as opposed to mental training induced responses per se. On the other hand, as in the case of this EN, the failure to achieve statistical gains in the intervention phase does not necessarily mean that mental training did not work, since physical and technical deficiencies may be so extensive that they cannot be overcome alone through psychological training (more on this later). Thus, at Level I in the evidence hierarchy, negative findings require that an athlete's performance be further investigated at higher evidentiary levels, while positive intervention findings must be validated in better controlled investigations that establish a more direct association between intervention-induced psychophysiological responses and objective sport-specific outcome measures.

Analyzing Technical and Focus Thresholds: A Season-Long Case Study

The following procedures, data, and analyses were applied to and derived from a regionally ranked junior male tennis tournament player. He was followed throughout his summer tennis season both during practice and competition. Virtually every tennis ball that he hit in the context of structured accountability drills was documented in terms of type of stroke and outcome. His practice sets and tournament matches were also analyzed.

Case Study: Player Athlete's Profile Overview

The CARLSTEDT PROTOCOL

Roland A. Carlstedt, Ph.D., Licensed Psychologist

ABSP-BRC INTERPRETIVE REPORT

Athlete: EN   Sport: Tennis

CSARCS-A

SUBLIMINAL ATTENTION (Hypnotic Susceptibility): 14

SUBLIMINAL REACTIVITY (Neuroticism): 18

SUBLIMINAL COPING (Repressive coping): 13

SUMMARY CLASSIFICATION: MEDIUM-HIGH-MEDIUM

ATHLETE'S PROFILE

Profile: MEDIUM-HIGH-MEDIUM

The above constellation of Medium Subliminal Attention/Hypnotic Susceptibility (SA/HS)–High Subliminal Reactivity/ Neuroticism (SR/N) and Medium Subliminal Coping/Repressive Coping (SC/RC is a 1 RED FLAG PROFILE).

This profile is associated with performance disruptions, especially when stress occurs or increases during competition (e.g., critical moments). Although athletes who are in the MEDIUM range of SA/HS have a slightly heightened ability to focus intensely on the task at hand, once stress in perceived, whether consciously or subliminally (as reflected in physiological measures that are being monitored), if concurrently HIGH in SR/N, there is a tendency to turn their focus inward toward intrusive thoughts that are generated by HIGH SR/N. These intrusive, negative, and catastrophic thoughts get in the way of the so-called just-do-it mode. Instead, thinking takes over, which can lead to a disruption of motor/technical skills.

SC/RC, which serves to suppress negative intrusive thoughts associated with high SR/N, is in the MEDIUM range for this athlete. Thus, it unlikely that SC/RC will have the strength/valence to subvert the potential detrimental consequences of High SR/N, during heightened competitive stress. This athlete is likely to experience an increased level of performance decrement during critical moments during competition, but not to the extent that athletes who exhibit the most performance-detrimental profile will.

Performance Statistics: Technical and Focus Threshold Outcome

Figure 7.2 reveals EN's total tennis stroke success and errors across all accountability sessions in the pre-intervention and intervention. Tennis stroke totals were obtained from numerous task iterations for basic strokes and foundational hitting patterns that are shown in Figures 7.3 to 7.6. It should be noted that success or error criteria are not only based on whether a particular shot landed where it was supposed to, but also on technical ratings. For example, if on a backhand down-the-line, a technical flaw was evident, an error would be noted, even if the ball landed in the target area. When employing technical and focus threshold training, technique and attention are analyzed in

TOTAL: ALL STROKES	Total Attempts-Success %	Total Success-Errors
Pre-Intervention	3366-72%	2442-924
Intervention	1730-57%	992-738
Combined (pre-post intervention)	5096-67%	3434-1662

FIGURE 7.2   Total strokes across all practice accountability sessions.

Forehands (FH: cross-court & down-the-line)	FH Total Attempts - Success%	FH Total Success -Errors	FH-cc Total Attempts - Success%	FH-cc Total Success -Errors	FH-dl Total Attempts - Success%	FH-dl Total Success -Errors
Pre-Intervention	854-73%	625-229	236-69%	164-72	164-69%	113-51
Intervention	696-60%	415-281	421-58%	244-177	63-57%	36-27
Combined (pre-post intervention)	1550-67%	1040-510	657-62%	408-249	227-66%	149-78

FIGURE 7.3   Total forehands across all practice accountability sessions.

Backhands (BH: cross-court & down-the-line)	BH Total Attempts - Success%	BH Total Success -Errors	BH-cc Total Attempts - Success%	BH-cc Total Success -Errors	BH-dl Total Attempts - Success%	BH-dl Total Success -Errors
Pre-Intervention	902-68%	611-291	363-67%	245-118	130-44%	90-40
Intervention	620-60%	373-247	385-58%	225-160	39-48%	19-20
Combined (pre-post intervention)	1518-65%	984-538	748-63%	470-278	169-64%	109-60

FIGURE 7.4   Total backhands across all practice accountability sessions.

Volleys (FH & BH cross-court & down-the-line)	Volley (FH & BH)Total Attempts - Success%	Volley Total Success -Errors	Volley-cc Total Attempts - Success%	Volley-cc Total Success -Errors	Volley-dl Total Attempts - Success%	Volley-dl Total Success -Errors
Tot pre int. drills	333-77%	255-78	69-84%	58-11	111-68%	75-36
Tot post int. drills	184-72%	132-52	106-75%	80-26	82-63%	52-30
Combined (pre-post intervention)	517-75%	387-130	175-79%	138-37	193-66%	127-66

FIGURE 7.5   Total volleys (FH & BH) across all practice accountability sessions.

Serves (First)	Serve: Attempts-Success %	1st Serves Made	1st Serves Missed
Tot pre int. drills	126-50%	63	63
Tot post int. drills	185-41%	75	110
Combined (pre-post intervention)	311-44%	138	173

FIGURE 7.6   Total serves across all practice accountability sessions.

an integrative manner. It is not sufficient to merely tally target or direct outcome success irrespective of technical flaws that need to be remediated. Testing an athlete's ability to perform a task successfully in relationship to both a direct (task result) and indirect (technical standard) outcome measure fosters integrative divided attention or focus. On one hand, an athlete has to be aware of a task's end goal, for example, making a basket from a position on the court, or sinking a putt or hitting a target area with a forehand; yet, doing so is not a sufficient success metric if success can be achieved despite technical deficiencies. For example, Shaquille O'Neal, a notorious poor free-throw shooter, still managed to make some free throws despite having poor technique for this particular basketball task. Since there are numerous subject and sport-technical variables in the task-technique-focus outcome equation, it is important to structure technical and focus threshold training in conjunction with an athlete's coach if a sport psychology practitioner does not have expertise in a particular sport.

Getting back to the aggregate data at first glance, it may be troubling to see that this player's pre-intervention success rate of 72% was significantly higher than in the intervention phase (72% vs. 57%). This disparity is addressed later in the chapter.

Figures 7.2 through 7.5 reflect a breakdown of basic foundational tennis strokes, including the forehand, backhand, volley, and serve success/error rates (note cc = crosscourt; dl = down-the-line).

Practice Strokes-Drills: Success Rates

The previous data and findings (Figures 7.2 through 7.6) on basic tennis stroke success rates emanate from more foundational or routine tasks. In theory, these tasks should be easier for advanced players. However, an easy technical task can evolve into a difficult focusing task if habituation leads to a reduction in motivation to succeed and concomitant fluctuating level of attention.

By contrast, the following data and findings (Figure 7.7) were derived from the so-called drills, or stroke tasks involving variable and random hitting patterns that were designed to simulate the way points evolve and end during actual competition. This Level II technical and focus threshold training has higher evidentiary stature and usually supersedes Level I results in terms of its predictive validity (although this must be determined empirically).

Commentary

What stands out regarding the preceding statistics is that the success percentage in the pre- or non-intervention stage of this EN's structured training was higher than in the intervention phase across all stroke and drill types. Such a finding could be disconcerting to sport psychology practitioners who are convinced of the power of their mental training techniques and ability to teach athletes

Pre-Intervention	Date	Time	Total Success	Total Error	Success %
	28-Jun		193	137	58%
	29-Jun		277	75	79%
	2-Jul		287	53	84%
	9-Jul		339	99	77%
	11-Jul		244	84	74%
	12-Jul	Off			
	16-Jul	10.00	161	78	67%
	16-Jul	14.00	185	98	65%
	18-Jul	13.00	147	43	77%
	19-Jul	14.00	279	58	83%
	20-Jul	Tourney			
	21-Jul	Tourney			
	22-Jul	Off			
	23-Jul	10.00	283	165	63%
	23-Jul	14.00	47	34	58%
	Total				**71%**
Intervention	24-Jul	13.00	109	143	43%
	25-Jul	10.30	192	86	69%
	26-Jul	No Drill			
	26-Jul	12.00	104	65	62%
	27-Jul	No Drill			
	27-Jul	No Drill			
	28-Jul	Off			
	29-Jul	Off			
	30-Jul	10.00	112	121	48%
	30-Jul	14.30	34	33	51%
	1-Aug	10.30	83	71	54%
	1-Aug	14.30	22	37	37%
	2-Aug	Tourney			
	3-Aug	Off			
	6-Aug	Sick			
	13-Aug	10.30	162	80	67%
	13-Aug	15.20	64	31	67%
	14-Aug	Tourney			
	15-Aug	10.30	110	71	61%
	Total				**57%**

FIGURE 7.7 Level II Match simulation drill accountability session: Successful completion.

to use and benefit from them. It also points to the danger of documenting performance and attempts to empirically establish a positive association between an intervention and objective performance outcome measures, especially when global statistics are used as the sole benchmark for improvement. Since negative findings are not that uncommon (even though they are rarely reported), they can call a practitioner's methods into question in the minds of athletes, coaches, consumers, and practitioners themselves, making efficacy testing a potentially perilous endeavor. Nevertheless, in the interest of best practices, ethics, and full disclosure, establishing the validity and reliability of a practitioner's assessment of a client and the efficacy of an intervention is critical to the credibility of the field of sport psychology and must be engaged in, irrespective of outcome results that do not support initial hypotheses or beliefs about an evaluative or mental training approach. It should not be about looking good, but learning as much as one can about an athlete's psychological tendencies and performance.

However, before one concludes that the intervention in this case did not work and may have even contributed to a decline in performance, alternative hypotheses that attempt to explain why a pre–post decline occurred need to be considered. Confounding person factors not relating directly to the intervention include: (1) the player's level of technical and physical ability and medical issues, (2) his level of fitness, (3) scheduling and practice continuity issues, (4) grade of difficulty of practice drills, (5) quality of coaching or remedial advice during drills, and (6) habituation to drills. Factors affecting the intervention include (1) the extent to which mental training could be expected to eradicate or diminish the impact of technical, physical, and medical deficiencies that can play a predominant role in the performance equation, (2) temporal dynamics relating to the learning, administration, and application (by the player) of the mental training method, and (3) insensitivity of the selected outcome benchmark to psychological gains that were made that could be attributed to an intervention but remained masked (e.g., using global practice statistics as a criterion measure to determine intervention effects when micro-level criticality are indicated).

In the case of this player, it should be known that, although a tournament tennis player (with a sectional ranking), he still had significant technical and physical issues that undermined his ability to play at an even higher level (commensurate with his goals), including foot speed and quickness problems. His movement issues were also exacerbated by an overall lack of fitness that in part or at times could be attributed to a medical condition (type 1 diabetes). Scheduling in the intervention phase was also a problem, since he was playing more tournaments in the intervention part of his program, resulting in less concerted technical and focus threshold training. In addition, the transition to the intervention phase was not immediate, with a 1-week vacation interrupting his training continuity. Consequently, upon returning (from the West to the East Coast), in addition to having to readjust his circadian rhythm (a significant issue, especially for a diabetic) he also had to regain his timing and rebuild an already suspect level of physical fitness. Relative to coaching, one must also consider that his drill instructors (tennis coaches) rotated regularly. As such, he was not assured of constant and consistent input from the same coach (coaches had varying levels of experience and knowledge). That, along with the fact that most structured training took place in groups of three players, with players in his group being of a higher or lower level (than him), depending upon who was available on a particular day, may have led to inconsistent coaching input regarding the types of drill, that were carried out, their level of difficulty, and what he should correct. Finally, relative to training issues, it was a long and arduous summer for this player, who had never trained extensively and intensively like he did that season, with burn-out and/or habituation to the redundancy of a full training and tournament schedule leading to less effort during practice sessions in the second segment (intervention phase) of the summer (see Figures 7.7 and 7.8).

A trend that supports this burn-out/habituation and related temporal explanation for his progressive statistical decline (pre- versus intervention) is evident in Figure 7.7. In the early days of technical and focus training, the player went from a low-level baseline threshold of 58% to as high as 84%, and went below 70% only after a day off.

By contrast (Figure 7.9), after EN's first tournament of the season on July 20th, he did not have an accountability session (and regular training) for 3 days. His first-day intervention threshold baseline was 43%. This was understandable, since learning to apply an intervention can be initially

FIGURE 7.8   Temporal differences: Best training phase.

Pre Intervention	Date	Time	Total Success	Total Error	Success %
	28-Jun		193	137	58%
	29-Jun		277	75	**79%**
	2-Jul		287	53	**84%**
	9-Jul		339	99	**77%**
	11-Jul		244	84	**74%**
	12-Jul	Off			
	16-Jul	10.00	161	78	67%
	16-Jul	14.00	185	98	65%
	18-Jul	13.00	147	43	**77%**
	19-Jul	14.00	279	58	**83%**
	20-Jul	Tourney			
	21-Jul	Tourney			
	22-Jul	Off			

Pre Intervention	Date	Time	Total Success	Total Error	Success %
	20-Jul	Tourney			
	21-Jul	Tourney			
	22-Jul	Off			
	23-Jul	10.00	283	165	63%
	23-Jul	14.00	47	34	58%
	Total				**71%**
Intervention	24-Jul	13.00	109	143	**43%**
	25-Jul	10.30	192	86	**69%**
	26-Jul	12.00	104	65	**62%**
	27-Jul	No Drill			
	27-Jul	No Drill			
	28-Jul	Off			
	29-Jul	Off			
	30-Jul	10.00	112	121	**48%**
	30-Jul	14.30	34	33	**51%**
	1-Aug	10.30	83	71	**54%**
	1-Aug	14.30	22	37	**37%**
	2-Aug	Tourney			
	3-Aug	Off			
	6-Aug	Sick			
	13-Aug	10.30	162	80	67%
	13-Aug	15.20	64	31	67%
	14-Aug	Tourney			
	15-Aug	10.30	110	71	61%
	Total				**57%**

FIGURE 7.9   Temporal differences: Declining performance.

disruptive. Consolidating a mental training technique in long-term procedural memory can take time before one engages in it automatically/subliminally without conscious effort. In EN, after a very poor intervention-phase baseline performance, strong strides were made the next 2 days, with his success rate going up to 62% and 69%, respectively. EN's self-report of liking the intervention provided anecdotal feedback that was consistent with his good performance during the initial days of mental training that unfortunately did not hold up. His subsequent decline was preceded by 4 days of having no accountability sessions and 2 full days off. When he resumed his threshold training, PPP ranged from 37% to 54%. Thereafter, he rebounded into the 60% range prior to the end of his season.

In light of his numerous confounding technical, physical, medical, training, and scheduling factors, it becomes apparent that there may have been too much to deal with that could be overcome by mental training alone. These moderating confounding variables may have rendered his global tennis statistics invalid and unreliable (in their aggregate) for the purpose of ascertaining the effects or true efficacy of mental training in this player.

Nevertheless, for the sake of argument, let us assume that derived performance statistics are valid and reliable. If so, how could other confounding variables affect the actual intervention process and lead to statistical findings that do not necessarily support the efficacy of mental training? As is always the case when it comes to interventions, one must be aware of the inherent limitations of mental training. In this individual, a tennis player with significant technical and physical flaws, could one really expect that any psychological performance gains would be reflected in global outcome measures that were designed to directly assess performance on an objective sport-specific task parameter (stroke success)?

A key limitation when using global statistics to criterion reference and evaluate intervention efficacy is not knowing how much of the performance equation in a particular athlete can be explained on the basis of psychological factors? For example, how much of what it takes to hit a forehand actually involves unique psychological factors and how much is strictly a technical or physical action? To answer this question one must first distinguish psychological from technical/physical measures, since in the extreme, one could argue that merely standing up is a psychological act or involves psychological processing. Hence, to answer such a vexing question, one must operationalize as precisely as possible those measures that one considers to be psychological and in the process decide whether more ambiguous constructs are actually of a psychological or physical nature (e.g., when deciding to classify a measure of reaction time or visuoperceptual processing as being psychological or physical). Assuming that the performance equation formula has been written[2] for a specific player and tested (using multiple linear regression and other modeling procedures), one would likely discover that when using a global sport-specific outcome statistic (like forehand success %), technical and physical predictor variables would account for more than 90% of the equation. Ten percent in the performance equation that can be attributed to all psychological variables has rarely been surpassed.

Here is what a performance equation analysis looks like (specific to EN):

Test Variable—Forehand in a combination, match simulation context: Technical Factors: Ready Position Rating (1–5 for all technical variables) Reaction Time + Split Step Action Initiation + Shoulder Turn Backswing + Movement to Ball + Swing-to-Contact + Follow-through + Directional Accuracy + Speed of Ball + Spin-of-Ball + (Measurable Psychological Factors) Pre-Shot Preparation (1–5 for all technical variables) + Pre-Shot Heart Rate Deceleration Inducement + Pre-Shot Heart Rate Variability + Visualization Component + Body Language Interpretation + Shots Completed as Required (Focus/Attention Metric) + Motor Control (Rating of Technical Replication) in Relationship to Performance Outcome Measure(s).

All of the included technical and psychological measures are predictor variables that were selected on the basis of their hypothesized influence on any number of macro- and micro-level criterion (outcome) measures; for example, Task Success Percentage. Once these variables have been quantified over at least 60 trials to attain sufficient statistical power, multiple regression and/or other related data analysis methods will generate a variance-explained coefficient that reflects the additive, integrative effects of any number or these variables (or in a worst-case scenario, no variables would emerge as having predictive validity) on selected performance outcome measures. This recent addition to the Carlstedt Protocol (CP) performance equation analysis system relies on ratings and actual measurement (where possible) of relevant technical, physical, and psychological/behavioral and psychophysiological (e.g., HRV/HD) responses to determine the technical/physical–psychological/behavioral balance of the individualized performance equation. While this new system was not incorporated into EN's technical and focus threshold training, coach, athlete, and sport psychology practitioner feedback clearly implicated technical and physical factors as being most crucial to his successful task performances. This suggests that in this player the road to mental toughness goes through the physical and technical game. However, this is not to imply that his technical/physical deficiencies can be remediated through training alone, since psychological traits and behavioral tendencies including motivation, conscientiousness, determination, and grit, among others that may impact an athlete's training duration, intensity, and quality.

Time to Achieve Change: Temporal Dynamics

Another major issue in the technical-focus threshold equation involves temporal dynamics or time that it takes to achieve enduring change (TAC). TAC can be operationalized as the amount of time that it takes to achieve neuronal consolidation of a technical skill, context-specific attention span, or any other performance-relevant psychological tendency or behavior. Neuronal consolidation can be determined directly through functional magnetic resonance brain imaging (fMRI), electroencephalography (EEG), and other brain imaging methods: less directly, using HRV and other psychophysiological measures; and indirectly, using neuropsychological-type approaches to imply consolidation on the basis of success-error rates and resistance to performance decrement as a function of temporal dynamics. This latter approach was used to evaluate EN's technical and threshold level and is more practical and less expensive than the aforementioned brain imaging procedures. The CP routinely uses HRV/HRD monitoring and analyses as part of its user friendly, inexpensive and criterion-referencing validation paradigm, a biomarker approach centering on measures that have known brain functional and anatomical correlates (e.g., HRD concomitant to the pre-action-to-action left-to-right brain hemispheric shift).

Relative to EN's poor technical and focus threshold training results, one must strongly consider TAC temporal dynamics as being at the heart of his inability to attain increasingly rising thresholds for motor control and attention and associated improved performance. A problem that besets all human helping services, including sport psychology, is establishing reliable and valid individualized time-to-change parameters. Without such guiding metrics, interventions are for the most part ad hoc attempts to "cure," reduce symptoms, and suffering, or in sport psychology, enhance performance. Unfortunately, the TAC issue will continue to persist as long as treatment or intervention paradigms are essentially practitioner-based, that is, structured to accommodate practical and financial realities that are associated with having a private practice and even in a TEAM CONSULTING context. Sessions with patients and athletes are sporadic, usually a few times a week at the most, when many sessions spanning many hours over consecutive days and weeks might be what it takes to reach the TAC threshold. By not reaching the TAC threshold for each individual athlete or patient, it is unlikely that issues and problems that may have taken a lifetime or career to develop can be ameliorated, let alone eradicated through perfunctory, cursory treatment, intervention, and/or training efforts that are administered devoid of an evidence-based temporal framework.

EN's eventual improvement in training and tournament competition ultimately may be predicated on determining his TAC for technical and attention deficits, an analytic pursuit on the part of coaches and sport psychology practitioners that can take much time and effort; yet it must be done in the interest of gold standard client services.

Criterion Referencing Threshold Training With Higher Evidentiary Outcome

While technical and associated focus/attention deficits and attempts to reduce or eliminate them in the context of training can be measured in a straightforward manner, one cannot be absolutely certain that gains or losses in a practice setting will transfer to actual official competition. For example, although EN displayed inconsistent threshold performance throughout his summer season indicative of a lack of technical acumen, motor control, and sustained attention (low thresholds), it is still important to engage in confirmatory analyses by criterion-referencing threshold results that were derived during training with his match performance. Conceivably, especially those epochs in which his technical/focus thresholds were relatively high and fairly stable (July 25 and 26 and two sessions on August 13) may reflect his best baseline or threshold range (Individual Optimum Threshold Zone [IOTZ]), a level of performance, that if and when accessed, may be associated with greater success during real competition. To determine if this is the case with EN, it is necessary to compare his training technical and focus thresholds with match outcome and related sport-specific (tennis) statistics. If his match performance turns out to be better than expected (compared to previous seasons and and in light of identified technical and focus problems) despite a poor threshold training record, one can assume that his IOTZ has been consolidated in long-term procedural memory and can be manifested even during competition where pressure is thought to be greater than in training. Such a positive scenario suggests that a player is a "match" player in contrast to a "training weltmeister" (training champ) who excels in practice but tends to falter during match play or official games. If no differences emerge across practice and competition, then technical-physical-focus thresholds are likely to be true or real, meaning that technical–physical, focus, and/or other deficits need to be remediated in their own right (independently) if it is to be expected that significant gains during competition can be made.

The following section contains findings pertaining to EN's practice and tournament sets and matches.

Match Performance Statistics With Criticality Analysis

PRACTICE SETS (FIGURE 7.10)

The findings depicted in Practice Sets (Figures 7.10 and 7.11) are consistent with EN's overall poor technical and focus threshold training results. It is again notable that his performance in the pre-intervention phase was better than in the intervention phase for the most important outcome measures, including Games Won, Games Lost, and Critical Moment level 4 points.

OFFICIAL TOURNAMENT MATCHES

EN did not fare better in official tournament matches, winning only one of four matches and considerably less than 50% of critical moment level 4 points.

COMMENTARY

On the basis of the practice sets and official match outcome findings, one can conclude that EN's actual performance equation is predominantly mediated by technical factors that need to be addressed before one can expect that psychological factors and mental training interventions will have an impact relative to his improvement as a tennis player. Thus, his technical and focus threshold levels are real or true indicators of where he stands as a player. In other words, his poor training threshold performance benchmarks are very likely not psychologically mediated, and indeed, EN has major physical and technical deficits that need to be reduced or eradicated before one can expect performance gains during matches and a climb in the rankings.

So what can be done to get EN to the next level? First of all, threshold training should be continued and intensified, albeit in a more customized manner and independent of group training drills into which his accountability sessions were incorporated. Moreover, he must be trained within a temporally structured, systematic TAC framework until technical and focus thresholds are incrementally reached and surpassed on a daily basis. This may require long, sustained, and intensive technical and focus threshold epochs to reach the TAC thresholds that are set as target levels. The failure to empirically attain TAC, even if an athlete trains for a long duration, will not lead to enduring neuronal consolidation in long-term procedural memory. Hence, threshold training is all about both quantity and quality and the documentation of the process statistically to determine if and when TAC occurs.

Match Performance Statistics with Criticality Analysis

Practice Sets

Date	SETS	GWON	GLOST	PTWON	PTLOST	PT %
2-Jul	3 sets	13	12	85	80	51
9-Jul	1 set	7	5	36	39	48
12-Jul	2 sets	12	6	65	50	52
18-Jul	3 sets	13	15	98	100	49
23-Jul	1 set	3	6	25	35	41
Intervention						
24-Jul	2 sets	12	10	87	73	55
26-Jul	1 set	6	2	28	16	63
27-Jul	1 set	3	6	37	42	47
27-Jul	2 sets	9	9	64	63	51
1-Aug	1 set	2	6	23	33	41
13-Aug	1 set	1	6	13	25	34
13-Aug	2 sets	1	12	31	62	33
15-Aug	1 set	7	6	51	45	53

Date	CM1WON	CM1LOST	CM2W	CM2L	CM3W	CM3L
2-Jul	11	6	5	11	45	41
9-Jul	1	8	14	20	10	9
12-Jul	4	8	31	23	24	15
18-Jul	43	34	16	16	6	10
23-Jul	9	13	0	1	12	14
Intervention						
24-Jul	8	4	22	32	47	30
26-Jul	5	3	12	10	10	3
27-Jul	7	8	7	13	18	16
27-Jul	12	8	22	33	24	16
1-Aug	1	8	6	5	10	11
13-Aug	5	0	2	12	2	6
13-Aug	3	4	7	24	11	19
15-Aug	2	5	16	11	23	21

Date	CM4WON	CM4LOST	CM5WON	CM5LOST
2-Jul	24	21	0	1
9-Jul	11	2	0	0
12-Jul	5	4	0	0
18-Jul	33	39	0	0
23-Jul	4	7	0	0
Intervention				
24-Jul	10	9	0	0
26-Jul	0	1	0	0
27-Jul	5	5	0	0
27-Jul	5	5	1	1
1-Aug	6	8	0	1
13-Aug	3	7	0	0
13-Aug	10	15	0	0
15-Aug	10	8	0	0

FIGURE 7.10   Practice sets and criticality statistics by date.

TECHNICAL AND FOCUS THRESHOLD TRAINING: STEP BY STEP

1. Comprehensive analysis of an athlete's technical and physical game

   Step 1 involves a coach or expert sport psychology practitioner in consultation with one another identifying an athlete's technical and physical strengths and weaknesses.

2. Design accountability sessions

   Step 2 involves designing accountability sessions (see Figure 7.12) in which sport-specific tasks are structured in the context of designated technical, physical, movement, reaction time and repetition (focus) predictor, and objective outcome measures; parameters and ratings that are

	GWON	GLOST	POINTWON	POINTLOST
TOTAL PRE-INTERVENTION	48	44	309	304
TOTAL INTERVENTION	41	57	334	359
TOTAL	89	101	643	663

CM1Won	CM1Lost	CM2Won	CM2Lost	CM3Won	CM3Lost
Pre-68	69	66	71	97	89
Interven-43	40	94	140	145	122
Total-111	109	160	211	242	211

CM4Won	CM4Lost	CM5Won	CM5Lost
Pre-77	73	0	1
Interven-49	58	1	2
Total-126	131	1	3

FIGURE 7.11   Practice sets total outcome and criticality statistics.

commensurate with an athlete's level of skill. Every identified technical and physical component of an athlete's game is tested. First or initial tests in an accountability session establish an athlete's baseline motor-control and focus threshold level. Subsequent accountability sessions require reaching and exceeding higher technical and focus thresholds. There are no set threshold ceilings, because the testing process is open-ended.

3. Determining outcome and threshold training efficacy

Step 3 involves calculating an athlete's PPP and threshold levels for sport-specific tasks. Once a PPP performance threshold plateau is attained and consistently sustained, Time-to-Achieve-Change (TAC) can be inferred. Training PPP and TAC results are cross-validated or criterion-referenced in the context of higher level evidentiary performance outcome measures, such as practice games/matches and official league/tournament games/matches.

Official Tournament Matches

Date	GWON	LOST	PTWON	PLOST	PT %
7-Jul	12	3	60	34	0.57
8-Jul	2	12	32	59	0.35
21-Jul	1	12	38	65	0.37
2-Aug	9	13	56	73	0.43

	CM1Won	CM1Lost	CM2Won	CM2Lost	CM3Won	CM3Lost
7-Jul	15	8	11	12	29	11
8-Jul			11	23	17	30
21-Jul				7	34	44
2-Aug	4	3	3	1	22	32
Totals	19	11	25	43	102	117

Date	CM4Won	CM4Lost	CM5Won	CM5Lost
7-Jul	5	3		
8-Jul	4	6		
21-Jul	4	14		
2-Aug	22	28	4	9
Totals	35	51	4	9

FIGURE 7.12   Official tournament match outcome and criticality statistics.

Threshold Training Matrix: Sport-Specific Samples

Figure 7.13 contains sample sport-specific threshold training drills with specified threshold goals. Drill operationalizations and iterations are almost endless and should be structured in accord with coach and sport psychology practitioner analyses of an athlete's technical/physical game and focus (attention and motor control). The aforementioned threshold levels (goals) are arbitrary. They should be customized/individualized (for each athlete) once baseline technical and threshold levels have been established for as many relevant sport-specific tasks and performance outcome measures that are deemed highly relevant to an athlete's game and eventual ability to improve.

Sample PPP-Threshold Level Calculation: Soccer Player Example

Task: Dribble from 25 m through an obstacle course of cones and then shoot on small goal target area after last cone (10 m from goal target area).

Trials: Ten trials must be successfully completed before Threshold Level 1 is reached (passed) and a GO is awarded (moving on to Threshold Level 2 trials).

Success: Success in relationship to this task is operationalized as completing the obstacle course in 15 sec or less with a culminating shot that goes through the small target goal. Both success metrics must be achieved (time and shot). Failure to complete the task results in a STOP or having to repeat the task again.

Calculation Sport-Specific Task PPP and Threshold Level: The first threshold trial is the baseline trial that establishes the initial threshold for a specific task. If an athlete successfully completes all trials within a defined task threshold level on the first attempt (in the case of a soccer player being evaluated within the aforementioned threshold testing paradigm: for 10 successful timed dribble/obstacle/shot trials [no errors in time or shot]), his or her PPP would be 100%, or 1.000. If it took two attempts to go error free, the PPP would be $(1/2)$, or 50% or .500. Ten attempts to achieve success would result in a PPP of 10%, or .100. Threshold level is expressed as follows: $8^1 = 8$ successful trials (out of 10 the upper threshold in round 1) $24^3 = 24$ successful trials extending into round three in which four successful trials were completed before an error occurred. Threshold can change continually, increasing or decreasing, and should be dated and entered into an Excel database.

Goal: The ultimate goal is to become as psychologically proficient in as many technical/focus threshold tasks as possible by completing designated/defined/delineated tasks in as few attempts as possible.

Summary

Technical and focus threshold testing is a low-tech method that is used to help determine the extent to which an athlete exhibits technical/motor control and concomitant focus or attention in the context of sport-specific task challenges of increasing level of difficulty. It is an important first step in on-the-playing-field assessment of technical/physical and psychological performance, allowing a coach and sport psychology practitioner to quantify technical–psychological balance or how much of an

Practitioner Challenge: Construct a technical and focus threshold testing model and hypothetical outcome data for a sport that you have advanced knowledge of or expertise in.

Sport-Specific Task	Threshold 1	Threshold 2	Threshold 3	Threshold 4	Threshold 5
Tennis: Combination Drill with Concluding Backhand Passing Shot	10 trials in a row with success outcome = GO	20 trials in a row with success outcome = GO	30 trials in a row with success outcome = GO	40 trials in a row with success outcome = GO	50 trials in a row with success outcome = GO
Golf: Drive Length and Accuracy with Technical Rating	10 trials in a row with success outcome = GO	20 trials in a row with success outcome = GO	30 trials in a row with success outcome = GO	40 trials in a row with success outcome = GO	50 trials in a row with success outcome = GO
Basketball: Movement, Dribble, and Shoot with Time Limit	10 trials in a row with success outcome = GO	20 trials in a row with success outcome = GO	30 trials in a row with success outcome = GO	40 trials in a row with success outcome = GO	50 trials in a row with success outcome = GO
Football: Lineman-Response-to-Snap with Play Response and Movement Requirement with Reaction Time	10 trials in a row with success outcome = GO	20 trials in a row with success outcome = GO	30 trials in a row with success outcome = GO	40 trials in a row with success outcome = GO	50 trials in a row with success outcome = GO
Soccer: Dribbling from 25 meters with cone obstacles and shot to small goal target with time limit	10 trials in a row with success outcome = GO	20 trials in a row with success outcome = GO	30 trials in a row with success outcome = GO	40 trials in a row with success outcome = GO	50 trials in a row with success outcome = GO
Alpine Ski Racing: Abbreviated slalom with time limit and technical rating	10 trials in a row with success outcome = GO	20 trials in a row with success outcome = GO	30 trials in a row with success outcome = GO	40 trials in a row with success outcome = GO	50 trials in a row with success outcome = GO
Baseball: Quality-of-at-bat (QAB) rating; Success Based on Positive Outcome QAB; Strike/Missing Ball Negates Trial	10 trials in a row with success outcome = GO	20 trials in a row with success outcome = GO	30 trials in a row with success outcome = GO	40 trials in a row with success outcome = GO	50 trials in a row with success outcome = GO

FIGURE 7.13   Threshold training as a function of sport and specific task.

athlete's performance equation can be explained on the basis of mind–body factors. It provides criterion-referencing for in-office self-report and psychological test scores as well as practitioner intuition.

This method should used by practitioners to not only assess baseline technical and focus performance, but as an intervention to shape technical changes and increase focus/attention within a more ecologically valid testing paradigm.

Notes

1. Note that the terms "taught" and "shaped" were used as opposed to "learned," since one cannot be certain that laboratory or office-based responses to mental training will transfer to the playing field or that they will be associated with improvements in performance. Intervention efficacy cannot be assumed without engaging in longitudinal repeated predictor-outcome investigations at the intra-individual level (in this case, determining how much of the variance in successful threshold training outcome measures can be attributed to HRV, or whether threshold training alone leads to performance gains).

2. The performance equation formula consists of all predictor variables that a coach or sport psychology practitioner hypothesizes to have a performance-influencing impact. It consists of any number of technical, physical, psychological, and other factors that are measurable repeatedly in the context of sport-specific statistical outcome measures.

Sport Psychological Performance Statistics and Analysis II: Criticality Analyses During Training and Competition

Critical Moment Testing Paradigm

The Critical Moment (CMT) testing paradigm (criticality analysis) introduces psychological stressors to practice settings by attaching physical, psychological, and material value to what would otherwise be routine moments during training. CMT brings accountability to practice sessions by documenting performance throughout a training period or on demand during specific testing epochs. This procedure was also designed to assess athletes' ability to master performance tasks while under induced pressure during training. It is a step up in the evidence hierarchy and augments initial office-based self-report test and laboratory-derived psychophysiological measures that purportedly reflect and predict responses to stress (mental toughness), using more ecologically valid outcome measures. As previously mentioned, while profiles and responses that were derived from the Athlete's Profile (AP) and heart rate variability-based stress test have a relatively high degree of predictive validity, group-derived validity and reliability coefficients do not always generalize to each unique individual athlete. Furthermore, although the ideal and worst APs are highly predictive of critical moment performance since they are only exhibited by a minority of athletes (with most having more ambiguous profiles), it is prudent to always approach athlete assessment from an integrative and multimodal/multifactorial perspective. Hence, ecological, on-the-playing-field testing should always be a culminating procedure in the evidence chain, even when previous findings are highly suggestive or predictive of stress responses, and especially when ambiguity and the possibility of false-positive and -negative findings exist.

CMT is the second assessment procedure in the ABSP-Carlstedt protocol (ABSP-CP) that takes place on the playing field during practice (preceded by or concurrent with Technical and Focus Threshold testing; see Chapter 7). It is a systematic, structured, and standardized test battery for determining athletes' performance and responses to psychological stressors that are introduced during training (randomly; athlete does not know when). The purpose of this test is to create psychological stress in a performance situation that otherwise might be perceived as routine and innocuous by an athlete. Performance on the CMS test results in a *Psychological Proficiency Quotient: Critical*

Moments (PPQ: CM-T; or Mental Toughness Quotient-T [MTQ-T, T = training context]) that quantifies the extent to which an athlete has mastered designated critical moments during training.

CMT paradigms are sport specific and can be customized so as to simulate important actions or tasks that are common and important to a particular sport. It requires that an athlete carry out a designated sport-specific task either spontaneously (when told to by a coach or sport psychology practitioner) or as part of a formal CM test component, as opposed to allowing athletes to practice whatever they want to work on all of the time. In the latter scenario, an athlete would be told that he or she can do what he or she wants to do for a certain period of time, like shoot jump shots from the perimeter (basketball) for 20 minutes. Normally, such an unstructured type of practice drill takes place without much oversight beyond occasional remarks by a coach, and there are usually no tangible consequences for missing shots and overall sub-par performance. Rarely is every task or action documented statistically. By contrast, in the CM testing situation, any coach-designated shot would be counted toward a player's CM psychological proficiency score (CMPPQ). In the CM performance-testing situation, all task outcomes are noted (successful or unsuccessful). At random times (unknown to the player, but known to the coach) a so-called *critical moment* is announced by designating a particular shot or task as a "money ball" moment. In football, a routine practice situation might involve a quarterback passing to a receiver who is running a particular route, a relatively easy task that could be made more stressful if it were structured to include a CM component. The required CM drill might be structured to involve 10 pass attempts, with three being randomly deemed money-ball passes that have to be completed. In both scenarios, missed money balls, either an errant shot in basketball or faulty pass in football, would have consequences. On the positive side, achieving a high aggregate CM money-ball percentage (successes divided by attempts) would be rewarded, whereas a low total CM proficiency score would result in punishment. For example, players who exceed their initial CM proficiency rating, in a subsequent practice session might receive tokens toward a dinner or movie ticket that could be redeemed at specific times during the season. By contrast, athletes who fail to exceed baseline CM benchmarks might be required to run extra laps after practice, or lose access to or not be allowed to do something for a day (e.g., not be allowed to send text messages or play video games). The goal of the CM testing is to regularly and randomly expose athletes to potential stressors in the context of mere training in an attempt to habituate or inoculate them to pressure over time (longitudinally). The hypothesis being (that always needs to be tested at the intra-individual level regardless of group findings) that athletes who continually are aware of and encounter or confront critical moments, will, over time, become less psychophysiologically reactive (i.e., less nervous), maintain greater mental and technical control, and perform better under pressure during real competition. Competitive stress inoculation is thought to function similarly to clinical situations in which patients are required to repeatedly confront their fears and phobias in an attempt to habituate to and eventually master stressors (like flying or avoiding elevators) that can have a negative impact on one's well-being. However, this premise must always be tested empirically to determine the extent to which pressure performance increases or decreases over time, and between money-ball performance during practice and simulated and real competition.

Critical Moment Testing Paradigms

The CP has created and validated test paradigms for numerous sports, including baseball–softball, basketball, football, ice hockey, soccer, tennis, and golf along with position-specific tasks (e.g., for a lineman in football). An overview of CMS testing along with a select case is presented next.

Overview: Step by Step

(A) Random CMS Testing:

1. Player/Athlete engages in a practice routine.
2. Coach or sport psychology practitioner observes practice (teammates can also be used to carry out testing). Since athletes have been informed that they may be randomly required to perform specific tasks, they must be ready to respond appropriately on demand.
3. Tester will attempt to interject pressure situations proportionately with about 10% to 15% of all sport-specific tasks being designated money ball/critical moments. For example, in tennis, where players frequently just hit in an unstructured manner, over the course of an hour, hundreds of balls can be hit. In such a hitting scenario, if 1000 balls were hit, about 100 to 150 balls hit should be designated money balls.
4. When money ball is called out, the athlete must generate a sport task-specific/technical response and achieve a required outcome, for example, hitting an immediate winner in tennis.
5. Designated sport/task-specific responses and outcome results are made known prior to a practice session so that an athlete is aware that at some point he or she must respond accordingly (e.g., drive a golf ball 200 yards to the left side of the course on demand).
6. Sport-specific/task iterations can be variable from money ball to money ball or kept constant (e.g., in tennis, having to hit an immediate winner each time money ball is called, or requiring an immediate winner, but designating a directional target [e.g., winner down the line]).
7. Operationalizations of money-ball designated responses are virtually limitless. They should be commensurate with the ability level of the athlete being tested.
8. Statistics must be kept: (a) the total number of a sport-specific task, (b) money-ball designated task(s) and response(s) should be noted in a computer template or scorebook. The key outcome statistics are: (1) total tasks (e.g., 1,000), (2) total successes (e.g., 750 out of 1000), (3) total money ball (e.g., 120), and (4) total money-ball successes (e.g., 80 out of 120). In this example, one would then compare routine-task success % with money-ball success %, which in this example would be 75% routine performance success rate versus 67% money-ball performance success, or Psychological Performance Proficiency Quotient: Routine Moments versus PPPQ: Critical Moments, also known as Mental Toughness Quotient.
9. Attaining the level of statistical power that balances the possibility of making a Type I versus Type II error (.80), at the individual (intra-individual) requires about 60 repeated measures. As such, if at least 60 repetitions cannot be achieved in one training session, CMS testing should be carried over to the next practice session. If the athlete's sport involves tasks with hundreds of repetitions (like tennis), 60 repetitions (money ball encounters) can easily be attained in one session, whereas in a sport like football, it is unlikely that sufficient repeated measures, for example, an offensive lineman (blocker), can be achieved in one session (multiple sessions would usually be required to arrive at PPPQ).
10. Pressure performance/Critical Moment/Money-Ball statistics should be entered into a database for comparative and other analytic purposes, including the eventual closing out of an athlete's money-ball bank for reward and punishment purposes. For example, over the course of a 6-month season, one could check on an athlete's money-ball account status and issue rewards and punishment accordingly monthly or even weekly. Accountability reinforcement need not only be based on having a greater money-ball success than routine-moment task performance success rate. One could also reward an athlete whose poor money-ball PPPQ improves in, for example, month 2, even though he or she still

falters more than succeeds during these critical moments. Nevertheless, there should also be a straightforward ranking of all players/athletes on a team (when entire teams are being worked with/tested), with a prize and punishment structure in place that is used to determine who gets what at the end of the season.

11. In addition to readily obtainable statistical comparisons that are derived from sport-specific routine tasks (critical moment/money ball versus routine task performance; intra- & inter-comparisons) from which one can infer or hypothetically implicate psychological processes in the performance equation, it is recommended that participating athletes are assessed for Athlete's Profile constellation (CSARCS-A), Serial 7s stress test responding, neurocognition, and, if possible, heart rate variability (HRV) using the BioCom and/or Polar systems and integrated Carlstedt Protocol HRV psychologically mediated heart deceleration (HRD/HRV) and autonomic nervous system (ANS) critical moment practice/training paradigms. HRV/HRD responses are analyzed prior to practice, during time-outs, and pre- and action phases of sport-specific tasks, as well as after training to determine the extent to which brain–heart–mind–body responses are associated with critical moment/money-ball responses and an athlete's CMS test-generated PPPQ-CM. Doing so can provide important insight into the psychological etiology of pressure performance at the individual level (in each athlete), which is important in the context of eventual interventional pursuits to enhance performance during critical moments.

Sport-Specific Critical Moment Testing: Baseball Paradigm Case Study

Players from an NCAA Division II baseball team were assessed on critical moment stress responding after having taken standard CP PHO-Athlete's Profile (CSARCS-A), BRC neurocognitive, and laboratory-based psychophysiological (HRV) tests. Players were scheduled individually to undergo CMST at an indoor training facility. Teammates were on hand to simulate game conditions and were told to act like opponents and fans by bantering and engaging in other disruptive behavior to create noise and distractions that are common at baseball games.

Players were told that they would participate in three rounds of hitting against a programmable pitching machine. Each round consisted of 10 swings or hitting attempts. Of the 10 attempts, one swing was randomly (unknown to the batter) designated as a critical moment or money ball (one money ball per round or three in total 1×3 rounds). Money balls or critical moments carry special weight in the evaluation process, since an athlete's success rate or batting percentage in these situations along with the *Quality of At Bat* (QAB) for critical moments are the determinants for the issuance of rewards or punishment. The critical moment or money-ball score supersedes the aggregate task success score or percentage (which includes money balls). However, in the case of a tie(s), the aggregate score/percentage acts as the tie-breaker (this fosters concentration throughout the entire task rounds since noncritical moment attempts have potential major importance).

Players had the option of not: swinging at a pitch to simulate dynamics of hitter-pitcher encounters that occur in real games; when players try to predict pitches in advance, base their swings on tactical and situational considerations, or don't swing if the pitch is bad (a ball or unexpected type of pitch). Each swing and resultant outcome was notated and attributed a QAB rating ranging from zero to seven points (Figure 8.1).

Since the critical moment task was carried out on a confined baseball training field, QAB ratings (as opposed to the real outcome that would occur in an actual game) were determined by the sport

Home Run = 7
Triple = 6
Double = 5
Single = 4
Lineout = 3
Fly Out = 2
Ground-out = 2
Pop Up = 1
Foul Ball = 1
Strike = 0

FIGURE 8.1   Quality of at-bat ratings.

psychology practitioner, a former high-level college player and mental training coordinator of a professional baseball team (Major League Baseball [MLB]) using the Carlstedt Protocol Quality of at-bat-Critical Moments Paradigm for baseball as a guiding framework. Such a constraint or limitation (indoor batting-range experimental format) obviously reduces ecological validity, but it is still much higher than in laboratory-based testing or on the basis of self-report assessments alone. It should also be noted that for research purposes, ideally one would use multiple expert raters to determine a quality of at-bat or other qualitative ratings of performance. However, in clinical or practice settings, this is not always necessary provided that a practitioner is a recognized expert in a specific sport. If not, practitioners should always administer CMST in conjunction with a coach or designated expert.

Reward incentives and punishment were gift certificates for dinners in a restaurant and having to run extra laps after practice, respectively. The top and second-highest scoring player would receive prizes while all other players would be required to engage in additional physical training commensurate with their scores (lowest scorer would have to run the most amount of laps).

Anecdotally, one will frequently observe that athletes of all levels also are motivated intrinsically to compete and want to perform well and win, even in intra-squad competitive events or tasks that are ancillary or irrelevant to real game statistical performance. As such, there often is an inherent feeling of tension among players who participate in CMST, with reward–punishment and spectator effects adding further to the generation of competitive stress. The fact that players only get one swing per scored event (each swing is analogous to one at-bat in a real game) in the CMST paradigm for baseball (as opposed to at least three swings per at-bat in a real baseball game) presents an additional challenge in that batters know that they have to make each swing count. The structure of the CMST for all sports demands successful performance in the moment, on demand.

As is often the case, an athlete's PHO Athlete's Profile can help a practitioner or coach forecast in advance, who in CMST situations is more or less likely to experience nervousness prior to action, with the ideal and worst profiles being the most predictive of such a tendency. Competitive stress responding can also be assessed within the actual testing paradigm by monitoring pre-action during and post-action neuropsychophysiological responses to validate anecdotal observations or suppositions about players, and to criterion-reference Athlete's Profile predictions with objective mind–body measures that reflect autonomic nervous system reactivity and motor control.

In this particular baseball paradigm and as is required in all ABSP student-researcher final project tests of the CP, at minimum, the measurement of HRV takes place throughout the CMST process. Specifically, players' heart activity is monitored for 2 minutes prior to the overall testing (before batting commences) and then for 2 minutes prior to the second and third rounds, followed by a final, post-CMST 2-minute monitoring session. Resulting HRV can then be analyzed prospectively and retrospectively in the context of a player's quality of at-bat for each round (micro-level analysis) and globally (association between and among pre- or post-CMST HRV and QAB score for each round or total QAB score). In addition to HRV, an athlete's relative cortical activation (i.e., cerebral laterality) was also determined using a *line-bisecting* (LB) test that was administered prior to batting and before each round. The LB test is elaborated elsewhere (see Carlstedt, 2001), but it essentially provides basic insight into emotional processing and visuoperceptual shifts that are associated with pre-action strategic planning and the transition to task-related motor action.

It should be noted that, at the most basic level, neuropsychophysiological monitoring need not be incorporated into the CMST process. HRV and LB procedures were mentioned for descriptive purposes. Their application is for the most part contingent on a practitioner's scope of training. Those who have special training in psychophysiology, applied neuroscience, and the methodologies that are advanced in this book, should also strive to incorporate high evidentiary procedures into the athlete assessment and intervention process personally, or collaborate with practitioners who have advanced training in applications and methods that are crucial to best practices in applied sport psychology. Nevertheless, CMST, in and of itself, can be very revealing and can be administered by virtually all practitioners provided that they have expertise in a specific sport.

Outcome Data Sets

The following outcome tables (Figures 8.2 and 8.3) present various levels of criticality analyses. At the most basic level, the quality of at-bat percentage can be compared with money-ball percentage in an attempt to discern if performance degrades as a function of the money-ball pressure condition or to what extent it may actually improve. Figure 8.2 reveals each tested player's critical moment performance in the context of quality of at-bat points accrued percentage (in the money-ball and non-money-ball condition) and in terms of straightforward batting average differences. Quality of at-bat metrics are designed to take luck and fielding factors out of the hitting equation by rewarding the strength of a struck ball (speed, power, intention, intentional direction; e.g., a successful sacrifice bunt or hit-and-run; a hard line-drive that is caught) and negatively quantify an unintentional weak hit (e.g., a "cheap" infield dribbler resulting in a single). Hence, in terms of analyzing pressure performance, in this paradigm, QAB%—CM-MB% changes carry more interpretive weight than mere BA/CM-BA% changes. Also depicted are each player's Athlete's Profile PHO factors and directional rating, that is, to what extent a player's QAB% versus QAB-Money-Ball% change was consistent with what would have been predicted based on these pressure performance relevant psychological/behavioral factors (see Chapter 4 for an in-depth explication of the Athlete's Profile).

Interpretations

Since all players were tested to determine their Athlete's Profile, using the CSARCS-A performance was analyzed in the context of each athlete's PHO constellation. This was done retrospectively by assigning a response consistency rating to each player. One can also prospectively attempt to predict how an athlete will respond under pressure using the CSARCS-A, because of its very high predictive validity, often being used for initial mental toughness screening. Interestingly, almost half of this team's players were high in subliminal reactivity (neuroticism-N) and on the cusp of having the most pressure-performance-hindering Athlete's Profile. As such, one could

NAME	QAB %	CM-Money Ball %	BA %	CM BA %	PPPQ-CM (rank)	SA	SR	SC	AP-PC
A	37	43	0.400	0.333	.37(11)	28	4	18	***
B	37	38	0.333	0.333	.37(10)	20	14	11	**
BM	38	33	0.333	0.333	.38(7)	23	17	13	****
BN	40	33	0.367	0.333	.40(2)	24	18	14	****
C	39	43	0.367	0.667	.39(4)	12	7	21	****
D	42	29	0.433	0.000	.42(1)	19	7	22	*
N	39	38	0.367	0.333	.39(4)	22	18	12	***
P	39	38	0.367	0.333	.39(4)	16	18	15	***
PL	38	52	0.300	0.667	.38(7)	24	11	18	***
S	38	57	0.333	1.000	.38(7)	26	12	17	***
SO	35	38	0.300	0.333	.35(12)	29	12	18	***
T	40	52	0.400	0.667	.40(2)	20	7	13	***

Operationalizations of Measures: QAB % = total number of points for three rounds of hitting (30 swings; 10 per round) divided by total possible points for three rounds of hitting (210; these include the money ball). Money Ball % = total number of points for the three money balls (three swings) divided by total possible points for three money ball swings (21). Athlete's Profile Predicted Performance Change (AP-PC): **** highly consistent *** consistent ** inconsistent * very inconsistent.

FIGURE 8.2   QAB and criticality performance.

expect this team to be more likely to falter in critical moments of real games. In this particular test/assessment paradigm, 10 out of 12 players performed consistently or highly consistently with what would be expected on the basis of their PHO constellation (SA-SR-SC) with high SR (N) players exhibiting declines and low SR (N) demonstrating gains in the money-ball condition, with the exception of player "D," a player on the verge of the Ideal Athlete's Profile who performed worse in the critical moment condition. Because, ultimately, group norms or findings should at best help guide player/team evaluations and eventual interventions, it is important to closely assess each athlete individually. In the case of player "D," one should repeat CMST to help determine to what extent an initial test finding holds up over the course of repeated measures and in the context of real competition.

It should be noted that there should usually be more trials or repeated measures than were obtained from this team. Time and facility usage constraints prevented the tester from carrying out the about 60 repeated measures (in this case swings) per player that are required to approach acceptable levels of statistical power that allows one to make statistical inferences with a higher level of confidence. Nevertheless, in the context of money balls, less may be more in the sense that having too many designated critical moments can lead to a habituation effect over time with players no longer registering cognitively the difference between a regular and a money-ball trial. To avoid or attenuate the habituation effect, it is important to make sure that athletes are continually made aware of the positive and negative consequences of money-ball performance so as to facilitate their motivation to perform well during critical moments.

Since this team's players were also assessed neurocognitively and psychophysiologically, it was possible to derive group performance associations between and among brain–mind–body measures and micro-level critical moment and macro-level performance outcome measures. They are presented as follows (Figure 8.3). It should be noted that sample size limitations preclude lending too much explanatory credence to these findings. Nevertheless, this data has exploratory relevance and will be entered into the American Board of Sport Psychology Universal Trial (clinical and sport and performance) database for sport/athlete specific analysis and meta-analytic purposes.

Neurocognition	QAB	CMQAB	BA	CMBA
N1			-.70	
N5			.69	
N6			.70	
N13		-.73		
N20			.76	
N27		-.65		
N31				-.71
N36	.71			

Key:N1 = (immediate recall) Frontal/Parietal; N5 = (learning rate) Frontal/Parietal; N6 = (intrusion errors) Frontal/Parietal; N13 = (sustained attention-reaction time) Pre-Frontal/Frontal/Parietal/Temporal/Basal Ganglia/Thalamus; N20 = (motor tapping) Motor/Basal Ganglia/Cerebellum; N27 = (verbal interference/color) Frontal/Parietal/Occipital/Anterior Cingulate; N31 = (maze-path learning time) Pre-Frontal/Frontal/Motor/Parietal/Occipital; N36 = (Go-no-Go/inhibition-false misses) Pre-Frontal/Frontal.

FIGURE 8.3 Group findings: Neurocognition and outcome.

The neurocognition measures in Figure 8.4 emanate from the Brain Resource Company's validated Internet-based neurocognitive test battery that is part of the ABSP-CP Athlete's Profile testing paradigm. The following neuro-anatomical/functionality chart (Figure 8.4; sample only; not from

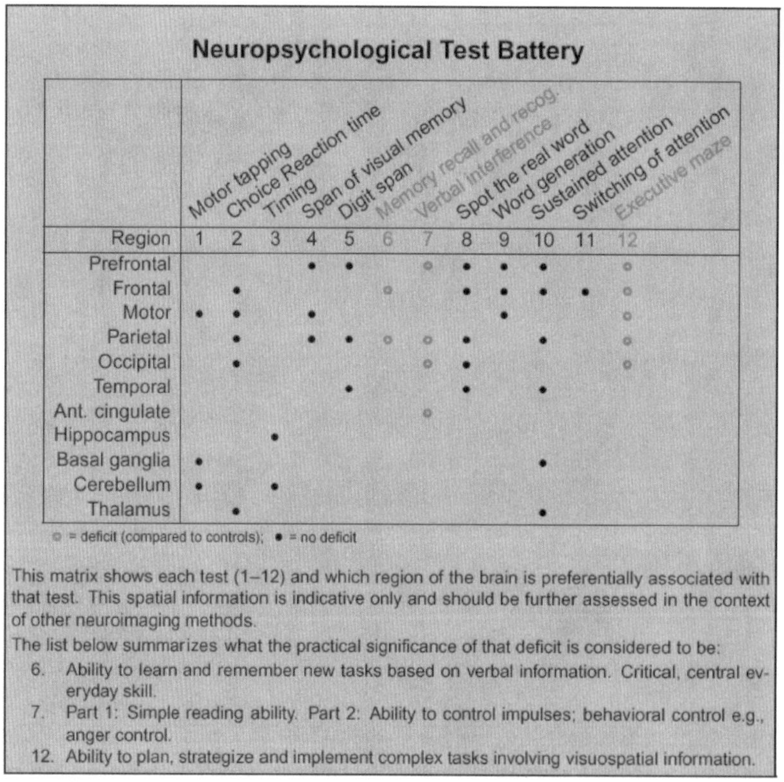

Neuropsychological Test Battery

	Motor tapping	Choice Reaction time	Timing	Span of visual memory	Digit span	Memory recall and recog.	Verbal interference	Spot the real word	Word generation	Sustained attention	Switching of attention	Executive maze
Region	1	2	3	4	5	6	7	8	9	10	11	12
Prefrontal				•	•		○	•	•	•		○
Frontal		•				○		•	•	•	•	○
Motor	•	•		•					•			○
Parietal		•		•	•	○	○	•		•		○
Occipital		•					○	•				○
Temporal					•			•		•		
Ant. cingulate							○					
Hippocampus			•									
Basal ganglia	•									•		
Cerebellum	•		•									
Thalamus		•								•		

○ = deficit (compared to controls); • = no deficit

This matrix shows each test (1–12) and which region of the brain is preferentially associated with that test. This spatial information is indicative only and should be further assessed in the context of other neuroimaging methods.

The list below summarizes what the practical significance of that deficit is considered to be:

6. Ability to learn and remember new tasks based on verbal information. Critical, central everyday skill.
7. Part 1: Simple reading ability. Part 2: Ability to control impulses; behavioral control e.g., anger control.
12. Ability to plan, strategize and implement complex tasks involving visuospatial information.

FIGURE 8.4 BRC neurocognitive tests and brain localization and functionality.

an athlete from this team) links neurocognitive test measures (see coded measures; e.g., N1) with brain region. The following findings emerged:

1. Batting average was associated with differential performance on neurocognitive measures (N1, N5, N6, and N20). N1, a measure related to the frontal and parietal brain regions, was negatively associated with batting average $(-.79)$. Conceptually, this suggests that greater recall, a verbal performance indicator, is associated with lower batting average, an interpretation that is consistent with the intrusive thoughts dynamics involved in high neuroticism. Conceivably, greater recall may be associated with neural pathways that facilitate the transfer of generated negative intrusive thoughts from the temporo-parietal regions to the frontal lobe where they are ruminated on, disrupting the seamless left-to-right hemispheric shifts and concomitant heart rate deceleration (HRD) that is associated with pre-action motor priming and subsequent enhanced performance (see Chapter 2). By contrast, N5, N6, and N20 measures (neurocognitive performance) were positively correlated with batting average (higher batting average), .69, .70, and .76, respectively. Neuro-measures N5, N6, and N20 implicate the frontal–parietal, motor/basal ganglia, and cerebellum regions of the brain, suggesting that a faster rate of learning that is associated with N5, less intrusions that are associated with N6, and faster motor tapping that is associated with N20, may facilitate better batting performance with mechanisms associated with less intrusions (N6 score), fostering the previously mentioned left-to-right shift, possibly being associated with neuro-circuitry underlying high repressive coping/subliminal coping and its associated ability to suppress negative intrusive thoughts. Thus, combine positively interacting neuropsychological and motor responses, in the absence or pressure and possibly even when under pressure, in players with the Ideal Athlete's Profile and performance will be facilitated.

2. Perhaps of greater interest in the context of CMT is the relationship between neurocognitive response tendencies and quality of at-bat and money-ball performance. Here N13 and N27 were negatively correlated with critical moment (money-ball) performance. Conceptually, N13 is a measure of sustained attention and reaction time within an attention test paradigm that implicates a host of brain regions, including the pre-frontal, frontal, parietal, temporal, basal ganglia, and thalamus. It could be expected that athletes who score low in sustained attention and attention-dependent reaction time will not perform well as competitive pressure increases $(N13 = -.73,$ when money ball is encountered), especially when coupled with high scores on verbal interference $(N27; -.65)$, even if color mediated. This finding is reconcilable with the Theory of Critical Moments and Athlete's Profile Models of Peak Performance (see Chapters 2 and 3), suggesting that attention and verbal interference can interact to mediate decrements in performance.

In addition to neurocognition, heart rate variability (HRV) was investigated in relationship to CMST outcome measures. HRV measures were obtained prior to each trial. In addition, the Serial 7s Stress Test was carried out prior to the on-the-field CMST.

The following group findings emerged:

HRV-Stress Test	CMQAB
1. Task-serial 7s VL frequency	.71
2. Differential Baseline/task VL freq.	.67

The first finding is that very-low-frequency heart activity, a measure that reflects predominance of the sympathetic nervous system (SNS), or a high level of physiological reactivity/activation was strongly correlated with Critical Moment (money-ball) Quality of At-Bats. This suggests that in this group of players, higher levels of intensity, independent of being temporally "time-locked" to actual at-bats, was associated with better performance, a finding that is not necessarily consistent with a lineup of players that were found to be high in neuroticism/subliminal reactivity. However, while greater S7s task condition VL frequency activity was associated with better CMQAB performance, this does not mean that CMQAB performance was consistently high, since the QAB range runs from 0 to 7, which was the case here.

Finding two revealed that the greater the difference in VLF between the baseline and task/stress condition of the S7 stress test, the greater the CMQAB, suggesting further that predominance of SNS activity impacted pressure performance positively.

Since the ABSP/Carlstedt Protocol advances a multifactorial and multimodal and integrative approach to athlete assessment and intervention, it is possible to determine the extent to which multiple variables impact pressure performance, both temporally isolated personality, behavioral, and neurocognitive trait and state measures, and in-the-moment, on-the-playing-field state psychophysiological, as well as time-locked brain–heart–mind–body measures impact critical moment performance. Here are regression findings from this team.

Multiple Regression: Variance Explained

1. Subliminal Attention (SA) explained 57% of the variance in QAB in a negative direction, that is, the greater the SA, the lower the QAB.

   Interpretation: In the presence of high neuroticism (SR), the focus facilitative component of high SA is thought to lock in and potentiate the negative intrusive thoughts that are associated with high SR, especially when stress increases, as is the case when critical moments are encountered by athletes who are high in SR. Since this cohort of athletes consisted of a disproportionate amount of athletes who were high in this trait and concurrently high in SA, it could be expected that brain–mind–body dynamics associated with high SA and SR would manifest themselves negatively to disrupt performance during critical moments.

2. Serial 7 Very Low HRV frequency explained 58% of the variance in CMQAB performance (the greater the VLF during backward counting, the better CM QAB).

   Interpretation: This finding is consistent with the earlier correlation findings and further point to the ability of trait levels of physiological reactivity to affect performance in line with the Individual Zone of Optimum Functioning (IZOF, Hanin, 2006) model of peak performance.

3. N29 (number of maze trials completed) explained 54% of the variance in BA (the greater the number of trials completed, the better the BA).

   Interpretation: N29, a neurocognitive measure associated with the pre-frontal, frontal, parietal, temporal, and occipital brain region activity when engaging in a complex mental and motor challenge (executive maze task), was strongly linked to better general, non-CM batting average. This suggests that the integration of multiple brain regions is associated with better performance on tasks that are not directly related to the cognitive test at hand, and that conceivably specific cognitive tests could be used to train the brain. However, this premise must be further tested in the context of gold standard research paradigms that are advanced in this book.

4. SDNN or the HRV Index explained 73% of the variance in CMBA (critical moment batting average; the greater the SDNN, the better the BA).

   Interpretation: The so-called HRV index (SDNN) was strongly associated with CMBA, a pressure performance metric. This could be expected in the context of Brain–Heart dynamics that have been linked to peak sport performance in which a left-to-right brain hemispheric shift prior to the commencement of action (pre-action) phase is time-locked to heart rate deceleration (occurring concomitantly), an HRV dynamic that is marked by greater SDNN (i.e., greater HRV). Greater pre-action HRD has been associated with better performance in numerous investigations of pre-action phase in a variety of sports, including baseball, tennis, and golf (Carlstedt, 2004a).

Sport-Specific Critical Moment Stress Testing Paradigms

Criticality test iterations are almost limitless. They should be structured in the context of individual athlete considerations. For example, a tennis player may exhibit good critical moment performance when the culminating money-ball shot is a forehand, but when a pressure situation task requires, say, a backhand down-the-line winner on demand, his or her mental toughness proficiency quotient goes down significantly. In such a scenario, it may be determined by a coach that the player's backhand is not technically proficient, and as such, it was revealed that an assumed psychological weakness was in fact driven by a specific technical deficiency.

Sample Tennis Critical Moment Test

Player engages in a baseline rally to establish consistency thresholds, that is, the player being evaluated attempts to hit as many balls as possible without making an error; his or her opponent just tries to keep the ball in play. Each shot is notated as is the player's last shot (e.g., 23 shots; last shot: forehand error crosscourt). Money ball is called out about 10% to 15% of the time (10%–15% of all trials). Money balls are predefined so that the player knows what to do or how to react when he or she hears "Money ball." Money ball response iterations are almost limitless. In this example, when "Money ball" is called out by the coach or sport psychology practitioner, the player is required to hit one set-up shot in any direction followed up by a winner (a ball that the opponent cannot reach and touch). If the set-up shot is unsuccessful, the money-ball response failed, and likewise if the winner shot is not made. Should the opponent make an error at any time, resulting in an incomplete threshold or money-ball trial, the trial is repeated.

Summary

Practitioner Challenge: Construct a technical and focus threshold test.

Practitioner Challenge: Design a criticality analysis model for a sport in which you have advanced knowledge of or expertise. Generate hypothetical data for analysis purposes (include test iterations, focus-comfort-control, money-ball, and HRV measures).

Threshold and money-ball CMS test training is a crucial final component of criticality testing and accountability sessions. They should be built into all training sessions and should last at least 30 minutes. They should be structured in advance, cognizant of technical and tactical strengths and weaknesses of an athlete, being sure to brief a player on the importance of money-ball CMS testing and reminding them of the reward and punishment consequences associated with money-ball performance outcome. CM testing introduces mental challenges that must be mastered in what would otherwise be routine practice situations, making athletes aware that they are always being monitored and will be held accountable for performance during CM and money-ball situations.

Acknowledgment

Some of the presented data were acquired by John Couture M.A., formerly of the Cleveland Indians (Mental Training Coach) and Amherst College baseball team as part of his American Board of Sport Psychology final project (leading to Board Certification). The data, procedures, conceptualizations and operationalizations as well as the findings and interpretations are the copyright of ABSP/Roland A. Carlstedt, Ph.D.

Heart Rate Variability Monitoring and Assessment During Training and Competition: A Window Into Athlete Mind–Body Responding

Over the course of the ABSP/Carlstedt Protocol (CP) validation process, heart rate variability (HRV) has emerged as the most potent psychophysiological predictor and outcome measure in the performance equation. HRV measures have been found to consistently predict macro- and micro-level sport-specific outcomes, including performance during critical moments as well as reflecting differential states of attention, intensity, and mental control (among other mind–body states; e.g., competitive stress/choking), especially when an athlete is under competitive pressure.

HRV is also the ideal psychophysiological measure for establishing an athlete's Individual Zone of Optimum Functioning (IZOF; Hanin 2006), since it is the only[1] physiological measure that can be reliably monitored during ecologically valid situations, including high movement-intensity training and even during official competition. Advanced user-friendly instrumentation allows for the monitoring of heart activity from which HRV measures are extracted for analysis in the context of both static (during time-outs) and dynamic (continuous, real time) assessment paradigms. HRV profiles or response tendencies are also central to the Athlete's Profile (AP) and Critical Moments (CM) models of peak performance as well as intervention efficiency and efficacy studies. The manipulation of mind–body–performance responses in the context of virtually any sport-specific and clinical intervention can also be guided and evaluated using HRV biofeedback (see Chapter 12). The CP uses HRV to initially assess both athletes and patients (determine baseline values for HRV), analyze treatment (clinical and wellness interventions and mental training in athletes), and to ascertain pre-versus post (intervention) changes in psychologically mediated autonomic nervous system responses (ANS).

This chapter will explore and explicate HRV in the context of pre-intervention assessment of athlete mind–body–motor and outcome responses and attempts to arrive at an athlete's IZOF, as well as criterion reference AP PHO constellations with ANS/psychophysiological measures in both training and real (official and practice) competition (e.g., real tennis matches or golf rounds; baseball games). A brief primer on HRV will precede the presentation of procedures, methodologies, and analyses of acquired data. The use of BioCom (BC) Technologies Heart Rate Scanner (HRS) and Polar HRV monitoring hard- and software systems will be explicated in the context of real case studies.

HRV: A Primer

Heart rate variability is a global measure of autonomic nervous system (ANS) functioning. It is composed of a number of measurement components that are derived through the monitoring of heart activity and subsequent analyses of inter-beat-interval/cardiac cycles (IBIs; using special algorithms; see Malik & Camm, 1995 for the definitive source on HRV) that are recorded. While heart rate (HR) is a well-known HRV measure, HRV also encompasses other measures that extend well beyond mere HR that are often more revealing than this basic measure in terms of providing reliable information on autonomic nervous system (ANS) balance, the extent to which the sympathetic nervous system (SNS) or parasympathetic nervous system (PNS) predominate in both clinical and performance contexts.

There are two sets of HRV measures: (1) time domain measures that include HR, SDNN, and RMS-SD, and (2) frequency domain measures that quantify the power spectrum (output) of ANS activity (see sample BioCom Heart Rate Scanner report and outtakes in Figure 9.1).

Heart rate (HR) is the most basic measure of HRV. As a stand-alone measure, it reflects how fast the heart is beating (beats-per-minute; bpm) and although there are known correlations between HR and other HRV measures (that are calculated on the basis of beat-to-beat fluctuations of HR), one should not be misled or arrive at conclusions regarding ANS functioning, athlete performance, or the impact of psychological factors on performance on the basis of HR alone, unless statistical analyses of sport-specific performance outcome measures reveal relationships between HR and performance (see the first case study later in the chapter; Figure 9.2).

The next time domain HRV measure of interest is SDNN or the standard deviation of each normal R to R wave of all cardiac cycles (IBIs) that are recorded/documented from the revolving or progressing mean (Figure 9.3). That is, as each heartbeat or cardiac cycle is recorded, the mean of all IBIs up to the point of the next or impending IBI changes, with the mean change of all IBIs from the revolving mean resulting in the final mean standard deviation, or SDNN, also known as the HRV-Index. SDNN is expressed in milliseconds (ms = 1000th of a second) and has important clinical and performance significance and implications, including cardiovascular integrity and psychological resiliency in medical, health psychology, and sport performance contexts. It has also been associated with pre-action strategic planning and focus (attention), as well as level of intensity and emotional control during sport competition (Carlstedt, 1998; Malik & Camm, 1995).

SDNN also reflects ANS balance or the extent to which SNS and PNS ANS activity interacts to differentially facilitate self-regulation or mediate dysfunctional ANS states. SDNN readings of under 30 (30 ms), if consistently documented, can signal or predict cardiologic problems, including, in the extreme, sudden death (Malik & Camm, 1995). Practitioners in the course of clinical and sport psychological assessments and interventions who monitor HRV should be cognizant of SDNN's relevance to cardiovascular functioning and make referrals to cardiologists when indicated (if consistent SDNN readings of less than 30 ms occur in a client/patient/athlete). SDNN is also frequently consistently lower (less than 40) in the obese, depressed, and anxiety-prone patients and can signal, in otherwise fit individuals, an impending cold or immune system–related illness onset (Malik & Camm, 1995). SDNN should be used to guide exercise therapy outcome and be routinely integrated into interventional pursuits that are designed to ameliorate psychophysiological and related disorders.

Over time (longitudinally), SDNN can also play an important role in determining the efficacy of an intervention. One would expect a compliant patient/client to make gains (symptom

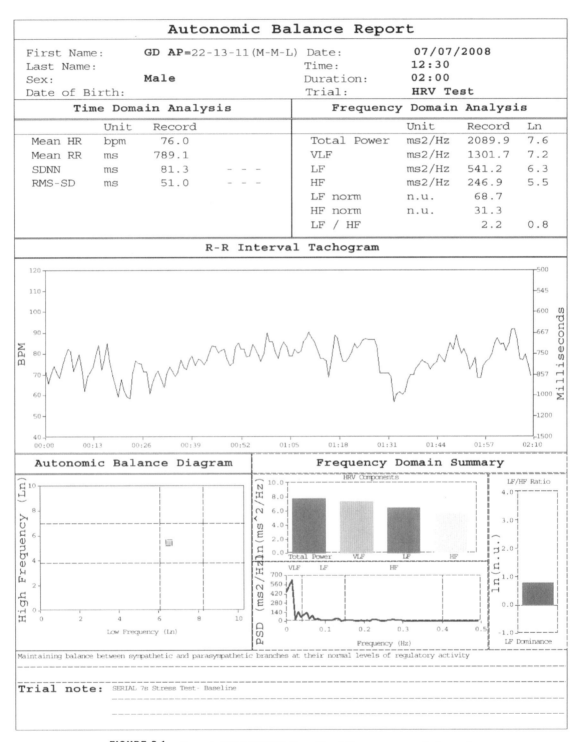

FIGURE 9.1   Sample HRV-ANS BioCom Heart Scanner generated report.

reduction/increase in physical/mental wellness) when engaging in a well-validated disorder-specific intervention. SDNN allows practitioners to go beyond clinical intuition and patient/client feedback that can be fallible to arrive at a reliable intervention efficaciousness metric or

Time Domain Analysis

	Unit	Record	
Mean HR	bpm	53.4	
Mean RR	ms	1123.2	
SDNN	ms	166.4	- - -
RMS-SD	ms	151.3	- - -

FIGURE 9.2   HRV time domain measures.

indicator on the basis of a measurable mind–body biomarker that is strongly linked to virtually all behavior, disorders, psychological issues, medical symptoms, and illness. SDNN truly is as close as there is to a universal biomarker of differential physical and psychological well-being, dysfunction, or distress. It is a very potent biomarker-predictor variable across many clinical and performance contexts.

Although SDNN is very revealing clinically, in terms of forecasting sport performance, its predictive validity can be variable, usually as a function of individual differences factors, including those that compose the Athlete's Profile PHO constellations. Consequently, it must again be stressed that all predictor measures of interest in the performance equation, regardless of their clinical potency or perceived stature (on the basis of positive group findings) must be assessed and tested at the intra-individual level to determine their impact, including SDNN.

It should be noted, though, that SDNN is very stable across most athletes when they are engaged in the pre-action phase of a sport-specific task (like a serve in tennis, putt in golf, or free-throw in basketball). SDNN tends to be higher during phases of linear heart rate deceleration (HRD), a species-wide response to an impending oncoming stimulus (like an oncoming baseball pitch) or internal cognitive preparation to initiate action (mental preparation leading up to a drive in golf). This can be attributed to the linear nature of HRD, in which each successive IBI during the pre-action preparatory phase increases, that is, each cardiac cycle is longer or slower than the previous one until the onset of action when HRD gives way to heart rate acceleration (HRA) and the HRD linear trend is broken. In the absence of HRD in the pre-action phase, often a psychologically mediated phenomenon (e.g., associated with having the least performance facilitative Athlete's Profile PHO constellation during a critical moment), one is more likely to observe differential levels of HRA (more constant and less variable heart activity; less HRV) and resulting lower SDNN. SDNN tends to decrease as a function of higher HR (greater than 90; see Chapters 2 and 12 for more on HRD; Malik & Camm, 1995).

SDNN is one of the most important HRV measures in and of itself, and should be analyzed within an integrative applied psychophysiological intervention approach to both off-the-playing field conditioning, recovery, sleep facilitation, immune functioning, jet lag/biorhythm regulation and general wellness, as well as on-the-playing-field peak performance–related assessment and manipulation of attention, intensity, cognitive preparation/mental coping (subliminal coping), and pre-action HRD.[2]

R   IBI   R

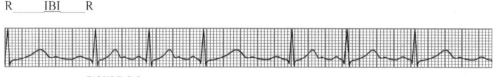

FIGURE 9.3   Electrocardiogram strip with extracted R to R wave.

Frequency Domain HRV Measures

Frequency domain measures (see Figures 9.4 and 9.5) reflect the power spectrum of the ANS and include the following measures: total power (TP), very low frequency (VLF), low frequency (LF), and high frequency (HF) activity and the ratio of low-to-high frequency (LF/HF, or L/H) activity. They are obtained using algorithms that are built into virtually all automated HRV software programs (see Malik & Camm, 1995, for technical details pertaining to the processing and analysis of Frequency Domain measures).

Total power (TP) reflects the total ANS output (all frequency ranges). TP is not routinely entered into correlation or regression-HRV performance analyses, since it is a conglomerate measure (can lead to inflated HRV measure intercorrelations) that contains other ANS frequency domain measures that tend to be more revealing independently. Nevertheless, it can be used for descriptive and exploratory purposes.

The frequency domain measure that is almost exclusively associated with SNS activity is VL frequency. SNS activity is linked to greater physiological activation or reactivity. It usually predominates under conditions of increased activation, including sports that demand consistent movement and higher levels of intensity and concomitant faster HR (over 100 bpm). SNS activation is an ANS response to increasing metabolic demands, whether as a result of exercise, performing, or the proverbial fight-or-flight reaction when real (or perceived) threats to one's safety and well-being are encountered. Evolutionarily, sudden SNS activation is seen as an adaptive response that is manifested to deal with normal mind–body and survival demands. However, as the human brain developed its neo-cortex and the pre-frontal and frontal lobes (and modern day neuroses, etc.), the phenomenon of psychologically mediated HRV evolved in which the ANS became susceptible to frontal-lobe generated cognitions, both adaptive ones but also maladaptive superfluous negative intrusive thoughts. In more vulnerable individuals (e.g., athletes possessing the most performance detrimental Athlete's Profile: H-H-L), the mind has developed the tendency to set off a cascade of ANS responses, including situational or context-inappropriate hyper-reactive SNS VL frequency

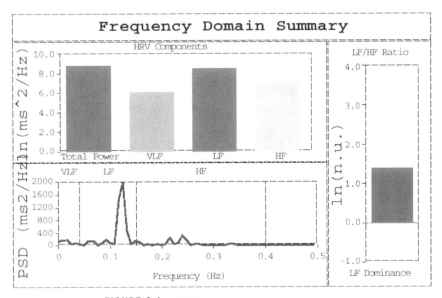

FIGURE 9.4   HRV frequency domain measures.

Frequency Domain Analysis

	Unit	Record	Ln
Total Power	ms2/Hz	6231.1	8.7
VLF	ms2/Hz	399.0	6.0
LF	ms2/Hz	4661.6	8.4
HF	ms2/Hz	1170.6	7.1
LF norm	n.u.	79.9	
HF norm	n.u.	20.1	
LF / HF		4.0	1.4

FIGURE 9.5   Additional frequency domain sample outtake.

activation, the kind that is seen during panic attacks, and in sports, during competitive anxiety (Malik & Camm, 1995; Andreassi, 1995).

Since VL frequency activity can be situationally appropriate or inappropriate, it can be difficult to discern to what extent it is impacting performance when taken at face value. Consequently, it is important that VL frequency activity is analyzed integratively. Relative to sports performance, it is important to establish baseline values of VL-SNS activity as a function of minimum and maximum levels of intensity that are common to a specific sport. Such baselines are established through straightforward analyses of performance during routine training or practice epochs that are devoid of pressure (e.g., just hitting tennis balls randomly, or driving golf balls on a driving range, or shooting free throws in basketball). Pre, during, and post-competition HRV readings/recordings of 1 or 2 min (usually 2 min for pre and post, and 1 min during [time-outs]) are taken to establish periodic levels of all HRV measures including VL frequency activity. Usually, one will observe a linear increase in HR and VL frequency activity as a function of increasing metabolic demands that are associated with greater physical effort that is required to perform sport-specific tasks (e.g., by the time a tennis player has hit the 20th consecutive ball, his or her level of HR and VL frequency activity should increase significantly compared to when the first ball was struck). Once an ANS physiological reactivity or VL frequency activity baseline has been established (based on routine practice tasks with no pressure [coach stresses that players should just take it easy or that it's a warm-up session, to mitigate pressure]), a second test condition (see Chapter 8 Critical Moment Stress Testing), containing pressure components (e.g., money-ball performance), should be administered for comparative purposes. Assuming that levels of intensity are held fairly constant between the baseline and pressure conditions, changes in VL frequency activity can be inferred to reflect the psychological mediation of HRV. In the case of VL frequency that reflects SNS activation, should it increase in the pressure condition, it can be assumed that any introduced pressure component (Money-Ball or Critical Moment) had a psychological impact that is reflected in differential HRV-VL frequency. Note, though, it still must be determined on the basis of about 60 repeated outcome measures, whether an increased level of VL is associated with better or worse performance. A potent clue as to whether, especially, higher levels of VL frequency activity under pressure conditions will be associated with enhanced or reduced performance outcome lies within an athlete's Athlete's Profile. The High-High-Low profile (high subliminal attention/hypnotic susceptibility–high subliminal reactivity/neuroticism and low subliminal coping/repressive coping; see Chapter 4) is more likely to be associated with greater VL frequency activity in the pressure condition and even at baseline. By contrast, the High/Low-Low-High Athlete's Profile is likely to be associated with less VL activation at baseline and in the pressure condition. However, athletes with this latter Ideal Athlete's Profile, should they exhibit greater VL frequency in the pressure condition, are still likely to perform better than their more psychologically burdened counterpart exhibiting a similar level of VL frequency. In cases where VL frequency is above or below what would be expected as a function of no-pressure versus pressure and Athlete's Profile, practitioners and coaches should try to determine to what extent unexpected fluctuations in VL frequency activity are physiologically or psychologically mediated.

Low frequency (LF or L) HRV, in contrast to VL frequency activity that reflects almost exclusively ANS SNS activation, is associated with activation of both branches of the ANS (SNS and PNS). LF activity is a measure of autonomic balance and is strongly correlated with SDNN and the L/H frequency ratio. As one inhales, HR increases, and as one exhales, it decreases. LF activity is in part generated from variations in an individual's inhale–exhale cycles (see the tachogram in the preceding full ANS report; Figure 9.1). The influence of LF in the performance equation, again, as with all HRV measures, must be established at the intra-individual level, since an athlete's IZOF is unique and can be highly variable from athlete to athlete (Carlstedt, 1998; Hanin 2006; Malik & Camm, 1995).

High frequency (HF or H) consists almost exclusively of PNS activity. It is an ANS response that predominates the most during states of extreme under-activation such as when dozing, presleep/sleep, or day dreaming while sitting or lying down. Irrespective thereof, HF is also constantly manifested during every exhale cycle. It serves an important regulatory purpose by preventing SNS responses from dominating to the point of an individual being incapable of "coming down" or relaxing. In fact, a dampened PNS response has been associated with a host of psychophysiological disorders, including malignant cardiac arrhythmias, which can be life-threatening (Malik & Camm, 1995).

LF and HF activity can interact in both clinical and performance contexts. These ANS measures comprise an important performance-relevant measure, the Low-High ratio (L/H). The L/H ratio reflects the extent to which a mixture of LF-HF and HF ANS activity predominates for any given measured epoch. In athletes, differential-directional changes in L/H ratio from a static baseline condition to the Serial 7s stress test condition (see Chapter 5) have been associated with variations in performance, with a lower L/H ratio being correlated with better subsequent actual sport-specific performance outcome (magnitude of directional change from more to less LH-HF activity and increasing HF activity; i.e., a lower L/F ratio, e.g., from 2.3 to .9; or conversely, a baseline L/H ratio with HF predominance of, say, .2 increasing to .8 in the stress condition [= more H frequency]).

The L/H ratio is also an important measure relative to intervention efficiency and efficacy, especially when breathing-based interventions are used to induce pre-action HRD. It can also be revealing in the context of multimodal intervention efficiency and efficacy testing (e.g., testing and using imagery-video and HRD breathing). It also frequently emerges (more so than individual HRV measures) as a predictor of performance outcome in both pre-intervention and intervention contexts and as a differentiator of ANS states between pre and post no-pressure versus pressure conditions, both in groups and individuals. As always, though, L/H ratio measures must be subjected to testing at the intra-individual level, cognizant of the IZOF and Athlete's Profile models of peak performance.

Instrumentation: The BioCom and Polar Systems

For the past 10 years, the BioCom Technologies HRV monitoring and analysis system has been used as part of the ABSP/Carlstedt Protocol athlete assessment and intervention process. The BioCom system consists of software and linked sensors (ear or finger sensor or full EKG electrode configuration). Its main limitation is the inability to monitor heart activity in real time during actual action phases of most sports. This has led to the validation of an alternative monitoring, measurement, and analysis methodology that will be addressed later.

Recently, the Polar RS800CX heart activity monitoring system has been incorporated into ABSP applied training and research.[3] The Polar system opens up new possibilities, including telemetry-based real-time recording that lends itself well to heart rate deceleration (HRD) experiments as well heart activity assessment during action phases of virtually all sports, from the beginning to the end of a competition, in which all inter-beat intervals are recorded. This latter capability is rather remarkable since most heart activity monitoring systems are very artifact prone (distorted and inaccurate HRV readings due to sensors losing contact with the skin) whenever subjects (athletes) engage in constant movement as well as upper-body rotations (as in baseball, tennis, golf and other sports). Polar has developed not only a robust recording system that links a chest strap to a computerized wrist watch, but a very user-friendly artifact correction function that can be used to normalize artifacts that are detected. To date, on the basis of mostly tennis and cycling data,

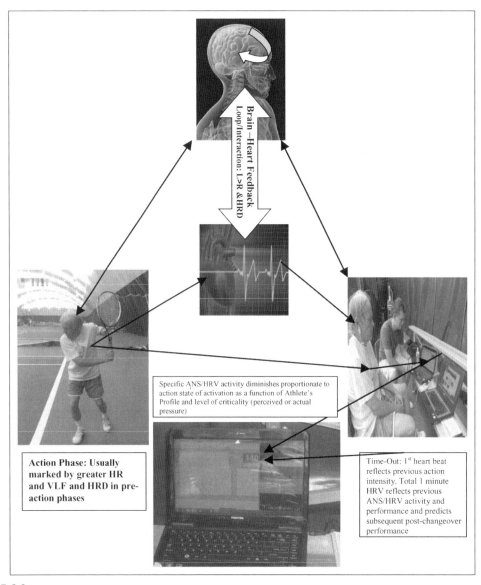

FIGURE 9.6 Heart rate variability-performance model: Temporally discordant version/temporally remote paradigm (TRP; above; see Figure 9.8 for explanation).

the incidence of artifacts across hundreds of thousands of IBIs has been less than 3% (unpublished ABSP database). Such a level of recording integrity despite the oftentimes "violent" upper body rotation and constant high intensity movement endemic to many sports allows for unprecedented insight into psychophysiological performance dynamics at the most micro-level (e.g., IBI trends during critical moment level 5 situations). Specific Polar assessment, intervention, research, and analysis paradigms are presented in the next section.

HRV Monitoring and Assessment Paradigms: BioCom System

Because of previous (pre-Polar RS800CX) technical constraints associated with attempts to monitor heart activity during actual training and real competition, a paradigm was developed in an attempt to determine to what extent, if at all, "down-time" (changeover/time-outs) heart activity (HRV), as opposed to time-locked, real-time HRV (during action) would emerge as not only a predictor of subsequent performance (after a changeover/time-out), but reflect performance prior to a changeover/time-out. The conceptual basis (construct validity) for using an indirect, non-time-locked or temporally distant approach to the monitoring, measurement, and analysis of heart activity (HRV) is based on the following model and rationale (Figures 9.6 and 9.7).

PROCEDURES

1. Athlete undergoes 2-minute pre-competition baseline assessment (HRV ear-sensor-computer; see preceding Model with tennis example and baseball example further on)
2. Athlete is monitored from 1 to 2 minutes (depending on sport) each time-out
3. Report is immediately generated: can be used for in-the-moment feedback
4. Sport-specific statistical outcome measures are documented: "scoring the game"
5. Critical moment statistics are documented
6. Athlete undergoes 2-minute post-competition assessment (within 5 minutes of end of play)
7. HRV and performance measures are transferred to athlete/group database (Excel)
8. HRV and performance statistics are analyzed to determine how much variance explained in an outcome measure can be attributed to HRV measure(s) or to what extent HRV reflects pre-time-out or predicts post, time-out performance
9. The derived pre-intervention findings guide subsequent interventions (mental training)

Baseball Inning Changeover HRV Assessment Paradigm

Batter or Pitcher upon arriving in the dugout or bench have sensor connected to his ear lobe. HRV is measured for 1 minute. Data is analyzed in the moment and post-competition (See Chapter 20 for complete baseball player-HRV study)

FIGURE 9.7   Procedures HRV temporally discordant/remote paradigm.

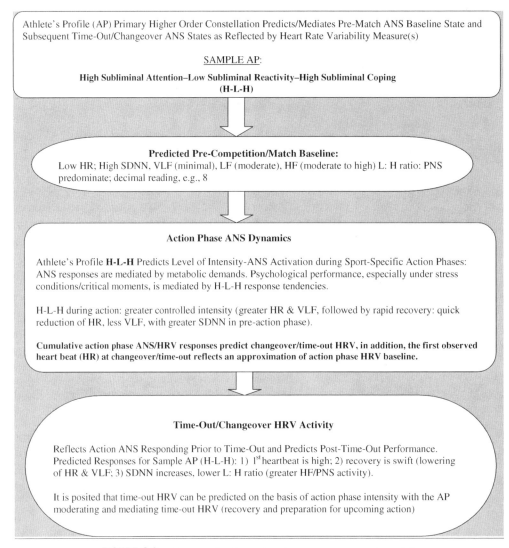

Athlete's Profile (AP) Primary Higher Order Constellation Predicts/Mediates Pre-Match ANS Baseline State and Subsequent Time-Out/Changeover ANS States as Reflected by Heart Rate Variability Measure(s)

SAMPLE AP:

High Subliminal Attention–Low Subliminal Reactivity–High Subliminal Coping (H-L-H)

Predicted Pre-Competition/Match Baseline:
Low HR; High SDNN, VLF (minimal), LF (moderate), HF (moderate to high) L: H ratio: PNS predominate; decimal reading, e.g., 8

Action Phase ANS Dynamics

Athlete's Profile **H-L-H** Predicts Level of Intensity-ANS Activation during Sport-Specific Action Phases: ANS responses are mediated by metabolic demands. Psychological performance, especially under stress conditions/critical moments, is mediated by H-L-H response tendencies.

H-L-H during action: greater controlled intensity (greater HR & VLF, followed by rapid recovery: quick reduction of HR, less VLF, with greater SDNN in pre-action phase).

Cumulative action phase ANS/HRV responses predict changeover/time-out HRV, in addition, the first observed heart beat (HR) at changeover/time-out reflects an approximation of action phase HRV baseline.

Time-Out/Changeover HRV Activity

Reflects Action ANS Responding Prior to Time-Out and Predicts Post-Time-Out Performance. Predicted Responses for Sample AP (H-L-H): 1) 1st heartbeat is high; 2) recovery is swift (lowering of HR & VLF; 3) SDNN increases, lower L: H ratio (greater HF/PNS activity).

It is posited that time-out HRV can be predicted on the basis of action phase intensity with the AP moderating and mediating time-out HRV (recovery and preparation for upcoming action)

FIGURE 9.8   Temporally discordant/remote conceptual model.

The above flow chart (Figure 9.8) contains components of the ABSP-CP *Heart Rate Variability-Performance Model: Temporally Discordant/Remote Paradigm* (based on a sample Athlete's Profile PHO constellation; H-L-H). The model assumes that baseline HRV measures during action phases of competition will attenuate or potentiate during time-outs as a function of the Athlete's Profile mediating impact on attention, intensity, and cognitive coping and responding to differential criticality (critical moments/competitive pressure; lawful changes over time with high test–retest reliability). Relationships are expected to emerge among pre-competition, competitive action, and post-competition HRV and time-out HRV measures, with time-out measures reflecting previous action (prior to the time-out) and predicting post time-out performance. Specific brain–heart–mind–body dynamics that heavily implicate the ANS are hypothesized to underlie differential athlete performance responses during both routine and critical moments of competition (see Chapters 8 and 20).

Case Study Analysis: Tennis Player Pre-Intervention HRV

The ABSP database of Brain–Heart–Mind–Body–Motor and Outcome (BHMBM-O) contains athletes whose HR is extremely low (normatively) during changeovers in tennis matches, which could suggest that players who exhibit such low HR (in the 50–60 range after reaching HR of 120–150 during games prior to changeovers) are either in very good cardiovascular shape (rapid recovery) and/or are impervious to psychological stress (no apparent competitive stress). By contrast, other players recover negligibly, maintaining HR during changeovers that is almost as high as when they were in action (e.g., a mean HR of 135 during games and a HR of 125 during 1-min changeovers). One might conclude that such a latter class of responses (game vs. changeover HR responses) are inconsistent with cardiovascular fitness or indicative of competitive stress that does not recede even in the absence of action (during changeovers).

One player in particular stands out as having anomalous, paradoxically low HR during numerous changeovers, dropping rapidly from, for example, 120 (first recorded heart rate upon sitting down for the changeover) to 55. Since this player, "DA," had reported having competitive anxiety, the reason he sought out a sport psychologist, his HR, in and of itself, suggested that he was in very good shape and in control psychologically. His very low changeover HR seemed highly inconsistent with competitive anxiety, a performance issue that is marked by excessively high HR during action and long recovery times. Had HR alone been used to guide the diagnostic process, one would not have recognized that this player's low HR was actually indicative of a paradoxical reverse competitive anxiety that was associated with a lack of intensity and concomitant movement (lack of effort). His extremely low action phase and changeover HR was strongly correlated with negative outcome in subsequent post-changeover games, lending initial support to the paradoxical competitive anxiety diagnosis.

Upon further analyzing his changeover HR retrospectively, that is, in the context of games leading up to changeovers, lower HR during changeovers were also correlated with poorer performance in those games. It was concluded that this player's competitive anxiety resulted in a sort of mind–motor paralysis whereby he would either try to win the point as quickly as possible without attempting to move and use tactics that required him to work for points and play defense as necessary, which can be laborious and taxing, but effective.

Practitioner Challenge: Locate HR in Figures 9.9 (pre-intervention) and 9.10 (intervention phase) and analyze this measure in the context of "paradoxical" competitive anxiety, paying special attention to pre- and post-intervention differences and the VLF measure.

Essentially, his fear of losing,[4] an emotion that is usually associated with higher HR, instead was reflected in freezing-up behavior and lack of movement. This player's low HR was not associated with greater PNS activity than would be expected (with an HR in the 50 beat-per-minute range), a finding that highlights the need to not only look at one global HRV measure in isolation (such as HR) when attempting to arrive at performance relevant conclusions on the basis of cardiac activity. Relative to DA, his low HR, at facevalue and without further analysis, could be very misleading. However, once it was determined that his predominant frequency domain measure was VLF, a measure that reflects SNS activity and is usually associated greater vasoconstriction (tightening of the vasculature [capillaries, veins, and arteries]) and excessive muscular

Practitioner Challenge: Identify components of the ABSP-CP, especially DA's Athlete's Profile constellation of PHO measures. Before reading beyond the cover page of the CSARCS-A, attempt to predict DA's response tendencies and outcome based on your knowledge of his AP.

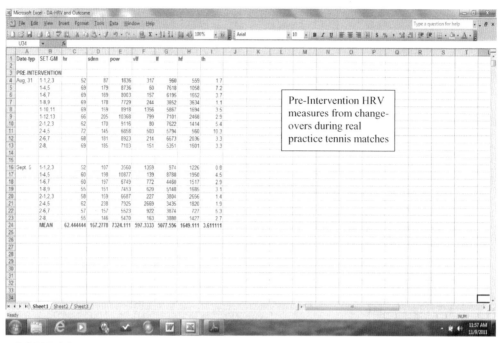

FIGURE 9.9   Case study DA's pre-intervention changeover HRV responses (practice matches).

tension, it was concluded that DA indeed exhibited a paradoxical manifestation of competitive anxiety.

DA's case report is presented in the following pages.

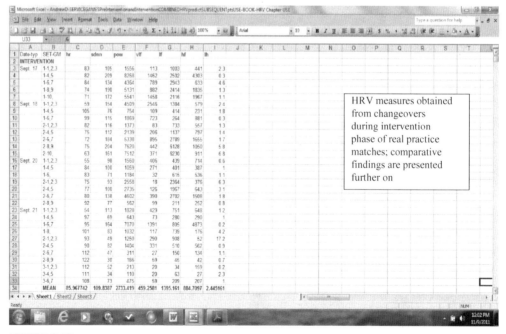

FIGURE 9.10   Case study DA's intervention phase changeover HRV responses (practice matches).

ABSP-BRC/Carlstedt Protocol
INTERPRETIVE REPORT

Athlete: DA   **Sport: Tennis**

Carlstedt Subliminal Attention, Reactivity and Coping Scale-Athlete Version (CSARCS-A)

SUBLIMINAL ATTENTION (ABSORPTION/Hypnotic Susceptibility): 20
Hypnotic Susceptibility Stanford Scale Hypnotic Susceptibility: A (SSHS-A): 6
(Medium Range)

SUBLIMINAL REACTIVITY (NEUROTICISM): 23

SUBLIMINAL COPING (REPRESSIVE COPING): 22

SUMMARY CLASSIFICATION: MEDIUM-HIGH-HIGH

Key: < = low range of classification   > = high range of classification

PLEASE READ INFORMATION and SEE CHARTS—ATHLETE'S ANALYSIS

Psychophysiological Responding: Match Heart Rate Variability and Outcome

Most Performance Relevant Statistically Significant Findings (r)

All Matches Combined HRV at Changeover and Subsequent Points

Heart Rate – Total Points Won	r = .37 (*p* value; all .05 or <)
Heart Rate – Total points Played	r = .33
Heart Rate – % Pts. Won	r = .26
Low-High Freq. Ratio - Critical Moment	r = .32
Level 3 Points Won	

<u>Pre-Intervention HRV at Changeover and Subsequent Points</u>

Heart Rate – CM Level 3 Points Won	r = .33

<u>Pre-Intervention HRV at Changeover and Points from Previous Game(s)</u>

Heart Rate – Games Won	r = .30
Heart Rate – Games Played	r = .32
Heart Rate – Points Won	r = .33
Heart Rate – CM Level 4 Points Won	r = -.30
SDNN (HRV Index) – CM Level 4 Points Won	r = .42
HF (High Freq. HRV) – CM Level 4 points Won	r = .40

<u>Intervention Induced HRV at Changeover and Subsequent Points</u>

Heart Rate – CM Level 4 Points Won	r = .40

<u>Intervention Induced HRV at Changeover and Points from Previous Game(s)</u>

Heart Rate – Games Played	r = .38
Heart Rate – Points Won	r = .38
Low-High Ratio – Points Lost	r = -.32
Heart Rate – CM Level 4 Points Lost	r = .44 (? Paradoxically)
SDNN – CM Level 4 Points Lost	r = -.43

<u>Strongest Regression Models: HRV and Outcome</u>

SDNN explained <u>18% of the variance (adjusted r^2)</u> in Critical Moment Level 4 Points Won (Pre-Intervention Phase HRV at Changeover and Subsequent Points).

SDNN explained <u>16% of the variance</u> in CM Level 4 Points Won (Pre-Intervention Phase HRV at Changeover and Previous Points).

Heart Rate explained 13% of the variance in Games Won (All Matches)

<u>Psychophysiological Responding: Match Heart Rate Variability and Outcome (cont.)</u>

<u>Comparisons with Saif (T-Tests) All Matches</u>

Heart Rate (mean):	High Frequency (mean):	SDNN(mean):
Saif = 104 (at changeover)	1848	77
AD = 89 (at changeover)	565	114
(p = .001)	(p = .007)	(p = .01)

Implications: Neuropsychophysiological responding (Mind-Body-Motor) during competition can be predicted by and reflect personality, behavioral, and cognitive influences, especially an athlete's constellation of CSARCS-A measures. What stood out in this athlete was a very low changeover heart rate, the lowest this practitioner-researcher has ever observed. The fact that heart rate stood out as the main measure of heart rate variability in the performance equation lends support to the hypothesis that this player likely was under-activated during matches and/or experienced fluctuations in intensity levels during games. Heart rate was found to positively influence numerous performance outcome measures in a linear manner and explained 13% of the variance in GAMES WON across all matches played. Thirteen %, while perhaps seeming low, is actually quite substantial when one considers how many variables make up the performance equation, especially when one considers that a temporally isolated mind-body measure retrospectively and prospectively predicted performance. It is also important to note that SDNN, the heart rate variability index that reflects autonomic balance and can be manipulated through HRV-Respiratory biofeedback (as was engaged in by this athlete), predicted 18% and 16% of the variance respectively in the pre-intervention phase CRITICAL MOMENT LEVEL 4 points, both retrospectively (points played prior to a change-over) and prospectively (points played after a changeover). This suggests that HRV-Respiratory biofeedback should be used routinely by this athlete in accord with what he was taught to facilitate greater HRV between points and heart rate deceleration immediately prior to action. Heart rate should be increased and sustained during points to boost effort and engagement.

Note that his primary practice partner (opponent) SA had a mean Heart Rate of 104 compared to 89 for AD. He also exhibited significantly more high frequency HRV (a marker of parasympathetic activation) than AD. High frequency HRV activity across a match probably reflects a recovery or return to baseline response after points. SA has a much more stable recovery profile, one that may allow him to quickly reactivate after down time (like a changeover) whereas, AD despite a significantly lower changeover heart rate is more activated at baseline than SA, suggesting less stable ANS activity in AD. ANS-HRV stability is emerging as an important marker of emotional or psychological consistency across competition.

Greater SDNN in AD compared to SA appears also to reflect greater HRV that may be associated with a lower level of intensity coming off the court, since SDNN linearly decreases as a function of increased heart rate.

Unfortunately, after leaving New York, the client has not remained compliant regarding the assessment and intervention protocol as evidenced by the failure to transmit HRV and other performance data to this practitioner. This could be predicted on the basis of the athlete's NEO score for CONSCIENTIOUSNESS, which was VERY LOW. Although this trait is not directly implicated in the performance equation, it can play a major ancillary role in driving motivation and practice habits and can adversely affect improving one's mental game. Other NEO interactions are also troubling when viewed in a global context (these charts are provided for scrutiny below). Low extraversion and high subliminal reactivity are also traits that have strong psychophysiological correlates. Very low extraversion may mediate under-activation/lack of sustained and consistent intensity, while high subliminal reactivity can lead to nervousness and negative intrusive thoughts during critical moments of competition.

> In concert, this athlete's neuoropsychophysiological tendencies, personality, and behavioral profile, along with objective heart rate variability data, appear to mediate and reflect significant psychological/competitive performance issues that need to be resolved in order to increase the probability that this athlete can achieve incremental goals as a tennis player. The failure to adhere to a clearly prescribed protocol in the absence of this practitioner can be considered a setback, and if not rectified may lead to a continuation of competitive "symptoms" and sub-par performance.

The cautionary tale here is the use of HR alone to make inferences about performance is not acceptable. Myths about mere HR abound and continue to be advanced, especially by sport commentators who frequently talk about getting one's HR down. Unfortunately, these myths have permeated the realm of practitioners and athletes who also tend to think in simplistic terms and the notion that HR alone is a very revealing mind–body metric. It can be, but such must be established at the intra-individual level over time. Note also, that HRD, an important HRV response, does not refer to mere slowing of HR. It is a specific pre-action mind-body response interaction that is marked by greater HRV (SDNN). HRD will be explicated later in this chapter.

Case Study 2: Professional Golfer

Golf is perhaps the most ideal sport for heart rate variability monitoring and assessment because of the sport's very limited motion during pre-action phases of training and competition, lessening the contamination of data due to motion artifact. In this case study, HRV response data emanating from a professional golfer is presented (Figure 9.11).

Prior to pre-intervention/HRV training rounds, a golfer (GV) was tested using the CSARCS-A and BRC neurocognitive assessment batteries. A summary of findings follows (Figure 9.12).

GV's Athlete's Profile constellation is Medium-Medium-Medium, although he is close to having one of the Ideal Athlete's Profiles of Low Subliminal Attention (SA)-Low Subliminal Reactivity (SR) and High Subliminal Coping (SC). Raw scores should always be checked to determine proximity to

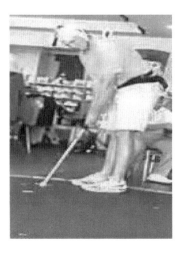

FIGURE 9.11   Photo depicting golfer wearing HRV/EEG telemetry monitoring equipment (Nexus 32).

CSARCS-A

Carlstedt Subliminal Attention, Reactivity and Coping Scale

Client: CARL-NORM-00011

The Carlstedt Subliminal Attention, Reactivity and Coping Scale-Athlete Version (CSARCS-A) contains measures that reflect the following neuropsychophysiological processes (Mind-Body processes):

I. **Subliminal Attention (SA):** this measure reflects an athlete's subliminal or unconscious focusing or concentration tendencies. It can be viewed as the "Zone" facilitator in athlete's who score high on this dimension (23-35). They possess an enhanced ability to focus intensely on task-relevant activities (sport-specific action/movement, etc). Paradoxically, low SA can also be performance facilitating.

II. **Subliminal Reactivity (SR):** this measure reflects an athlete's subliminal autonomic nervous system or "fight" or "flight" tendencies. It can be viewed as the "Great Disrupter" of peak performance in athletes who are high on this dimension (16-25). They are likely to exhibit increased psychophysiological reactivity (nervousness; muscle tension) that is mediated by catastrophic and negative intrusive thoughts, especially during critical moments of competition.

III. **Subliminal Coping (SC):** this measure reflects an athlete's subliminal or unconscious ability to fend off negative intrusive thoughts associated with high Subliminal Reactivity. It can be viewed as the "Great Facilitator" of "Zone" states and peak performance in athletes who are high in this measure (22-34).

Measure	Client Score	Range
Subliminal Attention	12	Medium
Subliminal Reactivity	10	Medium
Subliminal Coping	18	Medium

This client has a "**Neutral**" profile as measured by the CSARCS-A.

It should be noted that the above measures interact to affect performance as a function of the criticality of a competitive moment. In other words, the more critical the moment as established by the Carlstedt Critical Moment Analysis System (CCMAS), the greater the probability that an athlete's combination of the above measures will influence performance either positively or negatively. In isolation and outside the context of critical moments or competitive stress, singular measures are expected to exert their positive effects. Their negative influences will remain relatively dormant until actual or perceived critical moments or competitive stress are encountered (see Critical Moments During Competition: A Mind-Body Model of Sport Performance When it Counts the Most; Carlstedt [2004] Psychology Press for a complete analysis of the dynamics of the above constructs).

Follow-up Report Service: It is recommended that athletes, coaches, and practitioners who use this test battery consult with Dr. Roland A. Carlstedt to further inform the interpretation and implementation. Contact: RCarlstedt@americanboardofsportpsychology.org or DrRCarlstedt@aol.com. See the website: www.americanboardofsportpsychology.org

FIGURE 9.12   Golfer (GV's) CSARCS-A summary report.

cutoff scores. In GV's case, he is in the lower range for both SA and SR. His level of SC is in the high–medium range. This suggests that he is more likely to perform well under pressure than falter in critical situations, but this prediction is not unequivocal; hence, the need for further ecologically based critical moment testing.

Hole #	Par (yds.)	Score	Shot #	Scan	Direction	Distance (yds.)	Location	Quality	Shot Type (Club)	Focus	Comfort	Control	CM prob	CM sit.	HR	SDNN	VLF	LF	HF	LF:HF
Pre-round				Y											65.6	68.6	1397.5	334.8	83.9	4
1	4 (350)		1 Y		S	280	Fairway	5	Drive (D)	5	5	4	2	2	65.5	84.4	68.2	699.3	194.3	3.6
			2 Y		S	110	Green	4	Approach (SW)	5	5	4	3	3	956.9	72	956.9	1221	122.9	9.9
MB			3 N			25'	Green	4	Putt	5	5	5	3	4						
		4	4 Y		Z	2'	Green	4	Putt	5	5	5	3	3	69.8	49	309.8	158.1	111.3	1.4
2	4 (377)		1 Y		S	265	Rough	5	Drive (D)	5	5	4	2	2	67	73.9	40.6	933.9	126.5	7.4
			2 Y		S	115	Green	4	Approach (52)	5	5	4	3	3	67.4	62.1	374.6	333.4	62.7	5.3
			3 N			20'	Green	4	Putt	5	4	4	3	3						
		4	4 Y		1'		Green	4	Putt	5	4	4	3	3	66.3	99.5	592.9	495.3	273.9	1.8
3	3 (192)		1 Y		R	190	Sand	3	Tee Shot (5i)	5	4	4	3	3	67	79.1	92.4	618.9	111.4	5.6
MB			2 Y		S	25	Green	3	Sand Shot (SW)	4	4	3	3	3	71.7	106.2	577.5	689.8	296.3	2.3
			3 N			12'	Green	4	Putt	5	4	4	4	5						
		4	4 Y		6'		Green	4	Putt	5	4	4	3	3	67.1	101.9	79.8	248.3	108	2.3
4	4 (336)		1 Y		S	280	Rough	4	Drive (D)	5	5	4	2	3	63.9	58.3	78	273.8	36.4	7.5
			2 Y		S	64	Green	5	Approach (SW)	5	5	4	3	4	64.8	75.3	522.7	428.7	131.8	3.3
		3	3 Y		7'		Green	5	Putt	5	5	5	4	5	60.5	83.4	145.5	153.1	44.4	3.4
5	4 (379)		1 Y		S	280	Fairway	5	Drive (D)	5	5	4	2	2	70.3	78.7	77.2	395.3	67.7	5.8
			2 Y		S	100	Green	5	Approach (SW)	5	5	5	3	3	65.1	101.2	969.1	808.2	76.4	10.6
			3 N			8'	Green	5	Putt	5	5	6	3	4						
		4	4 Y		2'		Green	3	Putt	5	5	5	3	3	68.2	106.6	252.9	522.6	265.7	2
6	4 (420)		1 Y		R	240	Rough	2	Drive (D)	4	3	3	2	2	71.5	63.3	120.2	176.1	87	2
			2 Y		S	65	Rough	2	Approach (6i)	3	3	2	3	3	61.6	59.4	51.3	135	107.7	1.3
MB			3 Y		S	100	Fairway	3	Approach (SW)	4	4	4	4	5	68.2	49.4	517.3	323	71.2	4.5
			4 N			25'	Green	4	Putt	5	5	5	5	5						
		5	5 Y		1'		Green	5	Putt	5	5	5	3	3	64.4	90.3	153.2	587	115.3	5.1
7	5 (533)		1 Y		R	275	Rough	2	Drive (D)	5	4	3	1	3	65.3	57.3	341.7	123.3	72.2	1.7
			2 Y		S	163	Rough	3	Layup (5i)	4	4	3	2	3	74.5	33.9	56.7	43.6	28.7	1.5
			3 Y		S	95	Green	4	Approach (SW)	5	4	4	3	4	76.3	60	65.6	864.9	130.9	6.6
MB			4 N			16'	Green	4	Putt	5	5	5	4	5						
		5	5 Y		1'		Green	5	Putt	5	5	5	3	3	66.7	76.6	68.7	286.8	147.3	1.9
8	4 (332)		1 Y		S	265	Fairway	4	Drive (D)	5	4	4	2	3	70.8	138.9	465.5	3191.8	1725.9	1.8
			2 Y		S	75	Green	4	Approach (SW)	5	4	4	3	4	74.8	88.3	1133.6	448.3	803	0.6
		3	3 Y			20'	Green	5	Putt	5	5	5	4	5	61.2	51.8	140.7	318.8	104.2	3.1

FIGURE 9.13   "Psycho-Scorecard" containing predictor and outcome measures.

The Excel file (Figure 9.13) contains GV's golf performance data prior to the mental training phase of his performance analysis and enhancement program. The key predictor and outcome measures, some of which serve as both predictor and criterion measures, include:

1. Quality of Shot: ranges from 1 (worst) to 5 (best) and is based on distance and direction in the context of a hole's configuration: Outcome Measure.
2. Heart Rate Variability: see cells "P" through "U": Outcome measures that reflect psychological influences/responses prior to a shot and Predictor measures that predict impending shot (HRV measures after a shot [outcome measure] and HRV measures before a shot [predictor measure]).
3. Focus-Comfort-Control: Self-report CSARCS-A state analogue measure obtained after a shot via self-report upon prompting. Used as a predictor and outcome measure (predictor of HRV and/ or quality of shot in the context of level of critical moment prior to a shot and retrospectively [reflects mind–body state during previous shot; outcome measure]). Focus is hypothetically related to SA, Comfort to SR, and Control to SC.
4. Criticality: level of criticality (1–5 scale from least to most critical) is assigned to each shot; (1) Probabilistic Criticality (CMPROB) score is based on the probability that par or better can still be achieved, depending on where the ball is in relationship to the green and the number of the current shot (e.g., shot 2 within range of the green on a par 4 hole would have high par probability and a low CMPROB; less probabilistic-based pressure/criticality); (2) Situational

Criticality (CMSIT) takes additional factors into account when assigning criticality, including a golfer's Athlete's Profile, special strengths and weaknesses and current round score. Situational criticality can be raised or lowered as a function of such variables. Critical Moment (criticality) variables serve as predictor measures that are analyzed relative to quality of shot performance and psychophysiological responding (HRV responses).

5. Money ball (MB): an added in-the-moment test of responding to a stressor. Money-ball moments are introduced randomly across all trials or competitive actions (about 10%–30% of all trials). A golfer must achieve a 4 or 5 QoS rating to have mastered or won a money-ball moment. Money balls are notated in a money-ball bank. Periodically, one's money ball "balance" is checked and rewards or punishment are given based on Money Ball performance is a predictor variable.

Method

In the pre-intervention phase, the golfer's pre-round HRV was measured for 2 min about 15 min before his first tee shot and again, for 1 min immediately before his initial shot. The BioCom Technologies Heart Scanner program with a linked ear sensor was used to monitor HRV. A golf cart was used to get around the course. One-minute HRV measurements were taken while the player was seated in the golf cart and was driven to the location of the ball after each shot. The measures seen in the preceding Excel spreadsheet were notated after each shot with the exception of the HRV measures that were extracted from Heart Scanner Autonomic Balance reports after each round and then entered. The pre-intervention phase consisted of 36 holes and 150 shots (cumulative scores in the 70s each round = 150 shots).

Findings

Correlation analyses were run in an attempt to establish the extent of relationships between select predictor and criterion measures. SPSS output charts are further presented in Figures 9.14 to 9.19. Relevant findings are discussed.

Relationships Between Criticality, Quality of Shot, and HRV: Prospective (Figure 9.14)

What stands out in the preceding data set is the positive correlation between Probabilistic Criticality and Quality of Shot (QoS); $r = .19$, indicating that GV's performance increased as a function of level of criticality. While an r of .19 "only" explains about 4% of the variance in QoS that can be attributed to competitive pressure (CMPROB), comparatively, based on extensive studies of baseball and tennis players and golfers, positive correlations between criticality and performance outcome tend to rarely exceed .30 and are frequently well below .05, with only 2 out of 45 major league professional baseball players in a pilot study having attained a positive correlation between criticality and batting performance (Quality of At-Bat; Szuhany, Carlstedt & Duckworth, 2009). Hence, GV's criticality performance suggests that he is more likely to succeed or at least perform well than falter when under pressure, consistent with his Athlete's Profile (AP) constellation of M-M-M (raw scores: 12-10-18 putting him on the cusp of the Ideal AP of L-L-H).

In terms of the impact criticality had on HRV measures, very low frequency (VLF) was associated with CMPROB ($r = .21$) and CMsit (.21), suggesting that as the level of criticality increased,

Correlations

		QUALITY	CMPROB	CMSIT	HR	SDNN	VL	L	H	LH
QUALITY	Pearson Correlation	1.000	.190*	.146	-.233**	-.249**	.092	-.139	-.173*	.029
	Sig. (2-tailed)	.	.020	.075	.004	.002	.265	.090	.034	.722
	N	150	149	149	150	150	150	150	150	150
CMPROB	Pearson Correlation	.190*	1.000	.753**	.040	-.031	.206*	-.074	-.007	-.092
	Sig. (2-tailed)	.020	.	.000	.631	.708	.012	.371	.929	.265
	N	149	149	149	149	149	149	149	149	149
CMSIT	Pearson Correlation	.146	.753**	1.000	-.007	-.020	.214**	-.045	-.021	-.179*
	Sig. (2-tailed)	.075	.000	.	.932	.810	.009	.585	.795	.029
	N	149	149	149	149	149	149	149	149	149
HR	Pearson Correlation	-.233**	.040	-.007	1.000	.055	-.027	.096	.000	.074
	Sig. (2-tailed)	.004	.631	.932	.	.505	.741	.241	.995	.368
	N	150	149	149	150	150	150	150	150	150
SDNN	Pearson Correlation	-.249**	-.031	-.020	.055	1.000	.271**	.561**	.719**	-.153
	Sig. (2-tailed)	.002	.708	.810	.505	.	.001	.000	.000	.062
	N	150	149	149	150	150	150	150	150	150
VL	Pearson Correlation	.092	.206*	.214**	-.027	.271**	1.000	.104	.057	.119
	Sig. (2-tailed)	.265	.012	.009	.741	.001	.	.205	.490	.146
	N	150	149	149	150	150	150	150	150	150
L	Pearson Correlation	-.139	-.074	-.045	.096	.561**	.104	1.000	.460**	.225**
	Sig. (2-tailed)	.090	.371	.585	.241	.000	.205	.	.000	.006
	N	150	149	149	150	150	150	150	150	150
H	Pearson Correlation	-.173*	-.007	-.021	.000	.719**	.057	.460**	1.000	-.309**
	Sig. (2-tailed)	.034	.929	.795	.995	.000	.490	.000	.	.000
	N	150	149	149	150	150	150	150	150	150
LH	Pearson Correlation	.029	-.092	-.179*	.074	-.153	.119	.225**	-.309**	1.000
	Sig. (2-tailed)	.722	.265	.029	.368	.062	.146	.006	.000	.
	N	150	149	149	150	150	150	150	150	150

*Correlation is significant at the 0.05 level (2-tailed).

**Correlation is significant at the 0.01 level (2-tailed).

FIGURE 9.14 HRV and golf outcome measures.

sympathetic nervous system (SNS) responding as reflected in VLF may have contributed to better performance (QoS). It should be remembered that HRV measures, when using the BioCom paradigm, are obtained after the fact, that is, they are temporally distant to the moment of a shot. However, it is hypothesized that endocrinological responses (hormonal; stress hormone levels of cortisol, adrenaline, etc.) that are manifested concomitant to encountering stress (e.g., critical moments) will continue to exert their influence on HRV measures in the minutes after a competitive event (e.g., after a putt). Consequently, even temporally disparate measures of HRV can be considered viable ANS/psychophysiological snapshots of mental, emotional, or mind–body–motor states at the time of an actual competitive event or action, such as a golf shot, especially after pressure situations (either real-probabilistic or AP-mediated perceived pressure; critical moments). Thus, in this case, increased level of criticality led to enhanced ANS–SNS activity as reflected in greater VLF, that, while likely degrading slowly from the time the shot was completed to when the golfer's HRV was measured prior to the next shot, was sufficiently sustained to emerge as both a reflector of what just happened (retrospectively) and predictor of what will happen (prospectively; the next shot).

The extent to which such a temporally remote monitoring paradigm compares to a wireless in-the-moment paradigm (constant monitoring and measuring) using the Polar RS800CX system will be investigated in the near future (see pilot case study further on). Nevertheless, data from hundreds of intra-individual investigations across numerous sports supports usage of the Carlstedt Protocol 1- to 2-min pre-action or time-out HRV-monitoring paradigm with IZOF profiles being established on the basis of associations between and among HRV measures, level of criticality (competitive pressure), and performance (micro-level outcome measures) for these athletes. The Polar system will be explicated later in this chapter.

In addition to the VLF and criticality findings, Low: High-frequency ratio (LH) was negatively correlated with CMSIT ($r = -.18$). Low: High ratio reflects ANS balance or the extent to which the SNS and PNS interact to adapt to changing internal (mental) and environmental stimuli (criticality). Relative to GV, the greater the situational criticality, the lower his L: H ratio (greater low-frequency activity compared to high frequency activity), indicative of more of a PNS influence prior to and after shots having greater situational criticality. This response, as with GV's VLF response as a function of increasing criticality, is consistent with his AP.

While it would be expected that criticality will impact or mediate ANS responding as reflected in HRV, ultimately, it is all about outcome, that is, the extent criticality mediated HRV responses are associated with actual outcome, such as QoS in golf. With GV, whose QoS increased as a function of CMPROB, it was also observed that a number of HRV measures were associated with QoS, including HR ($r = -.23$), SDNN ($r = -.25$), and high frequency (HF; $r = -.17$), indicating that greater HR, SDNN, and HF resulted in lower QoS. This can be interpreted as follows. In GV, a preliminary IZOF profile emerged in which various HRV measures predicted quality of performance. Since, conceptually, heart rate deceleration (HRD) has been shown to predominate in pre-action phases of many sports, including golf, it can be expected that HRV parameters that are associated with the mitigation of HRD, including high HR and (at times) greater SDNN (HRD is *usually* associated with less HRV as reflected in lower SDNN, *depending upon the length or duration of the HRD response*), will be negatively associated with outcome (QoS). The HF finding, while inconsistent with the greater PNS activity that has been found to be associated with HRD trends, can be seen as anomalous here, since it would be expected that *less* HF activity would be associated with poorer QoS and not vice versa.

However, this latter HF finding can be explained in the context of temporal properties of HRV in which the accuracy of HRV measures are often contingent on the length of measured epochs. As a result, while time domain measures are more stable and not impacted by recording length, frequency domain measures are more sensitive to epoch duration. Hence, as pertaining to the time-locked HRD response that only lasts a few seconds, at most, it may not be possible to accurately assess the amount of any given frequency domain measure in a very short HRV epoch (HRD). This issue can only be resolved in future micro-studies of HRD using the Polar system (which are on the drawing board). By contrast, a 1-min recording can be used to establish the predictive impact of frequency domain measures on performance both retro- and prospectively. Alternatively, such an unexpected response may reflect IZOF components that are unique to this athlete.

State CSARCS-A Self-Report Analogue Measures and HRV Criterion Referencing (Figure 9.15)

In addition to HRV, criticality and QoS analyses, self-report of CSARCS-A (Athlete's Profile) analogue state measures were investigated. Focus (SA), comfort (SR), and control (SC) were moderately correlated with outcome (QoS); $r = .45$, 58, and .58, respectively. Essentially, GV's mental/emotional state as determined on the basis of his self-report immediately after a shot predicted performance on the next shot. This finding supports the temporal discordant hypothesis that proposes that an athlete's mind–body state after a competitive action or event will be reflected in HRV measures, even if they are obtained before or after the fact (i.e., are not time-locked or synchronized to the actual action or event).

Correlations

		QUALITY	CMPROB	CMSIT	FOCUS	COMFORT	CONTROL
QUALITY	Pearson Correlation	1.000	.190*	.146	.454**	.576**	.576**
	Sig. (2-tailed)	.	.020	.075	.000	.000	.000
	N	150	149	149	150	150	150
CMPROB	Pearson Correlation	.190*	1.000	.753**	.096	.279**	.424**
	Sig. (2-tailed)	.020	.	.000	.243	.001	.000
	N	149	149	149	149	149	149
CMSIT	Pearson Correlation	.146	.753**	1.000	.038	.130	.241**
	Sig. (2-tailed)	.075	.000	.	.648	.115	.003
	N	149	149	149	149	149	149
FOCUS	Pearson Correlation	.454**	.096	.038	1.000	.712**	.613**
	Sig. (2-tailed)	.000	.243	.648	.	.000	.000
	N	150	149	149	150	150	150
COMFORT	Pearson Correlation	.576**	.279**	.130	.712**	1.000	.869**
	Sig. (2-tailed)	.000	.001	.115	.000	.	.000
	N	150	149	149	150	150	150
CONTROL	Pearson Correlation	.576**	.424**	.241**	.613**	.869**	1.000
	Sig. (2-tailed)	.000	.000	.003	.000	.000	.
	N	150	149	149	150	150	150

*Correlation is significant at the 0.05 level (2-tailed).

**Correlation is significant at the 0.01 level (2-tailed).

FIGURE 9.15   Qualitative self-report and quality of shot relationships.

Probabilistic and situational criticality were associated with two of the three Athlete's Profile measures, comfort ($r = .28$ with CMPROB) and control ($r = .42$ with CMPROB and $r = .24$ with CMSIT), but not level of focus. Athletes are blind to criticality ratings in the moment.

That is, they are not told what level of criticality was assigned to the just-completed competitive action or event or the pending action or event (golf shot in this case). As such, they have no prior knowledge that their self-report will be analyzed in the context of objective measures of competitive pressure or stress. Consequently, level of criticality can be used to criterion reference self-report of AP analogue states to help determine to what extent a specific state (AP state constellation level; e.g., 4-5-4 [state focus-comfort-control]) predicts or reflects performance outcome. It can also be used to ascertain the extent to which trait AP constellations and associated behavioral and performance propensities mediate or manifest state behavior and performance that are consistent with what would be expected/predicted on the basis of their general trait AP.

In the case of GV, whose AP was M-M-M (but relatively close to L-L-H), his self-report (state AP measures) was consistent with the more ideal AP that he appears to approach. The concurrent or criterion-referenced validity of the AP trait constellation increases or decreases as a function of strength of association (correlation) between state AP measures (F-C-C) and criticality, more so than the relationship between and among F-C-C and outcome (QoS), since athletes are blind to criticality ratings but are well aware of what just happened (they know what the outcome was). Consequently, correlations between AP state measures (F-C-C) and outcome may be vulnerable to response sets (self-report being influenced by biases, social desirability, or direct knowledge of clear performance relationships) with higher or lower associations between F-C-C feedback and performance not being reflective of actual subliminal psychological processes that underlie the AP's conceptual and construct bases that are known to impact critical moment performance. Thus, when it comes to outcome, awareness of mental states that were "felt" or experienced in the moment may be more "conscious" and prone to distortion (e.g., rarely will an athlete after a successful sport-specific action report low F-C-C scores [e.g., 2-1-2]). By contrast, the subliminal or unconscious premise of the AP and Theory of Critical Moments is less likely to be consciously negated or overridden when the AP state measures are analyzed in the context of predictor and measures to which an athlete is blind (single- or double-blind methodology).

HRV is an outcome measure that can also be used to criterion reference and, further, blindly validate the self-report-based AP state analogue measures that may be subject to bias and response sets, especially when an athlete is high in subliminal attention (SA; HS = hypnotic susceptibility; Figure 9.16). Relative to GV, who is very low in SA, it is less likely that his self-report was contaminated by response sets.

GV's HR was negatively correlated with each AP state measure (F, $r = -18$, C, $r = -.23$ and C, $r = -.18$). This finding can be considered consistent with AP and theory of critical moments models of peak performance and pre-action HRD that is associated with enhanced focus, reaction time, and outcome, a psychophysiological measure that is marked by decreasing HR. The fact that VL frequency was positively correlated (.17) with F can be interpreted in the context of IZOF model and may indicate that GV needs a minimum level of physiological reactivity (SNS activity) to achieve peak levels of attention.

Finally, GV's L: H ratio was positively correlated with F-C-C (.21, .19, and .14, respectively). As with HR and AP state measures, this last finding is conceptually consistent in that one would expect level of autonomic balance (that the L: H reflects) to be associated with greater mind–body control. Overall, GV's HRV responses were consistent about his self-report of state level of focus-comfort and control.

Correlations

		FOCUS	COMFORT	CONTROL	HR	SDNN	VL	L	H	LH
FOCUS	Pearson Correlation	1.000	.712**	.613**	-.175*	.022	.169*	.122	-.055	.205*
	Sig. (2-tailed)		.000	.000	.032	.787	.038	.137	.503	.012
	N	150	150	150	150	150	150	150	150	150
COMFORT	Pearson Correlation	.712**	1.000	.869**	-.230**	-.139	.079	-.022	-.144	.191*
	Sig. (2-tailed)	.000		.000	.005	.090	.335	.791	.079	.020
	N	150	150	150	150	150	150	150	150	150
CONTROL	Pearson Correlation	.613**	.869**	1.000	-.181*	-.101	.100	-.012	-.122	.141
	Sig. (2-tailed)	.000	.000		.026	.219	.221	.888	.138	.086
	N	150	150	150	150	150	150	150	150	150
HR	Pearson Correlation	-.175*	-.230**	-.181*	1.000	.055	-.027	.096	.000	.074
	Sig. (2-tailed)	.032	.005	.026		.505	.741	.241	.995	.368
	N	150	150	150	150	150	150	150	150	150
SDNN	Pearson Correlation	.022	-.139	-.101	.055	1.000	.271**	.561**	.719**	-.153
	Sig. (2-tailed)	.787	.090	.219	.505		.001	.000	.000	.062
	N	150	150	150	150	150	150	150	150	150
VL	Pearson Correlation	.169*	.079	.100	-.027	.271**	1.000	.104	.057	.119
	Sig. (2-tailed)	.038	.335	.221	.741	.001		.205	.490	.146
	N	150	150	150	150	150	150	150	150	150
L	Pearson Correlation	.122	-.022	-.012	.096	.561**	.104	1.000	.460**	.225**
	Sig. (2-tailed)	.137	.791	.888	.241	.000	.205		.000	.006
	N	150	150	150	150	150	150	150	150	150
H	Pearson Correlation	-.055	-.144	-.122	.000	.719**	.057	.460**	1.000	-.309**
	Sig. (2-tailed)	.503	.079	.138	.995	.000	.490	.000		.000
	N	150	150	150	150	150	150	150	150	150
LH	Pearson Correlation	.205*	.191*	.141	.074	-.153	.119	.225**	-.309**	1.000
	Sig. (2-tailed)	.012	.020	.086	.368	.062	.146	.006	.000	
	N	150	150	150	150	150	150	150	150	150

* Correlation is significant at the 0.05 level (2-tailed).

** Correlation is significant at the 0.01 level (2-tailed).

FIGURE 9.16   AP state measures and HRV relationships.

Relationships Between Criticality, Quality of Shot, and HRV: Retrospective

It should be noted that the previous data sets, findings, and analyses are prospective, that is, mind–body responding and performance relationships were established on the basis of the effect of predictor variables such as criticality, money ball, state self-report, and HRV, on subsequent outcome (e.g., the effect of CMPROB on immediate outcome [QoS]). However, as previously mentioned, the preceding and other predictor measures can be investigated retrospectively to determine to what extent HRV measures that are documented prior to an impending shot not only predict subsequent outcome but are still reflective of what just occurred (as in the data set below, Figure 9.17). The retrospective analysis approach is also based on the assumption that although mind–body measures (such as HRV) may change (usually attenuate) over time, if the time lag is relatively short, endocrinological responses that can influence HRV will still be active and reflective (indirectly reflected in HRV) as well as predictive of what just happened. As such, HRV, after the fact, to a certain, and at times, large extent, may be mediated by prior psychological influences (e.g., emotions, attention, and psychophysiological responses [intensity]) as well as energy expenditure. Extensive research has confirmed the existence of retrospective IZOF and performance profiles. Retrospective analyses are an important part of comprehensive assessment of psychological performance (Unpublished ABSP database).

Interestingly, GV's QoS increased as a function of increasing criticality (CMPROB) to the same extent as in the prospective condition ($r = .19$), suggesting stability or test–retest reliability relative to performance under pressure in this athlete. Regarding HRV, HR and HF emerged as correlates of QoS in the retrospective condition as in the prospective condition (HR and QoS, $r = -.15$; HF and QoS $r = -.07$). In the retrospective condition, criticality was negatively correlated with HF (HF and CMPROB and CMSIT; $r = -.19$ and $.19$ respectively).

Correlations

		QUALITY	CMPROB	CMSIT	HR	SDNN	VL	L	H	LH	HHR	LHR
QUALITY	Pearson Correlation	1.000	.190*	.146	-.148	.052	.015	.087	-.066	.130	a	a
	Sig. (2-tailed)		.020	.075	.071	.531	.857	.292	.420	.114	.	.
	N	150	149	149	150	150	150	150	150	150	0	0
CMPROB	Pearson Correlation	.190*	1.000	.753**	-.038	-.093	.131	-.133	-.188*	.060	a	a
	Sig. (2-tailed)	.020		.000	.647	.261	.111	.105	.022	.464	.	.
	N	149	149	149	149	149	149	149	149	149	0	0
CMSIT	Pearson Correlation	.146	.753**	1.000	.080	-.072	.122	-.085	-.189*	-.008	a	a
	Sig. (2-tailed)	.075	.000		.333	.384	.138	.302	.021	.927	.	.
	N	149	149	149	149	149	149	149	149	149	0	0
HR	Pearson Correlation	-.148	-.038	.080	1.000	.057	-.015	.107	.001	.095	a	a
	Sig. (2-tailed)	.071	.647	.333		.491	.859	.193	.993	.248	.	.
	N	150	149	149	150	150	150	150	150	150	0	0
SDNN	Pearson Correlation	.052	-.093	-.072	.057	1.000	.300**	.542**	.718**	-.163*	a	a
	Sig. (2-tailed)	.531	.261	.384	.491		.000	.000	.000	.046	.	.
	N	150	149	149	150	150	150	150	150	150	0	0
VL	Pearson Correlation	.015	.131	.122	-.015	.300**	1.000	.117	.096	.034	a	a
	Sig. (2-tailed)	.857	.111	.138	.859	.000		.155	.245	.683	.	.
	N	150	149	149	150	150	150	150	150	150	0	0
L	Pearson Correlation	.087	-.133	-.085	.107	.542**	.117	1.000	.470**	.225**	a	a
	Sig. (2-tailed)	.292	.105	.302	.193	.000	.155		.000	.006	.	.
	N	150	149	149	150	150	150	150	150	150	0	0
H	Pearson Correlation	-.066	-.188*	-.189*	.001	.718**	.096	.470**	1.000	-.291**	a	a
	Sig. (2-tailed)	.420	.022	.021	.993	.000	.245	.000		.000	.	.
	N	150	149	149	150	150	150	150	150	150	0	0
LH	Pearson Correlation	.130	.060	-.008	.095	-.163*	.034	.225**	-.291**	1.000	a	a
	Sig. (2-tailed)	.114	.464	.927	.248	.046	.683	.006	.000		.	.
	N	150	149	149	150	150	150	150	150	150	0	0
HHR	Pearson Correlation	a	a	a	a	a	a	a	a	a	a	a
	Sig. (2-tailed)											
	N	0	0	0	0	0	0	0	0	0	0	0
LHR	Pearson Correlation	a	a	a	a	a	a	a	a	a	a	a
	Sig. (2-tailed)											
	N	0	0	0	0	0	0	0	0	0	0	0

*Correlation is significant at the 0.05 level (2-tailed).
**Correlation is significant at the 0.01 level (2-tailed).
a Cannot be computed because at least one of the variables is constant.

FIGURE 9.17 Retrospective analysis of post-golf-stoke-obtained HRV and outcome.

Self-report of AP state measures in the retrospective condition reveal an athlete's conscious awareness of mental states immediately after a competitive event. These states are reflective of what just happened. In contrast to the prospective condition, all F-C-C and criticality relationships were negative (F and CMPROB, $r = -.31$; C and CMPROB, $r = -.39$; C and CMPROB, $r = -.39$; F and CMSIT, $r = -.32$; C and CMSIT, $r = -.43$; C and CMSIT, $r = -.43$), suggesting that GV was fairly oblivious to the level of criticality associated (attributed) with the competitive event that just occurred. This could be expected of an athlete whose PHO constellation is on the cusp of being an ideal AP. As previously mentioned, ultimately, performance outcome supersedes assumptions and assessments pertaining to mental toughness. Consequently, GV's failure to recognize that a particular shot was determined to have a high level of criticality likely was/is performance facilitative. Essentially, and in line with his AP, GV may be/have been oblivious to changes in pressure as a function of rising criticality that athletes with more detrimental and worst APs would be highly aware of and more likely to falter when encountering greater probabilistic and situational criticality. In terms of outcome in the retrospective condition, GV's level of F-C ($r = .21$)-C ($r = .24$) as in the prospective condition, was positively correlated with QoS, albeit to a considerably lesser extent with the exception of F, which did not predict QoS in the retrospective condition (see Figures 9.16 [prospective condition] and 9.18 [retrospective condition]).

This suggests that self-report of F-C-C after a competitive event, if accurate, will be confirmed or can be criterion referenced by/using HRV measures/profiles that are likely to be conceptually consistent with what would be expected on the basis of an athlete's AP in the context of increasing criticality.

As previously noted, GV's self-report of F-C-C and HRV in the prospective condition could be considered conceptually consistent (Figure 9.16). However, in the retrospective condition (Figure 9.19), in which state F-C-C was negatively associated with level of criticality (CMPROB and CMSIT), no HRV measures emerged as reflective of these psychological states. Such a finding could be expected in a case where an athlete's self-report is inconsistent with "normal" (HRV) responses to objective indices of stress (criticality ratings); self-report, that, paradoxically, in an athlete with an ideal AP is not consistent with what one would expect, namely, greater SNS-VLF activation as criticality increases.

Hence, relative to GV (AP on the cusp of being ideal), whose self-report of state AP PHO measures was highly inconsistent with what one would expect, indicative of obliviousness to the

Correlations

		QUALITY	CMPROB	CMSIT	FOCUS	COMFORT	CONTROL
QUALITY	Pearson Correlation	1.000	.190*	.146	.080	.209*	.236**
	Sig. (2-tailed)	.	.020	.075	.332	.011	.004
	N	150	149	149	148	148	148
CMPROB	Pearson Correlation	.190*	1.000	.753**	-.310**	-.394**	-.388**
	Sig. (2-tailed)	.020	.	.000	.000	.000	.000
	N	149	149	149	147	147	147
CMSIT	Pearson Correlation	.146	.753**	1.000	-.324**	-.425**	-.431**
	Sig. (2-tailed)	.075	.000	.	.000	.000	.000
	N	149	149	149	147	147	147
FOCUS	Pearson Correlation	.080	-.310**	-.324**	1.000	.712**	.613**
	Sig. (2-tailed)	.332	.000	.000	.	.000	.000
	N	148	147	147	150	150	150
COMFORT	Pearson Correlation	.209*	-.394**	-.425**	.712**	1.000	.869**
	Sig. (2-tailed)	.011	.000	.000	.000	.	.000
	N	148	147	147	150	150	150
CONTROL	Pearson Correlation	.236**	-.388**	-.431**	.613**	.869**	1.000
	Sig. (2-tailed)	.004	.000	.000	.000	.000	.
	N	148	147	147	150	150	150

*Correlation is significant at the 0.05 level (2-tailed).

**Correlation is significant at the 0.01 level (2-tailed).

FIGURE 9.18   Retrospective AP state self-report and outcome.

Correlations

		FOCUS	COMFORT	CONTROL	HR	SDNN	VL	L	H	LH
FOCUS	Pearson Correlation	1.000	.712**	.613**	.060	.050	.034	.044	-.019	.063
	Sig. (2-tailed)	.	.000	.000	.470	.550	.685	.597	.822	.446
	N	150	150	150	148	148	148	148	148	148
COMFORT	Pearson Correlation	.712**	1.000	.869**	.102	.087	-.009	.120	.060	.105
	Sig. (2-tailed)	.000	.	.000	.217	.295	.911	.146	.467	.204
	N	150	150	150	148	148	148	148	148	148
CONTROL	Pearson Correlation	.613**	.869**	1.000	.108	.104	-.078	.125	.102	.029
	Sig. (2-tailed)	.000	.000	.	.191	.207	.347	.131	.217	.724
	N	150	150	150	148	148	148	148	148	148
HR	Pearson Correlation	.060	.102	.108	1.000	.057	-.015	.107	.001	.095
	Sig. (2-tailed)	.470	.217	.191	.	.491	.859	.193	.993	.248
	N	148	148	148	150	150	150	150	150	150
SDNN	Pearson Correlation	.050	.087	.104	.057	1.000	.300**	.542**	.718**	-.163*
	Sig. (2-tailed)	.550	.295	.207	.491	.	.000	.000	.000	.046
	N	148	148	148	150	150	150	150	150	150
VL	Pearson Correlation	.034	-.009	-.078	-.015	.300**	1.000	.117	.096	.034
	Sig. (2-tailed)	.685	.911	.347	.859	.000	.	.155	.245	.683
	N	148	148	148	150	150	150	150	150	150
L	Pearson Correlation	.044	.120	.125	.107	.542**	.117	1.000	.470**	.225**
	Sig. (2-tailed)	.597	.146	.131	.193	.000	.155	.	.000	.006
	N	148	148	148	150	150	150	150	150	150
H	Pearson Correlation	-.019	.060	.102	.001	.718**	.096	.470**	1.000	-.291**
	Sig. (2-tailed)	.822	.467	.217	.993	.000	.245	.000	.	.000
	N	148	148	148	150	150	150	150	150	150
LH	Pearson Correlation	.063	.105	.029	.095	-.163*	.034	.225**	-.291**	1.000
	Sig. (2-tailed)	.446	.204	.724	.248	.046	.683	.006	.000	.
	N	148	148	148	150	150	150	150	150	150

*Correlation is significant at the 0.05 level (2-tailed).

**Correlation is significant at the 0.01 level (2-tailed).

FIGURE 9.19   Post-golf-shot HRV and previous outcome: Retrospective analysis.

criticality of a competitive event/action, one could expect that his HRV profile or individual HRV measures would also reflect a lack of subliminal ANS responding, supportive of such conscious oblivion.

Money Ball versus No Money Ball

Another criticality or pressure metric is the money ball. Money balls are randomly induced or encountered (from the perspective of the athlete but known to a coach and/or sport psychology practitioner) situations that demand of an athlete peak technical and psychological responding and performance and an all-or-nothing outcome (the athlete must win the point or successfully complete an operationalized task; for example, make a "perfect" loft pass to a teammate in soccer). Money balls are intended to keep an athlete on edge during training and practice/simulated competition, requiring them to focus, perform, and succeed on command. Money balls are designated "MB" in the initial Excel score sheet shown in Figure 9.13. They usually compose 10% to 30% of all attempted actions (golf shots).

In this MB situation, performance was evaluated on the basis of QoS to determine whether GV performed better when he was made aware of a critical moment and had to succeed, compared to non-MB shots, CM-rated, and routine shots. Note, it has already been established that GV, based on his F-C-C self-report and HRV responses, seemed to be unaware of level of criticality throughout his golf rounds, consistent with his AP. Thus, it was important to determine if his repressive coping (RC, or state RC = C) mediated obliviousness to competitive pressure could be penetrated by making him aware of the heightened importance of a specific shot, and whether his MB performance would be worse than when more routine shots where encountered. Mean comparisons are shown in Figure 9.20.

GV's performance outcome and HRV responses were not significantly different in the MB versus non-MB situations. At first glance, this finding is inconsistent with his AP, and although

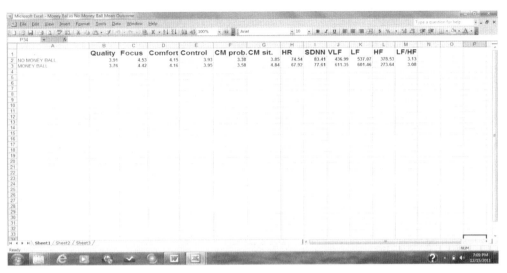

FIGURE 9.20   Money ball versus no money ball and outcome.

one might expect that a professional athlete who is on the cusp of the ideal AP would perform significantly better under pressure, in light of the fact that his QoS for all shots was fairly high to begin with (almost 4.0), his statistically *insignificant* drop in QoS in the MB condition may be a spurious finding. It should also be noted that there were only 19 MB compared to about 130 non-MB (although level 4 and 5 CRITPROB and CRITSIT is comparable to an MB) situations. Ideally, in consideration of statistical power requisites, it would have been better to carry out MB analyses after at least 40–50 MB had been encountered. Nevertheless, GV's MB performance and HRV responses were consistent with his overall general and especially CM performance, in line with his AP.

Summary

Prospective and retrospective analyses are important to helping establish test–retest reliability or psychophysiological stability (mind–body stability) at the intra-individual level. Stability or test–retest reliability should, however, not necessarily be interpreted in the context of performance unless measures of interest are positively or negatively correlated with a specific outcome measure(s). In the case of GV, performance increased (was better) at higher levels of probabilistic criticality in both the retrospective and prospective condition with level of criticality (independent of outcome) also being negatively correlated with the same HRV measures in both conditions, suggesting that the manifestation of greater pressure (higher criticality) elicited psychophysiological responses (HRV measures) that were sensitive to higher levels of competitive stress. When such associations are discovered, it then must be determined if they are conceptually consistent or spurious or reflective of an athlete's unique situational IZOF or AP (Hanin, 2006). In this case, it must still be ascertained if greater criticality is consistently associated with a reduction in high frequency ANS–PNS activity across numerous rounds of golf, since one might expect more of a deactivation response (greater HF activity) when encountering greater levels of competitive stress (high level of criticality) in a mentally tougher athlete, as GV appears to be or have been during rounds upon which these analyses were based. On the other hand, in line with the IZOF and AP tenets and predictions, disparate and counterintuitive mind–body responses can be differentially associated with outcome. That is, the same ANS-HRV response profile in two different athletes having the same level of ability or skill could result in diametrically opposite results; one might lose the other win despite exhibiting the same psychophysiological response profile.

Heart Rate Variability-Performance Model: Time-Locked Version-Polar Telemetry System I

Recently, the CP has incorporated the Polar RS800CX heart activity monitoring system into its assessment and intervention procedures. The Polar system allows for real-time wireless and telemetry HRV data acquisition and analyses opening up the possibility of isolating specific inter-beat intervals during action. Such a capability facilitates micro-analyses of HRV and HRD on an unprecedented level, especially since investigations of HRV/HRD can be carried out during high-intensity training and competition. It is now possible to identify a single heartbeat or series of heartbeats prior to a tennis player hitting a passing shot on the run or as a quarterback is about to unleash a pass. While the Polar system was designed for guiding and assessing physical training and fitness-related activities, it is readily adaptable for sport psychological evaluative, analytic, and even mental training purposes over the course of simulated and official competition.

This section provides an in-depth overview of the use of the Polar system in the context of a real tennis match in an attempt to analyze HRV during all action phases and HRD in pre-action phases of competition. The presented pilot study was undertaken to evaluate the feasibility of using the Polar system across most sports. Methodological and procedural approaches will be discussed, along with the analysis and interpretation of the acquired data and the issue of motion artifact resistance.

The following chart (Figure 9.21) depicts step-by-step procedures associated with use of the Polar system during a tennis match.

Photo 1 contains components of the Polar RS800CX system, including the watch/computer that stores data that is transmitted from the chest strap and attached monitoring and telemetry hardware piece (as seen in photos 2 and 3).

Photo 4 shows a procedural approach whereby a player's heart activity during a changeover is then isolated post facto (after the match) by time-locking all inter-beat-intervals in this 1-min time-out epoch. This procedure is analogous to the CP one-minute changeover protocol using the BioCom Technologies system that was described previously in this chapter. By contrast, the Polar system is wireless, meaning that an athlete is not tethered to a wire connecting an electrode to a computer. This allows for continuous monitoring from the beginning to the end of the competition. Note: most of the photos are computer screenshots that were derived from a video recorder that was synchronized with the competition's timeline. This is achieved by starting the Polar watch-computer/monitor and video recorder at the same time.

Photo 5 captures a part of the pre-action phase as it gives way to action as seen in photo 6. After-the-match pre-action, action, and changeover epochs of interest can be retrieved for analysis purposes. Data from isolated epochs are transferred from the Polar analysis program into an Excel file for special HRD/HRA trend and HRV analyses (see 7).

The isolated HRV/HRD data are further analyzed using SPSS to determine the extent to which HRV activity of interest predict or reflect psychological performance (e.g., HRV during action phases and level 4 critical moments or length of HRD trends prior to a point that was won or lost).

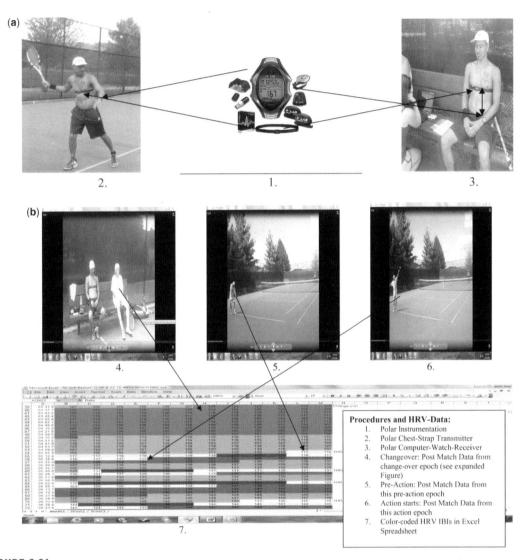

FIGURE 9.21   Illustrated (photos/screen shots) step-by-step overview of Polar components and use sequence.

HRV-Inter-Beat-Intervals: Expanded Excel Spreadsheet With Color Code Key

The following Excel chart (Figure 9.22) is an expanded version of item 7 in Figure 9.21 above.

This is a sample outtake of real match HRV-IBI data from the above-pictured player (wearing a shirt-Polar-chest strap that is concealed; Figure 9.22). The data was derived from Polar software that can be used to analyze basic HRV as well as HRD, HRA, and other allied measures that are time-locked to specific competition epochs. The above time-locked epochs represent pre-action, no-action (down-time), action, and time-outs (changeovers) during a tennis match as follows:

1. Yellow = heart rate deceleration trend
2. Red = heart rate acceleration trend
3. Blue Number-White Background = pre-action without HRD or HRA trend
4. Lavender = action phase

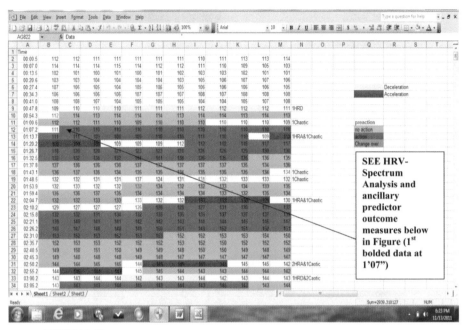

FIGURE 9.22   Color-coded HRV timeline with epochs of interest highlighted.

5. Light Orange = no action, prior to pre-action phase
6. Black Number-White Background = downtime (e.g., walking to the court before first point)
7. Green = changeover/time-out

HRV-Inter-Beat-Intervals: Expanded View of Match Sample Data Above

The following chart (Figure 9.23) contains examples of time-event epochs that correspond with the above photos in Figure 9.21 (4, 5, and 6; changeover and pre-action). The measures are expressed in beats per minute (although millisecond [msec] is usually preferred and can be used with the Polar system).

Once competition events of interest have been localized and color-coded, further analyses can be undertaken. For exploratory purposes, all action phases of the first set (up to 6 games all [6-6]) for the player of interest (CR = player) were isolated along with pre-action HRD/HRA and change-over HRV. There is no research on record documenting every IBI during an entire competition (any sport) in the context of pre-action and action phases and time-outs and subsequent HRV analyses on all action and time-out epochs.[5]

The following Excel file, Figure 9.24, contains a listing of a timeline of all action phases of the aforementioned set and the generated HRV analysis for each epoch. These epochs were isolated and extracted from the raw tachogram (seen in Figure 9.25), resulting in a chronological listing of every IBI in this 56-min tennis set.

A software function of the Polar system allows for any length of epoch to be delineated (see the blue line running from the left to the right of the tachogram in Figure 9.26) and then analyzed (in this case, HRV for the entire 56 min the first set took to complete). Such analyses can be performed for any epoch length.

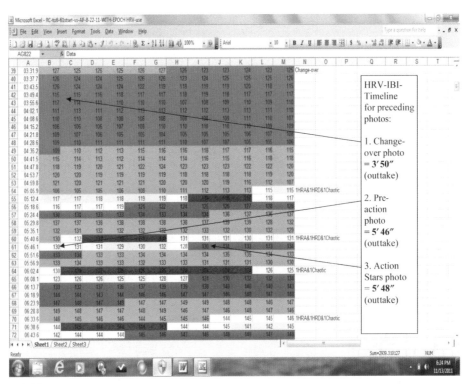

FIGURE 9.23 Additional color-coded sample HRV outtakes corresponding to preceding player photos.

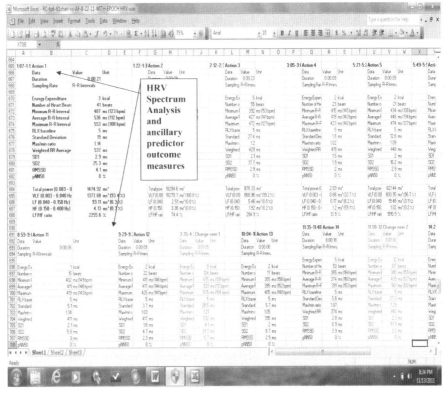

FIGURE 9.24 Spectrum analysis and ancillary predictor outcome measures.

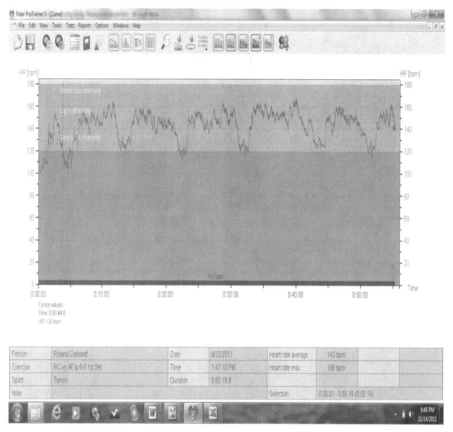

FIGURE 9.25   Tachogram from first set of sample tennis match.

Findings: CP Time Locked HRV Paradigm

METHOD, OPERATIONALIZATION OF HRD, AND "CHOKE" THRESHOLD

A former professional tennis player's (CR: AP of L-M-M) heart activity was monitored during a real practice match to determine whether pre-action phases of competition would be marked by specifically operationalized types of HRD trends. The entire match was also videotaped.

An HRD trend is considered to have occurred when the following or similar configuration of IBIs can be isolated during the pre-action phase of a point, from the moment a player commences his or her pre-action ritualistic movements, pre-ready position, and ready position: *one or more linearly slowing cardiac cycles leading up to the start of action (start of service windup when serving or start of the return split-step when returning), for example: 100, 98, 95 bpm* **action**. This would be an HRD trend of 3 (HRDt3). Since minute movements, such as even wiping one's face, can disrupt a linear HRD trend and lead to a brief acceleratory IBI as follows (same sample IBIs): 100, **102**, 98, **99**, 95 bpm, one can consider these accelerations as superfluous IBIs and of a metabolic nature and not psychologically mediated. Consequently, so long as the last IBI prior to action is a decelerating IBI, one can assume that pre-action HRD has occurred. Thus, in terms of how to analyze pre-action HRD, the following is recommended: (1) count all decelerating IBIs within the pre-action epoch commencing with the IBI corresponding with the video-synchronized/identified pre-action ritual onset and ending with the last HRD IBI prior to action to derive the total HRD IBIs in a pre-action epoch, (2) delineate the

FIGURE 9.26   HRV analysis of entire tennis set with time and frequency domain measures.

longest HRD IBI trend, that is, the number of consecutive (without interruption) linearly showing cardiac cycles (IBIs; if using the preceding example 100, 98, and 95 it would be a HRDt3, the longest of this pre-action epoch), and (3) finally, determine how many pre-action epochs end with a decelerating IBI. The same procedure is used to identify HRA trends. Thereafter, comparisons are made between HRD and HRA in the context of numerous outcome measures, including level of criticality (CM), points won or lost, and points won or lost when serving or returning. Since tennis outcomes can be strongly influenced by opponent factors, the mere manifestation of HRD does not guarantee successful performance or outcome, but at a minimum, is expected to prime an athlete to perform up to peak potential by helping set off a cascade of mind–body–motor responses that have been associated with enhanced attention (focus), faster reaction time, and motor (technical) preparation; thereby reducing the odds that an athlete will falter because of psychological factors. An athlete might lose a point immediately after pre-action HRD, but when this occurs, opponent factors and not "choking" could have contributed to negative outcome. Note: HRD appears to be a species-wide response to an impending stimulus or when expecting to respond to a stimulus like an approaching ball. This phenomenon (HRD) is pervasive across almost all athletes in pre-action phases of most sports. However, once the level of criticality reaches or exceeds an athlete's mental toughness, or "choke" threshold, psychologically mediated competitive anxiety is expected to disrupt pre-action performance preparatory HRD; instead, HRA predominates, an ANS response that is associated with left-frontal-lobe-based rumination, the generation of intrusive thoughts, and a failure to become technically primed to react. Vulnerability to HRA along with a lower choke threshold has been strongly linked to most performance detrimental AP PHO constellations (e.g., H-H-L; see Chapter 3).

Findings: Action Phase HRV

Each action epoch was isolated on the basis of the video timeline. The Polar software allows for the delineation of any epoch of interest and the subsequent automatic generation of HRV time and frequency domain measures for a specified epoch. CR's mean bpm (Mbpm) during action epochs was correlated with points won ($r = .30$), as was his low-frequency activity ($r = .27$). This finding suggests that greater HR during action epochs, a marker of greater effort or intensity, facilitated performance during points in this match. The LF activity and outcome finding is more ambiguous, although since this HRV measure can reflect ANS balance, a mind–body response may be associated with greater F-C-C in certain athletes (a specific IZOF biomarker response). However, this would need to be determined with greater statistical certainty over the course of additional matches.

The fact that maximum bpm during action phases explained 11% of the variance in points won supports the earlier interpretation of the Mbpm finding, namely, that greater action phase HR and associated higher levels of psychologically mediated intensity enhanced performance in this player. While this may make intuitive sense, this finding too must be validated across additional matches. In addition, data modeling of action epochs should be undertaken to determine whether relationships between HRV and outcome are influenced by a number of variables, including action epoch duration, number of shots during action phases, as well as the type of shots that were engaged in and how a point was won or lost.

Heart Rate Deceleration (HRD) and Heart Acceleration (HRA) Action Trends

Of major conceptual importance is to what extent HRD is present immediately prior to action. In this match's first set (for CR) consisting of 65 action epochs, HRD occurred 44 times prior to action (in which at least one or more decelerating IBI[s] preceded the onset of action).

Subsequent to these 44 HRD trends, 24 points were won and 20 were lost, resulting in a global HRD-win index (HRDgwi) of .545 (55%) and a global HRD-index (HRDgi) of .676 (68%).

While the win index may seem relatively low, it should be noted that the global win index encompasses all points, including opponent serve initiated points. The serve in tennis, as with pitching in baseball, can be very dominating to the extent of neutralizing any advantage pre-action HRD may bring in the moment. Thus, on one hand, HRD and the HRDgi, while hypothesized to reflect an in-the-moment peak performance state that is marked by optimum attention (focus), physiological reactivity (comfortable level of intensity), and technical/motor priming (control), opponent factors like a dominating serve or overpowering ground strokes can render HRD moot at times. This reality, however, does not diminish the importance of HRD as a potent performance biomarker (mind–body correlate of peak pre-action psychological readiness).

By contrast, HRA immediately prior to action may reflect a lack of pre-action F-C-C with the HRA global index (HRAgi), serving to quantify a lack of mind–body preparedness. CR exhibited 21 HRA trends prior to action (HRAgi of .477 [47%]) and an HRA global loss index (HRAgli) of .619 (62%). Norms for HRD and HRA trends (both group and individual averages) are being developed by the ABSP research consortium of board-certified practitioner/researchers, student certification final project research, summer fellowship programs, and other client/team athlete organization research. Nevertheless, irrespective of not yet having comprehensive HRD/HRA norms, intuitively, the higher the HRDgi and its converse (the lower the HRAgi), the more in control of mind–body performance processes an athlete is thought to be. Furthermore, relative to technical and physical ability, with all things being about equal in terms of player/athlete match-ups, ultimately, especially in the context of increasing criticality (competitive pressure), an athlete who manifests more HRD trends prior to action can be expected to win most games/matches and/or perform better than an opponent who exhibits a greater HRAgi (a greater HRAgi always indicated a lower HRDgi).

There was also one ancillary finding from this pilot HRD investigation, namely, HF HRV activity was correlated with total pre-action HRD IBIs ($r = .30$). This has conceptual significance in that HRD is PNS mediated and HF reflects, exclusively, PNS activity. When possible, micro-analyses and modeling of HRD trends should be performed, especially global win-and-loss indexes to determine to what extent an opponent or other factors that may be beyond the control of an athlete mitigate his or her HRDgwi. In addition, secondary operationalizations of HRD trends, including total HRD IBIs and longest HRD trend within a pre-action epoch, irrespective of whether the last IBI prior to action is a decelerating IBI, should be analyzed in the context of multiple sport-specific performance outcome measures.

These HRD findings are encouraging and are consistent with the first study of HRD during official tennis tournament matches that was carried out in 1997 using the first-generation Polar system (Carlstedt, 1998, 2001). They underscore the potential utility of using HRD trends to quantify in-the-moment comprehensive psychologically mediated mind–body–motor performance.

Heart Rate Variability-Performance Model: Time-Locked Version-Polar Telemetry System II

In addition to monitoring and analyzing HRV and HRD during actual competition, the Polar system has real-time telemetry data-acquisition capabilities that allow for numerous HRV/HRD experiments. Practitioners, researchers, and coaches can see cardiac activity live on a computer monitor, and capture and isolate HRV/HRD epochs of interest in the context of various research paradigms. The Polar telemetry option can also be used for biofeedback purposes, including the entrainment of HRD and validation of hypotheses relating to HRV/HRD and mental training (see the experimental configuration next).

Pilot HRD Validation Experiment: Description, Method, Issues, and Findings

An advanced tennis player ("PP"; male with AP of H-L-M) wearing the Polar chest strap and attached data collection and transmission component was linked to a telemetry-enabled computer (Polar Windlink) for real-time cardiac signal processing, display, and analysis of his heart activity (see the photos in Figure 9.27).

He was stationed in the service return area of a tennis court and was told to prepare for an impending serve (60 return trials), being sure to engage in any routine or preparatory ritual that he would normally do during real competition. A participating player (the server) was instructed to serve first serves (associated with more speed) into the deuce court service box/area. PP was told to focus on the service motion of the server and transition from mental preparation to action (do a split-step) once the server commenced his upward swing from the backscratcher position toward the ball.

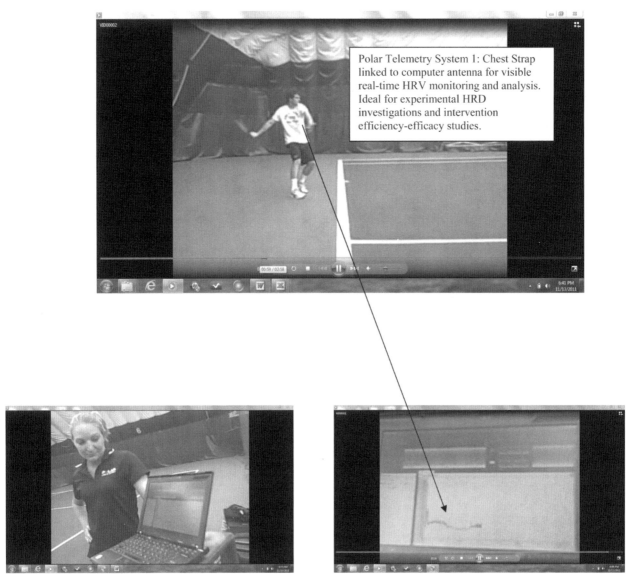

FIGURE 9.27 Screenshot photo series of Polar "live" telemetry-based HRV recording.

During the pre-action ritual and mental preparation phase, the visible cardiac cycle (IBIs) that could be seen in real time on the computer monitor were notated by a research assistant (pre-action HRD or HRA). The purpose of this experiment was to document all IBIs in the pre-action phase of the service return and analyze their properties after the experiment was completed. The lead researcher (a sport psychologist, pro-tour level tennis coach, and former professional tennis player) rated the quality of the return (QoS) on a 0-to-5 scale (from worst to best outcome) after each shot (return). The experiment consisted of 51 valid trials out of 60 that were attempted. Ten trials were rejected due to motion artifact.

Sixty trials is the approximate number of repetitions that is recommended when investigating single individuals in the context of a repeated-measures design and is methodologically comparable to having 60 subjects doing one trial each. Sixty trials is associated with a level of statistical power between .80 and .90 that balances the probability of making a Type I or Type II error during hypothesis testing. This type of design allows a researcher/practitioner to reach more empirically informed conclusions about the psychophysiological response and performance of an individual athlete. Findings pertaining to individual mind–body responses should always supersede group findings in terms of athlete assessment or evaluation and the interpretation of data/results provided by a repeated measures study's methodology/procedures replicate those of a group investigation (same study, but with a single case versus multiple subjects).

Since group study findings and interpretations, often, for the most part, are based on mean scores/results and are usually marked by wide variability relative to outcome or distribution of scores, in the context of applied sport psychological consulting, each individual athlete subject who participated in a group study should be analyzed separately or independently, irrespective of a group study's consolidated findings and interpretations. Decisions or expectations about athletes' performance should not be made on the basis of assumptions that are influenced by group findings, no matter how compelling the results may be. Group findings need to be replicated at the intra-individual level, cognizant of methodological and analytic issues, including statistical power. The 60- trial guideline is an important rule of thumb, and, as previously mentioned, provides a methodological framework that can render individual longitudinal investigations more meaningful and sensitive to predictor–criterion variable relationships, especially for the select athlete of interest and his or her coach and other stakeholders.

Findings

This experiment was interested in determining whether, and to what extent HRD, would occur immediately prior to action, and if such a response would be associated with a greater QoS (better return) than when no HRD or HRA was evident prior to action.

The following was found:

1. In 31 (61%) of 51 trials, HRD was documented immediately prior to action. By contrast, 20 of 51 trials were marked by HRA (39%).

   Interpretation: Conceptually, it would be expected that during routine moments of competition, HRD will be manifested prior to all action phases. The fact that this is rarely the case supports notions and hypotheses that many competitive actions or events will indeed be influenced by psychological factors, more so during critical moments of competition. Hence, questions that must be asked include why did HRD not occur prior to action every trial (service return) and what interfered with this well-established pre-action HRV response (HRD) that is expected to always occur in response to an impending/anticipated sport-specific stimulus (the ball when returning serve) or in conjunction with preparation to initiate action (e.g., when serving)? In addition to measurement error (a methodological issue, since it can be difficult to exactly synchronize heart beats at the millisecond level with the onset of action), psychological and physical factors, even during routine moments of a training experiment like this one (or during competition), can influence performance. For example, it is conceivable that peak levels of attention (focus) could not be maintained across 60 consecutive trials that were carried out consecutively without a break. Visual and cognitive fatigue could have led to a breakdown of the expected left-to-right cortical shift and concomitant HRD that has been associated with pre-action readiness, quicker reaction time, and successful outcomes. Since PP's AP of H-L-M is on the cusp of being the ideal PHO constellation, one would not expect him to choke in the context of a routine performance experiment that was not designed to test or assess his mental toughness per se. However, it is plausible that he (an athlete with a near ideal AP) was not challenged enough by an innocuous performance drill to the extent that his superior potential to focus intently through all trials was activated, leading to mental lapses and associated HRA across select pre-action epochs (39% of all trials). Additional assessment of PP should be undertaken to test the preceding possibility.

Nevertheless, irrespective of these interpretations, pre-action HRD occurred 61% of the time, a finding that tends to support and partially replicate the pre-action HRD hypothesis. In terms of global focus-comfort-control (F-C-C), PP's HRDgi of .61 is line with CR's match play HRDgi of .68. HRDgi is an exploratory/hypothetical emerging indicator of level of attention/focus (F), situational comfort/intensity/physiological reactivity (C), and coping/pre-action strategic planning/motor-technical priming and can be used to compare F-C-C at the intra-individual level across competitions and in relationship to other athletes.

2. Relative to QoS outcome at threshold level I (QoS of 3, 4, or 5), HRD was associated with a QoS I in 26 out of 31 trials (84%), whereas HRA was associated with a QoS of I 15 out of 20 trials (75%).

Interpretation: this is a critical outcome measure domain in that, conceptually, one would expect, predict, and want performance subsequent to pre-action HRD to be significantly better than performance after pre-action HRA. After all, if post pre-action HRD responses are not associated with a better performance that distinguishes HRD from HRA, then both measures are rendered relatively meaningless in terms of predicting or distinguishing performance. However, it should be cautioned that even in instances where HRA and not HRD is associated with better performance, numerous performance-related extraneous variables can possibly be implicated in driving poor performance after pre-action HRD, such as opponent variables, including personal skill level, technical weaknesses, and subliminal mind–body processes that are associated with specific AP constellations, as well as perceived stress or competitive anxiety, even in the absence of higher levels of criticality. Thus, in order to better illuminate the etiology of HRD-HRA performance outcome discrepancies or paradoxical outcomes, group studies are necessary (hundreds of athletes who are assessed across similar controlled experimental HRD paradigms and real competition), as well as extensive modeling of HRV (HRD/HRA) in the context of as many relevant performance outcomes mediating or moderating variables, as can be derived/extracted from a data set in individual athletes (e.g., HRD and criticality level 4 or 5; HRD and forehand returns [e.g., whether a return's quality is influenced by the type of stroke] or HRD and time of epoch's outcome [e.g., HRA occurring to a greater extent at the end of a series of trials to assess fatigue and attention decrement or boredom, lack of motivation]). All of these as well as other factors could undermine the HRD-enhanced performance hypothesis and even call into question the omnipresence of HRD as a pre-action biomarker.

The finding that HRD and Level I performance outcome only exceeded the HRA-Level I performance by 8% highlights the preceding concerns and issues. Conceptually, one would expect, predict, and, ideally, want pre-action HRD to result in greater Level I performance and performance decrement to be associated with HRA. It appears that individual differences factors that drive performance outcome can be capable of neutralizing the performance-enhancing mind–body–motor mechanisms associated with pre-action HRD. For example, even though an athlete may be highly focused, mentally prepared, and in control of his or her motor response system (F-F-C), and as such, manifest pre-action HRD and concomitant brain responses that lead to peak reaction time and an initial stellar response (e.g., a great service return), the positive cascade of brain–heart-mediated responses associated with HRD may not be sufficient to counter what is to come in the impending action phase (e.g., an opponent's backhand winner down the line; or a baseball pitcher's 95-mile-an-hour fastball). Ultimately, a psychophysiological response, even if initially associated with optimal focus, comfort, and control, can at most foster initial peak performance responses, but it will not necessarily always lead to successful performance throughout a subsequent action epoch. Individual variability in psychologically mediated pre-action HRV (HRD and HRA) and later action phase motor, technical, and strategic responses are likely to impact performance in both directions. Moreover, mind–body responses within the pre-action–action equation are expected to be influenced, to a large extent, by an athlete's AP constellation, especially during critical moments during competition.

3. HRD occurred 13 out of 31 times (42%) and HRA occurred 7 out of 20 times (35%) prior to QoS Level II outcome (QoS of 4 or 5).

   Interpretation: This finding can be interpreted similarly to the previous outcome analysis. Essentially, even in a controlled experiment in which the task is to try to return a serve as proficiently as possible (as determined by placement and power criteria that is assessed by an expert rater), variation in speed and direction of the oncoming serve, coupled with an athlete's technical strengths, weaknesses, and limitations, are potential extraneous variables that are capable of neutralizing the performance-facilitative HRD response. Relative to HRA during pre-action, while its manifestation and subsequent association with positive outcome (Level 4 or 5 QoS) would not have been predicted, it is possible that most serves in an HRA occurring pre-action epoch were very easy to return. As such, even a non-performance-facilitative pre-action response like HRA may not have a negative influence on *actual performance*. For example, further analysis and statistical modeling might determine that most HRA successes and HRD failures were associated with serves to this player's strength and weakness, respectively, increasingly the likelihood that the impact of pre-action HRV would be differentially lessened or increased when interpreted in the context of technically mediated, post, pre-action phase outcome. Statistical modeling requires more repeated measures to ensure adequate sample size relating to each variable of interest. As a result, an in-depth multifactorial micro-analyses can only be done after additional entire experimental trials (multiple 60+ serve return experiments; circa 10 additional trials per additional predictor/criterion variable).

4. Finally, worst performance (QoS level 1 or 2) was associated with HRA in 5 out of 20 trials (25%) and in 5 of 31 (16%) trials with HRD.

   Interpretation: This finding is more in line with expectations, with the difference between HRD and HRA being slightly greater than with the previous performance outcome categories (11% versus 8%, and 7% in favor of HRD). However, even this finding reveals far less outcome separation than one would have liked. Directional discrepant performance differences, as with the previous findings, may be attributable to numerous other psychological and technical factors, including some that were mentioned.

Summary

Heart rate variability measures have emerged as potent predictor and criterion variables that have been shown to influence performance. They have been found to reflect the immediate past and predict future performance on the basis of cardiac data that is derived during training games/matches and official/real competition. A submeasure of HRV, heart rate deceleration has also emerged as perhaps the most important objective indicator of crucial mind–body performance responses, including focus-comfort and control (attention, intensity, and mental and motor control).

Both HRV and HRD, specifically (prior to the onset of action and during action phases of competition), can be used to help establish an athlete's Individual Zone of Optimum Functioning as well as criterion reference mind–body response tendencies that would be predicted on the basis of an athlete's Athlete's Profile and the Theory of Critical Moments.

Because of the heart's robust signal properties, HRV is the psychophysiological modality of choice when it comes to ecological-based athlete assessment and intervention. It has many advantages over all other mind–body measures, including EEG, EMG, and EDR to name a few, since it is the only measure that can be reliably measured during real-official competition in the context of both temporally distant time-out and real time play-by-play monitoring paradigms, with resultant HRV measures capable of being directly and indirectly linked to performance outcome and/or by extrapolation, reflect, predict, and assess the impact virtually any intervention (ranging from cognitive-behavioral, visualization, and hypnosis to other biofeedback-based training, including neurofeedback) has on performance outcome.

HRV monitoring and assessment during training and real competition should be an integral component of applied sport psychological consulting and attempts to assess and enhance performance. It is strongly recommended that all practitioners obtain comprehensive training in the use of HRV and that training and degree programs in sport psychology mandate the inclusion of sport HRV into their curriculum.

In this book's section on Intervention/Mental training, it will be shown how HRV and HRV analyses can be further used to assess intervention efficiency (the extent to which an athlete is actually engaging in a prescribed mental training method), guide mental training, and help determine intervention efficacy (the extent to which an intervention impacts performance). Specific HRV/ HRD-based intervention protocols, procedures, and methodologies will be explicated.

Notes

1. HRV can be obtained during high movement-based, ecologically structured training and official competition using time-out based data acquisition and analysis paradigms, and wireless telemetry–based systems such as the Polar RS800CX. The cardiac signal is quite robust and can be easily obtained, and is much more artifact resistant than other physiological measures, most (e.g., EEG) that cannot be obtained reliably using telemetry and wireless approaches and are, as such, limited to static experimental paradigms.
2. RMS-SD (Root Mean Squared-Standard Deviation) has not been incorporated into ABSP research.
3. It should be noted that this author used the first Polar system in 1997 in an attempt to isolate HRD during official tournament tennis matches. The resulting Master's thesis, the first research of any kind to monitor heart activity during real competition, led to seminal findings on the HRD phenomenon. Since then Polar instrumentation has advanced considerably, most notably via the robustness of its chest strap system and artifact resistance.
4. DA was under tremendous pressure to win, since the failure to attain a higher ATP ranking within 6 months to a year would have led to a loss of sponsor funding, and that would have effectively ended his dream of becoming an established professional tennis player.
5. Carlstedt (1998, 2001) used a first-generation Polar system to document every IBI across three official tournament matches, but was not capable at the time of performing the comprehensive HRV analyses mentioned earlier. At the time, only HRD results were analyzed.

SECTION II

Mental Training and Intervention

* = empirical strength of intervention
the greater the *, the higher the evidentiary value of an intervention

This section presents a broad spectrum of well-known and specialized mental training (MT) and intervention modalities in the context of advanced evidentiary approaches, procedures, and methodologies that are crucial to the establishment of their reliability and validity. Case studies of athletes who have undergone extensive pre-intervention assessment and MT over the course of entire seasons of official games as well as elaborate MT efficacy testing are presented to highlight critical issues in MT.

The ABSP/CP approach to athlete intervention/MT that is predicated on cognizance of the existence of inherent flaws, oversights, and myths that are associated with the administration, analysis, and interpretation of MT and their effects, including the pervasive, overwhelming assumption that MT always works, is explicated.

The following is a verbatim excerpt from the American Board of Sport Psychology's original State of Applied Sport Psychology Position Paper that was later adapted for and presented at the 2011 annual convention of the American Psychological Association. It sums up crucial issues and observations that must be taken into account when engaging in MT with athletes:

> Athletes are taught visualization techniques, cognitive strategies, breathing, and other methods in the context of the intake or first session and then sent on their way under the assumption that a client has (1) *learned a mental training (MT) technique and is capable of practicing it*, (2) *that the temporal properties of an MT technique are such that they can be applied at any time and then work later or on command*, and (3) *that MT will generalize to the real world of competition*. Most MT techniques are designed to relax an athlete (or induce some sort of mental state); yet *NO* practitioner could be located who actually monitored athletes during training and competition to determine (1) *whether an athlete is/was engaging in the prescribed MT technique*, (2) *whether and what sort of psychophysiological responses are/were associated with engaging in MT prior to and during actual competition, and, importantly*, (3) *whether engaging in an MT training technique really improves/improved performance, and if so, to what extent this assumption of MT-efficacy can/could be validated* (on the basis of objective statistical outcome measures that are accrued longitudinally at the intra-individual level)?

Addressing these and other related issues, critiques, findings, and recommendations are central to countering blind anecdotal conjecture about an intervention's efficacy and, instead, determining to what extent an applied intervention or MT modality *really* demonstrates efficacy, if at all.

Critical Issues in Mental Training: Advancing Higher Evidence-Based Interventions

Construct Bases/Validity of Interventions and Mental Training

Practitioners should be aware of and critically appraise the conceptual bases and construct validity of an intervention or MT method. It is not sufficient to merely teach and advocate for a particular MT modality. Practitioners, coaches, and especially athletes need to know why an intervention or MT modality is being applied and how to evaluate the efficacy of MT pursuits, whether after each session and/or over the course of an entire season of games or matches. Athletes need to be involved participants who not only do MT but know as much as possible about the process, underlying mind–body responses that reflect intervention efficiency and how and what basis the efficacy of MT is determined.

The conceptual and construct bases of the ABSP-CP MT paradigm emanate from the Athlete's Profile (AP) and Theory of Critical Moments models of peak performance. They were elaborated earlier in the book. It is suggested that readers review these models.[1] Briefly, these models have isolated specific brain–heart–mind–body–motor response dynamics that are associated with better or worse performance, especially during critical moments of competition. What has been shown to occur in numerous sports in pre-action phases leading up to the commencement of action is a reduction in left-frontal brain hemispheric activity and an increase in cortical activity in right motor cortex areas. Concomitant to this brain hemispheric shift that is associated with strategic planning and subsequent motor priming is the onset of heart rate deceleration (HRD), which reflects heightened in-the-moment focus or attention and facilitates faster reaction time and technical control.

Thus, ultimately, the bottom-line goal of any intervention or MT pursuit should be to induce the above-described cascade of mind–body–motor responses and associated peak performance, something that all practitioners and athletes should be aware of and learn to assess, irrespective of their therapeutic orientation or biases.[2]

The conceptual basis and construct models that have been advanced throughout this book contain the driving components or mediators of peak psychological performance. As such, interventions should be designed to induce in-the-moment, during real, official competition, mind–body–motor responses that increase the probability that an athlete will maintain control over that which he or she can control; in other words, play up to peak potential. Playing up to peak potential does not necessarily mean that an athlete will win every point, sink every putt, and win every game or match; it means that an athlete will be less likely to falter because of psychological issues or negative mental states, especially during crucial pre-action-transition to action phases and encountered critical moments of competition.

The conceptually/construct model-based, biomarker approach to intervention-MT that the CP advances allows for the objective assessment of intervention efficiency and efficacy. Without a validated conceptual/construct model to guide MT, interventions tend to be an ad hoc and arbitrary exercise in which intervention efficiency and efficacy are assumed but rarely, if ever, demonstrated.

TEMPORAL PROPERTIES OF MT MODALITIES AND DOSE–RESPONSE–TIME TO ACHIEVE ENDURING CHANGE

Temporal properties refer to time frames in which an intervention is administered by a practitioner or engaged in independently by an athlete, an issue that has not received sufficient consideration in the context of MT paradigms. The vast majority of practitioners tend to teach and carry out interventions in their offices or when working with teams, en masse in group settings as part of workshops, or pre-season preparation sessions; the assumption being that an MT technique can and will be learned and then applied during real competition by all athletes who are exposed to and taught a particular method of MT. However, this assumption is faulty, and unless a practitioner systematically documents and analyzes, at the intra-individual level (i.e., every athlete), the time aspects of learning and eventually independently engaging in an intervention modality, one will not know to what extent an MT technique has been learned, let alone consolidated mentally or procedurally (long-term procedural memory) beyond practitioner conjecture and athlete self-report. The notion that visualizing a sport-specific scenario at night before going to bed or on the playing field prior to or during competition devoid of empirically derived time frames or temporal parameters will result in reliable or predictable outcomes is tenuous at best.

The bottom-line question in regard to temporal properties of an intervention is, how much time must be devoted to learning and consolidating its components in long-term procedural memory? Is an hour a week sufficient? Is five minutes before competition adequate? Does an athlete need to be prompted to engage in an intervention, or should he or she do so without being told or signaled to? Should not an athlete be so well-trained and subliminally primed that mind–body responses that are associated with peak performance are automatically induced after "x" amount of time through unconscious and/or consciously mediated MT procedures, techniques, and/or methods? Or, can individual temporal properties of an MT method even be determined and quantified?

Methodologies for indirectly establishing ideal temporal parameters of MT should center on experimentally manipulating time frames or the amount of time engaged in a particular intervention and then determine the impact of different time frames on performance outcome and whether such outcome can reliably be associated with the manifestation of specific biomarker responses. For example, one efficient short-term experiment pertaining to temporal properties of visualization could involve an athlete engaging in visualization of 1, 3, and 5 min prior to a performance task (putting from 15 ft) over the course of 180 attempts (trials). The visualization scenario should be related to technical aspects of putting and should be repeated as many times as possible within the prescribed epoch length. Immediately after the visualization trial comes to an end, the subject attempts a putt, being sure to engage in his or her pre-putt routine. Heart rate variability (HRV) should be monitored during each visualization period, and, if possible (using the Polar or other telemetry systems), during the putt (from pre-action to the end of the putt). The 1-, 3-, and 5-min visualization epochs should be counterbalanced (e.g., trial $1 = 5$ min, trial $2 = 1$ min, trial $3 = 3$ min, trial $4 = 5$ min, trial $5 = 1$ min, and so on until each of the 60 trials are completed for each time frame). The experiment should be carried out over the course of a week. Once all of the trials have been completed, correlation and regression analyses should be performed to determine to what extent, if any, differential time frames are associated with better or worse performance, to what extent a specific MT time epoch is associated with HRV that is distinct and different from another MT time epoch, and whether HRV responses during pre-action phases after an MT epoch differs as a function of MT time frame and the putt outcome. What emerges from such an MT temporal testing paradigm are MT efficiency metrics that reflect the extent to which the conscious manipulation of mental imagery as a function of time engaged in visualizing a performance/technical scenario impacts the autonomic nervous system (HRV measures), and whether specific visualization mind–body-mediated responses affect performance and outcome. It is hypothesized that each individual athlete has an Ideal Mental Training Temporal Zone (IMTTZ) that a practitioner should attempt to determine. This requires meticulous analyses over time and should include varying degrees of temporal distance or proximity, for example, testing whether (as has been anecdotally claimed) pre-sleep visualization the night before competition is beneficial to performance, or if it is better for a particular athlete to engage in a visualization session two hours or other time increment before competition. Critical to such analyses is also determining the amount of time an athlete engages in an MT session (see the preceding 1-, 3-, and 5-min examples). Iterations of temporal timeline experiments are almost limitless. Their design should be determined to a large extent on the temporal properties of specific sports. In general, the ABSP-CP recommends that MT should directly lead to or induce neuropsychophysiological responses that are known to be associated with enhanced performance and a successful outcome, that is, an in-the-moment (real/official competition) positive outcome, especially the heart rate deceleration (HRD) pre-action response. As such, MT that is engaged in well in advance of actual competitive moments may be superfluous exercises, or "doing sport psychology just to be doing something." Nevertheless, even this contention should be tested at the individual level, especially in cases where athletes have been previously exposed to or taught MT training routines that have not taken temporal properties into account. In the context of evidence-based practice, as little as possible should be left to chance. Consequently, attempts should be made to empirically establish an athlete's IMTTZ.

Dose–Response–Time to Achieve Enduring Change

Intervention dose–response relationships (IDRR) and time to achieve enduring change (TAEC) is a conceptual issue that is closely related to temporal properties of MT. The main difference is that IDRR and TAEC can be viewed as analogous to traits, whereas temporal properties can be viewed as time-delineated MT-mediated changes in ANS state responses that may not necessarily lead to permanent biomarker verifiable change. IDRR and TAEC can be impacted by temporal properties or MT.

The failure to reach time-to-achieve enduring-change thresholds as determined by IDRR that are established on the basis of extensive temporal testing is hypothesized to prevent or reduce the probability that athlete trait tendencies that hinder peak psychological performance can eventually be permanently eradicated or at least mitigated. In other words, if a practitioner and athlete have no real idea how much and intensely (dose) MT must be engaged in to perform up to peak potential, the entire intervention/MT process is nothing more than a random exercise in which one's beliefs and hopes influence perceptions of MT efficiency and efficacy, instead of high evidentiary data-driven outcome measures.

It is folly to assume that arbitrarily structured MT sessions devoid of temporal and dose–response considerations and potent guiding data are capable of overwriting maladaptive psychological and psychophysiological tendencies that may have taken a lifetime to develop. It defies credulity to think that a 1-hour MT session, once a week, followed by unsupervised and undocumented self-practice on part of the performance-troubled athlete, will be sufficient to achieve enduring change. While there may be anecdotal case studies of miraculous athlete turnarounds, evidence-based approaches to MT and intervention must take temporal and time to achieve enduring change parameters into account using the systematic methodologies that have been advocated throughout this book.

ECOLOGICAL VALIDITY-MT DELIVERY/APPLICATION MODEL

MT should for the most part be taught to and carried out by an athlete in a realistic as possible environment, one that at minimum simulates that which one will encounter during real competition and, ideally, during real-official competition. Simulated and real competition situations are examples of more ecologically valid MT contexts or environments. As previously mentioned, the vast majority of MT and intervention sessions are carried out in the office, with practitioners rarely going to the playing field to administer and assess the efficiency and efficacy of MT attempts. It is just assumed that MT or an intervention will work, that what has been taught and supposedly learned will generalize to and be self-applied by an athlete during actual competition. Although cursory attempts to observe and evaluate MT may be done occasionally, high evidentiary, gold standard MT delivery and analysis services must involve systematic pre-intervention–intervention phase comparisons on the basis of psychological/psychophysiological and performance outcome measures and data that is derived during simulation, practice, and ultimately real or official competition. Even if a practitioner is incapable of obtaining mind–body measures, such a pre-game/match, during game/match, and post-game/match HRV, for whatever reason (usually due to not being trained in applied psychophysiology) meticulous pre- versus post-criticality and other micro-sport-specific statistical analyses must be undertaken to bring accountability and clarity to the MT-intervention process.

Ecological validity is a vital prerequisite for high evidentiary athlete assessment and intervention. Athlete consulting that does not predominantly involve ecological approaches can be considered substandard.

CRITERION-REFERENCED VALIDITY: OUTCOME VARIABLE(S) INTER-RELATIONSHIPS

MT and interventions are designed to enhance performance. However, rarely do practitioners use applied psychophysiological methods to determine, observe, and gain insight into what an MT method actually does. An athlete is taught how to visualize, or "relax," yet how does a practitioner know that an MT technique has been learned or exerted an effect? Criterion-referencing methodologies are necessary for establishing an athlete's intervention efficiency, that is, the extent to which engaging in an MT method can be documented and assessed on the basis of an external outcome measure. Criterion-referencing methods have been extensively discussed throughout the book. They will be further elaborated in case studies later in this book section.

PREDICTIVE VALIDITY: VARIANCE EXPLAINED

The goal of most interventions and MT methods in sport psychology is to improve performance. Unfortunately, practitioners rarely carry out extensive efficacy testing analyses to determine to what an extent an intervention worked. MT or intervention efficacy testing is critical to just about all issues relating to interventions, including an MT's temporal properties, dose–response metrics, and intervention efficiency (criterion referencing). One important finding pertaining to efficacy testing is that the impact of MT or intervention usually varies significantly across individual athletes such that IZOF profiles emerge or can be established on the basis of relationships between HRV and micro-level performance outcome measures (e.g., level of criticality). Correlation and regression statistical procedures should be used to determine and/or predict the effect of an intervention or MT method on performance. Predictive validity is expressed in the variance, explained coefficient, either r^2 (correlation r squared) or adjusted r^2 (multiple regression). It reflects the amount of variance in an outcome measure that can be attributed to one or more predictor variables. In the context of MT, the intervention efficiency quotient is often used as the predictor variable, with macro- and micro-level sport-specific outcome measures serving as criteria (outcome measures). For example, if an athlete engaged in visualization for 5 minutes prior to a baseball game and his or her intervention efficiency as determined by changes in MT condition HRV (compared to baseline HRV) revealed that a change of $+10$ beats per minute that was found to be associated with Critical Moment (CM) level 4 quality of at-bat performance ($r^2 = .11$), he or she can conclude that 11% of the variance in performance outcome can be attributed to an intervention-induced psychophysiological change that was positively associated with a high-level competitive pressure situation. While 11% may seem low, in terms of a performance-mediated or associated effect, any positive relationship between psychological factors or processes, in this case an MT mind–body response, is of importance and should be highlighted and used to assess intervention efficacy.

The predictive validity–variance explained analysis paradigm is well suited to intervention efficiency and efficacy studies and should be used with all athletes to evaluate the course and progression of an intervention-MT regime. While changes from baseline to MT condition mind–body responses are only one indirect measure of MT efficiency, they have been found to reflect pre-action/game/match self-induced mental states (using MT) and predict performance outcome.

The Polar HRV/HRD paradigm allows for more extensive and time-locked predictive validity statistical analyses (see Chapter 12) so that in-the-moment MT over the course of entire official games/matches/competition can be delineated and quantified in terms of MT's predictive validity. Alternative intervention efficacy methods can also be used (such as t-tests of mean differences between pre- and intervention phases); however, they are less sensitive than linear regression that takes every data point into account, allowing practitioners to analyze every intervention epoch in terms of its impact on psychophysiological responding and micro-level outcome, in addition to pre- and post-MT efficacy.

The bottom line is that MT-interventions should never be administered in isolation, devoid of an accountability model or paradigm. Unfortunately, the norm is to just administer or engage in MT and hope for the best, a belief metric that is heavily influenced by placebo and dual-placebo beliefs that tend to mask the reality of what may actually be happening in terms of MT and its actual, as opposed to its assumed impact on performance.

Notes

1. The Athlete's Profile (AP) Model and its primary higher-order measures will be revisited throughout numerous chapters pertaining to intervention/mental training.
2. There are practitioners who ardently subscribe to schools of thought and apply methods with supreme confidence who have never observed the previously described mind–body dynamics in real time or in the context of intervention/MT, efficacy outcome data. Practitioners who eschew data-driven approaches to intervention efficacy testing, who instead rely on intuition or athlete feedback to determine the impact of MT, should at minimum be aware of advanced biomarker approaches to intervention efficiency and efficacy testing, as should hardcore empiricists entertain the prospect that many intervention modalities can lead to the cascade of performance-related mind–body responses that underlie zone or flow states.

11

Spectrum of Intervention and Mental Training Modalities in Sport Psychology: Perspectives and Practices

There are numerous intervention and mental training modalities to choose from, both as a practitioner and an athlete. What determines which intervention will be chosen? For the most part, practitioners tend to select interventions that they have been exposed to, either as a student in a training program or in a postgraduate training course or workshop, or perhaps even as an athlete. As a research assistant, they may have worked under a mentor who specialized or had expertise in a particular MT modality. Or, a practitioner, like students, athletes, and consumers, may have been influenced by oftentimes hyperbolic media reports on the efficacy of an intervention or a famous athlete's testimonial regarding a mental-training method. The literature is also replete with group-based positive outcome studies that attest to an intervention's efficacy, while negative findings go unnoticed, never making it to print. These latter factors influencing decisions to specialize in or select a particular intervention to try as an athlete, in and of themselves, should not be the basis for determining what MT procedure or method to use. Biases abound, research findings are often questionable and athlete and practitioner (Guru) testimonials, more often than not, cannot be trusted. Critical oversights in the intervention selection, amenability, compliance, and efficacy equations range from relying on group findings to guide individual intervention-MT to blind acceptance of misguided driving beliefs about many MT methods.

The selection of an intervention should be based on individual differences factors that influence the ability to engage in an MT method in an efficient and temporally sustainable manner. Moreover, and importantly, ultimately, an intervention must have demonstrated efficacy, otherwise it's back to the drawing board. Even then, interventions and MTs do not always work. That is the big secret that few practitioners will ever admit to. How could they, if they have never engaged in gold standard efficiency and efficacy-testing procedures? In terms of interventions, ignorance can be bliss so long as dual-placebo belief dynamics underlie a practitioner–athlete relationship, irrespective of any real outcome metrics that often are ignored. Unless interventions-MT are applied and rigorously scrutinized in the context of plausible conceptual-construct models and advanced investigative approaches, one can never be certain of an intervention's efficiency or efficacy. As previously mentioned, intervention efficacy must be determined using regression and correlation statistical procedures to ascertain the amount of variance in salient sport-specific micro–macro level outcome measures that can be attributed to intervention-based predictor variables. Doing so is an absolute prerequisite of advanced, highest evidentiary-applied sport psychology.

The ABSP-CP Approach to Intervention and Mental Training

The ABSP-CP approach to intervention and MT is based on the Athlete's Profile (AP) model of individual differences that has isolated key primary higher-order (PHO) factors that are intimately related to critical components of performance: attention, physiological reactivity (intensity), and strategic planning/coping, all of which play a mediating role in the intervention and MT process. AP PHO measures and/or profiles help determine which intervention or MT method to apply to an athlete. They predict with a high degree of certainty intervention amenability and compliance (AP constellation and intervention amenability match-ups can be found after the Intervention-MT Spectrum diagram further on).

Equally, if not more important than an athlete's AP PHO measures and constellation is intervention-MT outcome; that is, what MT eventually leads to in terms of mind–body responses (e.g., HRV changes) and efficacy (enhanced performance being the goal). Rather than just hope that some sort of transformative response will be induced by MT and result in the manifestation of a zone or flow state that leads to unbridled and unexpected success in a previously psychologically burdened athlete, the ABSP-CP approach attempts to systematically shape and induce mind–body–motor/technical responses that are known to be associated with greater focus, faster reaction time, and optimum mind–body control. Instead of using intervention-MT procedures in isolation and/or temporally distant to the immediate competitive challenge at hand, the ABSP-CP espouses an un-circumvented, direct interventional approach that leads to the most valid and reliable biomarker of an in-the-moment zone performance state, namely, pre-action heart rate deceleration (HRD), a mind–body HRV response that is unconsciously/subliminally mediated routinely during competition in the absence of pressure and even under pressure in athletes possessing the ideal AP (high or low HS/SA, low N/SR, and high RC/SC; see Chapter 3). Especially in vulnerable athletes who are most likely to admit to psychological performance frailties (those with the high HS/SA, high N/SR, and low RC/SC AP), it is important that an intervention demonstrate its efficacy. The probability of this occurring is likely to increase if an intervention-MT directly induces performance-enhancing mind–body responses. This can be best achieved using MT techniques that can immediately set off the mind–body response cascade that is associated with peak in-the-moment performance (see above on conceptual/construct bases). The most ecological method for inducing this dynamic is timed breathing, not to be confused with respiratory sinus arrhythmia (RSA) breathing, a clinical relaxation breathing procedure that is often mistakenly taught and misused (the CP HRD-timed-breathing technique is presented further on).

Essentially, the ABSP-CP approach to intervention-MT advances a systematic, step-by-step, mechanistic mind–body manipulation procedure that usurps and transcends all indirect and for the most-part temporally distant MT methods that are usually administered in an ad hoc manner, to get to the essence or heart of what MT must do, namely, induce a reliable in-the-moment, on-the-playing-field, pre-action mind–body response biomarker, the HRD response.

While the most common and some less-used interventions and MT methods that are presented further on can be, and are, in the context of the ABSP-CP, systematically administered, most still contain numerous underlying nebulous components, processes, and mechanisms that are hard to directly and objectively illuminate and/or quantify, rendering them lower-tier approaches that can be used, but not relied upon alone when attempting to enhance performance.

Mental Training Modalities

The following intervention-MT modalities constitute a spectrum of most used procedures and methods in sport psychology. The position of a specific modality in the "spectrum wheel" further on in no way conveys its usage status or potency as an intervention. What is clear, though, is that all roads lead to HRD (center circle), the ultimate MT mind–body outcome measure. Irrespective of MT modality and how it is taught or engaged in, once on the playing field, in sports that have a preaction phase (and most do, ranging from getting out of the block in track, off the line in football, or prior to setting up to return an oncoming volleyball to preparing to putt or hit an oncoming baseball or cricket ball) HRD has been shown to occur and is associated with heightened attention (focus), physiological reactivity/ideal level of intensity and motor primary (technical readiness). Essentially, regardless of how much time an athlete devotes to MT, in the end, it all comes down to what happens in the seconds and milliseconds prior to action when he or she must perform up to peak potential, marked by technical and motor responses that increase the probability that success, at least for that particular competitive moment, will be increased.

So, the maxim that "all roads lead to pre-action HRD" means that regardless of intervention modality (that is, administered or chosen on the basis of AP PHO constellation), it must prepare an athlete to confront a competitive situation effectively by helping suppress awareness of pressure or stress as well as negative or superfluous intrusive thoughts. Such effective preparedness will be marked by or reflected in greater pre-action HRD.

While one could argue that specific MT techniques involve diverse and divergent mind–body mechanisms and responses, which is indeed often the case, if an MT method is applied in a temporally too distant manner (e.g., the night before competition), the probability that performance will be enhanced may be greatly reduced. The ABSP-CP perspective goes so far as to contend that MT that is not individually customized in terms of its temporal administration and duration and then tested or validated in a pre-intervention phase in regard to its efficiency is an ad hoc superfluous exercise that has little, if any, basis in science. Thus, all interventions, whether applied individually or in a multi-modal format (multiple interventions applied in a hierarchical manner), must be administered and engaged in, in the moment, during actual competition and be associated with successful outcome metrics to ultimately demonstrate its worth to the specific individual athlete.

Intervention research has for the most part not considered these critical issues. As a result, many practitioners are unduly influenced by group-based intervention investigations that report positive outcomes on the basis of mean between-subject outcome comparisons. This has led to the proliferation of "pet" interventions, especially imagery-based MT, despite blatant methodological oversights. This is not to disparage visualization as an intervention. Rather, this critique is cautionary, with the ABSP-CP approach to interventions being crucial to advancing the state of applied higher evidentiary MT.

The following interventions will be addressed in the context of ABSP-CP perspectives, procedures, and methodologies, and, particularly, how a specific MT technique can be applied/used to facilitate in-the-moment peak performance as reflected in HRD.

The following MT spectrum (Figure 11.1) depicts a wide range of commonly used interventions as well as select advanced highly specialized MT methods that require extensive practitioner training and experience.

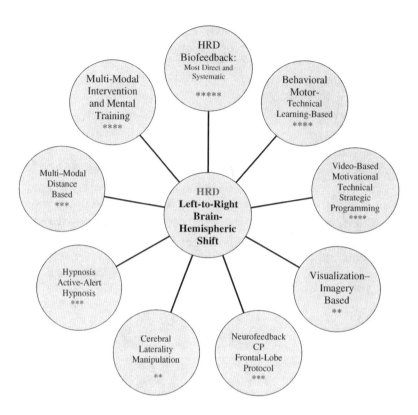

FIGURE 11.1   Intervention-mental training modality spectrum[1].

Mental Training Modality-Intervention Hierarchy

The following interventions and MT modalities are presented in order of the hypothesized probability that engaging in a select method will lead to a successful outcome per CP efficacy criteria (higher variance explained in objective sport-specific micro-outcome measures). This intervention-efficacy hypothesis is based on hundreds of case studies of athletes who used these MT methods. Nevertheless, it should be remembered that an intervention must be tested for efficacy at the intra-individual level, even in the presence of compelling group-based MT outcome findings.

Each intervention within the MT spectrum will be presented in the context of the following methodological considerations and components:

(I)   Intervention Amenability and Compliance: Athlete's Profile Ideal Compatibility: An athlete's AP constellation of measures, especially HS/SA and RC/SC, are associated with intervention modality amenability, that is, wanting and being able to engage in a particular mental training method and complying with prescribed MT protocols.

(II)   Conceptual-Construct Basis: how a specific intervention-MT method is associated with, linked to, and/or mediates or helps mediate cortical and HRD dynamics that have been shown to reflect optimum readiness to respond appropriately and subsequent peak performance, especially when under competitive pressure.

(III)   Description of Procedure: a step-by-step overview of how to administer (as a practitioner) and engage in an MT technique.

(IV)   Documentation-Accountability: MT efficiency-efficacy/outcome analysis: Case studies where available or within recommended intervention efficiency–efficacy group and case studies.

(V)   General Comments and Perspectives: will be interspersed throughout each subsection as necessary to highlight important issues and considerations, and present hypothesis and conceptual matters.

Note

1.   Rating System: Based on Group Acquired Intervention Efficiency and Efficacy Data (***** = highest; * = lowest). Note: ranking does not preclude that intervention efficacy will vary widely as a function of AP-mediated individual differences. Actual individual intervention efficacy outcome supersedes such a global rating system. The rating system primarily ranks the preceding interventions in terms of how directly the ultimate goal of mental training can be attained (namely: pre-action strategic and motor priming as reflected in pre-action HRD, and subsequent technical and tactical control during action, as also reflected in HRD and HRV).

12

Heart Rate Deceleration Biofeedback: Direct Pathways to Peak Performance Responses

Heart rate deceleration biofeedback (HRD BF) is a relatively unknown intervention whose origin can be traced to an extensive body of research on pre-stimulus or pre-action cardiac activity (see References at the end of the book). Nevertheless, HRD BF is a potent MT modality (perhaps the most potent intervention), one that facilitates the manifestation of key mind–body–motor responses preceding the onset of action. It is a validated intervention that is designed to induce in-the-moment peak performance responses irrespective of an athlete's AP and related psychological issues with which an athlete may be burdened. HRD BF is a very mechanistic approach, whose effects can be immediately documented independent of speculative interpretive components associated with more cognitively based interventions.

Readers are referred to Chapters 2 and 9, in which this brain–heart response phenomenon is elaborated.

The HRD Response

HRD just occurs. It can also be shaped and conditioned and is associated with a validated electro-cardiogram signature. The manifestation of HRD occurs concomitant to a cascade of performance facilitative brain–heart–mind–body–motor/technical responses. The HRD response occurs subliminally in well-functioning athletes but can also be volitionally induced, irrespective of an athlete's mental state prior to the initiation of a specific breathing pattern. By contrast, cognitive methods, including mental imagery, are MT approaches that contain nebulous processes that, at best, can only be indirectly linked to peak performance responses (e.g., mental imagery as a mediator of HRD), if at all. Consequently, HRD BF should be the primary intervention for in-the-moment facilitation of peak performance responses. All other interventions should be structured so that they lead to HRD prior to the onset of action, assuming that are even needed (which they may or may not be, depending on athlete individual differences factors).

Intervention Amenability and Compliance: Ideal AP PHO Constellation or Measure(s)

All forms of BF provide athletes with objective data and insight into psychological influences on the mediation of physiological responses and the impact mind–body interactions can have on performance. While athletes who are high in HS/SA are very attuned to bodily processes and are capable of using internal mental processes to manipulate psychophysiology independent of observable signal changes on a computer screen or via auditory feedback, athletes who are high in RC/SC tend to be almost oblivious to the mind–body connection. They are also skeptical of mental training and interventions, tending to believe that they are unnecessary or don't work. As such, athletes who are low in HS/SA and high in RC/SC can be best reached or influenced to engage in MT if they can be convinced that an intervention has merit and that the mind can indeed affect performance-relevant physiological responses. BF, by literally providing visual and/or auditory numeric-based feedback, can be used to show that a person can indeed self-induce mind–body performance facilitative responses. This can motivate the skeptical high RC/SC athlete to try MT. Eventually, to the high RC/SC athlete, BF may become a kind of competition in and of itself in which he or she wants to succeed (Figure 12.1).

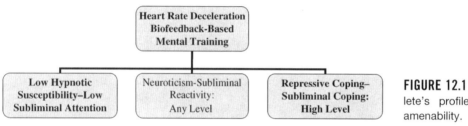

FIGURE 12.1   Intervention Athlete's profile and intervention amenability.

Conceptual Rationale

As has been made known throughout this book, HRD can be considered the most valid and reliable biomarker of pre-action psychological and psychophysiological readiness. It is the zone mind–body (HRV) measure that reflects optimum pre-action strategic planning, intensity, and mind–body–motor control (technical and motor priming). Ultimately, all interventions should lead to the HRD response in pre-action phases of competition, a response that is hypothesized to also occur throughout an entire competitive, sport-specific action (e.g., throughout an entire tennis point or from the point of getting off the mark and driving past an opponent to make a lay-up in basketball). HRD has been shown to occur in virtually all athletes in numerous sports that have preaction phases in which an athlete must either respond to an impending stimulus (like a ball being pitched or served) or initiate a response (e.g., a free throw). HRD can be disrupted or not be manifested during critical moments of competition when an athlete consciously or subliminally experiences competitive stress (as reflected in mind–body responses [e.g., specific HRV measures] that are incongruent with previously documented performance-facilitative HRV baseline or pre-action HRD readings).

The nonappearance of HRD prior to action when an athlete is under stress is more likely to occur in athletes who possess the worst AP (high HS/SA-high N/SR-low RC/SC). Athletes who are known to have more maladaptive AP tend to be aware of their performance-related psychological frailties. They are the athlete-subset that is also the most likely to seek out MT. Nevertheless, all athletes, regardless of AP, should be educated about pre-action HRD dynamics and their relevance to peak performance. They should also be taught how to volitionally set off the brain–heart–mind–body cascade that leads to the onset of HRD.

How Does BF Work?

BF attempts to induce or shape mind–body responses by first showing baseline autonomic and/or central nervous system activity as reflected in waveform oscillations or other representations that are observable on a computer screen (e.g., bar graphs), and then reinforcing prescribed performance or wellness-related target psychophysiological responses. The successful self-elicited or induced response is shaped subliminally over time through operant conditioning, whereby as one's response approaches the prescribed one that is usually associated with optimum self-regulation, attention, or physiological reactivity, visual scenarios (along with audio feedback at times) on a computer screen change incrementally. For example, if a practitioner prescribes the generation of more parasympathetic nervous system (PNS) activity via controlled breathing to reduce sympathetic nervous system (SNS) flooding associated with panic attacks, a patient will know if he or she is generating more or less or an ideal amount of PNS activity on the basis of feedback in the form of a rising bar and audio signal when a PNS activity threshold is reached. Parallel to this process, over time, the patient will feel the difference between extremes: a panic-like SNS-predominant mind–body state and a PNS-predominant relaxation psychophysiological state, first in the context of doing BF and receiving reinforcement for manifesting prescribed adaptive responses and then (hopefully) later, without BF, in the real world and in the presence of an actual panic attack, that a patient is capable of volitionally shutting down (Andreassi, 1995; Carlstedt, 2009; Wickramasekera, 1988).

Essentially, well-consolidated adaptive and/or health or performance-facilitative mind–body responses that were shaped in the lab, in theory, can then be self-induced in the presence of actual or perceived environmental or internal stressors to restore psychophysiological homeostasis.

Description of HRD BF Procedure I: ABSP-CP BioCom Paradigm

Initially, athletes should be educated regarding the cardiovascular mechanisms associated with HRD, commencing with inhalation/inspiration and exhalation/expiration breathing-mediated cardiac responses both in static/naturalistic and HRD BF in sport training and competition contexts. This can be done using the BioCom Technologies (BCT) Heart Tracker (HT), and Heart Scanner (HS) BF systems as follows.

Laboratory Familiarization, Observation, and Manipulation Training

1. The athlete is attached to computer via an ear sensor. A 2-minute HRV baseline is established using the BCT HS program.
2. Thereafter, while running the HT program, the athlete is instructed to just look at the screen and observe the breathing pacer bar and tachogram progression that shows each heartbeat, noticing how cardiac activity is influenced by normal breathing. The athlete should be made aware that inspiration leads to increasing heart rate (HR; HR acceleration-HRA) and expiration leads to decreases in HR (HRD; Figures 12.2 through 12.7).

FIGURE 12.2 Initial HRD education, familiarization, and observation session.

3. After about 2 minutes of observing heart activity, stop the initial session, save the data, and run a 2-minute HRV analysis using the BCT HS program.
4. Compare the two HS-generated HRV reports (baseline with no mental engagement compared to the initial observation condition).

FIGURE 12.3 HR prior to paced inhalation.

FIGURE 12.4 HR increases during breathing-pacer-guided inhalation.

The above screenshot (Figure 12.4) depicts the initial 2-minute baseline reading (familiarization and observation session). Notice the HR, SDNN, and LF/HF readings. These are important measures in the respiratory sinus arrhythmia (RSA)-HRD BF equation. They are very

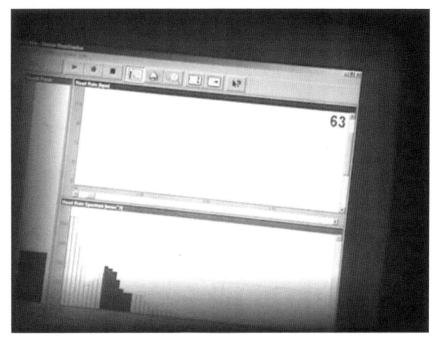

FIGURE 12.5 HR decreases during breathing-pacer-guided exhalation.

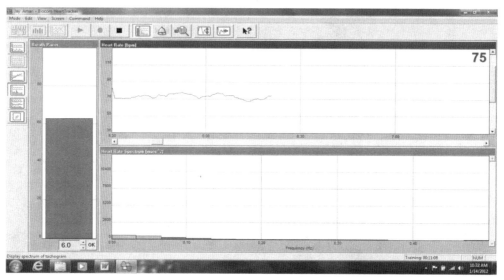

FIGURE 12.6   Screen shot of BioCom HT-based RSA-HRD training session.

sensitive to subliminal/unconscious changes in breathing as well as volitional manipulation of breathing, as was attempted after this initial baseline session.

5. Review inhalation–exhalation principles and their relevance to HRD before using HT to introduce the athlete to manipulated paced breathing.

6. Start with classic RSA training at a pace of 8 breaths/minute, instructing the athlete to synchronize his or her inhalation(s) with the rising pacer bar; do the same when exhaling (synched with the falling pacer bar). Continue this procedure for 2 minutes. Be sure to teach the athlete to inhale by gently compressing the stomach inward and simultaneously lifting the chest or

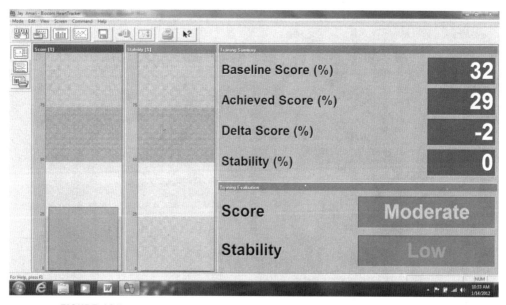

FIGURE 12.7   Qualitative rating of RSA training session: BioCom HT program.

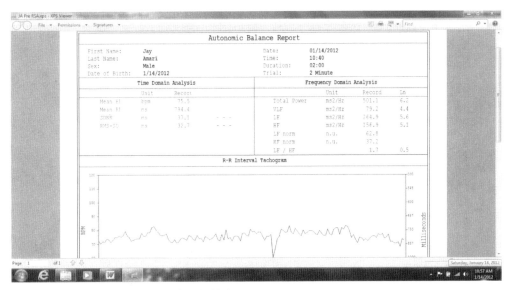

FIGURE 12.8   Baseline HRV report.

diaphragm and taking in air through the nostrils (not the mouth), being sure to complete the inspiration cycle by the time the pacer reaches its apex, and then gently expel the inhaled air through the nostrils, allowing the chest to drop and belly to protrude (relax controlling muscles), being sure to fully complete the expiration cycle by the time the pacer reaches the bottom (Figure 12.9).

7. Immediately run a 2-minute HRV scan using BioCom HS for comparison purposes (determine differences in HRV measures across the baseline (Figure 12.8 Baseline HRV), observation, and manipulation conditions).

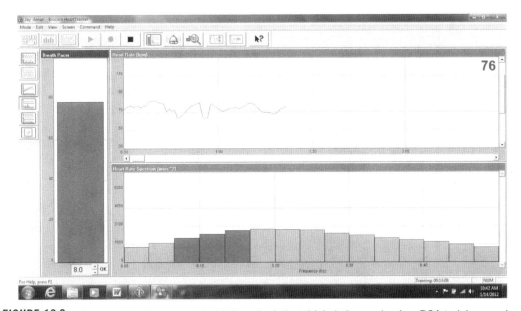

FIGURE 12.9   Screenshot of pacer-guided (8 breaths/minute) inhalation cycle of an RSA training session.

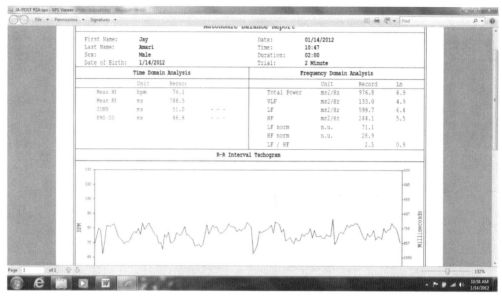

FIGURE 12.10   Spectrum analysis of HRV after a 2-minute paced breathing session.

Figure 12.10 depicts a spectrum analysis of HRV measures after a 2-minute paced breathing RSA training session. Note the changes compared to baseline. HR was almost the same. This is very illustrative and points to the need to take other more sensitive HRV markers of psychophysiological influences into account in the context of athlete assessment and intervention. HR is an overused and publicized cardiologic measure that in and of itself can be very misleading. A more sensitive performance-relevant biomarker, SDNN (the HRV index), increased significantly in the RSA training session, from 37 to 51 milliseconds. In addition, another important indicator of autonomic nervous system (ANS) balance, the low-frequency–high-frequency (LF/HF) ratio increased from 1.7 to 2.5 in the training condition, revealing significantly more low-frequency activity (a mixture of sympathetic [SNS] and parasympathetic nervous [PNS] nervous system activity) in the paced breathing condition. Breathing was paced to elicit 8 breaths/minute in the RSA condition that can later be reduced to 6 breaths/minute in an attempt to facilitate greater ANS balance for health and wellness purposes. Note again, though, RSA training in this scenario was used to help the athlete gain awareness of the impact breathing has on HR and HRV as a precursor to temporally guided, sport-specific pre-action HRD that is not based on RSA inhalation–exhalation dynamics (see Figure 12.9).

8. After analyzing and discussing the HRV reports, being sure to focus on HR, SDNN, and L/H ratio as a function of a select measuring condition, proceed to the playing field to introduce and operationalize HRD in the context of the pre-action temporal dynamics of a specific sport (in this case, tennis; Figure 12.11).

   Once the athlete's individual heart rate deceleration temporal zone (HRDtz = sport-specific preaction HRD trends) has been established, commence with sport-specific breathing-induced HRD BF that can then be practiced in accord with practitioner instructions. HRD training should always be documented and analyzed for efficiency and efficacy (Figure 12.12).

9. Sport-specific HRD BF training requires calibrating the HT breathing pacer with the length and duration of preaction epochs in which HRD should occur. Preaction HRD can be induced by consciously manipulating the inhale/exhale cycles. In tennis, when returning,

FIGURE 12.11 Tennis player's heart and brain responses being monitored using the Nexus 32 EEG/HRV telemetry system to determine HRD-brain response relationships and HRD temporal zone (can also be done without EEG brain wave acquisition instrumentation).

inhalation should commence in conjunction with the rise of the server's arm (e.g., the pacer bar of the HT program can be thought of or visualized as a server's arm), with exhalation occurring immediately and progressively until the oncoming tennis ball is struck. Athletes can use a tactile learning method to "feel" the inhalation–exhalation cycles by letting their cheeks fully expand with incoming air and then blowing it out, with all air being expelled by the time the ball is struck (this is associated with grunting that spectators often hear when tennis players hit the ball). Once the HRDtz parameters of a specific sport have been set for an individual athlete, HT can be calibrated to allow for practicing paced-breathing-induced HRD prior to competition.

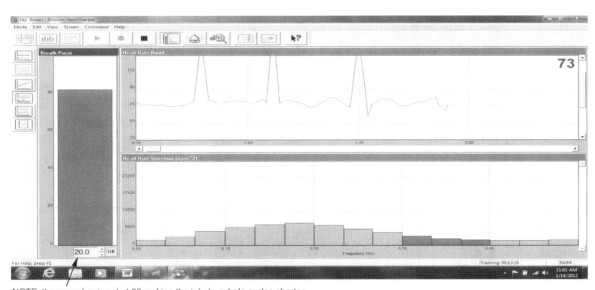

NOTE: the pacer bar is set at 20 making the inhale-exhale cycles shorter

FIGURE 12.12   Calibration of paced breathing for sport-specific HRD-BF.

10. Once it has been determined that an athlete has learned the basics of HRD and its inducement, he or she should be tested for intervention efficacy on the playing field, in the context of both experimental and competition paradigms. If using the BioCom system (that cannot be applied during actual action phases of competition, but can be during change-overs or time-outs during practice and official competition), indirect assessment of the manifestation of HRD and its impact can be done using the *temporally distant* method. In this paradigm, an athlete is taught and then instructed to engage in breathing-induced HRD cycles during change-overs/time-outs, and between action phases on the playing field during competition, usually within an A–B design (HRD on for one time-out cycle and nonaction phase and off for the next time-out/nonaction phase, etc.). This analytic approach to assessing HRD efficiency–efficacy will be elaborated in the documentation-accountability section further on.

Post-HRD and HRDtz Training on the Playing Field: ABSP-BioCom HS Procedure

In contrast to pervasive approaches to BF that are almost exclusively carried out in office or lab settings, the ABSP-CP BF protocols are designed to be administered and engaged in on the playing field during practice games/matches and real or official competition. The BioCom system can be used within a time-out or changeover paradigm whereby an athlete goes to a computer station on the sideline, dugout, bench, or other area to practice HRD and HRDtz BF prior to the initiation or continuation of a game/match or performance task. The temporal parameters of time-out and/or pre-action HRD BF should be established on the basis of pilot testing that determines the best time for MT onset (i.e., how soon or how close to game time should MT commence) and duration (i.e., how long should MT last). Recommendations regarding temporal parameters are made on the basis of variance-explained metrics that are derived from a longitudinal repeated-measures design during intervention training periods leading up to official or real competition (about 50–65 MT trials in which HRV measures are analyzed in the context of sport-specific macro- and micro-outcome measures, including situational criticality [level of critical moment]; an A-B-A design can also be used, with or without concurrent HRV monitoring [100–120 trials] to determine no-intervention/intervention differences as a function of temporal lag [time of intervention prior to start of competition]) using sport-specific outcome measures to determine intervention efficacy. Once competition has started, MT or intervention duration is usually determined by the progression of the game/match or event. In a sport like tennis, interventions are engaged in during changeovers and limited to 1 minute. In baseball, players do mental training prior to each at-bat within a three-phased paradigm (see Chapter 20). In basketball or other sports with similar time-out structures, players are instructed to engage in HRD or related HRV BF within 1 to 5 minutes of being made aware that they will return to the game; this requires coordination and communication with coaches to ensure that sport psychology practitioners and players alike know when to start and finish MT.

Step-by-Step HRD BF Procedures: Ecologically Based MT-Official Competition

1. Athletes in all sports engage in a sport-specific customized pre-action-oriented HRD BF mental training session, ranging from 2 to 5 minutes in duration within 10 minutes of competition onset or in accordance with pilot testing established temporal guidelines. Pre-competition MT time

frames can be modified as a function of ongoing intervention efficacy data. If initial intervention temporal properties before and/or during a match are associated with negative or minimal to no gain outcome, MT time lines can be modified, as can the intervention modality itself be tweaked. For example, multi-modal approaches that integrate HRD BF and HRV monitoring that will be presented later in this chapter can be used and tested for efficacy (Figure 12.13a and b).

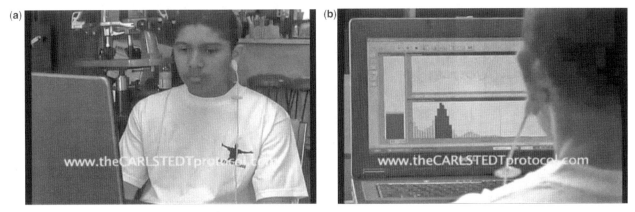

FIGURE 12.13   Tennis player engaging in pre-competition HRD BF.

2. The HRD BF session should be based on HRDtz parameters for sport-specific tasks or actions; for example, in tennis, the serve or return of serve and pre-shot pre-action time frame. In baseball, a batter's HRDtz is based on a pitcher's pre-action routine, with the inhale cycle coinciding with the wind-up and exhale cycle with the release of the ball (Figure 12.14a and b).

FIGURE 12.14   Softball batter pre-action HRDtz based on the pitcher's pre-action time line.

In sports, having self-initiation components that are not opponent dependent or based on an oncoming stimulus, time to initiate action can be highly variable, even open-ended, unless time to commence rules mandate the maximum amount of time allowed before action must start. Golf, downhill skiing, marksmanship, and even free-throw shooting in basketball or penalty shots in soccer and ice hockey are examples of sports and sport-specific actions that are self-initiated (Figure 12.15).

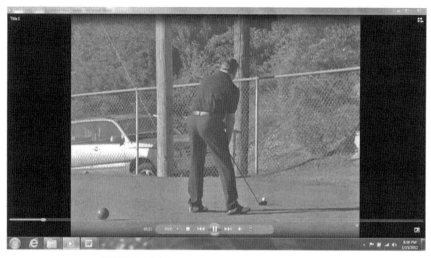

FIGURE 12.15   Preaction phase of golf drive.

3. An MT-intervention computer station should be set up in a private area on the sideline or in the dugout in baseball or bench in tennis. Golfers can use a golf cart in which to engage in HRD MT as they are driven to where their ball lies (see Figure 12.16 below).

FIGURE 12.16   Tennis player being prepped for HRD-HRV scan.

4. The player is called to the intervention station to start HRD MT in accord with sport-specific time lines and/or time restrictions by the sport psychology practitioner or independently in certain situations (when an athlete does not have a coach or assistant).
5. The player looks at the monitor (Heart Scanner screen; the HS program is used as a first step in weaning an athlete from the breathing pacer in the Heart Tracker program; it is possible, though, and can be beneficial in the initial phase of HRD BF intervention training, to use the HT program with a practitioner [see Figure 12.17a and b] to guide the pacing of the inhalation–exhalation

cycles [as in Figure 12.17b] until the athlete has mastered the procedure). In multi-modal HRD BF, video and visualization components are integrated into the MT process (see Figure 12.17). In the absence of video-augmented HRD BF, the athlete is told to focus intensely on the temporal dynamics of his or her HRDtz. Doing so is hypothesized to subliminally prime an athlete to carry out a sport-specific task independent of seeing or generating internal images of an impending sport-specific action, since time-locked preaction HRD that has been consolidated through extensive precompetition MT is expected to set off a precise cascade of brain–heart–mind–motor responses once an athlete steps on to the playing field. This process can be viewed as an inverse or reverse visualization dynamic in which technical-performance-related neuronal ensembles are primed for activation directly via motor pathways, independent of visual priming that can be contaminated, perceptually (how an athlete sees, perceives, or imagines his or her technique may be incongruent with how it should be) or by an inability to exploit potential performance facilitative aspects of mental imagery because of an athlete's low level of HS/SA, rendering the athlete unable to engage in structured visualization. Hence, the goal of direct HRD BF is to shut down or shut out visual and other mechanisms (e.g., negative intrusive thoughts) that cannot be controlled by directly manipulating and inducing brain–heart–mind–body responses that have been directly linked to optimum attention, reaction time, and technical control. Thus, if HRD occurs naturally, or is self-induced via BF-facilitated manipulation of time-locked breathing, superfluous and negative intrusive thoughts and images (even when supposed positive visualization scenarios are thought to be active) can be prevented from ever being manifested and hindering peak performance.

(a)

(b)

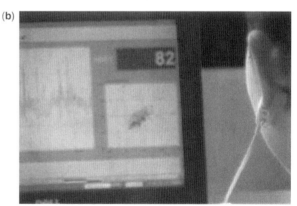

FIGURE 12.17   Practitioner-guided HRD BF.

The primary task when engaging in HRD BF is to practice one's HRDtz cycle up to 4 times per minute. This is done by inhaling in synchrony with the sport-specific pre-action routine of the task at hand. The inhale cycle is always longer or more protracted than the exhale cycle, which is usually short or quick in duration and forceful, especially in sports that have fast reaction time and strength demands of varying magnitude, such as tennis, golf, baseball, and football, to name a few. When inhaling, the goal is to progressively drive the digital HR reading that can be seen in the upper right-hand corner of the HS screen as high as possible (highest reading should occur at the apex of the inhalation cycle). For example, in this scene (Figure 12.17), the athlete, after having his inhale cycle guided upward by the practitioner using the HT program, exhales quickly and forcefully (HR decreases linearly to 82 bpm).

6. After the sport-specific time-out has expired either on the basis of rules stipulating its maximum duration, the progression of the game and its impact on time of performance (e.g., waiting to get up to bat in baseball or cricket), or being called into a game by the coach, the athlete must now perform. The previously practiced HRD BF and HT or HS guided, induced, and reinforced mind–body procedures and responses (HRD), if strongly consolidated in procedural memory, should be accessible and used once the task-specific technical or sporting action is encountered during actual competition, especially if and when an athlete faces critical moments or feels competitive stress anytime during the course of a game or match. While conscious efforts to engage in mental training constantly throughout an entire competition can have a paradoxical effect and negatively impact technical performance, eventually (must be documented), hypothetically, it is expected that athletes will, upon reaching a to-be-determined MT consolidation threshold, eventually engage in intervention routines subliminally or automatically. Thus, one can expect in the initial phases of learning, applying, and consolidating HRD BF and subsequent, noninstrument-aided attempts to induce HRD responses during competition, that more susceptible athletes (AP of high–high–low or non-MT modality amenable AP) will regress before making progress (note though that this observation and associated MT Onset Performance Decrement Hypothesis [MTOPDH] must be tested empirically on all athletes individually). Readers are reminded that mind–body responses, including pre-action HRD and mediated heightened attention, faster reaction time, and enhanced motor control, tend to occur in all athletes during routine moments of competition. As such, one might ask why risk disrupting specific phases of competition when an athlete feels comfortable and in control by coaching or prompting him or her to engage in MT of any kind, especially when it is obvious that an athlete is playing up to peak potential? Practitioners need to consider an athlete's schedule and the availability of sufficient amounts of time in which to intensively and systematically practice an intervention or risk failing to reach consolidation thresholds and paradoxically disrupting performance due to thinking about how to do an MT procedure instead of it just happening. As with technical training, ultimately, engaging in an MT technique should occur automatically without conscious effort. Extensive MT should lead to the neuronal consolidation of MT-facilitated mind–body–motor responses that can be switched on or off as needed, subliminally. Subliminal MT activation thresholds must be documented before one can be certain that an athlete is actually engaging in an intervention procedure independent of conscious efforts to do so, something that is much easier to do with direct MT procedures like HRD BF, since HRD is a known performance-facilitative biomarker response that routinely occurs during pre action phases of many sports in the absence of situational or perceived competitive pressure.

The photos that follow (Figures 12.18 through 12.25) depict a tennis player engaging in post-changeover HRD BF-training, on the court volitional-breathing-induced pre-action HRD extending from the moment his opponent makes contact with the ball to the onset of returning the oncoming ball. Note the protrusion of the cheeks showing the effect of the inhale cycle in the first photo and the subsequent exhalation of inhaled air in the second and third photos. This player was trained to transfer the paced breathing cycles associated with the inducement of sport-task-specific HRD BF off the tennis court in front of a computer monitor, to the court without the aid of instrumentation, the goal of BF (weaning an athlete off instrumentation under the assumption that lab-based BF-shaped mind–body responses will generalize to the playing field and critical situations that require optimum attention, physiological reactivity, and motor control).

FIGURE 12.19   Onset of heart rate deceleration.

FIGURE 12.18   End of pre-action inhale cycle inhalation cycle apex.

FIGURE 12.20   Exhale cycle and HRD in progress.

FIGURE 12.21   Exhale-induced HRD.

HRD BF Efficiency and Efficacy Testing

As readers may know by now, when it comes to athlete assessment and intervention, nothing should be based on beliefs. High evidentiary analytic methodologies must be used to determine to what extent responses that are assumed to have occurred at specific times really did, and if they are associated with better performance. With the BioCom system, HRV/HRD responses can only be analyzed within the *Temporally Remote Paradigm* (TRP; nonreal time monitoring), since heart activity can be

FIGURE 12.22   Exhale continues.

FIGURE 12.24   End of exhalation HRD.

FIGURE 12.23   Close-up–exhalation.

FIGURE 12.25   Close-up–end of exhalation.

monitored only before and after competition and during time-outs. Hence, in order to establish intervention efficiency and efficacy for HRD BF, it must be determined *if time-out/changeover, paced-breathing-guided HRD BF,* and resulting HRV measures are different from HRV measures that are derived during *time-outs in which no HRD BF is administered.* On a more ecologically valid level, one can also test for intervention efficacy using a structured experimental paradigm in which an athlete is instructed to engage in the previously practiced HRD-BF (off the playing field) and on the playing field prior to every competitive event, like the service return that is depicted in the preceding photos. After x amount of returns in which self-induced BF shaped HRD is attempted by a player prior to action (the pre-action phase of the service return), an HRV scan of the player's heart activity is administered. Thereafter, in a no-intervention phase of the same paradigm with same amount of service returns, another scan is obtained. The resultant intervention/no intervention HRV measures are then compared. Conceptually, if HRD exerts an enduring temporal effect on post-time-out-pre-action HRV that is significantly different from HRV occurring in the post-time-out-no intervention condition, then intervention efficiency has been established. Then, if HRD BF–associated HRV measures predict a specific macro- and/or micro-level outcome (e.g., level 5 critical moment success or points won versus lost), intervention efficacy will have been established. Again, intervention efficacy can exist on a continuum from very low to very high; as such, merely establishing intervention efficacy, while necessary, is not sufficient to unabashedly advocate for the universal application of a particular MT method. On the other hand, minute performance gains that can be attributed to an intervention may have major practical significance, for example, winning one additional game or match that impacts an athlete's world or national ranking.

HRD BF Intervention Efficiency and Efficacy Testing: Intervention versus No Intervention

In the context of the TRP, conceptually, intervention efficiency has been shown to exist if one or more HRV measures obtained during time-outs of the intervention (HRD BF) phase immediately after the last in a series of points have been played (during which HRD BF was also engaged in after each point) significantly differ from HRV measures obtained during time-outs of the no-intervention phase (also no intervention between points in this condition). In addition, the greater the conceptual consistency of such differences, the greater the intervention efficiency.

The following data emanates from an advanced senior-level tennis player engaging in an experimental paradigm to determine if on-the-bench HRD-BF, subsequent to self-initiated HRD using paced breathing after each point played between time-out HRV scans would be associated with conceptually relevant changes in HRV (as would be predicted) compared to HRV measures obtained during no-intervention time-outs, subsequent to points played after which HRD BF was not self-initiated. Each phase (no-intervention versus intervention HRD-BF) consisted of about 17 or 18 games of 11, in which each player attempts to win the point after two free "hits" (ball is introduced using a bounce-stroke and no winner can be hit on the first ball). A 1-minute HRV scan using BioCom HS was immediately administered after a game of 11s ended (first player to win 11 points by a margin of at least 2 wins the game).

The obtained data spanned three sessions over the course of 1 week.

Intervention Efficiency (Figures 12.26 and 12.27)

Two statistically significant, including one highly conceptually consistent, findings emerged. In the HRD-BF intervention condition, SDNN (the HRV index) was significantly different from the no-intervention condition. Since volitionally breathing–induced HRD (or attempts to induce HRD) via paced inhalation and exhalation cycles are associated with greater HRV (as reflected in intervention-associated HRD BF here) one can infer that the exhibited differences did not

Independent Samples Test

		Levene's Test for Equality of Variances		t-test for Equality of Means						95% Confidence Interval of the Difference	
		F	Sig.	t	df	Sig. (2-tailed)	Mean Difference	Std. Error Difference		Lower	Upper
MEASURE	Equal variances assumed	5.884	.019	-2.348	49	.023	-13.4785	5.7404		-25.0143	-1.9427
	Equal variances not assumed			-2.383	32.480	.023	-13.4785	5.6558		-24.9923	-1.9646

FIGURE 12.26   SDNN frequency HRV No HRD BF versus HRD BF.

Independent Samples Test

		Levene's Test for Equality of Variances		t-test for Equality of Means						95% Confidence Interval of the Difference	
		F	Sig.	t	df	Sig. (2-tailed)	Mean Difference	Std. Error Difference		Lower	Upper
MEASURE	Equal variances assumed	5.515	.023	-1.888	49	.065	-106.5754	56.4441		-220.0041	6.8533
	Equal variances not assumed			-1.923	27.496	.065	-106.5754	55.4281		-220.2086	7.0578

FIGURE 12.27   Very low frequency No HRD BF versus LF HRD BF.

happen by chance, at least, the probability is high (see Figure 12.29, $p = .023$) that this was not a random effect. SDNN is one of two most conceptually, HRD-relevant HRV measures (along with L/H ratio). As such, HRD-BF intervention efficiency was established for the specific athlete over the course of 1 week of testing trials. A second, borderline finding revealed less very low-frequency activity in the intervention phase. This finding is also conceptually consistent, since paced breathing and resulting HRD has a strong PNS component (VL frequency is a measure of SNS activation).

Practitioner Challenge: If no significant differences in HRV activity had emerged across monitoring conditions (no intervention versus intervention), what would that suggest?

This pilot investigation was undertaken in an attempt to preliminarily validate the temporally remote HRD and HRD BF no-versus-intervention paradigms by documenting changes in HRV across divergent and distant measurement occasions.

Intervention Efficacy (Figures 12.28 and 12.29)

In terms of intervention efficacy, the tested player won more and lost fewer games in the HRD BF compared to the no-intervention condition (PTS11W 7.9 versus 5.5, and 6.3 versus 8.1 PTS11L). These macro-level outcome findings, while encouraging, would have to be replicated across about 60 trials for statistical significance to be established. On the other hand, practical significance, a potentially important efficacy metric in some sports in which small differences in an outcome measure can impact global outcome measures such as games won or lost, can be considered in the intervention efficacy testing analytic process. This particular athlete, who previously lost about 80% of all 11 games against the same player who served as his opponent in this study, won close to 40% of all 11 games in the HRD-BF intervention condition, a 100% increase over his

Descriptive Statistics

	Mean	Std. Deviation	N
STRKNOIN	20.5294	5.5240	17
PTS11W	5.4706	3.6076	17
PTS11L	8.1176	3.6722	17
HR	125.1111	9.2093	18
SDNN	34.0000	5.7701	18
VL	31.1111	26.2205	18
L	47.4444	43.5947	18
H	63.5000	72.7819	18
LH	2.6556	3.8933	18
HHR	138.4444	8.3611	18
LHR	116.7778	9.5150	18

FIGURE 12.28   HRD BF No intervention: Points and HRV.

Descriptive Statistics

	Mean	Std. Deviation	N
STRKHRD	20.1579	8.1531	19
PTS11WHD	7.8421	3.4523	19
PTS11LHD	6.2632	2.8644	19
HRHD	119.7368	13.8156	19
SDNHRD	49.1053	30.8399	19
VLOWHRD	139.5263	298.7220	19
LOWHRD	608.6316	2221.1748	19
HIGHHRD	343.0526	1074.7273	19
LHIGHHRD	2.2000	2.1736	19
HIGHHRHD	133.2632	11.7324	19
LOWHRHD	113.7368	13.0973	19

FIGURE 12.29   HRD BF intervention: Points and HRV.

norm performance. His self-report was also supportive. He maintained that he felt more focused and less nervous during critical moments during the 11 games (e.g., when being close to arriving at game point). Although self-report has little, if any, empirical stature, if athlete feedback is consistent with actual performance and likely not high HS driven or placebo-mediated (this player's AP was M-L-M, a more ambiguous AP), it can serve a purpose.

Practitioner Challenge: What is the practical significance of this player's GIEQ, and what other intervention efficacy metrics might provide better or additional insight into whether HRD-BF works beyond such an experimental test?

Overall, intervention efficacy was established for HRD-BF in this athlete. His provisional Global Intervention Efficacy Quotient (GIEQ) for the 11s competition paradigm was .400% or 40%.

Intervention efficacy can also be investigated in the context of conceptually relevant mind–body measure; in this case, HRD-BF based intervention. The following SPSS correlation output charts (Figures 12.30 and 12.31) depict no-intervention and HRD-BF intervention HRV measures and their relationship with point and streak outcome (an ancillary continuous performance statistic [number of consecutive shots during an 11s point). There were no significant associations between HRV and outcome measures in the no-intervention condition (Figure 12.30).

By contrast, in the HRD-BF intervention condition (Figure 12.31, the HRV L/H frequency ratio; LHIGHHRD) was negatively correlated with points won ($r = -.47$, $p = .04$; PTS11WHD). This is another conceptually consistent finding attesting to intervention efficiency mediated intervention efficacy. Since a smaller L/H ratio usually contains more PNS-related HF activity, and greater HF activity is mediated by the exhalation phase of the HRD breathing cycle, brain–heart responses that have been associated with peak performance components, it could be expected that lower levels of L/H frequency activity would result in better performance (lesser L/H frequency ratio = more points won).

Summary: Temporally Remote HRD-BF Intervention Paradigm

The presented pilot investigation of the BioCom HS-based TRP was validated in this tennis player. Clear, conceptually consistent intervention efficiency and efficacy findings support its utility as an athlete assessment and intervention approach. Nevertheless, this paradigm is limited by its lack of

Correlations

		STRKNOIN	PTS11W	PTS11L	HR	SDNN	VL	L	H	LH	HHR	LHR
STRKNOIN	Pearson Correlation	1.000	-.095	-.237	-.110	.269	-.254	-.172	.174	-.195	-.028	-.046
	Sig. (2-tailed)		.717	.359	.675	.297	.326	.509	.504	.454	.914	.862
	N	17	17	17	17	17	17	17	17	17	17	17
PTS11W	Pearson Correlation	-.095	1.000	.585*	.240	.126	.203	.221	-.105	.351	.153	.139
	Sig. (2-tailed)	.717		.014	.354	.631	.435	.394	.687	.167	.557	.595
	N	17	17	17	17	17	17	17	17	17	17	17
PTS11L	Pearson Correlation	-.237	.585*	1.000	.092	.171	-.097	.266	-.053	.304	.030	.058
	Sig. (2-tailed)	.359	.014		.724	.512	.712	.302	.840	.235	.909	.824
	N	17	17	17	17	17	17	17	17	17	17	17
HR	Pearson Correlation	-.110	.240	.092	1.000	-.194	.242	.093	.222	-.171	.869**	.925**
	Sig. (2-tailed)	.675	.354	.724		.441	.333	.713	.376	.498	.000	.000
	N	17	17	17	18	18	18	18	18	18	18	18
SDNN	Pearson Correlation	.269	.126	.171	-.194	1.000	.101	.352	.297	-.110	-.200	-.255
	Sig. (2-tailed)	.297	.631	.512	.441		.691	.152	.232	.664	.426	.307
	N	17	17	17	18	18	18	18	18	18	18	18
VL	Pearson Correlation	-.254	.203	-.097	.242	.101	1.000	.558*	.605**	-.167	.251	.269
	Sig. (2-tailed)	.326	.435	.712	.333	.691		.016	.008	.509	.316	.281
	N	17	17	17	18	18	18	18	18	18	18	18
L	Pearson Correlation	-.172	.221	.266	.093	.352	.558*	1.000	.665**	-.191	-.061	.165
	Sig. (2-tailed)	.509	.394	.302	.713	.152	.016		.003	.447	.811	.513
	N	17	17	17	18	18	18	18	18	18	18	18
H	Pearson Correlation	.174	-.105	-.053	.222	.297	.605**	.665**	1.000	-.447	.192	.361
	Sig. (2-tailed)	.504	.687	.840	.376	.232	.008	.003		.063	.446	.141
	N	17	17	17	18	18	18	18	18	18	18	18
LH	Pearson Correlation	-.195	.351	.304	-.171	-.110	-.167	-.191	-.447	1.000	-.142	-.176
	Sig. (2-tailed)	.454	.167	.235	.498	.664	.509	.447	.063		.575	.484
	N	17	17	17	18	18	18	18	18	18	18	18
HHR	Pearson Correlation	-.028	.153	.030	.869**	-.200	.251	-.061	.192	-.142	1.000	.811**
	Sig. (2-tailed)	.914	.557	.909	.000	.426	.316	.811	.446	.575		.000
	N	17	17	17	18	18	18	18	18	18	18	18
LHR	Pearson Correlation	-.046	.139	.058	.925**	-.255	.269	.165	.361	-.176	.811**	1.000
	Sig. (2-tailed)	.862	.595	.824	.000	.307	.281	.513	.141	.484	.000	
	N	17	17	17	18	18	18	18	18	18	18	18

*Correlation is significant at the 0.05 level (2-tailed).

**Correlation is significant at the 0.01 level (2-tailed).

FIGURE 12.30   HRD BF-No intervention condition, macro-outcome (points and streaks) and HRV.

real-time monitoring of HRV and pre-action epoch-specific HRD analysis capabilities. These limitations, along with more advanced approaches to HRD BF using Polar telemetry instrumentation, are addressed in the next section.

Description of Procedure: Polar System

In terms of HRD BF efficacy testing, because of limitations associated with HRV monitoring systems that use wired as opposed to telemetry-based wireless data acquisition methods, until now, this MT modality and the HRD response that it is supposed to shape, could only be analyzed in the context of more static paradigms in which responses could not be isolated or time-locked to competitive situations or epochs of interest (as with the previously described BioCom HS system).

This limitation has been overcome with the advent of the ABSP-CP Polar system and its wireless monitoring capabilities.

While the BioCom system is excellent for educating and training athletes in HRD BF and can be reliably adapted for real competition-based efficiency and efficacy checks, ideally, one would want to observe and know when and to what extent HRD has occurred and whether the manifestation of HRD in a specific athlete is associated with better outcomes than when HRD is not manifested. The Polar RS800CX and allied *Windlink* telemetry systems allow for such time-locked analyses of HRD during competition as well as instrument-based in-the-moment pre-action HRV BF on the

Correlations

		STRKHRD	PTS11WHD	PTS11LHD	HRHD	SDNHRD	VLOWHRD	LOWHRD	HIGHHRD	LHIGHHRD	HIGHHRHD	LOWHRHD
STRKHRD	Pearson Correlation	1.000	-.080	.127	-.254	-.266	-.329	-.389	-.381	.015	-.146	-.204
	Sig. (2-tailed)		.745	.606	.295	.271	.170	.100	.108	.951	.552	.403
	N	19	19	19	19	19	19	19	19	19	19	19
PTS11WHD	Pearson Correlation	-.080	1.000	.763**	.286	.019	.171	.211	.228	-.471*	.214	.316
	Sig. (2-tailed)	.745		.000	.236	.939	.485	.387	.348	.042	.380	.187
	N	19	19	19	19	19	19	19	19	19	19	19
PTS11LHD	Pearson Correlation	.127	.763**	1.000	.146	.089	.246	.224	.232	-.242	-.025	.237
	Sig. (2-tailed)	.606	.000		.550	.717	.309	.356	.339	.319	.918	.328
	N	19	19	19	19	19	19	19	19	19	19	19
HRHD	Pearson Correlation	-.254	.286	.146	1.000	-.239	-.220	-.084	-.040	-.696**	.911**	.968**
	Sig. (2-tailed)	.295	.236	.550		.324	.366	.732	.870	.001	.000	.000
	N	19	19	19	19	19	19	19	19	19	19	19
SDNHRD	Pearson Correlation	-.266	.019	.089	-.239	1.000	.885**	.885**	.883**	.143	-.285	-.178
	Sig. (2-tailed)	.271	.939	.717	.324		.000	.000	.000	.559	.237	.467
	N	19	19	19	19	19	19	19	19	19	19	19
VLOWHRD	Pearson Correlation	-.329	.171	.246	-.220	.885**	1.000	.977**	.969**	.049	-.345	-.157
	Sig. (2-tailed)	.170	.485	.309	.366	.000		.000	.000	.844	.148	.520
	N	19	19	19	19	19	19	19	19	19	19	19
LOWHRD	Pearson Correlation	-.389	.211	.224	-.084	.885**	.977**	1.000	.998**	-.023	-.173	-.032
	Sig. (2-tailed)	.100	.387	.356	.732	.000	.000		.000	.926	.480	.898
	N	19	19	19	19	19	19	19	19	19	19	19
HIGHHRD	Pearson Correlation	-.381	.228	.232	-.040	.883**	.969**	.998**	1.000	-.071	-.132	.015
	Sig. (2-tailed)	.108	.348	.339	.870	.000	.000	.000		.772	.589	.952
	N	19	19	19	19	19	19	19	19	19	19	19
LHIGHHRD	Pearson Correlation	.015	-.471*	-.242	-.696**	.143	.049	-.023	-.071	1.000	-.543*	-.694**
	Sig. (2-tailed)	.951	.042	.319	.001	.559	.844	.926	.772		.016	.001
	N	19	19	19	19	19	19	19	19	19	19	19
HIGHHRHD	Pearson Correlation	-.146	.214	-.025	.911**	-.285	-.345	-.173	-.132	-.543*	1.000	.848**
	Sig. (2-tailed)	.552	.380	.918	.000	.237	.148	.480	.589	.016		.000
	N	19	19	19	19	19	19	19	19	19	19	19
LOWHRHD	Pearson Correlation	-.204	.316	.237	.968**	-.178	-.157	-.032	.015	-.694**	.848**	1.000
	Sig. (2-tailed)	.403	.187	.328	.000	.467	.520	.898	.952	.001	.000	
	N	19	19	19	19	19	19	19	19	19	19	19

*Correlation is significant at the 0.05 level (2-tailed).

**Correlation is significant at the 0.01 level (2-tailed).

FIGURE 12.31 HRD BF-Intervention condition, macro-outcome (points and streaks), and HRV.

playing field. Being able to engage in instrument-guided BF during official competition is a major breakthrough, since to-date practitioners worked on the premise that a BF-shaped response in the lab or office or on the sideline had to be well engrained or consolidated to reliably generalize to the playing field. Yet, practitioners and researchers alike have been unable to consistently demonstrate, if at all, that lab-based BF-generated-and-shaped mind–body responses could be reproduced by an athlete on command when necessary, and importantly, if such responses were actually associated with optimum performance and/or successful outcomes. Such ambiguity and the equivocal generalizability of lab-based BF-shaped psychophysiological responses to the playing field calls into question the utility and viability of BF as a reliable intervention, despite claims to the contrary by stakeholders in BF. Consequently, Polar-based/acquired HRV/HRD measures have leaped to the forefront of psychophysiological assessment and BF, since data can now be reliably obtained in real time and time-locked to all important competitive epochs, ranging from pre-action to specific moments during an action phase (e.g., the precise moment when a field-goal kicker's foot makes contact with the football). Importantly, since specific cardiac responses are strongly correlated with performance-relevant cortical (brain) responses, it is an ideal ersatz measure for criterion-referencing in-the-lab induced-and-shaped BF responses with HRV/HRD, a response that can be reliably induced, manipulated, and documented on the playing field.

> *Practitioner Challenge: Does intervention efficiency and efficacy validation in an individual athlete generalize to other athletes? Discuss validation in the context of individual vs. group findings.*

FIGURE 12.32 Preparing to use the Polar instrumentation.

The ABSP-CP Polar paradigm offers cross-validation capabilities (lab-based with in-the-field equipment during real competition data comparisons) because of the robustness of this system's instrumentation during extreme movement (resistance to motion artifact).

HRD BF On the Playing Field During Competition: Ecological Mental Training

The following photos depict step-by-step HRD BF procedures using the Polar RS800CX heart activity monitoring system. This instrumentation is emerging as the primary monitoring system for all ABSP-CP interventions and MT, since HRV and HRD trends can be isolated throughout competition in virtually all sports in real time as the athlete engages in MT, wirelessly. The ability to obtain time-locked mind–body response data during real competition offers unprecedented insight into comprehensive sport-specific psychophysiological response dynamics.

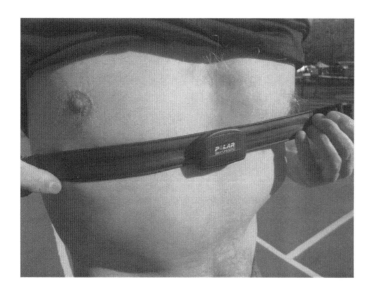

FIGURE 12.33 Polar chest strap with receiver.

FIGURE 12.34   Polar computer-watch-receiver.

1. The photo in Figure 12.32 shows the Polar chest strap and heart activity receiver/transmitter.
2. The chest strap is attached so that the receiver/transmitter is tightly secured over the breastbone (Figure 12.33). Wearing a chest strap is a nonissue for the vast majority of athletes who quickly adapt to wearing it.
3. Once the chest strap is in place, the watch, which functions as a data receiver and storage as well as a BF device, is started by the athlete (Figure 12.34). When engaging in HRD/HRV assessment

FIGURE 12.35   Player's HRV being monitored as he competes.

FIGURE 12.36   Post point HRD BF.

and BF, it is necessary to videotape training and competition sessions from beginning to end. The video recorder should be started in conjunction with the Polar watch/data receiver.

4. Here the player has just returned a serve (Figure 12.35). Heart activity signals are transmitted from the chest monitoring/receiver unit to the watch/computer receiver and stored over the course of the entire training or competition.

5. Player checks his post-action/post-point HR (Figure 12.36). The watch can also be used as a BF device. Here we see at 2′ 23″ of this tennis set an HR of 106 bpm (Figure 12.37). The depicted

FIGURE 12.37   HR at HRD BF onset (106).

FIGURE 12.38   Start of inhale-exhale cycles.

tennis player was previously trained in HRD BF and conditioned to check his HR by looking at the watch immediately after a point, in this case a service return that resulted in no further action, hence the relatively low HR.

6. Thereafter, the player commences breathing-based HRD BF prior to the next point (Figure 12.38). In tennis, players have about 20 to 25 seconds between points. This down time or part of this time is used, as necessary, to practice HRD and HRD BF for the purpose of priming automatic mind–body responses that a player then synchronizes to the task demands and temporal parameters of a specific sport, in this case, either the serve or return of serve. In this photo, the player is in his exhalation/expiration breathing phase. His goal is to induce HRD through a continuous, quick, and forceful exhale cycle that is time-locked to the impending onset of action; either the start of the upward racquet swing when serving, or swing of the racquet when returning a serve. Exhalation should be timed to be fully completed by the time contact is made with the ball.

7. The preceding HRD BF epoch lasted 12 seconds, from 2′ 23″ to 2′ 35″, resulting in a linear reduction in HR from 106 to 96 bpm (Figure 12.39).[1] The player successfully self-generated HRD through timed breathing that was initially learned and consolidated in the lab. The watch provides on-the-playing-field feedback and reinforcement by showing HRV changes over a prescribed amount of time in which an intervention is engaged.

It should be noted that 12 seconds, although possibly seeming to be too lengthy a time frame, was the mean time that the player's opponent took from the onset of the service-ready position to when the ball was struck. Consequently, the player was instructed to engage in a pre-return HRD BF routine for 12 seconds and then get into his service-return position, do one more HRD BF cycle if possible (dependent on whether the server who, per rule, can dictate the pace of play so long as the maximum between point time allowed [25 seconds] is not exceeded), and then, initially, on a conscious level, pace and time his inhalation–exhalation cycles to his opponent's 12″ service cycle. Over time, it is expected that a player will initiate pre-action HRD automatically, as most athletes do during nonstressful

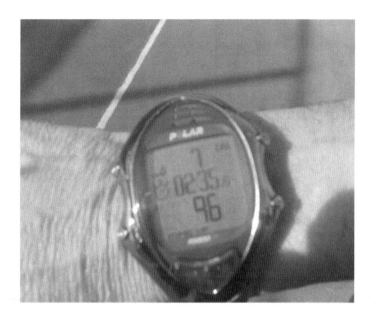

FIGURE 12.39   HR after HRD BF (from 106 to 96).

routine phases of competition, a performance-facilitative response that hopefully will be so well conditioned and consolidated that an athlete can depend upon it occurring naturally, without self-or external prompting by a coach or volitionally telling oneself to do the HRD BF routine whenever he or she feels competitive stress or is aware of the importance of or heightened criticality of a certain point or competitive situation.

Practitioner Experiment Challenge: See if you can feel the effects of inhalation and exhalation on your own heart rate. Find your pulse near your wrist, throat, or head. Proceed to inhale slowly and then exhale slowly. Can you detect an increase in heart rate when you inhale and a decrease when you exhale? Vary your inhale and exhale force and length. Culminate the experiment with a rapid inhale and protracted exhale cycle, or use an inhale– exhale rhythm that is timed to the pre-action phase of a sport in which you participate or have advanced knowledge of.

Documentation and Accountability-Intervention Efficacy

Readers are referred to Chapter 9 for a comprehensive explication of HRV and HRD monitoring and data analysis during training and competition, as well as Chapter 20, which presents an integrative assessment and intervention season-long study of official baseball games in which HRD BF was carried out on the bench prior to all starting players' at-bats using the ABSP-CP BioCom-based MT paradigm.

Note

1. It should be noted that reduction in HR also occurs as a function of decreasing metabolic demands. Consequently, it is important to observe HRD trends in the pre-intervention training phase in the context of natural metabolic-mediated HRD and breathing-mediated HRD, as well as orienting-response mediated HRD. Volitional breathing-based HRD and HRD BF should be distinct from metabolic-mediated HRD and marked by less of a linear HR slowing trend, whereas self-induced and stimulus-oriented HRD should exhibit linear trends consisting of two or more linearly slowing inter-beat intervals.

Behavioral–Motor–Technical-Based Mental Training

Behavioral–Motor–Technical (BMT)-based intervention attempts to help support an athlete's mental game using exposure, confrontation, threshold, and learning principles to improve attention, motor control, and self-confidence, as well as reduce nervousness associated with pressure moments of competition.

Intervention Amenability and Compliance: Ideal AP PHO Constellation or Measure(s)

BMT-based intervention is a direct approach to mental training (MT). It bypasses better-known modalities such as mental imagery and, instead, focuses on motor and technically oriented learning and drills to reinforce technical changes and/or corrections that need to be made, or for the purpose of developing better sport-specific skills. It also confronts pressure performance from a technical perspective using exposure approaches, for example, requiring an athlete to repeatedly maintain motor control and demonstrate peak technical ability in the context of simulated and actual pressure during real competition. It is a method that is well-suited to athletes who are in the high range for repressive coping/subliminal coping (RC/SC) and low range for hypnotic susceptibility/subliminal attention (HS/SA), primary higher order factors (PHO) constellation measures that tend to be resistant to most indirect MT modalities (like visualization or self-hypnosis). Athletes who are low in HS/SA and high in RC/SC tend not to believe in MT. They are most amenable to direct feedback training approaches that they might not even perceive as being MT. They like to see (in their own minds) direct (perceived) causal links that are often apparent with BMT-based MT, for example, being able to quickly discern that repeatedly practicing a new technical motion or sequence under pressure conditions results in a pressure-performance statistic that has meaning and documents peak performance or some level of improvement.

BMT MT is also a generic broad-spectrum intervention that can be used by all athletes at some point without them thinking of it as MT (irrespective of AP). What takes it into the realm of the mental game is the application of accountability methodologies that operationalize and quantify its diverse technical and motor procedures in the context of psychological and mind–body predictor and sport-specific performance outcome measures (Figure 13.1).

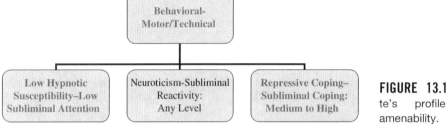

FIGURE 13.1 Intervention athlete's profile and intervention amenability.

Conceptual Rationale

Conceptually, BMT MT's utility and potential to enhance psychological performance is based on motor learning, technical repetition, and exposure/habituation principles. The premise being that the direct path to mental toughness or self-regulation and motor control, especially when competitive pressure situations arise, is through the technical and physical game. Rather than engage in indirect and circuitous intervention methods that can be nebulous in terms of their underlying mechanisms, efficiency, and efficacy, BMT MT is designed to systematically improve technical, motor, and physical skills to such an extent that they are unlikely to break down even when an athlete encounters critical moments during competition. Formulas can be used to guide, document, express, and analyze the BMT MT training process. For example, at the most basic level or initial MT iteration, an attempt would be made to establish global technical and motor performance thresholds, for example, the number of balls a tennis player can hit to a specified area on the court while exhibiting optimum form or technique. Scores of additional technical/motor/physical micro-iterations could also be added to the performance equation that are then analyzed in the context of specific operationalizations of attention, motor control, physical parameters (e.g., reaction time), and common psychological and mind–body measures such as critical moment and pressure/routine moment contrasted heart rate variability (HRV) responses.

A central tenet of BMT-MT is the exposure-confrontation hypothesis (ECH) that fears must be approached head-on. Competitive anxiety must be dealt with in a very direct and continuous manner. In other words, athletes who fear competition or pressure moments when competing must be repeatedly exposed to critical situations and competitive stress until it can be documented that maladaptive mind–body responses as reflected in HRV and/or other psychophysiological measures have attenuated or are eradicated and replaced with IZOF mind–body responses and enhanced performance. The goal of BMT-MT is to increase technical, motor, and physical thresholds as a function of linearly rising competitive pressure to the point of inoculation or habituation; that is, shaping and consolidating technical and mental responses under conditions of duress until pressure becomes the norm, but is no longer feared. Pressure becomes the routine, not a competitive moment in isolation that is rarely encountered. Within the BMT-MT paradigm, pressure is constantly encountered and confronted and is built in to all training sessions. Well-consolidated technical skills that were honed under constant pressure are hypothesized to lead to the manifestation of peak performance skills, not only during routine moments, but also when competitive pressure is encountered, even in AP vulnerable athletes. The central nervous system mechanisms that are thought to be associated with BMT-MT-induced habituation or inoculation to competitive stress are discussed under Brain-Based interventions of the AP brain–heart–mind–body conceptual model and construct bases.

Practitioner Challenge: How could IZOT be operationalized?

It is further hypothesized that each individual athlete has an attainable Individual Zone of Optimum Technique (IZOT) if competitive stress or pressure can be minimized or eliminated in terms of how they are perceived and dealt with behaviorally.

BMT-MT offers potential solutions to the vexing problem of how to play one's best when it counts the most. As with all MT modalities, they must be administered within an extensive pre- and intervention phase accountability framework (see below).

Description of Procedure

1. Player undergoes BMT-MT baseline threshold analysis (in this case, tennis ground strokes; forehand and backhand-outcome statistics presented in the accountability section that follows).
2. Player performance is rated relative to both outcome and technique.

FIGURE 13.2

3. This player had a protracted backswing on the forehand side with too little hip rotation and shoulder turn, leading to a late forward swing and reduced power and spin on the ball, especially when under pressure (Figure 13.2).

FIGURE 13.3

4. The player's ability to accelerate through the hitting zone was thereby hindered (Figure 13.3).
5. On the backhand side, the player had a tendency not to rotate his shoulders quickly enough and get his feet and hips into more of a sideways-closed position (Figure 13.4).

FIGURE 13.4

6. When the player had time, he could demonstrate an almost perfect one-handed backhand, but when under pressure and in matches his backhand technique tended to break down (Figure 13.5).

FIGURE 13.5

7. This former professional tennis player, who still competes at a high level and has ambitions, was tired of losing matches because of supposed mental performance issues. He was, however, very surprised to discover that the etiology of his performance issues and perceived tendency to choke had a technical etiology. Rarely over the course of his career was he able to see himself on video or film. As such, in his mind's eye his technique was very good, and, in fact, as a teaching pro, he was able to demonstrate perfect technique to his students. But, in reality, his technique had subtle flaws that were never adequately addressed over the course of his career, something that may have limited his ability to get to higher levels of the professional game.

8. The player was taken through full video diagnostics, and as an experienced teaching pro and coach, he was able to immediately recognize the aforementioned technical flaws relating to this forehand and backhand. He was actually stunned that he had gone years without realizing that the minor problems that were now obvious existed, and that perhaps he was not really a "choker," but had a technical foundation that was predestined to breakdown. For example, how could he really expect to hit a crucial backhand down the line if he always set up too late, leading to an excessively fast and forceful motion that caused him to over-rotate upon contact with the ball, away from the straight path the racquet needed to take to hit a precise shot down the line? This was almost an impossibility, especially during critical moments of competition.

This case description serves to illustrate how important broad-based technical competence is to the mental game. Hence, it is critical for sport psychology practitioners who do not have expertise or at least expert-knowledge in sports their athletes or clients play to involve a coach to thoroughly analyze the technical game of their players, in order to better delineate their performance in terms of Mental-Technical Balance (MTB). The MTB equation is a performance assessment formula that reflects how much of an athlete's outcome, whether successful or unsuccessful, can be attributed to a player's technical or mental game. MTB quotients that are skewed in one direction or the other (technical versus mental) help determine how and to what extent MT or an intervention is structured to improve in one area or ameliorate related issues (either technically or psychologically centered MT). In cases where there is a 50–50 balance, integrative approaches such as video-based programming (VBP) and BMT methods can be used (multi-modal) to, on one hand, attempt to improve technique, and on the other hand, use behavioral methods and motor-learning principles to consolidate technique procedurally, which may help prop up and enhance an athlete's level of mental toughness.

9. In the case of this athlete, once it became clear to him that certain technical parts of his game were not what he thought they were, he was committed to engaging intensively in MTB-MT (this athlete has a low-medium level of HS/SA, a trait associated with a diminished ability to feel or perceive mind-body processes and a reduced ability to generate and process internal images).

> *Practitioner Challenge*: What does such a diminished ability imply in the context of MTB-MT and other interventional options?

10. This athlete, over the course of multiple ABSP-Summer program sessions, engaged in numerous MTB-MT iterations in a systematic step-by-step manner in attempt to overwrite faulty technically consolidated "quirks" (see the following example).

11. The athlete initially engages in rudimentary, very easy technical drills that were designed to give him the time to think about and feel his technique and associated technical flaws.

12. In the following screenshots (Figures 13.6 and 13.7), a tennis-knowledgeable sport psychology practitioner tosses balls to the player's forehand side. The practitioner, who was cognizant of his technical flaws and recognizes the technique that should be modeled, provides auditory feedback using a 1–5 scale to rate, for example, in this case, the player's initial shoulder rotation. Later on in the process, the entire forehand is rated. Each shot rating is documented in a scorebook for later analysis.

Such other iterations of MTB-MT can involve hundreds of repetitions per session. The goal is to reach motor consolidation thresholds for, at first, technical phases of a sport-specific task and, eventually, an entire technical motion from beginning to end; in this case, exhibiting perfect forehand technical components ranging from the initial shoulder and hip rotation to the follow-through.

FIGURE 13.6   Initial forehand component: rotation and acceleration.

FIGURE 13.7   Completed forehand follow-through.

13. After the forehand session, the player starts to work on backhand technical corrections, starting with the initial rotation-backswing and ending with the follow-through (Figure 13.8).

FIGURE 13.8

FIGURE 13.9

Note: the opening-up of the shoulders in the above screenshot (Figure 13.9), indicative of the failure to make the desired technical correction. The video upon which this screen shot is based is systematically accessed and reviewed throughout the MTB-MT process. This correction drill is repeated as necessary until a sport-specific action in its entirety approaches perfection in practice and especially match contexts.

14. After weeks of MTB-MT within a comprehensive multi-modal intervention design, this modality was applied prior to matches in the context of money-ball drills in which the player's technique was rated on a 1–5 scale after each shot. Money-ball shots are randomly designated about 10% to 15% of the time. This is a simulated pressure-generating method that has been shown to elicit stress responses in AP vulnerable athletes and is used to rate pressure performance during training. In the context of MTB-MT, the money-ball method is used to determine if corrected techniques (like this player's forehand/backhand issues) are not only well consolidated in procedural memory during routine moments, but pressure ones as well.

15. The player is shown in action prior to a match after extended MTB-MT. In this picture (Figure 13.10), the player has exhibited a perfect backhand. Notice that his shoulders are parallel to the

FIGURE 13.10

sideline, indicative of optimum preparation, swing to contact, and racquet progression through the hitting zone.

16. After each 3-month training session involving multi-modal MT procedures, this player maintained that VBP and MTB-MT, especially, were the most efficacious type of mental training for him. He noted that he had much greater confidence in his technique during matches and pressure situations. His anecdotal assertions were scrutinized and are reported below in various contexts.

Note: HRV readings/scans were taken during all time-outs associated with the MTB-MT.

Findings are presented in the following section.

Documentation—Accountability—Intervention Efficiency and Efficacy

	Date	TRIAL	Game/Trial #	HR	SDNN	VL	Low	High	L-H	HiStreak	LoStreak	AvgStreak
2	6/1/2010	2min	Non Directional	125	43.6	33	85.7	204.7	0.4	22	1	7.72
3	6/1/2010	2min	Non Directional	126.9	72.6	123.6	127.3	202.4	0.6	47	1	12.06
4	6/2/2010	2min	Non Directional	115	53.9	64.3	25.7	87.6	0.3	24	1	10.08
5	6/2/2010	2min	Non Directional	122.2	103.1	86.2	280.4	569.7	0.5	36	1	12.67
6	6/2/2010	2min	Non Directional	127.7	44.3	27.8	142.1	132.2	1.1	36	1	10.15
7	6/3/2010	2min	Directional Drill	111.6	47	21.9	101.4	224.7	0.5	22	1	8.07
8	6/3/2010	2min	Directional Drill	121.8	67	80.8	67.2	257.5	0.3	33	3	15.67
9	6/8/2010	2min	Non Directional	106.1	53.4	5.3	27.2	91.2	0.3	41	3	10.38
10	6/8/2010	2min	Directional Drill	116.2	79	17.6	45	310.8	0.1	20	2	9.67
11	6/9/2010	2min	Directional Drill	106.9	57.4	53.9	187.4	231.5	0.8	17	2	8
12	6/9/2010	2min	Directional Drill	97.5	25.5	92.3	36.1	37.9	1	19	2	11.11
13	6/10/2010	2min	Non Directional	91.3	149.7	520.5	1024.3	1223.6	0.8	26	2	12
14	6/10/2010	2min	Directional Drill	107.5	83.3	96.5	139	391	0.4	12	3	8.14
15	6/10/2010	2min	Directional Drill	105.1	62.5	87.5	114.2	184.3	0.6	16	12	14
16	6/11/2010	2min	Non Directional	97.8	166.1	1656.9	2830.1	3215.7	0.9	41	7	19.4
17	6/14/2010	2min	Directional Drill	107.4	116.9	219.7	408.9	826.3	0.5	13	3	8.54
18	6/14/2010	2min	Directional Drill	126.5	71.5	61.2	301.6	375.4	0.8	27	11	17.75
19	6/15/2010	2min	Directional Drill	112.1	40.8	35.6	34.1	77.6	0.4	16	1	8.23
20	6/15/2010	2min	Directional Drill	110.1	125.3	258.9	487.4	1340.5	0.4	16	2	7.92
21	6/15/2010	2min	Directional Drill	97.3	68.9	180.5	190	55	3.5	30	1	7.13
22												10.9345

FIGURE 13.11   Documentation of technically-based streaks.

The above Excel data file (Figure 13.11) documents technically-based streaks. A streak is calculated on the basis of successfully hitting consecutive criteria designated shots (hit to a specific area of the court with specified spin, depth, power, and accuracy and at least a 4 technical rating). Attempted streaks take place over the course of 20- to 30-min time frames. The goal is to reach a continually higher streak threshold, sustain, or exceed longer streaks once upper thresholds have been achieved. Threshold consistency over time (within session/multiple trials and between session/multiple trials) serves as a strength of consolidation index or the extent to which developed or corrected technique is consistently manifested and is a measure of enduring change (initially during training) that must then be criterion-referenced during official competition. Technical threshold ratios can then be calculated to determine an athlete's MTB quotient. An athlete whose training attempt to success percentage for attaining an established upper technical threshold is 70% (7 out of every 10 threshold streak attempts resulted in reaching or exceeding the previously established highest threshold) but is only 50% in official competition (5 out of every 10 sport-specific technical actions receive a technical rating of 3 or less, or a 5 out of every 10 shots [in tennis] results in a technically mediated error), then such an athlete's MTB quotient would equal −20 (minus sign signifies a technically skewed MTB, meaning that such a score reflects a mental decrement during competition; if the results were opposite, MTB would be +20 indicative of better technical performance [exceeding training thresholds] reflective of enhanced mental performance during competition).

This player's training-based streak performance was fairly erratic and inconsistent over time. After reaching a streak threshold of 47 in the second trial, he could not exceed 24 consecutive criteria-designated and technical level 4 or 5 shots in trial 2, indicative of significantly less focus and concomitant motor control, suggesting that procedural consolidation is far from occurring (Figure 13.12).

> **Practitioner Challenge**: Analyze the preceding streak data in terms of increasing thresholds as a function of measurement occasion (how many trials or measurement days exhibited a higher threshold than the one before it?).

Correlations

		STREAKHI	STREAKOW	STREAKAV	HRPRE	SDPRE	VLPRE	LPRE	HPRE	LHPRE
STREAKHI	Pearson Correlation	1.000	−.063	.487*	.264	.130	.300	.296	.193	.164
	Sig. (2-tailed)		.791	.030	.260	.586	.198	.205	.414	.491
	N	20	20	20	20	20	20	20	20	20
STREAKOW	Pearson Correlation	−.063	1.000	.678**	−.072	.179	.259	.284	.249	−.053
	Sig. (2-tailed)	.791		.001	.762	.449	.270	.225	.289	.824
	N	20	20	20	20	20	20	20	20	20
STREAKAV	Pearson Correlation	.487*	.678**	1.000	.077	.366	.544*	.561*	.491*	−.117
	Sig. (2-tailed)	.030	.001		.746	.112	.013	.010	.028	.622
	N	20	20	20	20	20	20	20	20	20
HRPRE	Pearson Correlation	.264	−.072	.077	1.000	−.364	−.448*	−.411	−.368	−.355
	Sig. (2-tailed)	.260	.762	.746		.114	.047	.072	.111	.125
	N	20	20	20	20	20	20	20	20	20
SDPRE	Pearson Correlation	.130	.179	.366	−.364	1.000	.749**	.782**	.865**	−.016
	Sig. (2-tailed)	.586	.449	.112	.114		.000	.000	.000	.948
	N	20	20	20	20	20	20	20	20	20
VLPRE	Pearson Correlation	.300	.259	.544*	−.448*	.749**	1.000	.990**	.947**	.126
	Sig. (2-tailed)	.198	.270	.013	.047	.000		.000	.000	.598
	N	20	20	20	20	20	20	20	20	20
LPRE	Pearson Correlation	.296	.284	.561*	−.411	.782**	.990**	1.000	.964**	.091
	Sig. (2-tailed)	.205	.225	.010	.072	.000	.000		.000	.704
	N	20	20	20	20	20	20	20	20	20
HPRE	Pearson Correlation	.193	.249	.491*	−.368	.865**	.947**	.964**	1.000	−.039
	Sig. (2-tailed)	.414	.289	.028	.111	.000	.000	.000		.871
	N	20	20	20	20	20	20	20	20	20
LHPRE	Pearson Correlation	.164	−.053	−.117	−.355	−.016	.126	.091	−.039	1.000
	Sig. (2-tailed)	.491	.824	.622	.125	.948	.598	.704	.871	
	N	20	20	20	20	20	20	20	20	20

*Correlation is significant at the 0.05 level (2-tailed).
**Correlation is significant at the 0.01 level (2-tailed).

FIGURE 13.12   Streak Outcome and HRV.

The second BMT-MT outcome analysis attempts to discern whether streak performance is associated with or mediated by specific HRV measures. As with all interventions, HRV monitoring affords potential insight into mind–body processes and how they may impact performance, in this case in the context of technical streak and threshold training. Although there were numerous average streak-length associations with specific HRV measures, these may be spurious in terms of their practical significance relative to performance decrement or gain, since "mean" streak could be directionally skewed. A few moderate HRV and streak associations were found. However, it remains to be seen if they will hold up.

> **Practitioner Challenge**: What HRV measure, if it were to hold up over 60 trials, may have practical significance in terms of streak performance?

Another accountability metric that can be integrated into BMT-MT is the money ball, a designated situation that is designed to bring pressure into routine training, such as when attempting to establish and exceed technical thresholds. Money ball is called out at set or random times that are unknown to the athlete being tested. If a money-ball action or shot is missed, an entire threshold trial receives a score of zero, potentially nullifying a very high threshold score if, for example, an athlete made a technical or outcome error on the money-ball moment. A tennis player who at the time of the money ball made, for example, 45 technical level 4–rated shots with successful outcomes, would see his or her performance eradicated. Money ball performance should be documented over time and across MT modality efficacy testing in a money ball bank. Rewards and punishment can be issued periodically to keep athletes motivated to succeed when they hear this warning, ("Money-ball"), indicating that successful performance is paramount (Figure 13.13).

Date	Trial	Game/Trial #	HR	SDNN	VL	Low	High	L-H	MB	MBP/\	MBP/Lost
6/3/2010	2min	Directional Drill	111.6	47	21.9	101	224.7	0.5	3	1	2
6/3/2010	2min	Directional Drill	121.8	67	80.8	67.2	257.5	0.3	1	1	0
6/8/2010	2min	Non Directional	106.1	53.4	5.3	27.2	91.2	0.3	3	1	2
6/8/2010	2min	Directional Drill	116.2	79	17.6	45	310.8	0.1	3	2	1
6/8/2010	2min	Baseline Game to 11	106.5	103.3	62.8	646	928.4	0.7	4	3	1
6/9/2010	2min	Directional Drill	106.9	57.4	53.9	187	231.5	0.8	4	1	3
6/9/2010	2min	Directional Drill	97.5	25.5	92.3	36.1	37.9	1	2	1	1
6/9/2010	2min	Baseline Game to 11	109	67	98.1	216	244.3	0.9	6	4	2
6/10/2010	2min	Non Directional	91.3	149.7	520.5	1024	1224	0.8	1	0	1
6/11/2010	2min	Non Directional	97.8	166.1	1657	2830	3216	0.9	1	0	1
6/14/2010	2min	Directional Drill	126.5	71.5	61.2	302	375.4	0.8	1	1	0
6/14/2010	2min	Baseline Game to 11	125.4	89.1	200	617	592.3	1	5	1	4
6/14/2010	2min	Tiebreaker	120.4	88.4	48.7	148	555.4	0.3	3	3	0
6/14/2010	2min	Tiebreaker	99.4	47.5	54.8	79.2	202.7	0.4	3	1	2
6/15/2010	1min	Baseline Game to 11	111.4	110.1	111.1	111	970.4	0.1	3	2	1
6/15/2010	1min	Tiebreaker	118.8	59.9	40.9	103	267.8	0.4	3	2	1
6/15/2010	1min	Tiebreaker	131.4	62.8	32.8	19.6	334	0.1	4	2	2
										26	24

FIGURE 13.13

This tennis player's money ball performance was on the weak side. At 26 won and 24 lost, his MB quotient was barely over 50%. Such a score suggests that even though an athlete may be improving technically (as this player thought he was), a high streak threshold and other technical outcome metrics may not reflect mental toughness or the ability to demonstrate best technique and motor performance when it counts the most.

Practitioner Challenge: What is the next step in the evidence-hierarchy for determining whether money-ball performance in a threshold paradigm is an accurate reflection of an athlete's mental toughness?

Encountering competitive stress, whether real or perceived, can lead to changes in autonomic nervous system responses that are reflected in HRV measures. In this particular case, total or aggregate HRV spanning all frequency domain measures (HRV, Power measure) was negatively associated with money ball points won (MBW). This finding can be attributed to the low sample size and points to the need to structure intervention efficiency and efficacy pursuits in the context of pre-intervention, intervention training, and intervention accountability phases having around 60 repeated measures each.

Seventeen money balls only was well below prescribed statistical power and inferential sensitivity thresholds (Figure 13.14).

Correlations

		MBW	MBL	HRPRE	SDPRE	VLPRE	LPRE	HPRE	LHPRE
MBW	Pearson Correlation	1.000	-.094	.331	-.211	-.461	-.410	-.326	-.229
	Sig. (2-tailed)	.	.720	.194	.416	.062	.102	.202	.376
	N	17	17	17	17	17	17	17	17
MBL	Pearson Correlation	-.094	1.000	-.014	-.194	-.084	-.047	-.156	.275
	Sig. (2-tailed)	.720	.	.957	.455	.747	.858	.550	.285
	N	17	17	17	17	17	17	17	17
HRPRE	Pearson Correlation	.331	-.014	1.000	-.273	-.419	-.399	-.353	-.380
	Sig. (2-tailed)	.194	.957	.	.289	.094	.113	.164	.133
	N	17	17	17	17	17	17	17	17
SDPRE	Pearson Correlation	-.211	-.194	-.273	1.000	.757**	.809**	.882**	.159
	Sig. (2-tailed)	.416	.455	.289	.	.000	.000	.000	.541
	N	17	17	17	17	17	17	17	17
VLPRE	Pearson Correlation	-.461	-.084	-.419	.757**	1.000	.974**	.949**	.378
	Sig. (2-tailed)	.062	.747	.094	.000	.	.000	.000	.135
	N	17	17	17	17	17	17	17	17
LPRE	Pearson Correlation	-.410	-.047	-.399	.809**	.974**	1.000	.960**	.458
	Sig. (2-tailed)	.102	.858	.113	.000	.000	.	.000	.065
	N	17	17	17	17	17	17	17	17
HPRE	Pearson Correlation	-.326	-.156	-.353	.882**	.949**	.960**	1.000	.262
	Sig. (2-tailed)	.202	.550	.164	.000	.000	.000	.	.310
	N	17	17	17	17	17	17	17	17
LHPRE	Pearson Correlation	-.229	.275	-.380	.159	.378	.458	.262	1.000
	Sig. (2-tailed)	.376	.285	.133	.541	.135	.065	.310	.
	N	17	17	17	17	17	17	17	17

** Correlation is significant at the 0.01 level (2-tailed).

FIGURE 13.14

Summary

1. BTM-MT attempts to enhance an athlete's mental game using motor learning principles and procedures.
2. Threshold training guides the BTM process.
3. The goal of BTM-MT is to consolidate optimum technical and motor patterns in long-term procedural memory as well as repetitively attempt to demonstrate peak technical performance under greatest situational pressure, first in training (money-ball paradigm) and then during official competition.
4. Standard accountability methodologies should be employed to document time to achieve enduring change in technical and/or HRV markers as well as MTB ratio.

14

Video-Based Mental Programming

Video-Based Mental Programming (VBP) is a more direct intervention modality that accesses and uses visual processing to facilitate, especially motor and technical, performance; although it can also be used in attempts to increase motivation, emotional engagement, and attain IZOF (Hanin, 2006) established levels of physiological reactivity (intensity). In the MT hierarchy, it ranks tied for second with multimodal and Multi-modality Distance-Based approaches to psychological performance enhancement pursuits in terms of its hypothesized potency or ability to induce brain–heart–mind–body–motor responses that are associated with peak performance in a systematic and direct manner. While it may seem that VBP is just another form of visualization, this modality distinguishes itself from mental imagery through the use of high-tech visualization augmentation components and procedures. Whereas visualization is usually engaged in by accessing and activating internal image generation processing, recall, and performance techniques, independent of most high-tech training aids (or by being prompted by a practitioner via scripts and other activators to do so), VBP is a video-based/supported MT modality. While video-recording the training and competition of athletes is nothing new, it is often overlooked in the context of mental training techniques to consolidate the learning of motor skills and the development of new and better techniques/technical skills and for the purpose of on-the-playing-field priming of attention, reaction time, tactical preparation, and carrying out sport-specific action epochs with optimum motor and technical control.

Intervention Amenability and Compliance: Ideal AP PHO Constellation or Measure(s)

VBP can readily be engaged in regardless of an athlete's AP, but especially those whose cognitive style tends to be less visual in nature (athletes who are low in HS/SA and/or high in RC/SC). It is also expected to enhance athletes who are high in HS/SA, already superior ability to convert internal images into action in a focused, sustainable, and controlled manner. Basically, the vast majority of athletes like and need to view themselves in action for technical developmental and strategic analytic purposes. Watching video of oneself perform is fairly straightforward, with amenability to doing so extending across AP PHO constellations.

What may vary as a function of AP is the programming aspect of this visually based MT modality. The word programming in VBP implies that engaging in free-flow or structured viewing of self-performance using video input and feedback will help better consolidate technique,

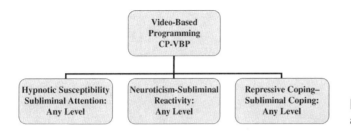

FIGURE 14.1 Intervention Athlete's Profile and intervention amenability.

technical changes, or corrections as well feel and make self-corrections of technical flaws during training and competition and facilitate the implementation of strategic or tactical instructions. Determining VBP intervention efficiency and efficacy as a function of AP is an empirical issue that should be addressed at the intra-individual level (see ways of doing this further on; Figure 14.1).

CONCEPTUAL-CONSTRUCT BASIS

The conceptual and construct bases and/or rationale for administering and engaging in VBP is primarily entrenched in motor-learning principles, shaping and consolidating one's technique, and using an improved technical game to carry out as many sport-specific or relevant tactical iterations as possible. This is especially important in athletes, who, while perhaps possessing an ideal AP, still have glaring technical flaws that limit their ability to perform on a technical and strategic level that is necessary for success within the age, skill, or division (e.g., little league or 3.5 player in tennis, or 15 handicap in golf) in which they compete. Without commensurate technical, physical, and motor skills and the ability to carry out tactics that increase the probability of a successful outcome, the mental game, in the classic sense (being the most important performance component) and its contribution to the performance equation (variance explained) will be negligible; unless (in the abstract) one considers the inability or failure to recognize or focus on known technical, physical, and tactical deficiencies as having a mental etiology (which is highly likely). Consequently, VBP can be viewed as a very direct MT approach, one that circumvents (like HRD BF) esoteric and extraneous intervention procedures that are more difficult to assess in terms of efficiency and efficacy (e.g., certain visualization and cognitive and other random methods like Eye Movement Desensitization and Reprocessing [EMDR], which some practitioners now use with athletes). VBP is thought to activate affective engagement and motivation through central nervous system (CNS) pathways, depending upon an athlete's in-the-moment mental state, which, if suppressed (being down and not motivated) can be positively activated ("getting psyched"). Intervention-induced changes in cortical responses, especially when emotional processes are involved, usually, simultaneously lead to differential activation of ANS responses compared to baseline, a neuropsychophysiological process that can be assessed via HRV monitoring to determine the impact VBP is having in the moment and over prescribed time frames. In cases of chronic under-activation (dampened pre-game/within game intensity) and lack of motivation, practitioners are advised to experiment with and vary the VBP timeline to establish temporal thresholds that are associated with real-time state changes before or during practice, and competition and longitudinally to determine time to achieve enduring biomarker verifiable change or approximations thereof (e.g., attaining positive motivation and pre-competition intensity 75% of the time).

Equally, if not more, important is using VBP to boost technical, physical, motor, and tactical performance, an approach, that if successful, can go a long way to enhancing athlete self-confidence; a secondary lower-order (SLO) factor, that while thought to be mediated by an athlete's level of RC/SC, even if it is high (high self-confidence), unless strong self-belief and esteem is backed by the reality of having advanced technical and motor skills and technical acumen, self-confidence can be illusory and not contribute anything of note to performance outcome. It's just a trait or state that may make an athlete feel superior, even in the face of poor performance realities. In and of itself, self-confidence, in the absence of top-notch sport-specific game-time skills and the ideal AP that usually mediates it (H or L-L-H), cannot overcome technical realities that are critical for successful outcomes, and highlights the pervasive myth of the mental game being the most important. The mental game, of course, is very important. However, such a catchphrase or slogan should not be parroted in isolation; instead, the mental game of each individual athlete should be quantified in terms of how much psychological/mental factors contribute to or predict performance outcome. In other words, how much of the variance in sport-specific outcome measures can be attributed to psychological and related mind–body predictor variables?

The royal road or best and most direct path to peak performance in many, if not most, athletes may initially go through the technical–physical–tactical game, a performance domain that first must be fully developed before psychological influences, per se, are addressed and analyzed in the context of their impact on pressure performance. Performance under pressure becomes more of an issue when an athlete with optimum sport-specific skills falters during critical moments of competition than in an athlete who has deficits in the technical–physical–motor realm.

Consequently, VBP should be the go-to MT intervention relative to attempts to develop, change, improve, and eventually reliably consolidate technical skills in long-term procedural/motor memory. Despite not being what might be thought of as an actual MT method, it is in that it requires that an athlete call upon a host of behaviors and responses that are psychologically mediated, ranging from intense focus, over, at times, protracted training epochs to emotional control that is necessary to successfully reach time to achieve change and enduring change in sport-specific technical actions and tasks.

The VBP process lends itself well to accountability methodologies, including the power law of motor learning (see Klemm, 1996), in which technical and motor skills can be broken down in numerous components that are then systematically practiced until each link in a technical chain is consolidated procedurally. For example, a basketball player with a dismal free-throw shot that can be traced to faulty arm-hand-wrist interaction would be instructed to look at an ideal technique that isolates the aforementioned part of the free throw on a video monitor or computer screen "x" amount of times (spanning "x" amount of minutes), initially without attempting to do the role-model free-throw technique. Thereafter, he or she would be summoned to the court and shoot free throws while being video-recorded anew. Free-throw percentage would be documented, as well as deviations from or in concordance with the ideal previously viewed free-throw technique; this would establish the technical success ratio (e.g., 20 technical deviations and 10 correct technical actions would result in a 2:3 success ratio, or a 33% success rate). Afterward, the player would return to the video-viewing station and see if there was any improvement from the first viewing session and a previously established baseline free-throw technical and success outcome measures (e.g., if the baseline success ratio was 5 out of 30, or 1:6 or 17%, then improvement was evident). This process would be repeated hundreds of times or however long it takes to document reliable enduring change (to be enduring, positive gains approaching the 100% mark in terms of technical proficiency, not to be confused with actual sport-specific outcome or success measures like games won or field goal percentage).

Once enduring technical change has been attained, a process that can take from weeks to years or never be achieved in full (or perhaps a minimal incremental technical advance is reached but cannot be exceeded after weeks of trying; low maximum threshold), a maximum but insufficient technical threshold has been reached. Baseline technical thresholds can be determined for global domains, for example, ground strokes in tennis or short-game in golf or macro-measures, such as backhand and forehand with topspin hit cross-court in tennis or 7-iron versus 9-iron shots in golf.

Baseline percentages or scores of any number of sport-specific technical actions allow for the later quantification of an athlete's mental game, since it can be expected that a fully consolidated technical ceiling or upper skills threshold or approximations thereof, in the absence of competitive pressure, will result in peak technical performance (commensurate with an athlete's level of achieved/attained and/or baseline skill set or technical threshold), but not in the presence of competitive stress (critical moments), where an athlete's AP will determine with a high degree of certainty to what extent an athlete's baseline technical threshold will hold up, be exceeded, or not be reached.

VBP can be a stand-alone intervention, but it is best used in the context of multi-modal intervention approaches since virtually all athletes, regardless of AP, are amenable to viewing themselves perform. It is a relatively low-tech MT modality that can rapidly make an athlete aware of his or her technical status and used within temporally guided time to achieve enduring technical change, dose–response, and mental versus technical physical comparative paradigms.

VBP can also be used as a stress test, whereby an athlete's underlying psychophysiology (HRV specifically) is monitored while watching his or her self-performance over the course of a complete game or match. HRV and HRD measures can then be analyzed in relationship to sport-specific macro and micro outcome measures, including critical moments of competition to ascertain whether merely viewing oneself perform leads to the elicitation of differential HRV patterns and HRD trends, especially as a function of recognized high-pressure situations. VBP can be used to augment HRD, HRV BF, and neurofeedback, whereby in a pre-intervention phase, psychophysiological responses establish a baseline profile for mind–body responses that are later correlated with actual performance during real competition. In an intervention phase in which an athlete attempts to induce performance facilitative and suppress performance detrimental ANS responses concomitant to the performance scenes that are being viewed, (assuming that ANS responses that an athlete wants to induce in such a VBP paradigm have been validated as performance-epoch-specific biomarkers), such induced responses can also be compared with real competition ANS responses in the context of intervention efficacy testing.

Description of Procedure: Step-by-Step

The following photo (Figure 14.2) depicts a professional tennis player engaged in pre-match VBP, primarily for motivational, intensity, and motor priming purposes. Readers will notice the ear sensor. When possible, all intervention sessions should include psychophysiological monitoring,

FIGURE 14.2 Pre-match video-based programming.

FIGURE 14.3 VBP hammer thrower scene.

either before training and competition and, if possible, during competition (time-outs or continuously [Polar system]. Baseline HRV profiles should be compared with intervention-induced HRV to establish intervention efficiency.

1. A variety of performance scenarios should be recorded, including:

   (a) Full matches, games, or competitions for ANS response comparisons (viewing versus actual match HRV), psychophysiological stress testing and athlete criticality debriefing (comparing coach–practitioner critical moment ratings with self-report of athlete thereto; Figure 14.3).
   (b) Structured action clips of varying lengths for motivation and intensity manipulation and technical training and/or correction sessions (Figure 14.4).
   (c) Structured sport-specific action scenes for technical/motor and tactical priming (Figure 14.5).
   (d) Video clips can also be narrated for use with multi-modal MT; for example, inclusion of hypnosis/self-hypnosis and active-alert hypnosis scripts; technical instructions and reminders; technical, tactical, and MT prompts and reminders (Figure 14.6).

FIGURE 14.4 VBP basketball clip.

FIGURE 14.5   Tennis technical VBP clip.

FIGURE 14.6   Tennis VBP clip for active-alert hypnosis.

Documentation and Accountability–Intervention Efficacy: Case Study

As always, interventions or MT must be tested for efficacy. The methodological and analytic procedures associated with doing VBP is virtually the same with all MT modalities. A real case study is presented to illustrate the VBP intervention process and an outcome associated with it (intervention efficiency and efficacy).

Background

A former professional and now senior international-level tennis player who is still capable of defeating much younger opponents participated in the 2010 ABSP Summer research practice-based fellowship/internship program, an on-going (annually since 2006) intensive and rigorous athlete assessment and intervention project. This particular player has participated in the program since its inception. Extensive data has been collected on him, including pre-intervention and intervention assessments (intervention efficiency) and intervention-based performance outcome measures (intervention efficacy). The player's AP constellation of PHO measures is L-M-M (low HS/SA, medium N/SR, and medium RC/SC); conceptually, this profile is associated with less amenability to visualization and hypnotic interventions. He also expressed general skepticism about mental training and said that, based on his experience, with over three decades of competitive tennis, the best way to deal with his admitted tendency to be nervous and choke during matches was by playing lots of matches and preparing extensively to hone his strokes, shots, and tactics. Over the course of his participation in the ABSP summer research and athlete training program, he stated that he felt most comfortable engaging in pre-match technical and tactical training, a method that he felt helped prime him to come "out of the gates running and ready to play." He compared himself to Ivan Lendl, Guillermo Vilas, and Rafael Nadal, players who were known for having to practice for protracted periods of time even on match days to feel right about their games.

Since all players in the ABSP summer program tennis cohort are taken through many of MT modalities listed in the preceding intervention spectrum, at first individually and then in the context of multi-modal approaches, this individual experienced procedures that he was not amenable to, such as visualization methods, hypnosis, and cognitive MT. He also asserted that HRD BF did not work for him. What he did like was VBP. He said that of all the interventions that he tried, the VBP best helped him deal with career-long technical issues that limited his success and exacerbated the nervousness that he experienced when playing real matches. He mentioned that watching clips of himself, especially repeatedly looking at video loops of his backhand, backhand passing shot, forehand drive, and serve, helped him immensely and gave him confidence and assurance that his strokes looked like those of a professional (which he was anyway), and that so long as his timing was on, he was less nervous. Indeed, independent ratings of the aforementioned specific strokes increased over the course of the summer, from being in the 3 to the 4 or 5 range by the end of the program. By having the same athletes in the program over the course of a few years, one can see what downtime does to players like this one, who have certain technical deficiencies. What happens is that they regress to technical baseline threshold states without constant intensive technical training. VBP is thought to help athletes surpass baseline technical thresholds in conjunction with prolonged on-the-court technical training so long as they understand all components of a technical action and notice or feel when their technique is not working and know what steps to take to make technical corrections. VBP is hypothesized to augment the self-correction and consolidation of new motor patterns at least temporarily, hence the need for constant visual reinforcement followed by on-the-playing-field indirect tactile and direct coach feedback (being told what is wrong and right about an athlete's technique).

While self-report about the efficacy of an intervention should always be viewed critically and even with skepticism, when placebo-prone athletes (high HS/SA athletes) are involved (and even when placebo-prone coaches and sport psychology practitioners are involved; see dual-placebo beliefs and effects), this particular athlete, who himself was very skeptical about MT in general, to the point of being nocebo-prone (extreme belief that an intervention will not work and even have a negative effect), his self-report feedback turned out to be consistent with the following macro-intervention outcome measures (efficacy testing outcome measures; see Figure 14.7).

In the pre-intervention phase, the player's match won-loss record was 4-3-1 (only two sets were played, split sets counted as a tie), in which 9 sets were won and 8 were lost. In intervention phase 1, in which HRD BF only was engaged in during changeovers, the player made minor gains, losing one less match and two fewer sets.

In intervention phase 2, multi-modal MT was administered that included self-generated tennis-match specific visualization and HRD BF. Here, too, gains were made with no loss of matches occurring, although 5 matches resulted in ties (split sets). Intervention phase 3, in which players were allowed to request the MT modality or modalities of choice, they picked the one(s) they liked the

Intervention Phase and Modality	Match Won-Lost	Sets Won-Lost
Pre-Intervention: None	4-3-1 (tie)	9-8
Intervention Phase 1: Change-over Breathing-based HRD BF	4-2-1	9-6
Intervention Phase 2: Self-Generated Visualization and HRD BF	3-0-5	9-5
Intervention Phase 3: Video-Based Programming Only	5-1-1	11-4

FIGURE 14.7 Intervention outcome comparisons.

most. In this phase, the player's match record, a correlate of overall micro-level performance, was better than in the pre-intervention and two other intervention phases. His 5-1-1 match and 11-4 set record supports the player's self-report contention that VBP helped him the most. It should be noted that the same opponents were encountered in each phase of intervention-efficacy testing. As such, experience could be a threat to the internal validity of the design of this approach to intervention efficacy testing, with familiarity of his opponent's strengths, weakness, and other tendencies playing a greater role than VBP in influencing outcome. Hence, rather than rely on macro-level outcome measures as benchmarks of intervention efficacy, it is preferable to use a variance-explained design that is based on repeated sport-specific micro-level outcome measures, including critical moment point ratings (level of criticality of each point in a match). Such an extensive analysis is beyond the scope of this case study. Readers are referred to a comprehensive baseball study that includes such analyses (see Chapter 20 of this book's intervention section).

Nevertheless, the preceding match findings have practical significance, an outcome and intervention efficacy metric that can transcend statistical significance alone, especially in instances where there are insufficient repeated measures to achieve the recommended statistical power upon which to make empirical inferences. During the ABSP summer program, players play about 30 matches and are ranked and reranked after each match. Thus, in the context of rankings, winning or losing a match within the pre- and any intervention phase can have a major impact on the final standings. Thus, winning more or fewer matches in a particular intervention phase, especially when the program/match series nears the end, can reflect macro-level pressure performance tendencies or mental toughness, irrespective of who one's opponent is. Thus, the experience and familiarization threats to internal validity may be greatly mitigated by the pressure that is inherent in the final intervention phase, making competitive pressure stand out as the most potent mediator or influencing factor impacting performance, a stressor that lessens the impact of opponent variables, since an opponent who one has previously encountered in more routine matches having less competitive pressure may play very differently from when under pressure, and viceversa. Consequently, an intervention modality like VBP that this tennis player found to be effective for priming technique may indeed have enhanced this player's performance when under pressure. It is also possible that opponents who this player beat or lost to in the pre- or first two intervention phases possessed APs that were more or less susceptible to performance decrement as a function of pressure that did not arise earlier in the program but did later, making them appear and play completely different from when at their worst or best. In essence, an opponent who one has frequently played against, can seem like a new opponent.

Summary

This player's VBP intervention phase 3 performance propelled him to the top of the standings and included wins against two players who had beaten him twice earlier, lending additional anecdotal support to the player's contention that VBP helped him play better. However, it must be pointed out that this player's opponents also engaged in interventions during changeovers. This gives rise to the paradox: if all athletes engage MT, how can anyone lose? This points to the need to analyze interventions from multifactorial/multidimensional perspectives and ultimately attempt to quantify the impact or efficacy of an intervention on the basis of how much of the variance in the performance equation can be attributed to an intervention. This can be best done by always linking an intervention to MT-induced psychophysiological measures that ideally can be acquired across entire real games, matches, and/or competitions, and determine the extent to which such measures predict micro-level outcomes, especially critical moments of competition (level of criticality of sport-specific moments/situations).

15

Multi-Modal Intervention-Mental Training I and II (Distance-Based Multi-Modal MT)

Multi-modal approaches to MT involve the incorporation of more than one intervention method in attempts to enhance performance. While one might wonder why there is even a need for any secondary interventions or other primary stand-alone MT methods if HRD BF in and of itself and the mind–body responses that it can shape is the most direct path to performance-facilitative self-regulation and subsequent peak performance, supportive, ancillary MT modalities may help establish a baseline psychophysiological state that is a necessary precursor for inducing in-the-moment HRD in certain athletes, especially those who are more burdened by a performance-detrimental AP. For example, an athlete with an AP PHO constellation of H-H-L (the worst AP) may experience extreme competitive anxiety going into a game or match, such that his or her underlying ANS cannot be balanced (excessive SNS activation), a state associated with very low HRV (low SDNN) even at baseline. Such may require pre-competition intervention to reduce SNS activation (increase low and high frequency HRV activity) in an attempt to eliminate potentially crippling nervousness that can impede the BF targeted pre-action HRD that is intended to set-off a cascade of brain-heart-mind-body-motor in pre-action epochs. HRD BF is not a clinical solution, and in most psychologically burdened athletes who tend to present the most (seek out consultation and help), their mental and concomitant psychophysiological states during competition may be so detrimental to performance that they are incapable of self-accessing and self-engaging in the HRD BF during time-outs and on the playing field. When this occurs, a secondary and possibly third intervention may be called for to prime an athlete and render him or her capable of remembering to and then actually engage in the primary-direct MT method (usually HRD BF). During periods of extreme duress during competition, an athlete's "racing" mind can lead to technical and motor breakdowns of such a magnitude that the afflicted individual feels and is helpless.

The above-described scenario can also be technically mediated, in which an athlete who possesses an ideal AP (H-L-H or L-L-H) and has a foundation for being mentally tough falters because of technical or physical deficiencies that have been ignored or overlooked and prevent his or her psychological strengths from ever being manifested. After all, if an athlete has a glaring technical weakness that can be continually exploited by an opponent, or it manifests itself too often in sports like golf where there is no direct opponent, mental toughness alone cannot eliminate the deleterious impact of poor technique or inability to carry out important tactical sequences. And, although HRD may occur in every pre-action epoch in athletes with an ideal AP, outcomes associated with this HRV response may not always be favorable or successful in the presence of technical and tactical deficiencies. Consequently, in cases in which consistent HRD prior to action is documented but performance outcome is predominately negative, it is highly likely that an athlete has technical and tactical deficiencies. Although such nonpsychological issues usually cannot be overcome during actual competition, prematch/game interventions can be used to reinforce and prime existing technical strengths and tactical patterns that can be reliably carried out, and at the same time help an athlete avoid falling into or initiating patterns that lead to his or her technical weaknesses being exploited.

Relative to the previously described, more clinical issues (as opposed to performance concerns per se), multi-modal secondary or ancillary, and in some cases primary, interventions could include or be limited to RSA BF, hypnotic-based MT, visualization, and cognitive or cognitive behavioral therapy that are designed to foster better self-regulation on the playing field and lead to a more automatic manifestation or volitional inducement of pre-action HRD, which might be otherwise difficult to do because of a level of ANS SNS activation that makes it very difficult to think clearly and gain mind–body control.

As far as the technical issues are concerned, ideal secondary/ancillary MT modalities are video-based programming, motor learning-based technical training, and behavioral approaches that include simulated exposure procedures, including money-ball and critical moment training with reward and punishment reinforcement schedules, along with technical–tactical threshold training.

Additional MT modalities can be incorporated into an intervention routine considerate of AP amenability and compliance tendencies. For example, VBP in an athlete who is high in HS/SA can be augmented with hypnosis, transitioning to active-alert hypnosis and self-hypnosis once competition commences.

Intervention Amenability and Compliance: Ideal AP PHO Constellation or Measure(s)

Intervention amenability and compliance relative to multi-modal MT, as when using singular modalities alone (independently), need to be seriously considered. Increasing the probability that an intervention will lead to the desired result can be maximized by tailoring a multi-modal battery to an athlete's AP. As such, MT methods should not be randomly or arbitrarily administered or mixed just because a practitioner knows how to teach and administer a particular MT procedure, which, by the way, is one of the most common reasons why an intervention is used in the first place. Intervention should be athlete-driven and not based on practitioner decisions alone, which can be limited in terms of competency and ability to teach, administer, document, and analyze MT efficiency and efficacy and, importantly, unawareness of AP-based intervention amenability and compliance tendencies. For example, most practitioners use visualization-imagery procedures as their go-to MT modality, but fail to consider that about only 15% to about 30% of all athletes are medium to high in HS/SA (10%–15% are high in HS/SA), significantly decreasing the probability that an athlete can relate to, access, learn, and/or effectively engage in imagery MT. Consequently, in the context of the preceding clinical and technical MT examples, the inclusion of visualization or mental imagery would be contraindicated as part of a multi-modal MT battery if the affected athletes were both low to low-medium in HS/SA. One would not augment RSA BF to ameliorate precompetition with mental imagery or technical threshold, motor learning, nonvideo-based facilitated visualization.

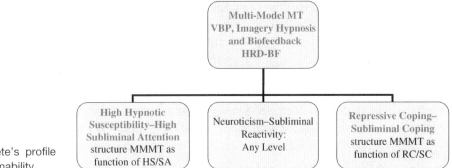

FIGURE 15.1   Athlete's profile and intervention amenability.

As one can glean from the intervention amenability and compliance chart (Figure 15.1), HS/SA tends to be the driving AP PHO measure in terms of ability to engage in, stick with a prescribed MT training schedule, and increase the probability that it may work (enhance performance), with low RC/SC and low HS/SA being associated with, across the intervention spectrum, general lack of intervention amenability (interest in and belief that MT works) with the exception of BF/NF, assuming that a practitioner can get an athlete with such a level of these two AP PHO measures to actually try BF/NF. Athletes who are high in N/SR are usually amenable to all interventions; however, their ability to successfully learn and then engage in an intervention will to a large extent be moderated by their concurrent level of HS/SA. Thus, an athlete who is high in N/SR (high N/SR is the AP PHO measure and part of the AP that presents the most for voluntary consultation) would be well-advised to learn and use RSA BF to reduce excessive ANS-SNS activation that tends to underlie high levels of this mind–body measure, but not add a visualization component to a multi-modal MT approach in an attempt to help such a person.

CONCEPTUAL-CONSTRUCT BASIS

As far as the construct basis of multimodal approaches to interventions are concerned, readers are referred to the individual MT modalities within this section for insight regarding the brain–heart–mind–body–motor responses an intervention is known to and/or hypothesized to induce, mediate, or influence. Readers should also review this book's chapter on Construct Validity (Chapter 2).

Conceptually, multi-modal MT is based on the hypothesis that if one primary go-to intervention is good, and will increase the probability that athlete weaknesses can be reduced with strengths being increased, and leading to their long-term consolidation and resultant overall manifestation of enhanced performance facilitative mind–body responses and subsequent successful sport-specific outcome, then two or three or four secondary and/or ancillary add-on interventions will be better and contribute to more of the variance in performance outcome that can be uniquely attributed to mental training alone or mental training enhanced technical training.

The need for multi-modal intervention and its eventual application is usually predicated on the existence of multiple psychological, mind–body, and/or psychologically and/or physical/motor-mediated issues, problems, and/or deficiencies that can best be addressed integratively, with specific MT modalities being selected for inclusion in a multi-modal battery on the basis of their known and hypothesized interventional potency (i.e., their ability to address, deal with, attenuate, or eradicate one or more specific performance issues, problems, or deficiencies). Readers are referred to the previous example in which RSA BF is recommended to help an athlete reduce excessive SNS activation associated with extreme competitive anxiety as a means to priming an athlete to subsequently engage in volitional breathing-based HRD, something that might not be possible if time-out HRD-BF was used as a stand-alone MT modality. RSA-BF is strategically employed to first reduce excessive SNS activation that can interfere with the ability to engage in HRD-BF and help self-induce the HRD response during pre-action phases of competition, a multi-modal approach involving two highly appropriate and complementary-integrative intervention modalities.

Intervention and MT are not only or all about psychological and mind–body performance relevant deficiencies. They can be used in attempts to enhance the performance of stable and even highly proficient and successful athletes—even mentally tough athletes—who want to exhibit peak performance potential more consistently. Although this latter example may seem oxymoronic, as previously pointed out, athletes with an ideal AP, who do not get nervous come crunchtime, still may lack certain skills that prevent a successful outcome from occurring the majority of the time, despite optimum mind–body responses such as pre-action HRD. Their developed mental toughness, if not complemented with the requisite physical, motor, and technical ability and skills, cannot be fully exploited. Multi-modal performance-facilitating approaches (with athletes with the Ideal AP) for example, HRD BF combined with VBP and behavioral-based/motor-learning threshold MT could be implemented to address both the mental and technical games of athletes having notable disparities (e.g., strong mental toughness but with technical flaws).

Multi-modal MT can also be very straightforward and designed to specifically address psychological or technical issues or goals independently. For example, attempts to increase attention thresholds might include on-the-playing-field task-specific repetition-focus conditioning threshold drills that are augmented with hypnosis in athletes who are high in HS/SA. In such a multi-modal intervention paradigm, a baseline attention threshold would be established on the basis of time to achieve or reach a technically based performance goal, say, number of consecutive shots before a technical and/or real error occurs. In the MT phase, after hypnosis and active-alert hypnosis, the athlete attempts to continually exceed newly established thresholds, for example, making 10, then 15, and then 25 consecutive free throws with a level 4-rated free throw technique. The intervention

Description of a Sample Multi-Modal MT Procedure

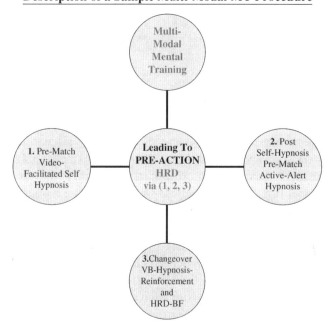

FIGURE 15.2   Sample multi-modal intervention configuration.

predictor variables are hypnosis and active-alert hypnosis HRV and active-alert hypnosis technical ratings, while the time to reach a threshold goal serves as one of the outcome/criterion measures. Other outcome measures could include technical rating for a threshold session/epoch and ratio of successful task completion to attempts. Such a multi-modal paradigm should be temporally delineated within A-B-A, intervention on-off design in place to compare intervention and non-intervention trials both on the basis of differential HRV between condition and their impact on outcome. In addition, non- and intervention outcomes can be compared using T-tests and Chi^2 analyses independent of HRV. Also of interest would be how much of the variance in performance outcome (shooting percentage, technical rating) can be attributed to hypnosis-associated HRV (i.e., hypnotic procedure) in both the non- and intervention condition (Figure 15.2).

Step-by-Step: Multi-Modal MT: VB-Hypnosis, Active-Alert Hypnosis-HRD BF

The following is an example of a select individualized multi-modal intervention. It was customized for a professional tennis player having an AP of high HS/SA-high N/SR and high RC/SC (H-H-H). This is the rarest AP, since seldom does an individual concurrently exhibit high neuroticism/subliminal reactivity and high repressive/subliminal coping. Conceptually, RC/SC has been shown to inhibit the inter-hemispheric transfer of negative affect that is associated with high neuroticism from the right-to-left brain hemispheres, a mechanism that is thought to be facilitative of the left-to-right pre-action cortical shift that is associated with pre-action HRD and subsequent heightened attention, faster reaction time, and enhanced motor control (Carlstedt, 2004a, 2004b; Tomarken & Davidson, 1994). It has not been established whether high levels of neuroticism have the neurophysiological strength to withstand the effects of high levels of RC/SC across all competitive stress situations, or if high RC/SC has the potency to suppress high N/SR during critical moments of competition. This is an intriguing empirical question that still needs to be resolved. As such, athletes who exhibit the H-H-H profile must be closely observed using the accountability methodologies that are advanced by the ABSP-CP on a case-by-case basis to determine if variations in individual performance and test responses are consistent or inconsistent with what would be expected on the basis of self-report N/SR and RC/SC scores. For example, alternate form tests that measure levels of N/SR can be used to see if scores for neuroticism are the same or similar (e.g., NEO-neuroticism scale or Eysenck Personality Inventory-N scale; BRC, 2007; Eysenck & Eysenck, 1975). The Serial 7s stress test, a step up in the evidence-hierarchy, can also be used to determine whether the aforementioned tests that are based on self-report/questionnaire and resulting scores can be criterion-referenced using stress-test generated HRV measures of SNS responses (VL frequency, the expected predominate response during heightened competitive stress in an athlete who is high in N/SR) or ANS balance (L:H frequency ratio, a lower ratio would be expected in a true high RC/SC athlete). If similar sample HRV changes are not elicited by the S7s test, self-report of N/SR may be called into question. Criterion referencing can also be done on the basis of ecological performance testing (e.g., money-ball and critical moment testing and actual competition criticality outcome measures), the highest evidentiary approach to validating pressure performance tendencies that correlate with N/SR.

One thing that is certain, though, is that this athlete's high level of HS/SA makes him a very good candidate for imagery and hypnotic-based interventions and assuming that his N/SR scores are valid and truly reflect underlying stress-response tendencies that are associated with high N/SR. As such, one would expect him to readily admit that he has psychological performance issues, like choking under pressure, and needs help. Such an admission could call into question whether his RC/SC score is accurate, since athletes who are high in this measure tend to be very skeptical of "therapy" and MT, believing that interventions are unnecessary, don't work, and that especially don't believe that they need assistance with their mental game.

Background

This player's background provides some clues as to whether he is a true high N/SR and RC/SC performer. First of all, he sought out a sport psychologist, admitting that his career, after brilliant junior results and high rankings, has stagnated as a professional, and lately he felt as though he was regressing. Such stark admissions would be unheard of in an athlete who was a true high RC/SC, even in the presence of obvious stress and poor performance. Moreover, his coach concurred, stating that his player's biggest problems were "mental." Based on such self-report and coach-based anecdotal feedback, it was preliminarily concluded that it was doubtful that the athlete was high in RC/SC and, in fact, he likely was very low in this trait. If that could verified on the basis of additional stress and other HRV and on-the-court critical moment/money-ball testing, he may actually have the least pressure performance facilitative AP (i.e., the worst AP of H-H-L). It should be noted that the predictive validity of the CSARCS-A from which the AP is derived ranges from about .46 to .70, which is extremely high relative to forecasting performance tendencies of athletes. Nevertheless, as with all self-report-based tests, there will be false positive and negative results along with parallel behavior and performance responses that do not jibe with what is known and expected about a particular AP. As a result, in cases where there is ambiguity about an AP, initial behavioral and personality assessments should be further scrutinized (hierarchically) so as to design MT and intervention approaches that an athlete is most likely to be amenable to and compliant with prescribed procedures.

As a result of multi-modal assessment, initial anecdotal, and clinical intuition, it was concluded that this athlete was low instead of high in RC/SC, and it was decided to commence with a multi-modal intervention approach consisting of the following MT modalities: (1) hypnosis leading to self-hypnosis and (2) active-alert hypnosis supported or augmented, with video-based programming and concurrent HRD BF during time-outs (Figures 15.3a and b).

PROCEDURE[1]

1. After a thorough assessment and preintervention phase involving at least 60 repeated measures for every predictor variable (e.g., pre-match HRV and outcome; time-out HRV and subsequent

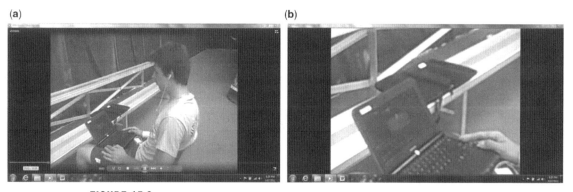

FIGURE 15.3 Video-based programming aided self- and active-alert hypnosis.

money-ball or match performance outcome) that lasted 2 wks, brain–heart–mind–body–technical–motor baselines were established and analyzed in the context of the intervention phase and goals related to MT.

2. Based on this athlete's high levels of HS/SA and N/SR, it was decided to use hypnotic procedures commencing with familiarization sessions (education and learning), progressing to pre-match video-based-programming-enhanced self-hypnosis with situation-specific verbal prompts (audio) and followed up with pre-match active-alert hypnosis along with changeover HRD BF.

3. The two preceding photos (Figure 15.3a and b) show the player engaged in pre-match VBP-enhanced or facilitated self-hypnosis containing context specific clips/scenes/scenarios. A clip or scene was/could be accessed on the basis of coach or sport psychologist recommendations or athlete input or pre-intervention HRV readings that were obtained (before every practice session, match/practice session, match/practice intervention session, and post-match/practice intervention session).

Baseline HRV can be very revealing over time (30–50 repeated premonitoring sessions are needed), leading to reliable precompetition IZOF (Hanin, 2006) profiles that can predict upcoming performance and guide pre-competition MT. In the preceding scenario, the player is engaging in a 5-minute motivational and technical priming self-hypnosis routine containing specific audio prompts that are synchronized with tennis shot scenes as they occur. For example, this player had a tendency to hold back and not accelerate and fully follow through when hitting ground strokes when under pressure. Thus, when he saw a ground stroke on the computer screen, he would hear the prompt "accelerate" to reinforce the fact that he had to be aggressive with every shot. While engaging in the self-hypnosis routine, the player's HRV was monitored to determine to what extent it changed as a function of the hypnotic intervention, compared to baseline. This allows practitioners, coaches, and players to gauge intervention efficiency and determine, over time (longitudinally), whether intervention-induced changes in HRV predict outcome and/or are associated with MT efficacy (Figure 15.4).

4. Immediately following the self-hypnosis session, an HRV ANS report is generated and analyzed and eventually discussed with the athlete (see the following Accountability section for a discussion of the generated HRV reports). The resulting self-hypnosis-associated HRV profile is used to predict performance outcome and intervention efficiency and efficacy, as well as help determine

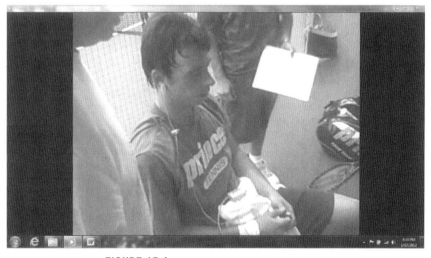

FIGURE 15.4   Post-self-hypnosis HRV scan.

to what extent self-hypnosis (as a motivational, correction, and technical priming intervention tool) carries over and facilitates the next MT phase (active-alert) hypnosis, and whether it predicts warm-up performance and match outcome. Self-hypnosis-induced HRV as a predictor variable is best analyzed in the context of an A-B-A design during pre-official match or tournament preparation training, to better illuminate on-off differences in HRV (no intervention versus intervention) and outcome (whether self-hypnosis-induced HRV is different from HRV with no intervention, and whether the intervention condition positively impacts performance to a significantly greater extent than the no-intervention condition).

5. After the self-hypnosis session that is intended to program the mind and prime the motor system, the player then engages in active-alert hypnosis, a hypnotic procedure that is designed to activate an athlete psychophysiologically and further reinforce technical and tactical patterns that will be carried out in the upcoming match (that were initially encountered via VBP self- hypnosis MT). Active-alert sessions can last from 5 to 30 minutes, depending on the availability of practice partners, time, and practice court constraints that can affect a tennis player's ability to carry out his or her normal full practice routine, or (importantly) the amount of time it takes an athlete to establish his or her IZOF (a temporal epoch that can be established using analytic methods and procedures that are advanced by the ABSP-CP throughout this book).

Figure 15.5 depicts the player engaging in active-alert hypnosis. A typical session involves starting off very slowly, carrying out shadow motions (shadow strokes in tennis) deliberately and with perfect form. After all sport-specific actions that one will need to perform in a competition have been actively rehearsed (all tennis strokes here), the session should transition to simulating entire action sequences and tactics that one will encounter or intends to carry out in the upcoming match at requisite levels of intensity on a point-by-point basis (e.g., start out serving, with a serve-and-volley sequence, or ground stroke, approach shot, volley, and overhead, resulting in a winner combination; the player should keep score and use the previously heard prompts accordingly). The entire active-alert session is designed to reinforce, consolidate, and prime motor and technical responses, tactics, and corrective measures, thereby activating performance-facilitative cortical neural pathways and suppressing superfluous and negative intrusive thoughts by deactivating brain pathways associated with their manifestation (see conceptual bases of brain-based volitional and subliminal MT modalities later in the chapter).

FIGURE 15.5   Active-alert hypnosis.

FIGURE 15.6   Active-alert hypnosis with coach prompts.

Active-alert hypnosis can also involve the coach or sport psychology practitioner who vocally administers the same prompts that the athlete was exposed to in the pre-active-alert self-hypnosis session (see Figure 15.6, coach stands in background).

6. In pre-competition training leading up to matches, self-hypnosis-engrained mental images of technique, tactics, and positive outcome scenarios, as well as performance-facilitating (audio and or verbalized by a coach/practitioner) prompts and reminders that are subsequently reinforced and further primed using active-alert hypnosis, should be further engaged in during actual competition and in sports where permitted, assessed, and practiced (simultaneously) during time-outs.[2]

An MT method, if well consolidated, is intended to transfer to the playing field. Consequently, to facilitate such consolidation, an MT routine should be practiced constantly in the context of advanced accountability methodologies until they are shown to exhibit efficiency and efficacy. In the case of this tennis player, after pre-match self- and active-alert hypnosis, VBP self-hypnosis was engaged in for 1 min during each changeover (time-out), along with concurrent HRD BF during all practice matches. Notice the split-screen in the following photo (Figure 15.7). On the right side of the screen the self-hypnosis VBP clip can be seen, while the left side contains a tachogram displaying heart activity and a digital heart rate indicator that is used to practice 3 to 4 HRD BF inhalation–exhalation cycles.

Documentation-Accountability-Intervention Efficiency and Efficacy

As with all MT modalities, multi-modal methods must be documented and scrutinized for efficiency and efficacy. Again, HRV is used as the primary agent of change that differentiates baseline ANS from intervention-induced or associated states. This player's pre-match routine was such that upon arriving at a training or tournament site, he would set up his laptop computer and commence with VBP-augmented self-hypnosis and with his mental preparation routine. In the hypnosis training phase, he was conditioned, using post-hypnotic suggestions (see the Hypnosis section further on), to re-enter a hypnotic state very quickly, and when in such a state, he became intensely focused on the video scenario and audio prompts to the point of being oblivious to any distractions.

FIGURE 15.7   Changeover reinforcement VBP and HRD-BF.

As his HRV was monitored for the duration of the self-hypnosis session, an ANS report was generated immediately after its completion. The following report emanates from a $10' \ 28''$ session. Session length always varies to a certain extent because of court time schedules and other factors that cannot be controlled. An attempt is made to hold them within 30 minutes of practice or match time.

HRV ANS reports are used to determine intervention efficiency and efficacy. Relative to MT efficiency, global change in any number of the preceding HRV measures across the intervention and change-assessment condition (a 2-minute assessment within 10 minutes of completion of an intervention condition) determines intervention efficiency. There are no group intervention efficiency norms for any MT modality. They must be established using a repeated measures design for each individual athlete. Consistent with the IZOF model, an intervention like self-hypnosis can lead to diametrically opposite ANS responses and changes across baseline and/or post-MT assessment conditions as a function of AP-based and other individual differences. The greater the difference between the baseline or post-intervention assessment condition and the intervention in ANS responses, the greater intervention efficiency is hypothesized to be.

This player's hypnosis-associated or -induced ANS response can be seen in Figure 15.8. Measures should be interpreted in the context of an athlete's AP, paying special attention to measures that one would expect to occur concomitant to high or low levels of a specific AP PHO measure. Relative to this athlete's H-H-H AP that was then revised to H-H-L (based on additional diagnostics and testing), one would predict HR to be elevated, SDNN reduced, more VL and less H frequency HRV to be generated, and a relatively high L:H frequency ratio (Figure 15.9).

Major unexpected or expected changes, for that matter, even in isolation, at a minimum attests to intervention efficiency for a specific MT session, as was the case here in which post-self-hypnosis SDNN (the HRV index) more than doubled from 60 to 130 msec with L frequency activity increasing more than 10-fold (from 454 to over 5000), resulting in a very high L:H ratio of 42.4 compared to 4.7 in the self-hypnosis condition. Conceptually, it is expected that an intervention will lead to changes in ANS responses since most interventions, especially those that have strong mental manipulative components, whether volitionally or subliminally induced (as with hypnotic procedures), will lead to differential increases or decreases in mind–body activation. Change is thought to be

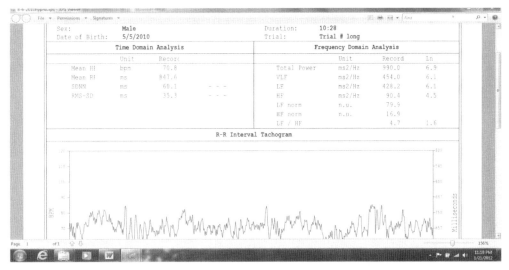

FIGURE 15.8   HRV ANS report after pre-match self-hypnosis session.

ongoing during an intervention. Such response variability is ideally captured or reflected in heart rate *variability*, with SDNN being the HRV index of direct marker of such change. Intervention-induced change is also expected to be enduring, that is, mind–body changes that are induced by MT will lead to ANS changes that are measurable over time, with the maintenance of, for example, ANS/HRV responses that are documented immediately after an intervention session (like self-hypnosis here), establishing a new functional intervention-mediated baseline that will be maintained over a certain amount of time as a function of the strength of difference in HRV measures between conditions and subsequent intervention-based reinforcement throughout competition. Hence, the greater the difference in ANS HRV-specific responses between the intervention

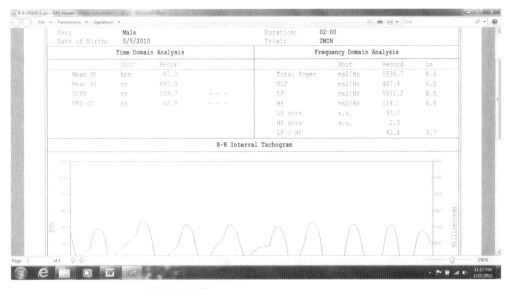

FIGURE 15.9   Post-self-hypnosis 2 min HRV.

and post-intervention assessment conditions, the greater the intervention efficiency and likelihood that such intervention-induced response differences will remain stable over time (e.g., the entire duration of competition). However, readers again should note that such intervention efficiency does not necessarily equate with or predict intervention efficacy, that it must be determined empirically using both variance-explained methodologies and macro-level pre-versus intervention-analytic procedures (e.g., T-test, Chi^2). Nevertheless, even in the absence of sufficient sample size (too few sessions for comparison purposes), intuition-based preliminary trend observations can be made to guide efficiency and efficacy appraisals.

The preceding two HRV reports (Figures 15.8 and 15.9) were associated with a 6-4, 3-6 outcome, (an incomplete match, split sets; two out of three sets constitutes a match) or 9 games won and 10 games lost, an equivocal outcome, that in this case (because the player usually beat this particular opponent) reflected relatively poor performance. These HRV reports were generated about 2 weeks into initial hypnosis/self-hypnosis training. As such, it remained to be seen whether such unexpected poor performance could be linked to the self-hypnosis intervention's efficiency. Note, just because an intervention is shown to exhibit efficiency does not mean that generated mind–body responses (HRV) are or will be conducive to optimum performance. Once sufficient sampling and power has been achieved, it may emerge that an intervention must generate more specific mind–body responses that are strongly associated with successful macro- and/or micro-sport-specific outcome measures. Since, as previously mentioned, *all* interventions are experimental, it can take time to determine whether, if at all, and what mind–body measures and parameters, if any, are associated with better performance and outcome.

The next two HRV reports (Figures 15.10 and 15.11) were obtained prior to another practice match the day after the aforementioned match and associated HRV scans. As one can see here, self-hypnosis-induced HRV over the course of an 11-minute session were fairly similar to the 10-minute session the previous day, although the L:H ratio dropped from 4.7 to 3.0 (less L and H frequency mixture). In contrast to the first match day post-self-hypnosis ANS report, in which an extreme change in L:H ratio was observed from 4.7 to 47.4, the second match day post-self-hypnosis

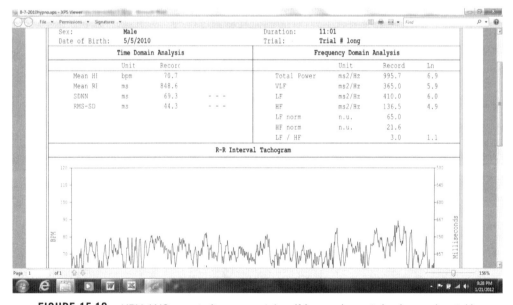

FIGURE 15.10   HRV-ANS report after pre-match self-hypnosis-next day (second match).

assessment revealed a smaller change from 3.0 to 10.7. Nevertheless, an increase from 3.0 to 10.7 is significant and may point to the activating influence of continuous VBP self-hypnosis involving action clips that are repeatedly shown and mentally processed. Moreover, SDNN increased greatly from 69 to 104 msec. Greater HRV (SDNN is the HRV index) in a static intervention condition may have later relevance to HRD BF and the elicitation of pre-action HRD. If that is the case, SDNN could be an important construct validity biomarker attesting to the utility and efficacy of this self-hypnosis MT paradigm and should be further investigated.

Unfortunately, this player, despite exhibiting good intervention efficiency, lost the subsequent match 0-6, 4-6, a very bad loss. As always, though, intervention efficiency does not necessarily translate to successful performance. On the other hand, macro-level outcome measures such as games, sets, and/or matches won or lost do not convey or reflect micro-level performance success that could exist even in the context of such apparently poor global outcomes. Moreover, in tennis, opponent factors and other extraneous variables like court surface and/or type of ball can influence outcomes, neutralizing even a professional tennis player's ability to mount strong resistance and win certain matches. Hence, it takes time and extensive analyses to disentangle many variables in the quest to determine the true impact of an intervention.

The following Excel file (Figure 15.12) contains self-hypnosis HRV-induced responses emanating from actual MT sessions, self-hypnosis-induced HRV responses obtained immediately after the pre-match self-hypnosis session and immediately after the match (inferred self-hypnosis-induced HRV response) along with global-macro outcome measures (games won-GW and games lost-GL). The data was derived prior to and after eight official professional tournament matches (ITF Future's Series Tournaments).

Outcome analyses were run, leading to preliminary evidence attesting to the efficacy of self-hypnosis as an intervention. The term "preliminary" is used since these findings are based on a very small sample size, and it remains to be seen whether they would hold up over the course of enough matches. Nevertheless, the following correlation coefficients suggest trends and patterns that are consistent with the preceding ANS-HRV training-match–derived reports and speak to

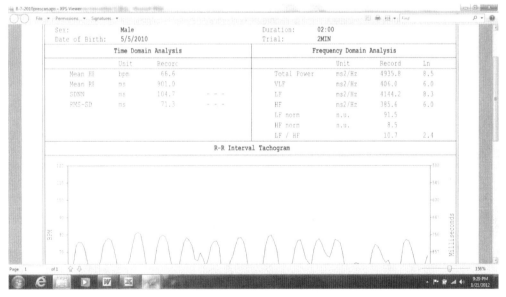

FIGURE 15.11   Post-self-hypnosis 2-min HRV-2nd match.

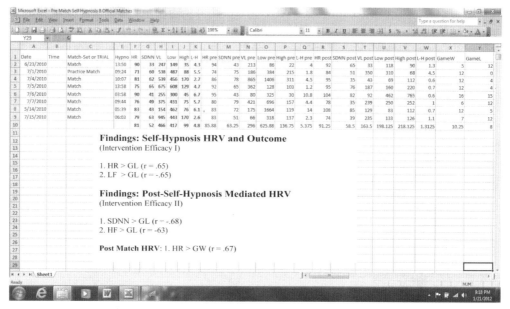

FIGURE 15.12　Self-hypnosis, HRV, and performance outcome.

the possibility that the following predictive HRV measures were not only influenced by the self-hypnosis process prior to and during matches, but performance as well and the establishment of intervention efficacy.

What was revealed is that pre-match self-hypnosis-associated HR predicted GL, meaning that greater heart rate across the preceding eight matches was correlated with more games lost. This suggests that self-hypnosis that generates a higher HR may be detrimental to performance over time, and suggests that what happens in 5- to 15-minute pre-match self-hypnosis can have an enduring effect (additional evidence of intervention efficiency and efficacy). Conceivably, pre-match self-hypnosis can generate both adaptive and maladaptive HRV responses that are then reinforced throughout the course of a competition (matches here) as an athlete continues to engage in a selected intervention (self-hypnosis here) during time-outs and/or on the playing field (changeovers and between points here). Alternatively, HRD-BF, the secondary multi-modal MT procedure that this player used, may have also shaped these emerging adaptive and maladaptive HRV responses.

Low-frequency HRV, in contrast to the time-domain HR, was negatively associated with GL, indicating that the greater the LF (HRV frequency domain measure), the fewer games lost. Greater low frequency is associated with more SNS-PNS interaction, a correlate of increased SDNN (the HRV index) and greater HRD. This finding is also consistent with the previously presented training match's self-hypnosis-induced, heightened SDNN in the post- and pre-match assessment conditions (2-minute HRV assessment), which more than doubled across matches on consecutive days, suggesting that low frequency may be an important self-hypnosis intervention efficiency-and-performance-facilitative efficacy biomarker. It should be noted that these two predictor measures (HR and LF) were derived from the HRV ANS report for the entire self-hypnosis session.

The post-self-hypnosis session was also revealing in a manner that was consistent with the pre-match self-hypnosis LF finding, suggesting further that initial intervention-induced or mediated HRV responses may exert a consistent enduring and replicable effect at the intra-individual level. Both SDNN and high frequency (HF) activity were strongly negatively correlated with GL, meaning that greater levels of these HRV time and frequency domain measures were associated with fewer games lost ($r = -.68$ and $-.63$ respectively). These findings from the 2-minute post-self-hypnosis session ANS-HRV report provide additional evidence of intervention efficiency and efficacy.

Finally, the ABSP/CP requires that a 2-minute post-competition HRV scan is performed for the purpose of discerning to what extent mind–body processes, including attention, physiological reactivity, and strategic planning and coping (AP correlates), as well as physiological effort, retrospectively predict outcome. In other words, to what extent does a post-game or match HRV still reflect psychophysiological processes after competition. Conceptually, it is thought that extreme and intensive mind–body states, physiological effort, and intensity can be inferred on the basis of post-competition ANS-HRV responses as well as reveal residual temporal effects of interventions that were engaged in prior to and over the course of an entire competition. The post-match HRV scans over eight matches revealed that greater HR was strongly correlated with games won ($r = .67$), an outcome that appears to negate the pre-match self-hypnosis HRV finding, associating HR at that point in time with more games lost. Both may be spurious findings, with HR being more a reflection of physiological effort in the post-match HRV reading than having psychological significance, which is highly likely, since post-match HR was 10 beats/min higher that self-hypnosis condition HR (91 versus 81).

The preceding data suggest that, in this player, both multi-modal MT methods, VBP-self-hypnosis, and HRD BF exhibited an efficiency effect and were efficacious, at least over the course of eight tournament matches. It is acceptable to analyze intervention efficiency and efficacy in the context of a series of matches or games, for example, an entire baseball season.

However, ultimately, the gold standard approach to MT efficiency and efficacy testing should be based on about 60 repeated measures. This can be done through an intra-individual meta-analysis that combines intervention data that is obtained in a fragmented manner (e.g., as with this tennis player over the course of multiple tournament series).

In conclusion, from the perspective of a practitioner, researcher, coach, and athlete, it is usually encouraging when intervention efficiency and efficacy can be established, despite, as in this case, that preliminary sample size may be too small since it is nevertheless possible that initial positive findings will hold up over time, especially if there is conceptual consistency across temporally divergent measurement occasions (e.g., two temporally spaced measurement occasions within the same competition result in conceptually related measures emerging as predictors of performance outcome or reflect the influence of an initial measure on a conceptually similar one in a second measurement occasion).

Multi-Modal II At-a-Distance Mental Training and Intervention

Multi-modal mental training (MMMT), as with any form of intervention that has established efficiency and efficacy, should be carried out independently by athletes who travel to competitions or are assisted by coaches and/or teammates in the absence of a sport psychology practitioner. Since repetition and repeated measures are necessary to constantly reinforce and consolidate interventions that have been shown to be efficacious, an athlete should be trained to self-administer and engage in mental training as well as document, manage, and analyze his or her performance.

The tennis player in the aforementioned case study who proved to be very compliant in participating in the prescribed specific multi-modal MT protocol was instructed and trained to carry out intervention-specific procedures when traveling around the world. Before arriving at a tournament site, his sport psychology practitioner would try to arrange for the tournament staff to recruit a tennis and psychology-knowledgeable individual to assist the player by video taping and scoring his matches for later criticality analyses. In addition, during practice matches or regular off-day training, the assistant would chart training drill and/or score point play (training sets or matches). Since it was not always possible to procure an assistant at every tournament, the player would videotape matches using a tripod set up for later match statistical analyses. He would also set up and run a pre-, during, and post-practice and tournament HRV monitoring and analysis station on the sideline, if possible, but at minimum always do a pre- and post-match HRV scan, as well as monitor HRV during any other preparation and/or wellness-related interventions (e.g., RSA recovery HRV BF).

Intervention Amenability and Compliance: Ideal AP PHO Constellation or Measure(s)

As far as intervention amenability is concerned, distance-based multi-modal MT should be conceptualized and structured in accord with an athlete's home-based protocol. In other words, the specific AP-based and chosen methods should remain the same. For some athletes, irrespective of intervention amenability issues, compliance can be problematic, especially those who are high in RC/SC, who are traveling alone. Fortunately, when it comes to team sports and at higher amateur and professional levels in individual sports (e.g., tennis and golf), an athlete will frequently at least be accompanied by a parent or friend, and/or oftentimes have a coach along as well who can help foster compliance and help with administering a multi-modal distance-based protocol. See the preceding Multi-modal training for an elaboration of AP and MT amenability/compliance (Figure 15.13).

Conceptual-Construct Basis

The conceptual and/or construct bases of distance-based interventions, whether multi-modal or single methods, such as visualization that are engaged in independently, have their own unique components, processes, and issues. They can be reviewed in each intervention's section within this chapter. There are, however, special conceptual considerations relative to interventions that are carried out at a distance.

First of all, it is erroneous to assume that it is sufficient to administer MT at home, in the context of a practitioner's office hours only, or occasionally on the practice field when he or she can get away and work with an athlete on the playing field. Unfortunately, though, the pervasive MT services

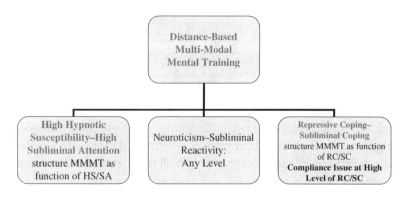

FIGURE 15.13 Athlete's profile and intervention amenability.

delivery paradigm tends to be structured on the basis of practitioner temporal and financial realities and constraints, and not the basis of scientific realities that drive performance enhancement that must be considered when working with an athlete, especially psychologically burdened ones whose maladaptive performance relevant performance tendencies that likely have a lengthy developmental history and complex etiology. Consequently, it is folly to think that sporadically engaging in MT to either attempt to enhance performance or ameliorate or eradicate negative behaviors and psychological tendencies that have taken a career to develop. A coach and serious athlete, for the most part, would not consider missing a day of physical or technical training, since repetition is an integral component for maintaining peak reaction time, power/strength, focus, motor control, and timing. Yet, practitioners can often be very *lackadaisical* when it comes to the mental game, somehow thinking, believing, and conveying to athletes that the MT methods they recommend, administer, and teach are so potent that they can alleviate performance-related psychological issues almost instantaneously. While some practitioners may acknowledge the complexity of performance issues and the mental game and attempts to improve it, such an admission does little to change the intervention process unless it is accompanied by high evidentiary approaches that especially address the previously mentioned time to achieve enduring biomarker-validated change and dose–response parameters that are associated with MT pursuits.

Essentially, theoretically, hypothetically, and conceptually, MT and interventions must be structured with time to achieve enduring change and dose–response considerations at the forefront, and that until it can be shown otherwise, empirically, more is likely to be better. MT should at least parallel time-of-engagement parameters that are associated with physical and technical training and, if possible, integrated into the training process, in vivo, during both simulated and real competition as well, using the multi-modal and integrative approaches to athlete assessment, intervention efficiency, and efficacy testing that the ABSP-CP advances throughout this book. This means extending MT and intervention beyond an athlete's home base as he or she travels and competes.

Distance-based multi-modal or a specific, independent, singular MT procedure, for that matter, are designed for repetition purposes, engaging in interventions, day in and day out, in an attempt to put in the time that is necessary to come even remotely close to overwriting faulty and maladaptive neuronal patterns that are reflected in behaviors and psychological tendencies that undermine peak performance that took years to develop. Or, to attempt to reinforce and maintain peak performance in less negatively impacted athletes and those competitors that have a technical and physical foundation that has not been fully exploited because of certain mental game issues.

Leaving home to compete should not mean an absence of MT or interventions. With effort and commitment, along with high evidentiary accountability methodologies, MT can be taken on the road in an attempt to increase the probability over time that an intervention may eventually lead to the full consolidation of adaptive psychological and behavioral responses that are crucial to an athlete's success.

Description of Procedure: Distance-Based MMMT

1. This screenshot (Figure 15.14) depicts the player engaging in self-initiated distance-based pre-match VBP-facilitated self-hypnosis with background HRV monitoring. The athlete was extensively instructed on a daily basis in how to carry out his full multi-modal MT protocol independently prior to his departure.

FIGURE 15.14   VBP-facilitated distance-based pre-match self-hypnosis.

2. Upon arriving at a tournament site, if an assistant had been procured, he would meet with the person and instruct him or her in the video, VBP computer-HRV monitoring procedures and how to keep score and criticality statistics per ABSP-CP.
3. Prior to every match or training session, the player would engage in a self-hypnosis epoch of varying length, usually for about 10 min, followed by 15 minutes or more of active-alert hypnosis (Figures 15.15 and 15.16).
4. Two-minute pre- and post-intervention HRV baselines and MT-impact scans were assistant- or self-administered. Two-minute pre- and post- HRV scans were similarly administered on before and after matches.
5. All matches and training sessions were videotaped, as were the MT epochs. Criticality and match statistical analyses were also performed, either by the assistant or later, retrospectively, by the player using the acquired video recording (Figure 15.17).

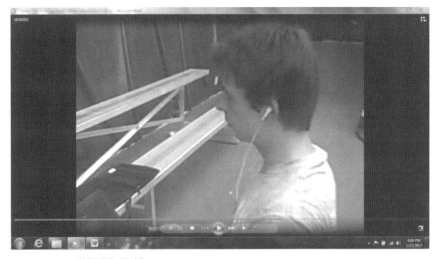

FIGURE 15.15   Unsupervised self-hypnosis at a distance.

FIGURE 15.16   Post-self-hypnosis active-alert hypnosis.

6. BioCom Technologies Heart Scanner ANS HRV reports were generated after each scan. Data from the reports were extracted for storage in an Excel template for later review.

7. The player also engaged in wellness and health-facilitating interventions using RSA breathing-based BF, which should not be confused with breathing-based HRD BF. This was done for 5 to 10 minutes in the morning (for activation and self-regulation purposes), for 20 minutes after a training session or match (for recovery purposes), and for 5 minutes or until the onset of drowsiness at bedtime to induce pre-sleep and/or reset biorhythm and reset bio-chronological state to offset or reduce the impact of jet lag.

8. In the evening, the player reviewed his ANS-HRV reports and emailed them along with edited video clips to his sport psychologist in the United States for analysis.

9. The player communicated with his sport psychologist prior to each training session or match and at other times when it was important to convey results of the data analyses and/or observations pertaining to interventions that could be observed on the received videotape.

FIGURE 15.17   Screenshot clips from videotaped match at a distance.

Documentation–Accountability–Intervention Efficiency and Efficacy

The preceding protocol was engaged in over the course of 9 months of away tournaments. The following screenshot (Figure 15.18) depicts his database files containing a repository of extensive assessment, intervention, and performance information. These were transmitted via email attachment to the player's sport psychologist after each match.

ACCOUNTABILITY: INTERVENTION EFFICACY

The following SPSS outcome charts contain multi-modal self-hypnosis, active-alert hypnosis-centered MT (with video-based programming augmentation) data. Self-hypnosis-associated (generated) HRV was obtained prior to matches, along with post-self-hypnosis-associated HRV (obtained within a couple of minutes after each self-hypnosis session of variable duration). In addition, 2-min post-match HRV was documented. Correlations between self-hypnosis, post-self-hypnosis, and post-match HRV were calculated.

Hypotheses:

1. It was predicted that pre-match self-hypnosis would be associated with an HRV signature that would predict performance outcome and thereby establish intervention efficacy in this specific tennis player.

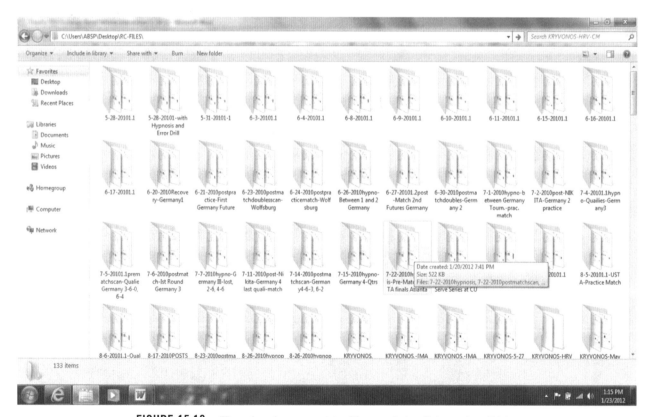

FIGURE 15.18　Files of performance data: Managed at a distance by athlete.

2. It was predicted that pre-match self-hypnosis-generated HRV would lead to significantly different post-self-hypnosis 2-min scan HRV and that such or other (noncorrelated with self-hypnosis responses) post-hypnosis HRV responses would be associated with performance outcomes.

3. Relationships between all HRV conditions (self-hypnosis and post-self-hypnosis HRV, and post-hypnosis HRV and post-match HRV were investigated for exploratory purposes; Figure 15.19).

FINDINGS

In terms of outcome, significant findings in Figures 15.20 and 15.21 may have conceptual and construct relevance relative to intervention efficiency. Generally, changes across intervention measurement occasions (either a baseline versus intervention condition or intervention versus

Paired Samples Statistics

		Mean	N	Std. Deviation	Std. Error Mean
Pair 1	HRHYP	75.4444	9	3.8442	1.2814
	PREHR	76.1111	9	6.2339	2.0780
Pair 2	HRHYP	75.6667	9	3.6056	1.2019
	POSTHR	92.0000	9	11.8954	3.9651
Pair 3	PREHR	77.3333	9	5.2202	1.7401
	POSTHR	90.4444	9	11.0126	3.6709
Pair 4	SDHYP	56.2222	9	11.1779	3.7260
	PRESD	75.0000	9	26.8561	8.9520
Pair 5	SDHYP	55.4444	9	11.1255	3.7085
	POSTSD	51.6667	9	23.5744	7.8581
Pair 6	PRESD	68.3333	9	17.6423	5.8808
	POSTSD	44.6667	9	23.1247	7.7082
Pair 7	VLHYP	344.3333	9	98.4911	32.8304
	PREVL	363.7778	9	239.6496	79.8832
Pair 8	VLHYP	353.3333	9	112.4733	37.4911
	POSTVL	102.4444	9	107.1892	35.7297
Pair 9	PREVL	335.6667	9	248.6167	82.8722
	POSTVL	100.0000	9	108.5207	36.1736
Pair 10	LHYP	409.2222	9	98.3651	32.7884
	PRELO	1560.1111	9	1792.2957	597.4319
Pair 11	LHYP	398.4444	9	101.3202	33.7734
	POSTL	152.6667	9	114.7628	38.2543
Pair 12	PRELO	1064.3333	9	1254.9971	418.3324
	POSTL	140.5556	9	122.0257	40.6752
Pair 13	HHYP	120.8889	9	72.0684	24.0228
	PREH	153.8889	9	101.2293	33.7431
Pair 14	HHYP	117.5556	9	74.3339	24.7780
	POSTH	207.8889	9	223.3072	74.4357
Pair 15	PREH	163.6667	9	101.5788	33.8596
	POSTH	189.5556	9	230.8658	76.9553
Pair 16	LHHYP	4.0333	9	1.5700	.5233
	PRELH	10.1667	9	12.7098	4.2366
Pair 17	LHHYP	4.1222	9	1.6338	.5446
	POSTLH	.9667	9	.5612	.1871
Pair 18	PRELH	5.7556	9	4.0921	1.3640
	POSTLH	.9889	9	.5533	.1844

FIGURE 15.19   Mean comparisons.

Paired Samples Test

		Paired Differences							
				Std. Error Mean	95% Confidence Interval of the Difference		t	df	Sig. (2-tailed)
		Mean	Std. Deviation		Lower	Upper			
Pair 1	HRHYP - PREHR	-.6667	3.9370	1.3123	-3.6929	2.3596	-.508	8	.625
Pair 2	HRHYP - POSTHR	-16.3333	11.9373	3.9791	-25.5092	-7.1575	-4.105	8	.003
Pair 3	PREHR - POSTHR	-13.1111	12.2622	4.0874	-22.5367	-3.6856	-3.208	8	.012
Pair 4	SDHYP - PRESD	-18.7778	26.4423	8.8141	-39.1031	1.5476	-2.130	8	.066
Pair 5	SDHYP - POSTSD	3.7778	28.6914	9.5638	-18.2764	25.8319	.395	8	.703
Pair 6	PRESD - POSTSD	23.6667	24.1609	8.0536	5.0949	42.2384	2.939	8	.019
Pair 7	VLHYP - PREVL	-19.4444	183.9783	61.3261	-160.8627	121.9738	-.317	8	.759
Pair 8	VLHYP - POSTVL	250.8889	164.6591	54.8864	124.3207	377.4571	4.571	8	.002
Pair 9	PREVL - POSTVL	235.6667	270.7393	90.2464	27.5580	443.7753	2.611	8	.031
Pair 10	LHYP - PRELO	-1150.89	1777.3531	592.4510	-2517.08	215.3057	-1.943	8	.088
Pair 11	LHYP - POSTL	245.7778	121.9946	40.6649	152.0044	339.5512	6.044	8	.000
Pair 12	PRELO - POSTL	923.7778	1271.9524	423.9841	-53.9314	1901.4870	2.179	8	.061
Pair 13	HHYP - PREH	-33.0000	130.6292	43.5431	-133.4105	67.4105	-.758	8	.470
Pair 14	HHYP - POSTH	-90.3333	246.5806	82.1935	-279.8720	99.2053	-1.099	8	.304
Pair 15	PREH - POSTH	-25.8889	222.8017	74.2672	-197.1495	145.3717	-.349	8	.736
Pair 16	LHHYP - PRELH	-6.1333	12.3889	4.1296	-15.6563	3.3896	-1.485	8	.176
Pair 17	LHHYP - POSTLH	3.1556	1.7444	.5815	1.8147	4.4964	5.427	8	.001
Pair 18	PRELH - POSTLH	4.7667	4.2172	1.4057	1.5250	8.0083	3.391	8	.009

FIGURE 15.20   Paired *T*-tests: self-hypnosis, post-self-hypnosis and post-match HRV.

post-intervention condition) can be interpreted to reflect intervention efficiency, more so if such changes are also associated with intervention efficacy. Changes may also diverge from conceptually expected changes, including those that were predicted earlier, since no previous hypnosis-related norms were established for this athlete and the possibility that no change is actually a sign of intervention response stability, a response that may be more consistent with sustained hypnotic depth and the impact of post-hypnotic suggestions. The following conceptually relevant intervention-associated significant changes in HRV were documented:

1. Self-Hypnosis SDNN and L frequency HRV were close to being significantly different ($r = .06$ and .08, respectively) than the post-self-hypnosis-generated HRV condition.

Paired Samples Correlations

		N	Correlation	Sig.
Pair 1	HRHYP & PREHR	9	.796	.010
Pair 2	HRHYP & POSTHR	9	.140	.720
Pair 3	PREHR & POSTHR	9	-.016	.968
Pair 4	SDHYP & PRESD	9	.245	.525
Pair 5	SDHYP & POSTSD	9	-.274	.476
Pair 6	PRESD & POSTSD	9	.321	.399
Pair 7	VLHYP & PREVL	9	.705	.034
Pair 8	VLHYP & POSTVL	9	-.123	.752
Pair 9	PREVL & POSTVL	9	.005	.989
Pair 10	LHYP & PRELO	9	.179	.645
Pair 11	LHYP & POSTL	9	.368	.330
Pair 12	PRELO & POSTL	9	-.091	.815
Pair 13	HHYP & PREH	9	-.111	.776
Pair 14	HHYP & POSTH	9	-.163	.675
Pair 15	PREH & POSTH	9	.298	.436
Pair 16	LHHYP & PRELH	9	.264	.493
Pair 17	LHHYP & POSTLH	9	-.032	.935
Pair 18	PRELH & POSTLH	9	-.162	.677

FIGURE 15.21   Self-hypnosis, pre- and post-conditions.

Interpretation: this finding can be interpreted in two ways: (1) in this athlete, self-hypnosis exerted an effect on SDNN and low-frequency HRV; or (2) self-hypnosis-generated HRV remained stable over time (few between-condition changes, a very plausible construct/conceptual tenet), since in this athlete all other HRV measures did not change significantly over initial recordings of HRV. It could be expected that self-hypnosis-induced ANS activity is more likely to remain stable over time, especially in the minutes immediately after a self-hypnosis session has ended.

> *Practitioner Challenge:* An earlier finding on L:H frequency in the self-hypnosis and post-hypnosis condition influenced the derivation of a part of *Hypothesis 2*, above. Locate and comment on this finding (earlier in this chapter).

2. Highly significant correlations (including the preceding ones) between the self-hypnosis and post-match HRV would suggest stability of the hypnosis-induced response and the potency of post-hypnotic suggestions. Low nonsignificant correlations across these conditions, however, could also be expected due to temporal distance and level of intensity changes, as reflected in post-match HRV that is obtained within 5 minutes of a match's completion (variations in intensity from the self-hypnosis to the post-match condition). The following was found (paired *T*-Tests): self-hypnosis HR, and post-match HR (.003), self-hypnosis and post-match VL frequency (.002), self-hypnosis and post-match L frequency (.000), and self-hypnosis and post-match LH ratio (.001) were significantly different; by contrast, self-hypnosis SDNN and H frequency were not significantly different across time and condition (.70 and .30, respectively).

Interpretation: in light of intensity differences between a pre-match self-hypnosis session and immediate post-match HRV that is obtained after an entire match of intense action, it would be expected that a pre-match intervention-induced ANS measure would change over time. Consequently, the fact that SDNN and H frequency activity did not change over time suggests that intervention efficiency was maintained over time, possibly as a result of post-hypnotic suggestions leading to subliminally induced pre-action HRD, since greater SDNN is a correlate of greater magnitude of HRD and H frequency activity increases in the context of extended-time exhale cycles that are associated with HRD.

3. Pre- versus post (post-self-hypnosis 2-minute HRV and post-match 2-minute HRV) relationships may also reflect self-hypnosis-induced HRV across an entire match. The following was found: all HRV measures across the pre- and post-condition, with the exception of H frequency activity, were significantly different ($p = .76$), again suggesting that H frequency PNS responses associated with HRD-related exhale cycles over the course of entire matches reflected ongoing posthypnotic suggestion mediation of performance (indicative of intervention efficiency).

> *Practitioner Challenge*: What major caveat must be taken into account when arriving at the preceding interpretations?

Intervention Efficacy

Pre-match self-hypnosis was found to lead to HRV changes across a post-self-hypnosis condition and over the course of an entire match as reflected in post-match HRV, suggestive of a high degree of intervention efficiency. However, as readers should know by now, intervention efficiency, without parallel intervention efficacy, diminishes the utility and value of an intervention.

Relative to intervention efficacy L frequency (LHYP in Figure 15.22), HRV was positively correlated with games lost as a macro-level outcome measure. Such a finding is antithetical to intervention efficacy, since it suggests that self-hypnosis-generated L frequency HRV may be, in this athlete,

Correlations

		GW	GL	TIMEHYP	HRHYP	SDHYP	VLHYP	LHYP	HHYP	LHHYP
GW	Pearson Correlation	1.000	-.260	.348	.201	-.103	.158	-.424	-.253	.346
	Sig. (2-tailed)		.440	.324	.577	.776	.662	.222	.481	.328
	N	11	11	10	10	10	10	10	10	10
GL	Pearson Correlation	-.260	1.000	.283	-.406	.201	.428	.636*	-.166	.242
	Sig. (2-tailed)	.440		.429	.245	.578	.217	.048	.648	.501
	N	11	11	10	10	10	10	10	10	10
TIMEHYP	Pearson Correlation	.348	.283	1.000	-.416	.206	.795**	-.018	-.233	.245
	Sig. (2-tailed)	.324	.429		.232	.569	.006	.961	.517	.496
	N	10	10	10	10	10	10	10	10	10
HRHYP	Pearson Correlation	.201	-.406	-.416	1.000	-.430	-.760*	-.045	.082	.136
	Sig. (2-tailed)	.577	.245	.232		.215	.011	.901	.823	.708
	N	10	10	10	10	10	10	10	10	10
SDHYP	Pearson Correlation	-.103	.201	.206	-.430	1.000	.213	.218	.760*	-.586
	Sig. (2-tailed)	.776	.578	.569	.215		.555	.545	.011	.075
	N	10	10	10	10	10	10	10	10	10
VLHYP	Pearson Correlation	.158	.428	.795**	-.760*	.213	1.000	.120	-.272	.237
	Sig. (2-tailed)	.662	.217	.006	.011	.555		.741	.448	.510
	N	10	10	10	10	10	10	10	10	10
LHYP	Pearson Correlation	-.424	.636*	-.018	-.045	.218	.120	1.000	.105	.287
	Sig. (2-tailed)	.222	.048	.961	.901	.545	.741		.773	.422
	N	10	10	10	10	10	10	10	10	10
HHYP	Pearson Correlation	-.253	-.166	-.233	.082	.760*	-.272	.105	1.000	-.810**
	Sig. (2-tailed)	.481	.648	.517	.823	.011	.448	.773		.004
	N	10	10	10	10	10	10	10	10	10
LHHYP	Pearson Correlation	.346	.242	.245	.136	-.586	.237	.287	-.810**	1.000
	Sig. (2-tailed)	.328	.501	.496	.708	.075	.510	.422	.004	
	N	10	10	10	10	10	10	10	10	10

*Correlation is significant at the 0.05 level (2-tailed).

**Correlation is significant at the 0.01 level (2-tailed).

FIGURE 15.22   Self-hypnosis and associated HRV and outcome.

an IZOF biomarker that remained active and potent over time and negatively impacted performance. This finding diminishes the previous intervention efficiency SDNN and H frequency HRV changes that were hypothesized to be associated with performance-facilitative HRD.

A second intervention efficacy relevant measure is post-self-hypnosis HRV (PRE in Figure 15.23), since it is hypothesized to reflect either the stability of self-hypnosis-generated HRV over the short term or the potency of self-hypnosis in mediating changes in ANS measures over the short and long

Correlations

		GW	GL	PREHR	PRESD	PREVL	PRELO	PREH	PRELH
GW	Pearson Correlation	1.000	-.260	.035	-.069	.399	-.180	-.340	-.024
	Sig. (2-tailed)		.440	.923	.849	.254	.618	.337	.947
	N	11	11	10	10	10	10	10	10
GL	Pearson Correlation	-.260	1.000	-.211	.339	.806**	.072	.320	-.039
	Sig. (2-tailed)	.440		.558	.339	.005	.843	.367	.915
	N	11	11	10	10	10	10	10	10
PREHR	Pearson Correlation	.035	-.211	1.000	-.745*	-.283	-.792**	-.582	-.535
	Sig. (2-tailed)	.923	.558		.013	.429	.006	.077	.111
	N	10	10	10	10	10	10	10	10
PRESD	Pearson Correlation	-.069	.339	-.745*	1.000	.367	.919**	.419	.820**
	Sig. (2-tailed)	.849	.339	.013		.297	.000	.228	.004
	N	10	10	10	10	10	10	10	10
PREVL	Pearson Correlation	.399	.806**	-.283	.367	1.000	.117	.144	.056
	Sig. (2-tailed)	.254	.005	.429	.297		.747	.691	.877
	N	10	10	10	10	10	10	10	10
PRELO	Pearson Correlation	-.180	.072	-.792**	.919**	.117	1.000	.473	.842**
	Sig. (2-tailed)	.618	.843	.006	.000	.747		.167	.002
	N	10	10	10	10	10	10	10	10
PREH	Pearson Correlation	-.340	.320	-.582	.419	.144	.473	1.000	-.042
	Sig. (2-tailed)	.337	.367	.077	.228	.691	.167		.909
	N	10	10	10	10	10	10	10	10
PRELH	Pearson Correlation	-.024	-.039	-.535	.820**	.056	.842**	-.042	1.000
	Sig. (2-tailed)	.947	.915	.111	.004	.877	.002	.909	
	N	10	10	10	10	10	10	10	10

*Correlation is significant at the 0.05 level (2-tailed).

**Correlation is significant at the 0.01 level (2-tailed).

FIGURE 15.23   Post-self-hypnosis-associated HRV and outcome.

Correlations

		GW	GL	POSTHR	POSTSD	POSTVL	POSTL	POSTH	POSTLH
GW	Pearson Correlation	1.000	-.260	.701*	.300	-.303	.108	-.024	-.347
	Sig. (2-tailed)	.	.440	.024	.399	.394	.766	.947	.326
	N	11	11	10	10	10	10	10	10
GL	Pearson Correlation	-.260	1.000	.108	-.222	.096	.563	.346	.161
	Sig. (2-tailed)	.440	.	.766	.538	.793	.090	.327	.657
	N	11	11	10	10	10	10	10	10
POSTHR	Pearson Correlation	.701*	.108	1.000	.581	-.231	.179	.107	-.312
	Sig. (2-tailed)	.024	.766	.	.078	.521	.621	.768	.381
	N	10	10	10	10	10	10	10	10
POSTSD	Pearson Correlation	.300	-.222	.581	1.000	.427	.342	.510	-.463
	Sig. (2-tailed)	.399	.538	.078	.	.218	.333	.132	.178
	N	10	10	10	10	10	10	10	10
POSTVL	Pearson Correlation	-.303	.096	-.231	.427	1.000	.664*	.795**	-.296
	Sig. (2-tailed)	.394	.793	.521	.218	.	.036	.006	.407
	N	10	10	10	10	10	10	10	10
POSTL	Pearson Correlation	.108	.563	.179	.342	.664*	1.000	.879**	-.156
	Sig. (2-tailed)	.766	.090	.621	.333	.036	.	.001	.666
	N	10	10	10	10	10	10	10	10
POSTH	Pearson Correlation	-.024	.346	.107	.510	.795**	.879**	1.000	-.384
	Sig. (2-tailed)	.947	.327	.768	.132	.006	.001	.	.273
	N	10	10	10	10	10	10	10	10
POSTLH	Pearson Correlation	-.347	.161	-.312	-.463	-.296	-.156	-.384	1.000
	Sig. (2-tailed)	.326	.657	.381	.178	.407	.666	.273	.
	N	10	10	10	10	10	10	10	10

*Correlation is significant at the 0.05 level (2-tailed).

**Correlation is significant at the 0.01 level (2-tailed).

FIGURE 15.24   Post-match HRV and outcome.

term (e.g., as reflected in post-match HRV). Relative to post-self-hypnosis, VL frequency activity was strongly correlated with games lost (GL, .81; $p = .005$), again suggesting that self-hypnosis-mediated ANS responses impacted performance negatively. On the other hand, caveats exist (see PRACTITIONER CHALLENGE).

Practitioner Challenge: Why is it possible that the advanced intervention efficiency thesis regarding SDNN, H, and the resulting HRD may still have merit, despite the L frequency activity intervention efficacy finding, and why must this latter finding be interpreted with caution?

Finally, post-match HRV, based on intervention efficiency findings (associations between self-hypnosis HRV and post-self-hypnosis HRV), may be influenced by these measures, revealed one strong correlation with a successful outcome, games won (HR and GW; $r = .70$; $p = .024$). This is an encouraging finding and suggests that self-hypnosis-induced greater HR over time may enhance performance. Nevertheless, it is also a more nebulous finding that needs to be further investigated in light of temporal distance intensity issues and the fact that in this data set, self-hypnosis HR, was significantly lower than in post-match HRV (see Figures 15.20 and 15.24).

Summary

1. Intervention efficiency appears to have been established, that is, hypnosis-elicited conceptually consistent mind–body responses as reflected in HRV stability and/or changes across conditions.
2. Intervention efficacy appears to be tenuous; however, there are issues and caveats that must be considered before reaching a final conclusion.

3. Importantly, this player was very amenable to and compliant with the prescribed multi-modal hypnosis and video-based-programming augmented mental training.

Notes

1 *See the Hypnosis/Active-Alert Hypnosis section for an elaboration of the hypnotic methods that are used within this sample multi-modal MT approach that was applied to numerous professional and developing athletes.*

2 Since there is no official rule in tennis that prevents an athlete from engaging in the aforementioned protocol on the sideline (as depicted in Figure 15.7, in which VBP self-hypnosis and concurrent HRD BF is practiced/reinforced on the bench). However, there have been occasions when officials have not permitted the use of computer stations during official tournament matches, so when it comes to *in vivo* tennis assessment and intervention paradigms, officials should be notified in advance and made aware that there is no rule stipulating that technology-based MT cannot be done on the bench, courtside. In most other sports, the use of computer/video assisted MT is a non-issue with, for example, most major league baseball teams, which have video analysis stations in or near the dugout. Also, an ABSP research group carried out an extensive multi-modal computer-assisted assessment and intervention protocol on the bench for an entire official season of youth baseball games (see Chapter 20).

Hypnosis-Active-Alert Hypnosis: Subliminal Mental Programming

Sport-specific hypnosis is a precursor, priming intervention that is designed to facilitate motor, technical, tactical ability as well as induce brain–heart–mind–body responses that are associated with IZOF (e.g., preaction HRD). In contrast to clinical hypnosis that usually attempts to relax a patient, sport hypnotic procedures should attempt to progressively raise levels of activation that are necessary to efficiently engage in sport-specific actions. Since it is beyond the scope of this book to provide a comprehensive overview of or train individuals in hypnosis, readers should access websites of the Society for Clinical and Experimental Hypnosis or Division 30 of the American Psychological Association (Psychological Hypnosis).

Intervention Amenability: Athlete's Profile and Ideal Mental Training Modality

Obviously, athletes who are high in hypnotic susceptibility (HS) are most amenable to hypnosis/self- and active-alert hypnosis. Practitioners of Ericksonian-based hypnosis and many others may be unaware of research showing that individuals who are high in HS have distinct neuropsychophysiological signatures at baseline in the absence of being inducted or hypnotized compared to individuals who are low in HS who also have a strongly diminished ability to even enter a hypnotic state (Fromm & Nash, 2003). Individuals who are high in HS also have been shown to exhibit differential cortical responses as a function of the stage of hypnosis (from induction to deep hypnosis; Fromm & Nash, 2003). Trait theorists appear to have the upper hand in the state-trait debate, and although hypnotic states are real, they can most readily and easily be accessed and sustained by people who have high trait HS (Fromm & Nash, 2003). Consequently, athletes should always be tested using direct validated measures of HS (Stanford Scale of Hypnotic Susceptibility; SSHS/HSHS; Weitzenhoffer & Hilgard, 1959), which requires training to administer and takes about 45 to 50 minutes to carry out. Alternatively, the Tellegen Absorption Scale (Tellegen & Atkinson, 1974; TAS) can be used to arrive at strong approximation of HS if an individual scores about 28 or higher. The CSARCS-A subliminal attention scale that strongly correlates with the TAS can also be used as an ersatz test of HS. Athletes who score in the high-mid range for HS, absorption,

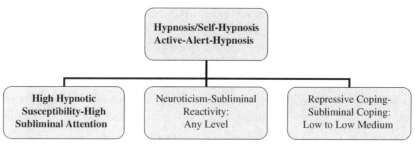

FIGURE 16.1   Athlete's profile and intervention amenability.

and/or SA are potential candidates for hypnotic-based MT, but as with all assessments, they must be further tested for intervention efficiency and efficacy using additional criterion-referencing and predictive validity methodologies that have been advanced throughout this book (Figure 16.1).

Conceptual-Rationale

The feeling that one has when under sport and performance-specific hypnosis is one of mental calmness. Inductions should be designed to reduce or eliminate the mental chatter that AP-vulnerable athletes (those who are high in N/SR and low in RC/SC) frequently experience prior to, and especially during, critical moments. Once alert-calmness has been attained using sport-specific inductions, as reflected in changes in ANS (SNS–PNS) responses from the baseline to hypnosis condition (which can vary as a function of individual differences), active-alert hypnosis is used to raise activation or intensity levels and prime motor-technical responses.

What practitioners, coaches, and athletes should know is that an athlete who is under hypnosis does not lose all volitional control. They can still communicate and respond as would be expected, that is, they can readily respond to coaching and other questions. Clinical and sport-specific inductions are not comparable to stage hypnosis where subjects are often prompted to do embarrassing and other nonperformance-related things. Hypnosis, when properly channeled by a well-trained and experienced practitioner, can help induce performance-facilitative response chains, ranging from mind–body strategic and motor preparation to completing a sport-specific task and requisite technical actions in a more controlled manner.

The ABSP-CP hypnosis/self-hypnosis/active-alert hypnosis process is usually carried out within an integrative multi-modal paradigm that includes Video-Based Programming and Motor-Technical-Based MT. The initial hypnotic induction is brief and prompt-oriented as opposed to lengthy and wordy, as clinical inductions can be. Readers should review the preceding multi-modal section that included hypnotic MT procedures (Chapter 14). In this section, numerous photos and screenshots show an advanced former college tennis player engaged in pre- and during competition self-hypnosis. Customized video-recorded feedback was not used as a primary induction method with this player. This athlete did not hear a conventional script; he was instead provided with task/action-specific short phrases or one-word prompts or reminders that were repeatedly conveyed by a sport psychology practitioner. For example, if an athlete is being trained to eliminate technical quirks, he or she will hear a prompt each time the specific technical action that is associated with such a technical problem is imagined, as part of the induction process or while engaged in active-alert hypnosis. A slalom skier who constantly takes too indirect of a route going into a gate might receive the prompt "direct" every time a gate is hypnotically envisioned or encountered when active-alert hypnosis is being engaged in.

Prompts and short phrases that are repeatedly heard in conjunction with imagined optimum technique (assuming it is of a high level and shown in a structured-guided manner so as to not contain technical/motor deficiencies that may exist). They serve to facilitate the consolidation of technical movements in procedural memory. A role model with technique and style that is similar to one's client athlete should be visualized to reinforce technical motions that the athlete is striving to replicate. Replicating or sequentially visually/internally reproducing perfect technical motions, giving way to subliminal self-repeated hypnotic-induced prompts during self and active-alert hypnosis, and eventually during training and actual competition, is hypothesized to facilitate the consolidation process by shutting off interfering intrusive thoughts, and overwriting, if only for a short period of time, well consolidated negative technical and motor actions that must be suppressed during competition.

The self-hypnosis course should be systematically structured, documented, and analyzed as follows. An athlete with performance psychological problems "a" and "b" and technical issue "c" that are known to manifest themselves, especially under pressure conditions, can be eradicated by "x_1" amount of pre-competition video-based self-hypnosis, and/or "x_2" amount of active-alert hypnosis and x_3 amount of post-hypnotic suggestion-situation prompt-induced mental–motor–technical corrective, performance-facilitative reinforcement pertaining to "a," "b," and "c."

The administration of the ABSP-CP hypnosis approach (as should any other approach to hypnosis and all interventions, for that matter) must be individualized and is always considered experimental. The onus is on the practitioner to demonstrate experimentally (empirically) both intervention efficiency and efficacy. This can be attempted on the basis of temporal intervention engagement parameters (when was a MT session started, how long was it engaged in, how many times was it reinforced), mind–body response changes from the baseline to intervention condition (as reflected in HRV), and how much of the variance in sport-specific macro- and micro-level outcome measures can be explained on the basis of hypnosis-based predictor measures.

Experientially, one can think of being hypnotized as being similar to the feeling that one gets when one is so absorbed or engrossed in a book, thought, or scene in nature or on television. In a more athletic context, the mental state that runners frequently report, that of mind–body dissociation, also captures the essence of an hypnotic state; although individuals low in HS/SA in reading may not be able to relate to these descriptions, even if they have experienced similar states. In other words, they would not associate intense attention or focus that they have experienced with hypnosis, per se, and likely, the level of intensity and dissociation that is experienced during actual hypnotic states seem to well exceed levels of absorption that are common to non-hypnosis-induced strong concentration.

Although it cannot be disputed that hypnotic states exist, it still must be determined to what extent performance can be enhanced as a result of hypnosis and/or active-alert hypnosis as a function of depth, strength, and duration of such states as well as induction scripts, prompts, and whether VBP can significantly reinforce sport-specific hypnotically induced responses.

As with all more nebulous interventions such as hypnosis that are marked more by experiential and subjective feelings and self-report feedback as to their perceived impact than objective and measurable responses, it is crucial to document their application and outcome as illustrated further on.

It should be noted that individuals who are high in HS have the ability to intensely focus on salient stimuli and tasks. In athletes, this ability should be channeled (practitioner-guided) to facilitate motor and technical control, and in the process suppress negative intrusive thoughts that are often manifested by athletes who are concurrently high in N/SR through diversionary procedures that result in absolute attention to sport-specific cognitions and actions that are continually reinforced via verbal/internal prompts and, where possible, video-based input. Over time, the constant repetition of auditory and/or visual feedback/prompts upon which the high HS athlete easily focuses is thought to result in enduring positive, performance-facilitative mental states, even when an athlete encounters previously unmanageable critical moments that resulted in technical, tactical, and psychological breakdowns. The two case-study athletes (the preceding and the following) reported that after a few days of intensive hypnotic MT, they started to hear the performance-specific prompts and see the VBP scenarios during matches, not randomly or context inappropriately (e.g., hearing a prompt to be aggressive after a point or envisioning a tactical pattern involving an approach shot when preparing to hit a serve), but in conjunction with what just happened, should be done, or how to improve or change something (e.g., completing a prescribed pre-return ritual, especially after a point was lost).

This feedback suggests that in athletes who are high in HS, auditory, and visual feedback in the form of prompts (external–internal) and actual technical–tactical–motivation video scenes are rapidly consolidated and surface subliminally as needed (situation relevant and performance facilitative). Of course, while such feedback appears to attest to intervention efficiency, intervention efficacy must be established on the basis of statistical relationships between hypnotic procedure-related predictor variables and sport-specific, macro- and micro-performance outcome measures.

Since athletes who are high in HS are extremely likely to also be placebo-prone, any self-report feedback regarding intervention efficiency, amenability, and efficacy must be viewed with caution, since merely feeling or believing that a MT procedure is having a mind–body effect (although it likely is) and working (it may not be), are insufficient benchmarks of efficiency of success. Practitioners, most who are hypothesized to be high in HS, can also be placebo-prone, leading to a dual-placebo belief system in which mutual belief systems drive the intervention efficiency and efficacy evaluation process. As such, for practitioners who are, as their athlete/client, high in HS, it is imperative that they call upon higher evidentiary methodologies to guide the athlete assessment and intervention process, even if this requires involving neutral third-party analysts to run data analyses.

Description of Procedure

1. As in the case of all athlete assessment and interventions, pre-competition HRV baseline recordings are obtained (2-minute duration). The athlete depicted below (far right; Figure 16.2) is being trained in hypnotic procedures. He is surrounded by his sport psychologist, his tennis coach, and a sparring partner.

FIGURE 16.2 Hypnosis training with HRV.

FIGURE 16.3   Hypnotic induction.

2. In the scene above (Figure 16.3), the player is undergoing an hypnotic induction (unaided by video-based programming). The induction does not involve a lengthy narrative. A scenario is set up for the player to imagine, in this case carrying out serve and return sequences. The player is asked to signal when he starts to vividly imagine the described tennis-specific sequence. Once the signal has been noticed by the practitioner, prompts take over for "x" amount of time. Prompts are tennis-action specific. For example, this player has some service-technical issues, including the failure to consistently extend his right arm and accelerate upward to the ball. In addition, once the ball was in play he tended to be too passive. Hence, he was told to imagine a serve scenario involving 3 shots (by him) after the serve (the average amount of shots associated with points that he won in 15 previous matches). The prompting was as follows: (a) "EXTEND," "ACCELERATE," "AGGRESSIVE," "AGGRESSIVE," "AGGRESSIVE." Prompts were conveyed in a strong voice, and they were timed to the temporal rhythm of the player's serve sequence and a point that would last 6 shots (3 by the player and 3 by the opponent). Time lines for numerous stroke, tactical, and point iterations were determined during the pre-intervention phase of this player's sport psychology/mental game program. This specific serve and 3-shot sequence was repeated numerous times, over the course of a 15-minute hypnosis session. The length of a hypnosis session, commencing with an induction and ending with post-hypnotic suggestions, should be based on depth of hypnosis parameters that can be established on the basis of measures that are derived from continuous HRV and/or EEG monitoring, or if such high-tech analysis possibilities are not available or a practitioner is not trained to administer and interpret data that emanates from such procedures, hypnotic-depth can also be inferred behaviorally (e.g., the extent [subjectively interpreted] to which an athlete appears to be in a trance-like focused state that cannot be disrupted through external attempts to do so [using noise or social distractions like the sudden appearance of an unexpected and unknown spectator]). In addition, objective performance tests can be used to discern hypnotic depth (e.g., using focus and technical threshold baseline versus test condition comparisons; sustainability of attention using technical and success outcome measures). It should be noted that without absolute expert knowledge of the specific

sport in which a practitioner's athlete participates, it would very difficult to carry out this or similar hypnosis leading to active-alert hypnosis, a possible reason why the literature is replete with negative or weak efficacy outcome studies (see Morgan in Van Raalte & Brewer, 1996). As such, practitioners should always involve expert coaches when designing interventions for athletes who specialize in a sport of which they do not have comprehensive knowledge (Figure 16.4).

FIGURE 16.4   Self-hypnosis.

3. Once the hypnotic induction was completed, culminating with post-hypnotic suggestions that are designed to subliminally or unconsciously prompt an athlete to engage in a specific hypnosis-guided performance-facilitative routines or actions/tasks during competition or independent of competition (e.g., a post-hypnotic suggestion to engage in RSA BF at 10 p.m. every day), the player (via a post-hypnotic suggestion) commenced to start unprompted self-hypnosis. A post-hypnotic suggestion can be thought of as being similar to an impulse, obsession, or compulsion to do something, without really knowing why. In the extreme and having nothing to do with hypnosis per se, checking to see if the gas for the stove is turned off multiple times before leaving one's apartment could also be programmed in a highly hypnotizable person. Or, readers may have recalled before harm could occur, checking to see if the crosswalk light turned green just before stepping off the curb, or realizing that one does not have their keys just before the door almost slams shut. These protective reactions show that the mind is virtually always on red-alert, even when sleeping (Wick-ramasekera, 1988). Post-hypnotic suggestions attempt to manipulate this subliminal activation phenomenon in the context of desired clinical or performance goals by first priming and then consolidating prompts and eventual actions that are to be setoff and engaged in both long- and short-term memory. Individuals who are high in HS appear to be very prone to manipulation, such that a programmed external or internal stimulus or visual, auditory, and/or event or situation encountered prompt or event (e.g., losing a point in tennis) leads to an impulse to engage in performance-facilitative or corrective action (like taking a full 20 seconds to regroup and systematically prepare for the next point, or engage in HRD BF prior to action the next point after a

poorly played point). Such post-hypnotic suggestions, if well consolidated, can remain dormant for extended periods, only to be manifested when needed. For example, a player with a good physical and technical game, who is high in HS, high in N/SR, and low in RC/SC may have long stretches in a match that go well, only to experience a breakdown when an initial critical moment is encountered. At that point, a well-consolidated post-hypnotic suggestion may manifest itself as a reminder to engage in three cycles of breathing-directed HRD training with RSA components to automatically stave off SNS flooding that can accompany the recognition of pressure situations during competition and lead to decrements in attention and reduced motor-technical control. Thus, the goal of post-hypnotic suggestion is for an athlete to recognize subliminal/unconscious prompts to engage in performance-facilitative MT techniques, analogous to suddenly recognizing that one had better go back to the house before driving off without one's driving license. A post-hypnotic suggestion in a competitive situation serves as a subliminal alert to engage in, immediately, what an athlete was trained to do, without thinking about the MT process (which can have an opposite paradoxical effect and actually exacerbate a problem, like competitive anxiety or trouble maintaining focus).

Being able to unconsciously setoff a cascade of brain–heart–mind–body–motor responses to avert performance decrement is perhaps the most important component of the hypnotic process, a subliminal ability that is associated with high HS. Athletes who are low in this AP PHO measure, on the other hand, often must think about what they have to do pertaining to an MT method, and until it is well consolidated and starts to come naturally (if ever), they may experience the "thinking it" instead of "just doing it" paradox, a phenomenon that may explain lack of intervention efficacy or even performance regression that has been found to occur in conjunction with conscious efforts to use an MT technique.

4. After the hypnosis and self-hypnosis sessions, the player proceeded to the tennis court to engage in pre-match active-alert hypnosis. Active-alert is a hypnotic activation and priming technique. It is used to reinforce visual components of hypnosis and self-hypnosis that involve action and technical and tactical motions by doing what had been previously imagined. While similar to shadow actions, in which an athlete mimics sport-specific movements, active-alert hypnosis involves a more systematic approach to mental preparation in which a wide variety of technical motions are actively practiced, initially slowly and in the end culminating with complete tactical sequences involving numerous technical components that are carried out at a level of intensity comparable to that which needs to be exhibited during actual competition. Active-alert hypnosis, in addition to priming motor and technical action, should also intensify the hypnotic state that was induced in the prior hypnosis and self-hypnosis sessions, whereby an athlete becomes even more absorbed in sport-specific actions, tasks, and tactics to the point of obliviousness to their surroundings. The brain mechanisms associated with active-alert-enhanced hypnosis are hypothesized to involve the pre-action shifts in cerebral laterality and concomitant preaction HRD that is advanced by the Theory of Critical Moments and Athlete's Profile models of peak performance, as well as the Transient Hypofrontality Hypothesis that is introduced to this book in the section on brain-based mental training further on (THH; Carlstedt, 2004a, 2004b; Dietrich, 2003).

The photos in Figure 16.5 show the tennis player engaging in the last stage of active-alert hypnosis containing an optional culminating ball toss drill in which the player transitions from shadow strokes only (no ball), to tactical combinations of shots (with ball) that simulate styles of play and patterns that are expected to be encountered or carried out during the upcoming match.

5. Once the match began, the player's sport psychologist and coach observed whether the post-hypnotic suggestions that were administrated in the hypnosis session would result in the intended

FIGURE 16.5 Active-alert hypnosis.

performance-facilitative self-administered procedures both on the court during match play and during changeovers.

FIGURE 16.6 Going to bench (changeover).

The above screenshot (Figure 16.6) shows the player heading to the bench for a changeover. In Figure 16.7, consistent with one post-hypnotic suggestion, the player proceeded to engage in self-hypnosis combined with imagery-guided breathing-based HRD BF (note the elevated chest, indicative of an in-progress inhalation cycle; the heart rate R-R wave tracer shows a rising line that signifies increasing heart rate through this cycle).

FIGURE 16.7 Self-hypnosis with post-hypnotic suggestion prompted HRD-BF.

6. Upon returning to the court, the player (see below, returning serve; Figure 16.8) engages in the self-induced pre-action breathing-mediated HRD BF that he had just practiced on the bench in the context of the hypnotic state that he was in.

FIGURE 16.8 Self-hypnosis continuation throughout match.

7. The player who was high in HS, low in N/SR, and medium in RC/SC continued to carry out the prescribed and hypnosis-supported MT procedures throughout the match.

Documentation–Accountability–Intervention Efficiency and Efficacy

In terms of intervention efficiency and efficacy, rather than be redundant, readers are referred to the section on multi-modal MT, in which hypnosis-related efficiency and efficacy data were presented and analyzed.

An additional overview of hypnosis-based intervention efficiency and efficacy testing is provided herewith:

1. Intervention efficiency is determined by comparing a baseline 2-minute HRV scan and resulting ANS measures with a 2-minute HRV scan after a hypnosis and/or self-hypnosis session and resulting ANS measures. Any significant differences that emerge are hypothesized to reflect a hypnotic state.

2. Hypnotic depth is thought to be measurable incrementally from minimal to very strong (hypnotic depth) on the basis of pre-hypnosis baseline HRV, hypnosis-associated HRV, and post-hypnosis HRV comparisons, with greater changes in one or more ANS measure being suggestive of greater hypnotic depth. The following HRV reports emanate from the multi-modal case study of a professional tennis player (Figures 16.9 and 16.10).

The following ANS-HRV reports reveal numerous highly significant differences between the hypnosis condition and post-hypnosis HRV scan. It should be emphasized that the post-hypnosis (2nd) report (Figure 16.10) was obtained under the influence of a continuing state of hypnosis that was induced, measured (HRV was monitored), and reflected in the first report (Figure 16.9). In other words, the induced hypnotic state is thought to have influenced or even mediated ANS responses that were captured by the second report. Numerous frequency domain response differences between the hypnosis induction and post-induction hypnotic-continuation conditions stand out, including a fivefold increase in total ANS power or the aggregate amount to all SNS and PNS ANS activity (from about 1000 to about 5000 ms^2/Hz), as well as a 10-fold increase in L:H frequency activity from the induction/hypnosis to the post-hypnosis continuation condition, reflective of proportional changes in VL, L, and H frequency changes.

These findings are strongly suggestive of a high level of hypnotic depth, and point to the sensitivity of ANS activity as reflected in HRV as a possible biomarker of hypnotic depth (validation and reliability studies should be undertaken on the basis of promising data that has emerged from ABSP research labs and study groups).

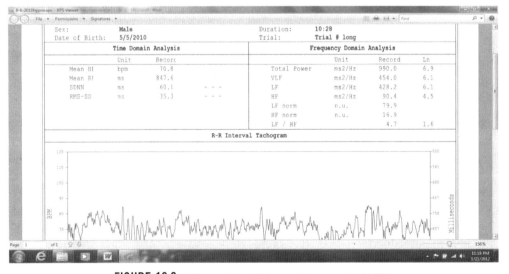

FIGURE 16.9   Pre-match self-hypnosis-generated HRV.

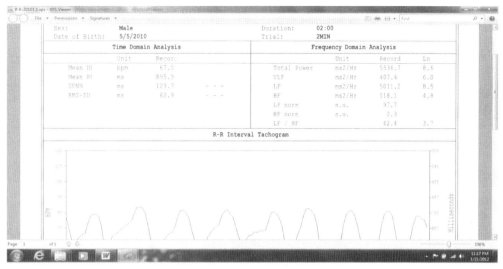

FIGURE 16.10   Two-minute post-self-hypnosis HRV scan to assess hypnotic depth and change.

Another potential clue and biomarker pertaining to hypnosis, hypnotic depth, and their influence on post-hypnosis continuation ANS-HRV measures (intervention efficiency) can be gleaned from the R-R interval cycles (as seen in the preceding tachograms). Note the chaotic ups and downs of these cycles during the hypnotic induction/hypnotic state transition condition and associated lower SDNN (about 60 msec). By contrast, in the post-hypnotic state continuation phase, the so-called RSA cycles can be observed. These are associated with higher SDNNs (here, about 120, compared to 60 msec) that are mediated by both protracted/extended inhale and exhale cycles at a rate of about six to eight breaths/minute, a breathing pace that is taught in clinical context to foster better self-regulation and general well-being. The preceding findings may have important implications for hypnosis-related intervention efficiency testing in both clinical and performance contexts.

It should be noted that the ABSP-CP approach to interventions uses HRV to test efficiency for all MT modalities and routinely assesses mental imagery/visualization ability, a correlate of HS/SA using HRV. The ABSP database happens to have the preceding tennis professional's visualization ability HRV reports. They will be reported on in the mental imagery/visualization intervention section (see Chapter 17).

Another way to assess or infer hypnotic depth and the impact of post-hypnotic suggestions is to simply chart the number or times an athlete who is under hypnosis can be observed engaging in a self-hypnosis/active-alert hypnosis-trained techniques that are reinforced by post-hypnotic suggestions. For example, if an athlete's hypnosis routine includes solution-oriented approaches to technical problems during competition, or prescribed ways to deal with critical moments along with post-hypnotic suggestion-based prompts, like "RESET" or "REGROUP" after a poorly played point or technical action, or the reminder "HRD" as part of a pre-action visually embedded post-hypnotic suggestion, and they can been seen engaging in these performance-corrective or facilitative procedures, then it can be assumed that subliminally planted post-hypnotic suggestions were indeed embedded.

Such could be quantified as follows: 30 performance-related incidents and/or situations calling for facilitative or corrective action, if then dealt with by an athlete as prescribed and reinforced by post-hypnotic suggestions 15 times would result in a PostHypnotic Suggestion Manifestation Rate (PHSMR) of 50% or .500, suggestive of weaker or fluctuating hypnotic depth and relatively poor consolidation of posthypnotic suggestions (individual norms would need to be established before one can qualitatively rate such a percentage).

Regarding intervention efficacy, in addition to the hypnosis-based multi-modal MT case study in which efficiency and efficacy findings were previously presented, the effectiveness of hypnosis can also be assessed as follows:

1. Pre-intervention macro-level and intervention (hypnosis) phase comparisons, for example, won versus loss record across conditions.
2. Same design using micro-level criticality measures as outcome variables.
3. A-B-A design, alternative, no intervention, and intervention across consecutive days in the context of macro- and micro-outcome measures.
4. Important: temporal experiments to determine depth of hypnosis (if any) as a function of the time it takes to become hypnotized and/or time engaged in active-alert hypnosis and quality of time-out self-hypnosis and effect on macro- and micro-outcome measures. Temporal parameters associated with hypnosis may vary widely as a function of level of HS.

Summary

Hypnotic procedures have much potential as a mental training intervention, provided that they are not applied indiscriminately. When contemplating their use, hypnotic susceptibility should first be assessed in athletes who are earmarked for these procedures.

Athletes who score high in HS or analogue measures, SA, or absorption are usually good candidates for self- and active-alert hypnosis. As always, although intervention efficiency may be easy to establish in athletes who are high in HS, mental training efficacy is another matter, and must be documented on the basis of extensive outcome testing.

17

Mental Imagery-Visualization Training

Mental imagery (MI) or visualization can be considered the go-to mental training (MT) method. It is used by the vast majority of sport psychology practitioners. The fascination with MI extends to researchers who have published hundreds of papers on this MT modality in the context of sport performance (see Imagery in Sports; Volume 2; *Coaching Science Abstracts*, 1997). The appeal of MI makes sense. Almost everyone can relate to imagination and the spontaneous generation of visual scenarios; visualizing is an omnipresent mental process. However, just as visualizing can be directed and controlled, images can also be random and disruptive. Consequently, one must question whether the status of MI as an intervention is justified and if the claims and promises regarding its efficacy that are made by its legions or proponents are valid.

The introduction to this section on interventions posed some crucial questions about MI efficiency and efficacy that readers should review. The notion that visualization is some sort of panacea and that it can be used by all athletes to enhance performance and that it will work is simplistic. Moreover, the mere presence of a multitude of investigations attesting to the efficacy of MI (for the most part group-based research) does not free practitioners from the obligation to test MI efficiency and efficacy at the individual level (each athlete individually in accord with ABSP-CP recommended methodologies).

Nevertheless, despite valid criticisms and concerns about MI, and especially the way it is often administered, visualization is integral to MT and is an important component of many interventions. Unfortunately, it can also be an uncontrolled extraneous variable, a nebulous state that cannot be seen, only inferred or believed to exist on the basis of an athlete's self-report. Consequently, it is difficult, if not impossible, to study in a more direct manner beyond just believing and actually knowing that script-guided or other means of inducing visualization really generates desired, performance facilitative images, and that their manifestation leads to successful performance. MI is rarely tested for efficiency and efficacy. For the most part, it is just assumed by practitioners, coaches, and athletes alike that MI works.

This mind-set must change. MI and visualization must be approached critically. Practitioners and athletes need to set aside beliefs about MI efficacy, especially dual-placebo-mediated notions (trait-based high HS/SA) that visualization works. The mere generation of images does not necessarily translate to enhanced performance. MI is a complex intervention procedure that should be systematically investigated, not only within formal research projects, but routinely as part of the consulting process.

Intervention Amenability: AP and Ideal Mental Training Modality

The ability to effectively engage in MI is strongly influenced by an athlete's level of HS/SA (see Figure 17.1). Athletes who are high in HS/SA are very amenable to visualization procedures, while athletes who are low in this measure and/or low in HS/SA and high in RC/SC not only have difficulty generating and sustaining internally manifested visual images, but are likely to not even try to, since they tend to have a developed skepticism and discount the need for MT in the first place. Since only about 15% to 30% of athletes are high in HS/SA, with another 15% being in the medium range, at best, only 45% of athletes (a very liberal estimate) are marginal candidates for this intervention method and only about 15% make excellent subjects (Carlstedt, 2001). Hence, practitioners should always screen for HS/SA and RC/SC to determine whether an athlete is likely to be amenable to MI. Athletes who are in the medium to high-medium range for HS/SA should augment MI with VBP. Video-based programming is well accepted across AP constellations and appears to help guide internal self-attempts to use MI or engage in well-structured sport-specific technical-motor approaches to visualization. In fact, MI may be most effective if used with a multi-modal intervention protocol, one that incorporates VBP. Note intervention amenability does not equate with intervention efficiency and efficacy.

As always, irrespective of an athlete's AP, criterion-referencing methodologies should be used to determine to what extent AP PHO measure predictions regarding MI amenability, compliance, efficiency, and efficacy extend to a practitioner's individual client, even if he or she is high in HS/SA.

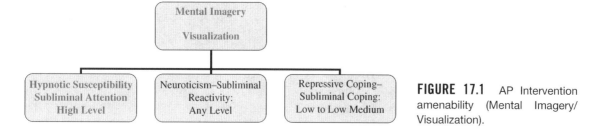

FIGURE 17.1 AP Intervention amenability (Mental Imagery/Visualization).

CONCEPTUAL-CONSTRUCT BASIS

There are numerous conceptual models that account for MI phenomena and its components. It is beyond the scope of this book to elaborate on them. Conceptually, MI is addressed in the context of the Theory of Critical Moments and AP models of peak performance construct bases and the brain–heart–mind–body–motor dynamics they advance in regard to intervention efficiency and efficacy. Original models and findings that touch on, overlap, or uniquely account for MI processes and outcome are as follows:

1. The ABSP-CP maintains that all interventions that are designed to enhance on-the-playing-field performance have an increased chance of succeeding if they take brain–heart–mind–body–motor processes that are associated with peak performance into account (this allows for higher evidentiary intervention efficiency and efficacy testing). These include brain hemispheric shifts associated with mental preparation (left frontal lobe-based), strategic and motor priming, and pre-action HRD and concomitant increases in right-hemisphere motor-cortex activation (see Chapters 2 and 9 for a review of these brain–heart processes). MI can conceivably facilitate these processes by preparing priming mechanisms associated with the initiation of pre-action

psychological preparation and eventual action. The ability of visualization to contribute to the manifestation of the peak performance responses is hypothesized to depend on how it is carried out. That is, (1) what scenarios are created for an athlete or are self-generated, (2) the temporal properties of an MI protocol, and (3) what systematic accountability methodologies that help establish time to achieve enduring biomarker-validated change and/or macro- and/or micro-performance outcome verifiable success metrics are used.

Due to the subjective nature of the visualization experience, one can at most infer that an athlete is actually experiencing a prescribed imagery scenario. Consequently, carefully formulated intervention efficiency and efficacy experimental paradigms should be integrated into the MI MT process (and all others as well).

An ABSP-CP-validated approach to the assessment of the MI process and intervention efficacy testing is presented further on. The MT efficiency and efficacy paradigm is psychophysiologically and ecologically based. HRV monitoring is central to discerning whether an athlete who engages in MI exhibits ANS responses that are conceptually consistent across baseline and visualization conditions. Visualization Responsivity Testing (VRT) using HRV as both a predictor and outcome measure is used to assess MI ability/intervention efficiency and to determine if ANS changes from baseline to the MI intervention condition prior to, during time-outs, and actual competition (between shots or points to other relevant sport-specific action) are associated with differential outcome and whether time-locked responses (using the Polar HRV monitoring system) can be isolated as a function of pre-action/task MI. If this latter function can be identified, conceptually one would predict, want, or expect that MI, as a priming intervention, would facilitate the consistent manifestation of pre-action HRD and its brain response precursor (relative left-to-right-hemispheric shift).

Although the more direct and mechanistic approach to setting off the desired cascade of brain–heart response is, the better, especially volitional, or entrained subliminal paced-timed breathing; mind-based manipulation interventions such as self-hypnosis and visualization may benefit athletes who are high in HS/SA and high in N/SR by activating visual pathways associated with the priming of technical-motor responses and in the process shut down temporal lobe-amygdala pathways associated with the generation of memory-experience-based negative intrusive thoughts in a manner that has been shown to occur neurophysiologically in individuals who are high in RC/SC (Tomarken & Davidson, 1994). Thus, conceptually, MI may have the potential to mediate RC/SC-like responses even more in vulnerable athletes (AP of H-H-L).

Integrative performance-facilitative brain–heart–mind–body processes may also involve the frontal brain lobes as proposed by the Transient Hypofrontality Hypothesis (Dietrich, 2003) that is discussed in Brain-Based Manipulation interventions (see further on). MI may have the potential to facilitate cortical responses that have been anecdotally associated with "just do it–don't think it," notions (e.g., THH model of aerobic thresholds, neuro-metabolic demands, and runner's high; Dietrich, 2003). The ABSP-CP proposes that specific brain-based manipulation interventions are capable of mediating frontal lobe metabolic changes that are associated with the proverbial, quiet-mind, or zone/flow states. MI has a place in the Carlstedt Frontal Lobe (CP-CFL) protocol, an adaptation of the THH that was conceptualized to explain reductions in frontal-lobe activation as a function of long and strenuous exercise. The CP-CFL proposes that macro-based (long duration and aerobic-mediated reductions in pre- and frontal lobe activation) brain dynamics can be volitionally induced in the moment (micro-level even very short duration sport-specific pre- and action epochs) to shut down intrusive cognitions that may potentially disrupt motor performance.

Again, HRV monitoring is central to MI efficiency and efficacy testing, since ANS responses are very sensitive to salient, emotionally charged visual images. As such, since HRV can be monitored during competition, it may emerge as a potent MI outcome measure and even supplant EEG as the ideal reflector of the visualization process in real-time ecological contexts (see case studies further on).

Description of Procedure

1. Athlete is initially tested for Visualization Responsivity (VR) using the Carlstedt Protocol Visualization Responsivity Test-Athlete Version (CPVR-A). This test of MI ability requires an athlete to imagine three sport-action, technical, intensity, or motivation visualization scenarios as prescribed. The test is administered daily prior to training during the pre-intervention phase of the consulting process (as a reminder, mental game programs and consulting should always include a pre-intervention and intervention phase; the pre-intervention phase is critical to eventually establishing intervention efficiency and efficacy).

   The following four consecutive ANS-HRV reports (Figures 17.2 through 17.5) emanate from a professional tennis player who was high in HS/SA. The first report is the baseline condition, followed by positive–negative and relaxation visualization scenario-based HRV responses.

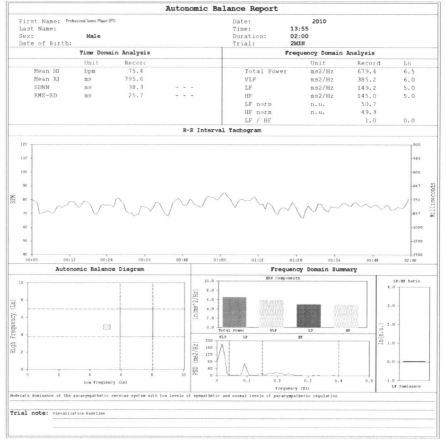

FIGURE 17.2   Visualization and HRV baseline condition.

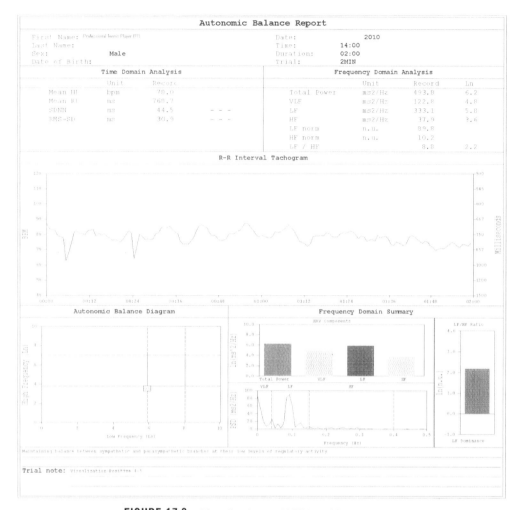

FIGURE 17.3 Visualization and HRV positive condition.

The methodology relating to this assessment procedure is discussed further on. Note the L/H frequency ratio changes as reflected in the bar graph on the lower right side of each report.

Since pre-intervention phases should last as long as it takes to acquire about 60 repeated predictor and outcome measures, the CPVR-A should be administered each day of the pre-intervention phase. If procuring 60 repeated measures takes 14 days, then there should be 14 visualization tests. HRV should be monitored concurrent to each CPVR-A test segment.

The CPVR consists of a 2-minute baseline HRV scan/reading. It is immediately followed (counterbalanced across multiple test occasions) by a 2-minute positive visualization segment in which the athlete is told to internally self-generate a prescribed positive scenario (e.g., seeing oneself engaged in successful sport-specific actions), followed by a 2-minute negative scenario (e.g., seeing oneself fail or falter in a sport-specific scenario) and culminating with a relaxation scenario (e.g., seeing oneself lying on a beach; nonsport-specific scenario). In the baseline condition, that athlete is told to just sit there and let thoughts occur as they may, just go with the flow and don't try to manipulate thoughts.

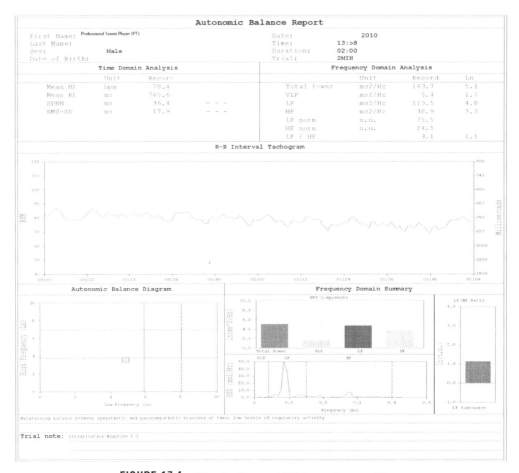

FIGURE 17.4   Visualization and HRV negative condition.

Note: Athletes must engage in visualization testing with their eyes open, under the assumption that guided or prescribed visualization should be challenging and tested in the presence of potential visual and auditory distractions.

Conceptually, it is hypothesized that select HRV measures will change as a function of visualization scenario conditions in a manner that would be predicted on the basis of an athlete's AP and/or expected changes in ANS responding, in the context of differentially emotionally charged visual input and processing. For example, one would expect negative visualization to generate greater levels of SNS-related HRV measures, such as VLF, than the relaxation scenario (significantly less SNS VLF activity, especially in athletes who are high in SR/N).

2. After visualization testing has established an athlete's MI efficiency and it is determined that he or she is amenable to visualization as an MT method, and are highly likely to comply with a prescribed MI program, an attempt is made to establish intervention efficacy. This is done after an extensive MT period (after the pre-intervention phase, before efficacy testing in the context of training experiments and actual competition), in which temporal parameters and time to achieve enduring biomarker-based visualization-facilitated mind–body changes and performance gains are delineated and documented.

Two case studies involving CPVR-A are presented next.

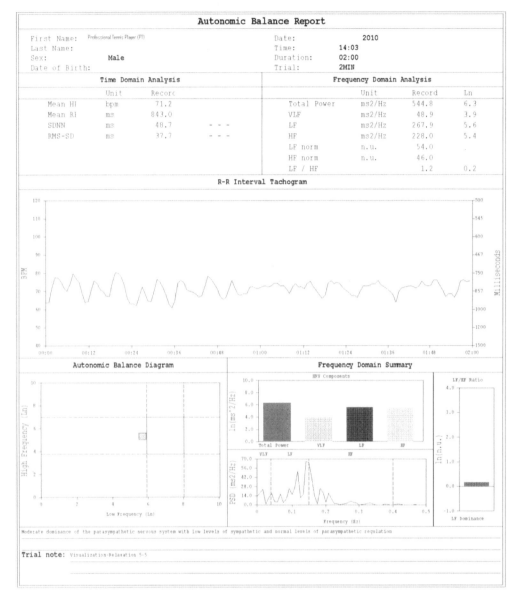

FIGURE 17.5   Visualization and HRV relaxation condition.

The following screenshot (Figure 17.6) depicts a tennis player engaging in pre-training technically-based MI.

Note: After visualization testing, athletes are free to close their eyes when visualizing.

A challenge associated with MI is accurately determining temporal time lines associated with the visualization process. How long should one engage in MI before it will have an effect? This is an empirical question that needs to be addressed. Initially, an athlete's self-report can be used to help guide the process. Too much visualization can lead to boredom and inattention and the inducement of an ANS-PNS state that may not be conducive to readiness to compete. On the other hand, too little time spent on visualizing prescribed scenarios may hinder the consolidation process and prevent an athlete from reaching requisite sport-specific imagery-mediated

FIGURE 17.6   Pre-match visualization.

mental-control thresholds that are necessary to facilitate performance. In the early stages of MI training, more is probably better. In fact, athletes should be encouraged to attempt to maintain image and thought control for as long as possible. Afterward, they should be debriefed and provide feedback on a 1–5 scale (from least to most) on imagery vividness, intensity, and sustainability. Since self-report can be biased and influenced by response sets, HRV (which should always be monitored for entire MI sessions) can be used to assess visualization-influenced changes in ANS responses across baseline, and imagery conditions and their degradation or enhancement as a function of time. For example, if it is determined that a guided (script-based) technical-tactical scenario that an athlete claims he or she can generate elicits a strong SNS response up to 10 min into the MI process, but then drops into the PNS realm, indicative of possible boredom, habituation and loss of image (mental) control, then 10 min may be the initial and possible upper threshold for such a scenario. Moreover, if ANS-HRV responses that are associated with an MI training epoch are then found to impact sport-specific outcome (either positively or negatively), the established MI scenario-specific threshold will have established intervention efficacy (variance explained in a sport-specific outcome measure that can be attributed to visualization scenario-influenced/mediated HRV).

However, it must be cautioned that intervention efficacy, both in experimental and competitive contexts, takes time to establish (requiring about 60 measurement occasions, that is, the preceding 10-minute epoch would have to be tested 60 times to attain sufficient statistical power). As such, establishing reliable temporal time-of-engagement time lines or epochs of MI or any intervention can be a long and even tedious process. Nevertheless, gold standard intervention efficiency and efficacy testing demands extensive experimentation to establish valid and reliable temporal thresholds. This methodological tenet points to the need to always divide the performance enhancement consulting process into a pre-intervention assessment period, followed by an intervention training and validation phase and a culminating intervention efficacy testing phase that encompasses real or official competition and, as necessary, follow-up testing, intervention revision or tweaking, and continued MT with accountability methodologies in place.

3. After an initial technical-tactical MI session (depicted earlier), an athlete should engage in active-alert visualization, a variant of active-alert hypnosis. Similarly, as with active-alert

hypnosis, progressive shadow stroke (in tennis), or other sport-specific technical routines should be carried out for imagery quality control purposes. For example, the shown tennis player who just engaged in technical-tactical visualization, to demonstrate (to her coach) technical knowledge and competence performs specific shadow strokes or tactical patterns (in this case, serve-related). This particular player, who was prescribed a serve-based technical-tactical scenario, in order to convince her coach that she could really internally visualize a "perfect" motion (even though she had technical glitches with her serve) attempted to do so in the post-MI active-alert phase.

It is critical that athletes do not visually (via MI or even VBP) reinforce faulty technique and tactical patterns by seeing or visualizing sport-specific technical patterns and components that are counterproductive to improvement. Having a coach rate on a 1–5 scale the extent to which an athlete can demonstrate a perfect role-model technique or tactical patterns after a visualization session, even if they have yet to master optimum technical-tactical responses when playing, at least conveys to a coach that he or she understands and can imagine and initially replicate excellent technical form after a visualization session. Thereafter, in the context of a multimodal intervention approach, visualization-facilitated technical correction and improvement attempts can be reinforced using video-based programming and behavior-technical-tactical methods in an attempt to enhance performance (Figure 17.7).

One might ask, "how is visualization different from hypnosis?" Since hypnotic susceptibility can be considered to be a psychophysiological trait that is associated with a neurophysiological signature that is distinct (diametrically different in individuals who are high in HS compared to people who are low in HS), hypnosis can be thought of as a method for entering vastly enhanced states of attention and visual retention of imaged and/or video or auditory-prompted performance-facilitating scenarios that cannot be readily accessed (if at all) by individuals who are low in HS. Thus, visualization can be thought of as hypnosis "light," an MT technique that can be engaged in by most people and athletes, on some level (thresholds must be determined on an individual basis) that, however, does not lead to externally and within-subject perceptible alteration of one's mental state. Visualization can be used to induce hypnotic states in susceptible individuals, whereas, people who are low in HS, assuming that they can effectively engage in MI will rarely, if ever, reach the hypnotic threshold that is biomarker verifiable. Remember though, hypnosis-induced

FIGURE 17.7   Reinforcement of technical visualization.

altered states may or may not help an athlete perform better. The same can be said of MI, their efficacy must be established at the individual level. Their application is also predicated on an athlete's AP constellation of PHO factors, especially level of HS/SA and RC/SC.

Documentation–Accountability–Intervention Efficiency and Efficacy

Two case studies pertaining to MI intervention efficiency are presented and discussed, followed by an MI intervention efficacy case study in the context of actual competition using a repeated A-B-A design.

Intervention Efficiency: Case Studies

Subject I: Female College Rugby Player
Subject II: Female former High School Softball Player

CASE STUDY I (FIGURE 17.8)

A female college rugby player with an AP of H-L-H underwent VRT using the CPVR protocol for a period of nine consecutive days. The procedures were the same as described above. A 2-minute baseline was followed by three measurement conditions (visualization scenarios; 2 minutes, positive, negative, and relaxation; counterbalanced across daily administrations). HRV was monitored for comparison purposes (within and between subjects). It was hypothesized that athletes who are high in HS will generate significantly more and greater magnitude HRV responses than athletes who are medium to low in HS; especially as they pertain to most conceptually appropriate responses (ANS, SNS vs. PNS responses as a function of MI scenario). (Figures 17.9 and 17.10)

Findings: 15 general statistically significant differences in the same HRV measure as a function of baseline and/or MI condition were found. In terms of greatest conceptual consistency (the extent to which HRV changes are consistent with expected ANS-HRV responses as a function of MI-emotionally charged condition [e.g., positive versus negative scenario]), the following findings are strong:

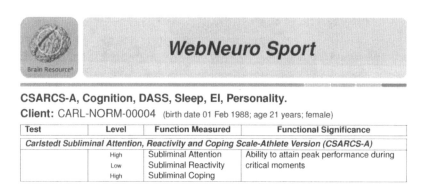

CSARCS-A, Cognition, DASS, Sleep, EI, Personality.
Client: CARL-NORM-00004 (birth date 01 Feb 1988; age 21 years; female)

Test	Level	Function Measured	Functional Significance
Carlstedt Subliminal Attention, Reactivity and Coping Scale-Athlete Version (CSARCS-A)			
	High	Subliminal Attention	Ability to attain peak performance during
	Low	Subliminal Reactivity	critical moments
	High	Subliminal Coping	

FIGURE 17.8 Case study Athlete's Profile.

Descriptive Statistics

	N	Minimum	Maximum	Mean	Std. Deviation
HR	12	55.00	71.00	62.6667	5.9442
HRVP	11	59.00	72.00	65.0909	4.2061
HRVN	12	60.00	72.00	66.6667	3.9619
HRR	12	53.00	69.00	62.5000	5.7918
SDNN	12	57.00	108.00	73.8333	15.7817
SDNNVP	11	56.00	92.00	73.8182	12.7814
SDNNVN	12	47.00	82.00	61.2500	12.5924
SDNNR	12	47.00	109.00	75.5000	21.2624
VL	12	103.00	812.00	526.1667	214.4307
VLVP	11	155.00	1329.00	728.8182	402.8553
VLVN	12	55.00	673.00	374.9167	220.0233
VLR	12	73.00	993.00	524.1667	271.9679
L	12	141.00	796.00	436.5000	241.5305
LVP	11	117.00	538.00	248.0000	143.7553
LVN	12	69.00	1134.00	401.3333	374.7007
LR	12	84.00	889.00	319.3333	268.4502
H	12	262.00	923.00	471.0000	182.4136
HVP	11	98.00	430.00	161.6364	96.0492
HVN	12	49.00	222.00	111.0000	56.5814
HRELAX	12	137.00	1391.00	411.8333	346.3474
LH	12	.20	2.20	1.0250	.6552
LHVP	11	.40	4.10	1.7909	1.2934
LHVN	12	.20	6.30	3.1583	1.8928
LHR	12	.20	1.60	.7333	.4830
Valid N (listwise)	11				

FIGURE 17.9 Descriptive statistics HRV and visualization condition.

1. HRV Measure: heart rate (HR = baseline): baseline HR differed significantly from HRVN (heart rate in the negative visualization condition), $p = .024$; approached significance in the HRVP (positive visualization condition), .077, but remain unchanged in the relaxation condition (HRVR), $p = .905$. Since the athlete's baseline HR was in the low 60s, it could be expected that a negatively charged MI scenario would result in greater HR. By contrast, a positive and relaxation scenario would not be expected to significantly raise an already low HR. The HR-HRVP finding also suggests that the positive scenario probably lacked motivational and action scenes that could have increased ANS-SNS activity and concomitant greater HR.

   Relative to HR in the negative versus positive MI condition, statistical significance was approached (.072, but zero was crossed in the confidence interval, rendering this finding tenuous; that could change, however, with a greater sample size [measurement occasions]). HRVP versus HRVR revealed no differences, a conceptually consistent finding, whereas, HRVN versus HRVR revealed significant differences, which is also a conceptually consistent finding ($p = .022$).

   Conceptual Consistency Score: Domain HR = 5 out of 6, or .83 (83%)

2. HRV Measure: SDNN (the HRV Index): baseline SDNN was significantly greater than in the SDNNVN condition (.039), a conceptually consistent finding, but did not differ compared to the SDNNVP and SDNNVR conditions, additional conceptually consistent findings. Moreover, SDNNVP was significantly greater compared to SDNNVN. By contrast, SDNNVN was less than

Paired Samples Test

		Paired Differences							
					95% Confidence Interval of the Difference				
		Mean	Std. Deviation	Std. Error Mean	Lower	Upper	t	df	Sig. (2-tailed)
Pair 1	HR - HRVP	-1.7273	2.9014	.8748	-3.6765	.2219	-1.974	10	.077
Pair 2	HR - HRVN	-4.0000	5.2915	1.5275	-7.3621	-.6379	-2.619	11	.024
Pair 3	HR - HRR	.1667	4.7450	1.3698	-2.8482	3.1815	.122	11	.905
Pair 4	HRVP - HRVN	-1.3636	2.2482	.6779	-2.8740	.1467	-2.012	10	.072
Pair 5	HRVP - HRR	1.7273	4.1010	1.2365	-1.0278	4.4824	1.397	10	.193
Pair 6	HRVN - HRR	4.1667	5.3908	1.5562	.7415	7.5918	2.677	11	.022
Pair 7	SDNN - SDNNVP	-1.1818	17.3079	5.2185	-12.8094	10.4458	-.226	10	.825
Pair 8	SDNN - SDNNVN	12.5833	18.5740	5.3618	.7820	24.3847	2.347	11	.039
Pair 9	SDNN - SDNNR	-1.6667	18.6076	5.3715	-13.4894	10.1560	-.310	11	.762
Pair 10	SDNNVP - SDNNVN	11.6364	12.3957	3.7375	3.3088	19.9639	3.113	10	.011
Pair 11	SDNNVP - SDNNR	-1.8182	23.3659	7.0451	-17.5156	13.8792	-.258	10	.802
Pair 12	SDNNVN - SDNNR	-14.2500	16.8530	4.8650	-24.9579	-3.5421	-2.929	11	.014
Pair 13	VL - VLVP	-221.9091	454.3528	136.9925	-527.1475	83.3293	-1.620	10	.136
Pair 14	VL - VLVN	151.2500	217.9646	62.9210	12.7619	289.7381	2.404	11	.035
Pair 15	VL - VLR	2.0000	322.7380	93.1664	-203.0579	207.0579	.021	11	.983
Pair 16	VLVP - VLVN	381.0000	429.5519	129.5148	92.4231	669.5769	2.942	10	.015
Pair 17	VLVP - VLR	188.2727	505.7719	152.4960	-151.5095	528.0549	1.235	10	.245
Pair 18	VLVN - VLR	-149.2500	274.4429	79.2249	-323.6227	25.1227	-1.884	11	.086
Pair 19	L - LVP	162.2727	242.3997	73.0863	-.5736	325.1191	2.220	10	.051
Pair 20	L - LVN	35.1667	408.1245	117.8154	-224.1433	294.4766	.298	11	.771
Pair 21	L - LR	117.1667	332.4490	95.9698	-94.0613	328.3947	1.221	11	.248
Pair 22	LVP - LVN	-172.1818	422.9898	127.5362	-456.3502	111.9866	-1.350	10	.207
Pair 23	LVP - LR	-51.0909	272.2379	82.0828	-233.9828	131.8010	-.622	10	.548
Pair 24	LVN - LR	82.0000	519.7781	150.0470	-248.2512	412.2512	.546	11	.596
Pair 25	H - HVP	298.9091	109.0206	32.8709	225.6681	372.1501	9.093	10	.000
Pair 26	H - HVN	360.0000	218.2925	63.0156	221.3035	498.6965	5.713	11	.000
Pair 27	H - HRELAX	59.1667	335.0888	96.7318	-153.7386	272.0719	.612	11	.553
Pair 28	HVP - HVN	45.0000	127.5657	38.4625	-40.6998	130.6998	1.170	10	.269
Pair 29	HVP - HRELAX	-229.5455	359.5242	108.4006	-471.0771	11.9862	-2.118	10	.060
Pair 30	HVN - HRELAX	-300.8333	376.5151	108.6905	-540.0596	-61.6071	-2.768	11	.018
Pair 31	LH - LHVP	-.7818	1.1771	.3549	-1.5726	8.989E-03	-2.203	10	.052
Pair 32	LH - LHVN	-2.1333	1.5663	.4522	-3.1285	-1.1381	-4.718	11	.001
Pair 33	LH - LHR	.2917	.7879	.2275	-.2090	.7923	1.282	11	.226
Pair 34	LHVP - LHVN	-1.2909	2.0912	.6305	-2.6958	.1139	-2.047	10	.068
Pair 35	LHVP - LHR	1.0636	1.1351	.3423	.3010	1.8262	3.108	10	.011
Pair 36	LHVN - LHR	2.4250	2.1558	.6223	1.0553	3.7947	3.897	11	.002

FIGURE 17.10 Paired *T*-test and visualization scenario.

in the SDNNVR condition. These are all conceptually consistent findings that point to the sensitivity of SDNN as a reflective biomarker of visualization-induced changes as a function of emotional valance or scenario-activating impact.

Conceptual Consistency Score: Domain SDNN = 6 out of 6, or 1.000 (100%)

3. HRV Measure: VLF (ANS-SNS marker): baseline VLF did not differ from VLVP activity but did differ from VLVN activity ($p = .038$). In addition, VLVP activity was significantly different from that exhibited during VLVN ($p = .015$). There were no significant differences between VLVP and VLVR and VLVN and VLVR conditions. These were the only conceptually consistent findings for the VLF domain. It should be noted, though, that a VLF SNS response can be generated in both positive and negative visualization scenarios. However, one would have expected a rebound in the relaxation situation in which, especially compared to the negative condition,

less VLF would be generated (there was less VLF in the relaxation condition compared to the positive condition, suggesting that the positive MI condition contained excitatory images).

Conceptual Consistency Score: Domain VLF = 2 out of 6, or .333 (33%)

4. HRV Measure: Low frequency (HRV frequency domain measure of ANS-balance): baseline LF was almost (.051) significantly different from the LFVP condition but not the LFVN and LFVR conditions. It also did not significantly change in the LFVP compared to LFVN and across all LF relaxation scenario conditions.

   Since LF HRV contains a mixture of SNS and PNS activity, as such it may not be as sensitive to central nervous system–generated visual input. However, since there were mean differences across all LF conditions, were they to hold up in a larger sample size, these changes may reach statistical significance. Since LF appears to be a more ambiguous HRV measure in the context of MI, it is not rated in terms of conceptual consistency.

   Conceptual Consistency Score: Domain LF: NOT COUNTED

5. HRV Measure: High frequency (HRV-ANS marker of PNS activation; associated with exhale cycle of breathing-based HRD MT and HRD-BF MT): baseline HF was significantly different compared to both the HFVP and HFVN conditions ($p = .000$) but not in the HFVP versus HFVN condition. However, both HFVP and HFVN activity differed significantly from HFVR.

   Although four of six comparison conditions were significantly different, the HFVP and HFVP and relaxation differentials could be considered conceptually inconsistent in that the relaxation condition was associated with less HF activity, a PNS response that one would expect to increase as a function of a relaxation-based MI scenario. However, this points to the nebulous nature of MI, since it is possible that the subject's visualization scenario was such that it was not "relaxing" enough to generate levels of HF activity to exceed the level of HF activity associated with the positive and negative conditions. In fact, baseline HF activity exceeded HF in all other visualization conditions. This latter finding supports the hypothesis that MI will be associated with changes in HRV across numerous conditions of varying degrees of conceptual potency (most meaningful changes relative to expected relationships between an HRV and MI mediating emotionally charged visualization scenarios).

   Conceptual Consistency Score: Domain HF = 4 out of 6, or .667 (67%)

6. HRV Measure: Low:High frequency ratio (L:H ratio is another HRV marker of ANS balance-SNS/PNS balance and is also associated with HRD inhale–exhale cycles): baseline LHF was significantly different from the LHVP and LFVN conditions ($p = .052$ and .001, respectively). LHVP versus LHVN revealed no significant differences, but both LHVP and LHVN activity differed from LH activity in the relaxation condition.

   These findings are highly conceptually consistent with what one would expect the LH frequency ratio to reflect, and are supportive of the MI-HRV change hypothesis. LH ratio increased from the baseline condition in the positive and negative scenarios (the highest level was in the negative scenario to 3.17, or about 3 times as much low-high than high frequency activity, suggesting that a negative scenario was the most activating: least ANS balance, as would be predicted). The LH ratio was also consistent with what a relaxation scenario should do, namely, lessen SNS and increase PNS activity (the relaxation response), dropping from a high of 3.17 (negative SNS/SNS-PNS ANS-HRV mixture) to .73, a relatively predominant PNS response.

   Conceptual Consistency Score: Domain L:H = 5 out of 6, or .833 (83%)

Intervention Efficiency Summary

Statistically Significant Changes in MI Associated HRV = 15 out of 36 (.422; 42%)
Conceptual Consistency Score (CCS) = 22 out of 30 (.733; 73%)
Aggregate Intervention Efficiency Quotient (IEQ-A) = 37 out of 66 (.560; 56%)

Conclusion: This player's IEQ-A of .560 (56%) is moderately high, but importantly, his CC score reflects strong congruence between predictor measures (visualization scenario) and mind–body outcome measures (HRV-ANS responses), and provides suggestive, supportive evidence in support of the ABSP-CP, MI-HRV Hypothesis, and AP model intervention amenability predictions. This athlete, who possessed one of the two Ideal AP and its intervention mediating trait, high HS/SA, exhibited highly conceptually consistent ANS responses, as would be expected (73% of the time).

Intervention amenability as predicted by an athlete's AP is expected to also predict intervention efficiency. For comparison purposes, a second intervention efficiency case study in abbreviated form is presented below. This former softball player has an AP of M-M-M. An intervention efficacy summary will be calculated, but it will be left up to the reader to do an in-depth analysis of this case study and compare it to the preceding one. Since this is a practitioner-researcher and student's manual, readers, especially those in the American Board of Sport Psychology certification and training programs, are encouraged to test their knowledge of the ABSP-CP and allied procedures and methodologies that are central to higher evidentiary applied sport psychology. Readers who complete this exercise should submit their analyses to rcarlstedt@americanboardofsportpsychology.org for evaluation. Submitted work count toward the enrolled student's practicum. Future enrollees will also be credited for this work (Figures 17.11–17.13).

CASE STUDY II

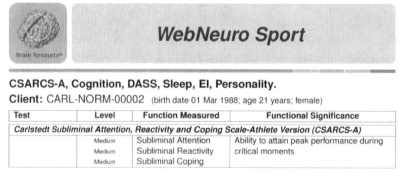

FIGURE 17.11   Case study II Athlete's Profile.

Intervention Efficiency Summary (Athlete II; AP = M-M-M)

Statistically Significant Changes in MI Associated HRV = 5 out of 36 (.138; 14%)
Conceptual Consistency Score (CCS) =1 out of 30 (**.033; 03%**)

Descriptive Statistics

	N	Minimum	Maximum	Mean	Std. Deviation
HR	7	71.00	78.00	75.2857	2.4976
HRVP	6	71.00	79.00	74.6667	2.5820
HRVN	7	71.00	80.00	75.2857	3.1472
HRR	7	72.00	80.00	74.7143	2.6904
SDNN	7	27.00	58.00	38.2857	12.2572
SDNNVP	6	23.00	40.00	32.0000	6.1644
SDNNVN	7	23.00	36.00	30.0000	5.4772
SDNNR	7	22.00	41.00	32.5714	7.9970
VL	7	20.00	558.00	173.2857	181.9365
VLVP	6	17.00	132.00	83.5000	48.9030
VLVN	7	13.00	150.00	61.0000	48.4218
VLR	7	12.00	345.00	114.7143	121.7699
L	7	31.00	116.00	55.7143	27.9506
LVP	6	37.00	61.00	54.1667	9.7040
LVN	7	37.00	195.00	103.5714	53.2098
LR	7	24.00	235.00	78.1429	71.9616
H	7	16.00	126.00	81.5714	42.4612
HVP	6	45.00	82.00	66.3333	16.5005
HVN	7	19.00	100.00	58.8571	29.4360
HRELAX	7	53.00	284.00	134.8571	77.2041
LH	7	.40	2.70	.9571	.7997
LHVP	6	.60	1.20	.8333	.2066
LHVN	7	1.20	3.50	1.9429	.9947
LHR	7	.40	.80	.5429	.1397
Valid N (listwise)	6				

FIGURE 17.12   Descriptive statistics HRV and visualization condition.

> *Practitioner-Researcher-Student Challenge: Use the above (Figure 17.12) descriptive statistics to determine if directional changes in HRV values as a function of visualization scenario are consistent with what would be expected.*

Aggregate Intervention Efficiency Quotient (IEQ-A) =6 out of 66 (**.090; 9%**)

Intervention Efficiency Summary (Athlete I; AP=H-L-H)

Statistically Significant Changes in MI Associated HRV = 15 out of 36 (.422; 42%)

Conceptual Consistency Score (CCS) = 22 out of 30 (**.733; 73%**)

Aggregate Intervention Efficiency Quotient (IEQ-A) = 37 out of 66 (**.560; 56%**)

Summary and Additional Practitioner-Researcher-Student Challenge Questions

The preceding differences are stark. They highlight response differences that are hypothesized to be differentially mediated by AP mind–body response tendencies that have been explicated throughout this book. As would be expected, an athlete who is high in HS/SA should demonstrate greater intervention efficiency than an athlete who is lower in this measure. Intervention efficiency is expected to degrade linearly as a function of a linear reduction in HS/SA score. Athlete I had a raw score of 34

Paired Samples Test

		Paired Differences							
					95% Confidence Interval of the Difference				
		Mean	Std. Deviation	Std. Error Mean	Lower	Upper	t	df	Sig. (2-tailed)
Pair 1	HR – HRVP	.1667	2.5626	1.0462	-2.5226	2.8559	.159	5	.880
Pair 2	HR – HRVN	.0000	1.5275	.5774	-1.4127	1.4127	.000	6	1.000
Pair 3	HR – HRR	.5714	1.7182	.6494	-1.0177	2.1605	.880	6	.413
Pair 4	HRVP – HRVN	.1667	2.4833	1.0138	-2.4394	2.7727	.164	5	.876
Pair 5	HRVP – HRR	.8333	1.9408	.7923	-1.2034	2.8701	1.052	5	.341
Pair 6	HRVN – HRR	.5714	1.2724	.4809	-.6054	1.7482	1.188	6	.280
Pair 7	SDNN – SDNNVP	6.5000	15.8335	6.4640	-10.1162	23.1162	1.006	5	.361
Pair 8	SDNN – SDNNVN	8.2857	12.0238	4.5446	-2.8344	19.4059	1.823	6	.118
Pair 9	SDNN – SDNNR	5.7143	15.2065	5.7475	-8.3494	19.7780	.994	6	.359
Pair 10	SDNNVP – SDNNVN	3.0000	8.7178	3.5590	-6.1488	12.1488	.843	5	.438
Pair 11	SDNNVP – SDNNR	.3333	7.5277	3.0732	-7.5665	8.2332	.108	5	.918
Pair 12	SDNNVN – SDNNR	-2.5714	7.1614	2.7068	-9.1946	4.0518	-.950	6	.379
Pair 13	VL – VLVP	115.3333	176.5941	72.0942	-69.9908	300.6574	1.600	5	.171
Pair 14	VL – VLVN	112.2857	201.5612	76.1830	-74.1273	298.6987	1.474	6	.191
Pair 15	VL – VLR	58.5714	118.7474	44.8823	-51.2516	168.3945	1.305	6	.240
Pair 16	VLVP – VLVN	37.3333	69.0295	28.1812	-35.1086	109.7753	1.325	5	.243
Pair 17	VLVP – VLR	-29.3333	105.8559	43.2155	-140.4223	81.7556	-.679	5	.527
Pair 18	VLVN – VLR	-53.7143	136.1772	51.4702	-179.6572	72.2286	-1.044	6	.337
Pair 19	L – LVP	-8.5000	16.1462	6.5917	-25.4444	8.4444	-1.290	5	.254
Pair 20	L – LVN	-47.8571	35.1066	13.2691	-80.3254	-15.3889	-3.607	6	.011
Pair 21	L – LR	-22.4286	76.0895	28.7591	-92.7997	47.9425	-.780	6	.465
Pair 22	LVP – LVN	-34.1667	40.9068	16.7001	-77.0957	8.7624	-2.046	5	.096
Pair 23	LVP – LR	-26.5000	74.3418	30.3499	-104.5169	51.5169	-.873	5	.423
Pair 24	LVN – LR	25.4286	84.6086	31.9791	-52.8214	103.6785	.795	6	.457
Pair 25	H – HVP	9.3333	34.1682	13.9491	-26.5240	45.1907	.669	5	.533
Pair 26	H – HVN	22.7143	59.8880	22.6355	-32.6729	78.1014	1.003	6	.354
Pair 27	H – HRELAX	-53.2857	82.3887	31.1400	-129.4826	22.9112	-1.711	6	.138
Pair 28	HVP – HVN	6.8333	43.4576	17.7415	-38.7727	52.4393	.385	5	.716
Pair 29	HVP – HRELAX	-63.1667	75.5445	30.8409	-142.4457	16.1124	-2.048	5	.096
Pair 30	HVN – HRELAX	-76.0000	75.5579	28.5582	-145.8794	-6.1206	-2.661	6	.037
Pair 31	LH – LHVP	.1167	.8353	.3410	-.7599	.9932	.342	5	.746
Pair 32	LH – LHVN	-.9857	1.4218	.5374	-2.3006	.3292	-1.834	6	.116
Pair 33	LH – LHR	.4143	.7988	.3019	-.3245	1.1531	1.372	6	.219
Pair 34	LHVP – LHVN	-.8500	.8191	.3344	-1.7096	9.641E-03	-2.542	5	.052
Pair 35	LHVP – LHR	.2667	.2582	.1054	-4.30E-03	.5376	2.530	5	.053
Pair 36	LHVN – LHR	1.4000	1.1030	.4169	.3799	2.4201	3.358	6	.015

FIGURE 17.13   Paired *T*-tests and visualization scenario.

> *Practitioner-Researcher-Student Challenge:* Use the above paired T-test table (Figure 17.13) to evaluate conceptual consistency relative to this athlete and her Athlete's Profile.

(34 out of 36 for HS/SA), one of the highest scores on record, whereas Athlete II had a score of 18. These contrasting levels of HS/SA were associated with conceptually consistent intervention efficiency within this MI-HRV test paradigm.

Intervention Efficacy: MI and Performance Outcome: A Case Study

Although intervention efficiency should be established to better guide the MT process, especially when indirect approaches such as MI and hypnotic procedures are used, a high AIEQ does not guarantee strong intervention efficacy. As such, athletes need to undergo intervention efficacy testing in the context of pre-intervention-intervention training and intervention phases to determine to what extent actual performance outcome and associated psychophysiological predictor and outcome measures (usually HRV/HRD measures) are influenced or even mediated by an intervention or multiple MT methods (multi-modal). This CP-tenet should be very clear by now.

The following case study includes pre-during and post-sport-specific outcome measures from the initial MI phase of a multi-modal intervention protocol that was applied to a former tennis player who still competes on a high level.

PROCEDURES

1. Pre-intervention phase: MT modality #1: MI.
2. A series of matches were played.
3. A pre- and post-2-minute match HRV scan was administered.
4. At each changeover, the player was seated and scanned for 1 minute (HRV scan)
5. The pre-intervention phase (modality #1; MI) was terminated after about 35 HRV scans were obtained (10 game pro set matches).
6. MI intervention training commenced after the pre-intervention phase.
7. Player was taught a technical–tactical guided visualization protocol. Scenarios were constructed so as to fit within a 1-min changeover time frame and thereafter on the court between every point.
8. Player practiced the visualization protocol over the course of five additional pro set matches. HRV was obtained during changeover periods but was not used as part of the final data analysis; it was, however, evaluated in the context of intervention efficiency. The player's AIEQ was in the very low range (7%). His intervention efficiency score was even lower than would be expected based on his medium level of HS/SA.
9. After the 5-match MI training phase, the intervention efficacy accountability phase was started, the pressure phase of intervention efficiency, and efficacy testing in that the sport psychology practitioner, coach, and athlete all want the intervention to work (mutual expectation pressure). This phase of the process is the accountability phase, in which subjective and anecdotal impressions are validated or called into question.
10. The procedures during the intervention phase are similar to the MT training phase, with the exception being that an athlete is expected to produce and perform better and is aware that the intervention (in this case, MI) is expected to work.
11. After about 35 changeover HRV scans (4–5 pro set matches), intervention phase #1 is completed.
12. Thereafter, the data is analyzed and the intervention efficacy quotient is established.
13. The preceding cycles/phases are repeated with the addition of multi-modal MT method #2 (e.g., MI and HRD BF concurrently).

OUTCOME: PRESENTATION OF THE DATA, DATA ANALYSIS, AND DISCUSSION

Intervention efficiency findings for this M (low M)- M (high M)- M (low M) are presented first.

The following descriptive statistics (Figure 17.14) compare HRV in the intervention versus no intervention ("no") condition (pre- versus intervention phases). It remained to be seen whether intervention efficiency would be impacted by higher levels of activity that are usually associated with greater ANS-SNS activity (initial intervention efficiency is usually tested in resting contexts; see earlier case studies).

As one can discern, there was only one statistically significant finding: the last lowest heart rate in the intervention compared to last lowest heart rate in the pre-intervention (no intervention) phase ($p = .039$; Figure 17.15). Note: an HRV monitoring component is the documentation of the first highest heart beat that is immediately noted when an athlete is seated after coming off the playing field or tennis court, in this case, and the lowest heartbeat at the end of the time-out/intervention epoch (1 minute here).

This player's lowest heart rate was significantly higher after a time-out-based MT epoch in the intervention phase than in the no-intervention phase (6.4 beats/minute). This is a suggestive finding, but not necessarily a conceptually consistent one, since heart rate usually reduces significantly from time-out onset to its conclusion. On the other hand, a heart rate response that is inconsistent with the norm may actually reflect an intervention's impact, in this case, an MI-mediated

Paired Samples Statistics

		Mean	N	Std. Deviation	Std. Error Mean
Pair 1	HR	112.8718	39	10.1182	1.6202
	HRNO	108.3077	39	15.1365	2.4238
Pair 2	SDNN	66.0000	39	49.5549	7.9351
	SDNNO	53.7692	39	33.7463	5.4037
Pair 3	VLF	101.0256	39	413.2569	66.1741
	VLNO	87.0513	39	153.3060	24.5486
Pair 4	LF	247.2564	39	663.2935	106.2120
	LNO	185.6410	39	393.0178	62.9332
Pair 5	HF	536.3333	39	1518.7758	243.1988
	HNO	281.0256	39	468.8149	75.0705
Pair 6	LH	1.4692	39	2.7814	.4454
	LHNO	2.0205	39	5.2102	.8343
Pair 7	HHR	127.9211	38	10.3725	1.6826
	HHRNO	123.1053	38	22.2453	3.6087
Pair 8	LHR	108.0263	38	11.6352	1.8875
	LHRNO	101.5526	38	14.4852	2.3498
Pair 9	PW	3.4211	38	1.8400	.2985
	PWNO	3.8158	38	2.3807	.3862
Pair 10	PL	3.0263	38	1.7162	.2784
	PLNO	3.4211	38	2.4008	.3895
Pair 11	GW	.6216	37	.4917	8.083E-02
	GWNO	.5405	37	.5052	8.306E-02
Pair 12	GL	.3784	37	.4917	8.083E-02
	GLNO	.4595	37	.5052	8.306E-02
Pair 13	CM4W	2.0000	2	1.4142	1.0000
	CM4WNO	3.5000	2	3.5355	2.5000
Pair 14	CM4L	1.4000	5	.5477	.2449
	CM4LNO	2.8000	5	2.3875	1.0677

FIGURE 17.14   Visualization versus no visualization HRV intervention efficiency.

Paired Samples Test

		Paired Differences							
				Std. Error Mean	95% Confidence Interval of the Difference				
		Mean	Std. Deviation		Lower	Upper	t	df	Sig. (2-tailed)
Pair 1	HR - HRNO	4.5641	15.6235	2.5018	-.5005	9.6287	1.824	38	.076
Pair 2	SDNN - SDNNO	12.2308	44.3844	7.1072	-2.1570	26.6185	1.721	38	.093
Pair 3	VLF - VLNO	13.9744	438.8235	70.2680	-128.2757	156.2245	.199	38	.843
Pair 4	LF - LNO	61.6154	755.1581	120.9221	-183.1786	306.4093	.510	38	.613
Pair 5	HF - HNO	255.3077	1445.6553	231.4901	-213.3195	723.9349	1.103	38	.277
Pair 6	LH - LHNO	-.5513	6.1263	.9810	-2.5372	1.4346	-.562	38	.577
Pair 7	HHR - HHRNO	4.8158	25.2371	4.0940	-3.4794	13.1110	1.176	37	.247
Pair 8	LHR - LHRNO	6.4737	18.6775	3.0299	.3345	12.6128	2.137	37	.039
Pair 9	PW - PWNO	-.3947	2.9089	.4719	-1.3509	.5614	-.837	37	.408
Pair 10	PL - PLNO	-.3947	3.0804	.4997	-1.4072	.6178	-.790	37	.435
Pair 11	GW - GWNO	8.108E-02	.7218	.1187	-.1596	.3217	.683	36	.499
Pair 12	GL - GLNO	-8.11E-02	.7218	.1187	-.3217	.1596	-.683	36	.499
Pair 13	CM4W - CM4WNO	-1.5000	4.9497	3.5000	-45.9717	42.9717	-.429	1	.742
Pair 14	CM4L - CM4LNO	-1.4000	2.0736	.9274	-3.9748	1.1748	-1.510	4	.206

FIGURE 17.15   Visualization versus no visualization and intervention efficiency.

increase in heart rate and can be considered conceptually consistent. Borderline findings, including higher SDNN and HR in the intervention condition, are suggestive but do not cross the consistency threshold.

Aggregate Intervention Efficiency Quotient = .07 (7%)

Note: Further investigations of intervention efficiency paradigms in the context of high energy/ activity sports are necessary to establish individualized comparative MI-induced change norms as a function of baseline/inactivity context and coming off the field (time-out) post–high activity ANS responses.

Nevertheless, on the basis of this player's AIEQ, one could predict that his intervention efficacy quotient for MI will also be inordinately low. In other words, for this player, visualization may not work.

Intervention Efficacy Data and Findings

PRE-INTERVENTION PHASE

In the pre-intervention (no intervention), phase in which athlete HRV was measured for 1 min during each changeover of tennis matches (38 measurement occasions-repeated measures), VL, L, and LH frequency were associated with points won ($r = .34, .36$, and $.42$, respectively). These baseline HRV measures suggest a presence of preliminary IZOF profile that an intervention should attempt to manifest or maintain and even increase. If, for example, MI leads to increases in these HRV measures and points won (higher correlations), such would indicate intervention efficacy. However, it is also possible that MT can disrupt an apparent performance-facilitative IZOF. As such, one must be cautious in the first place and use such baseline IZOF profiles to determine if an intervention is indicated, at least interventions that have the potential to disrupt what is actually a stable mind–body response profile (Figure 17.16).

The next SPSS output chart depicts HRV time-domain and outcome measure relationships. SDNN, the HRV index, approached statistical significance ($r = -.56$; $p = .09$) in relationship to

Correlations

		PWNO	PLNO	GWNO	GLNO	CM4WNO	CM4LNO	VLNO	LNO	HNO	LHNO
PWNO	Pearson Correlation	1.000	.364*	.601**	-.601**	-.066	-.360	.338*	.375*	-.066	.415**
	Sig. (2-tailed)		.023	.000	.000	.857	.227	.036	.019	.690	.009
	N	39	39	38	38	10	13	39	39	39	39
PLNO	Pearson Correlation	.364*	1.000	-.474**	.474**	.610	.005	.224	.258	-.075	.276
	Sig. (2-tailed)	.023		.003	.003	.061	.986	.170	.113	.650	.090
	N	39	39	38	38	10	13	39	39	39	39
GWNO	Pearson Correlation	.601**	-.474**	1.000	-1.000**	-.482	-.254	.169	.153	.026	.175
	Sig. (2-tailed)	.000	.003		.000	.159	.402	.309	.359	.878	.292
	N	38	38	38	38	10	13	38	38	38	38
GLNO	Pearson Correlation	-.601**	.474**	-1.000**	1.000	.482	.254	-.169	-.153	-.026	-.175
	Sig. (2-tailed)	.000	.003	.000		.159	.402	.309	.359	.878	.292
	N	38	38	38	38	10	13	38	38	38	38
CM4WNO	Pearson Correlation	-.066	.610	-.482	.482	1.000	.631	-.420	-.554	-.537	.172
	Sig. (2-tailed)	.857	.061	.159	.159		.128	.227	.097	.109	.635
	N	10	10	10	10	10	7	10	10	10	10
CM4LNO	Pearson Correlation	-.360	.005	-.254	.254	.631	1.000	-.194	-.211	-.084	-.198
	Sig. (2-tailed)	.227	.986	.402	.402	.128		.525	.490	.785	.517
	N	13	13	13	13	7	13	13	13	13	13
VLNO	Pearson Correlation	.338*	.224	.169	-.169	-.420	-.194	1.000	.811**	.464**	.627**
	Sig. (2-tailed)	.036	.170	.309	.309	.227	.525		.000	.003	.000
	N	39	39	38	38	10	13	39	39	39	39
LNO	Pearson Correlation	.375*	.258	.153	-.153	-.554	-.211	.811**	1.000	.209	.888**
	Sig. (2-tailed)	.019	.113	.359	.359	.097	.490	.000		.203	.000
	N	39	39	38	38	10	13	39	39	39	39
HNO	Pearson Correlation	-.066	-.075	.026	-.026	-.537	-.084	.464**	.209	1.000	-.162
	Sig. (2-tailed)	.690	.650	.878	.878	.109	.785	.003	.203		.325
	N	39	39	38	38	10	13	39	39	39	39
LHNO	Pearson Correlation	.415**	.276	.175	-.175	.172	-.198	.627**	.888**	-.162	1.000
	Sig. (2-tailed)	.009	.090	.292	.292	.635	.517	.000	.000	.325	
	N	39	39	38	38	10	13	39	39	39	39

*Correlation is significant at the 0.05 level (2-tailed).
**Correlation is significant at the 0.01 level (2-tailed).

FIGURE 17.16 HRV frequency domain measures and performance outcome: Pre-intervention phase.

CM level 4 points won, a measure of situational pressure, suggesting that greater HRV (that SDNN reflects) a correlate of HRD may negatively impact pressure performance in this athlete. Remember, the HRV-obtained measures are temporally distant (not time-locked to an actual competitive event) reflectors and possible mediators of in-the-moment mind–body responses that are capable of influencing performance after a time-out (changeover). Thus, relative to this finding, one can infer that if greater SDNN was evident after the 1-min time-out scan (a result that could also have been influenced by activity-induced or mediated HRV in the game prior to the 1-minute HRV scan), it may have negatively affected critical moment performance subsequent to the 1-minute scan. Since this finding emanates from the pre-intervention phase, it is conceivable that this player developed a negative pressure response mechanism, marked by greater SDNN (which would be paradoxical since it is related to HRD inhale-exhale cycles that are known to facilitate pre-action readiness), which reduced pressure performance. On the other hand, the finding could be spurious because of the small sample size (only 10 CM4W). Moreover, even though greater HRV was associated with the fewer CM level 4 points won, that does not detract from the possibility that pre-action SDNN-mediated HRD did not occur prior to all or most such and other points in the match, since opponent factors can have a major effect on outcome independent of optimum preparatory responses (Figure 17.17).

Intervention Phase

The following chart (Figure 17.18) depicts relationships between intervention phase outcome measures and ANS-HRV frequency domain responses. The only conceptually relevant finding is that low-frequency ANS activity was highly correlated with level 4 critical moment (CM4L)

Correlations

		PWNO	PLNO	GWNO	GLNO	CM4WNO	CM4LNO	HRNO	SDNNO	HHRNO	LHRNO
PWNO	Pearson Correlation	1.000	.364*	.601**	-.601**	-.066	-.360	-.160	-.099	-.249	-.198
	Sig. (2-tailed)	.	.023	.000	.000	.857	.227	.331	.549	.132	.233
	N	39	39	38	38	10	13	39	39	38	38
PLNO	Pearson Correlation	.364*	1.000	-.474**	.474**	.610	.005	.026	-.080	.069	.013
	Sig. (2-tailed)	.023	.	.003	.003	.061	.986	.874	.629	.682	.940
	N	39	39	38	38	10	13	39	39	38	38
GWNO	Pearson Correlation	.601**	-.474**	1.000	-1.000**	-.482	-.254	-.216	-.003	-.320	-.218
	Sig. (2-tailed)	.000	.003	.	.000	.159	.402	.193	.985	.053	.195
	N	38	38	38	38	10	13	38	38	37	37
GLNO	Pearson Correlation	-.601**	.474**	-1.000**	1.000	.482	.254	.216	.003	.320	.218
	Sig. (2-tailed)	.000	.003	.000	.	.159	.402	.193	.985	.053	.195
	N	38	38	38	38	10	13	38	38	37	37
CM4WNO	Pearson Correlation	-.066	.610	-.482	.482	1.000	.631	-.192	-.567	-.381	.200
	Sig. (2-tailed)	.857	.061	.159	.159	.	.128	.595	.087	.278	.581
	N	10	10	10	10	10	7	10	10	10	10
CM4LNO	Pearson Correlation	-.360	.005	-.254	.254	.631	1.000	.126	-.132	-.017	-.182
	Sig. (2-tailed)	.227	.986	.402	.402	.128	.	.682	.667	.958	.571
	N	13	13	13	13	7	13	13	13	12	12
HRNO	Pearson Correlation	-.160	.026	-.216	.216	-.192	.126	1.000	-.077	.816**	.873**
	Sig. (2-tailed)	.331	.874	.193	.193	.595	.682	.	.640	.000	.000
	N	39	39	38	38	10	13	39	39	38	38
SDNNO	Pearson Correlation	-.099	-.080	-.003	.003	-.567	-.132	-.077	1.000	.205	-.246
	Sig. (2-tailed)	.549	.629	.985	.985	.087	.667	.640	.	.217	.136
	N	39	39	38	38	10	13	39	39	38	38
HHRNO	Pearson Correlation	-.249	.069	-.320	.320	-.381	-.017	.816**	.205	1.000	.703**
	Sig. (2-tailed)	.132	.682	.053	.053	.278	.958	.000	.217	.	.000
	N	38	38	37	37	10	12	38	38	38	38
LHRNO	Pearson Correlation	-.198	.013	-.218	.218	.200	-.182	.873**	-.246	.703**	1.000
	Sig. (2-tailed)	.233	.940	.195	.195	.581	.571	.000	.136	.000	.
	N	38	38	37	37	10	12	38	38	38	38

*Correlation is significant at the 0.05 level (2-tailed).

**Correlation is significant at the 0.01 level (2-tailed).

FIGURE 17.17 HRV time domain measures and performance outcome: Pre-intervention phase.

Correlations

		PW	PL	GW	GL	CM4W	CM4L	VLF	LF	HF	LH
PW	Pearson Correlation	1.000	-.083	.754**	-.754**	.353	-.149	-.227	-.252	-.209	-.111
	Sig. (2-tailed)	.	.616	.000	.000	.151	.643	.164	.121	.202	.503
	N	39	39	39	39	18	12	39	39	39	39
PL	Pearson Correlation	-.083	1.000	-.667**	.667**	-.067	.782**	.072	.123	.050	-.114
	Sig. (2-tailed)	.616	.	.000	.000	.791	.003	.664	.457	.764	.490
	N	39	39	39	39	18	12	39	39	39	39
GW	Pearson Correlation	.754**	-.667**	1.000	-1.000**	.378	-.535	-.199	-.277	-.180	-.008
	Sig. (2-tailed)	.000	.000	.	.000	.122	.073	.223	.088	.274	.961
	N	39	39	39	39	18	12	39	39	39	39
GL	Pearson Correlation	-.754**	.667**	-1.000**	1.000	-.378	.535	.199	.277	.180	.008
	Sig. (2-tailed)	.000	.000	.000	.	.122	.073	.223	.088	.274	.961
	N	39	39	39	39	18	12	39	39	39	39
CM4W	Pearson Correlation	.353	-.067	.378	-.378	1.000	-.098	.077	.005	-.016	-.266
	Sig. (2-tailed)	.151	.791	.122	.122	.	.775	.761	.985	.951	.286
	N	18	18	18	18	18	11	18	18	18	18
CM4L	Pearson Correlation	-.149	.782**	-.535	.535	-.098	1.000	.077	.784**	.269	.178
	Sig. (2-tailed)	.643	.003	.073	.073	.775	.	.811	.003	.398	.580
	N	12	12	12	12	11	12	12	12	12	12
VLF	Pearson Correlation	-.227	.072	-.199	.199	.077	.077	1.000	.954**	.970**	-.068
	Sig. (2-tailed)	.164	.664	.223	.223	.761	.811	.	.000	.000	.676
	N	39	39	39	39	18	12	40	40	40	40
LF	Pearson Correlation	-.252	.123	-.277	.277	.005	.784**	.954**	1.000	.971**	-.083
	Sig. (2-tailed)	.121	.457	.088	.088	.985	.003	.000	.	.000	.608
	N	39	39	39	39	18	12	40	40	40	40
HF	Pearson Correlation	-.209	.050	-.180	.180	-.016	.269	.970**	.971**	1.000	-.131
	Sig. (2-tailed)	.202	.764	.274	.274	.951	.398	.000	.000	.	.422
	N	39	39	39	39	18	12	40	40	40	40
LH	Pearson Correlation	-.111	-.114	-.008	.008	-.266	.178	-.068	-.083	-.131	1.000
	Sig. (2-tailed)	.503	.490	.961	.961	.286	.580	.676	.608	.422	.
	N	39	39	39	39	18	12	40	40	40	40

**Correlation is significant at the 0.01 level (2-tailed).

FIGURE 17.18 HRV frequency domain measures and performance outcome: Intervention phase.

performance ($r = .78$). This suggests that MI-associated or mediated LF activity (a mixture of SNS/PNS ANS activity) negatively impacts pressure performance. Although one might consider attempts to manipulate LF activity using MI in such a way that an amended or new visualization scenario reduces LF activity in hopes that doing so will improve critical moment performance, in an athlete like this one, who has a very low MI efficiency quotient, it may be prudent to integrate a more direct interventional procedure such as HRD-BF that can more readily, in-the-moment exert a targeted effect on ANS measures that one wants to manipulate. Interestingly, in the pre-intervention phase, LF HRV activity was negatively correlated with CM4 points won (approaching significance), a finding that inversely, concurrently validates, that in this athlete, over the course of a pre- and intervention phase, LF emerged as being detrimental to successful critical moment performance. It remains to be seen if this LF effect can be traced to the applied visualization scenario and MI implementation protocol while on the court and during changeovers.

The next output chart (Figure 17.19) reveals HRV time domain and performance outcome measures and their relationships. The only intervention-related finding relative to time-domain measures was the strong correlation between the lowest heart rate at the end of 1-min changeover HRV scans and subsequent CM level 4 points won ($r = .74$, or about 14% of the variance in this pressure performance outcome measure that could be attributed to this heart rate response). Conceptually, this suggests that HRV deactivation as reflected in a lower post–time-out beats-per-minute reading may have been intervention-induced or facilitated, leading to a carryover effect and subsequent continued engagement in the prescribed visualization intervention between points that were played immediately after the previous HRV scan and resultant mind–body responses associated with enhanced performance under pressure (e.g., preaction HRD being mediated or facilitated or sustained by the changeover intervention [MI] and pre-game psychophysiological state [lower heart rate]. This finding needs to be

Correlations

		PW	PL	GW	GL	CM4W	CM4L	HR	SDNN	HHR	LHR
PW	Pearson Correlation	1.000	-.083	.754**	-.754**	.353	-.149	.223	-.127	.011	-.007
	Sig. (2-tailed)		.616	.000	.000	.151	.643	.173	.441	.946	.967
	N	39	39	39	39	18	12	39	39	39	39
PL	Pearson Correlation	-.083	1.000	-.667**	.667**	-.067	.782**	-.079	.066	-.041	.015
	Sig. (2-tailed)	.616		.000	.000	.791	.003	.632	.691	.804	.926
	N	39	39	39	39	18	12	39	39	39	39
GW	Pearson Correlation	.754**	-.667**	1.000	-1.000**	.378	-.535	.221	-.137	-.005	-.034
	Sig. (2-tailed)	.000	.000		.000	.122	.073	.176	.406	.978	.838
	N	39	39	39	39	18	12	39	39	39	39
GL	Pearson Correlation	-.754**	.667**	-1.000**	1.000	-.378	.535	-.221	.137	.005	.034
	Sig. (2-tailed)	.000	.000	.000		.122	.073	.176	.406	.978	.838
	N	39	39	39	39	18	12	39	39	39	39
CM4W	Pearson Correlation	.353	-.067	.378	-.378	1.000	-.098	.066	.036	.101	.035
	Sig. (2-tailed)	.151	.791	.122	.122		.775	.795	.886	.690	.889
	N	18	18	18	18	18	11	18	18	18	18
CM4L	Pearson Correlation	-.149	.782**	-.535	.535	-.098	1.000	.131	.145	.253	.742**
	Sig. (2-tailed)	.643	.003	.073	.073	.775		.686	.652	.427	.006
	N	12	12	12	12	11	12	12	12	12	12
HR	Pearson Correlation	.223	-.079	.221	-.221	.066	.131	1.000	-.545**	.532**	.653**
	Sig. (2-tailed)	.173	.632	.176	.176	.795	.686		.000	.000	.000
	N	39	39	39	39	18	12	40	40	40	40
SDNN	Pearson Correlation	-.127	.066	-.137	.137	.036	.145	-.545**	1.000	-.337*	-.372*
	Sig. (2-tailed)	.441	.691	.406	.406	.886	.652	.000		.034	.018
	N	39	39	39	39	18	12	40	40	40	40
HHR	Pearson Correlation	.011	-.041	-.005	.005	.101	.253	.532**	-.337*	1.000	.330*
	Sig. (2-tailed)	.946	.804	.978	.978	.690	.427	.000	.034		.037
	N	39	39	39	39	18	12	40	40	40	40
LHR	Pearson Correlation	-.007	.015	-.034	.034	.035	.742**	.653**	-.372*	.330*	1.000
	Sig. (2-tailed)	.967	.926	.838	.838	.889	.006	.000	.018	.037	
	N	39	39	39	39	18	12	40	40	40	40

*Correlation is significant at the 0.05 level (2-tailed).

**Correlation is significant at the 0.01 level (2-tailed).

FIGURE 17.19 HRV time domain measures and performance outcome: intervention phase.

replicated in this specific player to conclude with better certainty whether visualization leads to a lower heart rate and subsequent better pressure performance across at least 50–60 CM level 4 points. Nevertheless, positive efficacy findings are always encouraging, but practitioners and athletes alike must always consider limitations to findings, methodological issues, and alternative explanatory hypotheses and models before crying "Eureka, we have succeeded; efficacy has been established." It should be noted that, as with intervention efficiency, intervention efficacy exists on a continuum and, as such, should be analyzed and interpreted in this context and with caution.

In addition to the aforementioned micro-level predictor and outcome measures (HRV and criticality measures) and their relationships, it is also important to look at important global macro- outcome measures in a pre- and post-intervention context, since there are cases in which no revealing micro-level predictor-outcome measure relationships emerge.

In this case, the important Games Won and Games Lost metric across the no versus intervention condition revealed no significant changes. In other words, the intervention (MI) was not associated with more games won or fewer games lost. Such a finding can be discouraging; they are, however, more common than many practitioners would admit to, assuming that they are even aware of these and other intervention-efficacy measures that should be routinely derived. On the positive side, though, as already revealed, was the lowest heart rate and CM-level 4 points won relationship, a finding that documented intervention efficacy that permits a preliminary case to be made that in this athlete, the MT intervention (MI-visualization) was associated with better situational pressure performance, establishing an Intervention Efficacy Quotient of .140, or 14%, for this athlete in the context of an intervention phase. Again, intervention efficacy is fluid and can rapidly change over time as a function of increasing sample sizes. As such, intervention analyses should be performed regularly in conjunction with sport-specific seasonal and other schedules (e.g., tournament series).

Summary

1. Visualization, or MI, is the most widely used MT intervention.
2. However, its status as an intervention may be more myth-driven than evidence-based.
3. Subjecting it to higher evidentiary accountability methodologies can help clarify its status.
4. As such, all athletes who engage in MI need to be assessed relative to this modality's intervention efficiency and efficacy.
5. A factor that is critical to increasing the probability that MI will enhance performance is the *time to achieve enduring biomarker-based mind–body change metric*.
6. As such, visualization scenarios must be tested in varying time contexts within a repeated measures design over the course of an intervention training period, culminating with ecological efficiency and efficacy testing (during real competition).
7. Macro- and micro-outcome measures should be used to establish intervention efficacy.
8. Variance explained in a visualization-based or associated outcome measure should be the intervention efficacy benchmark. This allows for the assessment of an intervention on a continuum. An initial intervention efficacy rating, for example, .140, or 14% of the variance in a level 4 critical moment measure, can be used to evaluate and guide future intervention phases.
9. Intervention efficiency and efficacy testing should be ongoing and determined within seasonal contexts; for example, during a summer series of games or competitions, then again in the fall series, and so on. Such testing should also be done during training for comparison purposes (training versus actual competition intervention efficacy).

10. Visualization scenarios should be structured in accord with specific goals, whether motivational, technical, or tactical in nature, and then analyzed to determine to what extent a supposed performance issue actually contributes to performance detriment. For example, if unknown to a practitioner, a technical issue drives poor performance, yet visualization is engaged in by the athlete in an unstructured manner devoid of technical scenarios and remediation imagery, then it cannot be expected that MI will demonstrate much, if any, efficacy.

11. MI should be administered primarily to athletes who are high in HS/SA. If an athlete has lower levels of HS/SA, it is imperative that extensive efficiency testing prefaces its use during competition, and then at least one 60-repeated-measures-intervention-efficacy testing phase should be carried out for confirmatory purposes (determining whether it likely can be successfully engaged in and demonstrate efficacy).

18

Brain-Based Manipulation: Neurofeedback

Although it could be argued that all interventions are "brain-based" since neuronal processes are always active, even more so during mental imagery, cognitive restructuring, and other MT methods that have extensive visual, auditory, and stimulatory components, for the purpose of distinguishing intervention modalities, "brain-based" MT (in this book) identifies methods and procedures that attempt to directly manipulate and shape cortical responses in the context of the enhancement of sport performance. Such methods are usually highly tech-based and require advanced brain-monitoring instrumentation. One such emerging intervention modality, neurofeedback (NF), is a brain-based procedure that has made its way into the sport performance MT arena. While NF is well-established in some clinical circles, it is still underused in the realm of applied sport psychology. This can be attributed to the fact that the vast majority of sport psychology practitioners have not been trained in brain-based biofeedback (NF). In addition, NF instrumentation is not inexpensive. Importantly, there also is a dearth of high-quality research attesting to its efficacy that could move practitioners to be trained in and adopt this method as a primary intervention approach.

This latter contention about questionable research will most certainly not go uncontested by practitioners who use NF with athletes, and there are numerous studies that attest to the efficacy of NF and advocate for its across-the-board use as the go-to MT modality to enhance sport performance. However, the ABSP-CP still takes issue with pervasive approaches to NF that are fraught with the same oversights and deficiencies that have been discussed throughout this book. While NF has much potential, because it indeed exerts a direct effect on brain functioning that can be seen, documented, and analyzed in real time, the cart is still ahead of the horse in terms of protocols and methodological approaches that predominate today and claims of efficacy that pervade.

It is beyond the scope of this chapter to comprehensively review most relevant sport-specific NF research and findings. Readers are encouraged to access reference sources and obtain training in NF via the Biofeedback Certification International Alliance (BCIA) and/or International Society for Neuronal Research and endorsed training organizations. Training in NF is absolutely vital to not only use it properly, but also understand conceptual and construct bases of this intervention modality before eventually applying NF to athletes. Even then, it is crucial that NF be administered in the context of the procedures, methodologies, and accountability approaches that the ABSP-CP has recommended throughout this book.

Intervention Amenability: Athlete's Profile and Ideal Mental Training Modality

In terms of intervention amenability, NF is likely to appeal most to athletes who are low in HS/SA and high in RC/SC. This subset of athletes, who tend to be skeptical of MT in general, are nevertheless, at times, willing to engage in procedures that provide objective data-based outcome information like NF does. Biofeedback-based MT is frequently seen almost as a competition in and of itself by athletes who are high in RC/SC. They like that they can manipulate HRV and/or brainwaves, and see themselves doing so via direct feedback on a computer screen. Since NF can still be considered an experimental MT modality, practitioners can also test it on athletes with other AP PHO constellations as well (Figure 18.1).[1]

CONCEPTUAL RATIONALE

NF is based and justified as an intervention modality on the idea that optimum health, wellness, and performance are associated with specific brain states that can be quantified (as reflected in specific configurations of brainwaves), and that such states can be achieved or attained by individuals who do not routinely exhibit context-specific optimum brain functioning parameters (verifiable by clinical [qEEG] or performance evaluations) through operant conditioning of brain responses. In the extreme, NF has been shown to ameliorate symptoms associated with traumatic brain injury, allowing even paralyzed individuals to improve their quality of life by being able to use brainwave manipulation to move a wheelchair or write an e-mail (see Thorton & Carmody, 2009). In the context of attention deficit/hyperactivity disorder (AD/HD), validated NF protocols have been developed to shape brainwave activity associated with enhanced attention (Little, Lubar, & Cannon, 2009). Athlete-specific NF protocols have also been used in an attempt to enhance performance (Edmonds & Tennenbaum, 2012). It is indisputable that brainwaves can be manipulated and shaped, but what is not so clear is whether specific manipulations are universally enduring and efficacious, especially in the context of sport performance.

Operant conditioning of brainwaves/brain functioning is attempted by having a patient or athlete client sit in front of a computer screen while connected to electrodes attached to his or her scalp over brain areas of interest (a brain region[s]; that is conceptually associated anatomically and functionally with optimum and/or deficient brain contextual responses; Figure 18.2).

After baseline brainwave responses of interest have been acquired and evaluated in terms of their distance from or similarity to what are hypothesized to be ideal brainwave parameters, NF commences (e.g., a golfer preparing to putt or ADD patient at baseline may exhibit what are considered maladaptive or performance-facilitative brainwave profiles that need to be altered or enhanced). The practitioner sets or calibrates brainwave threshold levels for delta, theta, alpha, and/or beta brainwave activity that are thought to reflect optimum functioning (contextually); the client then, subliminally (since one cannot physically, say, flex a neuron like one can flex a muscle), is

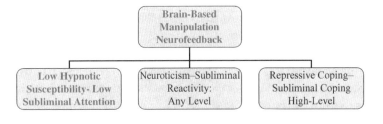

FIGURE 18.1 Athlete's Profile and intervention amenability.

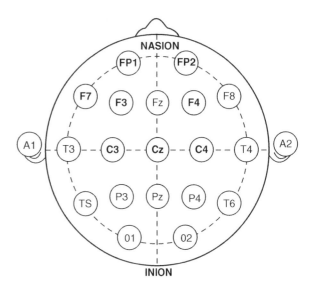

FIGURE 18.2   EEG electrode placement map per international 10–20 system (Andreassi, 1995).

capable of changing in-the-moment brainwave activity to approach and eventually reach brainwave thresholds that were set. Reaching prescribed thresholds are then reinforced via an auditory signal or visually apparent changes on a screen in a presented scenario (e.g., the color of a flower changes as a function of reductions in beta-wave power). These changes are NF mediated (subliminal operant conditioning).

Theoretically, it is thought that, over time, such operant conditioning of brainwaves will lead to enduring change and better contextual functionality, like being able to perform better when under pressure. The assumption being that lab-based NF-induced (operant conditioning–shaped) brainwave activity that supposedly is associated with optimum functioning will generalize to the playing field and be manifested subliminally to help an athlete master a sport-specific situation (e.g., better deal with a critical moment during competition; see Andreassi, 1995; Carlstedt, 2009; and Edmonds & Tannenbaum, 2012 for an overview of brainwave psychophysiology and NF procedures).

Operant conditioning of brainwave activity has been shown to occur as a real brain manipulation phenomenon. However, there are conceptual and methodological issues and problems associated with NF, more so in sport performance contexts. One major concern is the conceptual validity of most sport-specific NF protocols, or the notion that a peak performance or optimum attention/focus and/or emotional control biomarker/brain-biomarker "signature" exists for any of the aforementioned performance descriptors (e.g., optimum attention = "x" amount of theta, alpha, and beta activity over F_1 and F_3 electrode locations). Moreover, if such signatures exist and an athlete's brainwave responses can be shaped and reinforced in the lab, can they be replicated during real competition, and, if yes, are alleged performance-enhancing brainwave responses reliable predictors of key sport-specific macro- and micro-performance outcome measures (e.g., does a NF protocol lead to better critical moment performance)?

NF also tends to be administered within a practitioner-based delivery paradigm. Insufficient attention is paid to time-to-achieve-enduring-biomarker verifiable change. Efficacy testing is rarely performed and espoused NF protocols have not been validated using higher evidentiary procedures and methodologies. It is improbable that an athlete with major brain-based (mental) performance issues that may have taken a career to develop can, within a few 30- or 40-minute sessions spread over weeks, make notable performance gains that can be reliably attributed (validated) to these NF sessions. Rather, from the onset, it would be more reasonable to assume that a more efficient approach would be to have intensive NF sessions daily spanning 4 to 6 hours (with breaks) in an attempt to overwrite EEG verifiable maladaptive brainwave patterns that probably took years to develop and are now too well consolidated neuronally to be overwritten on the basis of weekly sessions of short duration. At least, such a deductive approach should guide NF and not temporal and financial realities that might preclude a practitioner from ever being able to test differential time lines in the context of enduring EEG change and outcome considerations.

As such, NF remains a highly experimental MT modality, albeit one that has much potential. Advancing and lifting NF to prominence as a sport-specific intervention modality is predicated on the development of strong conceptually sound brainwave BF (NF) protocols, ones that are cognizant of sport-specific, pre-action and subsequent brain–heart–mind–body–motor dynamics associated with successful outcomes, responses that increase the probability of peak performance, especially when an athlete experiences competitive pressure. It is faulty to assume that clinically based protocols like the standard and overused C3–C4 approach (analogous to using RSA-HRV BF instead of HRD BF, in an athlete) is a cure-all for sport-specific performance problems or for the purpose of enhancing performance without prior extensive validation testing at the group and individual level. Conceptually sound also means testing NF protocols for efficiency and efficacy on the playing field. Ecological validity is central to establishing the utility of any intervention, especially MT modalities like NF that are almost always temporally removed from the playing field.

The current state of NF mirrors that of the field of sport psychology in general. It tends to be a claim-based MT method, a cool approach that is capable of showing and manipulating brainwaves and impressing the uninformed, but is it all smoke and mirrors?

The ABSP-CP perspective is that NF can be much more and eventually emerge, perhaps, as one of the most potent interventional approaches to the remediation of performance issues and/or enhancement of performance in general, provided that this MT procedure is advanced and used systematically in the context of highest evidentiary methodologies.

CONCEPTUAL-CONSTRUCT BASES OF THE ABSP-CP NF PROTOCOL

The ABSP-CP advances an NF protocol that is based on known *ecologically* derived brain–heart–mind–body–motor responses that are associated with peak performance and the mastering critical moments of competition. They are as follows:

1. Relative left frontal brain lobe-based increased activation pre-action pre-paration-strategic planning transitioning to . . .
2. . . . relative left frontal brain lobe-based deactivation . . .
3. . . . followed by right-motor cortex relative increased activation with . . .
4. . . . concomitant heart rate deceleration.

THESE (# 1-4) ARE KNOWN AND DOCUMENTED RESPONSES ACROSS NUMEROUS STUDIES AND SPORTS

In addition to the preceding pre-action dynamics, it is hypothesized that additional cortical responses occur during action phases and downtime of most sports, especially those that involve high levels of energy expenditure for sustained periods of time (with or without breaks, time-outs, or substitutions), or sports that have extreme short-duration energy requirements. These hypothesized specific brain responses are elucidated in Dietrich's Transient Hypofrontality Hypothesis (THH; Dietrich, 2003) and summarized further on and explained in the context of the Athlete's Profile and Theory of Critical Moments models of peak performance and the ABSP-CP NF protocol.

The THH: An Overview

According to the THH, the brain must make do with a finite amount of metabolites and blood flow. As such, cortical functioning is fluid and in a state of flux as a function of ongoing and ever-changing mental and physical demands. Depending upon what sort of psychological or mental activity is occurring, brain regions or areas that are anatomically and functionally associated with specific mental activity and neuronal processing, will, as necessary, "recruit" metabolic resources from other brain region ensembles of neurons that are relatively inactive and not vital (at the time) for other regional processing to occur. This mechanism, a feedback loop, allows the brain to adapt to a changing "neuro-environment." For example, when engaged in a memory task sitting down, the motor cortex will require significantly less regional cerebral blood flow (rCBF) than when an individual is walking and trying to remember something at the same time. In the former situation, specific areas of the temporal lobes will require relatively more rCBF for memory-related processing, metabolic demands that can easily be met. By contrast, in the latter scenario, the act of walking, if strenuous enough, may lead to reduced memory-related performance due to insufficient rCBF. In essence, in this situation, the temporal lobes may have lacked sufficient metabolites to function optimally in a memory-related context because of the motor cortex's disproportionate metabolic demands associated with high-intensity walking. Such blood flow and oxygenation response dynamics can be captured using advanced brain imaging techniques such as positron emission tomography (PET) and functional magnetic resonance imaging (fMRI; see Dietrich, 2003).

The THH was originally conceptualized to account for findings associating endurance-based exercise, including long-distance running with decreased frequency of clinical depression (Dietrich, 2003). The THH also challenges the endorphin-mediated "runner's high" thesis that attributes feelings of flow, dissociation, and euphoria that runners have reported to elevated levels of the so-called pleasure neurotransmitters. Dietrich contends that runner's high and zone-state phenomena can be traced, not to endorphin levels, but to pre-frontal and frontal-lobe-based changes in metabolic activity that is initiated by the motor-cortex and the necessity of recruiting cortical resources in order to sustain high-intensity aerobic activity for lengthy periods of time from other brain regions. To do so, other areas of the brain that are not needed to maintain motor activity can go offline, and in the process, available cortical metabolites are drawn away from the pre-frontal and frontal lobes to the motor cortex. Experientially, this shift in cortical resources (rCBF, glucose/oxygen redistribution) can be explained in terms of feelings of nothingness, dissociation, blissfulness, and being stress- and worry-free. Essentially, when the frontal brain regions go "offline," so does higher cognitive functioning that has also been associated with stress, fear, and awareness of negative consequences (mediators or correlates of depression and anxiety). When a reallocation threshold has been reached suddenly, a stressed-out executive or mom enters a worry-free and pleasant state, even in the presence of intense exercise (running) and associated pain that may not even be registered once the THH zone–threshold has been reached.

Validating the THH

The THH can be difficult to test due to motion artifact issues associated with most brain imaging instruments, including PET and fMRI. However, EEG proved to be a viable option for investigating this explanatory model. Carlstedt (2008) investigated the model as follows:

FIGURE 18.3   Athlete undergoing THH testing.

FIGURE 18.4   Telemetry-acquired EEG waves.

A hobby tennis player and professional musician was instructed to pedal on a stationary bicycle until being told to stop, while wearing a 20 channel EEG electrode cap. The Nexus 32 EEG telemetry system was used to monitor brain activity (Figures 18.3 and 18.4).

The acquired EEG was observed over time and evaluated in regard to large changes in various brainwave frequencies as a function of passing time.

The following EEG (Figure 18.5) outtakes contain, to the trained eye, noticeable changes in brain activity across time. Differential increases and decreases in overall EEG power specific to the pre- and frontal lobes and motor cortex helped determine when to stop the trial (cessation of pedaling), which occurred around the 42-minute mark (Figure 18.6).

Consistent with the THH, this experimental investigation predicted that there would be significant differential changes in specific brain-regional location total EEG power and amplitude (sum of all brainwave activity) as a function of elapsed time. It was expected that the frontal brain areas would exhibit decreased total power/amplitude over time while motor cortex areas would be marked by an increase in total power, indicative of a reallocation of cortical resources from the frontal lobes to the motor cortex to sustain high-intensity aerobic activity. Findings are provided in Figure 18.7.

The initial chart in Figure 18.7 depicts changes in total brain amplitude over EEG regionally placed electrodes (per International 10–20 system; Andreassi, 1995). − = a reduction in total amplitude over time (the first 10 minutes of the cycling experiment compared to the last 5 minutes of pedaling). + = an increase in specific brain regional total amplitude.

Consistent with the THH, relative pre-frontal and frontal-lobe activity decreased as a function of time (in location **FP1, FP2** [pre-frontal] **F7, F3,** and **F4** [frontal-lobe area]). Total amplitude increased in F8 and Fz. However, since F8 is in close proximity to the motor cortex, this finding may reflect the start of metabolic reallocation from the front of the brain toward the motor cortex. The increase in Fz may be associated with the interhemispheric transfer of metabolites via the corpus callosum (Fz is located above the corpus callosum near the motor cortex [Figure 18.8]).

Increases in total amplitude over motor cortex areas **C3, Cz,** and **C4** lend additional support to the THH. Increases in activation over temporal (T), parietal (P), and occipital (O) areas need to be further investigated since they are not directly addressed by the THH.

The preceding qualitative directional ratings are supportive findings, however, additional quantitative evidence of significant changes in brain activity in the frontal and motor regions

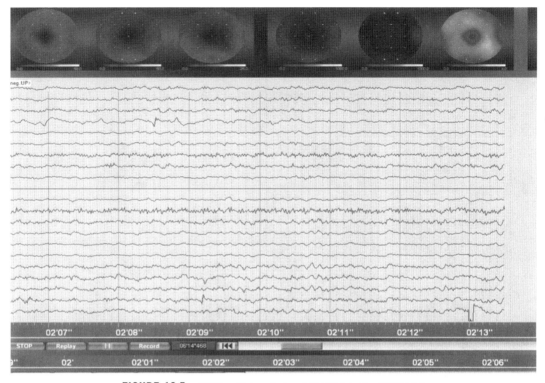

FIGURE 18.5   EEG outtake at about 2′ 07″ into the THH trial.

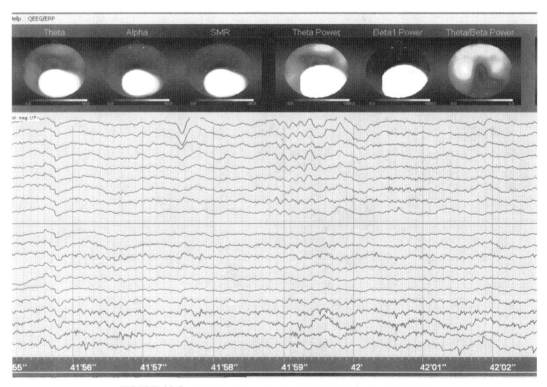

FIGURE 18.6   EEG outtake at about 41′ 55″ into the THH trial.

Change in Mean Total Amplitude
as a Function of Time (First 10
Minutes vs. Last 5 Minutes)

[FP1]	-	PF
[FP2]	-	PF
[F7]	-	
[F3]	-	
[Fz]	+	
[F4]	-	
[F8]	+	6-8 motor area proximity
[T3]	-	
[C3]	+	MOTOR AREA
[Cz]	+	MOTOR AREA
[C4]	+	MOTOR AREA
[T4]	+	
[T5]	+	
[P3]	+	
[PZ]	+	
[P4]		
[T6]	+	
[O1]	+	
[O2]	+	

FIGURE 18.7   Change in EEG activity as a function of time.

could help make a stronger case for the validity of the THH. Such evidence exists. The following T-tests provide additional insight into EEG change dynamics over time.

There were numerous "extremely" significant findings; in fact, changes were observed across all sites as a function of time. Of greatest conceptual significance were decreases in total amplitude at FP1, FP2, F4, and F7 (raw score bases for previous direction sign results) and increases at C3, C4, and Cz (Figure 18.9).

An additional Fold Function test (Figure 18.10) showed that the greatest conceptually relevant changes involved FP1 and C3. Total amplitude in the pre-frontal area (FP1) was associated with about a threefold decrease, whereas C3 motor cortex activity increased 10-fold. The greater-than-40-fold drop in T6 activity (temporal lobe) stands out and should be further investigated.

This experiment was the first known attempt to use EEG to test-validate the THH. Overall, in their totality, the preceding findings are consistent with the THH prediction that pre- and frontal-lobe activity will decrease and motor cortex activity will increase as a function of time. Although

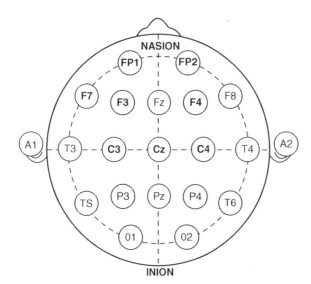

FIGURE 18.8   Localized change in total EEG amplitude. See FP1, FP2 [pre-frontal] F7, F3, and F4 [frontal-lobe area]).

T-Tests: First 10 Minutes Compared to Last 5 Minutes for 10-20 Sites

Electrode	First 10	Last 5	Electrode	Delta	N [602|296]	N [308224|151552]	N [10|5]
						t test (means, SD, n)	
[FP1]	4151	-9844	[FP1]	-3.3712	ES	ES	ES
[FP2]	-7222	-15788	[FP2]	1.18614	ES	ES	ES
[F7]	-4450	-12302	[F7]	1.76467	ES	ES	ES
[F3]	-11391	-17822	[F3]	0.56454	ES	ES	ES
[Fz]	12143	19895	[Fz]	0.63838	ES	ES	ES
[F4]	-5496	-7055	[F4]	0.28373	ES	ES	ES
[F8]	-16108	-5645	[F8]	-0.6495	ES	ES	ES
[T3]	-10399	-5771	[T3]	-0.445	ES	ES	ES
[C3]	-499	-5524	[C3]	10.0627	ES	ES	ES
[Cz]	16801	20921	[Cz]	0.24522	ES	ES	VS
[C4]	-5073	792	[C4]	-1.156	ES	ES	ES
[T4]	-2320	-7691	[T4]	2.31542	ES	ES	ES
[T5]	-11910	-7179	[T5]	-0.3972	ES	ES	ES
[P3]	-9143	-9635	[P3]	0.05383	ES	ES	NS
[PZ]	21727	37264	[PZ]	0.71512	ES	ES	ES
[P4]	0	-52	[P4]	#DIV/0!			
[T6]	11826	22798	[T6]	0.92783	ES	ES	ES
[O1]	197	-8308	[O1]	-43.159	ES	ES	ES
[O2]	-2883	-4674	[O2]	0.62106	ES	ES	ES
[A1]	17540	11050	[A1]	-0.37	ES	ES	ES
[A2]	2508	3487	[A2]	0.39014	ES	ES	ES
					Seconds	Seconds x 512	Minutes

296*512 = 151552
602*512 = 308224

ES –The two-tailed P value is < 0.0001, considered extremely significant.
VS – The two-tailed P value is 0.0042, considered very significant.
NS – The two-tailed P value is 0.4383, considered not significant.

FIGURE 18.9 Changes in total amplitude across brain location.

this experiment involved only a single case, consistent with ABSP-CP perspectives on athlete assessment and intervention methodology, a rigorously designed single case study with repeated measures has higher evidentiary status than group-based investigations that report mean scores for multiple athletes, especially when neuropsychophysiological measures are involved. AP individual differences factors have been found to significantly influence, effect, and even mediate brain–heart–mind–body responses to such an extent that they are capable of rendering many group-based findings unreliable. Consequently, although the preceding experiment should be performed on as many

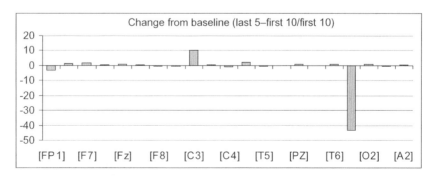

FIGURE 18.10 Change in total amplitude across locations: Fold test.

individual athletes as possible (to achieve requisite statistical power), acquired data should be analyzed in both and group contexts, and that requires repeating the experiment up to 60 times in single/individual athletes (to reach statistical power levels that allow making inferences at the intra-individual level). Thus, in terms of the tested athlete, his specific brain activity data can be used to guide NF irrespective of group findings that may be inconsistent with this (the tested athletes).

Critical to whether the THH is a viable guiding model for NF is establishing at the intra-individual level whether the predictive mechanisms that are advanced by this model are evident, and eventually, whether attempts to shape specific pre-frontal/frontal-lobe motor cortex dynamics (decreases and increases over time) using NF enhances performance (as operationalized) are associated with more successful outcomes.

The results of this test of the THH warrants its integration into sport-specific NF protocols. Considering that the conceptual bases of the most prevalent NF protocol, especially the C3–C4 universal approach that has not been validated in the context of comprehensive higher evidentiary methodological approaches in sports, it is recommended that NF practitioners test, validate, and eventually apply protocols that attempt to shape and manipulate brainwave activity in directions that are conceptually directly associated with pre-action mental preparation (AP and Theory of Critical Moments models of peak performance cortical dynamics) and subsequent action (the THH).

Description of Procedure

So how does one shape or entrain the pre-action left-to-right hemispheric shift that is associated with optimum mental preparation, motor/technical priming, and subsequent mind–body control upon the commencement of action? Or, if more concerned with what happens during action, what needs to be done to suppress frontal-lobe generated intrusive-disruptive thought and facilitate peak technical performance? How are conceptualized NF protocols administered?

1. The *Carlstedt Frontal Lobe Neurofeedback Protocol* (CP: FLNFP) is an experimental approach to brain-based manipulation, training, and operant conditioning. Its conceptual bases can be traced to the AP-TCM and THH models (previously elucidated). It is again stressed that all intervention modalities, pursuits, and individual sessions are experimental, a fact that all practitioners need to recognize; more so when it comes to NF.

2. Once an athlete has been briefed on the background of NF, what it is supposed to do, and its experimental nature, he or she is hooked up to the electrodes. NF is usually limited to two electrode sites and electrodes are placed bilaterally over two 10–20 locations of interest: brain areas that are targeted for manipulation and operant conditioning.

3. Assuming that an athlete has documented and/or verifiable pre-action anomalous brain–heart–mind–body responses the CP-FLNFP-pre (pre = pre-action) AP-based approach would be indicated. Verification of such a problem can be achieved on the basis of ecological, on-the-playing-field telemetry EEG recording and analyses, along with concurrent Polar RS800CX system HRV/HRD readings for the purpose of cross-validating (indirectly) left-to-right brain hemispheric shifts (changes in activation) that have been shown to occur prior to action (HRD concomitant to increases in right motor cortex activation). Such a pre-NF validation process is analogous to clinical qEEG analyses that are used to guide conventional clinical NF (Thorton & Carmody, 2009).

4. Additional HRV/HRD and outcome analyses that emanate from real competition should be performed to criterion-reference telemetry-based EEG and HRV/HRD activity that is obtained

within an experimental simulated competition (pre-action and action phases) or infer with a high degree of certainty, on the basis of such competition-derived HRV/HRD data, that pre-action and action phase maladaptive responses exist when it counts the most (when under pressure during real games/matches), even if simulation EEG and HRV/HRD findings reveal performance-facilitative responses.

5. When it is determined that NF is indicated two electrode placements are selected: the first one is placed at F3, the second at C4 (frontal and motor areas, respectively). Rather than attempt to manipulate specific brainwave responses using generic screen-scenarios, the CP-FLNP-pre- procedure uses video clips of the athlete that depict a sport-specific pre-action and action phase that is replayed over the course of the NF session. F3 and C4 brainwave activity bars are made visible above the video-screen viewing area.

6. The athlete is instructed to imagine that he or she is ready to respond to or initiate action, being sure to focus as the scene is presented and also look at the brainwave feedback bars before and after each clip cycle. The athlete is told to attempt to raise the F3 bar prior to action (as seen in the video clip); he or she is told that the bar will go up (reflecting greater total power/amplitude over F3) as a function of increasing attention, focus, and/or strategic planning. Just prior to action (as seen in the video), the athlete is told to "switch off" and "let go," that is, stop focusing and just watch the screen leading up to action. At that point, the F3 bar should start falling (decreases in total amplitude) and the previous motor area baseline total amplitude level (C4) should rise (increase in amplitude in the pre-action phase) and reach an apex (highest level of total amplitude) at the end of the action phase (as seen on the video screen).

7. The NF training goal is to, over time (numerous trials over sessions of up to an hour or longer) condition or entrain an F3 to C4 shift that is synchronized to the temporal pre-pre-action, pre-action, initiation of action, and action time line of each video clip (each clip is of a different duration); a shift that is marked by initial progressively increasing F3 total beta wave amplitude and stable-baseline differential C4 total beta amplitude until immediately before action starts, at which point F3 total beta amplitude should drop precipitously and C4 total beta amplitude should increase well above initial baseline levels (see Figure 18.15). In addition to visual feedback via the EEG total amplitude bar graphs above the video-viewing area, once a prescribed brain shift dynamic has occurred, as reflected in differentially appropriate total F3 and/or C4 beta amplitude, an auditory signal is emitted to reinforce that brainwave changes have taken place, along with changes in total amplitude as a function of the pre-pre-action and action video clip time line.

8. Since norms for total amplitude as a function of video-clip scenario and AP individual differences mediated-focusing ability within such an MT paradigm must be established for each individual athlete, this specific and other NF protocols must be carried out about 60 times. Sixty repeated measures can be segmented on a trial-by-trial basis; for example, 60 clips, viewed over the course of 2 hours, could serve as 60 repeated measures, and, as such, norms could be established in one

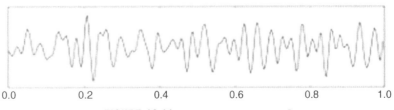

FIGURE 18.11   Sample beta waves.[2]

prolonged session. Such baseline norms can then be used for comparative purposes, since time to achieve an NF-mediated, biomarker-verifiable-enduring change can only be established longitudinally. In other words, NF should be administered and engaged in by an athlete over many weeks to determine whether a prescribed protocol is associated with positive, biomarker-mediated change, and to what extent, and if not, then it is necessary to tweak or even discard a protocol that has little, if any, performance-facilitative efficiency and efficacy.

The AP-TCM based NF paradigm as described earlier was primarily designed to help an athlete achieve better self-regulation and subsequent enhanced performance by entraining optimum brain responses as reflected in changes in total brainwave amplitude in the context of pre-pre-action and initiation of action phases of sport-specific competition. While achieving optimum NF-mediated neuro-marker verifiable responses and response-changes (shifts) in this sport-situational epoch may facilitate attention, reaction time, and pre-action motor/technical priming, it is not certain that optimum responses in these phases will extend throughout an entire action phase.

Conceivably, different brain–heart responses will occur during action than pre-action phases of competition, or maybe not, at least not when successful technical performance and outcome can be documented. So rather than assume that action phase response dynamics will be diametrically different from pre-action phases, action phases can be viewed as multiple mini pre-action phases within action phases. In other words, once action commences, there is an ebb and flow that resembles the temporal dynamics of the pre-action phase but on a micro-level in which heart rate and intensity elevates in accord with sport-specific metabolic demands, but then recedes after a sport-specific action that is marked by micro-level downtime that is followed by pre-action within an action phase (along with concomitant HRD that is seen prior to action) until action continues (if it continues). For example, in tennis there is a pre-pre-action epoch between or before a point downtime epoch. Then a player starts his or her pre-action routine; thereafter action is initiated or a player responds to a stimulus (oncoming serve) and action takes place until the point is over. During action phases, especially when numerous balls are hit back and forth, it is hypothesized that response chains (brain hemispheric shifts and HRD) that occur prior to action will also be manifested on a micro-level, even at high heart rates and levels of intensity (in a millisecond time frame) and will be reflected in cardiac inter-beat-interval (IBI) changes, including HRD prior to an action response within an action phase. HRD is further hypothesized to reflect (or correlate with; occur concomitant to) the action phase, pre-action epoch within an action phase brain hemispheric shift that has been documented in static experimental paradigms.

So what disrupts this known and, in the context of action, hypothesized performance facilitative brain–heart response chain? According to the AP and TCM models, it is an athlete's AP-mediated vulnerability (worst AP-H-H-L) to competitive stress or critical moments of competition that is reflected in a breakdown of the previously described facilitative brain–heart dynamics (see Chapters 2 and 3). THH-based NF may have the potential to reprogram or program performance adaptive brain–heart responses in athletes who are burdened with the worst AP by taking the frontal lobes out of the performance disruption equation. Here is how it could conceivably be done. Again, NF is an experimental procedure. However, the more conceptually plausible a NF protocol is, the greater the possibility that it may exert a positive effect, and the THH melds well with the AP and TCM models and identified brain–heart responses that have been associated with peak performance. Moreover, it has been preliminarily validated at the intra-individual level in terms of its conceptual temporally mediated EEG change dynamics.

The following two photos (Figures 18.12a and 18.12b) depict a tennis player being assessed prior to NF. The first picture shows the player on the bench. Her HRV is being monitored in the context of

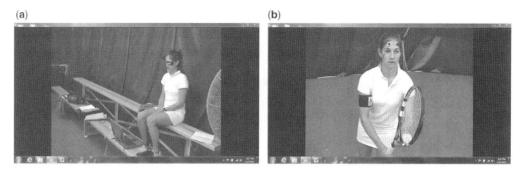

FIGURE 18.12   Ecological on-the-court telemetry-based Frontal Lobe Assessment.

manipulation of cerebral laterality. The second photo shows the player on the court. Her brainwave activity over F3 and F4 is being monitored and measured using the Brainquiry telemetry EEG system prior to NF. An initial EEG assessment is being performed to determine how these frontal brain lobe areas respond in the pre-action phase of the serve. Findings may be used to guide eventual NF (Figures 18.12 and 18.13).

Figures 18.14a and b show a tennis player and baseball player, respectively connected to the Nexus 32 EEG telemetry system that can be used for guiding and carrying out NF. All of the photos are shown for illustrative purposes only.

THH-Based NF

1. THH-guided NF is based on the premise that the frontal lobes are the generator of intrusive cognitions that predominate during critical moments of competition in athletes who have the worst AP (H-H-L). Although the frontal lobes are also involved in performance facilitative processes, including strategic planning and motor priming their facilitative involvement in the

FIGURE 18.13   Screenshot depicts EEG frequency bar graphs and raw signals above it (from player in Figures 18.12a and 18.12b).

(a)

(b)

FIGURE 18.14 Using Telemetry EEG-EKG to document pre-action brain–heart responses: Pre-NF assessment.

performance equation, can be disrupted whenever competitive stress thresholds are reached that can no longer be subliminally or volitionally managed. At that point, the previously described brain–heart response dynamics can break down and lead to performance decrements and the inability to perform up to peak potential.

2. The THH also proposes that the frontal lobes go offline as a function of sustained intensive physical activity, at which point zone or flow feelings have been reported. This response dynamic was demonstrated in the previously discussed test of the THH, in which it was shown that pre-frontal and frontal lobe activity decreased and motor cortex activity increased significantly over time.

3. Unfortunately, most sports do not involve sustained, uninterrupted high intensity action or constant movement. As such, thresholds associated with the reallocation of cortical resources away from the frontal lobes to the motor cortex that have been observed in conjunction with endurance sports and resultant zone states may not be reachable in sports that have less lengthy continuous action or have frequent time-outs. Nevertheless, the CP: FLNFP-action (action phase protocol) is based on the hypothesis that micro-level variations in rCBF and the acquisition, generation, or utilization of specific metabolites (in the frontal and motor

cortex areas) occur continuously in the context of sport-specific actions and tasks that have on and off cognitive and physical components of a shorter duration (e.g., strategic planning, followed by intensive action, followed by a cessation of action, followed by renewed strategic planning, all in a matter of seconds or a few minutes). This explanatory model maintains that "micro-bursts" or "micro-duration" frontal lobe deactivation occurs differentially, as does motor cortex activation and deactivation, and that these dynamics can be conditioned and contextually enhanced and volitionally or subliminally accessed after engaging in sufficient amounts of NF (as determined by time to achieve enduring biomarker [neuro-marker] verifiable change that is associated with enhanced performance and successful outcome metrics).

4. CP:FLNFP-action, THH-guided NF is structured similarly to the CP-FLNFP-pre-action approach, with the exception that manipulation thresholds are established in the context of visually encountered action phases (via the match-video embedded within the NF computer screen).

5. The CP:THH guided action protocol should also be administered after NF pre-action brainwave responses have been well consolidated. If this is the case, running EEG should change subliminally in pre-pre-action, pre-action, and initiation of action phases of the viewed video. Consequently, the CP-THH action NF protocol can be used for test-retest reliability checks, that is, to determine to what extent brainwave responses in the pre-action phases are stable across all pre-action phases over time (on separate days or measurement occasions). What one would hope to see is heightened cortical activation over F3, leading up to action, followed by immediately observable relative reductions in total amplitude (especially beta activity) and possible increases in delta and theta wave activity (increases in these slow brainwave measures is associated with reduced regional brain activity [e.g., cognitive processing; strategic planning]) over F3 and simultaneous increases over C4, along with concomitant HRD in the pre-action phase up to the initiation of action.

6. Once the athlete observes action (and even anticipates an action phase as would occur during actual competition), THH-based NF shaping and conditioning would commence. For example, relative to tennis, amplitude thresholds over F3 would be reduced once the player initiates action. Amplitude thresholds for beta brainwave activity would progressively and rapidly be reduced simultaneous or parallel to exhalation-induced HRD, such that by the time the player makes contact with the ball (as seen in the video clip), beta activity over F3 would almost be extinguished. By contrast, increased beta activity over C4 would be reinforced from the onset of action to the end of action (completed stroke follow-through). This threshold and reinforcement rhythm is repeated until the point is over.

7. Once a point is over, NF ceases, however, EEG monitoring over F3 and C4 continues while the player watches the downtime, pre-pre-action and pre-action leading up to the initiation of action scenario. Once action commences again, F3 and C4 thresholds are reinforced as described in number 6 above.

8. The goal of such CP-THH-guided NF threshold conditioning and reinforcement is to, at the micro-level, subliminally turn on and turn off specifically operationalized and manipulated levels of frontal (F3) and motor cortex (C4) brainwave activity (associated with underlying mental-psychological processes and processing) in the context of pre-action, action, and downtime, in an attempt to induce zone states that have been reported by endurance athletes concomitant to brain hemispheric shift dynamics that are predicted by the THH, and were demonstrated in the previously reported experimental test of the THH using telemetry-EEG.

9. Once it has been established that target brainwave responses have been conditioned, it must be determined whether the preceding synchronized on-off and cortical shift cycles are manifested in the context of a simulated experimental paradigm on the playing field in which pre-pre-action, pre-action, and initiation of action brain responses are monitored and analyzed. Since

EEG is extremely motion artifact-prone, sport-specific actions must be limited to the onset of action. However, this should be sufficient to demonstrate whether video in-the-lab NF-entrained EEG responses can be replicated experimentally during structured-guided sport-specific pre-action/action epochs.

10. If lab-generated NF responses are found to generalize to the playing field, experimental paradigm higher-order intervention efficiency will have been demonstrated. However, in this case, third-order intervention efficiency must be documented and show that lab-based NF-shaped F3 and C4 brainwave response parameters occur as predicted during actual action phases of competition. This is a difficult but necessary research task. It is best approached using HRV and HRD analyses, a validated biomarker correlate of relative right-hemisphere motor cortex activation leading up to action (using the Polar RS800CX system).

A competition would have to be videotaped with telemetry-based heart activity being synchronized to the video time line. Thereafter (as previously explicated in Chapter 9), pre-action, action, time-outs, and downtime would be identified along with HRD trends within these phases. It is predicted that HRD, one or more IBI leading up to the initiation of action, and at the end of an action phase, will mark the CP-THH NF hypothesized F3-C4 deactivation–activation dynamics. Third-order intervention efficiency would then be quantified as follows: pre-action and action phase HRD divided by the number of pre-action and action phases encountered = Neurofeedback Level 3 Intervention Efficiency Quotient (NF3-IEQ).

11. Finally, intervention efficacy must be established based on macro- and micro-level sport-specific outcome measures. This is a longitudinal task that must be undertaken within a pre-intervention and intervention phase encompassing about 60 repeated measures in each phase. An intervention training phase consisting of 60 measurement occasions (60 NF sessions) must also be completed between the pre-baseline and intervention-outcome phase.

CP-THH-NF: Hypothetical Model and Procedures (Figure 18.15)

Summary

The two presented NF protocols, on one hand, highlight the potential of NF to directly shape brain responses, and reinforce and consolidate them in the context of sport performance. It is easy to see why so many practitioners are enamored with this approach to interventions. The Svengali-like power that an NF practitioner can exert on a person's brain can seem impressive to many, and yes, NF can and does lead to momentary changes in brain responses. However, how enduring and potent are such changes, and can they really enhance performance? These are empirical questions that every practitioner needs to answer for any NF protocol that is under consideration. NF is a complex process. It is a procedure that should not be administered within a practitioner-centric delivery model, one that is influenced by practice and financial realities that may preclude extensive intervention efficiency, efficacy, and validation testing that is vital to an NF protocol's credibility and the best interests of athlete clients. Unfortunately, NF in sports is for the most part administered in an ad hoc manner, devoid of advanced accountability methodologies.

The CP-FLNF-pre-action/action and CP-THH NF protocols advances an approach that attempts to shape and condition sport-specific brain functioning that has been shown to occur prior to action that increases the probability of enhanced performance and successful outcomes. The CP-THH protocol extends NF through action phases using video-based and concurrent EEG

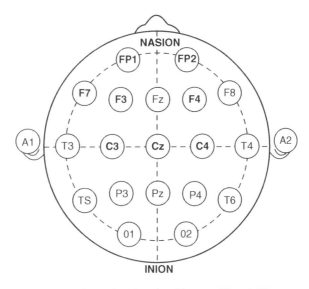

1. Electrodes Placed on Player at F3 and C4

2. Video-and EEG Guided THH-NF   3. Telemetry F4-C4 Validation   4. NF Generalizes to
Competition?

**CP-THH-Based NF Hypothetical Threshold as Function of Pre-Action to Action Phase
Change: Audio Reinforced F3 and C4**

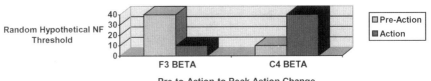

5. Intervention Efficiency Testing (2 versus 3 and F3 and C4 Conceptual Congruence Analyses
and HRD analyses for 4)

FIGURE 18.15   Steps 1 to 5 of the CP-THH-NF conceptual model and procedures.

visual and auditory feedback to entrain/synchronize brain responses to the time lines of sport-specific actions/motions/tasks in an attempt to eliminate brainwave-verifiable correlates of mental chatter that has been isolated in the left-frontal region (F3), and prime/enhance motor readiness in the C4 region of the motor cortex in an attempt to facilitate optimum technical–motor–tactical performance that intrusive thoughts are known to disrupt.

While the presented NF models have highly plausible conceptual and construct bases, they, too, must be validated before they can be used with confidence. Readers are encouraged to view NF critically (all other interventions as well). If one is interested in this modality, it is crucial that an individual receives advanced training in NF, applied neuroscience, and intervention efficiency and efficacy-testing accountability methodologies.

Training in NF without exposure to opposing perspectives about its utility that deserve serious consideration will ultimately limit a practitioner's effectiveness and do a disservice to clients. NF has great promise, but it must be subjected to rigorous testing and scrutiny.

Notes

1. Remember, conceptually, from the ABSP-CP perspective, *all* intervention sessions (each administered session) are experimental pursuits regardless of supportive research findings; since ultimately, wide response variability exists as a function of any MT method; as such, intervention efficiency and efficacy must be established anew, in each individual athlete, with *every* intervention session.

2. Beta waves (Figure 18.11) span a frequency range from about 13 to 30 Hz. They are associated with greater contextual activation, such as increased cognitive activity in the pre-frontal and frontal brain regions (e.g., F3) or motor priming and motor neuron firing when observed in motor cortex areas (C4). Sport-specific NF protocols should be conceptually based and then validated before manipulations of specific brainwave frequencies should be routinely used. If frequency-prescribed NF is not associated with intervention efficiency and efficacy after extensive testing, a protocol should be tweaked, amended, or discarded. It should never be assumed that specific brainwave frequencies and electrode placements will be associated with intervention efficiency and efficacy; such must always be demonstrated at the intra-individual level (see Andreassi, 1995).

Cerebral Laterality Manipulation: Inducing Shifts in Brain Hemispheric Activation

The manipulation of cerebral laterality is a validated brain-based experimental procedure that can be used to induce rapid changes in emotional states associated with potentially disruptive AP constellations as well as brain hemispheric shifts in the preaction to action transition. It is a low-tech method that can be easily administered after some initial assessments that will be presented.

Intervention Amenability: Athlete's Profile and Ideal Mental Training Modality

In terms of intervention amenability, since the manipulation of cerebral laterality cannot be prevented once visual-input is directed through one or the other visual field, it can be applied to all athletes regardless of AP Primary Higher Order factor (PHO) constellation. The likelihood, though, that it will be used or requested hinges for the most part on whether an athlete admits to the need to alleviate performance impacting emotionally based symptoms. Such an admission is most likely to come from athletes who are high in Neuroticism/Subliminal Activity (N/SR; Figure 19.1).

Conceptual Bases: Rationale

The origins of Cerebral Laterality Manipulation (CLM) as an intervention can be traced to the finding that highly skilled athletes were overwhelmingly relative left-brain-hemispheric predominant as determined by performance on a line-bisecting (LB) test, a validated clinical and research instrument that is routinely used to assess basic cortical functioning (Carlstedt, 2001, 2004a, 2004b). It has recently been adapted for use on the playing field to assess relative brain hemispheric predominance in athletes prior to CLM, in conjunction with special glasses that were designed to induce differential brain states through targeted visual input.

The goal of CLM is twofold. First, in an athlete with known performance issues, such as competitive anxiety or who possesses the worst AP (H-H-L; high N/R), hemispheric predominance

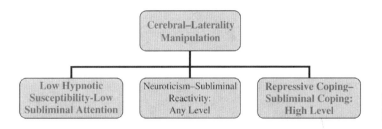

FIGURE 19.1 Athlete's Profile and intervention amenability.

would be manipulated to activate the brain hemisphere that is contralateral to the hemisphere that is associated with a high negative affect valence by directing a visual stimulus via optic pathways to the target hemisphere to activate positive and suppress negative affect, assuming that one hemisphere has an established positive affectivity valence (which is not always the case). Brain Hemispheric Emotional Valence (BHEV) is assessed using the Schiffer paradigm, a procedure that uses visual input in conjunction with patient/client feedback (using an amended Positive Affect-Negative Affect Schedule [PANAS test]; Watson et al., 1988) to arrive at brain hemispheric state and/or trait affectivity valence. Schiffer (1997) has called into question the dichotomous notion of cerebral laterality and the localization of affect, especially the pervasive belief, that is well entrenched in the literature, that negative affect is a right and positive affect a left-hemisphere-based trait. He provides compelling fMRI and CLM evidence in support of his "Dual-Brain" model of BHEC (Schiffer, 1997).

The second goal of CLM (which could be the primary approach for select athletes) does not address emotional issues and the manipulation of cerebral laterality to enhance positive affect; instead, it directly and mechanistically (similar to HRD BF) attempts to volitionally set off the known cascade of brain–heart responses that have been associated with peak performance in which relative left hemispheric (left frontal lobe) activation predominates in the pre-action phase, followed by immediate left frontal deactivation once action is initiated, along with simultaneous increasing relative right hemispheric activation.

Priming or stimulating the right visual and blocking the left visual field using special goggles/glasses is an experimental CLM intervention that has been associated with demonstrated intervention efficiency and efficacy (see Crews further on).

Description of Procedure: Pre-CLM Intervention Assessment

1. The athlete initially takes a Line-Bisecting (LB) test using the Drake Paradigm (see Carlstedt, 2004a, 2004b). A 2-minute HRV baseline test is administered prior to the test. Thereafter, the athlete is told to commence and mark the center of eight lines of varying length that are shown in an off-set, top-to-bottom configuration on a blank piece of paper (using a pencil and no aids such as a ruler). There is no time limit for doing the LB task per se, but it should not take more than a minute to bisect all eight lines. With the advent of the Polar RS800CX system, as of 2012, HRV and HRD are analyzed throughout the procedure.

2. A second 2-minute HRV test is administered immediately after the initial LB test and prior to a second LB stress test in which all bisections must be completed within 10 seconds. The purpose of the LB stress test is to further criterion-reference other ABSP-CP stress tests as well as determine if relative state/trait brain hemispheric predominance will be disrupted and/or change as a function of stress both in and in relation to an athlete's AP-PHO constellation. Polar-acquired HRV/HRD data is used to analyze cardiac response dynamics during the LB stress test.

3. The Schiffer Brain Hemispheric Emotional Valence (SBHEV) test is also administered to assess cerebral laterality affective-tendencies and guide CLM in the context of nonmechanistic volitional pre-action to action hemispheric shifts (Schiffer et al., 2007). The SBHEV is administered as follows:

(a) Athlete puts on safety glasses or special goggles that are covered or painted over so that forward sight or visual input from the front is not possible (Figure 19.2).

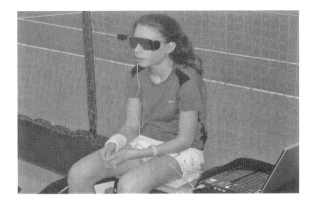

FIGURE 19.2   NeuView glasses, right flap up for left hemispheric stimulation.

(b) Athlete is instructed to (using either left or right eye as prescribed), for a period of 2 minutes, look out toward the left or right side of the glasses or goggles, respectively, depending upon which eye is being used, and straight ahead with the nonused eye, trying to blink as little as possible (Figure 19.3).

FIGURE 19.3   Right flap up with concurrent telemetry EEG response validation.

This screenshot (Figure 19.3) depicts an athlete with the right goggle-flap in the up position, leading to right visual field stimulation as she looks to the right, resulting in activation of the contralateral left-brain hemisphere (frontal-lobe area).

(c) After each trial, the athlete is debriefed, using the amended PANAS test to determine brain hemispheric valence (quantification of differential affect).

(d) After the first 2 minutes are up, the same procedure is used with the other eye.

(e) An optional trial in which the athlete looks straight ahead can also be administered; this trial serves as a baseline.

Practitioner Challenge: *Which brain hemisphere should be stimulated to activate positive affect based on the information in Figure 19.4? How would this be done?*

(f) HRV is monitored during all trials.

(g) All data is entered into a spreadsheet, including brain hemispheric valence scores (see Figure 19.4).

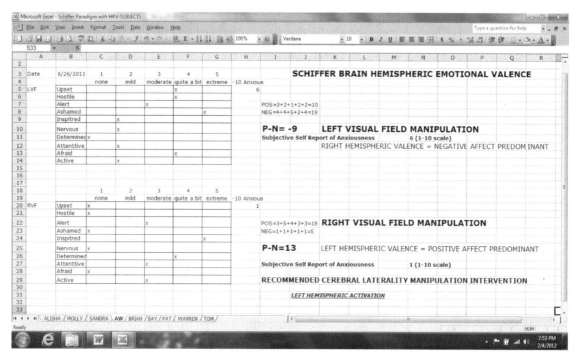

FIGURE 19.4   Assessment of emotional valence using Schiffer cerebral laterality manipulation paradigm: Outcome (Schiffer et al., 2007).

CLM Intervention Procedures

(a) Emotional Valence-Based CLM

  1. Athlete puts on the glasses or goggles. If he or she has a clearly predominating negative hemispheric valence, CLM is designed to stimulate the brain hemisphere that is contralateral to it (assuming that the opposite hemisphere has a positive affect valence). For example, if an athlete's left hemispheric valence is highly negative (−25) and his or her right hemisphere has a positive valence of +5, then CLM would attempt to induce a general state of right hemisphere–mediated positive affect by restricting visual input to the right hemisphere (remember the contralateral activation effect, in which the opposite hemisphere is activated as a function of stimulation of a specific visual field; right activates left and vice versa). Thus, in this case, the left visual field should be stimulated to activate the right hemisphere that in this athlete is associated functionally with positive affect.

  Note: Since this CLM paradigm is experimental (as are all, something that must be repeatedly stressed; although the degree of experimental level does vary as a function of validation ranking; see Accountability Challenge, Chapter 3), it must be determined at the individual level to what extent hemispheric valence ratios will impact the ability of visually based CLM to differentially increase positive or decrease negative affect, and whether induced positive states are enduring. For example, how long is targeted visual-field manipulation necessary in a +5 positive valence hemisphere to keep a 22-negative-affect hemisphere dormant since, obviously, it would be difficult to wear vision-restricting glasses or goggles all day long. It must also be determined if visually based CLM-state-induced changes in affect correlate with trait PANAS and other measures or correlates of positive and negative affect. It must also be ascertained to what extent hemispheric manipulation impacts mind–body measures, including HRV/HRD and EEG. Finally, can intervention efficiency be demonstrated, something that is fairly straightforward with visual-field stimulation; but do automatically in-the-moment visually induced changes in hemispheric affect persist and positively impact performance (intervention efficacy).

2. Assuming that the preceding issues can be satisfactorily addressed, CLM can be carried out during training and competition in most sports that have clear time lines that include downtime and time-outs.

3. In tennis, an athlete upon arriving at the bench would initially and quickly do the LB test. One would then put on the CLM glasses or goggles, raising the valence-indicated flap to stimulate the visual field that is contralateral to the brain hemisphere with a positive emotional valence. If safety glasses are being used, the athlete would look toward the left to, for example activate the right hemisphere if it has a positive valence. A tennis player would have about 1 minute to engage in visually based CLM. Currently Hypnotic Susceptibility (HS-HRV) or Polar HRV monitoring serves to assess intervention efficiency over time and for criterion-referencing validation purposes of CLM.

4. Athletes can further attempt to engage in CLM during competition, for example, between points in tennis or golf, using gaze manipulation (see Drake, 1987). If wearing unobstructed goggles with darkly tinted glasses that still allow and even enhance sight, athletes can lift the CLM-appropriate flap prior to the pre-action phase, or put on and take off the taped-over safety glasses for a quick dose of facilitative stimulation. These on-the-playing-field procedures are highly experimental and would have to be validated in each individual athlete. Conceptually, CLM is expected to work in a similar way to Neurofeedback (NF), with the key to performance-enhancing responses generalizing to the playing field being dependent on the enduring-change induced conditioning of the activation of pre-action positive affect, based on reliable evaluations of brain hemispheric valences. If such conditioning and consolidation has occurred, theoretically, performance-facilitative positive affect or the suppression of negative state responses should be manifested throughout competition. However, this explanation and associated mechanisms must be validated and eventually shown to demonstrate intervention efficacy.

(b) Mechanistic CLM

1. Alternatively, CLM manipulation can also be directly applied to facilitate the well-documented pre-action relative to left-to-right hemispheric shifts associated with peak performance responses, especially in athletes who have an ideal AP or more ambiguous hemispheric valence profiles (e.g., positive or negative valences in both hemispheres).

2. With this subset of athletes, an intervention is more about inducing known performance facilitative in-the-moment brain and heart responses, since their developed mind–body and other psychological propensities and tendencies are less likely to be disrupted by intrusive cognitions and behaviors than in their negative affect-burdened compatriots. As such, they need to enhance or fine-tune motor and technical brain-facilitated responses within

a micro–time line instead of ameliorating or shutting down negative predispositions they do not possess. Thus, approaches to CLM are dependent on an athlete's AP and/or hemispheric valences. The emotional valence approach conceivably could require visual stimulation and cortical manipulation that runs contra to what is known about and prescribed for pre-action–action performance facilitation (e.g., right hemispheric activation first). This is not necessarily an issue, though, if emotion-based CLM leads to a stable affect that fosters the in-the-moment left-to-right mechanistic CLM effect. Again, these are issues, questions, and hypotheses that need to be addressed and tested when using CLM.

3. The mechanistic application of CLM should be done with glasses or goggles, initially, within an experimental conditioning experiment with advanced accountability mechanisms in place for determining intervention efficiency and efficacy and level of consolidation. If well consolidated, performance in an intervention phase should surpass that of the pre-intervention phase. That would indicate the manipulation of pre-action laterality (from left to right) is occurring, a response chain that is associated with performance-enhancing mechanisms.

Documentation–Accountability–Intervention Efficiency and Efficacy

The use of visual field-specific covered glasses and visual-field-impeded goggles have been shown to exert an effect in activating the contralateral brain hemisphere, a conceptual prerequisite for the viability of CLM as an MT method for athletes.

The screenshot below (Figure 19.5) shows greater alpha brainwave activity in the left hemisphere as a function of right visual field stimulation (Crews, 2005). It could not be discerned when the observed alpha wave occurred (e.g., in the pre-action phase, or in the waning portion of this phase or in conjunction with the initiation of action). Nevertheless, it is clear that the manipulation of visual-field input leads to activation of the contralateral brain hemisphere and unequivocal evidence of intervention efficiency that is hard to demonstrate for most MT modalities.

The same study also revealed degrees of intervention efficacy as a function differential visual input. However, best performance was associated with both goggle flaps being down, a condition

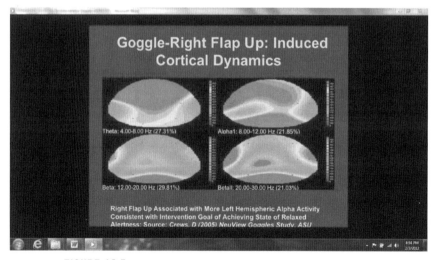

FIGURE 19.5   EEG study: Validation of right-flap-up condition.

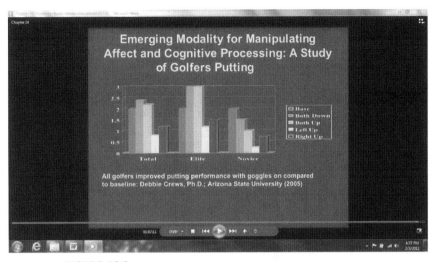

FIGURE 19.6   Outcome as a function of Goggle flap position.

that essentially is the same as wearing sunglasses, since the goggles, in contrast to covered safety glasses, allow for forward vision. More relevant to mechanistic CLM is the finding that in both novice and elite golfers, they each performed better with the right flap up compared to the left flap up (Figure 19.6). Overall though, these findings are conceptually muddled, since the right- and left-flap-up (i.e., both up condition) was associated with better performance than the only the right-flap-up condition. Consequently, enhanced performance may be attributable to having full (both eyes) forward vision a normal condition, since outside such an experiment golfers do not wear goggles that attempt to induce changes in differential hemispheric activation. As such, Schiffer (personal communication) questions the use of goggles that allow for forward sight.

While performance differences were found between the two most conceptually relevant conditions (left versus right flap up) they were positively exceeded by flap conditions (both up or down), and even the baseline condition (putting with no goggles on). As a result, conceptually consistent intervention efficacy was minimal.

These findings suggest that the utility of CLM may be limited to the manipulation of hemispheric affect prior to and during competition. It may not facilitate actual sport-specific actions like putting, in the moment, where vision, perception, and their interplay should not be impaired or manipulated.

Summary

1. CLM is a potent intervention associated with the manipulation of hemispheric affect.
2. Intervention efficiency can always be demonstrated, since visual-field manipulation always leads to differential hemispheric activation in intact human beings.
3. However, its intervention efficacy must be established in each athlete individually as well as time to achieve enduring biomarker-verifiable change.
4. The CLM goggle paradigm demonstrated that during an actual sports-specific action, the manipulation of visual field input did not lead to performance that was better than the normal baseline and forward vision conditions suggesting that goggle-based CLM does not

block or stimulate a visual field as is conceptually required (allows too much superfluous stimulation of both visual fields if forward vision is not blocked).

5. As such, it may be best to limit CLM to attempts to change hemispheric emotional valence using safety glasses only.

6. CLM has a highly experimental rating and still must undergo extensive testing. However, CLM is an interesting area that graduate students might consider for thesis or dissertation research in the context of sport and performance.

Integrative Athlete Assessment and Intervention: Team Case Study of Mind–Body Assessment and Biofeedback During Official Competition

This chapter presents a validated multifaceted assessment and intervention protocol (Carlstedt Protocol; CP, 2004a, 2004b, 2007a, 2007b, 2009) that has been used on hundreds of athletes over the last 15 years. It is conceptually based on an integrative individual-differences model of peak performance that is supported by strong construct validity and an extensive evolving database of psychophysiological and performance relationships and findings across numerous sports. The CP stresses ecological validity, real-time psychophysiological monitoring, biofeedback-based multi-modal intervention, and, importantly, extensive efficacy testing. The protocol involves a step-by-step hierarchical evidence-based approach that is predicated on the comprehensive assessment of athlete mind–body–motor response tendencies in pre-intervention and intervention phases prior to, during, and after practice and *official competition* (real games/matches). The goal of the protocol is to establish statistical relationships between interventions and objective macro- and micro-outcome measures of a specific sport, the benchmark for determining whether a mental training method works and to what extent. It was designed to bring accountability to the assessment and intervention process in the fields of sport psychology and biofeedback.

Readers will be exposed to specific components of the CP that were applied to starting players on an elite youth baseball team. Group data and findings will be presented, along with contrasting case studies that demonstrate wide variability in terms of outcome or intervention efficacy. Procedural and methodological issues and considerations that are crucial to higher evidentiary athlete assessment and mental training will be featured. It should be noted that this is the first study on record in which athletes' psychophysiological responses were monitored and measured *during official league games* over the course of an entire season. Pre-intervention assessment and intervention phases (biofeedback) were carried out prior to every at-bat (over 1200 data points/repeated measures; about 100–150 at-bats per player). Complete data sets of psychometric, behavioral, psychophysiological (heart rate variability; HRV), and critical moment (CM) performance statistics (predictor and macro–micro-criterion measures) were generated for analysis and athlete (client) feedback purposes.

In addition to discussing group and case study findings, particular attention will be paid to critical issues in applied sport psychology/sport psychophysiology and biofeedback. A goal of this chapter is not only to present data and findings on athletes who have experienced the CP, but also advocate for the integration of procedures and methodologies that are vital to evidence-based applied sport psychology, and the credibility of the field of sport psychology/biofeedback and its practitioners. Consequently, points of critique and rationale for doing specific things within the protocol will be discussed throughout the chapter. As I progress through specific procedures of the CP, player data will be inserted along with comments regarding their relevance. Certain procedures, methods, and response outtakes (e.g., heart rate variability reports) will also be shown and discussed.

A Hierarchical Evidence-Based Step-by-Step Ecological Protocol

Note: To assist the reader, the Athlete's Profile Model will be thoroughly reviewed in this chapter.

ASSESSMENT OF PRIMARY HIGHER-ORDER PSYCHOLOGICAL FACTORS: THE ATHLETE'S PROFILE

The first step of the CP involves establishing an Athlete's Profile, which is derived from the Carlstedt Subliminal Attention-Reactivity-Coping Scale-Athlete version (CSARCS-A). This test measures validated approximations of hypnotic susceptibility/subliminal attention (HS/SA) neuroticism/subliminal reactivity (N/SR) and repressive coping/ subliminal coping (RC/SC) as attested to by its moderate-to-high convergent validity coefficients with the Tellegen Absorption Scale (TAS), Stanford Scale of Hypnotic Susceptibility (SSHS), NEO-Neuroticism subscale, and Eysenck Personality Inventory and Marlowe-Crowne Scale ($r = .85 - .90$; see Carlstedt, 2004a, 2004b for a complete overview of these tests). The CSARCS-A has also exhibited high predictive validity across numerous replication and extension investigations (up to adj. r^2 .70).[1]

KEY PERSONALITY AND BEHAVIORAL CONSTRUCTS IN THE PERFORMANCE EQUATION

Hypnotic susceptibility/subliminal attention, neuroticism/subliminal reactivity, and repressive/ subliminal coping are considered traits and behaviors that have distinct mind–body correlates and dynamics. Research has localized them in specific brain regions and functionally with distinct patterns of EEG, heart rate variability, and muscle tension (Carlstedt, 2004a, 2004b, 2006; Davidson, 1984; Davidson, Schwartz, & Rothman, 1976; Tomarken & Davidson; 1994; Wickramasekera, 1988). These measures are emerging as *Primary Higher Order* (PHO) factors in mediating performance, especially during critical moments of competition when the perception of threat and competitive stress are thought to be the greatest instances when certain athletes are expected to be most vulnerable to negative intrusive thoughts. When interacting together, these measures have been shown empirically to supersede all other psychological variables in affecting and predicting psychological performance in athletes, especially during critical moments of competition (Carlstedt, 2001, 2004a, 2004b, 2007a, 2007b). These isolated PHO measures have been found to be intimately linked to key components of peak performance, including attention (focus), intensity (physiological reactivity), cognitive processing/strategic planning, motor readiness, and emotional control. A recent longitudinal study of tennis (spanning 5 years) and baseball players (season-long; presented herein) has found these traits and behaviors to be strongly associated with objective performance outcome measures as well as neurocognitive responses that have well-established functional and anatomical

	Outcome	N	N	N	N	N	N & HRV	N & HRV	HRV	HRV
HS/SA	.36	-.68 N13	-.58-N21	-.68-N25	.58-N21	.52-N22	-.55 N36	-.57 N44	.28 HR-sdnn/pre	.31 L/H-post
N/SR	.48	.52-N12	-.52-N14	.79-N17	-.40-N30	-.62-N34	-.31 HR-pre	.41 VL-pre	-.24 Hr-post	-35 HR-pre
RC/SC	-.41	-.72-N12	.89-N14	-.54-N17	.73-N30	.53-N30	.43 HR-pre	.35 L/H-pre	.37 LF-post	.29 Power-post

Outcome Measures: statistical performance measure (games lost); N12-pre-frontal/parietal/occipital; N13-pre-frontal/frontal/parietal/temporal/basal ganglia/ thalamus; N14-same as 13; N17-frontal; N21-pre-frontal/parietal/occipital/anterior cingulate; N22-same as 21; N25-same as 21; N30-pre-frontal/frontal/motor/parietal/occipital; N34-pre-frontal/frontal; N36-same as 34; N44-same as 34 and anterior cingulate.   HRV Measures: HR=heart rate; VL = very low frequency; LF = low frequency; L/H = low/high frequency ratio. NOTE: N measures are associated with implicated brain regions.

FIGURE 20.1   Sample outtake of correlations between primary higher-order factors and performance outcome, neurocognition, and heart rate variability.

cortical concomitants. In addition, they have been found to influence pre- and post-competition heart rate variability responses. In one form or another (interacting or singularly), HS/SA-N/SR-RC/SC have accounted for up to 70% of the variance in specific neurocognitive and HRV criterion measures, and up to 40% of the variance in the performance equation that can be attributed to psychological factors (personality traits, behaviors, and psychophysiological responding; Carlstedt, 2001, 2004a, 2004b, 2007; Figure 20.1).[2]

These statistics are but a handful of a plethora of revealing findings that strongly support the contention that HS/SA-N/SR-RC/SC are the most potent psychological mediators of performance under pressure. I recommend that all athletes should be assessed on these measures prior to starting a biofeedback or any other intervention regime. In addition to guiding biofeedback, the established Athlete's Profile is a strong predictor of intervention amenability and compliance tendencies, pain thresholds, attentional control during competitive stress, coachability, and the placebo–nocebo effects (Carlstedt, 2004a, 2004b; 2009; Wickramasekera, 1988).

PRIMARY HIGHER-ORDER FACTORS AND THEIR RELEVANCE TO BIOFEEDBACK

(A) *Hypnotic susceptibility* (Subliminal Attention; HS/SA) can be considered the zone trait in that peak performance experiences (e.g., zone or flow) have been described in similar terms as certain components of the hypnotic response (Carlstedt, 2004a, 2004b). It is marked by intense but effortless focus. It should be emphasized that hypnotic susceptibility is an omnipresent mode of information processing independent of actually being hypnotized. In other words, one does not have to be formally induced to experience a hypnotic response or state. HS/SA is a cognitive style that can occur unconsciously and lead to intense periods of attention. Knowing an athlete's level of HS/SA is important to predicting intervention amenability and compliance. Athletes who are high in this measure are more amenable to visually based interventions like mental imagery and hypnosis. Consequently, biofeedback should be structured to contain strong visual components or feedback when used with athletes who are in the high range for HS/SA to foster better compliance (Fromm & Nash, 2003).

(B) *Neuroticism* (Subliminal Reactivity; N/SR) can be viewed as the "zone buster." This trait is associated with excessive negative and catastrophic thinking and hyper-intensity (excessive physiological reactivity), especially when a person is under stress. Individuals who are high in N/SR also tend to have elevated physiological reactivity, even at baseline and in the absence of apparent stress and when taking standardized stress tests (e.g., Serial 7s). While heightened reactivity at baseline may facilitate activation levels that are necessary for competition, athletes who are high in this measure have also been shown to be more vulnerable to negative intrusive thoughts that can disrupt motor performance (Carlstedt, 2004a, 2004b). Athletes who exhibit high levels of this trait are amenable to and can benefit from biofeedback, but tend to need intensive and extensive training to overwrite faulty or dysfunctional psychophysiological response tendencies that may have taken a lifetime to develop. Of athletes who participated in various HRV biofeedback intervention studies in the context of my work with teams and private clients, those who scored high to very high in neuroticism/subliminal reactivity had the most difficulty generating high scores on the Stress Eraser device, and also took the longest to achieve shifts from very low (excessive sympathetic nervous system [SNS] reactivity at baseline) to high-frequency HRV (relaxation response). They also had the highest levels of change in physiological reactivity between the baseline and mental challenge conditions of the Serial 7s stress test (greater shifts toward sympathetic nervous system predominance [SNS]; Carlstedt, 2004a, 2004b, 2007).

(C) *Repressive coping* (Subliminal Coping; RC/SC) can be considered the "great facilitator" of zone states in that it functions to block the negative effects of high neuroticism/subliminal reactivity, thereby facilitating focus on the task at hand (e.g., needing to get a big serve in, or sinking a crucial putt when it counts the most). Individuals who score high for RC/SC have been shown to functionally inhibit the interhemispheric transfer of negative affect (N/SR) from the right to the left frontal brain hemispheres (Tomarken & Davidson, 1994). Athletes who are high in this behavior seem impervious to (or don't even generate) negative intrusive thoughts and are more likely to successfully master critical moments during competition than athletes who are low in RC/SC. Athletes who are high in RC/SC also tend to have high self-esteem and confidence. Nevertheless, despite its performance-facilitative properties, athletes who are high in RC/SC can be difficult to coach. They often are so convinced of their ability and (self-perceived) superiority that they may fail to recognize technical and physical deficiencies and not listen to constructive criticism to remediate them. They tend as well to be skeptical and noncompliant when it comes to participating in interventions. Overall, though, mentally tough athletes score high in RC/SC. Nevertheless, even mentally tough athletes falter at times and can benefit from mental training techniques to enhance attention or motor performance. Consequently, when working with athletes who are high in RC/SC (who can be resistant, skeptical, and noncompliant), one must convince them of the potential benefits of a mental training method. This can be achieved by providing them with evidence that an intervention works and show them how it affects mind–body–motor responses to enhances performance. Biofeedback is an excellent procedure for convincing the unbelieving, skeptical athlete that the mind, indeed, can influence the body and motor control, since self-generated response tendencies are readily apparent on a screen or in the form of audio feedback (Carlstedt, 2001, 2004a, 2004b). The high RC/SC athlete may actually view the biofeedback process as some sort of internal or personal competition at which they want to succeed (e.g., readily demonstrate a prescribed biofeedback response).

Construct Validity of the Carlstedt Protocol Athlete's Profile and Critical Moments Model of Peak Performance

Independently, the aforementioned PHO measures all have potential performance facilitating or disrupting effects. While they usually are relatively dormant during routine phases of competition, when critical moments are encountered, these measures have been shown to *interact* to exert a potent influence (positive or negative) on psychological performance as a function of their specific constellation (combination). Here is how they are hypothesized to work together to influence performance.

The mind–body dynamics (heart rate deceleration [HRD] and cortical shifts) that are depicted in the following chart (Figure 20.2) have been well documented in numerous studies of athletes performing during routine phases of competition (irrespective of an Athlete's PHO profile), whereby spectral analyses of total power (brain frequencies and their amplitudes) have revealed differential levels of activation between brain hemispheres as a function of internal or external focus or task orientation (e.g., strategic planning versus visuoperceptual attending). An observed seamless relative left-to-right brain hemispheric shift just prior to the commencement of action has been associated with faster reaction times, motor/technical control, and better outcomes (see Carlstedt, 2001, 2004a, 2004b for a review of EEG studies on athletes; Landers et al., 1994).

By contrast, in negatively predisposed players (high HS/SA, high N/SR, low RC/SC), whenever critical moments occur or when stress increases (whether real or self-perceived), this seamless left-to-right brain hemispheric shift that usually takes place during routine moments in all athletes (athlete populations and species-wide response) is disrupted. A cascade of emotional responses that is hypothesized to originate in the amygdala (the brain's repository for emotions, fear, and failure memory); is thought to set off a fight-or-flight response (excessive [SNS] physiological activation)

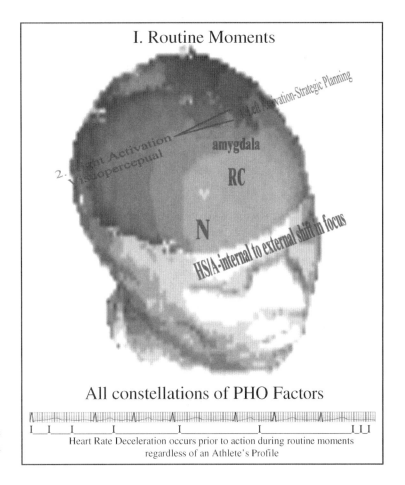

FIGURE 20.2 Cortical dynamics and heart rate variability during a routine pre-action phase.

that is mediated by negative, catastrophic, and chaotic thinking. Negative affect (right frontal region-based neuronal ensembles) that normally remain dormant during routine moments of competition become active and infiltrate the left frontal region of the brain. This occurrence is thought to disrupt an athlete's strategic planning phase and the subsequent shift to more right frontal hemispheric and motor cortex brain activity that is associated with focusing and visuoperceptual demands of a particular impending technical action (priming of task-specific motor pathways).

These negative intrusive thoughts (e.g., "I hope I don't lose this point") take over, leading an athlete to fixate on negative emotions and images instead of preparing for action. As a result, one no longer observes the previously described relative left-to-right shift in brain activity. Instead, sustained increased activation (varying levels of beta EEG activity) in the left frontal hemisphere has been found to occur. Essentially, athletes who are burdened with high neuroticism/subliminal reactivity and low repressive coping/subliminal coping remain stuck in the ruminative left-brain hemisphere and are often rendered incapable of exhibiting peak motor or technical ability. If they are concurrently high in hypnotic susceptibility/subliminal attention, their potentially superior ability to concentrate suddenly is directed inward toward negative thoughts and images, and not on competitive tasks at hand. Such athletes are likely to see their games fall apart (see the following illustrations, Figures 20.3 and 20.4).

On the other hand, athletes who thrive on and actually look forward to critical moments during competition usually have high levels of repressive/subliminal coping (left hemisphere based), are low in neuroticism/subliminal reactivity, and either high or low in hypnotic susceptibility/subliminal attention (Carlstedt, 2004a, 2004b). These athletes have developed a protective psychological mechanism over the course of their career. Rarely, if ever, do they experience

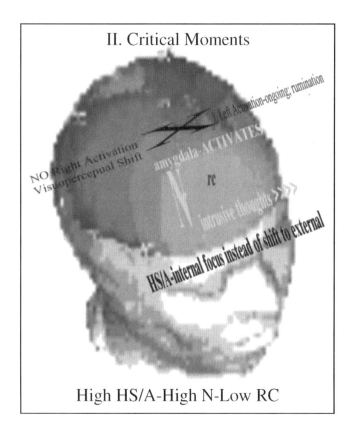

FIGURE 20.3   Brain heart response tendencies as a function of critical moments in most negative PHO profile.

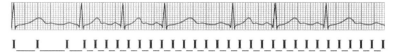

Heart Rate Deceleration does not occur during critical moments prior to action in athletes who possess the least performance facilitative Athlete's Profile. Heart Rate Acceleration occurs, instead indicative of greater relative left-hemispheric activation that reflects rumination on negative intrusive thoughts

FIGURE 20.4   Heart rate acceleration as a function of "Worst" Athlete's Profile during critical moments of competition.

negative or self-defeating intrusive thoughts. They are self-assured and confident even in the most precarious of situations. If they are also concurrently high in hypnotic susceptibility/subliminal attention, their focus on task demands can be so intense they may not even recognize that a critical moment is imminent (indicative of flow, or being "in the zone"), allowing them to play free from constraining pressure and associated negative intrusive thoughts and general lack of focus. In such athletes, the left-to-right shift that is observed during routine moments also occurs during critical moments. The fight-or-flight response is suppressed and negative thoughts are not generated. These athletes remain in total mind–body control that is marked by focused strategic planning (left frontal region activation) followed (immediately prior to action) by visuoperceptual attention to the impending task and motor priming (right frontal and motor cortex activation). This dynamic increases the probability that athletes will perform to their maximum physical and technical capabilities, even during critical moments (Carlstedt, 2004a, 2004b; Figures 20.5 and 20.6).

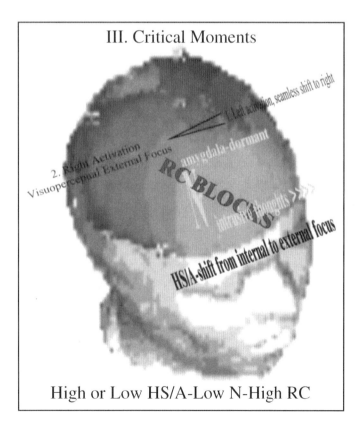

FIGURE 20.5   Brain–heart response tendencies as a function of critical moments in ideal PHO profiles.

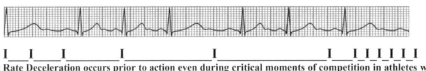

Heart Rate Deceleration occurs prior to action even during critical moments of competition in athletes who possess the Ideal Athlete's Profile indicative of the seamless left to right brain hemispheric shift

FIGURE 20.6   Heart rate deceleration as a function of an "Ideal" Athlete's Profile during critical moments of competition.

Athletes possessing the ideal constellation of high repressive/subliminal coping, low neuroticism/subliminal reactivity, and high or low hypnotic susceptibility/subliminal attention appear to be less vulnerable to negative intrusive thoughts, whereas athletes who are low in repressive/subliminal coping, high in neuroticism/subliminal reactivity, and high in hypnotic susceptibility/subliminal attention are more vulnerable to disruptive cognitions, especially during critical moments of competition (Carlstedt, 2004a, 2004b).

Concomitant to shifts in brain hemispheric activity are specific parameters of heart rate variability. Most notably, during routine phases of competition, athletes in most sports exhibit heart rate deceleration (HRD) immediately prior to action (e.g., before serving, putting, or shooting a free throw, batting, and pitching in baseball) regardless of their constellation of PHO measures. By contrast, during critical moments, athletes possessing the most negative or disruptive constellation of PHO factors exhibit heart rate acceleration (HRA) prior to action, while those having the most facilitative or protective constellation continue to demonstrate HRD. HRA is associated with cognitive activity (e.g., thinking; intrusive thoughts), whereas HRD is associated with visuoperceptual processing or orienting on or toward an important stimulus (like the ball). HRD is also more pronounced when right brain hemisphere and motor cortex activity increases after motor priming and strategic planning have taken place in the left frontal region (see heart activity tracers in the brain illustrations). Negatively predisposed athletes also exhibit increased muscle tension in secondary muscles that are not relevant to a specific technical demand (e.g., increased frontalis muscle activity when batting; see Carlstedt, 2004a, 2004b for a review and references pertaining to the aforementioned mind–body dynamics).

Applying the CP to Elite Youth Team Baseball Players: Assessment, Intervention, and Findings

STARTING PLAYER ATHLETE'S PROFILE PHO CONSTELLATIONS

The Carlstedt Subliminal Attention, Reactivity and Coping Scale-Athlete version (CSARCS-A) and the Brain Resource Company (BRC)–validated Internet-based neurocognitive test battery were administered to all starting players (position players and key pitchers). The CSARCS-A is embedded in the comprehensive BRC online test package. The following table depicts the resulting CSARCS-A, Athlete's Profile (PHO constellations) of the players. The "PHO Rank and Rating" cell contains the predicted, expected pressure response rating ranging from ***** (strongest) to − − − (weakest) that is associated with the corresponding PHO constellation (**bold** = case study player; Figure 20.7).

An interesting group finding regarding PHO profiles is that eight players scored low for neuroticism. That usually bodes well for a team when all things are about equal in the physical and technical realm. The predicted individual CM and psychophysiological (HRV) response tendencies can be compared to actual responses and performance in additional analyses further on

Player	HS/SA	N/SR	RC/SC	PHO Rank and Rating
K	19 high-medium	8 low	6 low	8; **
R	18 high-medium	15 high	13 medium	10; ----
M	20 high-medium	8 low	18 high-medium	7; ***
JV	18 high-medium	6 low	24 high	3; ***
Y	5 low	3 low	23 high	1; *****
G	22 high	13 high-medium	11 low-medium	9; - - - -
MC	23 high	7 low	19 high-medium	4; ****
RJ	18 high-medium	2 low	17 medium	6; ***
S	21 high-medium	6 low	23 high	2; ****
J	15 medium	4 low	25 high	5; ***

Key: HS/SA = hypnotic susceptibility/subliminal attention; N/SR = neuroticism/subliminal reactivity;
RC/SC = repressive coping/subliminal coping; High = high levels of trait; Med = medium levels;
Low = low levels; Rating: ***** = Ideal; - • - - - = Worst; + = positive tendencies; - = negatively tendencies;
N = neutral tendencies; PHO Rank indicates status of Athlete's Profile from 1, most performance to least facilitative

FIGURE 20.7   Starting player Athlete's Profile PHO constellations.

(Serial 7s stress test, CM performance; HRV pre-versus intervention responses and HRV and performance outcome).

IN-THE-LABORATORY PSYCHOPHYSIOLOGICAL STRESS TESTING

Once an Athlete's Profile and neurocognitive tendencies have been established, it is desirable to go up a level in the evidence hierarchy. Since an athlete's constellation of Primary Higher Order Factors (PHO = hypnotic susceptibility/subliminal attention; neuroticism/subliminal reactivity; repressive/subliminal coping) is differentially associated with physiological reactivity, mostly as a function of one's level of neuroticism/subliminal reactivity, it is important to concurrently validate or criterion-reference predicted with actual responses on standardized or commonly used stress tests. The Serial 7s backward counting test is used while measuring heart rate variability. Preliminary findings suggest that increases/decreases in specific heart rate variability measures from baseline to the test condition recording is a reliable predictor of physiological reactivity and subsequent critical moment performance tendencies (Carlstedt, 2007a). Especially baseline/test condition differences in low-frequency/high-frequency ratio have been found to be associated with critical moment performance. These differences tend to increase as a function of an athlete's level of neuroticism/subliminal reactivity, with the greater the low/high ratio being associated with subsequent poorer CM performance. Reactivity tendencies can also be teased out by using video feedback of an athlete's actual real competitive performance, with variable differential heart rate trends being observable as a function of an athlete's profile. For example, athletes who possess the most detrimental constellation of PHO factors (high HS/SA-high N/SR-low RC/SC) tend to exhibit more reactive HRV responses when they watch themselves encounter critical moments during competition. While this line of research is ongoing and Serial 7s stress testing needs to be validated, preliminary results are promising and correspond with reactivity tendencies that one would expect on the basis of an athlete's PHO profile (Carlstedt, 2007a).

Starting Player Stress Test Responses

PROCEDURE

Players were individually administered the Serial 7s Stress test prior to the commencement of the baseball season. Players were told to sit still and try to keep their minds blank while heart activity was recorded for 2 minutes. Thereafter, players were instructed to count backwards out loud from 1000 by seven for 2 minutes (e.g., 1,000, 993, 876 . . .). Players were told to pick up the count if they stopped or made a (real or perceived) mistake in subtraction from the point of any error.

INSTRUMENTATION

The Biocom Technologies Heart Scanner software program was used for all HRV recordings and subsequent HRV monitoring and biofeedback procedures. Heart Scanner is a user-friendly hard- and software system containing automatic artifact correction and report generation capabilities. A standard ear-lobe sensor is used to generate a cardiac signal that can be depicted in varying forms on different screens for monitoring, biofeedback, and analysis purposes. Recording time can be set from 1 to 30 minutes. Heart Scanner and other Biocom HRV programs meet research standards for reliability that were established by the *Task Force of the European Society of Cardiology and the North American Society of Pacing and Electrophysiology*, (1996).

STRESS TEST OUTCOME: FINDINGS ON STARTING PLAYERS

The first two charts (Figure 20.8) contain baseline and stress condition heart rate variability responses for starting players. A third chart lists differences in HRV responses across the baseline and stressor task, and the players are ranked in order of greatest HRV Low/High-frequency differences. Signs (e.g., + or -) in the third chart indicated whether stress responses can be considered consistent with what would be expected on the basis of a player's CSARCS-A, PHO constellation, and to what extent ($+++$ = highly consistent; $++$ = moderately consistent; $+$ = consistent; $---$ =highly inconsistent; $--$ = moderately inconsistent; $-$ =inconsistent; $1-9$ = change rank; ? = unsure due to ambiguous PHO profile).

Practitioner Challenge: On the basis of Figure 20.8, HRV responses in the backward-counting stress condition (S7s Chart) arrive at a Blind-Reverse based Athlete's Profile PHO constellation assessment/validation for each listed player. Then look at the HRV Differential chart in Figure 20.8 to determine whether your blind reverse AP validation attempt matched each player's actual AP (see 3rd Chart in Figure 20.8). Try to account for any mismatches.

Three players' stress responses (L/H) were highly consistent with what would have been expected on the basis of their Athlete's PHO profile, and two were highly inconsistent with what would have been expected. High neuroticism (the second value in the Player cell) is usually associated with a greater shift to sympathetic activation as reflected in a positive L/H value (e.g., +0.9). Negative L/H values are indicative of relative parasympathetic predominance (less physiological reactivity). While the change from baseline to the stress condition has been associated with better critical moment (CM) performance at the group level, consistent with the IZOF model, ultimately, micro-ecological statistical outcome measures will reflect actual CM performance. The PHO Athlete's Profiles and stress test responses (Figure 20.8) are illustrative, but interpretations about their significance should be made with caution. Ultimately, one needs to rely on a multi-faceted macro- and micro-statistical outcome measures to guide athlete assessment,

Baseline

Player	HR	SDNN	VL	LOW	HIGH	L/H
K: HM-L-L	71	149	251	670	5460	0.1
R: HM-H-M	80	66	652	967	298	3.2
M: HM-L-HM	74	78	171	415	1032	0.4
JV: HM-L-H	76	169	79	6879	1420	4.8
Y: L-L-H	85	55	227	498	281	1.8
G: H-HM-LM	73	74	58	340	339	1.0
MC: H-L-HM	68	54	151	452	369	1.2
S: HM-L-H	85	116	63	3407	728	4.7
J: M–L–H	82	142	1684	289	236	1.2

Stressor: Serial 7s Backward Counting Condition   **PRACTITIONER CHALLENGE DATA**

Player	HR	SDNN	VL	LOW	HIGH	L/H
K	83	66	81	575	847	0.
R	90	50	282	298	235	1.3
M	96	53	383	223	176	1.3
JV	79	108	197	1812	1638	1.1
Y	102	43	171	170	250	0.7
G	85	57	98	534	446	1.2
MC	92	62	596	439	252	1.7
S	95	46	116	488	172	2.8
J	85	60	132	468	305	1.5

HRV Differential and Athlete's Profile Concordance

Player	HR	SDNN	VL	LOW	HIGH	L/H	PHO
K (19,8,6)	+12	–83	–170	–25	–4613	–0.1	5+
R(18,15,13)	+10	–15	–370	–669	–63	–1.9	4 – – –
M (20,8,18)	+22	–13	+212	–192	–856	+0.9	9–
JV (18,6,24)	+3	–161	+118	–5067	+218	–3.7	1 +++
Y (5,3,23)	+17	–12	–56	–328	–31	–2.5	2 +++
G(22–13–11)	+13	–17	+40	+134	+107	+0.2	6?
MC(23,7,19)	+24	+8	+445	–13	–117	+0.5	8--
S(21–6–23)	+10	–70	+53	–2919	–556	–1.9	4 +++
J (15,4,25)	+3	–72	–1552	+179	+69	+0.3	7–

FIGURE 20.8   Serial 7s stress test baseline, stress condition, and differential HRV.

with actual real situational performance, in the end, being the gold standard benchmark for establishing the criterion referenced and predictive validity of an assessment instrument.

Procedures During Official Games: Pre-Intervention Phase

A psychophysiological monitoring station was set up in the dugout at each game site. The station consisted of two laptop computers that were loaded with Biocom Technologies Heart Scanner software. An ear sensor was connected to each computer. A trained analyst from the American Board of Sport Psychology (ABSP) summer Fellowship/Internship program was assigned to each computer for monitoring and intervention purposes. Another analyst was assigned to score the game in accord with standard baseball scoring and ABSP Critical Moment and Quality-of-at-bat/Quality of Pitch Psychological Proficiency methodologies. Coaches and players were briefed regarding the following procedures: (1) at the end of a defensive inning, as players headed to the dugout to prepare to bat, the

FIGURE 20.9   Sample photo of the data collection (pre-intervention) phase on the bench prior to batting.

names of three players were called out; the first batter to hit that inning, the second (on-deck) batter and the third (in the hole); (2) the first two players were called to one of the computer stations, were connected (hooked up) to the computer via the ear sensor, and then monitored and measured for HRV activity for 1 minute[3]. In the pre-intervention phase of the investigation, players were told to "just sit there and try to remain still" while they were being monitored (Figure 20.9, view of the computer monitor was blocked); (3) after the 1 minute was up, the players were disconnected from the computer and they proceeded to the plate or on-deck circle as indicated; (4) thereafter, players who were in the three, four, or five batting order for that inning were alerted and told to be ready to report to the station for monitoring; this procedure was repeated until the inning was over. Pitchers were measured in a similar manner, once immediately upon coming off the mound, and approximately 90 seconds to 3 minutes before returning to the mound to pitch the next inning, depending upon the progression of the inning.

The pre-intervention phase lasted for 13 games and was exclusively concerned with determining players' psychophysiological (HRV) response tendencies (IZOF) prior to batting or pitching as a function of differential criticality (situational pressure).

PROCEDURES DURING OFFICIAL GAMES: INTERVENTION PHASE

The logistics of the intervention were very similar to the pre-intervention phase, with the exception that the monitor was viewed by players (to observe their own HRV activity) for shaping/inducing a specific biofeedback response.

THE INTERVENTION: "LOCK-IN"-HRD/HRV BIOFEEDBACK PROTOCOL

Players were briefed on the mind–body–motor relevance of HRD. They were told to think in terms of learning to regulate or induce specific levels or states of activation, in this case, timed breathing to set off the HRD cascade of mind–body–motor responses that have been linked to peak performance. Consequently, position players were trained to time their inhale and exhale cycles with the impending onset of the pitch from the pitcher. Inhalation was timed to coincide with the pitcher's wind-up, with exhalation occurring rapidly (and linearly) as soon as the pitcher releases the ball toward the plate (batter). By contrast, pitchers were trained to time their inhale cycle with the onset of their windup-and-exhale cycle with the release of the ball. In both instances, conceptually, inhalation is associated with heart rate acceleration (HRA is known to occur when cognitively engaged such as during the preaction strategic planning and motor priming that takes place prior to preaction when hitting or pitching) and exhalation with HRD (see the HRD section above). HRD prior to the onset of action is expected to suppress intrusive/superfluous thoughts and facilitate focus, technical priming, and subsequent coordinated motor responses.

To increase awareness of this cardiac dynamic and practice the HRD "Lock-In" breathing cycle, players were taken through three stages of mental training commencing with (1) HRD-breathing biofeedback at the computer station in the dugout for 1 minute, followed by (2) a continuation of the prescribed breathing process in the on-deck circle while taking batting swings (cuts) that were timed to the pitcher's pitching rhythm (practicing the HRD protocol while watching the pitcher pitch to the current batter). Finally, players attempted to apply the entrained HRV-biofeedback technique when batting, timing their inhale–exhale cycles with the pitcher's rhythm (during a real at-bat). While conscious efforts to induce specific psychophysiological responses can have a paradoxical effect initially (and lead to performance decrements), over time, it is expected that HRD will be set off independent of any conscious efforts to do so (see the preceding PHO-HRD charts as a function of criticality) due to repetition and the eventual consolidation of long-term procedural memory. It should be noted that HRD and concomitant cortical responses occur routinely, anyway, independent of conscious attempts to control it, especially in the absence of competitive stressors in virtually all athletes. However, more vulnerable athletes who are negatively predisposed (with the most negative PHO constellations), when facing increasing criticality (or pressure; whether real [based on objective statistical metrics] or perceived) are more likely to exhibit mind–body–motor responses that are incongruent with the HRD (e.g., HRA and reduced motor control, slower reaction time). It is thus expected that this subset of negatively predisposed athletes will need mental training the most. Nevertheless, in this investigation, all players engaged in the protocol throughout the intervention phase of the season.

THE "LOCK-IN"-HRD BIOFEEDBACK: STEP BY STEP

Consistent with the team's schedule (comprised almost exclusively of official league games and no formal practice/training sessions between games) the prescribed HRV-biofeedback protocol could only be formally practiced under controlled and supervised conditions before each game for about 5 to 10 minutes, as feasible. Training was augmented using the *Stress Eraser* device to further help entrain the prescribed breathing pattern (each player was given this instrument to use on their own for the entire season). The intervention was designed to induce a so-called lock-in state immediately prior to action, whereby players attempted to induce heart rate deceleration (HRD) that is associated with enhanced attention, faster reaction times, and improved motor/technical performance (review the preceding text on PHO measures and HRD-cortical responses). The goal of this form of mental training is to circumvent hard-to-assess and document interventions like mental imagery or generic biofeedback procedures like progressive relaxation or respiratory sinus arrhythmia (RSA; that have not been validated in sport), with a method that has been directly associated with the initiation of a cascade of performance facilitative mind-body-motor responses that have been shown to underlie peak performance.

1. Player goes to Lock-In Monitoring and Biofeedback station.
2. Player is hooked up to ear sensor and computer.

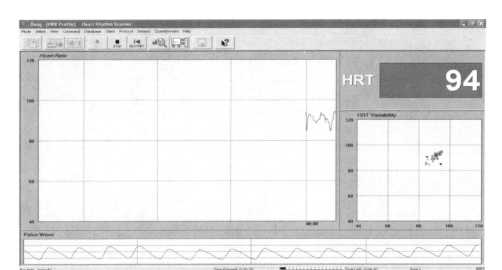

*Notice the rising line or curve on the far-right side of the tachogram that is associated with inhalation-mediated heart rate acceleration

FIGURE 20.10   Inhalation cycle of heart rate deceleration biofeedback.

3. Player is instructed to breathe in and attempt to raise the digital heart rate indicator on the computer screen to as high as possible (e.g., from 75 bpm to 100 bpm) with one long breath (inhalation cycle; see the screenshot, Figure 20.10).

4. Player is then instructed to rapidly exhale once the HRA apex has been attained, until the lowest
heart rate number has been reached (HRD); the exhale cycle should be fast and progressive to
induce the uninterrupted, linear cardiac cycle slowing trend (e.g., 100, 95, 90, 85 bpm) that
has been associated with faster reaction time and improved performance (Figure 20.11).

5. Player is instructed to pause for a few seconds after each HRD timed breathing cycle and then
repeat until the 1-minute monitoring epoch is over.

6. Player is instructed to attempt to time HRD breathing cycle with the pitching rhythm that will be
encountered, and to visualize the impending at-bat and pitch sequences.

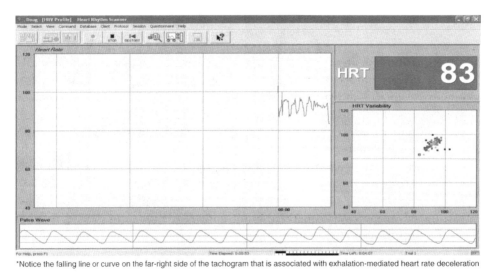

*Notice the falling line or curve on the far-right side of the tachogram that is associated with exhalation-mediated heart rate deceleration

FIGURE 20.11   Exhalation cycle of heart rate deceleration biofeedback.

7. Player is instructed to go to the on-deck circle after the on-bench HRV biofeedback and assume a stance that allows for the observation of the pitcher's pitches to the batter who is hitting (while waiting to go to bat); during the on-deck phase, the player is instructed to take timed cuts (practice swings) with concomitant HRD-timed breathing (timed to pitcher that is being observed while taking practice swings); that is, when the pitcher starts the windup (precursor to actual pitch), the player is told to calibrate the inhale cycle and start the exhale cycle as soon as the pitcher's hand starts to release the ball. Note: the on-deck HRD practice phase is a crucial step in establishing and synchronizing the HRD inhale–exhale cycles to the pitcher's pitching rhythm.

8. Player is instructed to implement the HRD-Lock-In breathing procedure when in the actual batter's box when at bat, remembering to inhale and exhale as a function of the pitcher's pitching rhythm.

9. Steps 1 to 8 are repeated throughout the game's batting cycles for each player.

CRITICAL MOMENT ANALYSES

An integral and crucial component of the CP is the measurement and assessment of psychological performance as reflected in critical moment statistics. Critical moments (CM) are operationalized as increasing levels of sport-specific situational importance. Criticality levels range from 1 (lowest level of importance in terms of being able to impact match/game outcome) to 5 (highest level of importance), with increasing level of criticality expected to induce greater competitive stress or pressure/stress responses in athletes especially as a function of an athlete's PHO profile. A criticality rating (CM) is assigned to each competitive moment of a specific sport (e.g., each point in tennis, shot in golf, or at-bat in baseball). The level of criticality of a competitive moment is determined by expert raters. Validation research has shown that increasing criticality in baseball is overwhelmingly associated with decreased performance. The linear relationship between heightened criticality and performance decrement has been established in numerous sports, including soccer, basketball, golf, tennis, and baseball (an initial baseball validation study involved an analysis of over 600 major league baseball games and 2000 at-bats; Szuhany et al., 2009). An ideal Athlete's Profile constellation can mitigate this decrement, but in studies of criticality in baseball mental toughness is associated more with the degree of lesser performance decrement (less of a negative correlation). Only two major league baseball players exhibited a positive correlation between criticality and quality of at-bat in the aforementioned study. *All* other players performed differentially worse as a function of increasing criticality (Szuhany, Carlstedt, & Duckworth, 2009).

Critical moment performance statistics were used to assess psychological performance in the context of pre-intervention and intervention-based batting and pitching (quality of at-bat and quality of pitch) and psychophysiological measures (HRV). Intervention efficacy was determined on the basis of micro-level predictor measures (e.g., level of criticality) and their statistical relationship with micro-level criterion/outcome measures (e.g., quality of bat; batting average with men in scoring position). Micro-outcome measures (performance statistics of a specific sport) are usually much more sensitive than more global or macro-level criterion variables in establishing relationships between psychological, behavioral, psychophysiological and personality measures and performance (Carlstedt, 2004a, 2004b). Nevertheless, global, macro-outcome measures such as batting average were also analyzed in the context of pre- and intervention phases of this study.

Critical Moments were investigated as follows (pre-intervention and intervention phases):

1. The effect of level of criticality on quality of at-bat
2. The effect of level of criticality on HRV

The following relationships were also investigated:

1. The effect of HRV and intervention-induced HRV on conventional baseball batting outcome measures and quality of at-bat as a function of level of criticality
2. Performance differences between pre-intervention and intervention as a function of level of criticality and HRV differences between pre-and intervention performance as a function of biofeedback and level of criticality

FINDINGS

The following initial charts reveal macro-level team outcome findings across pre- and intervention phases. Thereafter, criticality, Athlete's Profile, and Individual Zone of Optimum Functioning and performance relationships and findings are presented.

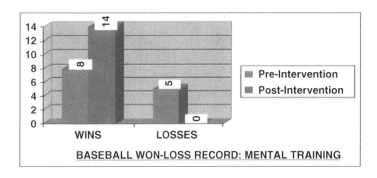

FIGURE 20.12   Team won-loss record as a function of intervention.

TEAM BASEBALL STATISTICS: PRE-INTERVENTION VS. INTERVENTION

Games won versus games lost are the first and most noticeable, and arguably the most important outcome measure in a team sport (Figure 20.12). It is thus tempting on the basis of the vast improvement from the pre- (nonintervention) to the intervention phase to attribute such success to the HRD, Lock-In biofeedback protocol. While this team's performance leap is highly suggestive, it does not establish causality between the intervention and outcome. Nevertheless, it is much better (and motivating) to observe statistical improvement over time in a quasi-controlled and ecological intervention paradigm, especially since formal training or practice (working on baseball skills) was virtually non-existent throughout the season due to the team's demanding game schedule (a game or two 6–7 days a week), than have a team exhibit a worse record after an mental training phase. Although playing lots of games over a concentrated period may have had a psychologically stabilizing effect and enhanced batting skills, the only controlled difference between the pre- and intervention phases was the actual intervention. As such, one could maintain that the Lock-In component of the CP had a positive effect on overall team performance. Additional macro-level baseball-specific performance statistics lend further support to this preliminary conclusion. For example, team batting average and on-base and slugging percentage were higher in the intervention phase (Figure 20.13).

Although the conventionally used p value threshold for determining statistical significance may have not been met when comparing some of the preceding macro-level batting statistics, statistical significance frequently takes a back seat to practical significance in sports, and especially baseball, where an absolute numeric gain can speak volumes and even impact the value of a player's contract or the security of a manager or coach's job. Relative to this team's aggregate batting average, going from .327 to .351 could mean the difference between winning or losing two or three more games and finishing in first as opposed to second place in the standings. Nevertheless, irrespective of the

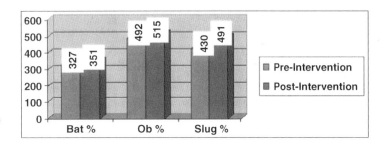

FIGURE 20.13 Team performance as a function of intervention.

statistical versus practical significance issue, additional findings further on reveal performance gains in the intervention phase that have both statistical and practical significance.

More micro-level findings include the so-called crunch-time statistics that, anecdotally, are thought to reflect mental toughness, another overused and under-operationalized sport psychological buzz phrase. Yet, if we accept common notions about clutch or mental toughness, the following team findings also revealed impressive gains in the intervention phase. Batting average and on-base and slugging percentage with runners in scoring position went up significantly in the mental training phase (Figure 20.14).

Team Mental Toughness Statistics: Pre-Intervention Versus Intervention

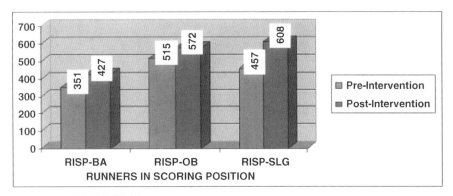

FIGURE 20.14 Mental toughness as a function of intervention.

Case Studies: Relationships Between Heart Rate Variability Components and Batting Performance and Pre-Intervention Versus Intervention Batting Performance

Although conceptually, the construct validity for the Lock-in HRD intervention is based on research that has isolated key cognitive (mind) and heart–brain–motor interactions prior to and as action commences, and would be the preferred predictor measure for determining real-time associations between HRD and performance outcome, the aggregate HRV data that is generated over a 1-minute monitoring period during time-outs (on-the-bench before batting or pitching) has emerged as a predictor of performance in its own right. In other words, although the Lock-in intervention, if carried over into the batting box (from the computer station on the bench) was designed to set off a cascade of performance facilitative mind–body–motor events related to breathing-mediated HRD, total HRV, and its time and frequency domain components that are acquired on the bench for 1 minute, have been shown to predict performance and explain "x" amount of the variance in the performance equation that can be attributed to a psychophysiological measure (pre-intervention phase) or biofeedback-shaped psychophysiological response (intervention). Even though nonintervention HRV or manipulated HRV biofeedback response profiles within this methodological paradigm are temporally isolated outside the context of actually batting, that is, not time-locked to the real pre-action pitching–batting epoch, these measures have exhibited predictive strength and emerging player Individual Zone of Optimum Functioning (IZOF, Hanin, 2006) profiles as a function of nonintervention baseline and biofeedback-induced responses. I propose that this 1-minute period of autonomic nervous system (ANS) responding (IZOF HRV response profile) can generalize to the playing field and may influence eventual pre-action response tendencies (entrainment of HRD response that was practiced using biofeedback). Consistent with predictions from the IZOF, pre-action response tendencies can be quite disparate across individuals, with athletes who manifest even diametrically opposite 1-minute HRV response profiles, performing differentially from what might be expected (e.g., heart rates of 70 and 120 being associated with an equally good performance outcome or vice versa; Figure 20.15).

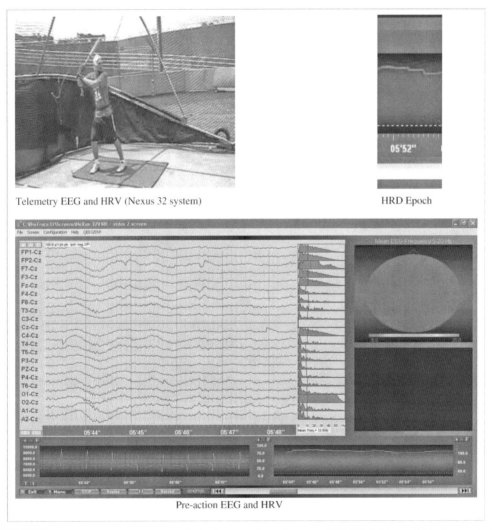

Telemetry EEG and HRV (Nexus 32 system)   HRD Epoch

Pre-action EEG and HRV

FIGURE 20.15   Validation of HRD in baseball players using telemetry EEG/EKG (Nexus 32 instrumentation).

Determining Intervention Efficiency and Efficacy

The following charts (Figures 20.16–20.19), contain player response data pertaining to intervention efficiency and efficacy.

Intervention Efficiency

Intervention efficiency can be operationalized as the magnitude of change in key HRV measures between a nonintervention and intervention condition. Relative to the Lock-in HRD protocol, the prescribed timed breathing cycles are expected to initially induce an HRA phase (linearly increasing heart rate), followed immediately by HRD and its concomitant linearly decreasing heart rate. As such, it is hypothesized that an individual engaging in this protocol correctly will exhibit a significantly greater heart rate variability index (SDNN) than individuals who are breathing in accord with their natural or developed situational breathing patterns. Thus, SDNN (Sd further on) is expected to be the predominant pre- versus post-HRV change measures in the context of this biofeedback protocol. Other HRV measures may emerge individually as a function of a person's IZOF (Hanin, 1996). However, irrespective of biofeedback-induced changes in HRV measures, ultimately, intervention efficacy must be determined independently of hypothesized efficiency parameters (see subsequent charts). Nevertheless, it is important to determine to what extent an athlete actually engages in a biofeedback technique, as reflected in changes from the baseline to intervention condition. It should be noted that intervention efficiency is expected to be affected by an individual's PHO constellation. Previous research suggests that individuals who are lower in hypnotic susceptibility (subliminal attention) and higher in repressive coping (subliminal coping) are more likely to induce

Player	Sdpre	Sdpo	Sddif	L:Hpre	L:Hpo	L:Hdif	PHO
K: HM-L-L	76	94	+18 (6)	.74	4.1	+3.36 (4)	+22.1 – 6
R: HM-H-M	74	79	+5 (7)	.93	3.0	+2.07 (6)	+7.1 + 7
M: HM-L-HM	57	88	+21 (4)	1.5	3.9	+5.40 (3)	+26.4 + 4
JV: HM-L-H	63	82	+19 (5)	2.3	8.1	+5.80 (2)	+24.8 +++ 5
Y: L-L-H	51	92	+41 (1)	6.3	7.4	+1.1 (7)	+42.1 +++ 2
G: H-HM-LM	44	71	+27 (3)	2.2	4.9	+2.7 (5)	+29.7 -- 3
MC: H-L-HM	67	64	-3 (9)	1.6	2.5	+0.9 (8)	–2.1 - 9
S: HM-L-H	127	117	-10 (10)	3.3	2.8	–0.5 (10)	–10.5 - 10
J: M-L-H	66	103	+37 (2)	2.5	9.6	+7.1 (1)	+44.1 +++ 1

Key: pre = pre-intervention; po = intervention; dif = difference pre versus post-intervention; Sd = SDNN; L:H = low-high frequency ratio; PHO = primary higher order constellation with magnitude of change between pre- and intervention (sum of Sd and L:H change). Signs (e.g., + or -) in the third chart indicated whether stress responses can be considered consistent with what would be expected on the basis of a player's CSARCS-A. PHO constellation and to what extent (+++ = highly consistent; ++ = moderately consistent; + = consistent; - - - - = highly inconsistent; - - = moderately inconsistent; - = inconsistent; 1-9 = change rank; ? = unsure due to ambiguous PHO profile).

FIGURE 20.16 Intervention-induced HRV changes: Hypothesized key measures related to HRD entrainment: Efficiency as a function of PHO constellation.

greater psychophysiological changes when engaged in biofeedback. The player's PHO constellation is listed next to their identifying initial, and their biofeedback-mediated total change in HRV measures is notated in the PHO column along with a consistency notation (degree of concordance with what would be expected on the basis of PHO constellation; Figure 20.16).

An intervention efficiency index was arrived at by adding the difference in responding in two HRV measures that are expected to vary (increase) the most from the pre-intervention baseline state to the intervention, namely, SDNN (the HRV index; Sd above) and L:H frequency ratio. Shifts toward greater change HRV (SDNN) and less of an L:H ratio are hypothesized to reflect greater autonomic nervous system control and the likelihood that the HRD Lock-in protocol will be successfully generalized to the batting box. Six out of nine players demonstrated a level of intervention efficiency that would have been predicted on the basis of their Athlete's Profile PHO constellation. It should be again noted that intervention efficiency does not necessarily predict intervention efficacy. While it might be expected that players who have learned and demonstrated specific biofeedback responses prior to a sport-specific task will be capable of exhibiting them prior to action (e.g., when batting), one cannot determine with certainty whether this is the case, and even if they are, that performance gains will be achieved and to what extent. Such must be determined using the CP intervention efficacy methodology that attempts to explain the amount of variance in various performance-outcome measures that can be attributed to an intervention-entrained or induced predictor measure like HRD or some other HRV measure (e.g., SDNN, see next section).

Intervention Efficacy

Intervention efficacy can be established both on the basis of more global macro-level (nonpsychophysiological, pre-intervention versus intervention gains in sport-specific statistical categories) and micro-level associations between 1-minute HRV biofeedback-manipulated response profiles and CM-mediated sport-specific statistical categories. It should be noted that an HRD study during an official tennis tournament using Polar instrumentation clearly delineated pre-action HRD and linking greater amounts and magnitude of HRD to enhanced performance (Carlstedt, 1998, 2001b). This study supported the hypothesis that a 1-minute HRD biofeedback intervention that is engaged in prior to returning to the playing field will increase the likelihood of successfully self-inducing HRD prior to action through a timed breathing technique, and that the efficacy of such attempts will be reflected in macro- and micro-level statistical outcome measures. Obviously, ultimately, a more direct real-time measurement of HRD during actual batting is desirable. A real-time HRD paradigm for baseball and tennis using the Nexus 32 telemetry EEG system has been piloted (see above) and plans are in place to attempt to validate real-time HRV/HRD responses in official baseball games in 2011 using the Polar system. Nevertheless, the extant CP HRD paradigm still allows for the objective quantification of mind–body response tendencies during time-outs (in the dugout or on the bench) and determining their subsequent impact on performance on the basis of associations between 1-minute HRV epoch ANS response profiles (Figure 20.17).

In the pre-intervention phase, five out of nine players performed as would have been predicted on the basis of their Athlete's Profile PHO constellation as a function of CM. In contrast to major league baseball players, these elite youth players, overall, performed better than their professional counterparts when under pressure (CM), with most players being over the zero threshold (less than 0 = negative association between association between criticality and quality of at-bat). This can likely be attributed to the dominance of pitching in professional baseball. Nevertheless, even with this youth team, performance decreased significantly in all players as a function of rising

Player/Profile	Pre-Intervention (CM→QAB)
K (19,8,6) 8	.232 +
R (18,15,13) 10	.205 ---
M (20,8,18) 7	.164 ++
JV (18,6,24) 5	.162 ++
Y (5,3,23) 1	.134 ++
G (22,13,11) 9	.130 ---
MC (23,7,19) 4	.079 +
S (21,6,23) 2	-.074 ---
J (15,4,25) 3	-.175 ---

Key: Pre-Intervention Criticality (CM) and Quality of at-bat (QAB); numbers 1-10 = ranking of PHO constellation from most to least performance facilitative with actual Athlete's Profile PHO scores in parentheses Signs (e.g., + or -) in the third chart indicated whether stress responses can be considered consistent with what would be expected on the basis of a player's CSARCS-A, PHO constellation and to what extent (+++ = highly consistent; ++ = moderately consistent; + = consistent; - - - = highly inconsistent; - - = moderately inconsistent; - = in-consistent; 1-10 = change rank; ? = unsure due to ambiguous PHO profile).

FIGURE 20.17 Pre-intervention criticality (CM) and quality of at-bat (QAB).

criticality compared to macro-level (more routine at-bats), more global batting performance, and outcome categories in which performance improved as a function of the intervention (Figures 20.18 and 20.19).

Player	Intervention (CM→QAB)
MC (23–7–19)	.218 +++
S (21–6–23)	.184 +++
K (19–8–6)	.165 +
G (22–13–11)	.090 +
JV (18–6–24)	.024 – – –
R (18–15–13)	.020 ++
J (15–4–25)	–.022 +++
Y (5–3–23)	–.052 – – –
M (20–8–18)	–.102 – –

Key: Intervention Criticality (CM) and Quality of at–bat (QAB): Signs (e.g., + or –) in the third chart indicated whether stress responses can be considered consistent with what would be expected on the basis of a player's CSARCS–A, PHO constellation and to what extent (+++ = highly consistent; ++ = moderately consistent; + = consistent; – – – = highly inconsistent; – – = moderately inconsistent; – = inconsistent).

FIGURE 20.18 Intervention phase criticality (CM) and quality of at-bat (QAB).

Player	Differential (pre-post)
J (15-4-25) +++	.153
MC (23-7-19) +++	.139
S (21-6-23) +++	.11
G (22-13-11) ++	-.04
K (19-8-6) +++	-.067
JV (18-6-24) ---	-.138
R (18-15-13) +	-.185
Y (5-3-23) ---	-.188
M (20-8-18) --	-.266

Key: Change differential as a function of Outcome Measure = **Quality of at-bat** from pre- to intervention phase as expressed in "r" (correlation coefficient). Signs (e.g., + or -) in the third chart indicated whether stress responses can be considered consistent with what would be expected on the basis of a player's CSARCS-A, PHO constellation and to what extent (+++ = highly consistent; ++ = moderately consistent; + = consistent; - - - = highly inconsistent; - - = moderately inconsistent; - = inconsistent; 1-10 = change rank; ? = unsure due to ambiguous PHO profile).

FIGURE 20.19 Pre-intervention versus Intervention differential: Criticality (CM) and quality of at-bat (QAB).

Since one expects that an intervention will help athletes master CM, it can be disconcerting to athletes, coaches, and sport psychologists when that is not the case. For example, with this team, only four players made pre- versus post-(intervention) gains in quality of at-bat as a function of increasing criticality. However, performance decrements in the intervention phase, especially in the context of micro-level measures like criticality (CM) can happen, yet, such instances do not necessarily call into question the validity or potential potency of an intervention. There may be explanations for unexpected intervention effects. With this team, variability of CM was quite limited, with significantly more CM level 1, 2, or 3, than levels 4 or 5 (the highest levels that are conceptually associated with the greatest amount of competitive stress) occurring. Thus, in order to arrive at a more accurate assessment of CM performance, a sufficient N of CM level 4–5 at-bats are needed (statistical power). Hence, in cases where there is an insufficient amount of a particular micro-level measure to arrive at valid statistical inferences, one must revert to more macro-outcome measures such as batting average and other conventional batting statistical changes in order to arrive at interpretations of intervention efficacy.

Select Case Studies: Pre- Versus Post-HRV and Outcome

PLAYER R (FIGURES 20.20 and 20.21)

Intervention Efficiency: + 7.1 (ranging from −2.1 to +44)
Pre-Intervention (CM → QAB): .205
Intervention (CM → QAB): .020
Differential (pre-post): − .185
Pre-Intervention (CM → SUC): .116
Intervention (CM → SUC): − .035
Differential (CM → SUC pre-post): − .151

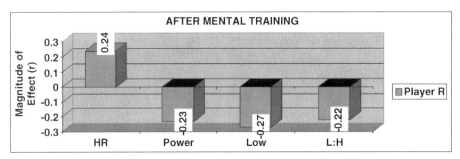

FIGURE 20.20   HRV and performance outcome: intervention phase.

Player Criticality and HRV Response and Outcome Association Findings (Micro-level):

PRE-INTERVENTION: CM AND POW .31; CM AND LF .33

Player "R" had no HRV measures associated with the performance outcome measure "Success" during the pre-intervention phase of the season. "Success" is operationalized as a hit of any kind (single, double, etc.). Relationships between HRV measures and outcome are investigated using correlational and regression statistical methods. Having no HRV components associated with the "Success" outcome measure means that no statistically significant correlations could be found between the predictor and criterion measures (HRV and Success). From an interpretive perspective, in such a case where no relationships emerged in the pre-intervention baseline phase but did in the intervention phase, one can at minimum assume that the prescribed intervention routine indeed changed a player's underlying psychophysiology. This was further substantiated in the previous pre- and intervention (efficiency and efficacy charts). As to whether such changes were associated with enhanced performance and to what extent must then be determined on the basis of the variance-explained metric (micro-level direct relationship between HRV and outcome) and macro-level pre- versus post-comparisons of sport-specific statistical outcome measures ("R's" baseball stat can be found in Figure 20.21).

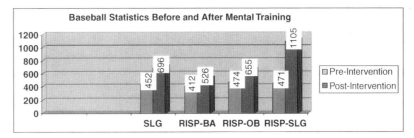

FIGURE 20.21   Batting outcome as a function of intervention.

In the mental training phase, player R's HR was associated with better outcome ($r = .24$, Figure 20.20) and explained about 6% of the variance in successful hitting. This means that in the 1-minute Lock-in mental training epoch, the HR component of the HRV response profile predicted subsequent actual batting performance, with greater heart rate during the intervention being associated with better performance. One should be aware that although an r of .24 and 6% of the variance may seem to not reflect a strong association, when viewed in the context of variance explained in sport performance that can be attributed to all psychological variables combined (whether, trait, behavioral, or psychophysiological measures) that have yet to exceed 10% of the variance (Carlstedt, 2001, 2004a, 2004b), 6% for one HRV component is quite impressive, especially in light of its temporal distance from the actual performance event (a measure obtained 1 to 3 minutes before batting).

Three other HRV components were associated with poorer performance, including total frequency domain Power (P), Low frequency activity (L), and the ratio of low to high frequency (L:H), meaning, the greater amount of these measures, the lower the rate of success. Disparate findings in which one or more HRV component is associated with successful performance and others with negative outcome may seem paradoxical, however, they can be explained on the basis that overall low success rates that occur in baseball where a 30% batting average is considered good. Hence, with significantly more failure being the norm, it is possible that specific HRV components emerge to negatively impact performance independent of positive associations between HRV and outcome. While correlational and regression relationships reflect linear associations, the ultimate goal of an intervention is to shape or enhance IZOF HRV response components that are associated with successful performance and suppress IZOF HRV response components that are shown to have a negative impact on performance. In the case of player R, his IZOF HRV profile suggests that HRA may have been predominant in the on-the-bench intervention, leading to the generation of more sympathetic nervous system (SNS) activation and subsequently more HRA when actually batting, especially when he did not get a hit (when unsuccessful).

Relative to Criticality (Critical Moments) in the pre-intervention phase, Power and Low frequency HRV were positively correlated with Criticality ($r = .31$ and $.33$, respectively, explaining about 10% and 11% of the variance in HRV that could be attributed to criticality).

ATHLETE'S PROFILE: Subliminal Attention: MEDIUM; Subliminal Reactivity: MEDIUM; Subliminal Coping MEDIUM.

These findings and all other case study findings were based on over 60 at-bats (greater than 60 on-the-bench intervention sessions prior to batting), lending good statistical power to R's data.

PLAYER M (FIGURES 20.22 and 20.23)

Intervention Efficiency: $+26.4$
Pre-Intervention (CM → QAB): .164
Intervention (CM → QAB): $-.102$
Differential (pre-post): $-.266$

Pre-Intervention (CM → SUC): .228
Intervention (CM → SUC): $-.233$
Differential (CM → SUC pre-post): $-.461$

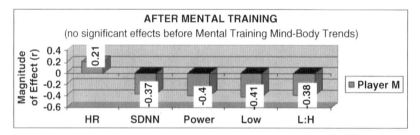

FIGURE 20.22 HRV and performance outcome: intervention phase.

Player Criticality and HRV Response and Outcome Association Findings (Micro-level): Pre-Intervention: CM and SDNN $-.309$; CM and HF $-.283$

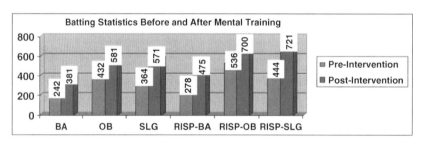

FIGURE 20.23 Batting outcome as a function of intervention.

This power hitter struggled in the first half of the season. During mental training, his slugging performance increased significantly, especially with runners in scoring position consistent with his high intervention efficiency rating $+26.4$. Increasing heart rate (HR) in the intervention phase was associated with better performance. By contrast, four other HRV measures emerged as having a negative effect on performance during the intervention phase. Again, disparate influences of HRV on performance (some positive, others negative) can be attributed to the overall low success rates associated with batting, increasing the likelihood that specific psychophysiological response tendencies will impact this hitting adversely.

Relative to criticality CM influenced SDNN $(-.309)$ and HF $(-.283)$; about 10% and 8% of the variance in these HRV measures in pre-intervention phase, respectively, that could be attributed to criticality. No HRV measures emerged in the intervention phase as effected by CM.

ATHLETE'S PROFILE: Subliminal Attention: MEDIUM; Subliminal Reactivity: LOW; Subliminal Coping: MEDIUM.

PLAYER J (FIGURES 20.24–20.26)

Intervention Efficiency: $+44.1$
Pre-Intervention (CM $\rightarrow$ QAB): $-.175$
Intervention (CM $\rightarrow$ QAB): $-.022$
Differential (pre-post): .153

Pre-Intervention (CM $\rightarrow$ SUC): $-.069$
Intervention (CM $\rightarrow$ SUC): $-.154$
Differential (CM $\rightarrow$ SUC pre-post): $-.185$

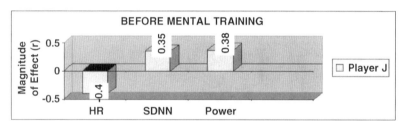

FIGURE 20.24   HRV and performance outcome: intervention phase.

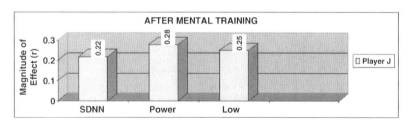

FIGURE 20.25   HRV and performance outcome: intervention phase.

Player Criticality and HRV Response and Outcome Association Findings (Micro-level):
Pre-Intervention: CM and SDNN .59
Intervention: CM and HR $-.253$

This player is on the cusp of having the best Athlete's Profile and, despite not being as physically and technically developed as some of his teammates, made major gains in all statistical categories, especially pressure performance during the mental training phase of the program. True to predictions, he performed as one would expect of a player with this Athlete's Profile PHO constellation. Mental training can still help even positively predisposed athletes enhance their performance, especially in baseball, where pitching can be very dominating and capable of negating any

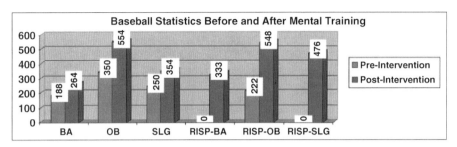

FIGURE 20.26 Batting outcome as a function of intervention.

psychological advantage that a player may have. As such, the Lock-in HRD protocol that is designed to not only facilitate focus, but faster reaction time may assist the mentally tough athlete help enhance attention and reaction time and to a certain extent mitigate the advantage pitchers tend to have, responses that are crucial to successful hitting. By locking in on the ball and priming the motor system for action, a mentally tough player possibly becomes tougher, especially ones who still are developing technically. Note also that this player had HRV measures emerge as being associated with better performance during the mental training phase and in the context of CM during the nonintervention phase (Mental training phase: SDNN, Power and Low frequency HRV). The strong correlation between pre-intervention SDNN was consistent with what would be predicted on the basis of this player's PHO profile and suggestive of a naturally or developed timed-breathing pace, which is synchronized to the temporal properties of the pre-action pitching-batting epoch in baseball ($r = .59$), independent of consciously attempting to generate a specific breathing pattern. A correlation coefficient of .59 equals about 35% of the variance in batting success that can be attributed to a psychophysiological measure, in this case SDNN, the HRV index. This is a remarkable finding that lends further support to the Athlete's Profile, Critical Moments, and IZOF models of peak performance.

Relative to Criticality, in this player, HR was negatively correlated with increasing criticality in the intervention phase ($r = -.25$), suggesting that a certain number of mental training sessions (one-minute on-the-bench sessions) in which lower heart rate was manifested were associated with subsequent decreased performance (in the following at-bat). This finding points to the need to closely monitor this player's Lock-in session and reduce the occurrence of longer periods of low heart rate (possible state of insufficient arousal or physiological reactivity). Engaging in the Lock-in HRD protocol as precisely as possible should prevent lower HR from predominating and eventually carrying over into the batting box.

ATHLETE'S PROFILE: Subliminal Attention: MEDIUM; Subliminal Reactivity: LOW; Subliminal Coping: HIGH.

PLAYER S (FIGURES 20.27 and 20.28)

Intervention Efficiency: -10.5
Pre-Intervention (CM → QAB): $-.074$
Intervention (CM → QAB): .184
Differential (pre-post): .11

Pre-Intervention (CM → SUC): $-.086$
Intervention (CM → SUC): .049
Differential (CM → SUC pre-post): .135

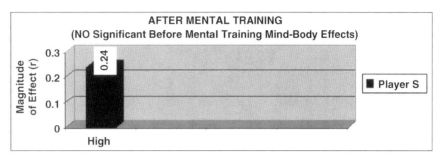

FIGURE 20.27   HRV and performance outcome: intervention phase.

Player Criticality and HRV Response and Outcome Association Findings (Micro-level): Intervention: L: H and CM .288

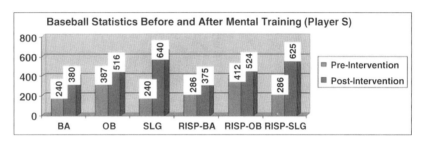

FIGURE 20.28   Batting outcome as a function of intervention.

This player is another power hitter whose performance was subpar in the first half of the season. However, he made strong gains in the intervention phase, especially in mental toughness categories. His improvement could be attributed in part to the 1-minute Lock-in HRD protocol in which High frequency HRV activity contributed about 6% of the variance in batting success. High-frequency activity is associated with parasympathetic nervous system predominance that is hypothesized to occur on an enhanced level during the exhale cycle of this protocol. Whenever an attempt is made to entrain (using biofeedback) a psychophysiological response that is temporally isolated or removed from an actual task or performance condition (e.g., when actually batting), any evidence of a response having an impact is crucial to establishing a procedure's potency or validity (criterion-referenced validity; predictive validity of a biofeedback protocol). In this player, as with the previous and subsequent case studies, regression analyses provide practitioners and researchers important insight regarding the effect, non-effect, or negative effect of an intervention as expressed in a variance explained. This important methodological component of the CP attempts to bring accountability to the assessment and intervention process and establish intervention efficacy on the basis of the extent a baseline or induced psychophysiological response is associated with macro- and micro-level statistical outcome measures of a sport.

Relative to Criticality, in Player S, the Low-frequency, High-frequency ratio (L:H), an HRV measure that can easily be manipulated through prescribed breathing, was associated with increasing criticality ($r = .288$; ca. 8% of the variance).

This player also had an Athlete's Profile on the cusp of being the most performance facilitative and, as expected, he performed well under critical moments pressure conditions. Like Player J, he encountered more of these in the second portion of the season (higher-level criticality).

ATHLETE'S PROFILE: Subliminal Attention: MEDIUM; Subliminal Reactivity: LOW; Subliminal Coping: HIGH.

PLAYER G (FIGURES 20.29–20.31)

Intervention Efficiency: 29.7
Pre-Intervention (CM → QAB): .13
Intervention (CM → QAB): .09
Differential (pre-post): −.04

Pre-Intervention (CM → SUC): −.063
Intervention (CM → SUC): .041
Differential (CM → SUC pre-post): .078

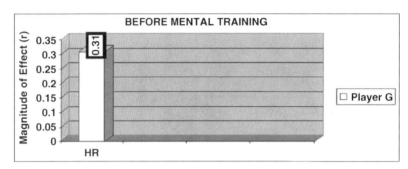

FIGURE 20.29   HRV and performance outcome: intervention phase.

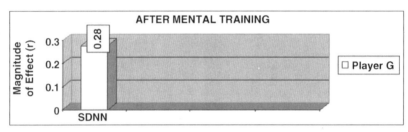

FIGURE 20.30   HRV and performance outcome: intervention phase.

Player Criticality and HRV Response and Outcome Association Findings (Micro-level):
Pre-Intervention: CM and HRV .292; CM and LF −.278

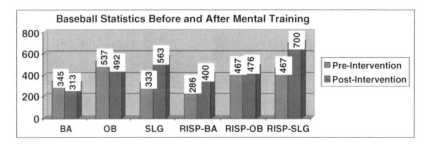

FIGURE 20.31   Batting outcome as a function of Intervention.

This is a very talented and physically imposing player; however, he has a more vulnerable Athlete's Profile, being in the high range for subliminal attention and high–medium range for subliminal reactivity and low range for the performance protective subliminal coping measure. As such, Player G is likely to be more psychologically vulnerable during critical moments of competition. HR stood out as being performance facilitative in the pre-intervention phase, accounting for 9% of the variance in batting success. This player made significant gains in slugging performance, both in routine and RISP-critical moments situations in the intervention phase. The fact that SDNN emerged as being associated with batting success in the intervention phase suggests that Player G had a higher degree of intervention efficiency (which he did, +29.7), since SDNN is expected to be the most responsive or likely to change as a function of the Lock-in HRD HRV protocol.

Relative to Criticality, HR was positively associated with increasing level of CM ($r = .292$; ca. 9% of the variance) and Low frequency was negatively associated with increasing level of CM ($r = -.278$; ca. 7% of the variance). This can be interpreted similarly as previously, whereby, those Lock-in HRD trials (intervention sessions) that generated greater heart rate (beats-per-minute; bpm) being linked to better Criticality performance and those that generated more Low-frequency activity being associated with poorer critical moment performance. Again, such discrepancies or possible inconsistencies in HRV responses in relationship to outcome may reflect differences in intervention efficiency across mental training sessions.

ATHLETE'S PROFILE: Subliminal Attention: HIGH; Subliminal Reactivity: MEDIUM/HIGH; Subliminal Coping: LOW.

PLAYER MC (FIGURES 20.32–20.34)

Intervention Efficiency: −2.1
Pre-Intervention (CM → QAB): .079
Intervention (CM → QAB): .218
Differential (pre-post): .139

Pre-Intervention (CM → SUC): .248
Intervention (CM → SUC): .030
Differential (CM → SUC pre-post): −.218

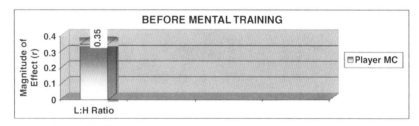

FIGURE 20.32   HRV and performance outcome: intervention phase.

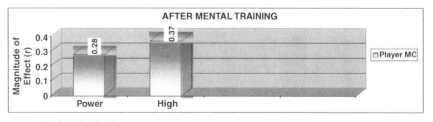

FIGURE 20.33   HRV and performance outcome: intervention phase.

Player Criticality and HRV Response and Outcome Association Findings (Micro-level):
Intervention: CM and HR − .459

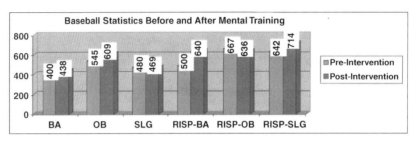

FIGURE 20.34   Batting outcome as a function of intervention.

This is a very talented player who is also on the cusp of having one of the two best Athlete's Profiles. His pre-mental training statistics were very good and he performed even better during the intervention phase, especially when it came to mental toughness statistics. His pre-intervention L:H ratio and the fact that is was positively correlated with batting success (explaining 12% of the variance in batting success that could be attributed to L: H ratio HRV) is consistent with his Athlete's Profile PHO constellation. In the intervention phase, Power (sum of all frequencies) and High frequency activity emerged as being performance-facilitative with this latter parasympathetic predominant response, explaining about 14% of the variance in batting success. Relative to Criticality, in the intervention phase, greater HR was associated with poor CM Performance, suggesting that those intervention sessions in which higher HR predominated (associated with less HRV [more HRV should occur in the Lock-In HRD HRV protocol] resulted in similar higher HR responses as when batting and subsequent poorer performance, especially as level of criticality increased).

ATHLETE'S PROFILE: Subliminal Attention: HIGH; Subliminal Reactivity: LOW; Subliminal Coping: MEDIUM.

PLAYER JV (FIGURES 20.35–20.37)

Intervention Efficiency: +24.8
Pre-Intervention (CM → QAB): .162
Intervention (CM → QAB): .024
Differential (pre-post): − .067
Pre-Intervention (CM → SUC): .165
Intervention (CM → SUC): .035
Differential (CM → SUC pre-post): − .13

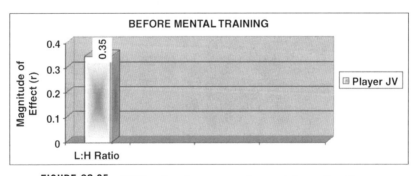

FIGURE 20.35   HRV and performance outcome: intervention phase.

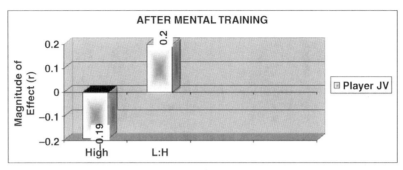

FIGURE 20.36   HRV and performance outcome: intervention phase.

Player Criticality and HRV Response and Outcome Association Findings (Micro-level): No CM and HRV relationships pre- or post-.

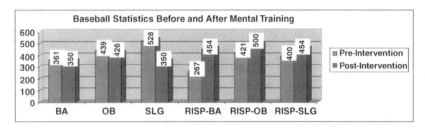

FIGURE 20.37   Batting outcome as a function of intervention.

Although this player's pre-intervention statistics were higher than those during the intervention phase, the differences were not statistically significant. However, importantly, this player's mental toughness statistics improved across the board, which suggests that the intervention impacted macro-level pressure performance positively. In terms of HRV changes at baseline, Player JV's L:H ratio was associated with batting success, explaining about 12% of the variance in performance that could be attributed to his baseline IZOF. By contrast, in the intervention phase, High-frequency HRV activity emerged as a performance-hindering measure ($r = -.19$), whereas, the L:H ratio maintained its performance facilitative effect, albeit to a lesser extent (4% of the variance in batting success could be attributed to the intervention generated L:H frequency). Such a pre–post discrepancy can be linked to a reduced intervention efficiency rating (however, this was not the case, as JV had a high rating). It is also possible that in well-functioning athletes (positive baseline psychophysiological measures/performance facilitative HRV) with an ideal or positive Athlete's Profile PHO constellation, an intervention may not be necessary and can actually change a natural zone state that positively predisposed athletes have developed, one that manifests itself during competition, into a less performance facilitative state.

Relative to Criticality and HRV, no relationships emerged in this player.

ATHLETE'S PROFILE: Subliminal Attention: MEDIUM; Subliminal Reactivity: LOW; Subliminal Coping: HIGH.

Summary: Critical Issues in Sport Psychophysiology and Biofeedback

This chapter was meant to not only present components of a validated athlete assessment and intervention protocol along with team and individual case-study findings, but also highlight important issues that have emerged pertaining to high evidentiary applied sport psychology and biofeedback (or lack thereof) that all practitioners need to be cognizant of, including:

1. Assessments and interventions are often administered in an ad hoc manner devoid of any underlying construct validity and coherent and integrative conceptual context.

   This point of critique was addressed in the context of a multi-dimensional conceptual framework that integrated relevant research from the domains or personality, behavior, neuropsychology/ applied neuroscience, applied psychophysiology, and biofeedback in the context of testable hypotheses to arrive at high levels of predictive validity, the ultimate benchmark for determining the strength of a relationship between predictor and criterion measures.

2. The need for ecological data that is procured during actual competition. It is no longer tenable to carry out biofeedback sessions in the office only and without prior additional real-world psychophysiological monitoring, and then merely assume that a protocol will work or generalize to the playing field, or believe an intervention works on the basis of fallacious notions like practitioner and athlete beliefs about efficacy (see Dual Placebo Effect, Carlstedt, 2010) or cursory outcome measures like winning a match after a biofeedback session.

   This chapter presented a comprehensive applied psychophysiological and biofeedback paradigm that was designed to be applied during real competition (official games). Such an ecological protocol is crucial to establishing dose–response and temporal parameters and the efficacy of an intervention (see item 3 next).

3. Athletes are taught visualization techniques, cognitive strategies, biofeedback, and other methods in the context of the intake or first session (often in group settings) and then sent on their way under the assumption that a client has (1) *learned a mental training (MT) technique and is capable of practicing it*, (2) *that the temporal properties of an MT technique are such that they can be applied at any time and then work later or on command*, and (3) *that MT will generalize to the real word of competition*. Most MT techniques are designed to relax an athlete; yet *NO* practitioner (other than myself and ABSP-trained and certified practitioners) could be located who actually monitored athletes during official competition to determine (1) *whether an athlete is/was engaging in the prescribed MT technique*, (2) *whether and what sort of psychophysiological responses are/were associated with engaging in MT prior to and during actual competition*, and importantly (3) *whether engaging in an MT training technique really improves/ improved performance, and if so, to what extent this assumption of MT-efficacy can/could be validated* (on the basis of objective statistical outcome measures that are accrued longitudinally at the intra-individual level)?

   Issue 3 is perhaps the most critical issue in applied sport psychology and biofeedback, since establishing dose–response, temporal, and criterion-referenced relationships between predictor and criterion measures are absolutely vital to efficacy testing and ultimately determining the amount of variance explained in an outcome measure that can be attributed to an intervention. The preceding findings clearly reveal how complex intervention efficacy can be. On one hand, a macro-outcome measure may suggest that mental training made a huge impact, especially at the team level (group level), yet when individual players are analyzed in the context of micro-outcome measures like critical moments, the seemingly clear association between an intervention and outcome becomes more muddled.

Conclusions

1. Construct validity: a strong conceptual framework will increase the likelihood that higher levels of variance explained in an outcome measure can be attained and directly linked to brain–mind–body–motor processes that are hypothesized to mediate peak performance.

2. The Individual Zone of Optimum Functioning (IZOF) model, one of the dominant models of peak performance, was supported in this study. Individual HRV response profiles emerged as a function of baseline, intervention, and criticality conditions.

3. Interventions do not always work: while macro-global statistics such as pre- versus intervention batting average may suggest that performance gains resulted from mental training, an in-depth analysis of multiple micro-outcome measures may reveal differential performance gains of decrements in the same player. Consequently, an evidence or interpretive hierarchy should be constructed to evaluate the impact of an intervention in terms of the magnitude of association between an intervention and most important micro-level outcome measure of a specific sport; usually, level 4 or 5 Critical Moment events during competition.

4. Intervention efficiency should be assessed to determine to what extent an athlete is engaging in a prescribed intervention (e.g., HRD of the Lock-in protocol), especially when there is a temporal lag between when an intervention is practiced (entrained) and applied when it counts (e.g., when actually batting).

The presented protocol is proprietary and copyrighted, not to prevent the dissemination of its procedures and methodologies, but to control its use or prevent the misuse of a protocol that has been validated at great expense over the last 15 years. Practitioners are invited to become trained in the CP protocol and participate in an ongoing project to better assess athlete functioning during competition and document the efficacy interventions. The goal of the American Board of Sport Psychology is to develop an international cadre of practitioners who are seriously interested in engaging in a systematized, high evidentiary approach to applied sport psychology, one that eschews simplistic solutions, guruism, the misuse of technology and biofeedback, one that is dedicated to valid and reliable procedures, one in which information and accountability reign and athletes, coaches, and organizations are provided with individualized data on performance, even if it reveals negative associations between an intervention and subsequent performance.

For more information on the American Board of Sport Psychology, please contact rcarlstedt@ americanboardofsportpsychology.org or visit www.americanboardofsportpsychology.org

Notes

1. The CSARCS-A test battery can be accessed via the American Board of Sport Psychology test center (email rcarlstedt@americanboardofsportpsychology.org; Key Word: CSARCS-A for access instructions, test codes, and passwords; the CSARCS-A and clinical analogue tests can also be accessed through the same email address).

2. Variance is explained on the basis of numerous combinations of PHO factors, neurocognition and heart rate variability (predictor variables) in objective statistical performance outcome measures, which ranged from circa .30 to .70 (adjusted r).

3. While conventional clinical heart rate variability assessments are usually obtained from recordings that are not less than 5 minutes, HRV assessment can be adapted to the temporal parameters or constraints of a sport (e.g., length of a time-out when HRV measuring takes place). As such, in baseball, 1-minute recordings are used. Although this is not an optimum time period (2 minutes is the minimum recommended recording period), shorttime recordings can be used. However, the very-low-frequency HRV domain may be inaccurate when recordings last less than 2 minutes (Perlstein, 2007, personal communication). This limitation was taken into account when analyzing the data.

The Intake and Initial Evaluation: A Sample Case Study From A to Z

The initial intake and evaluation session is an important first step in the evidence chain. It presents an athlete with the opportunity to discuss issues that are related to performance and can provide practitioners basic insight into an athlete's style of communication, behavior, personality, and the overall case at hand.

One of the goals of the intake process is to establish rapport with an athlete, a psychological dynamic that facilitates trust and motivation to participate in eventual assessments and interventions. It provides a practitioner with an opportunity to educate and inform an athlete about sport psychology and specific approaches to assessment and intervention, as well as convey expectations one may have regarding an athlete's participation and involvement. It is a time to address many of the issues that were raised in the introductory chapter, including what can be expected in terms of intervention efficacy, amenability, and compliance and their relevance to successful outcomes. It is also a chance to address myths and misunderstandings about sport psychology.

A successful intake session can go a long way toward making a practitioner appear more credible in the eyes of an athlete. Notice that the operative word in the previous sentence is "appear," since credibility should not hinge upon subjective impressions that an athlete may have of a practitioner (and vice versa), but, instead, be based on the use of valid and reliable assessment and intervention approaches, competency in administering procedures, and bringing accountability to the consulting and training process in the form of objective outcome measures and evidence of intervention efficacy.

While there is an art to the intake process, in an evidence-based context, human interactional and communication components should be delivery vehicles but not central to the ultimate goal of obtaining valid and reliable information on an athlete. Good rapport between an athlete and practitioner, although very important, can also mask deficiencies and competencies and convey to both parties that all is well even though something is wrong. For example, practitioners, in working hard to establish rapport and credibility, may focus too much on personal image and issues that are superfluous to the actual consulting process. Rather than realistically discuss the potential limitations of a particular intervention, practitioners may exaggerate their own successes in the past, but conveniently ignore that they may lack training in certain procedures or methodologies that are crucial to high evidentiary practice. Yet, they are capable, in part because of the trust they have instilled in an athlete, of diverting attention from a potent procedure that should be used but cannot because of a training gap (and possibly making a referral to another practitioner) that in the end limits an athlete's possibilities. Rapport can trump evidence. It can be used to manipulate, deflect, and conceal practitioner weaknesses, even if there was no conscious intent to do so.

The failure to practice within a standardized evidence-based template or system, including the intake process, exposes athletes to practitioner variables (education, training, and experience gaps) and biases (e.g., the belief that visualization works for every athlete) that can prevent athletes from receiving the highest level of services.

Personality and behavioral variables that may underlie and facilitate the development of rapport may also hinder critical thinking about the consulting process on the part of both athletes and practitioners. Since in most cases, especially in private practice settings, athletes voluntarily seek help for their performance problems or to enhance their play, they are usually highly motivated to succeed, just as a practitioner wants to demonstrate his or her ability to enhance an athlete's performance. The very nature of this "motivation to succeed" dynamic can lead to the dual-placebo effect, in which both the athlete and practitioner mutually convince themselves that a consulting relationship and mental training is working, often in the absence of any objective data that supports such a conclusion (Carlstedt, 2009).

A central measure in the Athlete's Profile triad of primary higher-order traits (PHO) and behaviors, hypnotic susceptibility has been strongly implicated as a primary mediator of openness (e.g., to new experiences, self-exploration, psychoanalysis, therapy), a trait that human service practitioners (psychologists, sport psychologists, etc.) tend to be high in (i.e., score high on tests of hypnotic susceptibility, Carlstedt, 2009). Hypnotic susceptibility and its behavioral and sport-specific analogues, absorption, and subliminal reactivity play a key role in interpersonal communication, dialogue, team building, and the establishment of rapport in a therapeutic or consulting context (e.g., in sport psychology consulting). Patients and athletes who are high in hypnotic susceptibility are very amenable to intervention and mental training pursuits, especially those that are imagery or hypnosis based. These individuals are open to new perspectives; they are quick to uncritically accept a therapist, physician, or consultant as a credible expert and authority, one who holds the key to their improvement, symptom amelioration, or success as an athlete. They believe in self-help, are frequently on the lookout for new cures and procedures, and are willing to expend much time and effort at mastering an intervention or mental training technique. They want to benefit from the wisdom and therapeutic or performance enhancement skills of their doctor or consultant, who often becomes their guru. An individual who is high in hypnotic susceptibility makes an ideal client or patient; he or she wants something to work, is overwhelmingly amenable to most therapies and training, will be compliant in practicing them, and, importantly, really believes that an intervention will work and readily argue and attempt to convince him- or herself, the therapist-consultant, and especially doubting skeptics, that it does. Couple a patient or athlete who is high in hypnotic susceptibility with a like-minded therapist or sport psychology practitioner who is also usually high in this cognitive and information-processing style, and you will have the optimal team, full of rapport, positive energy, goal orientation, and the utmost belief that an intervention or mental training modality will work. Practitioners of this disposition will swear by their methods, convinced that the mental imagery procedure or cognitive restructuring that was just administered will ameliorate a patient's symptoms or enhance an athlete's performance.

Statistically, about 15% to 30% of the population has been found to be in the high medium-to-high range for hypnotic susceptibility, although more cautious estimates tend to cap these levels in the 10% to 12% range (Wickramasekera, 1988). Thus, considering that individuals who are high in hypnotic susceptibility are more likely to voluntarily seek help for psychological or performance issues than individuals who are in the low-to-medium range for this trait, self-report feedback regarding experiences and perceived benefits of psychological interventions or mental training may be positively skewed or biased. Add to the equation the fact that most human services practitioners (including psychologists, social workers; but not physicians) have been found to be high in this measure and unlikely to think that their procedures do not work, and one has the perfect collusion; a dual-placebo prone and believing patient-client and a confident and assured expert-guru (in the eyes of the high hypnotizable) who also believes that what he or she does will unequivocally help his or her patient-athlete.

The point to be made here is not whether an intervention or mental training method works, rather that there are potent individual differences factors that can significantly influence the practitioner–athlete relationship. If these are unknown or left undetected, it can lead to the selection and use of unsuitable interventions and an overall lack of critical analysis and evidence-based pursuits during the intake assessment and intervention process. This can result in interpretations and impressions that may be anecdotal, skewed, biased, and placebo-mediated. Hence, an intake session should transcend mere conversation, self-report, and good rapport. It should be structured to facilitate the derivation of valid and reliable information about an athlete's psychological propensities and behavioral tendencies, preferably through preliminary testing prior to the first meeting with an athlete. The intake session needs to be data driven and cognizant of crucial psychological variables that can strongly affect the evaluative process. Practitioners, especially, also need to be aware of the extent to which their own constellation of PHO factors can bias and influence the manner in which they interact, analyze, and advise an athlete. They must realize that self-report can to a large extent be influenced by hypnotic susceptibility mediated cognitive and information processing style, often making athlete feedback regarding intervention efficacy unreliable. Moreover, if practitioners themselves are high in hypnotic susceptibility, they must temper any blind enthusiasm about the efficacy of their methods, deferring instead to objective outcome measures for determining whether a mental training method is having a positive impact, if at all.

The intake or interview process should not be an exercise in free association or undisciplined banter. While eclectic interviewing or questioning may help establish initial rapport and address what it is that will be done with an athlete, unstructured approaches usually lack substantive investigative components that transcend mere self-report. The generation of crucial information, data, and insight regarding an athlete's personality, behavior, and subliminal brain–mind–body–motor and performance tendencies hinges on evidence-based approaches. In an evidence-based approach, the initial intake session is structured and standardized. It recognizes that rapport or the therapeutic alliance is an important ingredient for a successful practitioner–athlete relationship, but that good rapport cannot replace validated methods and procedures that lead to potent data, findings, and outcomes that make up credible and evidence-based athlete assessment and intervention.

Components of Evidence-Based, Structured Intake Sessions

Components of the intake include the initial response to a client who is interested in sport psychological services, preintake assessment test battery, the first face-to-face contact and discussion of the initial test results, on-the-playing-field evaluation, and the culminating consulting and intervention strategy.

1. THE INITIAL CONTACT AND FOLLOW-UP

This is an actual initial email inquiry regarding sport psychological services:

From: lf@potentialclient.com
To: rcarlstedt@americanboardofsportpsychology.org
Subject: Sport Psychological Services

Dear Dr. Carlstedt:

I'm very interested in participating in your sport psychology protocol. I'm a 5.0 rated tennis player, former college player and am interested in working on my mental game. I have terrible lack of confidence during important moments on the tennis court. I think that if I fix my lack of confidence on the tennis court, results will also follow. I look forward to hearing from you.

Sincerely,
LF

Clients should be made aware of the consulting process by email prior to a phone conversation or intake session. Doing so will make clear to a potential client the practitioner's approach to practice, client expectations, consulting plan and time line, and fee structure. Initially, follow-up communication by email is preferable to phone conversations that can be protracted and unfocused and take up valuable time. Here is the follow-up email.

From: rcarlstedt@americanboardofsportpsychology.org
To: lf@potentialclient.com
Subject: Sport Psychological Services

Dear LF:
The first step in determining the extent to which I can work with an athlete is finding out whether an individual is willing to commit to participating in an extensive protocol that I have validated. I am a vociferous critic of simplistic approaches to the mental game that unfortunately are pervasive in our field. To help you gain better insight into my perspectives and methods, I am attaching a paper that I delivered at an international conference that is relevant to all sports. It also contains an overview of my protocol's assessment tools and mental training procedures.

Undertaking a sport psychological protocol should be seen as a long-term endeavor, and if you have performance issues they must be dealt with over time. There are no quick fixes; only procedures that must be selected on the basis of initial assessments that will establish an **Athlete's Profile** *of mind–body–motor functioning. Hence, any working relationship should be looked at in the context of long-term performance and success goals and not as a Band-Aid, quick-fix. Mental skills take time to be developed and overwriting maladaptive tendencies (if any) during competition requires effort and practice and the documentation and analysis of attempts to enhance performance.*

The starting point of my protocol is an initial pre-intervention evaluation and assessment, including an Internet-based test battery, additional office-based tests, and analyses of practice, training, and psychological tendencies during actual performance. This process helps reveal baseline pre-intervention mind–body propensities and their relationship to long-term objective performance outcome measures (e.g., the effect of level of intensity on batting success during critical moments). The acquired measures are then revisited in the context of intervention pursuits (mental training—pre- and post-comparisons to determine intervention effectiveness). These baseline measures are also helpful for determining the basis of slumps or subpar performance, quantifying mind–body–motor responses and performance changes over time, and whether one actually performs better in practice than during real competition.

Eventually, mental training techniques that are prescribed are tested to see to what extent they are affecting performance. If you are interested in further exploring my protocol, I could arrange an intake/information session with some preliminary testing. Prior to that you should take an Internet-based neurocognitive and personality-behavioral battery (if interested, please request an access code and password; this should be taken before any face-to-face consultation). An initial intake session, including the associated tests, costs ___. Fees must be paid in advance. Thereafter, at least ten sessions are required to complete Phase I of the protocol, the pre-mental training, comprehensive evaluation phase.

The vast majority of these sessions will take place on the playing field during training and actual competition. The fee for Phase I is __. I do not work with athletes who cannot commit to Phase I of my protocol, since comprehensive assessment is vital to an informed, evidence-based intervention phase. Phase II is the intervention component of the protocol. Mental training is administered in the context of real training and actual competition. It is heavily data-driven, meaning that pre-intervention mind–body–motor responses are compared to mental training–induced responses and changes in performance outcome measures (pre- versus intervention).

The protocol brings accountability to the intervention process by determining to what extent an intervention impacts performance. This is determined statistically. Be wary of practitioners, especially "guru" types who offer quick solutions to complex problems; especially someone who sees clients for one or two sessions and does not leave the office, yet is full of claims and guarantees success. As part of the evaluation process, it is also critical that you are observed and analyzed when you perform and compete, on multiple occasions. A fee-based telephone information session, independent of and prior to the other consultations as described, can also be arranged in case you want additional advice and information regarding the protocol before making a decision to make a full commitment. The entire protocol can also be carried out under a more economical retainer arrangement.

I look forward to hearing from you in the near future.
Sincerely,
Dr. Roland A. Carlstedt

The preceding email is intended to inform a potential client in an honest and open manner about the consulting process. An initial communication should not be used to seduce a potential client to become an actual client. On the contrary, the preceding letter makes clear how involved serious evidence-based applied sport psychology can be. It makes a few things quite clear. For one, it is evident that athlete assessment and intervention take time, possibly a long time. It cannot be expected that maladaptive psychological performance tendencies that usually have taken years to develop can be eradicated in a few sessions, nor can performance deficiencies be gleaned or discerned on the basis of mere self-report, practitioner intuition, or context-inappropriate tests. Moreover, the reliability of an initial assessment can be validated only on the basis of ecologically based follow-up assessments that are carried out during actual practice and competition. Similarly, in order to determine the efficacy of an intervention, it must be analyzed in the context of objective sport-specific statistical outcome measures. This takes time, and potential clients must be made aware that mental training starts with a comprehensive, reliable, and valid evaluation, and ends only when an athlete's Individual Zone of Optimum Functioning (IZOF; see Hanin, 2006) and intervention efficacy has been established. The notion that there are brief, quick fixes for complex performance issues is flawed and to imply such is unethical. Unfortunately, prevalent applied sport psychological paradigms are structured more to fit the time demands or constraints of a practitioner than those of the client and fail to consider and accommodate scientific necessities that are central to evidence-based performance enhancement pursuits. Athlete assessment and intervention paradigms need to individualized and cognizant of complex multifactorial and multidimensional methodological and procedural issues. The temporal properties of evidence-based assessment and intervention should foremost be about the science of performance and its enhancement. This means that the consulting time line or framework must be customized to deal with any number of empirical challenges that will be encountered when attempting to learn more about an athlete's performance tendencies, his or her ability to apply a mental training technique during competition, and the efficacy of an intervention. Simplistic, office-based approaches to assessment and intervention and the artificially constrained 60-minute session are no longer tenable. Evidence-based consulting sessions can be open-ended, lasting anywhere from two to six hours in the case of, say, a marathon tennis match or baseball game.[1]

The email also makes clear that an athlete has to invest in the mental game in terms of time and effort and monetarily. Athletes and those who support them are often all too willing to invest in special coaches, training, and consultants, yet, when it comes to the mental game, many seem to think that there is some economical magic solution or method that will make them mentally tough, like having a psychologist teach them to visualize or relax, or reading a book on how to get into the "zone." The field of sport psychology has also helped perpetuate this myth by feeding the media with anecdotal stories of sudden and great success or improvement in mental toughness that are erroneously, casually attributed to, for example, reading a particular book, working with some guru, or practicing some technique (like yoga or meditation). This has fostered a mind-set in many athletes, coaches, and teams that psychological improvement or mental toughness can be gotten on the cheap; that learning a few "mind-secrets" will lead to quick, positive results, when in fact, positive psychological change that can be demonstrated objectively to improve or enhance performance takes time, can be expensive (especially for private clients), and may, in many instances, never occur. Potential clients must be made aware of these facts in the initial email or phone communication.

2. CLIENT PRE-INTAKE TEST BATTERY

The preceding individual became a client and agreed to participate in the comprehensive protocol. Prior to the initial face-to-face intake session, the client took the prescribed Internet-based test battery. Some of her results are discussed as they were conveyed to her during the actual intake session. Before moving on to the intake session conversation, some additional information on the Internet-based test battery and its relevance to the consulting process is presented.

Background Information: Internet-Based Test Battery

A central component of the intake process is establishing a client's Athlete's Profile, using the Carlstedt Subliminal Attention, Reactivity, Coping Scale-Athlete (CSARCS-A; see Chapter 4) to determine an athlete's constellation of PHO measures (hypnotic susceptibility/subliminal attention [HS/SA]; neuroticism/subliminal reactivity [N/SR]; repressive coping/subliminal coping [RC/SC]; see Chapter 4 for a comprehensive review). The following chart (Figure 21.1) contains all of the possible PHO constellations and the extent that they are performance facilitative or disruptive, especially as a function of increasing criticality:

A/HS	NA/N	RC	Critical Moments and Ideal Intervention
Low	Low	Low	Neutral to Positive: Biofeedback
Low	Low	Medium	Positive Tendencies: Biofeedback
Low	Low	High	**Ideal:** Biofeedback
Low	Medium	Low	Neutral: Biofeedback
Low	Medium	Medium	Neutral: Biofeedback
Low	Medium	High	Neutral to Positive: Biofeedback
Low	High	Low	Red Flags (2): Biofeedback
Low	High	Medium	Red Flags (1): Biofeedback
Low	High	High	Red Flags (1): Biofeedback
Medium	Low	Low	Neutral to Positive: Cog-Behavioral
Medium	Low	Medium	Neutral to Positive: Cog-Behavioral
Medium	Low	High	Positive Tendencies: Biofeedback
Medium	Medium	Low	Negative Tendencies: Cog-Behavioral
Medium	Medium	Medium	Neutral: Cog-Behavioral
Medium	Medium	High	Neutral: Biofeedback
Medium	High	Low	Red Flags (2): Cog-Behavioral
Medium	High	Medium	Red Flags (1): Cog-Behavioral
Medium	High	High	Red Flags (1): Biofeedback
High	Low	Low	Positive Tendencies: Imagery-based/hypnosis
High	Low	Medium	Positive Tendencies: Imagery-based/hypnosis
High	Low	High	**Ideal:** Biofeedback/Imagery/hypnosis
High	Medium	Low	Red Flags (2): Imagery-based/hypnosis
High	Medium	Medium	Positive Tendencies: Imagery-based/hypnosis
High	Medium	High	Positive Tendencies: Biofeedback/hypnosis
High	High	Low	**Least Desirable:** Imagery-based, hypnosis
High	**High**	**Medium**	**Red Flags (1): Imagery-based/hypnosis**
High	High	High	Red Flags (1) Biofeedback/hypnosis

FIGURE 21.1   Athlete's Profile PHO constellation and ideal intervention.

In addition, the last cell contains the intervention modality that is best suited to the corresponding Athlete's Profile.

A thorough understanding of the Theory of Critical Moments and its conceptual model and construct validity is necessary to best interpret the relevance of a client's Athlete's Profile constellation of PHO measures (see Chapter 4). Athletes and coaches should also be thoroughly schooled and tested regarding their understanding of the Athlete's Profile model and their specific profile (or that of their athlete/player).

Essentially, PHO constellations in the high or low ranges are the most revealing in terms of their predictive validity (i.e., stronger statistical associations with sport-specific outcome measures). Specific Athlete's Profile PHO constellations have strong empirically established relationships with:

• Physiological reactivity at baseline and as a function of increasing situational competitive pressure (criticality; critical moments)
• Differential attention thresholds
• Differential cognitive control/strategic planning ability (also as a function of competitive stress/pressure)

- Differential vulnerability to intrusive thoughts
- Differential motor control (ability to exhibit peak technical/motor performance as a function of competitive pressure)
- Differential pain, exertion, fatigue thresholds
- Differential levels of self-confidence, self-esteem, belief in ability
- Differential level of belief pertaining to intervention utility and efficacy
- Differential intervention amenability
- Differential intervention compliance
- Differential coachability

Establishing an Athlete's Profile prior to a first in-office or on the playing field intake session is important for gaining insight into psychological and behavior tendencies that have been associated with important outcome measures. An athlete's PHO constellation predicts with a high degree of probability whether an athlete is more or less likely to falter as a function of increasing competitive pressure (criticality, critical moments; see Chapter 2). Knowledge of an Athlete's Profile is also crucial for guiding the selection of interventions with an athlete's PHO constellation being a strong predictor of eventual intervention amenability. Athletes who are high in HS/SA are most amenable to visually based mental training modalities such as imagery, hypnotic, cognitive-behavioral, or biofeedback procedures. By contrast, those who are low in HS/SA, even more so if they are concurrently low in repressive/subliminal coping, can be very resistant to mental training in general (especially visually based interventions). However, the low HS/SA-RC/SC athlete can eventually be persuaded to participate in mental training if he or she can be persuaded to help out[2] or take a look (in the interest of research or helping the team) at how their mind can influence their physiology-motor performance, which can be best achieved using biofeedback and practical on-the-playing-field interventions that directly link mental tasks to technical performance and outcome (performance-feedback).

It should be noted that the vast majority of athletes who voluntarily seek out a sport psychology practitioner will have Athlete's Profile PHO constellations that have "red-flag" tendencies (see the preceding chart, Figure 21.1) that are marked by higher levels of HS/SA and N/SR. While athletes who have positive critical moment (pressure) performance propensities (facilitative or ideal PHO profiles) may not always be the greatest athletes in the physical or technical sense, they more often than not believe that they are (the greatest) and will rarely if ever admit that they falter psychologically, which is usually the case (indeed, they tend not to waiver psychologically when under pressure). However, incongruence between high self-esteem or confidence and actual technical ability is frequent in athletes who have a more ideal Athlete's Profile. This disconnect can lead to faulty self-perceptions about one's game or physical capabilities and hinder technical development. Such athletes will not necessarily overcome technical problems merely because they possess an ideal Athlete's Profile, and think that they are the best.

The preceding chart (Figure 21.1) contains the Athlete's Profile of one initial case (highlighted in bold font). This athlete has a one red-flag PHO constellation (high HS/SA-HN/HSR-MRC/SC) with raw scores of HS/SA 29-N/SR 18-RC/SC 17, providing more precise insight into the strength or psychophysiological intensity of each measure (more so than the qualitative descriptors [high, medium, or low] alone). This athlete's very high level of HS/SA, high level of N/SR, and medium level of RC/SC suggests that she does have performance-related psychological issues and complaints (consistent with self-report; see further on). Especially in cases where high levels of neuroticism/subliminal reactivity are evident, it is highly probable that an athlete will exhibit excessive psychologically mediated sympathetic nervous system (SNS) reactivity as competitive stress increases (situational criticality) along with concomitant diminished technical/motor control, and even in innocuous baseline conditions (e.g., just sitting there).

Discussing the Pre-Intake Report: Face-to-Face Intake

Once an athlete's pre-intake test battery has been analyzed, it should be discussed face to face at the intake session. Here is how this athlete's test findings were conveyed.

Practitioner: *Hello, "L", it's nice to finally meet you. Before I go over test results, tell me about yourself and the performance issues that you mentioned in your email.*

Client: *Well, I am a former nationally ranked junior and still have play at a high level. While I no longer compete full-time, I still play quite a bit recreationally and am often recruited to play doubles and am expected to carry the team. What has happened recently and inexplicably is that I frequently get very nervous and am afraid of letting my partner down. You'd think that an experienced player would not get intimidated, especially in meaningless social tennis matches, but I do. I play with some high-powered, well-known partners and I guess I am fearful of not living up to their expectations, and believe me, these people take these matches very seriously. Even though I have much better strokes and played at a level my usual opponents will never attain, it's me who is nervous and I am sick of it. I am tired of being stressed-out during what should be a fun activity. Anyway, that's why I am here. I want to get my confidence back and have fun again.*

Practitioner: *Interesting, you appear to be a very good player, and from your account I would not expect you to have problems with an average hobby player, since the level that you played at should inoculate you from stress and worries when you play down. On the other hand, you may have some developed traits that are strong enough to disrupt your motor and technical skills, rendering you incapable of playing to the best of your ability. Your test battery might reveal something along those lines. But tell me first, did you experience similar episodes of competitive stress or anxiety when you competed in national and international tournaments as a junior player?*

Client: *Now that you mention it, yes I did. I grew up in a relatively small country that really is not known for its tennis. There was only a small circle of girls who played at a high level and I was better than all but one of them; at least I usually lost to her, even though my coach told me that I had a better technical game. But I would also on occasion lose to players who were not ranked and much less skilled than me. And, yes, come to think of it, I never felt totally comfortable during official tournament matches; I always had the feeling that I was going to blow it, even if it was clear that I was the better player. So yes, I guess that I always was on the verge of choking. I might mention that there were very few good coaches in my country at the time, so I never could really turn to someone for advice or get the kind of training that would help me overcome my nerves. I guess I still have the same issues.*

Practitioner: *Yes, having good coaching during an athlete's formative years can be critical. Systematic training that integrates psychological components early on when a player is developing can actually help shape performance facilitative brain–mind–body functioning that becomes permanent, that is, stays with you for a lifetime or career. By contrast, if a young athlete exhibits maladaptive tendencies such as excessive nervousness and subsequent* *choking and nothing is done to counter faulty responses, these too can become permanent or very difficult to eliminate. This is not to imply that nothing can be done to help you. On the contrary, since we now know what happens prior to and during action phases of competition and how to facilitate motor and technical control using psychological techniques, affected athletes at least have methods that can be learned, practiced, and used during competition. In fact, even though you are complaining about competitive anxiety, it is highly likely that you experience phases of competition that are free from stress, in which you are actually functioning on a high level. When this occurs, you are demonstrating responses in a manner similar to the most mentally tough tennis player; the difference being, the mentally toughest players stay in the peak performance mode throughout an entire match and especially during critical moments of competition. Nevertheless, you can take comfort in knowing that you indeed are capable of setting off positive response chains free of stress. I'll demonstrate this once we get to the intervention phase of the protocol. One thing that I also need to do is take a good look at your game, your strokes, match play, fitness, and level of raw talent, as well as current motor skills and fitness parameters. At times, even good players may overrate their games and ability. For example, maybe your volley could be better. Since your problems are showing up when you play doubles, maybe a technical fault with your volley that was glossed over due to poor coaching when you were a junior has come back to haunt you. If you miss volleys and overheads or have a weak serve, your confidence can erode quickly. You might also not be playing or training enough to maintain a solid technical level. So we are going to need to do a comprehensive analysis of your game on the court, where we will also assess concentration, technical, and tactical thresholds to see to what extent your mind is in control of your motor system. The process will be much more about doing and experimenting and evaluating during training and competition than just talking and speculating about your problems.*

Client: Sounds good; I look forward to getting started.

Practitioner: Ok, let's first go over your test results and discuss what your Athlete's Profile tells us about your psychological tendencies, or mental toughness, especially when the going gets tough, during those critical moments. I want to be frank when analyzing your profile; I don't want to hold back or sugarcoat things, so be prepared to deal with potentially negative information or feedback, since knowledge can be empowering and you are here for a reason, namely, to try to improve your mental toughness and demonstrate peak technical skills when it counts the most, free from stress or worrying about the consequences. So, let's get started.

Practitioner: The following important performance-relevant psychological measures function to regulate focus, intensity, and thought processes, key elements of athletic success. They can work independently or in combination to exert an influence on the way you respond during various competitive situations. During more routine moments of competition, these measures manifest themselves more subtly and are not likely to overly facilitate or disrupt performance. However, when competitive stress increases or critical moments are encountered, they can interact or work together to enhance or hinder performance, depending upon their combination or constellation. These measures that comprise your Athlete's Profile will also help determine what mode of mental training will suit you best. So, let's go over the three key measures underlying peak psychological performance and see where you stand.

Hypnotic Susceptibility/Subliminal Attention (HS/SA)

Practitioner: *Hypnotic susceptibility or subliminal attention is a psychological trait or behavioral tendency associated with the way we attend to external (real-world) and internal (our thoughts) stimuli. It can be considered a cognitive style relative to the way we perceive the environment, people we encounter, how we focus on tasks at hand, and our own thoughts. In the context of sports, HS/SA can be considered the focus, or zone factor. High levels of this measure have been shown to facilitate intense attention or concentration on what needs to be done. It helps athletes enter that just-do-it mode, especially in the absence of neuroticism or high levels of subliminal reactivity, which I will discuss shortly. It works to direct focus toward sport-specific actions and away from distractions. Research has shown that athletes who are high in HS/SA are capable of concentrating intensely throughout a game or match.*

Neuroticism/Subliminal Reactivity (N/SR)

Practitioner: *Neuroticism or subliminal attention is associated with emotional reactivity and intensity. It can be considered the great disrupter of zone states in that negative intrusive thoughts that are associated with high levels of this measure tend to disrupt sensitive mind–body processes that occur during sports (e.g., waiting to serve or hit a pitch; putt; shoot a free-throw). Especially in athletes who are high in hypnotic susceptibility, high levels of neuroticism can lead to a shift in focus away from important tasks at hand, onto internal intrusive thoughts (e.g., fear of losing or failing). This is most likely to occur during critical moments during competition, when athletes who are high in neuroticism are more likely to exhibit symptoms of competitive anxiety.*

Repressive Coping/Subliminal Coping (RC/SC)

Practitioner: *Repressive coping or subliminal coping can be considered the great protector of focus or zone states in that it has been shown to shut down negative intrusive thoughts associated with neuroticism. Studies have demonstrated that repressive coping actually inhibits the inter-hemispheric transfer of negative intrusive thoughts from the right-to-left brain hemisphere, thereby facilitating the mind–body dynamics associated with peak performance.*

Practitioner: *Together, the preceding measures interact to exert their influence on mind–body–motor processes to impact performance, especially when pressure during competition increases. Your Athlete's Profile is a potent predictor of critical moment performance. Since you sought out a sport psychology practitioner it is likely that your profile will reveal some negative psychological performance tendencies; that is to be expected. On the other hand, it is good to know that even champion athletes can possess the most negative Athlete's Profile, and vice versa. However, there is a clear association between one's Athlete Profile and critical moment performance tendencies. As such, if your profile shows that you are negatively predisposed, it is likely that you are more apt to falter come crunch time; and that may be why you are here. You want to address and alleviate your performance issues.*

Practitioner: *Here's what the test tells us about your Athlete's Profile.*

ABSP-CARLSTEDT PROTOCOL: ATHLETE'S PROFILE

INTERPRETIVE REPORT

Athlete: LF   **Sport: Tennis   Level: Former Top 5 National Junior Ranking**

CSARCS-A

SUBLIMINAL ATTENTION/Hypnotic Susceptibility (HS/SA): 29

SUBLIMINAL REACTIVITY/Neuroticism (N/SA): 18

SUBLIMINAL COPING/Repressive coping (RC/SC): 17

SUMMARY CLASSIFICATION: HIGH-HIGH-MEDIUM

Practitioner: Your Athlete's Profile is on the cusp of being the least-performance-facilitative one. Two things stand out: (1) your level of HS/SA is quite high, which can be a very good thing during routine moments of competition and (2) your level of N/SR, unfortunately, is also high. People who are concurrently high in these measures usually have trouble when the going gets tough, when critical moments are encountered. What happens is that in stress-laden situations, athletes with this profile tend to use their superior ability to focus to lock in on internal chatter. This generates, usually, negative intrusive thoughts that disrupt the normally seamless shift from strategic planning and motor preparation that occurs in the brain of all athletes during routine moments during competition, allowing them to exhibit peak technical performance. When competitive stress increases and an athlete's stress threshold or tolerance level has been reached, this mind–body–motor dynamic is disrupted, usually leading to a technical error. Since your level of RC/SC is in the medium range, you don't quite have the most negative Athlete's Profile. Now before you fixate on this finding, which someone with your profile might easily do, be aware that tendencies that are associated with your profile will not manifest themselves constantly and that there are absolute elite athlete champions who have a similar or even less facilitative Athlete's Profile. One way to strongly mitigate negative psychological influences is to train hard and continually stay in form or improve one's technical game. Doing so is a form of mental training in its own right. That's why it is important to thoroughly assess your technical-physical game so that we can determine how close or far away you currently are from playing to the best of your ability. Psychological issues that are associated with your Athlete's Profile are less likely to be manifested if your technical-physical game is at its highest level. Being in the peak performance range will help you stave off critical moments during competition and resultant competitive anxiety. An athlete who can dominate tech-nically and physically is less likely to get in trouble psychologically. Thus, we have to get out to the courts soon and take a good look at your game. I tend to think that since you are no longer a full-time player, you could use some good training to help recapture the level of technical proficiency that you probably once had. You should also be aware that, even if you continue to falter psychologically, once you feel that your technical game is in order, there are still things that can be done to increase the probability that you will perform under pressure. We will discuss your mental training plan once we have completed Phase I, the assessment component of the protocol.

IMPORTANT CAVEAT

Practitioner: *The preceding predictions associated with various combinations/ constellations of these key performance measures are most likely to hold-up in the context of critical moments during competition or when competitive stress arises or is perceived. It should be noted that predictions are fallible, that is, they are never 100% accurate. These predictions are used for assessment purposes only and in the context of a comprehensive protocol. This means that just because you have a certain profile does not mean that you are doomed, or even that your Athlete's Profile is a totally accurate reflection of your performance tendencies. There are false positives and negatives when it comes to psychological testing. Although the test battery that you took is highly accurate in predicting critical moment performance propensities, ultimately, what you do on the playing field will be the final benchmark of performance. The same applies to interventions or mental training. I will never guarantee that a procedure will work, as should no other practitioner. At best, an attempt will be made to increase the probability that your psychological performance issues can be remediated and performance will be enhanced, something that will be determined on the basis of sensitive empirical methodologies.*

STRESS TEST: CONGRUENCE OR INCONGRUENCE BETWEEN VERBAL REPORT AND MIND–BODY RESPONSES

Once a client's Athlete's Profile has been established and discussed, it is important to go up one layer in the evidence hierarchy by criterion referencing an athlete's PHO constellation to an external measure or measures that are conceptually related to this profile. Relative to self-report-generated psychological profiles, it is important to ascertain whether behavioral, psychophysiological, or performance tendencies that would be expected or predicted on the basis of what is hypothesized or known about an Athlete's Profile are indeed consistent or congruent. For example, an athlete who scores high for neuroticism or subliminal reactivity would be expected to be highly reactive in both baseline and stress conditions. Highly reactive can be operationalized as a level of sympathetic nervous system (SNS) activation as reflected in very low frequency (VLF) heart rate variability (HRV) at baseline (while just sitting there doing nothing) or under stress conditions, that exceeds normatively established levels of this measure of autonomic nervous system (ANS) functioning. Excessive reactivity may also be reflected in changes in the ratio or low frequency (LF) to high frequency (HF) HRV activity from baseline as a function of a stress condition (stressor). One validated stress test paradigm, the Serial 7s backward counting task, reliably measures psychophysiological changes across a baseline and stressor condition (backward counting; see Chapter 5). It is used to concurrently validate an Athlete's Profile using HRV measures to determine the extent to which psychological factors mediate ANS reactivity and eventually impact performance.

The Serial 7s Stress Test consists of a 2-minute baseline condition in which the client is told to sit still and do or think nothing in particular. Thereafter, the client is told to count backward from 1000 by 7 continuously for 2 minutes. Sudden and unexpected cognitive demands such as doing arithmetic in an unfamiliar setting while being watched, usually elicits a psychophysiological response. Greater increases in specific ANS SNS activity across conditions has been associated with performance decrement as a function of increasing criticality (critical moments; competitive pressure), an occurrence that is more likely in individuals, including athletes who are high in neuroticism/subliminal reactivity.

This test is usually carried out immediately after discussing a client's Athlete's Profile (see continuing Case Study dialogue below). Concordance between neuroticism/subliminal reactivity is very high, in the greater than .85 range, indicating that the Serial 7s Stress Test is a valid and reliable psychophysiological marker of neuroticism/subliminal reactivity. Moreover, its predictive validity exceeds that of the Athlete's Profile predictive validity of around .70 − .80 (still very high for a self-report-based test battery; see Carlstedt, 2004a, 2004b). Consequently, the Serial 7s is also a very good stand-alone test and should be routinely used on athletes who have a more ambiguous Athlete's Profile (PHO constellations that are not at the extremes of the normal curve; circa 40% to 70% of the population will not exhibit ideal or worst Athlete's Profiles).

STRESS TEST: CLIENT DISCUSSION-CASE CONTINUATION

Practitioner: *Since your Athlete Profile was derived on the basis of your feedback, or self-report answers to a series of questions, there's always a chance that it may be inaccurate to a certain extent. To better determine whether your profile is indeed accurate, I will now administer a so-called psychophysiological test that will capture certain response tendencies. If your responses are consistent or congruent with what would be expected on the basis of your profile and what you have told me so far, that would be additional evidence attesting to the validity of your Athlete's Profile.*

Client: *What do I have to do?*

Practitioner   *It's a very simple and painless test. I will hook you up to a sensor that is connected to your ear lobe and a computer containing special software that monitors heart rate variability (HRV), a sensitive measure of mind–body interaction, especially stress states. There will be two parts to this test. First of all, we will measure your HRV activity for a 2-minute baseline period while you are sitting very still and not thinking of anything in particular. Then you will carry out a task while being monitored. I'll tell you about it as soon as we have completed the baseline monitoring.*

After the 2-minute baseline:

Practitioner: *Ok, now follow my instructions. When I say start, count backward from 1000 by 7s until I say stop (after two minutes). If you feel that you have made a mistake, just pick up from where you left off. Ok, start.*

Client: *1000, 993, 987, 980, 973, 967, 961, 954, 946, 939, 932 (time's up). That was embarrassing. I can't believe how bad I did.*

Practitioner: *Don't worry about it. Most people make lots of errors. Let's see what your HRV responses tell us.*

Practitioner note: That is a typical comment from someone who is high in N/SR, they tend to be overly concerned with failure, usually get very nervous as soon as they are told what to do, and frequently have a high error rate when subtracting even if they are normally good at math. This test is usually administered in the presence of an assistant, since the social situation in which the test is carried out tends to generate greater levels of stress levels in people who have high in HS/SA-N/SR as reflected in various HRV measures than individuals who have the ideal profile (high or low HS/SA- low N/SR and high RC/SC). The test attempts to simulate the crowd effect in sports, that is, performing in front of strangers.

STRESS TEST FINDINGS

Practitioner: *Ok. L, let's see what you stress test tells us.*

Client: *I can't wait. It probably will say that I need to take remedial math.*

Practitioner: *Fortunately, it's not about the math, or maybe not so fortunately. It's actually about you responding to a sudden and unexpected task that puts you on the spot and forces you to perform in front of people, analogous to having to get your first serve in during a critical moment in front of a crowd. The greater your mind–body responses deviate from a baseline level that is devoid of stress in the task condition, when performance is required while under pressure, the greater the likelihood that you will experience a decline in performance (Figure 21.2).*

Practitioner: *Your baseline HRV measures reveal an apparently very good resting heart rate (HR; 59 beats per minute), which suggests a good level of cardiovascular fitness. However, while heart rate, in popular or lay circles, is frequently used to infer a host of things ranging from level of fitness to state of relaxation, there is much more to HRV than is revealed in its other so-called time and frequency domain measures. Consequently, SDNN, which is referred to as the HRV index, is actually a more robust indicator of cardiovascular fitness than mere HR, and should be used to evaluate fitness, general cardiac functioning, psychophysiological responding, and even to screen for certain cardiac disorders. Your SDNN is in the 30s, which is on the low side for an athlete, and suggests that you may not be as fit as you could be. Low SDNN can also emerge after a protracted illness that limits physical activity, like the flu. Your very low frequency activity (VLF), an indicator of sympathetic nervous system (SNS) responding (associated with activation, nervousness, stress) is about 82 in the baseline condition, indicating that you were relatively calm when just being monitored (no task) and your Low to High frequency ratio was .6, a reading that indicates that you were generating more parasympathetic nervous system (PNS; associated with the relaxation or deactivation response) than SNS activity (Figure 21.3).*

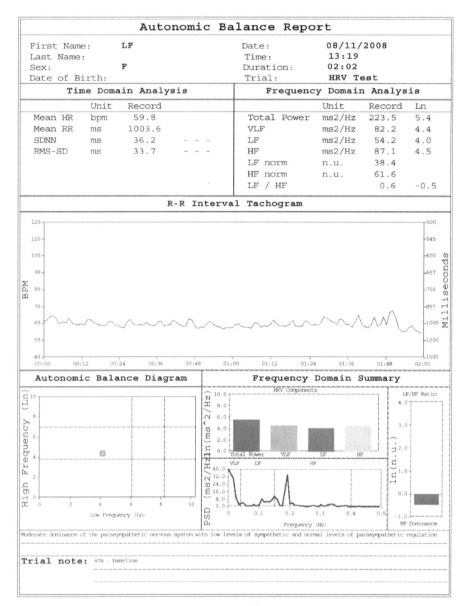

FIGURE 21.2   Baseline condition of the Serial 7s stress test.

Practitioner: *Here are your stress responses in the task condition: your heart rate was 69;
your SDNN, or so-called heart rate variability index, was also 69. Your very low frequency
(VLF) HRV activity was 649. In the stress condition, your L:H ratio was .7, indicating that
you exhibited more HF than LF activity when doing the backward-counting task. So what do
the differences in HRV across the two conditions reveal?*

Client: *So what does this mean?*

Practitioner: *There's actually some good news. Your response profile is to a certain
extent paradoxical. Although your HR increased 10 bpm in the stress condition, your*

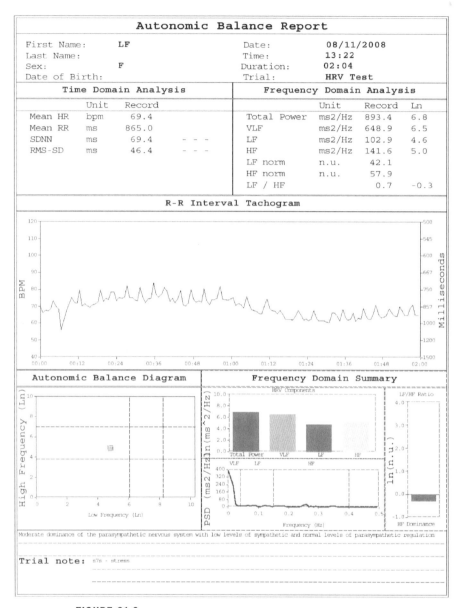

FIGURE 21.3 Stress-task condition of the serial 7s stress test.

SDNN, or HRV index, also increased, a sign of both psychological and cardiovascular resiliency. And, while you exhibited significantly more VLF frequency activity in the stress condition, this was tempered by greater overall autonomic nervous system (ANS) power (P; activity across all frequency ranges), such that, in the end, your L: H ratio was actually lower in the stress condition by .1 (.7 in the stress condition versus 6 in the baseline condition). What this means is that in their totality, your stress or task response measures were consistent with what one would expect to observe in a more mentally tough athlete, one who actually has a profile that is quite different from yours; one of the two ideal Athlete's Profiles (high or low HS/SA-low N/SR & high RC/SC). One explanation for the incongruence between your Athlete's Profile and your stress test ANS responding is that your level of RC/SC is in the medium high range. Thus, your level of RC/SC may mitigate the negative impact of your high N/SR.

It is also possible that you are exhibiting a false-positive response for high N/SR, in which case you may have a better Athlete's Profile than indicated. However, it is also possible, that in your case, the Serial 7s stress test is not sensitive enough to elicit a more extreme SNS response, one that may occur during actual matches, something that you reported to be the case. As a result, we will have to do additional on-the-court testing.

IS IT REALLY PSYCHOLOGICAL: ON-THE-PLAYING-FIELD TESTING

An office-based intake session, while important, is not always sufficient for accurately determining whether athlete self-report regarding psychological performance issues has credence. Just like self-report is often incongruent with underlying psychophysiology, indicative of a disparity between self-perceptions and subliminal mind–body processes that can impact health, well-being, and performance, so, too, are athletes' accounts of mental problems while competing frequently incongruently with the reality of their games. In other words, athletes are often quick to attribute their performance woes to psychological factors when, in reality, technical and/or physical deficiencies are at the heart of their inability to perform as well as they think they should. This is more likely to occur in amateur or hobby athletes who are less capable than well-trained and technically proficient athletes who have a better understanding of the technical parameters and demands of their sport. Nevertheless, this mental-technical incongruence syndrome can also occur in elite athletes in a more nuanced manner (e.g., a golfer not realizing that a subtle swing flaw prevents accurate tee shots). Such incongruence is also more likely to manifest itself in athletes who are high in repressive/subliminal coping. The incongruence phenomenon also applies to other in-office tests like the Serial 7s stress test, in which an athlete exhibits stress test responses that are incongruent with what would have been expected on the basis of one's Athlete's Profile, as with our case study (above). When incongruence pervades the evidence-hierarchy, additional ecological diagnostics must be undertaken on the playing field and in the context of realistic performance tests.

It is crucial that the intake session extend itself beyond the office and onto the playing field and involve expert coaches to help determine to what extent performance issues are actually psychologically mediated. Especially when practitioners lack expertise or at least significant knowledge regarding the technical and physical dynamics of a specific sport, it is important to bring a coach into the intake process. One cannot assume that athlete self-report about performance deficiencies have validity. As such, athletes need to be evaluated technically and physically in the context of structured training that is designed to determine the extent to which performance issues have a psychological or nonpsychological etiology. For example, a tennis player would have his or her strokes evaluated by a practitioner with expertise in tennis or a consulting coach to assess the probability that he or she will hold up in a match. For example, a tennis player with a poor backhand cannot expect to hit backhand passing shots in a match; yet, he or she might attribute his or her inability to do so to a tendency to choke when a backhand is encountered. But, did this player really choke? Is the self-report of choking congruent with the reality of his or her game, or specifically, a poor backhand that could not possibly generate a game-saving or winning passing shot? So, is it really psychological? This is a critical question that all practitioners must ask in the intake session and, if necessary, find the answer in the context of real training. And, if necessary, when a practitioner lacks expertise in a particular sport, a coach or other expert rater must assist in arriving at a valid and reliable technical evaluation that may confirm or call into question an athlete's self-report regarding psychological performance.

Another approach to disentangling psychological from technical/physical factors in the performance equation that is more relevant and sensitive to the games of advanced, elite, or professional athletes is to compare performance in simulated performance versus real performance contexts. At higher levels, technical issues are less pronounced, with most athletes being on fairly equal ground in terms of technical and physical ability. However, once pressure enters the equation (increasing criticality), breakdowns in technique or physically mediated skills may manifest themselves, which can be determined statistically (see Chapter 13).

On-the-playing-field evaluation is a mandatory component of the intake process. It is the most direct and ecologically valid approach for determining to what extent psychological factors are impacting performance, if at all. While one could argue that the incongruence phenomenon is a psychological factor (which it indeed is) that needs to be addressed, since faulty perceptions can hinder technical and physical improvement, incongruence between verbal report and actual performance can only be substantiated through higher evidentiary procedures that require additional ecological testing. Once incongruence has been documented, the issue of faulty perceptions can be addressed in the context of increased technical and physical training. Doing so usually leads to improvement and an athlete and practitioner eventually recognizing that previously incongruent perceptions were faulty. This can only occur if a practitioner, routinely, goes beyond the office when doing an intake.

The failure to extend the intake evaluation process to the playing field can have lasting deleterious consequences for an athlete and negatively impact a practitioner's effectiveness and credibility. What can occur is a situation in which an athlete, after revealing self-perceptions about his or her psychological performance issues (that are actually incongruent, but unknown to both the athlete and practitioner who never leaves the office), is given a "diagnosis" or some sort of analysis and mental training remedy that, in the end, is unlikely to have an impact. How could it, when a technical issue is really at the heart of an athlete's performance problems? Being told to apply some generic visualization intervention or engage in progressive relaxation or a patterned breathing routine is unlikely to improve a tennis player's poor backhand.

Hence, it cannot be stressed enough that an intake session must extend beyond the office and in many cases primarily take place on the playing field.

LF: ON-THE-COURT PSYCHOLOGICAL TESTING

Practitioner: *At this point, it has been determined that your expected Athlete's Profile tendencies were not manifested during the stress test task; in fact, your stress test performance was actually more consistent with a more performance-facilitative psychological profile. That does not, however, negate what you told me about your recent choking tendencies. So let's take a look at your game, strokes, tactics, and match play, among other things, on the court. I want to see if there are technical and physical factors that may be negatively impacting your game and contributing to your psychological performance issues.*

Note: In this case, the practitioner (the author), in addition to being a sport psychologist is a certified tennis instructor, is a former professional tennis tour coach and professional tennis player, rendering the need to consult with an expert (coach) unnecessary. However, when deciding to take on an athlete as a client whose sport a practitioner does not have expertise in or advanced knowledge of, it is imperative to involve an expert coach or the client's actual coach throughout the initial assessment process, and in many cases for the duration of a consultation.

> **Client:** *Sounds good. What exactly are we going to do?*
>
> **Practitioner:** *As a former tour coach and professional player, I have a good sense of what a player can do technically, that is, determine their talent and ability level fairly quickly, especially when there are glaring technical deficiencies that will impact performance. Technical and physical issues have to be brought to light in order to determine to what extent a player's problems are in the technical as opposed to the psychological realm. So what we will do initially is just rally or hit for about 15 to 20 minutes. I will shout out a number between one and five that is a technical rating for each stroke. Each rating will be noted. After the initial hitting session, we'll crunch the numbers and come up with a preliminary technical profile.*
>
> After about 20 minutes . . .
>
> **Practitioner:** *Okay L, let's see what we come up with. Ana, have you done the math?*
> **Research Assistant:** *Yes, here are the technical ratings.*

TECHNICAL FINDINGS

All Around (all strokes): 3.3
Forehand: 4.0
Backhand: 3.5
Forehand Volley: 3.0
Backhand Volley: 3.0
Overhead: 3.0
Serve: 3.0
Footwork: 3.5
Speed: 3.0
Power: 3.5

> **Practitioner:** *This hitting session was very revealing. Your game is just not where it should be at this point. This is understandable, considering that you are no longer a full-time tennis player and practice only 1 to 2 hours a week. I suspect that, in your prime, you were training at least 15 to 20 hours a week, right?*
>
> **Client:** *Sometimes more!*
>
> **Practitioner:** *While your forehand is still pretty good, the rest of your strokes, footwork, speed, and power are lacking, not because of not having the talent or potential, but because it is clear that you are not practicing nearly enough to maintain the technical level that you*

probably once had. Although I am certain that you overall will hold up against most hobby players and especially your doubles opponents, if you are under pressure, I can envision you, as you told me you do, faltering when the going gets tough. In addition, in contrast to your forehand and backhand, which are foundational strokes, your volleys, overhead, and serve have technical problems. Since these strokes are central to good doubles, I could imagine you missing volleys and overheads during critical moments in doubles, where net play is at the tactical forefront. Your footwork, power, and speed needs to improve, something that would happen if you could train more often. All in all, I think that your royal road to mental toughness is through your technical game. You can't expect to hit the shots that you once did when they count the most if your game is not where it should be. Moreover, if your Athlete's Profile stands as being accurate, you will have few technical or stroke weapons to hit your way out of trouble or avert being under psychological pressure in the first place.

Client: *So what do you suggest?*

Practitioner: *Let's discuss what I have in mind in the Intervention phase of the protocol. First I'll go over some mental training methods that can be applied in the context of technical and physical training or practice. Parallel to or in conjunction with your practice sessions or practice matches (singles and doubles), we analyze the matches using psychological performance statistics and HRV measures to see to what extent your mind–body responses are impacting performance and eventually changing, if at all, as a function of performance outcome and intervention effectiveness.*

Note: It is critical that athletes undergo a technical-physical evaluation under the auspices of a coach or other expert. It should not be assumed that an athlete (potential client) will provide an unbiased appraisal of his or her actual game, and the lower the skill level of an athlete, the greater the incongruence between self-report of skill and actual skill, especially in athletes who purport to have psychological performance issues. In the case of L, accepting her self-report about her technical game, or assuming that as a former internationally ranked player she would be technically proficient without doing follow-up on-the-court, a technical evaluation could negatively impact the entire subsequent assessment and intervention protocol. Practitioners who do not have sport-specific *expertise* who blindly accept an athlete's self-report regarding technical proficiency may expose themselves and their clients to the influence of technical artifact and false-positive/negative dynamics in the context of athlete assessment and intervention efficacy testing. Being unaware of an athlete's true technical competency also has ethical implications when clients are charged for services that are blind to variables that can invalidate psychological assessments and undermine interventions that supposedly will help an athlete overcome assumed psychological issues that are actually technically mediated.

MENTAL TRAINING METHODS FOR LF

Practitioner: *Here are few mental training methods that we will consider. They were selected on the basis of your Athlete's Profile. Ultimately, the goal of mental training is to get an athlete to unconsciously set off a cascade of brain–heart–mind–motor events that* *occur without any effort or thought when things are going well, regardless of the situation (whether routine or critical moments). This can be achieved directly or indirectly. The direct route to the "zone state" involves a simple timed breathing procedure that sets off simultaneous brain and heart responses that are associated with strategic planning and motor preparation, and the priming of an impending motor response and eventual commencement and completion of quick, targeted, and coordinated motor-technical responding. I should caution you though that this is not about yoga, meditation, or other relaxation-inducing breathing techniques; instead, it is very specific and time-locked to the pre-action–action cycles of specific sports. Once you learn, train, and eventually engrain this breathing pattern, that, like I said, occurs naturally when competitive stress is absent, it can be called upon during critical moments of competition. One important thing to remember is that even though I'll teach you the protocol's direct zone-facilitating timed breathing technique, learning and applying it will at most help you play up to your peak technical and physical potential; but, if your technical and physical game still has deficiencies that preclude playing at a level that is necessary to beat a specific opponent, this and any other mental training method cannot overcome them. Since I have identified deficiencies in your game, these have to be mitigated or eradicated before you can best utilize and eventually benefit from mental training methods that are most potent when an athlete's technical game is fully in order, that is, as good as it can be.*

Practitioner: *There are also more indirect mental training methods that are cognitively or mentally-based or mediated. They can be used to help get you to or set off the more direct mind–body procedure that I just described. Since you are high in HS/SA, you should be able to use imagery-based techniques to better self-regulate. With these methods, it's more about the management of mental activity so that you remember what it is you should be doing prior to action.*

IDEAL MENTAL TRAINING METHODS FOR H–H–M ATHLETE'S PROFILE

1. Imagery-Based Mental Training: pre-action motor priming

   Practitioner: *Prematch imagery training will be used to help prime your technical game for action. It is especially useful if an athlete can't practice on the court or playing field prior to action. This will be your primary mental training method in conjunction with increased technical and physical training. Again, remember, at this point, initially, it's about improving your technical and physical game. Doing so will go a long way to stabilizing psychologically, although, keep in mind the vulnerabilities that are predicted by your Athlete's Profile. Once technical and physical improvement have been achieved, you should be better positioned to reduce the frequency that you encounter in stress-inducing critical moments, especially in the context of hobby-player doubles, a setting in which you should eventually be able to dominate technically.*

2. Active-Alert and Self-Hypnosis for dealing with excessive thinking and intrusive thoughts

Practitioner Active-alert hypnosis is a form of hypnosis that combines physical activation and motor priming with psychological prompts that are intended to unconsciously remind or induce an athlete to do or not do something at a particular time or moment during competition, like setting off the mind–body pre-action–action cascade that I mentioned. It is also a method that someone like yourself who is high in HS/SA can use to better consolidate technical motions, like specific tennis strokes in long-term motor memory. For example, as you attempt to improve your volley with on-the-court training, you can augment and potentially expedite the consolidation process with post-training and pre-training active-alert hypnosis, something that can be done virtually anywhere that there is enough space. Once you play a match, depending upon the hypnotic depth that an athlete achieves through a self-guided induction and strength of post-hypnotic suggestions, an athlete like yourself may be able to go through an entire match or competition and have the feeling that it's just a practice match, devoid of fear and stress. The ability to engage in forms of hypnosis can be a major advantage for an athlete who is high in HS/SA, even if they are concurrently high in N/SR like you are, provided you are trained in this technique by a highly skilled practitioner who is also committed to efficacy testing, that is, using research methods to determine to what extent hypnosis is working. Always keep in mind and I'll always remind you, that components of this and other mental training methods cannot overcome faulty techniques or physical issues, so the absolute priority at this stage is to primarily use the methods that you will be taught to facilitate technical or motor consolidation. Then apply them when you compete in an attempt to reach your peak potential.

3. Heart Rate Variability-Respiration Biofeedback: to induce pre-action heart rate deceleration, a key mind–body marker of focus and motor priming.

   Practitioner: I already mentioned this "direct" mental training method that can be used independently of any other procedure to induce underlying mind–body responses that have been shown to occur prior to action in most sports, responses that are associated with greater focus, faster reaction times, coordinated motor responses, and successful outcomes. The timed breathing method that has been validated will be used to augment your psycho-technical training; however, once your game is back where it should be, it will become the primary mental training method, especially when encountering critical moments.

4. Threshold and Critical Moment Training for technical, tactical, and strategic issues; regulation of thought processes during competition.

   Practitioner: We will also use a behavioral conditioning technique in an attempt to desensitize you to competitive stress by continually training you in the context of ever-increasing levels of pressure or criticality with reward and punishment components. Over time, it can be expected that your sensitivity threshold will go up, that is, it will take much greater levels of pressure or criticality to set-off the fear and competitive anxiety that you have experienced. Threshold training will also be used to expedite the technical motor memory process.

Practitioner I think that I have a much clearer picture about you, your psychological tendencies, and, importantly, your game. Here's an outline of what we'll do over the coming weeks:

PRE-INTERVENTION PHASE[3]

1. Technical Threshold Testing
2. Focus Threshold Testing
3. Critical Moment Testing
4. Prematch Technical Preparation Tests
5. Match Play: Psychological Statistics
6. Comprehensive Analysis

Note: HRV monitoring will take place throughout each procedure in accord with validated methodological guidelines.

INTERVENTION PHASE

1. Pre-training Visualization and Active-Alert Hypnosis Technical Facilitation
2. Post-intervention Efficacy Testing (various paradigms)
3. Pre-match Visualization and Active-Alert Hypnosis Technical Facilitation
4. Post-intervention Efficacy Testing (HRV and critical moment statistics)
5. Comprehensive Analysis

Note: HRV monitoring will take place throughout each procedure in accord with validated methodological guidelines.

Practitioner: As you can see, the protocol is quite extensive. There will be two phases, the pre-intervention and intervention phase. There will be about 60 measurement occasions or repeated measures for each test. This is necessary for attaining an adequate level of what is referred to as statistical power to help ensure more accurate interpretation of the data. The pre-intervention process takes anywhere from a minimum of 15 to 20 sessions. It will help determine your Individual Zone of Optimum Functioning as well as reveal specific strengths and weaknesses. HRV monitoring along with structured mind–body response experiments will help delineate responding under pressure (e.g., critical moment–money ball paradigm) and serve as baseline comparison parameters once the intervention phase starts. You will also play anywhere from 6 to 10 matches in which changeover HRV is monitored for one minute. Time-out HRV has emerged as a potent reflector of mind–body responses during action phases prior to a changeover and predictor of subsequent performance in the next two games after a changeover. Again, I will need about 60 HRV measurement occasions to increase interpretive accuracy.

Once your IZOF has been established in the pre-intervention phase, we will start the intervention phase. You will be taught a technical visualization procedure, self-induced and administered active-alert hypnosis, and the CP-timed-structured breathing method for inducing pre-action brain states and shifts and concomitant heart rate deceleration that has been associated with heightened focus, quicker reaction, and enhanced performance. These mental training procedures will be practiced on the court or in a practice area prior to going on the court and throughout training and matches. Importantly, your ability to reliably use or engage these methods will be monitored throughout practice and matches along with the efficacy or effectiveness of these interventions in actually improving performance. This sort of accountability is critical, since just doing sport psychology (i.e., mental training) for the sake of doing something is not sufficient. Mental training must be systematically analyzed. It must be measurable and ultimately associated with performance gains. Be aware, though, that despite your and my efforts, an intervention may not work. If that's the case, it may be back to the drawing board. I cannot stress enough that psychological performance issues usually have taken a career to develop, just like it has taken a lifetime for your personality traits to set-in and influence your behavior and human interactions. Consequently, it would be folly to think that you can eradicate firmly entrenched negative performance tendencies in a matter of weeks. It may take a few years or more to overwrite maladaptive performance propensities, just like it would to change, say, your service motion or one-handed to a two-handed backhand. Thus, you really have to commit and work on your mental game like you did with your technical and physical game. There are no magic solutions. There is, however, a systematic evidence-based approach to the evaluation and mental training process, one that at minimum will reveal things about your psyche and how it impacts performance, along with one very direct mental training procedure that has been shown to facilitate pre-action technical priming and subsequent action.

Client: *Wow, this is quite extensive. I never realized how complex mental training is. I hope that I have the time to devote to the protocol.*

Practitioner: *You really need to make the time if you are serious, otherwise it would be best not to go forward. The notion that you can see a sport psychologist in his or her office once a week, be told to visualize or relax, or learn some generic breathing technique and presto, you will suddenly demonstrate mental toughness, is faulty. Sure, you'll find many practitioners who work this way, in the office consulting, stereotypical mental training with no accountability, just claims; they may make you feel good in the moment, but unless they can demonstrate empirically the efficacy of their methods, you will be participating in a mutual belief dynamic (seduction) that is placebo-driven (dual placebo-effect), but without the gains that mark the placebo effect. In other words, talk is cheap. It may make you feel good and get you motivated, but once actual outcome measures are brought into the equation, there may be no gains of note. Remember, demand accountability and realize that there are no quick-fixes.*

Client: *I see your point, and now can see how my high level of hypnotic susceptibility may be behind my belief that mental training will work, and quickly, and that I probably could be seduced by a quick pitch promising quick success. On the other hand, I am not sure that I can devote the time that is necessary to do the protocol correctly. I am going to have to think about this and will get back to you.*

Practitioner: *That is fine, I'd rather lose a client than have them commit but not follow through. Research on hundreds of athletes has shown that only a subset of these athletes* *will participate in the protocol from A. to Z. Those who do gain tremendous insight into performance-relevant psychological processes and tendencies and the effect they have on their game. They also experience an intensive and extensive intervention process that is quantified in terms of its impact on performance. My athletes, in the end, don't convey subjective impressions like "Yeah it works," or "No, it didn't really work" or "The method helped me relax,"; instead, they can tell a coach that mental training explained 14% of the variance in level-5 critical moments batting average. They will know whether and to what extent, say, Heart Rate Deceleration biofeedback, had an effect on level 4 critical moment success (points won in tennis). That is what they are working toward, the accumulation of valid and reliable information pertaining to psychological performance tendencies and their impact on performance and attempts to enhance performance through mental training.*

Note: This individual completed Phase I of the protocol but has yet to start Phase II (intervention phase).

Summary

The intake process in the context of the presented comprehensive athlete assessment and intervention protocol should go well beyond getting to know someone on a cursory level and establishing initial rapport. It should also not be seen as a mere opportunity to seduce an athlete into becoming another client through slogans, buzzwords, and tenuous claims of intervention efficacy (practitioner, subjective self-report claims of success). It should not be limited to an in-office intake and the arrival of a diagnosis on the basis of practitioner intuition or tests having limited, if any, predictive validity (e.g., using the Myer-Briggs test typologies to predict performance, or assuming that the TAIS style of attention will transfer to the playing field and predict actual performance outcome; it may, but that has to be determined empirically at the intra-individual level using gold standard investigative methodologies. See Chapter 3).

A high-level evidence-based intake session should include:

1. Pre-intervention validated psychological tests having established high predictive validity
2. Office-based face-to-face interview to assess congruence between self-report and test results (whether client agrees with Athlete's Profile)
3. Follow-up stress test in case of a more ambiguous Athlete's Profile, or when there is strong incongruence between self-report and Athlete's Profile
4. On-the-playing-field technical and physical evaluation for further congruence testing; is it really psychologically mediated?
5. On-the-playing-field focus, technical, motor control threshold testing
6. Critical moment analysis: practice sport-specific paradigm
7. Game-match critical moment analysis
8. Comprehensive analysis and report with discussion
9. Discussion of assessment results

10. Discussion of full pre-intervention assessment and intervention phases of the protocol
11. Discussion of all professional matters, including practitioner, client expectations and obligations, time line, schedule, homework, fees, and working agreement document.

Notes

1. While many practitioners may balk at the idea of leaving the office and open-ended consulting sessions, ultimately, a comprehensive athlete assessment and intervention framework will not only benefit an athlete, but also, justifiably, extend a working relationship with an athlete, and that can increase a practitioner's bottom-line.
2. Assist a coach or sport psychologist; find out why they are mentally tough by appealing to their heightened vanity (see Trojan Horse approach, Wickramasekera, 1988).
3. In case the reader has skipped ahead to this chapter, all of the assessment and intervention procedures that are mentioned in this chapter were elaborated in preceding chapters, in a step-by-step manner. Practitioners should thoroughly become familiar with the conceptual basis, construct validity, research, and findings pertaining to these procedures as well as how to apply them. Thereafter, practitioners should undergo training and certification in the protocol.

22

Critical Issues in Applied Sport Psychology

In contrast to the physical and technical game about which there is an abundance of scientific information and data along with large volumes of objective performance statistics, when it comes to the mental side, there is a paucity of valid and reliable information about its dynamics. The field of applied sport psychology remains mired in a paradigm that is based in part on weak data, questionable assessment methods, and interventions that are not validated at the intraindividual level. It continues to overemphasize findings that were derived from group studies as justification for the continued indiscriminant use of many of its procedures and interventions, despite the fact that such findings do not necessarily generalize to the individual athlete. This is ironic, especially since the most prominent theory of peak performance (Individual Zone of Optimum Functioning [IZOF]) stresses the need to establish individual profiles of athlete peak performance (Hanin, 2006). If the field is to make serious and lasting inroads and provide athletes, coaches, and organizations with best practices and methods, a paradigm shift needs to occur. It must be based on rigorous scientific applications and methods, similar to those seen in certain clinical realms where important advances have been made pertaining to patient diagnosis and treatment. New approaches to the evaluation of athletes must produce meaningful and useful information regarding an athlete's psychological performance that has a high degree of ecological validity and reliability. Just as a professional scout or coach knows an athlete's vertical jumping ability, foot speed, performance averages, technical propensities, body-fat index, and oxygen uptake, the time has come to develop individualized normative databases of psychological and neuropsychophysiological functioning in athletes for assessment/diagnostic, comparative, and intervention purposes. Practitioners should know an athlete's "attention threshold," "brain processing speed and reaction time," "frontal-lobe error rate," "emotional reactivity and valence," "critical moment psychological proficiency," "heart rate variability and deceleration response parameters," and "movement-related brain-macro potentials," to name a few important psychophysiological performance responses if they are to effectively advise athletes, coaches, and teams. The era of just telling athletes "to relax" or "just imagine" or "shut out negative thoughts" needs to evolve into a new one in which just relax means "generate more high-frequency heart rate variability" prior to critical moments, or engage in focus threshold training to improve concentration or manipulate cerebral laterality to suppress intrusive thoughts. The current cliché-laden "just do it" approach needs to be replaced with methods that define numerous nebulous constructs that pervade applied sport psychology today (e.g., "zone," "mental toughness," "focus"). It is time to delineate the IZOF theory and postulates using instruments and methodologies that allow for the operationalization of states of intensity or physiological reactivity it refers to.

It is no longer tenable for practitioners to speak in vague subjective terms such as "he doesn't concentrate" or "she's a choker," or "he's not mentally tough" or recommend interventions just because they are the thing to do. "You've got to visualize" or "get your intensity up," or "watch your body language" as slogans to somehow involve a person in mental training are insufficient. Athletes and coaches need to be provided with standardized assessment and intervention methods along with measures and parameters of performance-relevant psychological and neuropsychophysiological functioning. The time has come for sport psychologists to use new language, methods, and procedures that are based on empirically derived data and operationalizations of psychological processes and their effects on performance.

Claims and Promises

All it takes is a cursory search of the Internet using key words like *mental training, mental game*, or *sport psychology*, and one will come up with scores of websites of systems of mental training and practitioners that promise athletes the key to success. Usually, these sites and the businesses, services, or individuals that they represent have catchy names like *Peak Performance Consulting, Brain Game*, or *Ultimate Mental Training* with their very titles implying that the answer to an athlete's mental woes or goals can be found there. Looking a little further, one will find descriptions of a system or method that was developed by a key personality who runs the *practice*, who claims to have found *the* approach to the mental game, a system that is so unique and powerful that it will help struggling athletes or make them better. The more insidious systems make grand proclamations. For example, Brain Typing claims to be an infallible method for determining within minutes not only an athlete's psychological tendencies, strengths, and weaknesses, but also the neuroanatomical and neurofunctional underpinnings of a diagnosed athlete's mental game, and all this merely by just looking at an athlete.

A web search will also result in the discovery of former athletes, who, based on their experience and psychological struggles and self-methods for overcoming them, claim to have a major advantage over practitioners who were not top athletes. Less extreme, but just as troubling, are credentialed practitioners, many holding doctoral degrees or certification who claim unequivocally that *their* procedures work and will lift an athlete to new performance heights. Frequently, such practitioners advertise expertise in a particular method like hypnosis, mental imagery, motivation, or goal setting. Others may utilize biofeedback, with neurofeedback practitioners (a form of biofeedback) being notorious for claiming that achieving a certain brain wave functional profile in an office setting will take hold and transfer to the playing field to greatly enhance performance. In all cases, you will find a list of endorsees or testimonials from athletes, all professing to having discovered the *holy grail* for achieving peak psychological performance.

The guru-driven nature of sport psychology has contaminated the field and how it is perceived, evaluated, and valuated by coaches, athletes, and decision makers in organizations who may want to utilize the services of sport psychology practitioners. Yet, on the basis of what criteria are decisions being made as to who will be hired or retained, and on the basis of what and how much should they be paid? In a claim-ridden market, unlike one that is data, fact, or evidence driven, decision making is made difficult. Claims are not associated with transparency or accountability; hence, they can not be valuated. What is their worth? Does the claim that one's special visualization or neu-rofeedback protocol have inherent value, such that an athlete or team should pay a certain fee or offer a major consulting contract on the basis of what is promised? Does the fact that a practitioner has used a "special" procedure with hundreds of athletes carry any empirical weight? After all, how does the prac-titioner behind a mental training system demonstrate its efficacy; on the basis of having applied it to scores of athletes? Should not the benchmark for efficacy be data and not testimonial or endorsement driven, or experience in delivering services that upon close scrutiny are substandard and devoid of accountability? Can we expect administrators such as general managers of professional sport teams and athletic directors at schools and colleges, as well as coaches and athletes to make informed decisions as to who will be their sport psychology practitioner on the basis of personal pitches that to a great extent rest on claims, experience in practicing the procedures that led to a candidate's unjus-tified claims, and attestations of efficacy by current and former clients? Are such claims to be trusted, and should they be at the heart or center of a professional field of disciplined inquiry and practice?

The following critique provides a foundational and fundamental rationale for advancing evidence-based and validated athlete assessment and intervention protocols. Although highly criti-cal of the field, the points of contention that are raised were not intended to insult or be condescend-ing toward serious and ethical practitioners, most who are apt to have recognized, themselves, weaknesses and limitations of the field and many of its current practices.

The American Board of Sport Psychology: Position Paper on the State of Applied Sport Psychology

The American Board of Sport Psychology (ABSP) initially presented its *Position Paper on the State of Applied Sport Psychology* at the American Psychological Association's (APA) annual convention in 2008 in a poster session. It was expanded and redelivered in a paper at the 2011 APA convention as part of a broader symposium on the state of applied sport psychology (Carlstedt, 2008, 2011).

Background

The ABSP position paper advances the perspective that, compared to practice and evidentiary stan-dards in numerous allied human services fields, the field of applied sport psychology and its prac-titioners are for the most part engaging in antiquated and substandard practices at the lowest level in the evidence hierarchy. The initial basis of this critique emanated from

1. Anecdotal experiences and encounters with practitioners in the context of the ABSP certification training programs:

    The ABSP holds an annual summer visiting fellowship and internship training program in evidence-based applied sport psychology, going back to 2006. Dozens of participating prac-titioners and students were extensively questioned about their experiences as a sport psychology practitioner in the context of previous education and training. Undergraduate and graduate stu-dents and/or student-athletes in the program were asked about their experiences as recipients of sport psychological services. This line of ongoing research provided experiential feedback sup-porting most of the relevant points of critique in the ABSP position paper. Respondents fre-quently mentioned that they did not experience systematic approaches to mental training or were not taught how to administer higher evidentiary procedures with both practitioners and student/student-athletes having little if any awareness of accountability methodologies.

2. Accounts of sport psychology practices in the media and practitioner websites:

A review of scores of sport psychology-related websites of practitioners revealed that they contained unsubstantiated claims and testimonials and no cautionary language regarding intervention efficacy. Instead of just listing services in a neutral manner, the vast majority of websites used misleading language and guaranteed successful outcome was usually implied. Interventions were often touted on the basis of misinterpretation or embellishment of self-generated research with inflated claims of success without verifiable documentation pervading. No practitioners, regardless of credentials or academic degree, could be found that advertised, let alone engaged in, gold standard assessment and intervention efficiency and efficacy procedures. This is alarming, a discovery that led to the inception of the ABSP in 2000, and its quest to advance high evidentiary approaches to athlete assessment and intervention and attempts to educate the public regarding deficiencies in applied sport psychology.

3. Importantly, the largest database of practitioner-acquired brain–heart–mind–body responses in the context of real and simulated competition calls into question claims of universal intervention efficacy. While intervention efficiency showing mind–body changes as a function of mental training was frequently documented, intervention efficacy varied highly as a function of three key isolated individual differences measures (Athlete's Profile constellations, see Chapter 4) with more negative or no change findings emerging than performance gains that could be attributed to an intervention. This suggests that something is amiss in light of field-wide claims of across-the-board high intervention efficacy and almost nonexistent reports of negative outcome. As a result, one could conclude that

1. Group findings reporting high efficacy do not generalize to the individual athlete as is often assumed by practitioners.
2. Or, there are design and methodological flaws in many positive group studies (e.g., lack of ecological validity).
3. Or, negative findings are not being reported.

As a result, due to a lack of extension or validation studies or practitioner-generated high evidentiary data (usually none), claims of high intervention efficacy can be called into question, claims that in the end can mislead athletes, coaches, the public, and the field of sport psychology into believing that sport psychology consistently offers intervention solutions that are potent, reliable, and universally replicable.

ABSP-generated data suggests that nothing could be further from the truth when gold standard methodologies are applied longitudinally, with consistent high intervention efficacy being very difficult to demonstrate at the intraindividual level.

More non- and negative than positive results emerge when high evidentiary approaches to efficacy tested are used.

IDENTIFIED ISSUES AND SHORTCOMINGS IN APPLIED SPORT PSYCHOLOGY: OVERVIEW

- Prevalent approaches to athlete assessment and intervention are based on weak or incomplete data and even myth (e.g., lack of ecological data on mind–body performance responses during actual competition; notion that body language predicts performance).

- Assessment and intervention strategies are antiquated and often administered in an ad hoc manner, devoid of underlying construct validity or a coherent and integrative theoretical context.
- Little is known about psychophysiological responding during actual training and real competition, and whether attempts to induce supposed performance-facilitative intervention responses occur and, importantly, are they really associated with positive outcome? Moreover, the vast majority of practitioners have not been trained to engage in applied psychophysiology.
- Interventions are assumed to work; however, where is the accountability? Do they really work and how do we know (see Chapter 3)?
- These shortcomings have resulted in part from a failure to validate many of the theories, hypotheses, assumptions, and myths that drive prevalent approaches to practice, with untenable and unsupported approaches continuing to persist as though they were valid.

How Sport Psychology Is Not Being Practiced

Prevalent practice approaches are marked more by what they do not than do include and involve the following:

EVALUATION SESSIONS ARE OFTEN CURSORY

Practitioners rely to a large extent on an athlete's input or answers to questions about performance issues or context-inappropriate test instruments to arrive at a "diagnosis" or insight regarding performance issues. Important subliminal mind–body response tendencies that often transcend conscious awareness are usually not assessed. They are frequently overlooked despite their relevance to predicting performance, explaining etiology of performance issues, and determining intervention amenability and compliance. Coaches are rarely involved in the interview/evaluation process. Sessions usually last for an hour and resemble clinical or counseling sessions in their content and progression, with plans rarely being laid for later ecological evaluations and longitudinal follow-up and analysis.

PRACTITIONERS RARELY LEAVE THE OFFICE

On-the-playing-field observations and evaluation are not engaged in by the vast majority of practitioners, with many never leaving their office to actually observe a client perform. Major discrepancies between athlete in-office self-report and actual responses during training and competition thereby go unnoticed. Such incongruence between athlete feedback and practitioner impressions and actual underlying psychophysiology, psychological performance tendencies, and their effect on objective outcome measures (obtained in the field) frequently render in-office "diagnostic" conclusions incomplete, inaccurate, and/or flawed.

PRACTITIONERS RARELY MAKE REFERRALS

Practitioners, regardless of limitations in education, training, and expertise in a specific sport, tend to take on every case. Most seem very confident that they can handle any performance issue. What is troubling, though, is that very few practitioners are aware of what they do not know, including performance specificities and technical and tactical dynamics of many sports.

PRACTICE APPROACHES ARE ECLECTIC, AND LACK DOCUMENTATION AND ACCOUNTABILITY

Select 10 practitioners at random, and one is likely to find 10 different approaches to the evaluation and mental training of athletes. The lack of a systematic evidence-based approach to applied sport psychology can significantly hinder athletes from achieving peak psychological performance and obtaining valid and reliable information on their psychological response tendencies and mental performance during training and competition. Unfortunately, many practitioners are not aware that something may be missing from their practice repertoire, training/education, and knowledge base, or are reluctant to admit to such (even more so among highly credentialed or "experienced," "star," or supposed stalwart practitioners). Yet, the field and many of its practitioners continue to tout and promote their methods with utmost confidence to the extent of guaranteeing the validity and efficacy of their methods or approach. Such a state of affairs would be untenable in the medical arena, where procedural competence and data-driven accountability are demanded and the scope of practice is limited to specialty domains, a concept that is foreign to applied sport psychology where a "wild west" state of affairs pervades.

PRACTITIONERS FAIL TO UTILIZE ADVANCED TECHNOLOGIES AND METHODOLOGIES

Most practitioners lack training in applied psychophysiology, applied neuroscience, ambulatory monitoring, and use of psychophysiological instrumentation/software, procedures, and methodologies for real-time ecological in vivo monitoring and analysis of athletes. Most also lack training in biofeedback and knowledge pertaining to its utility as an on-the-playing-field intervention that can be used in an attempt to manipulate or shape desired psychological or mind–body responses (attention, physiological reactivity, and cognitive processing) and then determine the extent to which such attempts are achieved as reflected in fluctuations in the frequency and amplitude of wave forms that are visible on a computer monitor (e.g., EEG or ECG). These advanced technologically based procedures allow for the documentation of athlete responding, bringing accountability to the assessment and intervention process in the context of ecologically valid settings and situations, namely, real-official competition. Most practitioners also fail to employ single-case longitudinal statistical analysis strategies and generate performance-specific databases in follow-up to or in conjunction with every training session and competitive event that an athlete engages in. These are crucial high-level evidentiary procedures/methods that should be used by all serious, conscientious, and ethical practitioners or outsourced to specialists who are trained to use these methods and instruments. The failure to utilize the above methods, technologies, and information can be considered malpractice and is no longer tenable. Athletes, coaches, teams, and organizations who are not being exposed to these evidence-based approaches (the vast majority) that are critical to informed and best practices are being short-changed. Clients often unknowingly select (hire) or encounter practitioners under the assumption that there is indeed a systematic or universal and validated approach to athlete assessment and intervention that all practitioners are trained in and that they apply these and other important procedures. However, these assumptions are faulty with the vast majority of practitioners lacking training in these advanced evidence-based methods and procedures.

INTERVENTIONS ARE APPLIED IN A HAPHAZARD, AD HOC MANNER

Athletes are taught visualization techniques, cognitive strategies, breathing, and other methods in the context of the intake or first session, and then sent on their way under the assumption that a client has (1) *learned a mental training (MT) technique and is capable of practicing it*, (2) *that the temporal properties of an MT technique are such that they can be applied at any time and then work later or on command,* and (3) *that MT will generalize to the real word of competition.* Most MT techniques are designed to "relax" an athlete; yet, *no* practitioner could be located who actually monitored athletes during training and competition to determine (1) *whether an athlete is/was engaging in the prescribed MT technique,* (2) *whether and what sort of psychophysiological responses are/were associated with engaging in MT prior to and during actual competition* and importantly, (3) *whether engaging in an MT training technique really improves/improved performance, and if so, to what extent this assumption of MT-efficacy can/could be validated* (on the basis of objective statistical outcome measures that are accrued longitudinally at the intraindividual level)?

SPORT PSYCHOLOGY SERVICES DELIVERY APPROACHES ARE PRACTITIONER- AND NOT ATHLETE-CENTERED

The prevalent approach to applied sport psychology is practitioner-centered. It is driven by financial and practice realities that supersede what is known about developmental processes and the remediation of performance problems or the enhancement of performance. Yet, promises are made, guarantees are given, and claims pervade. It is disingenuous to ever make the claim that a psychological performance issue that probably took a lifetime to develop can be eradicated or performance can be improved on the basis of cursory, time-constrained sessions with a sport psychology practitioner that usually take place once a week for an hour. At worst, such a contention is a seductive claim and could be considered malpractice. Just as physical and technical training has ideal temporal parameters that facilitate technical maintenance and improvement, so too can it be expected that achieving enhanced psychological performance will also be contingent on intensive training over the course of time. Coaches and athletes know that technical proficiency and physical fitness require hours of training each day. Consequently, for example, a 1:10 ratio of mental to physical training is highly likely to be insufficient to improve an athlete's mental game. Just as a developing athlete or technically/physically deficient athlete requires supervised coaching for extended time periods, so does the psychologically vulnerable, burdened athlete who is trying to develop mental skills. An athlete's improvement or remediation program should not be constrained or dictated by a practitioner's temporal, financial, and other practice realities. This is a critical ethical issue as well, since developmental realities pertaining to behavioral change cannot be ignored in light of what is known about psychological remediation and improvement processes. It takes time to ameliorate sport-specific psychological problems or improve an athlete's mental game. Psychological interventions and mental training frequently must be carried out for hours to achieve consolidation. Ultimately, time-to-achieve enduring biomarker-verifiable change parameters must be established for each individual athlete. Doing so requires a structured athlete-centered delivery of services paradigm, even if it means that a practitioner must leave the office and work with an athlete for four hours a day for three weeks straight.

Toward a Gold Standard Approach to Applied Sport Psychology

If the field of applied sport psychology is to provide athletes, coaches, and organizations with best practices, fundamental changes in the way athletes are assessed and trained need to be instituted. New standardized and validated approaches to the evaluation of athletes must produce meaningful and useful information regarding psychological tendencies and performance that has a high degree of ecological and predictive validity and reliability. Sport psychology practitioners, athletes, and coaches need to be provided with evidence-based assessment and intervention methods that generate measures and parameters of performance-relevant psychological and neuropsychophysiological functioning for the purpose of predicting performance, guiding interventions, and determining their efficacy. The time has come for sport psychologists to engage in a new practice paradigm, one that is based on:

An integrative conceptual and systematic, evidence-based methodological framework for athlete assessment, intervention, and efficacy testing that leads to:

1. Group and *individualized* norms for attention, physiological reactivity, and cognitive responding that have a high degree of predictive and ecological validity.
2. Validation of standardized, ecological protocols that are designed to assess and manipulate attention, psychophysiological responding, and cognitive processing, as well as determine the efficacy of interventions on the basis of objective statistical performance and "mind–body" (e.g., HRV) outcome measures.
3. Operationalizations and measurement of psychological performance (e.g., Zone, or Flow states; IZOF) beyond self-report, anecdotal, and mythical descriptions.
4. Longitudinal databases of athlete psychological performance and psychophysiological responding that are derived from microanalyses of training and actual competition (before, during, and after) and include intervention efficacy testing information (outcome data).

Points 1–4 will not be elaborated here. They were extensively explicated throughout this book. Readers are referred especially to Chapters 2 and 3.

ABOUT THE AMERICAN BOARD OF SPORT PSYCHOLOGY

The ABSP was founded in 2000. Its mission is to advance practice, education, and training standards in the field of applied sport psychology as well as provide licensed psychologists the opportunity to achieve board certification in sport psychology. It also provides training and certification for other qualified individuals commensurate with their educational and occupational background and licensure status. Nonpsychologist practitioners who have earned board certification, consistent with state title and scope of practice laws, practice under the supervision of ABSP-licensed psychologists. In addition, all ABSP board-certified psychologists and consultants are continually linked to the ABSP database of athlete brain–heart–mind–body–motor and performance outcome responses. This has resulted in a network of practitioners who have been trained in comprehensive high evidentiary approaches to athlete assessment and intervention who continually submit data and findings to the ABSP psychological performance database, allowing for ongoing analyses of the ABSP construct and conceptual bases.

The ABSP certification roadmap is extensive and rigorous and is comparable to graduate-level education. Certification cannot merely be attained by a review of credentials, past education, degree or licensure status, and previous accomplishments, or based on an individual's background or experience as a sport psychology practitioner or on the basis of one's stature.

The default position of the ABSP is that unless a practitioner can demonstrate to the board that he or she is trained in all of the ABSP-identified advanced higher evidentiary methodologies, procedures, assessment approaches, intervention modalities, and comprehensive intervention efficiency and efficacy testing approaches, and provide evidence attesting to such and the fact that he or she actually uses gold-standard approaches to athlete assessment and intervention, practice deficiencies are assumed to exist that need to be addressed through advanced continuing education and training. Hence, mere experience, in light of the contemporary state of applied sport psychology and the field's pervasive practices, is not sufficient to be granted board certification or allow for a waiver of the ABSP entry-level training program on the basis of an candidate's extant credentials, background, and experience.

All candidates for board certification must complete the ABSP training roadmap, commencing with topic-specific study and task modules that lead to an applied practicum and culminating final project that must be of a publishable quality (analogous to a master's thesis). Completion of the entry-level board certification requisites results in Board-Certified Consultant status. Every candidate *must* complete the initial education and training program irrespective of licensure status or educational background. Entry-level board certification (Board-Certified Consultant) is a terminal credential for any candidate who does not possess a master's degree in psychology or field closely related to psychology (e.g., sport psychology, sport science, or physical education with a sport psychology emphasis or specialization). The Board-Certified Consultant credential was developed in order to preemptively reach people who were interested in sport psychology and intended to either practice applied sport psychology in its own right in the context of a consulting practice, or augment and enhance their work with athletes in other contexts, like coaching (as in coaching a team or individual athlete) or other sub-master's level human services professions, such as coaching (as in personal coaching), physical training, or even as a physician. Again, it must be stressed that ABSP Board-Certified Consultants usually, in light of state scope of practice laws governing the practice of psychology, must practice under supervision.

For master's degree holders in the level allied human services field, an advanced credential, Board-Certified Master Consultant, can be attained and is the terminal; psychologists' terminal certificate is the Board-Certified Sport Psychologist credential.

Postentry Board-Certified Consultant terminal credential attainment is based on accrued supervised experience as follows:

Board-Certified Consultant > Board-Certified Master Consultant: 25 complete or approved partial athlete assessment and intervention case consultations with comprehensive Athlete's Profile-guided evaluation, intervention efficiency, and intervention efficacy testing with preintervention and intervention phases using the ABSP-Carlstedt Protocol. Total approximate experience hours: 250 hours.

Board-Certified Master Consultant > Board-Certified Master Consultant–Diplomate: 50 complete or approved partial athlete assessment and intervention case consultations with comprehensive Athlete's Profile-guided evaluation, intervention efficiency, and intervention efficacy testing with preintervention and intervention phases using the ABSP-Carlstedt Protocol. Total approximate experience hours: 500 hours.

Board-Certified Consultant > Board-Certified Master Consultant > Board-Certified Sport Psychologist: 75 complete or approved partial athlete assessment and intervention case consultations with comprehensive Athlete's Profile-guided evaluation, intervention efficiency, and intervention efficacy testing with preintervention and intervention phases using the ABSP-Carlstedt Protocol. Total approximate experience hours: 750 hours.

Board-Certified Sport Psychologist > Board-Certified Sport Psychologist–Diplomate: Diplomate status can be earned or attained on the basis of professional accomplishments, including research and other publications that advance ABSP advanced methodologies and procedures; consulting appointments with professional, Olympic, or collegiate teams and/or athletes; case study data contributions to the ABSP database; or as determined by the ABSP board of directors on the basis of outstanding contributions to the field of applied sport psychology.

Hours include prepracticum study and research, practicum, and final project time during the mandated entry-level training program leading to the ABSP: Board-Certified Consultant certificate as well as other documented experience hours that are approved by the ABSP board of directors.

The American Board of Sport Psychology Training and Certification Roadmap: 2012[1]

OVERVIEW: DISTANCE-BASED AND RESIDENTIAL VISITING FELLOWSHIP AND CERTIFICATION PROGRAM

Candidates are given a reading list and provided study guides. Once all assigned reading is completed, work on content modules begins. There are 10 modules that are completed one at a time. Module completion requires doing tasks and answering questions related to a module topic. Completed work is sent to a candidate's mentor by email attachment for evaluation and feedback. Once a module is successfully completed, the student progresses to the next module and so on until seven modules have been completed. At that point, modules 8–10, a combined applied/experiential/practicum module (three in one), is undertaken. This module involves applying the ABSP evidence-based athlete assessment and mental training protocol to athletes. Once the applied module is successfully completed, a candidate designs a final project that entails carrying out prescribed research and data collection under the supervision of his or her mentor. The final project is heavily mentored and designed to expose students to the pitfalls, limitations, and testing aspects of applied sport psychology, as well as the potency and predictive capabilities of the ABSP athlete applied practice model.

Modules

Candidates may eliminate any one of the following two modules (1 or 9; see below). When all modules have been completed, the applied practicum module can be started.

1. History and Overview of Sport Psychology

Course Content:

1. History of Sport Psychology
2. Theories of Performance
3. Assessment of Athletes
4. Interventions and Mental Training

2. Behavioral-Motor-Technical Based Learning

Course Content:

1. Cognitive Motor Learning and Skills Acquisition
2. The Cognitive Advantage
3. Symbolic Versus the Connectionist Perspective
4. Expertise
5. Direct Perception Approaches
6. Applied Motor Learning
7. Technical Parameters of Popular Sports
8. Tactile Learning
9. Assessment of Motor Learning
10. Working with Coaches to Improve Athlete Technique

3. Neuropsychology/Physiology and Cognitive Sport Psychology

Course Content:

1. Neuropsychology and Sport: An Overview
2. Information Processing
3. Reflex Action and Reactions
4. States of Consciousness
5. Cognition
6. Attention
7. Neural Learning and Memory
8. Neuropsychological and Neurophysiological Research in Sport
9. Subliminal Neurophysiological Markers of Motor Learning
10. Applied Neuropsychology in Sport

4. Assessment in Sport Psychology

Course Content:

1. Assessment Instruments in Sport Psychology: A Critical Overview
2. Psychometric Issues: Ecological Validity, Criterion Referenced Validation, Predictive Validity
3. The Athlete's Profile and Theory of Critical Moments Assessment Models
4. Psychophysiological Assessment
5. Neurocognitive and EEG Assessment
6. Ecological Assessment of Athlete Psychological Performance
7. Critical Moment Analyses: Quantifying Mental Toughness
8. Quantifying Zone or Flow States
9. Systematic Advanced Multimodal Assessment
10. ABSP Experiential Ongoing Projects (in 2012 MLB Critical Moment Analysis and Reporting)

5. Applied Sport Psychophysiology and Biofeedback

Course Content:

1. An Overview of Sport Biofeedback and Psychophysiology
2. Psychophysiological and Autonomic Correlates of Imagery, Attention, and Intensity
3. Heart Activity and Heart Rate Deceleration/Variability Biofeedback
4. Neurofeedback
5. Critical Issues in Sport Applied Psychophysiology and Biofeedback
6. Methodological Issues in Applied Psychophysiology and Biofeedback
7. Critical Thinking in Sport Applied Psychophysiology and Biofeedback
8. Getting Started: Basic Applications
9. Professional Issues, Advanced Training Sources, Instrumentation

6. Interventions in Sport Psychology

Course Content:

1. An Overview of Traditional Approaches to Mental Training
2. Heart Rate Deceleration and Heart Rate Variability Biofeedback
3. Video-Based Intervention Augmentation
4. Motor and Technical-Based Intervention

5. Multimodal Intervention-Distance-Based Multimodal Intervention
6. Hypnosis-Based Intervention-Active-Alert Hypnosis
7. Mental Imagery
8. Brain-Based Manipulation: Neurofeedback-Cerebral Laterality Mental Training
9. Intervention Amenability and Compliance
10. Intervention Efficiency and Efficacy Testing

7. Research Methods in Sport Psychology

Course Content:

1. Construct Validity, Conceptual Bases and Accountability in Applied Sport Psychology
2. Research Methods and Applications in Sport Psychology
3. Microoperationalizations of Predictor and Criterion Measures
4. Advanced Single-Case Repeated Measures Design
5. Advanced Assessment and Intervention Validation and Efficacy Testing Methods
6. Statistical Analysis
7. Advanced Databasing
8. Experiential Task: Design an Assessment Validation or Intervention Efficacy Study

8. Ethics and Critical Thinking in Sport Psychology

Course Content:

1. An Overview of Ethical Issues in Sport Psychology
2. The APA Code of Ethics in the Context of Applied Sport Psychology
3. Abstract and Overlooked Ethical Issues in Applied Sport Psychology
4. Vignettes: Ethical Scenarios

9. Clinical Sport Psychology

Course Content:

1. Clinical Assessment of Athletes: HRMTP-Based
2. Psychopathology in Athletes
3. Promoting General Wellness in Athletes
4. Exercise Psychology–Exercise Therapy
5. RSA-Biofeedback to Facilitate Recovery and Sleep
6. Drug Abuse in Athletes: Doping
7. Psychotherapeutic Approaches
8. Clinical Intervention Efficiency and Efficacy Testing

10. Practicing Applied Sport Psychology

1. Establishing a Client-Athlete-Centered Practice
2. Ethical Marketing, PR, and Media Work
3. Working with Coaches and Teams
4. Collaborating with Coaches, Physicians, and Other Professionals
5. The Universal Athlete Database Practitioner-Researcher Project
6. Competencies, Referrals, and Fee Structuring

7. ABSP-Certification Continuing Education and Credential Upgrade and Renewal
8. ABSP: Special Ethical and Copyright Stipulates
9. General Ethics

Practicum Module

OVERVIEW: APPLIED SPORT PSYCHOLOGY, ASSESSMENT AND INTERVENTIONS

Experience is crucial to becoming a sport psychology practitioner. The ABSP practicum module emphasizes critical thinking in the context of applied assessment, diagnosis, and intervention efficiency and efficacy testing. Mastery of tasks is evaluated on the basis of knowledge assessment and intervention protocols, their appropriate administration, including psychophysiological monitoring, statistical analyses, and structuring and performing efficiency/efficacy studies. An integrative approach that incorporates research on assessment and interventions from other domains of psychology is utilized to broaden a candidate's perspectives of applied sport psychology and expose them to advanced methodologies and procedures. Knowledge of statistical and research designs is required and is evaluated in the context of all written assignments relating to a candidate's final project culminating paper that must be of publishable quality.

Learning Goals

1. Critically analyze assessment and intervention research in applied sport psychology and apply assigned preintervention assessments to a self-acquired athlete population.
2. Select and apply an assigned individual differences-based intervention approach to arrive at the ideal mental training modality (method that is best suited to a particular client).
3. Implement intervention efficacy studies to determine intervention efficiency and efficacy.
4. Document and assess athlete psychophysiological functioning during competition and in relationship to administered interventions.
5. Evaluate emerging intervention methods in applied sport psychology, including heart rate variability analysis and heart rate deceleration biofeedback, neurofeedback, and manipulation of cortical states in an attempt to enhance attention (focus) and manipulate affect.
6. Design a comprehensive assessment and intervention program for athletes, teams, and coaches based on the ABSP-CP protocol.
7. Create and manage individual athlete database of brain–heart–mind–body–motor and outcome responding.
8. Deliver a culminating report and deliver it to client-athletes.
9. Document the entire process: video documentation.

Practicum Subject and Content Areas

1. An introduction to athlete assessment and intervention: ABSP-CP
2. Assessing athletes: comprehensive evaluation from the lab to the playing field
3. Assessing athlete-intervention amenability
4. Video-based programming; motor/technical-based mental training

5. Multimodal-based mental training
6. Multimodal distance-based training
7. Biofeedback I: heart rate variability assessment and training
8. Biofeedback II: heart rate deceleration training; neurofeedback, cerebral laterality manipulation
9. Hypnotic procedures: Active-alert hypnosis
10. Mental imagery: New empirically based perspectives on and approaches to mental imagery efficiency and efficacy testing
11. Assessing intervention efficiency and efficacy (strongly HRV-based)
12. Accountability, psychological statistics, database management, data analysis reports

Practicum: Administering the ABSP-Carlstedt Protocol

Practicum DVD; HRV software (provided to candidate on loan for practicum and final project); HRV monitoring sensor; Polar RS800CX system; safety glasses; ABSP-BRC test center (one access code); Line-Bisecting Test (provided); database templates (provided); statistical analysis (ABSP analyzes the data); video recorder (must have access to digital recording device to document practicum and final project process); access to Skype for online training and discussion sessions. Participating athletes must be recruited.

Required material, instrumentation, software and hardware, and participants:

1. *Assessment of primary higher-order psychological factors using the Carlstedt Subliminal Attention, Reactivity, Coping Scale and related tests to measure an athlete's level of hypnotic susceptibility, neuroticism, and repressive coping*
2. *Neurocognitive testing using the brain resource Internet-based test battery for assessing subliminal brain responses (www.americanboardof sportpsychology.org link to test center)*

Informed consent must be obtained from each participant or parent of participant if under 18 years of age.

Applied Assignment: Take the ABSP-BRC Internet-based test battery. Locate your CSARCS-A Athlete's Profile PHO constellation. Analyze it in the context of what your AP predicts about your psychological performance tendencies. Administer the document-based CSARCS-A and clinical analogue tests (TAS, PANAS, and MC) to 10 athletes. Analyze each athlete's AP and write a brief report.

3. *In-the-laboratory psychophysiological stress testing with video stimulus/stress paradigm: checking for stress responding*

Applied Assignment: Obtain an HRV baseline on 10 athletes (after CSARCS-A testing) followed by a Serial 7s Stress Test using the provided HRV software and sensor. Thereafter, make a video of the most and least psychophysiological reactive athlete relative to his or her Serial 7s test (changes from baseline to the stress condition) engaging in sport competition. The video should last 10 min and show continuous action. Analyze HRV changes across the baseline, Serial 7s stress test, and video viewing. If necessary, recruit the help of a coach to conceptualize and shoot the video, being sure to depict critical moments that should be apparent to a viewer or made known that what is being watched contains critical moments.

Discussion Assignment: Based on each individual athlete's HRV across conditions, how many results could be considered consistent with what would have been expected or predicted on the basis of each athlete's individual AP constellation of PHO traits and behaviors?

4. *Quantitative EEG (qEEG, brain mapping) using the Brain Resource Paradigm for assessing subliminal brain responding: a sophisticated testing methodology that could reveal long-term effects of mental training*

5. *On-the-playing-field assessment of brain responding using blue-tooth-based wireless EEG: measuring actual brain responses come crunch time*

Applied Assignment: Athlete Database Management, Analysis, and Interpretation
Take and administer the line-bisecting (LB) test to the same 10 athletes being sure to prescreen athletes for handedness using the Edinburgh Handedness Inventory (EHI). Analyze the results in the context of cortical activation/laterality theory. Report your results and analyses.

Applied Assignment: Revisit the ABSP-BRC test results that you took and locate your BRC neurocognitive test scores. Analyze your neurocognitive performance in the context of your LB scores and Athlete's Profile.

Discussion Assignment: What neurocognitive measure(s) would you expect to reflect, measure, or be associated/correlated with your AP PHO (e.g., what/which neurocognitive measure(s) corresponds with hypnotic susceptibility, neuroticism, and repressive coping). What measures reflect relative left, right, or bilateral brain hemispheric predominance (i.e., in which hemisphere are the obtained neurocognitive measures thought to be located anatomically and functionally). What are their relevance to an athlete's level of physiological reactivity, attention, and style/speed of cognitive processing and vulnerability to intrusive thoughts, to mental toughness, and mastery of critical moments?

6. *On-the-playing-field assessment of heart rate variability: Time-out paradigm*

7. *Actual competition wireless monitoring of heart activity and postcompetition heart rate deceleration analysis*

Applied Assignment: Read Chapter 9 in Evidence-Based Applied Sport Psychology. Replicate the presented HRV monitoring paradigms in the context of a sport (1 athlete) in which you have advanced knowledge of or expertise, or design a replication paradigm with the assistance of a coach using the BioCom and Polar systems. Do an HRD analysis on the Polar data. Enter all data into the appropriate database template. Be sure to video record the process. Acquire at least 10 repeated time-out measures (or preaction HRV using the ABSP-BioCom system). Extract and time-lock the ABSP-Polar system-acquired data to sport-specific preaction, action, and other psychologically relevant epochs. Analyze the data and report on the findings.

8. *Critical moments analysis: an objective method to analyze how an athlete performs during critical moments*

Assignment: Observe five athletes competing (at least three different sports). Score each athlete's performance in the context of available sport-specific validated critical moment analysis criteria and/or develop a sport-specific critical moment analysis system (ABSP has validated critical moments analysis criteria and systems for baseball, football, basketball, soccer, ice hockey, rugby, tennis, cricket, and golf). Provide a statistical analysis of critical moment performance in the context of structured experimental paradigms during training, being sure to integrate "money balls" and during actual competition. See Chapter 8 for guidance.

9. *In-the-field technical and focus threshold analysis: used to analyze mind–body–motor control and ability to concentrate during practice and competition*

Assignment: Design a technical and focus threshold training system for athletes/sports in which you have advanced knowledge or expertise, and carry it out with five athletes. Report your results. See Chapter 7 for guidance.

10. *Mental training as a function of Athlete's Profile of primary higher-order factors, including:*
   (a) *Heart rate variability/heart rate deceleration biofeedback*

   Applied Assignment: Replicate HRV and HRD biofeedback mental training approaches in Chapter 12, or adapt them for a sport of your choice using BioCom and Polar equipment. *This assignment requires preparatory training via Skype. Arrange an appointment with your mentor.*

   (b) *Neurofeedback using Carlstedt Frontal Lobe Protocols: a means of directly shaping brain wave activity associated with peak-performance components such as attention/focus, motor control, and intensity. Used to manipulate key brain responses associated with zone states, responses that are vital to performance*

   Design Assignment: Using Chapter 18, adapt the Carlstedt Frontal Lobe NF protocols to a sport of your choice, being sure to consider the temporal properties of preaction, action, and other important performance epochs (this is a methodological/procedural design task; submit your work via email attachment).

   Applied Assignment: If you own or have access to neurofeedback hardware and software systems, apply a CP-NF frontal lobe protocol to one athlete, preferably one of the five previously tested athletes who has the most detrimental AP. *This assignment requires preparatory training via Skype. Arrange an appointment with your mentor.*

   (c) *On-the-field glasses-laterality manipulation training: teaches an athlete to induce immediate shifts in brain activation that have been found to underlie transition from strategic planning to perceptual preaction preparation; left to right brain shift facilitation and relative shutdown or idling of the frontal lobes, which can interfere with focus, keeping intrusive thoughts at bay*

   Applied Assignment: I. Using the obtained safety glasses, administer the Schiffer Cerebral Laterality Emotional Valence test paradigm to the five previously tested athletes while concurrently monitoring HRV (ABSP-BioCom system) for the purpose of establishing relative predominance of brain hemispheric localization of affect (emotional valence); a precursor to Cerebral Laterality Manipulation. II. Teach one athlete to induce a shift in cerebral laterality by manipulating his or visual field of choice to either induce positive affect or to facilitate the left to right hemispheric shift associated with concomitant HRD and subsequent enhanced attention, reaction time, motor control, and outcome. See Chapter 19 for guidance. *This assignment requires preparatory training via Skype. Arrange an appointment with your mentor.*

   (d) *Active-alert hypnosis: used with athletes who are high in hypnotic susceptibility to intensely focus and prime motor or technical responses, while shutting out intrusive thoughts and external distractors*

   Applied Assignment: Replicate the hypnotic procedures in Chapter 16. *This assignment requires preparatory training via Skype. Arrange an appointment with your mentor.*

   (e) *Mental imagery per Carlstedt Protocol: special mental imagery protocols customized to an athlete's profile and time demands of a sport*

Applied Assignment: Replicate the imagery procedures in Chapter 17. Be sure to carry out mental imagery or visualization intervention efficiency testing on the five previously tested athletes. *This assignment requires preparatory training via Skype. Arrange an appointment with your mentor.*

(f) *Tactile motor and technical learning: using motor learning principles to consolidate training and technique into long-term motor memory; used in athletes with the most negative psychological profile to override mental influences; strength and confidence, though dominating physical and technical ability*

Applied Assignment: Design motor/technical learning-based intervention for your sport of choice for one developing and one advanced athlete. See Chapter 13 for guidance.

(g) *On-the-field focus threshold training: to enhance focusing ability*

Applied Assignment: Replicate the procedures and analytic methods in Chapter 7.

(h) *Multimodal intervention; distance-based multimodal intervention:* Replicate methods and procedures in Chapter 15. Regarding distance-based multimodal intervention, video record yourself teaching an athlete how to self-administer sport-specific interventions, document the process, and transfer the data. Document the athlete process using video as well.

11. *Intervention efficacy testing: designed to ascertain to what an extent an intervention impacts performance*

Applied Assignment: Select one of the interventions that is covered and design an abbreviated intervention efficacy study. It should have a preintervention, intervention training, and intervention phase. Phases I and III should have 10 repeated measures. The intervention training phase should be taught and trained for two hours over two days.

Document the process statistically, analyze the data, report the results, discuss with the athlete; video record the process. See all intervention chapters for guidance. *This assignment requires preparatory training via Skype. Arrange an appointment with your mentor.*

12. *Comprehensive athlete database creation and management: documenting assessment and training measures over time; databases are used for comparative purposes, for example, preslump versus postslump could be used to test doper pre- and postdoping and effects on numerous performance measures*

13. *Psychological performance statistics: statistics on the mental game that can be used to document psychological performance in real time, game to game, like with regular statistics such as batting average*

14. *Comprehensive report: the culmination of a complete analysis of a player's mind–body–motor performance*

Applied Assignment: Numbers 12–14 involve an integrated assignment. Acquired psychological, HRV, neurocognitive, and other related predictor and performance outcome measures should be entered and stored in context-specific database files and analyzed as follows: (1) validation of assessments, (2) intervention efficiency, (3) intervention efficacy, and (4) general brain–heart–mind–body–motor and performance relationships. Review data and data entry templates across all chapters. Prepare an analysis-specific report on one of your athlete participants.

Practicum Final: Skype-based evaluation of practicum performance with your mentor.

Additional Practicum Assignment: Complete all Practitioner Challenges in Evidence-Based Applied Sport Psychology

Final Project: Applied Final Assessment, Intervention, and Research Project

   (I) Administer the following:
- **(A)** 15 ABSP-BRC CSARCS-A and Web Neuro Sport Tests
- **(B)** 15 Visualization HRV-Based Efficiency Tests
- **(C)** 15 Line-Bisecting Tests and Brain Hemispheric Valence Tests (Schiffer Paradigm)
- **(D)** 15 Serial 7s Stress Tests
- **(E)** 15 Sport-Specific Performance Tests

  (II) Comprehensive Assessment and Intervention Efficacy Case Study
Sample size: 60 repeated measures in the context of assessment and outcome, 60 in a preintervention phase, 60 in an intervention training/efficiency testing phase, and 60 in an intervention phase. *This assignment requires preparatory discussion via Skype. Arrange an appointment with your mentor.*

The final project may be modified or amended as a function of participant count, specific sport, and/or research/experimental design.

ABSP Certification: Resulting Competencies and Mandated Responsibilities

Sport psychologists and sport psychology practitioners must distinguish themselves from coaches and other practitioner-advisors who work with athletes. ABSP-certified practitioners must demonstrate the following competencies and be committed to ABSP-mandated client and practice responsibility dictates:

    (I) Priority 1. Thorough knowledge of construct validity, conceptual bases, and accountability methodologies relating to assessment instruments and procedures that are used with athletes. Priority 1 also applies to intervention modalities that are taught and administered to athletes.

   (II) The ability to validate and establish the reliability of assessment measures, instruments, and tests that are not part of the ABSP-CP athlete evaluation suite; includes being able to establish a test battery's criterion-referenced and predictive validity at both the group and individual levels.

  (III) The ability to establish the extent of intervention efficiency and efficacy for ABSP-CP advanced intervention modalities and other mental training methods at the group and individual levels.

  (IV) The ability and responsibility to convey to clients, athletes, coaches, parents, administrators, and other stakeholders "practice realities" that are associated with applied sport psychological assessment and intervention, making clear in no uncertain terms that assessment can be fallible and that interventions do not always lead to positive or successful income. The guiding mantra of an ABSP-certified practitioner is that "attempts are undertaken to accurately assess athletes using advanced evaluative methodologies as well as increase the probability that an athlete can benefit from mental training." ABSP practitioners also make known that individual differences factors and temporal and financial realities can greatly impact the intervention process and that there are no quick fixes. ABSP practitioners discourage consulting arrangements that do not allow for the accommodation of the comprehensive ABSP-CP. They make clear to potential clients that reliable athlete assessment and high evidence-based mental training take time, and as such, especially in the initial phases of a working relationship, more is better. ABSP practitioners strive to adhere to an athlete-centered applied sport psychological services delivery paradigm.

(V) The ability to use psychophysiological instrumentation for assessment and intervention purposes, including heart rate variability and heart rate deceleration monitoring and analysis systems.

(VI) The ability to carry out ABSP-mandated accountability methodologies across all assessment and intervention sessions, the vast majority of which must be carried out on the playing field, including the acquisition of brain–heart–mind–body–motor/technical and sport-specific outcome measures; managing the acquired responses in individual and group databases, analyzing the acquired data and providing comprehensive written and oral reports to client-athletes and other stakeholders as permitted by informed consent regarding confidentiality.

(VII) The ability to fully train athlete clients, coaches, and other potential "assistants" in distance-based multimodal assessment, intervention/mental training, and data management so as to facilitate seamless, ongoing applied sport psychological activities in the absence of the primary sport psychologist/sport psychology practitioner, especially when an athlete is away from his or her home base for training or competition purposes.

(See Chapter 15 of Evidence-Based Applied Sport Psychology).

(VIII) *Specific assessment and intervention mental training procedural competence*
See Numbers 1–14 of the Practicum section above. All ABSP-certified practitioners can carry out the listed procedures commensurate with their licensure status (either independently as a licensed psychologist or under supervision if not a licensed psychologist or in accord with state-by-state scope of practice laws governing the practice of psychology).

What Client–Athletes Should Demand of a Sport Psychologist/Sport Psychology Practitioner

1. Comprehensive assessment or evaluation of psychological and mind–body tendencies in the context of a longitudinal repeated measures design with training and official competition analytic components consisting of at least 60 repeated predictor measures that are related to global one-shot personality or behavioral measures and 60 repeated macro- and micro-outcome measures.

   Insufficient and cause for concern: receiving a test score, personality profile, or other type of analysis or verbal feedback from a practitioner without extensive follow-up on-the-playing-field cross-validation or criterion-referencing of office-based evaluation.

2. Comprehensive written report that is orally presented to an athlete client face-to-face or via telephone/Skype in which initial office-based assessments and responses are compared with ecologically based/obtained responses during training and competition using advanced validation methodologies that are advanced by the ABSP-CP.

   Insufficient and cause for concern: practitioner does not design ecologically based testing, does not leave the office to carry out training-competition-based validation and related psychological performance testing using validated approaches, procedures, and methodologies.

3. Transition to mental training or intervention only occurs after sufficient psychological performance testing has been carried out (60–60 repeated measures rule) to help determine an athlete's mental to technical/physical game ratio and/or the impact of state psychological measures on performance.

> *Insufficient and cause for concern: if a practitioner within the first or second session immediately starts with mental training, even more concerning if intervention amenability assessment is not done (which most practitioners are unaware of) and teaches a specific mental training technique(s); worse yet, he or she then sends the athlete off to try them and have an athlete report back in a week.*

4. Immediate mental training can be requested in some cases, for example, leading up to an important competition in the near future.

> *Insufficient and cause for concern: however, if a practitioner recommends and administers a specific mental training method without intervention amenability testing, an athlete may attempt to engage in an intervention technique that they are incapable of learning and exploiting, for example, trying to use hypnosis if an athlete is low in hypnotic susceptibility; moreover, if a practitioner fails to do intervention efficiency and efficacy testing during training and does not test intervention efficacy during competition or instruct his or her athlete to arrange for psychological statistical analyses to be performed during competition (if the athlete is traveling and the practitioner cannot attend a competition), gold standard practice standards are not being adhered to.*

5. Ideally, the intervention phase should commence after meticulous preintervention and intervention training phases that are carried out with ABSP-recommended accountability methodological paradigms.

> *Insufficient and cause for concern: being taught a mental training method and then being told to practice it without initial constant supervision in the context of an experimental efficiency and efficacy testing paradigm.*

Questions Athlete Clients, Coaches, and Other Stakeholders Should Ask Their Practitioner[2]

1. What is my Athlete's Profile? If a practitioner does not know what an Athlete's Profile is, suggest that they look into the ABSP-CP.
2. Alternatively, if your practitioner labels or analyzes you or types you according to any test results, ask what the predictive validity of any score, measure, or profile is (based on group studies) and, importantly, ask if there are analogous state measures that can be obtained that can be tested in the context of training and competition to see if any obtained psychological measures (based on group studies) are meaningful and predict psychological tendencies and your expected performance outcome.
3. If not, then ask the practitioner to verify or validate any test measure obtained by initial assessments by evaluating you during training and competition over time (at least 10 competitions).
4. If the practitioner then merely watches you play or compete and then tells you what he or she thinks about your psychological performance or mental toughness, ask them to quantify your mental game using validated paradigms. If they do not know of any, tell them to contact ABSP.
5. If a practitioner asks you to learn a specific or multiple mental training techniques, ask them why those were chosen, what they are expected to do, how long should they be trained, and how effective they are. If your practitioner *gives you* clear and *definitive answers* to these

questions, that is a major red flag, more so if he or she claims that a mental training method almost always or even usually works.

6. Ask your practitioner to demonstrate the selected intervention's efficiency and efficacy. Tell him or her that you want to know how much of the variance in micro-level outcome measures can be attributed to your mental training efforts. If this question cannot be answered or is avoided or brushed off, an athlete should have major concerns about a practitioner's competence.

7. Ask your practitioner about his or her background as an athlete and whether they have expertise or advanced knowledge of the sport in which you participate. If he or she does not have verifiable expertise or advanced knowledge of your sport, request that a coach attend your initial intake session and ask for an on-the-playing-field analysis of your mental and technical games, to determine the extent to which purported psychological issues are real and not more technically/physically based, which is often the case with lower-level athletes.

8. Ask for a referral if your initial practitioner does not have advanced knowledge of your sport or can arrange for a coach to participate in the assessment and mental training process.

9. Thoroughly read this book, become familiar on a basic level with all of the recommended procedures, and ask your practitioner to apply them and importantly require that they adhere to all of the recommended accountability methodologies. An educated athlete is an empowered athlete, one who can benefit or learn from evidence-based approaches to athlete assessment. Obtaining valid and reliable information is at least as important as engaging in mental training, more so, if mental training is not tested for efficiency and efficacy. Tell your sport psychology practitioner that you want to know as much as possible about your mental game; a request that can only be honored if he or she is capable of carrying out the procedures and methods that are advanced in this book.

10. Importantly, as a client, remember there are no quick fixes. High evidentiary applied sport psychological approaches to the mental game must be carried out over time in a systematic manner; they can be time consuming and involve extensive testing and intensive mental training sessions that must be documented and analyzed. The notion that merely talking to a practitioner occasionally is flawed and bogus and inconsistent with what is known about developmental processes, learning, procedural consolidation, neuronal change, and the remediation of performance psychological problems and the enhancement of an athlete's mental game. If you practice or train many hours a day to reach and maintain peak performance, you cannot expect to make major enduring and biomarker-verifiable psychological gains if the mental game is not approached in a manner similar to your technical game. Anything less is folly, and, as such, be wary of practitioners who portend otherwise. Consequently, an athlete has to invest in the mental game, there are no shortcuts. Do not fall into the practitioner-based paradigm trap, one in which an athlete must structure his or her schedule to that of the practitioner; the once- or twice-a-week office-based approach is not a tenable one, unless a practitioner can unequivocally demonstrate high-level evidence-based intervention efficacy that can be attributed to abbreviated approaches to the mental game.

Of course, gold standard approaches can be expensive and need to be funded. However, once an athlete becomes fully trained in the ABSP-CP, he or she should be capable of self-administering and documenting the protocol with a little bit of effort. Proficiency in the distance-based multimodel protocol allows for ongoing documentation, intervention efficiency, and efficacy testing, an approach practitioners and their athlete clients should carry out collaboratively in the context of a mutually acceptable fee structure.

The Professional, Olympic, and Elite Athlete and Teams

Sport psychology offers practitioners of highly disparate education, training, experience, and credentials an unparalleled opportunity to break into the elite strata of sports. Just about anyone who talks a good game, has inside contacts, and can sell themselves can work with elite athletes at the professional level and they do. This is not necessarily a good thing. In fact, one could contend that professional sports has been contaminated by an influx of practitioners who possess woefully inadequate training and are incapable of delivering gold standard services. Yet, teams and individual athletes continue to hire practitioners on the basis of personal contacts, previous experience, and anecdotal beliefs that a particular individual will provide a team or individual athlete with that nebulous edge. The ABSP surveys professional sports annually and has found that about 60% of all teams contacted trust their "mental game" departments to individuals who broke into "sport psychology" in a manner that could be considered highly irregular. Many practitioners talked their way into positions because a team wanted to start a sport psychology department and a particular person was at the right place at the right time; an individual may have had a few psychology courses, others were former athletes who sold the argument that if anybody understands what athletes are going through it is an ex-athlete, and some physicians and psychiatrists inherited the role of chief performance enhancer, despite having no specific training to do so.

The ABSP has had applicants who then did not follow through with pursuing its certification and training program, who were suddenly hired to direct sport psychology and related programs in the NBA and MLB. Such occurrences suggest that aspiring practitioners, while recognizing that something is missing in terms of what they can do, what they know, or in regard to their education, training, and credentials, will not stop them from bypassing high-level education and training that is mandated by all serious professions in the human services fields and take any job that they can get in professional sports. They are not going to miss out on a possible once-in-a-lifetime opportunity to work with elite athletes just because they lack knowledge and are incapable of delivering high-standard athlete assessment and intervention methods and procedures, since it is highly unlikely that a general manager would have a clue as to what constitutes high-standard athlete assessment and intervention. These sorts of accounts are plentiful. They range from the flight attendant who was earmarked by a Major League Baseball team to develop and direct a sport psychology program for its entire minor league operation, apparently because this individual was a former minor league player, was pursuing a master's degree in sport psychology, and was recommended by the team's current mental training practitioner. To this person's credit, he recognized that he was not prepared to take on this assignment without extensive additional training and collaboration. But he is the exception and not the rule, with scores of practitioners and "wannabe" practitioners trying to seduce professional sport teams and individual athletes into hiring or working with them, despite not offering much credible substance. The very fact that obtaining a position in professional sports or working independently with elite athletes, devoid of oversight, scrutiny, and objective accountability approaches in place, diminishes the field of applied sport psychology. It is inconceivable that a professional sport organization or individual elite athlete would hire or seek out a mere EKG technician or well-informed medicine aficionado to perform cardiologic clinical evaluations or hire as their team psychiatrist a practical nurse. Yet, in sport psychology, an individual, a few months out of college with a degree in marketing, or a guru of note could find themselves at the helm of a performance-enhancement department and entrusted with "working" with elite athletes. This dismal and even dangerous state of affairs can be attributed to the field's inability to police itself and regulate the practice of applied sport psychology. Instead, the field has effusively promoted unrealistic positive outcome expectations to the masses of potential consumers of sport psychological services, whether the high school athlete or professional sports team general manager; both and others have essentially been seduced by myths that pervade the field and as such have no idea about the many pitfalls of applied sport psychology (athlete assessment and intervention).

In all serious and mature subfields in psychology and related disciplines, progression through the ranks is predicated on extensive and supervised education, initial training, formal internships, residencies, and postdoctoral fellowships that are followed by years of acquiring experience under oversight before a practitioner/clinician can rise through the ranks. Yet, when it comes to applied sport psychology, within days it is possible for an individual without *any* formal training or background to go right to the top of the field and earn millions of dollars.[3] While this may make some ambitioned readers salivate, serious, concerned, and ethically driven practitioners and future practitioners should be alarmed by what can be considered a crisis in applied sport psychology and try to reverse this continuing trend.

Unfortunately, the problem of quality control in hiring decisions extends throughout the credential, training, and experience hierarchy, with even supposed stalwart doctorate holder and certified practitioners with years of experience in applied sport psychology continuing to engage in substandard practices, and it is not about specific methods or systems of applied sport psychology per se that continue to be propagated as the gold standard by influential and highly visible "star" practitioners, it is about an utter lack of accountability metrics that allow just about any assessment and intervention system to pass as credible or highly efficacious, despite this not being the case when assessments and interventions/mental training is subjected to rigorous validation methodologies.

In light of highly eclectic, diverse, and personality (guru)-driven approaches to applied sport psychology, can it be expected that decision makers in professional sports as well as elite athletes can make informed decisions about hiring and evaluating the work of their sport psychology departments? Who should be hired? On the basis of what criteria? What should a pro team GM expect to get or learn from a sport psychology practitioner? What should high-level decision makers in professional and elite sports know about applied sport psychology? What should they expect and *demand*?

Who Is Competent to Practice Applied Sport Psychology in Professional Sports?

The ABSP practice qualifications and competencies template is presented in Figure 22.1. Aspiring and active practitioners need to take these recommendations into account when pursuing or advancing a career in applied sport psychology. Competencies supersede credentials alone, irrespective of a certified practitioners experience and educational background if a highly degreed and credentialed practitioner fails to become trained in and applies athlete assessment and intervention procedures and analytic methodologies that are crucial to best practices and high evidentiary applied sport psychology. Ideally, however, in light of scope of practice laws that can restrict what a nonlicensed practitioner can actually do with an athlete, professional sport teams and elite individual athletes should hire licensed psychologists who are trained in, certified by, and possess the ABSP-recommended competencies or are available to supervise and collaboratively work with board-certified practitioners who have all of the ABSP-recommended competencies, unless an unlicensed practitioner obtains a waiver or dispensation from a state board of psychology on the basis of opinions regarding what constitutes the practice of psychology. Nevertheless, in cases where a master's level or lower-degreed practitioner possesses more ABSP-recommended competencies, such an individual should

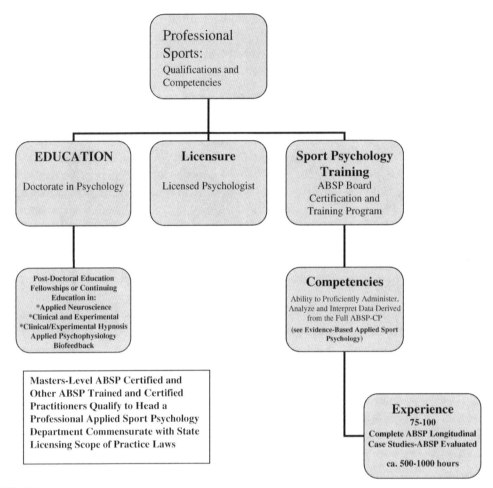

FIGURE 22.1 Qualification and competencies for heads of pro sport-applied sport psychology departments.

or can head a professional team's applied or related sport psychology department in an administrative, analyst, and researcher capacity, leaving licensed psychologists to carry out prescribed assessment and intervention procedures within ABSP accountability guidelines.

What Professional Sport Team Executives Should Know and Demand of Practitioners

1. Documented assurances from the state board of psychology of said professional sport team's state that a practitioner is permitted to practice applied sport psychology as an independent licensed psychologist, other related licensed profession, or is determined to be exempt from psychology scope of practice laws or can practice applied sport psychology under the supervision of a licensed psychologist.

2. Documentation that team's practitioner is an ABSP Board-Certified Sport Psychologist the highest level credential in applied sport psychology, since it denotes that a practitioner is a licensed psychologist and thus can practice psychology independently with assurances that such an individual is capable of administering the entire ABSP-validated athlete assessment and intervention protocol, including its advanced high evidentiary accountability methodologies.

3. Master's degree-level practitioners or lower and/or nondegreed practitioners who are not ABSP board-certified consultants are not trained in the extensive and validated ABSP-mandated athlete assessment, intervention, and accountability procedures and methodologies, and as such cannot be expected to provide highest-standard best applied sport psychological services.

4. Team executives should have their applied sport psychology departments evaluated by the ABSP. If the following gold standard components are lacking, a team and its athletes cannot be assured that they will be receiving high-standard applied sport psychological service:

   (a) Is your team's sport psychology practitioner a licensed psychologist? (yes = pass)

   (b) Is your sport psychology practitioner ABSP certified? (yes = pass)

   (c) Is your sport psychology practitioner certified by another agency or body? (yes = provisional pass)

   (d) If non-ABSP certified, but certified, is your practitioner trained in: Applied Neuroscience; Clinical and Experimental; Clinical/Experimental Hypnosis; Applied Psychophysiology; Biofeedback, Experimental Assessment and Intervention Validation Methods and Intervention Efficiency and Efficacy Testing Methodologies per ABSP recommendations? (yes = pass)

   (e) Does your sport psychology practitioner maintain a comprehensive database of brain–heart–mind–body–motor responses on athlete clients in the context of actual official sport-specific micro-level performance outcome measures derived from official competition, and would such data hold up to independent scrutiny or auditing? (yes = pass)

   (f) Does your practitioner have competency in and carry out most of the following procedures on all athletes within an accountability framework?

      1. *Assessment of primary higher-order psychological factors using the Carlstedt Subliminal Attention, Reactivity, Coping Scale and related tests to measure an athlete's level of hypnotic susceptibility, neuroticism, and repressive coping*

      2. *Neurocognitive testing using the brain resource Internet-based or related neuropsychological test batteries for assessing subliminal brain responses (www.americanboardofsportpsychology.org link to test center)*

      3. *In-the-laboratory psychophysiological stress testing with video stimulus/stress paradigm: checking for stress responding*

      4. *Quantitative EEG (qEEG, brain mapping) using the Brain Resource Paradigm or related EEG paradigms for assessing subliminal brain responding*

      5. *On-the-playing-field assessment of brain responding using wireless EEG*

      6. *On-the-playing-field assessment of heart rate variability: Time-out paradigm*

      7. *Wireless monitoring of heart activity, heart rate variability, and heart rate deceleration analysis during real competition*

      8. *Critical moments analyses during training and competition*

      9. *In-the-field technical and focus threshold analyses to analyze mind–body–motor control and ability to concentrate during practice and competition*

      10. *Mental training as a function of Athlete's Profile of primary higher-order factors, including:*

         (a) *Heart rate variability/heart rate deceleration biofeedback*

         (b) *Neurofeedback using Carlstedt Frontal Lobe Protocols: a means of directly shaping brain wave activity associated with peak-performance components such as attention/focus, motor control, and intensity. Used to manipulate key brain responses associated with zone states, responses that are vital to performance*

         (c) *On-the-field glasses-laterality manipulation training: teaches an athlete to induce immediate shifts in brain activation that have been found to underlie transition from strategic planning to perceptual preaction preparation; left to right brain shift facilitation and relative shut-down or idling of the frontal lobes, which can interfere with focus, keeping intrusive thoughts at bay*

(d) *Active-alert hypnosis: used with athletes who are high in hypnotic susceptibility to intensely focus and prime motor or technical responses while shutting out intrusive thoughts and external distractions*

(e) *Mental imagery efficiency and efficacy testing*

(f) *Tactile motor and technical learning: using motor learning principles to consolidate training and technique into long-term motor memory; used in athletes with most negative psychological Athlete's Profile in an attempt to override negative mental influences and enhance self-confidence on the basis of stellar physical and technical ability*

(g) *On-the-field focus threshold training*

(h) *Multimodal intervention; distance-based multimodal intervention*

11. *Intervention efficacy testing: designed to ascertain to what extent an intervention impacts performance*

12. *Comprehensive athlete database creation and management: documenting assessment and training measures over time; databases are used for comparative purposes, for example, preslump versus postslump could be used to test doper pre- and postdoping and effects on numerous performance measures*

13. *Psychological performance statistics: statistics on the mental game that can be used to document psychological performance in real time, game to game, like with regular statistics such as batting average*

14. *Comprehensive reporting: the culmination of a complete analysis of a player's mind–body–motor performance*

(yes to all = pass)

If your practitioner (i.e., applied sport psychology department) does not fulfill each "pass" criterion, then, in the context of professional sports, he or she can be considered substandard.

ABSP-Recommended Educational and Training Curricula: Applied Sport Psychology

Each year the ABSP holds a summer visiting fellowship and training/internship program. Participants from across the nation, including university professors as well as undergraduate students and even non-ABSP-certified sport psychology practitioners, are questioned regarding their experiences with sport psychology as an athlete recipient of services, student in a degree or certification program, or an instructor/professor or coach of athletes. The vast majority of these participants noted that they were not sure of what it was they were supposed to do, whether a procedure worked, and none systematically used mental training methods on their own, once team-based seasonal relationships with a sport psychology practitioner ended. On the other hand, all active athletes religiously adhered to physical and technically oriented training programs. Relative to instructors in sport psychology as well as practitioners seeking additional training in the ABSP summer program, all said that they were dissatisfied with educational approaches in applied sport psychology, especially experiential components that are lacking in many degree programs. A common theme was that graduates, certificate holders, and athletes themselves really did not know what to do when it came to competently administering or engaging in applied psychological procedures. A sort of learn-as-you-go attitude seemed to pervade with on-the-job training, guiding and eventually shaping practitioners' approach to athlete assessment and mental training. In the end, if 10 practitioners from the same graduate or certification program were surveyed, a few years later, regarding their practices, one likely would find 10 different approaches to applied sport psychology.

ABSP contends that the vast majority of applied sport psychology education programs are substandard and do not prepare graduates to become competent practitioners and practitioner-researchers. This may be in part attributable to the fact that sport psychology is a field, which since its inception has been dominated by and almost exclusively housed in physical education and kinesiology departments. Beyond a few distance-based sport psychology degree programs in psychology departments, sport psychology per se tends to be offered as a specialization or emphasis area within a physical education or kinesiology degree program. Master's degrees in sport psychology are also offered, but these are associated with potential practice constraints associated with state scope or practice and title laws.

By being housed in physical education and kinesiology departments, sport psychology degree programs for the most part are being taught by nonpsychologists. That in itself is not necessarily a negative thing. However, it is unlikely that ABSP-recommended competencies that are crucial to eventual high evidentiary practice will be considered and taught by a faculty whose background lacks crucial psychologically based educational and training components. Unless the previously mentioned competencies and educational and training program are part of a degree program or sport psychology emphasis area, a graduate will be incapable of delivering gold standard applied sport psychological services. Moreover, if legal realities governing scope of practice and title usage laws are not considered, graduates with degrees that are not associated with licensure will be seen as rogue practitioners if they choose to work with athletes but are not sanctioned by the state in which they reside. Current master's and lower-level practitioners who engage in procedures that fall within the scope of practice purviews of licensed professions, including Association of Applied Sport Psychology (AASP) consultants who are not licensed, are at risk. Hence, until (if and when) state laws regarding the practice of psychology or other laws exempt sport psychology practitioners from scope of practice laws, the entire education and certification infrastructure is in serious jeopardy, since a strong case could be made that people are being charged tuition, and given degrees and certification that in the end do not allow graduates and certificate holders to legally practice many, if not most, sport psychological procedures.[4]

Consequently, the time has come for university and college psychology departments to adopt sport psychology and play an important role in reshaping and defining sport psychology in the context of highest-standard education, research, and especially applied training programs that lead to degrees and credentials that permit eventual licensure and unrestricted, independent practice.

Recommended Curriculum

In addition to standard coursework and requirements for a major in psychology, master's, or doctorate in psychology, along with all experience and licensure components, the ABSP practicum roadmap should be integrated into the aforementioned degree and training programs (review ABSP practicum content above). It is also recommended that all psychology courses are augmented with a sport psychology component. For example, a course in neuropsychology consisting of three written papers, three quizzes, and/or a final examination or paper would require (for a sport psychology major, minor, or degree) one paper and/or quiz to be sport psychology topic-specific, along with an option to write one's final paper on, in this case, sport neuropsychology. Curriculum iterations leading to advanced knowledge and eventual applied competencies in sport and applied sport psychology are numerous. However, ultimately, the discipline of psychology, that is, its knowledge base, subject domains, and especially its evidence-based procedures, methodologies, and analytic approaches should guide the study of sport and applied sport psychology. The goal of psychology department-based sport psychology education, training, and degree programs is to produce a cadre of future practitioners who possess competencies that are crucial to the advancement of scientific applied sport psychology, best applied sport psychological practices, and the credibility of the field.

Collaborating With ABSP

The ABSP seeks to collaborate with colleges and universities that are interested in advancing its mission of higher standards in sport and applied sport psychology. In conjunction with its annual summer visiting fellowship/internship and training/research program in evidence-based applied sport psychology, ABSP offers students experience for institutional degree programs that count toward board certification in sport psychology and college credit. Faculty members and athletic department coaches are also invited to attend the ABSP program as visiting fellows. Eventually, ABSP would like to hold short courses at affiliated colleges/universities and certify psychology department-based sport psychology degree programs.

It must be again emphasized that to legally practice sport psychology and call oneself a sport psychologist, state licensure must be achieved. This can only be done through licensure track professional psychology-specific education, degree, training, and experience acquisition programs that the ABSP maintains should start at the undergraduate level and continue through graduate and professional degree programs in the context of a systematic competencies-based training roadmap, and that legal practice realities must be made known to all students who are interested in becoming sport psychologists. As such, applied sport psychology should go through psychology departments and eventually transition into professional psychology degree and training programs, and culminate with board certification as a Board-Certified Sport Psychologist or competence to practice sport psychology under supervision as a Board-Certified Consultant.

The ABSP-Carlstedt Protocol: Copyright Considerations

The ABSP-Carlstedt protocol is a validated proprietary system of athlete intervention. It should only be administered after extensive training that can be obtained in the ABSP certification, intern, and visiting fellowship programs.

Notes

1. References to this book's chapters appear throughout this chapter, since much of its content is part of the official American Board of Sport Psychology certification information document.
2. Alternatively, these questions and the issues they address should be preemptively discussed by practitioners to better inform their client-athletes, assuming a practitioner possesses ABSP requisite competencies.

3. See Brain Typing and the story of Jon Niednagel, a multilevel marketing executive, who was uncritically lifted to prominence by the media and eventually hired by numerous professional sport teams on the basis of a system of athlete evaluation that was sold as "brain science," whereby athletes were given neuro-psychological profiles on the basis of merely looking at an athlete and then predicting performance outcome (see Sandbek, 2012, *Pseudoscience of Brain Typing*).

4. Nonlicensed ABSP sub-doctoral-degreed practitioners must practice under the supervision of a licensed professional. ABSP advances a competency model. As such, if competency can be demonstrated as defined by the ABSP-applied practice template, a practitioner should be able to practice applied sport psychology. However, until the scope of practice laws is amended to accommodate nonlicensed practitioners in the context of independent practice, they must make formal arrangements to work under the supervision of a licensed psychologist.

References

Addis, M. E. (2002). Methods for disseminating research products and increasing evidence-based practice: Promises, obstacles, and future directions. *Clinical Psychology: Science and Practice*, 9(4), 367–378.

Akselrod, S., Gordon, D., Ubel, F. A., Shannon, D. C., Barger, A. C., & Cohen, R. J. (1981). Power spectrum analysis of heart rate fluctuation: A quantitative probe of beat-to-beat cardiovascular control. *Science, 213*, 220–222.

Anastassi, A. (1988). *Psychological testing* (6th ed.). Upper Saddle River, NJ: Prentice-Hall.

Andreassi, J. L. (1995). *Psychophysiology: Human behavior and physiological responding* (3rd ed.). Hillsdale, NJ: Erlbaum.

Anshel, M. H. (2006). *Applied exercise psychology: A practitioner's guide to improving client health and fitness.* New York: Springer Publishing Company.

Anshel, M. H., Reeves, L. H., & Johns-Wommack, R. (2009). *Concepts in fitness: A balanced approach to good health.* Boston: Pearson Education.

Armour, J. A. (1994). *Neurocardiology.* New York, NY: Oxford University Press.

Barbaez, A. (1983). Restricted environmental stimulation and the enhancement of hypnotizability: Pain, EEG alpha, skin conductance and temperature responses. *International Journal of Clinical and Experimental Hypnosis, 31,* 235–238.

Becker, M. B. (1986). *An investigation into the cognitive and personality dimensions of basketball athletes.* Unpublished dissertation. Dissertation Abstracts International, 42–02B, 739.

Bonanno, G. A., Davis, P. J., Singer, J .L., & Schwartz, G. E. (1991). The repressor personality and avoidant information processing: A dichotic listening study. *Journal of Research in Personality, 25,* 386–401.

Boutcher, S. H., & Zinsser, N. W. (1990). Cardiac deceleration of elite and beginning golfers during putting. *Journal of Sport and Exercise Psychology, 12,* 37–47.

Brain Resource Company. (2007). *International brain database project.* Sydney: Brain Resource Company.

Cannon, W. B. (1932). *The wisdom of the body.* New York, NY: Appleton Century-Crofts.

Carlstedt, R. A. (1998). *Psychologically mediated heart rate variability: A single case study of heart rate deceleration and a spectrum analysis of autonomic function during tournament tennis.* Master's thesis, Saybrook Graduate School, San Francisco.

Carlstedt, R. A. (2001). *Line-bisecting test reveals relative left brain hemispheric predominance in highly skilled athletes: Relationships among cerebral laterality, personality, and sport performance.* Doctoral dissertation, Saybrook Graduate School, 2001. Dissertation Abstracts International, 62, 4264B.

Carlstedt, R. A. (2004a). *Critical moments during competition: A mind–body model of sport performance when it counts the most.* New York, NY: Psychology Press.

Carlstedt, R. A. (2004b). Line-bisecting performance in highly skilled athletes: Does preponderance of rightward error reflect unique cortical organization and functioning? *Brain and Cognition, (54),* 52–57.

Carlstedt, R. A. (2005). *Mentales tennis.* Munich.

Carlstedt, R. A. (2006). *Relationships among neurocognition, heart rate variability personality, behavior and performance outcome measures: Findings from longitudinal investigations.* Research report, NY: American Board of Sport Psychology (submitted for publication in multiple papers).

Carlstedt, R. A. (2007a). Mind–body measures and sport performance. A cyber-symposium. *Journal of the American Board of Sport Psychology,* I, www.americanboardofsportpsychology.org

Carlstedt, R. A. (2007b). Integrative evidence based tennis psychology: perspectives, practices, and findings from a ten-year validation investigation of the Carlstedt Protocol. In S. Miller & J. Capel-Davies (Eds.), *Tennis science and technology III* (pp. 245–254). London, UK: International Tennis Federation.

Carlstedt, R. A. (2008). *A test of the transient hypofrontality hypothesis using telemetry EEG.* Presentation: Harvard Medical School-MIT-Massachusetts General Hospital Martinos Center for BioMedical Imaging.

Carlstedt, R. A. (2009). Integrative diagnosis and intervention: The high-risk model of threat perception revisited. In R. A. Carlstedt (Ed.), *Handbook of integrative clinical psychology, psychiatry and behavioral medicine: Perspectives, practices and research.* New York, NY: Springer Publishing.

Carlstedt, R. A. (2011). *American Board of Sport Psychology position paper on the state of applied sport psychology: Perspectives, practices and future directions.* American Psychological Association Annual Convention in Washington, DC.

Chaves, J. F., & Brown, J. M. (1978). *Self-generated strategies for the control of pain and stress.* Presented at the Annual Meeting of the American Psychological Association, Toronto, Canada, August, 1978.

Coaching Science Abstracts (1997). *Imagery in Sports;* Vol. 2, retrievable via http://coachsci.sdsu.edu/csa/vol26/table.htm

Crews, D. (2005). New View glasses: Investigation of glasses-based visual field manipulation in golfers. Commissioned study; retrievable via http//www.americanboardofsportpsychology.org.

Crowne, D. P., & Marlowe, D. (1960). A new scale of social desirability independent of psychopathology. *Journal of Consulting Psychology, 24,* 349–354.

Daino, A. (1984). Personality traits of adolescent tennis players. *International Journal of Sport Psychology, 16,* 120–125.

Davidson, R. J. (1984). Affect, cognition, and hemispheric specialization. In C. E. Izard, J. Kagan, & R. Zajonc (Eds.). *Emotions, cognition, and behavior* (pp. 320–365). New York, NY: Cambridge University Press.

Davidson, R. J., Schwartz, G. E., & Rothman, L. P. (1976). Attentional style and the self-regulation of mood-specific attention: An electroencephalographic study. *Journal of Abnormal Psychology, 85*(6), 611–621.

Dietrich, A. (2003). Functional neuroanatomy of altered states of consciousness: The transient hypofrontality hypothesis. *Consciousness and Cognition* (12), 231–256.

Dixon, N. F. (1981). *Preconscious processing.* Chichester, UK: Wiley.

Drake, R. A. (1987). Effects of gaze manipulation on aesthetic judgments: Hemisphere priming of affect. *Acta Psychologica, 65,* 91–99.

Edmonds, W. A., & Tennenbaum, (2012). *Case studies in applied psychophysiology: Neurofeedback and biofeedback treatments for advances in human performance.* Oxford, UK: Wiley-Blackwell.

Egloff, B., & Gruhn, A. J., (1996). Personality and endurance sports. *Personality and Individual Differences, 21,* 223–229.

Evans, F. J. (1977). Hypnosis and sleep: The control of altered states of consciousness. *Annals of the New York Academy of Sciences, 296,* 162–174.

Eysenck, H. J. (1960). *The structure of human personality* (2nd ed.). London, UK: Methuen.

Eysenck, H. J. (1983). Psychophysiology and personality. In A. Galse & J. A. Edwards (Eds.), *Physiological correlates of human behavior.* London, UK: Academic Press.

Eysenck, H. J., & Eysenck, S. (1975). *Manual of the Eysenck Personality Questionnaire.* San Diego, CA: Educational and Industrial Testing Services.

Eysenck, H. J., Nias, D. K., & Cox, D. N. (1982). Sport and personality. *Advances in Behaviour Research and Therapy, 4,* 1–56.

Flor, H., Turk, D. C., & Birbaumer, N. (1985). Assessment of stress-related psychophysiological reactions in chronic back pain patients. *Journal of Consulting and Clinical Psychology, 53,* 354–364.

Fortino, D. (2001). *Affect regulation, emotional intelligence and addiction: A five-factor personality model to predict treatment outcome, and efficacy in heroin abusers. Doctoral dissertation.* San Francisco: Saybrook Graduate School.

Fox, N. A., & Davidson, R. J. (1984). Hemispheric substrates of affect: A developmental model. In N. A. Fox & R. J. Davidson (Eds.), *The psychobiology of affective development* (pp. 353–381). Hillsdale, NJ: Erlbaum.

Fromm, E., & Nash, M. R. (2003). *Contemporary hypnosis research.* New York, NY: Guilford.

Galin, D. (1974). Implications for psychiatry of left and right cerebral specialization. *Archives of General Psychiatry, 31,* 572–581.

Gallwey, T. (1974). *The inner game of tennis.* New York, NY: Random House.

Geen, R. G. (1997). Psychophysiological approaches to personality. In R. Hogan, J. Johnson, & S. Briggs (Eds.), *Handbook of personality psychology* (pp. 269–285). San Diego, CA: Academic Press.

Geron, E., Furst, D., & Rotstein, P. (1986). Personality of athletes participating in various sports. *International Journal of Sport Psychology, 17*(2), 120–135.

Hall, R., de Antueno, C., & Webber, A. (2007). Publication bias in the medical literature: A review by a Canadian Research Ethics Board. *Canadian Journal of Anaesthesiology, 54*(5), 380–388.

Hanin, Y. L. (2006). Individual zones of optimal functioning (IZOF) model: Emotion-performance relationships in sport. In Y. L. Hanin (Ed.), *Emotions in sport.* Champaign, IL: Human Kinetics.

Harris, R. M., Porges, S. W., Clemenson-Carpenter, M. E., & Vincenz, L. M. (1992). Hypnotic susceptibility, mood state, and cardiovascular reactivity. *American Journal of Clinical and Experimental Hypnosis, 36*(1), 15–25.

Hatfield, B. D., Landers, D. L., & Ray, W. J. (1984). Cognitive processes during self-paced motor performance: An electroencephalographic profile of skilled marksmen. *Journal of Sport Psychology, 6,* 42–59.

Hatfield, B. D., Landers, D. L., & Ray, W. J. (1987). Cardiovascular-CNS interactions during a self-paced, intentional attentive state: Elite marksmanship performance. *Psychophysiology, 24,* 542–549.

Heslegrave, R. J., Olgilvie, J. C., & Furedy, J. J. (1979). Measuring baseline treatment-differences in heart rate variability: Variance versus successive differences mean square and beats per minute versus inter-beat interval. *Psychophysiology, 16,* 151–157.

Hogan, R., Johnson, J., & Briggs, S. (1997). *Handbook of personality psychology.* New York, NY: Academic Press.

House, J. S., Landis, K. R., & Umberson, D. (1988). Social relationships and health. *Science, 241,* 540–545.

Ingram, R. E., Saccuzzo, D. P., McNeil, B. W., & McDonald, R. (1979). Speed of Information processing in high and low susceptible subjects: A preliminary study. *International Journal of Clinical and Experimental Hypnosis, 27*(l), 42–47.

Jammer, L. D., Schwarz, G. E., & Leigh, H. (1988). The relationship between repressive and defensive coping styles and monocyte, eosinophil, and serum glucose levels: Support for the opiode peptide hypothesis of repression. *Psychosomatic Medicine, 50,* 567–575.

Kilhstrom, J. F. (1987). The cognitive unconscious. *Science, 237,* 1445–1452.

Klemm, W. R. (1996). *Understanding neuroscience.* St. Louis: Mosby.

Krantz, D. S., & Manuck, S. B. (1984). Acute psychophysiologic reactivity and risk of cardiovascular disease: A review and methodologic critique. *Psychological Bulletin, 96*(3), 435–464.

Lacey, J. I., & Lacey, B. C. (1964). *Cardiac deceleration and simple visual reaction in a fixed foreperiod experiment.* Paper presented at the meeting of the Society for Psychophysiological Research, Washington, DC.

Lacey, J. I., & Lacey, B. C. (1970). Some autonomic-central nervous system interrelationships. In P. Black (Ed.), *Physiological correlates of emotions* (pp. 205–227). New York: Academic Press.

Lacey, B. C., & Lacey, J. L. (1977). Change in heart period: A function of sensiomotor event timing within the cardiac cycle. *Physiological Psychology, 5,* 383–393.

Lacey, J. L., & Lacey, B. C. (1978). Two-way communication between the heart and the brain: Significance of time within the cardiac cycle. *American Psychologist, 33*(2), 99–113.

Landers, D., Han, M., Salazar, W., Petruzzello, S., Kubitz, K., & Gannon, T. (1994). Effects of learning on electro-encephalographic and electrocardiographic patterns in novice archers. *International Journal of Sport Psychology, 25,* 56–70.

Lane, R. D., Merikangas, K. R., Schwarz, G. E., Huang, S. S., & Pushoff, B. A. (1990). Inverse relationship between defensiveness and lifetime prevalence of psychiatric disorder. *American Journal of Psychiatry, 147,* 573–578.

Langer, E., & Imber, L. G. (1979). When practice makes imperfect: Debilitating effects of over-learning. *Journal of Personality and Social Psychology, 37,* 2014–2024.

Lederbogen, F., Gernoth, C., Weber, B., Colla, M., Kniest, A., Heuser, I., & Deuschle, M. (2001). Antidepressive treatment with amitriptyline and paroxetine: comparable effects on heart rate variability. *Journal of Clinical Psychopharmacology, 21*(2), 238–239.

Lepore, S. J., Mata, K. A., & Evans, G. W. (1993). Social support lowers cardiovascular reactivity to an acute stressor. *Psychosomatic Medicine, 55,* 518–524.

Lindsley, D. (1969). Average evoked potentials: Achievements, failures and prospects. In E. Donchin & D. Lindsley (Eds.), (NASA Sp-191), *Average evoked potentials: Methods, results and evaluation.* Washington, DC: NASA.

Little, K. D., Lubar, J. F., & Cannon, R. (2009). Neurofeedback: Research-based treatment for ADHD. In R. A. Carlstedt (Ed.), *Handbook of Integrative clinical psychology, psychiatry and behavioral medicine: Perspectives, practices and research* (pp. 807–822). New York, NY: Springer Publishing.

Malik, M., & Camm, A. J. (1995). *Heart rate variability.* Armonk, NY: Futura Publishing.

McGrady, A., Lynch, D., Nagel, R., & Zsembik, C. (1999). Application of the High Risk Model of Threat Perception to a primary care patient population. *Journal of Nervous and Mental Diseases, 187*(6), 369–375.

McCraty, R., & Watkins, A. D. (1996). *Autonomic assessment report: A comprehensive heart rate variability analysis.* Boulder Creek, CA: Institute of Heart Math.

Moss, D., McGrady, T. C., Davies, T. C., & Wickramasekera, I. (2003). *Handbook of mind-body medicine for primary care.* Thousands Oaks, CA: Sage Publications.

Nideffer, R. M. (1976). *Test of attentional and interpersonal style.* New Berlin, WI: Assessment Systems International.

Nowlin, B., Eisdorfer, C., Whalen, R., & Troyer, W. G. (1970). The effect of exogenous changes in heart rate and rhythm upon reaction time performance. *Psychophysiology, 7,* 186–193.

Oeppen, J., & Vaupel, J. W. (2002). Broken limits to life expectancy. *Science, 296*(5570), 1029.

O'Leary, A. (1990). Stress, emotion, and human immune function. *Psychological Bulletin, 108*(3), 363–382.

Pennebaker, J. W. (1985). Traumatic experience and psychosomatic disease: Exploring the roles of behavioral inhibition, obsession, and confiding. *Canadian Psychology, 26,* 82–85.

Phillips, C. (1977). A psychological analysis of tension headache. In S. Rachman (Ed.), *Contributions to medical psychology.* Oxford, UK: Pergamon Press.

Piedmont, R. L., Hill, D. C., & Blanco, S. (1999). Predicting athletic performance using the five-factor model of personality. *Personality and Individual Differences, 27,* 769–777.

Pribam, K. H., & McGuinness, D. (1975). Arousal, activation, and effort in the control of attention. *Psychological Review, 82,* 116–149.

Ravizza, K. (1977). Peak experiences in sports. *Journal of Humanistic Psychology, 4,* 35–40.

Rosenthal, R. N. (2004). Overview of evidence-based practice. In A. R. Roberts & K. R. Yeager (Eds.), *Evidence-based Practice Manual: Research and Outcome Measures in Health and Human Services* (pp. 20–29). New York: Oxford University Press.

Saccuzzo, D. P., Safnan, D., Anderson, V., & McNeil, B. (1982). Visual information processing in high and low susceptible subjects. *International Journal of Clinical and Experimental Hypnosis, 30,* 32–44.

Sandman, C. A., Walker, B. B., & Berka, C. (1982). Influence of afferent cardiovascular feedback on behavior and the cortical evoked potential. In J. T. Cacioppo, & R. E. Petty (Eds.), *Perspectives in cardiovascular psychophysiology* (pp. 189–222). New York, NY: Guilford.

Schiffer, F. (1997). Affect changes observed with right versus left lateral visual field stimulation in psychotherapy patients: Possible physiological, psychological and therapeutic implications. *Comprehensive Psychiatry, 38,* 289–295.

Schiffer, F., Teicher, M. H., Anderson, C., Tomoda, A., Polcari, A., Navalta, C. P. et al. (2007). Determination of hemispheric emotional valence in individual subjects: A new approach with research and therapeutic implications. *Behavioral and Brain Functions, (3),* 13.

Schwartz, G. E. (1990). Psychobiology of repression and health: A systems approach. In J. L. Singer (Ed.), *Repression and dissociation: Implications for personality theory, psychopathology, and health* (pp. 405–434). Chicago: University of Chicago Press.

Shields, J. (1962). *Monozygotic twins brought UD apart and brought up together.* New York, NY: Oxford University Press.

Sifneos, P. E., Apfel-Savitz, R., & Frankel, F. H. (1977). The phenomenon of 'alexithymia'. Observations in neurotic and psychosomatic patients. *Psychotherapy and Psychosomatics, 28*(1–4), 47–57.

Sternbach, R. A., Janowsky, D. S., Huey, L. Y., & Segal, D. S. (1976). Effects of altering brain serotonin activity on human chronic pain. In J. J. Bonica, & D. Albe-Fessard (Eds.), Proceedings on the First World Congress on Pain: Vol. 1, Advances in pain research and therapy. New York, NY: Raven Press.

Surwillo, W. W. (1971). Human reaction time and endogenous heart rate changes in normal subjects. *Psychophysiology, 8,* 680–682.

Szuhany, K. L., Carlstedt, R. A., & Duckworth, A. (2009). *Coming through in the clutch: Quantifying pressure performance in baseball.* Senior Honors Thesis Presentations. Philadelphia: University of Pennsylvania.

Task Force of the European Society of Cardiology and the North American Society of Pacing and Electrophysiology. (1996). Heart rate variability standards of measurement, physiological interpretation, and clinical use. *Circulation, 93,* 1043–1065.

Taylor, J. (1996). Intensity regulation and athletic performance. In J. L. Van Raalte, & B. W. Brewer (Eds.), *Exploring sport and exercise psychology* (pp. 75–106). Washington, DC: American Psychological Association.

Tellegen, A., & Atkinson, G. (1974). Openness to absorbing and self-altering experiences ("absorption"), a trait related to hypnotic susceptibility. *Journal of Abnormal Psychology, 83,* 268–277.

Thorton, K. E., & Carmody, D. P. (2009). Quantitative electroencephalography in assessment and rehabilitation of traumatic brain injury. In R. A. Carlstedt (Ed.), *Handbook of integrative clinical psychology, psychiatry and behavioral medicine: Perspectives, practices and research* (pp. 463–508). New York, NY: Springer Publishing.

Tomarken, A. J., & Davidson, R. J. (1994). Frontal brain activation in repressors and nonrepressors. *Journal of Abnormal Psychology, 103,* 339–349.

Van Raalte, J. L., & Brewer, B. W. (1996). *Exploring sport and exercise psychology.* Washington, DC: American Psychological Association.

Waller, S. (1988). *Alterations of consciousness in peak sports performance.* Doctoral dissertation. San Francisco, CA: Saybrook Graduate School.

Walter, G. F., & Porges, S. W. (1976). Heart rate and respiratory responses as a function of task difficulty: The use of discrimination analysis in the selection of psychologically sensitive physiological responses. *Psychophysiology, 13,* 563–571.

Watson, D., & Clark, L. A. (1984). Negative affectivity: The disposition to experience aversive emotional states. *Psychological Bulletin, 96,* 465–490.

Watson, D., Clark, L. A., & Tellegen, A. (1988). Development and validation of brief measures of positive and negative affect: The PANAS scales. *Journal of Personality and Social Psychology, 54,* 1063–1070.

Weinberger, D. A. (1990). The construct validity of the repressive coping style. In J. L. Singer (Ed.). *Repression and dissociation: Implications for personality theory, psychopathology, and health* (pp. 337–386). Chicago: University of Chicago Press.

Weinberger, D. A., Schwartz, G. E., & Davidson, R. J. (1979). Low-anxious, high-anxious, and repressive coping styles: Psychometric patterns and behavioral and physiological responses to stress. *Journal of Abnormal Psychology, 88,* 369–380.

Weitzenhoffer & Hilgard (1959). *Stanford hypnotic susceptibility scales, Forms A & B.* Palo Alto, CA: Consulting Psychologists Press.

Wickramasekera, I. E. (1988). *Clinical behavioral medicine.* New York, NY: Plenum.

Wickramasekera, I. E. (2003). The high-risk model of threat perception and the Trojan horse role induction: Somatization and psychophysiological disease. In D. Moss, A. McGrady, T. C. Davies, & I. Wickramasekera (Eds.), *Handbook of mind-body medicine for primary care* (pp. 19–42.). Thousands Oaks, CA: Sage Publications.

Wickramasekera, I. E., Davies, T., & Davies, M. (1996). Applied psychophysiology: A bridge between the biomedical model and the biopsychosocial model in family medicine. *Professional Psychology: Research and Practice, 27*(3), 221–233.

Wolk, C., & Velden, M. (1987). Detection variability within the cardiac cycle: Toward a revision of the "baroreceptor hypothesis." *Journal of Psychophysiology, 1,* 61–65.

Index